The Illustrious Impact of Luminarias on the Law

The **Illustrious Impact** of **Luminarias** on the **Law**

The Legal Handicraft of the First Latina Article III Judges, State Supreme Court Justices, and Public Interest Litigators

Dolores S. Atencio

CAROLINA ACADEMIC PRESS
Durham, North Carolina

Library of Congress cataloging-in-publication data
is available at **catalog.loc.gov.**

LCCN 2025031978
ISBN 978-1-5310-3060-5
eISBN 978-1-5310-3061-2

Carolina Academic Press
700 Kent Street
Durham, North Carolina 27701
(919) 489-7486
www.cap-press.com

Printed in the United States of America

Contents

Introduction

In 2015, the national legal history project, *Luminarias de la Ley | Luminaries of the Law*™ ("Luminarias Project") was created to identify the first Latina lawyers in the country from 1880 to 1980 ("Luminarias") and document their contributions to law and society. The *Luminarias Study* involved a retrospective record review of archived material of 167 law schools accredited by the American Bar Association (ABA) to produce the first baseline empirical data captured in *Luminarias: An Empirical Portrait of the First Generation of Latina Lawyers, 1880–1980* ("Luminarias Article").[1] The study found approximately 1,400 Latinas earned law degrees over the study period of 100 years, most during the decade of 1970–1980. The 1,200 Luminarias admitted to the bar were the first to enter most segments of the legal profession, as solo practitioners, law firm partners, corporate counsel, public interest and government attorneys, law professors. and, later in their careers, as the first Presidential Appointees requiring U.S. Senate confirmation (PAS).

Among the Luminarias are the first Latina jurists who served at each level of the judiciary, from justices of the peace to Associate Justice of the U.S. Supreme Court. The Luminarias study found 164 Latinas became jurists, each laying brick-by-brick the foundation upon which Justice Sonia Sotomayor ultimately would preside. Of the 1,200, 17 were/are Article III judges, and eight served as a state Supreme Court Justice or judge on a court of last resort.[2] Crafting law alongside them were Luminaria civil rights litigators.

The story of the first Latina Article III judges is the unrecorded history of women in the law. In 1789, the federal judicial system was created during the Constitutional Convention. One hundred forty-five years later, women began shaping law with the appointment of Florence Allen in 1934 to the Sixth Circuit Court of Appeals. It would be another 46 (or 191) years for Latinas to emboss their juridical mark.

Why, how or does the work of these Luminarias matter to Americans in their everyday lives? Few are aware that it was a Luminaria litigator-turned-administrator who interpreted Title IX as requiring equal opportunity for girls and women. Legally interpreted and taking hold on the country as equal funding, the resulting exponential rise of girls' and women's sports profoundly altered the country's social fabric and impacts the lives of Americans daily. It was a Luminaria judge who "saved baseball" by ending the national strike of 1995 and another who recognized the equal

1. UCLA Chicana/o Latina/o Law Review, 39:1, https://escholarship.org/uc/item/43f12635.
2. *Id.*, Table 9 at 66.

rights of LGBTQ Americans on the island of Puerto Rico. It was a Luminaria who successfully sought amendment of the Voting Rights Act of 1965 to ensure the rights of language-minorities—never recognized in federal voting law—and Luminarias who secured the right to an integrated public-school education for Latino children and fought for equal funding of their schools, impacting all children in low-wealth districts. Luminaria federal judges interpreted and applied immigration law that resonates today alongside fierce opinions issued by the sole Luminaria Supreme Court Justice. The import of their work and influence on U.S. jurisprudence and American society is worthy of examination. The current legal climate accentuates the durability of their decisions, and their legal reasoning, adopted years ago, is ever more relevant to today's issues.

Perhaps the passage of one hundred years was essential to developing and publishing the Luminaria story, a process akin to vinification. Mimicking the symmetry of winemaking, it took decades for Luminarias to cultivate their education, ferment their intellect, and harvest their legal skills before rising to the bench. As noted in the *Luminarias Article*,

> Being collectively unrecorded through the decades does not diminish their successes; to the contrary. The contributions of Luminarias irradiate through the ages because they were the first and succeeded during segregation and at the dawn of integration. Only when viewed through the lens of history does this properly contextualize the significance of their accomplishments.[3]

3. As originally published in the *Luminarias Article, supra* note 1 at 9.

Timeline of the First Luminaria Article III Judges and State Judges of Last Resort, 1980–2024

1972	Wayne County Circuit Court (Michigan): Dorothy Comstock Riley Puerto Rico Superior Court, Bayamón: Carmen Cerezo
1973	Puerto Rico Solicitor General: Miriam Naveira Merly
1975	Supreme Court of the United States (SCOTUS): Naveira Merly 1st Latina to Present Oral Argument
1976	Michigan State Court of Appeals: Dorothy Comstock Riley Puerto Rico Intermediate Court of Appeals: Carmen Cerezo SCOTUS: Vilma Martinez 2nd Latina to Present Oral Argument
1978	New York City Criminal Court: Carmen Beauchamp Ciparick
1979	Florida State District Court, Fifteenth Judicial Circuit: Rosemary Barkett
1980	Article III Judge, District of Puerto Rico: Carmen Cerezo
1981	New Mexico District Court, Santa Fe: Petra Jimenez Maes SCOTUS: Vanessa Ruiz 4th Latina to Present Oral Argument
1982	Michigan Supreme Court (appointed): Dorothy Comstock Riley, New York Supreme Court (elected): Carmen Beauchamp Ciparick
1983	Article III Judge, Southern District of Florida: Lenore Carrero Nesbitt
1984	Michigan Supreme Court (elected): Dorothy Comstock Riley Judge/Chief Judge, Florida Fourth District Court of Appeals: Rosemary Barkett
1985	Puerto Rico Supreme Court: Miriam Naveira Merly Florida Supreme Court: Rosemary Barkett
1987	Chief Justice, Michigan Supreme Court: Dorothy Comstock Riley
1991	San Diego Superior Court: Irma Gonzalez Philadelphia County Court of Common Pleas (elected): Nitza Quiñones Alejandro

1992	Article III Judge, Southern District of New York: Sonia Sotomayor Article III Judge, Central District of California: Lourdes Baird Article III Judge, Southern District of California: Irma Gonzalez Chief Justice, Florida Supreme Court: Rosemary Barkett Puerto Rico Court of Appeals: Liana Fiol Matta Connecticut State Court, New Britain: Carmen Espinosa
1993	Article III Judge, District of New Mexico: Martha Vazquez
1994	Article III Judge, Eleventh Circuit Court of Appeals: Rosemary Barkett Judge, District of Columbia Court of Appeals: Vanessa Ruiz Judge, New York Court of Appeals: Carmen Beauchamp Ciparick
1998	Article III Judge, Southern District of Texas: Hilda Tagle Article III Judge, Ninth Circuit Court of Appeals: Kim McLane Wardlaw Article III Judge, Second Circuit Court of Appeals: Sonia Sotomayor New Mexico Supreme Court (elected): Petra Jimenez Maes
2003	Chief Justice, New Mexico Supreme Court: Petra Jimenez Maes Chief Justice, Puerto Rico Supreme Court: Miriam Naveira Merly
2004	Article III Judge, Eastern District of New York: Dora Irizarry Article III Judge, Middle District of Florida: Virginia Hernandez Covington Puerto Rico Supreme Court: Liana Fiol Matta
2008	Article III Judge, District of Colorado: Christine Arguello
2009	Associate Justice, U.S. Supreme Court: Sonia Sotomayor
2011	Connecticut Court of Appeals: Carmen Espinosa
2012	Chief Justice, New Mexico Supreme Court: Petra Jimenez Maes
2013	Connecticut Supreme Court: Carmen Espinosa The Hague, Iran-U.S. Tribunal: Rosemary Barkett Article III Judge, Eastern District of Pennsylvania: Nitza Quiñones Alejandro
2014	Chief Justice, Puerto Rico Supreme Court: Liana Fiol Matta

Part One

Luminaria Activistas (Activists), 1973–2023

One

The Litigators, 1973–2023

This chapter explores the first Luminaria litigators and their crucial role in shaping the legal landscape for Mexican Americans, Latinas and the Latino community. Delving into the journeys of five trailblazing Latina litigators—Vilma Martinez, Antonia Hernández, Norma Cantú, Irma Herrera, and Deborah Escobedo—reveals their work in civil rights and social justice as activists—*activistas*,[1] who set legal precedents for the country. Their entrée into the courtroom created the optical of Latina litigators, who, in applying their extraordinary talent and novel legal theories, caused the profession to acclimate (some *albeit* grudgingly) to their presence. Collectively, their tenures, and those of other Luminaria litigators, paved the juridical road for Luminarias to ascend to the bench. Through examination of their formative years, the influence of racial and social consciousness on their careers, their major legal battles, and the lasting impact of their contributions, the legacy they created for future generations can now be installed into the historical indices of the legal profession.

A social justice propinquity fused the interests of the Luminaria activistas. They exemplify the 7% of Luminarias who served the country's public interest from the 1970s through 2023.[2] Except Martinez, all are members of the largest group of Luminarias to earn law degrees during the decade of 1970–1980, when admissions to law schools expanded with equal opportunity/affirmative action programs. In that one decade, the number of Luminarias admitted to the bar increased nearly fivefold from 300 in 1970 to 1,400 by 1980.[3]

Four of the five were Baby Boomers born by 1954 to working-class parents who raised them in the culturally rich Mexican American communities in California and Texas. Their racial and social consciousnesses were etched in segregated cities, notwithstanding these same cities consisted of a majority or significant percentage of Mexican Americans. Three were native Texans: Vilma Martinez grew up in San Antonio, Irma Herrera in Alice, Texas, and Norma Cantú in Brownsville, Texas. Antonia Hernández was born in Torreon, Mexico, to a U.S. citizen and grew up in East Los Angeles, while Deborah Escobedo was being raised in Lynwood, California. As

---

1. Irma Herrera describes herself as a social justice *activista*, which aptly and best describes these Luminarias. https://www.irmaherrera.com/.

2. Dolores S. Atencio, *Luminarias: An Empirical Portrait of the First Generation of Latina Lawyers*, 1880–1980, (Luminarias Article), UCLA Chicana/o Latina/o Law Review, 39:1, https://escholarship.org/uc/item/43f12635. Introduction, at 68.

3. *Id.*, Luminarias Article at 33.

first-generation law school graduates (most were also first-generation college graduates), they came of age during the turbulent domestic politics of the late 1960s and 1970s that propelled college activism by women and minority students. Their birthrights and earliest life experiences fertilized the activism, with Martinez being a prime example.

A. Vilma Martinez

1. Martinez's Formative Years

Vilma Martinez was born to Marina and Salvador Martinez, a construction worker, as the oldest of five siblings. Raised speaking Spanish, she grew up in a segregated world—having to sit in the back of the theatre and play at segregated parks, and enduring taunting for being Mexican American. Salvador predicated and vocalized a traditional future for his daughter though he introduced her to legendary attorney Alonso Perales[4] at the age of 15. Martinez knew then she would become a lawyer, having developed a strong and determined spirit nurtured by her mother. Dismissing her honors standing, high school counselors discouraged college, prompting Martinez to write to the University of Texas at Austin for information about college. Martinez was thereafter admitted and worked in the biochemistry lab, befriending a professor who encouraged her to apply to east coast law schools. Upon graduating in three years, she moved to the East Coast and earned her law degree in 1967 from Columbia Law.[5]

2. MALDEF and Martinez, 1973–1982

The social justice and quasi-legal organizations created by the Mexican American community during this period provided the Luminaria activistas opportunities to seek equality through litigation. Attorney Pete Tijerina[6] founded the Mexican American Legal Defense and Education Fund (MALDEF) in 1967 to secure equal rights for Mexican Americans. On August 1, 1968, MALDEF opened its doors in San Antonio and expanded into one of the nation's leading public interest organizations.[7] Mario

4. Michael A. Olivas (ed.), *In Defense of My People: Alonso S. Perales and the Development of Mexican-American Public Intellectuals* (Arte Publico Press, 2013).

5. Martinez's background was compiled from numerous sources, correspondence, and information from Martinez on file with author and other published sources.

6. MALDEF documents, M0673 (1967–1985), Dept. of Special Collections, Stanford University Libraries, Stanford, Calif. (MALDEF Archives), available at https://oac.cdlib.org/findaid/ark:/13030/tf9f59p0b2/entire_text/; Claudia Luther, *Pedro Tijerina, 80; Founder of the Civil Rights Group MALDEF*, Los Angeles Times, May 17, 2003, http://articles.latimes.com/2003/may/17/local/me-tijerina17.

7. MALDEF, https://www.maldef.org/history/; MALDEF: A Progress Report at 1, Record Group (hereafter "RG" are references to MALDEF Archives) 1, Box 47.

Obledo[8] was MALDEF's first general counsel. In 1970, MALDEF moved headquarters to San Francisco and opened regional offices in Washington, D.C., Albuquerque, Chicago, Denver, and Los Angeles, which became its permanent headquarters in 1986. MALDEF was established during the formative years of the Chicano movement, *El Movimiento* (the Movement). Started in the late 1960s, the Movement was rooted in universal principles of equity and through it, Mexican Americans—Chicanos, sought justice to overcome decades of oppression. It included the infamous farmworker strikes led by Cesar Chavez and Dolores Huerta through the United Farmworkers Union (1962). *La Alianza Federal de Mercedes* was created by Reies Lopez Tijerina in 1963 in New Mexico to address, *inter alia*, land grant rights. In 1966, the Brown Berets appeared in Los Angeles, and the Crusade for Justice was established in Denver by Corky Gonzales. *La Raza Unida* Party (the "united race" party) was started in 1970 by Jose Angel Gutierrez in Crystal City, Texas.[9] In the 1970s, the Movement exploded onto college campuses with the creation in 1969 of MEChA—*Movimiento Estudiantil Chicanos de Aztlan* (Student Movement Chicanos of Aztlan)—alongside the rise of feminism and infusion of Chicana[10] feminism into the Movement.[11] Amid this backdrop, Martinez became MALDEF's first female president and CEO in 1973 and the first Luminaria—at age 29—to lead a national public interest organization becoming, as history would have it, *la Madrina* (the Godmother).[12]

MALDEF was Martinez's second public interest job. From 1967 through 1970, she cut her teeth as a New York attorney for the Legal Defense and Education Fund of the National Association for the Advancement of Colored People (NAACP). Reflecting on her decision to become a litigator, Martinez stated,

> I became a litigator even though I was counseled that this was not a suitable job for a woman lawyer. It wasn't easy. It was important to find the right tone of voice in court. If you were perceived as too aggressive, the judge could take it out on the client. So, the key was to focus on the facts and the case and represent the client to the very best of our ability.[13]

---

8. Douglas Martin, *Mario Obledo, Hispanic Rights Leader, Dies at 78*, New York Times, August 20, 2010, https://www.nytimes.com/2010/08/21/us/21obledo.html.

9. *See, e.g.*, Rodolfo F. Acuña, *Occupied America: A History of Chicanos* (8th ed.); Mario T. Garcia (ed.), *The Chicano Movement: Perspectives from the Twenty-First Century* (Routledge Press, 2014).

10. The Merriam-Webster dictionary defines Chicana as an American woman or girl of Mexican descent, but the word is deeply rooted in the political activism of the Chicano movement of the late 1960s–1970s. "It is a proactive identifier with political implications." *See* Susana L. Gallardo, *Who Are Chicanas?* http://chicanas.com/.

11. In her 2008 article on MALDEF's Chicana Rights Project, Dr. Lori Flores captured the era into which Martinez stepped into as a newly minted Chicana lawyer, *A Community of Limits and the Limits of Community: MALDEF's Chicana Rights Project, Empowering The 'Typical Chicana' and the Question of Civil Rights*, Journal of American Ethnic History 27, no. 3 (Spring 2008):81.

12. Annette Oliviera, *MALDEF Diez Años* (MALDEF, 1978).

13. *Celebrating a History of Women Leaders at MALDEF*, MALDEF, March 27, 2021, at 2–3, https://www.maldef.org/2021/03/celebrating-a-history-of-women-leaders-at-maldef/.

Martinez was part of the legal team in *Griggs v. Duke Power Co.*, 401 U.S. 424 (1971), serving as attorney for the petitioner. In *Griggs*, the U.S. Supreme Court (or SCOTUS) unanimously adopted the disparate impact legal standard in Title VII employment cases, later codified in the Civil Rights Act of 1991. The Court held that a company's practices or policies could have a discriminatory effect, even if racial imbalance was not intended. In 1970, Martinez left the NAACP and became an equal opportunity counselor for the New York State Division of Human Rights, formulating new rules and procedures governing employee rights. That experience led to private practice in 1971 as a labor lawyer at Cahill, Gordon and Reindel. During this time, she joined MALDEF's Board of Directors alongside Luminaria Graciela Olivarez, the first woman and first Latina law graduate of Notre Dame Law School (J.D. 1970).[14] Two years later, Martinez became MALDEF's first female president and CEO and one of few female lawyers of color leading national litigation organizations. Immediately, Martinez was required to juggle management duties with significant legislative advocacy while tending to MALDEF litigation filed before her tenure. In that vein, Martinez became the second Latina attorney in 1976 to present argument before the Supreme Court.[15]

East Texas Motor Freight Sys. v. Rodriguez, 431 U.S. 395 (1977), dealt with class certification. The plaintiffs were three Mexican American city drivers who were denied transfers between terminals or to line driver jobs. Drivers were required to resign their jobs before they sought line driver positions. Seniority was established through separate collective bargaining agreements (CBAs), some of which ran only from the date an employee entered a particular CBA, discounting time spent in other jobs within the company. After being denied line driver jobs, the plaintiffs filed a Title VII claim with the Equal Employment Opportunity Commission (EEOC) and received right to sue letters.[16] Plaintiffs filed claims on behalf of all "Negroes and Mexican Americans who had been denied equal employment opportunities" and further asserted that the class should consist of all the employers' city drivers. Significantly, "the parties stipulated that before 1970, [employer East Texas Motor Freight] had never employed a black or Mexican American as a road driver in the Texas-Southern Conference area." *Rodriguez v. East Texas Motor Freight Sys.*, 505

14. Olivarez was the first Latina law professor on the mainland (1972–1975). Olivarez resume, May 14, 1973, Letter informing Olivarez of second Board term, RG 1, Folder 11, Former Director Files, Box 47: Folder 11.

15. Maria G. Mendoza, *The Fifteen Known Latina Advocates Before the Supreme Court of the United States*, *SSRN* (April 3, 2011), https://ssrn.com/abstract=1802008.

16. Title VII, 42 U.S.C. § 2000e-5(e), Act of July 2, 1964, Pub. L. 88-352 § 701, 78 Stat. 253, Codified at 42 U.S.C. §§ 2000e–2000e-17; § 2000e-2 states, (a) "It shall be an unlawful employment practice for an employer (1) to fail or refuse to hire or to discharge any individual or otherwise to discriminate against any individual with respect to his compensation, terms, conditions, or privileges of employment, because of such individual's race, color, religion, sex or national origin; or (2) to limit, segregate, or classify his employees or applicants for employment in any way which would deprive or tend to deprive any individual of employment opportunities or otherwise adversely affect his status as an employee, because of such individuals' race, color, religion, sex, or national origin." Plaintiffs also filed a claim under 42 U.S.C. § 1981.

F.2d 40, 48 (5th Cir. 1974) (Obledo then representing MALDEF). The trial court dismissed their suit after trial, concluding plaintiffs did not qualify as line road drivers and did not file the requisite motion to certify the class pursuant to Federal Rule of Civil Procedure 23(c)(1)[17]. The Fifth Circuit Court of Appeals reversed, ruling that the trial court had an independent obligation to determine whether certification was proper. With the full proceedings before them, the Fifth Circuit held the plaintiffs met the requirements of Rule 23(a) and established a proper class action. East Texas Motor Freight appealed to the Supreme Court, which Martinez argued as MALDEF's counsel. The Court reversed the Fifth Circuit's decision holding the Fifth Circuit erred in certifying the class and further ruled by the time of trial, the plaintiffs were not proper class representatives. The question whether a Court of Appeals should certify a class in the first instance remained open. *Rodriguez*, 505 F.2d at 403.

3. 1975 Amendments to the Voting Rights Act of 1965

With the impending reauthorization of the Voting Rights Act of 1965 (VRA), Martinez turned her attention to the voting rights of Mexican Americans in the Southwest. Martinez paid her NAACP experience forward. Under Martinez's leadership, MALDEF secured expansion of federal voting rights through the 1975 Amendments to include, for the first time, "language minorities," a term coined by Martinez that included all persons with none or limited English proficiency that prevented them from voting because they could not read English-only ballots. The amendments proposed by MALDEF extended beyond the rights of Spanish speakers/Mexican Americans to others, such as the Asian community—a strategy that revealed the depth of her political perspicacity.[18] Numerous voting rights cases and the cultural climate of the time ripened the cause for change. A pivotal case was litigated just prior to the beginning of Martinez's tenure that impacted decisions during her tenure. MALDEF had filed suit against the state of Texas and won its first major voting rights case in *White v. Regester*, 412 U.S. 755 (decided June 18, 1973, oral argument on February 26). MALDEF challenged the Texas 1970 House reapportionment plan because: (1) it contained constitutionally infirm deviations from population equality, and (2) the multimember districts drawn for Bexar and Dallas counties invidiously discriminated against racial and ethnic communities. The Supreme Court upheld the lower court ruling finding multimember voting districts were discriminatory and ordered they be redrawn so that Latinos and African Americans had the ability to elect their own representatives. By 1974, the VRA was up for renewal. MALDEF was contacted for assistance in extending the act to the Southwest

---

17. Rule 23(a) provides "(a) Prerequisites to a Class Action. One or more members of a class may sue or be sued as representative parties on behalf of all only if (1) the class is so numerous that joinder of all members is impracticable, (2) there are questions of law or fact common to the class, (3) the claims or defenses of the representative parties are typical of the claims or defenses of the class, and (4) the representative parties will fairly and adequately protect the interests of the class."

18. Public L. No. 94-73 amending the Voting Rights Act, 42 U.S.C.A. §§ 1973 to 1973bb-1 (Supp., Oct. 1975).

to diffuse and turn the tide on initiatives designed to disenfranchise (principally) Mexican American voters.

MALDEF attorney Albelardo I. Perez was working in the Washington, D.C. office when contacted by the U.S. Commission on Civil Rights seeking MALDEF's assistance in extending the VRA into the Southwest, specifically Arizona, California, New Mexico, and Texas.[19] Perez took the idea to Martinez who created a Voting Rights Task Force, designating Perez as lead. He gathered statistical data in California, Colorado, and Texas on voter discrimination of Spanish-speaking persons. As the U.S. Census Bureau did not officially recognize "Hispanics" until 1980, there was no data on Mexican Americans, but data gathered on Spanish-speaking residents was used to buttress MALDEF's case of voter dilution.[20] Initially, the African American community was concerned that the amendments proposed by MALDEF would dilute their rights under the VRA. MALDEF worked to convince them that the legislation's extension in the Southwest would increase—not dilute—their rights. MALDEF sought amendments to the VRA, specifically Section 4 to include that the states had a "test or device" to exclude Mexican Americans from voting and Section 5 to expand its jurisdiction to include the Southwest.

On July 24, 1975, Congress extended voting rights protections to language minorities (for seven years to 1982) adopting MALDEF's proposed changes:

> SEC. 203. Section 4 of the Voting Rights Act of 1965 is amended by adding the following new subsection: "(f)(1) The Congress finds that voting discrimination against citizens of language minorities is pervasive and national in scope. Such minority citizens are from environments in which the dominant language is other than English. In addition, they have been denied equal educational opportunities by State and local governments, resulting in severe disabilities and continuing illiteracy in the English language. The Congress further finds that, where State and local officials conduct elections only in English, language minority citizens are excluded from participating in the electoral process. In many areas of the country, this exclusion is aggravated by acts of physical, economic, and political intimidation. The Congress declares that, in order to enforce the guarantees of the fourteenth and fifteenth amendments to the United States Constitution, it is necessary to eliminate such discrimination by prohibiting English-only elections, and by prescribing other remedial devices."

The law defined language minority to include persons who are American Indian, Asian American, Alaskan Natives, or persons of Spanish heritage. Jurisdiction was

19. Voces, *Albelardo I. Perez*, University of Texas at Austin, Voces Oral History Center (Voces), https://voces.moody.utexas.edu/collections/stories/albelardo-i-perez.

20. *Supra*, note 2, Luminarias Article at 17–21, discussion on U.S. Census Bureau pertains to data on Hispanics.

expanded to include Alaska, Arizona, Texas, and South Dakota, and parts of California, Florida, and New York, among others.[21] Section 203(e) imposed a permanent nationwide ban on literacy tests and other mechanisms as prerequisites to registration and voting. Section 203(b) and (c) enacted a bilingual election requirement to provide ballots and voting information in the language of the language minority group and prohibited state and local governments from enacting any voting procedure designed to deny or abridge the voting rights of any citizen because s/he is a member of a language minority group. Section 203(f)(3) established procedures to determine if a jurisdiction employs such tests or devices. Originally set to expire after 10 years, Congress reauthorized Section 203 in 1982, expanded and reauthorized the section in 1992 for 15 years, and reauthorized it again in 2006 for 25 years.[22]

4. The Chicana Rights Project, 1974–1982

In 1974, Martinez created the Chicana Rights Project (CRP or the Project)—the first national legal project orchestrated to address the rights of Mexican American women in education, employment, health care, and housing.[23] In June 1974, Martinez hired the first CRP attorneys to implement her vision. Luminaria Patricia Vasquez was hired director, coordinating the Project from San Antonio (1974–1979), while Carmen A. Estrada worked in San Francisco (1978–1980). When Vasquez resigned, Estrada became director (1979–1980), and Luminaria Norma Solis was hired as staff attorney in MALDEF's San Antonio office. Estrada was succeeded by Luminaria Virginia Martinez (1980–1983).[24]

The Project was organized into three sections, research, community education, and litigation.

> (1) Disseminating civil rights *information* more broadly among women... especially crucial because many guarantees of equal opportunity and treatment in employment, education, day care and other important areas remain unknown to many Chicanas....

---

21. 42 U.S.C. § 1973(b), amended Pub. L. 94-73, title II, § 206, Aug. 6, 1975, 89 Stat. 402; Pub. L. 97-205, § 3, June 29, 1982, 96 Stat. 134.

22. *See Shelby County v. Holder*, 570 U.S. 529 (2013), ruling unconstitutional Congress's decision to reauthorize the preexisting coverage formula of Section 4(b) to determine which jurisdictions are subject to the preclearance requirement of Section 5, and violated the Fifteenth and Tenth Amendments and Article IV of the U.S. Constitution.

23. The Equal Rights Advocate which Herrera later led, was addressing the legal rights of Latinas through its Women of Color Project. *See* Judy Scales-Trent, *Equal Rights Advocates: Addressing the Legal Issues of Women of Color*, Berkeley Women's L.J. 13 (1998): 34–80 (hereafter ERA Article), https://digitalcommons.law.buffalo.edu/journal_articles/853.

24. Luminarias Study, research on the careers of Luminarias on file with the author: Vasquez J.D. 1972 Washington College, Adm. 1973 District of Columbia; Estrada J.D. 1977 UC-Hastings, Adm. 1977 California; Solis J.D. 1979 Houston Law Adm. 1978 Texas; Martinez, J.D. 1975 DePaul Law-Chicago, Adm. 1975 Illinois.

(2) Identifying specific practices which most unfairly burden Chicanas and increase the number of potential claimants; and

(3) Formulating a litigation strategy on the basis of information complied by the [CRP].[25]

CRP compiled U.S. Census data on Mexican American women, specifically in education and employment, but encountered difficulty in obtaining the data as it did not exist.[26] Similarly, the Luminarias Study required original research to ascertain the number of Latina lawyers in the country between 1880 and 1980 because law schools did not record the ethnicity of law students. Further complicating the research for CRP and the Luminarias Study, the U.S. Bureau of the Census did not add "Hispanic" to the census until 1980. CRP was required to cull data taken on Spanish-speaking women.

From this statistical composite, CRP created a profile of "a low-income, disempowered woman who nonetheless possessed the potential to discover her feminist identity and fight for her legal rights ... the 'typical Chicana.'"[27] Vasquez masterfully spun the statistical analysis into a tangible litigation blueprint that supported CRP's decision to focus on undereducated and underemployed Chicanas as its target clientele. Research became a vital tool to educate from within—Chicanas and the Chicano community—and outwardly, to generate funding from donors, compel the public and legislators to effectuate public policy change, and gather data to support and plan litigation. In litigation, CRP prioritized education and employment in the states of California and Texas, relying on the Equal Pay Act of 1963,[28] Title VII,[29] Title IX of the Education Act of 1972,[30] and the Comprehensive Employment Training Act (CETA).[31] CRP initially pursued individual civil service cases (due to client demand) and worked to obtain federal administrative action that, in many cases,

25. Patricia M. Vasquez, *Establishing Litigation Priorities to Secure Chicana Rights*, UCLA Chicana/o Latina/o L. Rev. (1976) at 38–39, https://escholarship.org/uc/item/9nv5820m.

26. CRP May 1975 Proposal to The Ford Foundation at 1, fn. 1, RG #4, Box 71: Folder 8. The lack of data on Latinas (and Latinos) is a recurring theme and one the author experienced in identifying the first Latina lawyers; *supra*, note 2, Luminarias Article, Introduction, at 18, 43–46,

27. CRP Brochure, RG #5, Box 57: Folder 1.

28. The Equal Pay Act of 1963, 29 U.S.C. § 206(d)(1), was promulgated "[t]o prohibit discrimination on account of sex in the payment of wages by employers engaged in commerce or in the production of goods for commerce."

29. *Supra* note 16, Title VII.

30. Title IX, Act of June 1972, Act Pub. L. 92-318, Title IX, § 901, June 23, 2972, 86 Stat. 372, 20 USC §1681, *et seq*., 34 CFR Part 106.

31. CETA, Act of Dec. 28, 1973, Pub. L. 93-202 § 2, 87 Sta. 839, codified at 29 U.S. § 800 *et. seq.*; amended Pub. L. 93-567, 88 Stat. 1845 (December 31, 1974). Section 848(f) provides: "The Secretary shall not provide financial assistance for any program under this subchapter unless the grant, contract, or agreement with respect thereto specifically provides that no person with responsibilities in the operation of such program will discriminate with respect to any program participant or any applicant for participation in such program because of race, creed, color, national origin, sex, political affiliation, or beliefs." *Supra* note 20 at 48–63.

was quicker than prolonged litigation. This approach was taken not only to comply with the federal mandate to exhaust administrative remedies, but also to develop and build administrative records of systemic patterns of discrimination that were reviewable by courts.

5. Select Chicana Rights Project Successes

In the nine years of its existence, CRP achieved remarkable success. The Project conducted original research to compose a statistical profile that formed and supported its legal strategy and litigation. Starting in 1975 and continuing through 1980, CRP produced 10 educational monographs that included one of the first bilingual guides for Chicanas on federal and state laws, Texas Women's Legal Rights Handbook and Chicana Legal Rights Handbook. Other pamphlets included Profile of the Chicana, A Statistical Fact Sheet (1975, 1978); Chicanas: Women's Health Issues (1978), on abortion and sterilization abuse; CETA: An Economic Tool for Women (1979); Chicanas and Mental Health (1979), which dealt with cultural sensitivity in mental health practices; Hispanic Women: Immigration Issues (1979) on the preference system, deportation hearings, voluntary departures, and immigrant rights; Hispanic/Women's Employment Rights (1980) addressing employment issues; and The 1980 Census: Impact on Hispanics and Women.[32] Concurrently, CRP built a national network and clearinghouse that by 1981 included "70 Chicana organizations, 77 legal and women's groups and coalitions, 71 prominent individuals."[33]

CRP filed administrative cases of first impression, employing unique litigation strategies to secure and expand the rights of Mexican American women.[34] It achieved results, even in cases where it did not prevail on the merits. From 1976 through 1981, CRP initiated administrative complaints, filed individual or class actions suits and provided legal assistance in approximately 100 cases, primarily in California and Texas. Amicus curiae briefs were filed in significant lawsuits including *Fernandez v. Wynn Oil Co.*, 653 F.2d 1273 (1981), a sex discrimination case that challenged whether the employer's preference of hiring male vice presidents, because South American clients preferred working with males over females, constituted a bona fide occupational qualification; and *Deans & Directors et al. v. California Board of Registered Nursing*, No. SF/81/6 (Cal. Sup. Ct., S.F. 1981), filed with the Asian Law Caucus. CRP joined the American Civil Liberties Union and Mexican American Equal Rights Project to conduct a Texas Grand Jury Study from 1959 to 1974, analyzing 88 grand juries, that established the gross exclusion of Chicanas. Significantly the study established Mexican Americans comprised less than 1% of all grand jurors though they

32. March 30, 1981, Memo from Virginia Martinez (V. Martinez Memo) at 2-3, RG #4, Box 125: Folder 1 at 6-7; CRP Brochures, RG #5, Box 57: Folders 1, 5, 10.

33. *Id.* V. Martinez Memo at 3.

34. January 10, 1977, Memo from Vasquez to Vilma Martinez *et al.*, RG #4, Box 71, Folder 1.

constituted 25% of the total population.[35] The Project's litigation advocacy extended the rights of working Chicanas. For example, in *Lee v. State Board of Education*, No. 716-916 (S.F. Sup.Ct. N., 1974), CRP successfully sought to enjoin implementation of statewide regulations governing the eligibility for publicly subsidized day care services that were adopted without public hearings. Regardless of their income, the regulations would have substantially excluded two-parent families and have a disparate impact on Chicanas. A temporary restraining order (TRO) was granted, and at defendants' request, the TRO was continued to allow the regulations to expire. The state abandoned any plans to readopt the more restrictive regulations.

a. Significant CRP Cases: Employment

The strategic plan to pursue equal rights for Chicanas propelled the Project to initiate litigation in the traditional occupations and by filing Title VII discrimination cases. Starting with the national "manpower" program (as it was then called), CETA was created in 1973 to provide job training and employment opportunities for economically disadvantaged, unemployed, and underemployed persons.[36] Starting in February 1976, CRP began monitoring CETA services to Mexican women in San Antonio. CPR filed *Hernández, et al. v. Cockrell*, et. al., No. SA-76-10 (1976), against CETA alleging gender discrimination. On March 12, 1979, CRP entered into a consent agreement that produced a 30% increase in the number of women and minority members in the San Antonio program. CRP conducted analyses of 29 CETA prime sponsor programs throughout the United States, establishing that it was underserving Hispanics and women. "The Secretary of Labor, Ray Marshall, concurred with many of MALDEF's recommendations and took action to recruit more women and minorities . . . in 11 geographical areas containing large concentrations of Hispanics, including: Los Angeles, San Francisco, Sacramento, Dallas, Houston, Fort Worth, Chicago and Toledo." CETA programs were restructured to designate women as a priority group.[37] The litigation continued due to ongoing discrimination of CETA training and nontraditional jobs to women and Chicanas.[38] *CRP v. Secretary of Labor* (CETA Project), No. SF/80/5 (1976).

In the class action lawsuit *Montejo, et al. v. Texas Employment Commission* (TEC), No. SA/76/1 (W.D. Tex. 1976), CRP sought to enjoin TEC under Title VII from denying unemployment benefits and referral services to pregnant women after their sixth month of pregnancy until six weeks after birth. TEC changed its policy in April 1975, but suit was filed as it continued to discriminate against pregnant women. Upon complaint by a Chicana bank employee, the Project consulted with the U.S.

---

35. MALDEF CRP Year End Report, May 1, 1975, RG #4, Box 71: Folder 6 at 9.

36. CETA was replaced with the Job Training Partnership Act of 1982, 29 U.S.C. § 1501 *et seq.*

37. March 1, 1978, Docket Update SA/10 from Rebecca Garcia to Tyler Kelly, RG #5, Box 16: Folder 1.

38. April 24, 1976, Memo from Vasquez to MALDEF Board, RG #2, Box 28: Folder 4; *supra* note 33 at 4–5.

Department of Treasury's Equal Employment Office (EEO). CRP obtained EEO forms, affirmative action plans, and other relevant documentation on five of the largest banks in the San Antonio area. The documents showed the underemployment of Chicanas in low-paying jobs and the absence of Chicanas in higher-paying positions in a city population comprised of more than 50% Mexican Americans. CRP filed a complaint against the five banks with the U.S. Department of Labor's Office of Contract Compliance alleging noncompliance with Executive Order 11246—Equal Employment Opportunity (Sept. 24, 1965) that prohibits sex and race discrimination by federal contractors.[39] CRP obtained compliance reviews and desk audits of the banks to assure equal employment opportunities for Chicanas.

The Project also filed actions to secure opportunities for Chicanas in nontraditional jobs. *Lopez v. Crosland*, No. SF/79/18 (S.D. Cal. 1979), was a class action employment discrimination complaint filed against the Immigration and Naturalization Service (INS) alleging it failed to hire Hispanic women by imposing a pretextual agility test. Applicants were required to scale an eight-foot-high wall. Out of a border patrol force of 2,045, 18 were women and only 4 were Mexican American. The INS eliminated the climbing test, and the women excluded by the test were given an opportunity to become border patrol agents.[40] In *Wickenhoefer v. Golden Gate Transit District*, No. SF/80/6 (N.D. Cal. 1980), CRP filed a class action suit on behalf of Hispanic women that alleged the Transit District discriminated in hiring bus operators based on sex and national origin. At the time, Hispanic women comprised less than 1% of all bus operators. Shortly after the suit was filed, Wickenhoefer (a Chicana) was hired as a bus operator and a consent decree was entered into by the parties that impacted California's Sonoma and Marin counties.[41] *Montano v. New Mexico Joint Apprenticeship Training Committee* (NM JATC), No. SA/80/16 (D.N.M. 1980), was a statewide class action challenge seeking easier access for Chicanas to one of the three electrical apprenticeship programs in New Mexico. Of 226 apprentices, only four were women and one of those four Chicana. At the time, women comprised 4.9% of the state's electrical apprentices. The plaintiff, Elaine Montano, scored in the "mid-to-high levels" on the required aptitude exam and underwent a "5-minute interview focused almost exclusively on her personal life: whether she planned to have more children, her husband's feelings about her job, etc."[42] The National Apprenticeship Act of 1937 (NAA) was created by Executive Order 10925 "to provide for more uniform training of apprentices and to promote equal opportunity in apprenticeship." The Department of Labor was charged with adopting and imple-

---

39. 30 FR 12319, 12935, 3 CFR, 1964–1965.

40. November 30, 1981, Memo from Virginia Martinez at 5, RG #4, Box 125: Folder 1.

41. *Id.*

42. November 19, 1980, press release, MALDEF CHARGES SEX DISCRIMINATION Files Lawsuit Against State Apprenticeship Program," RG #4, Box 125: Folder 1.

menting regulations to achieve the purpose of the NAA.[43] In 1978, the regulations were amended to require inclusion of female apprentices in NAA affirmative action plans.[44] Estrada said "[MALDEF] decided to take the case because... 22 Hispanic women have been rejected from the electrical apprenticeship program in the past year."[45] The law suit was filed upon issuance of a probable cause letter by both the New Mexico Human Rights Commission and EEOC.

b. Significant CRP Cases: Health Care

In a strategic plan that involved advocacy, networking, and litigation, the Project elevated a health care issue involving family planning services that disproportionately impacted Chicanas[46] The Informed Consent Program addressed the rights of Chicanas in cases of reproductive rights, especially non-English speakers, which were being violated. In May 1975, CRP joined other women's legal and medical organizations and filed petitions with the California Department of Health to ensure informed consent for sterilizations and greater accessibility to birth control information.[47] CRP filed lawsuits in California and Texas to challenge sterilization abuses and cutbacks in health services, for example, as intervenors in *California Medical Association v. Lackner*, No. 78-2 (Cal. Ct. Appls., 1978), to enjoin the California Department of Health Services from implementing sterilization regulations. In *Madrigal v. Quilligan*, No. CV-75-2057-EC (C.D. Cal., June 7, 1978), *aff'd*, 639 F.2d 789 (9th Cir. 1978), [48] CRP joined Hernández at the Center for Law and Justice as co-counsel in a landmark health care sterilization case. Despite losing on the merits, the hospital created bilingual consent forms and enforced a 72-hour waiting period before performing operations. *See discussion infra*, Hernández. CRP secured the right to affordable prenatal and general heath care for low-income and immigrant pregnant women in *County Health Alliance v. Board of Supervisors*, No. LA/81 (Cal. Sup. Ct., 1981). An administrative complaint was filed with the U.S. Department of Health and Human Services upon refusal by a public hospital to admit low-income Chicanas. In *MALDEF v. Madera County Hospital*, No. SF/79/9 (1979), the Project secured obstetric and maternity services for indigent women.

From inception of their efforts, Martinez and the CRP went on record in support of Chicanas' right to choose, which was a tough political stance among the largely Catholic and traditional Mexican American community. Women's reproductive freedom was placed in controversy by federal and state congressional leaders (pri-

---

43. Sec. 1, 50 Stat. 664, as amended, 29 U.S.C. 50; 40 U.S.C. 276c; 5 U.S.C. 301), parts 29 and 30 (Dec. 18, 1963).

44. 43 FR 20760, May 12, 1978.

45. Arley Sanchez, *Woman Plans Fight for Job*, Albuquerque Journal, November 21, 1980.

46. April 1976 CRP Report to the Ford Foundation, RG #4, Box 19 and Box 72: Folder 7 and *supra* note 44 at 5–6.

47. April 1976 CRP Report to The Ford Foundation, RG #4, Box 19 and Box 72: Folder 7.

48. Former MALDEF President Mario Obledo was a named defendant in his capacity as the California Secretary of Health.

marily male). Passed in September 1976, the Hyde Amendment prohibited the use of federal funding, including Medicare and Medicaid, to pay for abortions. It passed on a vetoed vote overriding the funding bill for the Department of Health, Education, and Welfare (HEW).[49] In the California Budget Act of 1978, the state legislature restricted Medi-Cal funding for abortions for victims of rape, including statutory rape, incest, pregnancies that threatened the life of the mother, and pregnancies that would result in severe physical and/or abnormal health of the child. The Department of Health estimated that the restrictions would cause a decrease in "Medi-Cal abortions by 95%, from an estimated 70,000 per year to only 3,500 per year." Martinez wrote to President Carter who supported the Hyde Amendment, urging him to reconsider on behalf of Chicanas who received Medi-Cal funded abortions[50]:

> Since the Supreme Court decided in *Roe v. Wade* that the decision to have an abortion is a determination to be made by the pregnant woman and her doctor, the recent Congressional action, which apparently you approve, will result in denying poor pregnant women the ability to make this choice. The action will have a significant impact on Mexican American women since in 1975 the median income... was $2,750.... Forcing poor women to continue unwanted pregnancies while those women financially able to do so [will] have a judicially recognized right to terminate such pregnancies, is grossly unfair. It is true, as you have stated, that many things in life are not fair.... However, to perpetuate unfairness in a situation which so easily can be made fair demonstrates a lack of concern for the interest of the welfare of all.... The constitutionally recognized right of privacy requires this decision to be hers alone.[51]

Joining the American Civil Liberties Union (ACLU), Equal Rights Advocates, and the Youth Law Center, CRP filed a writ of mandamus and brief in support of state-funded abortions in *Comisíon Feminil v. Cory*, No. SF/78/2, (Cal. Ct. Appls., 1978). In 1980, SCOTUS announced *Williams v. Zbaraz*, 488 U.S. 358 (1980), ruling that states had the right to promulgate their own versions of the Hyde Amendment. The CRP filed an amicus brief in this case. In *Committee to Defend Reproductive Rights v. Myers*, 29 Cal. 3d 256 (1981), CRP joined the ACLU and the Youth Law Center to successfully challenge the constitutionality of state legislation prohibiting state-funded abortions, on the heels of the Supreme Court's decision in *McRae v. Matthews*, 448 U.S. 297 (1980). In *McRae*, the SCOTUS considered the constitutionality of the Hyde Amendment and held that states participating in Medicaid under Title XIX of the Social Security Act[52] were not required to fund medically necessary abortions. It concluded the plaintiffs did not constitute a suspect class based on their

---

49. Pub.L. 105-119, § 617, Nov. 26, 1997, 111. Stat. 2519, 18 U.S.C. § 3006A.

50. July 19, 1978, MALDEF Litigation Memo by Estrada to Martinez, Vasquez and Mike Baller, RG #5, Box 57:16.

51. *Id.*, August 22, 1977, Letter from Martinez to President Jimmy Carter.

52. 42 U.S.C. § 1396 *et seq.* (1976 Ed. and Supp. II).

poverty and ruled that the Hyde Amendment did not violate their constitutional rights. In 1980, the Hyde Amendment was amended to include an exception for Medicaid funding where the life of the mother was endangered and remained substantially the same from 1981 to 1993.[53] In *Myers*, the California Supreme Court decided that *McRae* did not resolve their issue—the "much narrower question of whether the state, having enacted a general program to provide medical services to the poor, may selectively withhold such benefits from otherwise qualified persons solely because such persons seek to exercise their constitutional right of procreative choice in a manner which the state does not favor and does not wish to support." *Myers*, 29 Cal. 3d at 257. At the outset, the Court determined the majority in *McRae* differed "substantially from the analysis mandated by the controlling California authorities" and could not be followed in the instant case. *Myers*, 29 Cal. 3d at 258. In applying the three-prong test, the Court held that restricting state-funded abortions on poor women's right of procreative choice bore "no relation whatsoever" to the purpose of the Medi-Cal program. "Any attempt to reconcile Medi-Cal objectives with abortion limitations on the theory that the latter protect the fetus, however, impermissibly denigrates the woman's right of choice." *Myers*, 29 Cal. 3d at 274. Citing as authority *Roe v. Wade*, 410 U.S. 113 (1973), the Court reasoned the state failed to establish the proper balancing of protecting the state's interest in first and second trimester abortions ("protection of a nonviable fetus is not a state interest") resulting in a manifest impairment on the constitutional right to reproductive rights; nor did the state prove the unavailability of less offensive alternatives. The Court noted the legislative history "belied the state's proffer that the legislation was aimed at aiding poor women who had already chosen to bear a child, declaring it was all the more invidious for depriving poor women that which is guaranteed to rich women." *Myers*, 29 Cal. 3d at 286.

6. MALDEF Luminaria Litigators: Education, Civil Rights, and Employment

CRP's litigation was, at times, tried by MALDEF attorneys who were hired by Martinez. During her tenure, Martinez hired three Luminaria activistas (non-CRP attorneys) who litigated or directed litigation from 1979 to 2004, including the second female MALDEF leader, Antonia Hernández. Four of the Luminaria activistas worked for MALDEF with overlapping tenures:

Martinez	1973–1982
Norma Cantú	1979–1993
Irma Herrera	1980–1983
Antonia Hernández	1981–2004

53. Pub.L. 103-112, 107 Stat. 1082 (1993); Pub.L. 96-123, § 109, 93 Stat. 926 (1976).

Martinez and Antonia Hernández led MALDEF for a combined 28 years of its 55-year history.[54] Irma Herrera and Deborah Escobedo worked together for four years, from 1991 to 1995, at Multicultural Education, Training, and Advocacy (META). Escobedo was co-counsel and/or in partnership with MALDEF on cases and initiatives. The work of the activistas started before the first Luminarias were appointed judges to courts of last resort and the federal bench.

Starting with Martinez, education, civil rights, and employment became the razor-sharp focus—the strategic litigation fields of choice for the Luminaria activistas. Martinez was lead and co-counsel in two landmark education cases that changed American society and the lives of Mexican Americans and other communities of color: *Serna v. Portales Municipal Schools*, 499 F.2d 1147 (10th Cir. 1974), and *Plyler v. Doe*, 457 U.S. 202 (1982). *Portales* established the right to a bilingual education for non–English-speaking students. In 1972, Romana Serna filed the lawsuit on behalf of her daughter Judy, who attended the majority-white school district that had a significant Spanish-speaking student population. At the time of the suit, there were no teachers or other staff at any of the district's public schools who were Spanish surnamed, spoke Spanish, or could teach in Spanish, though 34% of the students in the district's four elementary schools were Spanish speakers, as were 29% of the junior high schools and 17% at senior high schools. The trial court's ruling in favor of the plaintiffs was affirmed in *Serna v. Portales Municipal Schools*, 351 F. Supp. 1279 (1972). While on appeal, *Lau v. Nichols*, 414 U.S. 563 (1974), was issued—a decision that expanded the language rights of public-school children. In 1971, San Francisco integrated their school system that included nearly 3,000 students of Chinese ancestry who were not proficient in English; classes were taught exclusively in English. SCOTUS held that the failure to provide supplemental English classes constituted an unequal and unconstitutional educational opportunity in violation of the Fourteenth Amendment and the Civil Rights Act of 1964. The *Lau* case mandated schools, not students, to bear the responsibility of addressing the students' language needs; bilingual education was a mere suggestion. The *Serna* case made explicit the right of minority language students to be taught at school not only in English, but in their home languages as well. In addition, the case affirmed the students' right to a culturally relevant curriculum and to have competent adults—teachers, administrators, and other school staff—whose cultural and linguistic identities reflected those of the schools' minority students. The ruling was enforceable in all states within the Tenth Circuit: Colorado, Kansas, New Mexico, Oklahoma, Utah, and Wyoming.

Plyler v. Doe, *supra*, was MALDEF's federal challenge that resulted in the Supreme Court decision guaranteeing a free K–12 public education to all children in Texas, regardless of immigrant status. At the time, James Plyler was superintendent of Tyler Independent School District (Tyler ISD). The "Doe" plaintiffs were siblings from the same family, some born in the United States, who did not have to pay tuition and

---

54. *Supra* note 12, *MALDEF Diez Años* at 2.

others undocumented who had to pay.[55] In 1977, Tyler ISD began assessing a $1,000 tuition fee to each child attending district schools who failed to provide documentation of U.S. citizenship based on the 1975 law, Section 21.031 of the Texas Education Code. The section permitted public school districts to deny admission or charge tuition to undocumented schoolchildren, making free public education accessible only to children residing legally within the state's borders. According to the state, undocumented children were not "within the jurisdiction" of the state and thus they were disqualified from public education. Tyler ISD concluded the charging of fees simultaneously saved money for the schools and discouraged illegal immigration. Martinez led the legal challenges to the Texas law by filing a class action lawsuit on November 11, 1981, requesting injunctive relief that was temporarily granted. Federal Judge William Wayne Justice rejected the state's rationale and declared Section 21.031 unconstitutional. Tyler ISD appealed to the Fifth Circuit which reaffirmed the lower court's decision by finding the imposition of fees violated the Equal Protection Clause of the Fourteen Amendment. Tyler ISD appealed to the Supreme Court. On June 15, 1982, the Supreme Court struck down the Texas law as unconstitutional. A divided SCOTUS (5–4) ruled all children—regardless of their citizenship—were entitled to free public education under the Equal Protection Clause of the Fourteenth Amendment. Writing for the majority, Justice Harry Brennan found Texas's rationale of denying or charging admission to undocumented children unpersuasive, writing, "By denying these children a basic education, we deny them the ability to live within the structure of our civic institutions and foreclose any realistic possibility that they will contribute in even the smallest way to the progress of our Nation." *Plyler v. Doe*, 457 U.S. at 223. The Court held states could not deprive children of a publicly funded education, request citizenship papers, or hold children liable for their parents' relocation into the country without the proper documentation. Later, California would attempt to overturn the effect of the decision by a state constitutional amendment known as Proposition 187 (*see discussion infra*). MALDEF's litigation in education, civil rights, and employment was expanded by the Luminaria activistas who proffered new legal theories on behalf of the Mexican American communities, which impacted other communities of color.

---

55. Texas State Historical Association (TSHA), Michael Olivas, *Plyler v. Doe*, https://www.tshaonline.org/handbook/entries/plylervdoe#:~:text=Peter%20Roos%2C%20MALDEF's%20national%20director, origin%20persons%20in%20subordinate%20status.

B. Antonia Hernández

1. Hernández's Formative Years

"[She] went to law school for one reason: to use the law for social change."[56] Antonia was born in Torreon, Mexico, to Manuel and Nicolasa Hernández, the oldest of seven children.[57] Her father, a U.S. citizen born in Mexico, and grandparents were forced to relocate to Mexico during the Mexican Repatriation of the Great Depression,[58] when her father was eight. En route, Antonia's grandfather passed. The Hernández family returned to the United States in May 1956 when Antonia was eight. They lived in the Maravilla Housing Projects of East Los Angeles. Antonia started school at Reagan Elementary School with little English proficiency but excelled in her classes under the guidance of teachers who recognized her potential. To help with family finances, Antonia worked alongside her father and helped her mother selling tamales. She later worked at a local produce and grocery market, the money she earned going toward the family's down payment for a home.

Through affirmative action programs, Hernández was admitted to and graduated from UCLA, earning both her undergraduate and law degrees. In 1974, she launched her public interest legal career as staff attorney at the Los Angeles Center for Law and Justice. Some four years later, Hernández and Charles Nabarrete co-counseled the health care sterilization case, *Madrigal v. Quilligan et al., supra.*[59] A whistleblower alleged doctors at USC Hospital, some who held eugenics beliefs, were sterilizing Latinas without their consent. The class action lawsuit was brought on behalf of 10 Mexican American women (some monolingual Spanish speakers) who were sterilized (tubal ligations) either without informed consent, upon limited knowledge, or through coercion. Hospital staff pressured the women to sign the consent forms, at times while in labor or under heavy medication, misrepresenting the risk and danger to the women. They also threatened loss of welfare benefits if they did not sign consent forms. Some of the women were unaware they had been sterilized until the suit was initiated. Defendant Dr. James Quilligan, hospital administrators, and California state officials were sued. In an unpublished opinion, Judge Jesse Curtis ad-

---

56. National Women's History Museum, Mariana Brandman, *Women's History, Antonia Hernández*, https://www.womenshistory.org/education-resources/biographies/antonia-hernandez.

57. Jocelyn Y. Stewart, *THE ADVOCATE: As the President of the Mexican American Legal Defense and Educational Fund, Antonia Hernandez Speaks for Millions,* Los Angeles Times, September 12, 1999, https://www.latimes.com/archives/la-xpm-1999-sep-12-tm-9130-story.html.

58. The Mexican Repatriation, triggered by decreased labor demands in the United States, occurred during the years 1929–1936 when nearly two million Mexicans (of those, 1.2 million Mexican Americans) were forced into Mexico. California State Apology Act for the 1930s Mexican Repatriation Program, Stats. 2005, Ch. 663, Sec. 1, effective January 1, 2006.

59. For a detailed discussion of the case and proceedings, *see* Karina Cardenas, *Who Makes the Decision to Sterilize Mexican Women?: The Doctor-Patient Debate in Madrigal v. Quilligan in the 1970s,* Cal. State LA, Perspectives 45, no. 63 (1974).

opted the doctor's defense and found the women at fault, concluding their cultural background heightened the alleged trauma suffered. The judge ruled:

- The doctors had the best interests of the plaintiffs in mind when conducting the procedures and did nothing wrong;
- The procedure was not objectionable if a physician believed a tubal ligation could improve a perceived overpopulation problem if the physician did not try to "overpower the will of his patients";
- The plaintiffs could not charge doctors of sterilizing without consent when some of the women signed the consent even though others had not signed consent forms; and
- The women's emotional breakdowns were attributable to their cultural value of desiring larger families rather than the actual sterilizations.

Though plaintiffs lost on the merits, the case produced positive results. The hospital was required to provide consent forms printed in multiple languages and impose a 72-hour waiting period for patients under 21 to consider before signing the consent forms. Welfare benefits were not terminated for those refusing sterilization. CRP joined the suit on appeal to the Ninth Circuit.

2. Hernández's Advocacy and Cases at MALDEF, 1985–2004

Hernández rose through the ranks at MALDEF, from staff attorney to president and general counsel. She led the organization for nearly 20 years, serving as president and general counsel from 1985 to 2004. During her tenure, MALDEF took on groundbreaking legal battles in education—some litigated by Norma Cantú under Hernández's leadership—immigrant rights, and voting. Like Martinez, Hernández understood the basic but profound importance of education:

> Education... continues to be the cornerstone of our work. The issues of funding for all levels of education concern us.... We are concerned with the whole issue of language. How language is being used—the English-only rules. We are trying to establish bilingualism or trilingualism as an asset in this county. You know, it's the only country in the world where being educated doesn't require you to speak more than one language.[60]

Hernández directed MALDEF's effort to defeat Proposition 187 ("Prop 187") working in collaboration with other legal and community organizations. *See Gregoria T. v. Wilson*, 54 F.3d 599 (9th Cir. 1995). Prop 187 (dubbed "Save Our State" by the proponents) was a California statewide initiative on the November 8, 1994, ballot. The referendum sought adoption of a state law to bar undocumented immigrants

60. Steve Proffitt, *Antonia Hernández, Working for the Latino Cause with Soft-Spoken Determination*, Los Angeles Times Interview, December 13, 1992.

from using public health care services (except in emergencies), other social services, and public school education at elementary, secondary, and postsecondary levels, unless verified as a U.S. citizen or legally allowed entry as a permanent or temporary resident. The measure made it a felony to manufacture, distribute, sell, or use false citizenship or residence documents.[61] It required designated state and local agencies to report "suspected residents in violation of immigration law" to the California attorney general and U.S. Immigration and Naturalization Service (INS). The measure passed with 58.93% of the vote.[62] On November 11, 1994, MALDEF and other groups filed a federal lawsuit seeking injunctive relief prohibiting the state from enforcing Prop 187. MALDEF argued the proposition violated *Plyler v. Doe*, which guaranteed a public education to undocumented children and asserted immigration was a federal, not a state, issue. Finding Prop187 unconstitutional under the Equal Protection Clause, the trial court granted a temporary injunction. Pending trial, a federal injunction then was issued. In 1997, the state of California asked for dismissal because federal immigration law had changed; the motion was denied. The state did not appeal the decision, leaving the permanent injunction standing. The case never proceeded to trial. In March 1998, U.S. District Court Judge Mariana Pfaelzer issued a final ruling confirming the federal government's exclusive authority over immigration and declared Prop 187 unconstitutional. On July 29, 1999, a court-approved mediation ended the legal battle over the proposition.

EEOC v. Tortillia La Mejor, 758 F. Supp. 585 (E.D. Cal. 1991), was the first case testing whether undocumented workers were covered by federal civil rights law, specifically Title VII of the 1964 Civil Rights Act (Title VII) as interpreted by EEOC regulations. The EEOC Compliance Manual provided that the legal status of a complainant did not dictate the acceptance or rejection of a Title VII complaint. Castrejón, an undocumented immigrant, sought to return to work upon exhaustion of employer-approved pregnancy disability leave. Refusing to reinstate Castrejón, Tortillia asserted Castrejón had no legal rights under Title VII as it did not apply to undocumented workers. *Tortillia* further asserted, *albeit* ironically, that the Immigration and Control Act of 1986 (IRCA)[63] would be undermined, specifically those provisions forbidding employers from hiring undocumented workers. MALDEF joined Equal Rights Advocates and the Asian Legal Caucus as co-counsel. Together, they successfully defeated the employer's motion to dismiss the case while acquiring permission on behalf of plaintiff Alicia Castrejón to intervene in the pending case.

---

61. California Ballot Propositions and Ballot Initiatives, Voter Information Guide for 1994, General Election, UC Hastings Scholarship, at 51–54, Repository, https://repository.uclawsf.edu/cgi/viewcontent.cgi?article=2090&context=ca_ballot_props.

62. Library of Congress, *1994: California's Proposition 187*, https://guides.loc.gov/latinx-civil-rights/california-proposition-187.

63. *Supra*, Title VII note 16, and Immigration Reform and Control Act of 1986, Pub. L. No. 99-603, 100 Stat. 3359 (codified as amended in 8 U.S.C. § 1324a (1988)).

Throughout Hernández's tenure, MALDEF filed voting rights lawsuits, prevailing in some—not in others—but each case successful in augmenting the country's political literacy about the emerging Latino electorate. *See e.g., Hastert v. State Bd. of Elections*, 777 F. Supp. 634 (N.D. Ill. 1991), which created a majority-Hispanic congressional district, upheld in *King v. Illinois State Board of Elections*, 979 F. Supp. 582 (N.D. Ill. 1996), and *Cano v. Davis*, 211 F. Supp.2d 1208 (C.D. Cal. 2002), an unsuccessful redistricting case challenging two congressional districts and one state legislative district. No matter the outcome, each case presented Hernández and MALDEF with the opportunity to test voting rights theories for the benefit of the Latino community. In MALDEF's hometown, Los Angeles, Hernández co-counseled a landmark reapportionment case that resulted in the creation of the first Latino-majority seat on the Los Angeles County Board of Supervisors ("Board"), *Yolanda Garza v. County of L.A. Board of Supervisors*, 756 F. Supp. 1298 (D.C. Cal. 1990), *aff'd.* 918 F.2d 763 (9th Cir. 1990), *cert. denied* 111 S. Ct. 681 (1991). On behalf of Yolanda Garza, a resident of Supervisorial District 1, MALDEF initiated a lawsuit alleging violation of Section 2 of the VRA. The U.S. government joined the lawsuit. Among the volume of evidence introduced at trial, was the Board's plan that was agreed to during a secret meeting. They planned to adopt a map shifting of "a group of 'lily white' voters into a white supervisor's district" to prevent creating a majority-Latino district"—all of which was memorialized in a memo. At a September 1981 public meeting, the map was approved without public input or discussion.[64] During trial, MALDEF successfully proved the five supervisors intentionally split the Latino communities of East Los Angeles and the San Gabriel Valley to avoid creating a majority-Latino district. MALDEF further established this gerrymandering existed for decades including in 1959, 1971, and 1981, perpetually disenfranchising the Latino community. The trial court stated:

> The Court has spent the past several weeks since the conclusion of this trial on April 10, 1990, immersed in what the Supreme Court in *Thornburg v. Gingles* referred to as a "searching evaluation of 'past and present reality' and on a 'functional' view of the political process." 478 U.S. 30, 45, 106 S. Ct. 2752, 2764, 92 L. Ed. 25 (1986) *citing* S. Rep. at 30, n. 120 U.S. Code Cong. & Admin News 1982, pp. 177, 208. The conclusion this Court reaches is that, on a fundamental level, the Hispanic community has sadly been denied an equal opportunity to participate in the political process and to elect candidates of their choice to the Board of Supervisors for this burgeoning County. *Yolanda Garza v. County of L.A. Board of Supervisors*, 756 F. Supp. at 1304.

Ruling in favor of the plaintiffs the trial court ordered a new map to be drawn based on total population figures—adopting MALDEF's strategy. It found the Board fractured the geographically compact and politically cohesive Latino community

64. MALDEF website, https://www.maldef.org/2019/07/the-garza-case-maldef-lawsuit-created-first-latino-majority-seat-on-los-angeles-county-board-of-supervisors/.

and diluted its vote in violation of the VRA.[65] The Board appealed unsuccessfully, first to the Ninth Circuit which concluded the Board intentionally discriminated against the Hispanic community, and then to the U.S. Supreme Court, which summarily rejected the appeal in one word, "Denied." The Ninth Circuit Judge Alex Kozinski captured the egregiousness of the case:

> Which brings us to what this case *does* stand for. When the dust has settled and local passions have cooled, this case will be remembered for its lucid demonstration that elected officials engaged in the single-minded pursuit of incumbency can run roughshod over the rights of protected minorities. The careful findings of the district court graphically document the pattern—a continuing practice of splitting the Hispanic core into two or more districts to prevent the emergence of a strong Hispanic challenger who might provide meaningful competition to the incumbent supervisors. The record is littered with telltale signs that reapportionments going back at least as far as 1959 were motivated, to no small degree, by the desire to assure that no supervisorial district would include too much of the burgeoning Hispanic population.
>
> But the record here illustrates a more general proposition: Protecting incumbency and safeguarding the voting rights of minorities are purposes often at war with each other. Ethnic and racial communities are natural breeding grounds for political challengers; incumbents greet the emergence of such power bases in their districts with all the hospitality corporate managers show hostile takeover bids. What happened here—the systemic splitting of the ethnic community into different districts—is the obvious, time-honored and most effective way of averting a potential challenge. Incumbency carries with it many other subtle and not-so-subtle advantages... [citation omitted] and incumbents who take advantage of their status so as to assure themselves a secure seat at the expense of emerging minority candidates may well be violating the Voting Rights Act. Today's case barely opens the door to our understanding of the potential relationship between the preservation of incumbency and invidious discrimination, but it surely gives weight to the Seventh Circuit's observation that "many devices employed to preserve incumbencies are necessarily racially discriminatory." *Garza*, 918 F.2d at 778.

On March 3, 1991, Gloria Molina was elected to the seat and sworn in as the first Hispanic to hold a seat on the Los Angeles Board of Supervisors. Supervisor Molina

---

65. For an analysis of the case, specifically, the application of total population figures vs. voting population (one person-one vote), *see* Dennis L. Murphy, *Garza v. County of Los Angeles: The Dilemma over Using Elector as Opposed to Total Population in Legislative Reapportionment*, Case W. Rsrv. L. Rev. 41 (1991); and Aide Cristina Cabeza, *Total Population: A Constitutional Basis for Apportionment Reaffirmed in Garza v. Los Angeles County*, UCLA 13 Chicano-Latino L. Rev. 74 (1992-93), https://escholarship.org/content/qt1pj950s4/qt1pj950s4_noSplash_5744b2d17d20829814585ba64be06aea.pdf?t=olo639.

served for 23 years from1991 to 2014.[66] Twenty-five years later in *Evanwel v. Abbott*, 578 U.S. ___, 136 S. Ct. 1120 (2016), SCOTUS (Ginsberg, J.) held the one person-one vote principle permitted the use of total population, not just total voting-eligible population, in state and local jurisdictions to measure equalization. The case adopted the approach successfully argued by Hernández some 26 years earlier. By the end of Hernández's tenure, MALDEF had sufficiently refined a national litigation strategy on behalf of the Latino community, such that is recognized as one of the country's leading voting rights experts.

C. Norma A. Cantú

1. Cantú's Formative Years

Norma Cantú was born on November 2, 1974, in Brownsville, Texas, to Federico "Kiko" and Gregoria (*nee* Garza) Cantú, the second of seven children and first of four daughters (an earlier-born brother died in infancy). Federico was a Korean War veteran and lifelong post office employee. Gregoria was the first in her family to earn a bachelor's and master's degree from the University of Texas-Rio Grande Valley. Gregoria taught at Webb and Longoria Elementary Schools and retired as an assistant principal. Norma credits her family's influence and emphasis on education for her success.[67] The decision to become a lawyer arose after she "walked into the Cameron County, Texas courthouse... at nine years old looking for a sip of water. Appreciating the air-conditioning and surroundings, the fourth grader decided she would pursue a law career."[68] The precocious student skipped grades twice in elementary school, graduating from Brownsville High School at age 16 as its "Outstanding Graduate." Attending the University of Texas–Pan American where she was a Pre-Law Society member, Norma earned a B.A. in English and graduated *summa cum laude* at age 19. She returned home and briefly taught English at her alma mater before applying to law school. Norma (Cantú) earned her law degree from Harvard Law School, graduating at age 22.[69] Litigation was her career pursuit, which first started at the Texas Attorney General's Office, followed by MALDEF.

---

66. Molina, the first Chicana elected to the California legislature, passed in 2023. *See* Gustavo Arellano, *Former Los Angeles County Supervisor Gloria Molina Dies*, Los Angeles Times, May 14, 2023, https://www.latimes.com/obituaries/story/2023-05-14/gloria-molina-dead.

67. Voces, *Norma Cantú*, https://voces.moody.utexas.edu/collections/stories/norma-cantu.

68. MALDEF Board of Directors, Norma Cantú Board Chair, https://www.maldef.org/about/board-of-directors/.

69. *Id.*

2. Cantú's Tenure at MALDEF, 1979–1993

Hired by Martinez in 1979, Cantú was a trial and appellate attorney who later served as MALDEF's national director and regional counsel/education director. She litigated educational cases at the intersection of education, civil rights, and public policy. Cantú's cases were among the most novel and difficult with great precedential value in the field of education law, school financing and desegregation lawsuits.

Edgewood Independent School District et al. v. Kirby, 777 S.W.2d 391 (Tex. 1989) (*Edgewood ISD*), is the seminal case on Texas public school financing. Cantú represented low-income students in low-wealth schools who successfully challenged the district's finance system. This case prompted the Texas legislature to reform its school funding laws and appropriate approximately $1 billion to property-poor school districts. The significance of *Edgewood ISD* must be understood in the context of the preceding "decade of legal inertia on public school financ[ing]" following the ruling in *Rodríguez v. San Antonio School District*, 337 F. Supp. 280 (D.C., W.D. Texas, 1971). At issue in *Rodríguez* was the state's public-school financing that perpetuated the gross disparity in funding between high and low-wealth public schools in the district.[70] The plaintiffs argued that the fundamental right to an education should be extended to the state's public school finance system and that failure to do so violated the Equal Protection Clause of the Fourteenth Amendment. In response to the 1968 filing, a three-judge federal panel provided Texas an opportunity to remedy the problem during its legislative session, which it failed to do. The federal district court, thereafter, ruled in favor of Rodríguez declaring education a fundamental right and the Texas school finance system unconstitutional under the Fourteenth Amendment. Texas appealed to the U.S. Supreme Court. On a 5–4 ruling (Powell, J.), the Court found the plaintiffs had no constitutional right to an equal education and that there was no infringement of their rights. *San Antonio School District v. Rodríguez*, 411 U.S. 1 (1973). The Court further held that the jurisdiction and management of Texas's public-school financing was reserved entirely to the state. Justices Brennan, William O. Douglas, Byran White, and Thurgood Marshall dissented. Justice Brennan thereafter penned an article for the *Harvard Law Review*, interpreted as urging plaintiffs to litigate constitutional claims before their respective state supreme courts.[71] Over 10 years later, *Edgewood ISD* was filed.

In *Edgewood ISD*, Cantú was co-counsel initially to eight school districts and twenty-one parents. The lead plaintiff in the *Rodríguez* case, Demitrio Rodríguez, joined *Edgewood ISD* as a plaintiff as did sixty-seven additional school districts plus more parents. *Edgewood ISD* was filed against then Commissioner of Education William Kirby in Travis County (Austin), alleging violation of the state's constitution

70. *MALDEF's Landmark Fight for Education Equality in Texas*, https://www.maldef.org/2021/01/maldef-landmark-fight-for-education-equality-in-texas/.

71. William J. Brennan, *State Constitutions and the Protection of Individual Rights*, 90 Harv. L. Rev. 90 (1977): 491.

resulting in discrimination against students, primarily Mexican American. Specifically, MALDEF claimed the state's method of financing public schools violated the Texas Constitution, Article I, §§3 and 19, and Article VII, §1.[72] The latter section known as the "Efficiency Mandate" provides: "[a] general diffusion of knowledge being essential to the preservation of the liberties and rights of the people, it shall be the duty of the Legislature of the State to establish and make suitable provision for the support and maintenance of an efficient system of public free schools." The plaintiffs contested the state's reliance on local property taxes to finance its system of public education. They argued the ad valorem taxation system was intrinsically unequal because property values varied greatly from district to district, creating an imbalance in funds available to educate students equally throughout the state.

In June 1984, the Texas legislature approved a school reform plan. MALDEF amended its complaint to incorporate that legislation and trial proceeded in Austin, Texas, between January 20 and April 8, 1987, before state district judge, Harley Clark. At trial, MALDEF presented evidence of disparity that ranged from $38,854 in property taxes per student in the poorest district, Edgewood ISD, to $570,109 per student in the wealthiest district, Alamo Heights. MALDEF established that property-poor districts had to set a tax rate that averaged 74.5 cents per $100 valuation to generate $2,987 per student, while richer districts, with a tax rate of half that much, could produce $7,233 per student. These differences produced disparities in the districts' abilities to hire good teachers, build appropriate facilities, offer a sound curriculum, and purchase such important equipment as computers. In its original 1984 brief, MALDEF declared such gaps amounted to the denial of equal opportunity in an "increasingly complex and technological society," and asserted that this was contrary to the intent of the Constitution's Texas Education Clause. Ruling in favor of the plaintiffs on April 29, 1987, the trial court concluded the school financing system violated the state Constitution: the equal rights guarantee of Article I, §3, due process Article I, §19 and the Efficiency Mandate in Article VII, §1. The trial court ordered the Texas legislature to adopt another school reform plan by September 1989.

The State appealed. On December 14, 1988, the appellate court reversed the trial court by a two-to-one decision on the grounds that education was not a basic right and that the present system of public-school financing was constitutional. *Kirby v. Edgewood Independent School District*, 761 S.W.2d 859 (1988). The Texas Court of Appeals recognized the "'patched up and overly cobbled' system of administration and finance," concluding, "[t]he opinion and judgment of this Court should not be viewed as an affirmation that the present school financing system is desirable or that it should continue without change; rather, our conclusion is solely that the system is

---

72. Art. VII, §1 (the efficiency mandate) provides: "A general diffusion of knowledge being essential to the preservation of the liberties and rights of the people, it shall be the duty of the Legislature of the State to establish and make suitable provision for the support and maintenance of an efficient system of public free schools."

not in violation of the Constitution of Texas." *Edgewood ISD*, 761 S.W. 2d at 867. In 1989, the plaintiffs appealed to the Texas Supreme Court which analyzed the case under the Efficiency Mandate in Article VII, § 1, of the Texas Constitution, noting the appellate court ignored this provision. On October 2, the court issued a unanimous 9–0 decision in favor of *Edgewood ISD*, ordering the state legislature to implement an equitable system by the 1990–1991 school year. Noting the "glaring disparities" in the ad valorem taxation system proven at trial, the court wrote:

> The amount of money spent on a student's education has a real and meaningful impact on the educational opportunity offered that student. High-wealth districts are able to provide for their students' broader educational experiences including more extensive curricula, more up-to-date technological equipment, better libraries and library personnel, teacher aides, counseling services, lower student-teacher ratios, better facilities, parental involvement programs, and drop-out prevention programs. They are also better able to attract and retain experienced teachers and administrators... The differences in the quality of educational programs offered are dramatic. For example, San Elizario I.S.D. offers no foreign language, no pre-kindergarten program, no chemistry, no physics, no calculus, and no college preparatory or honors program. It also offers virtually no extra-curricular activities such as band, debate, or football. At the time of trial, one-third of Texas school districts did not even meet the state-mandated standards for maximum class size. The great majority of these are low-wealth districts. In many instances, wealthy and poor districts are found contiguous to one another within the same county. *Edgewood ISD*, 777 S.W. 2d at 393.

Decades later as pro bono counsel, Cantú joined MALDEF attorney Nina Perales in the first adequacy case in Texas, *West-Orange-Cove I.S.D. et al. v. Neeley et al.*, No. GV-100528 (250th Dist. Ct., Travis County, Tex., Nov. 30, 2004). (By this time, Cantú was teaching at UT-Austin and received permission to co-counsel the case.) Wealthy school districts challenged the state's public school financing system (equalization provisions). The school districts asserted the property tax cap prevented them from meeting state accreditation standards and from exercising meaningful discretion in setting their tax rates, thereby constituting an illegal taxation. MALDEF intervened by representing 22 low-wealth school districts. As its theory of the case, MALDEF argued that the current system remained inequitable and inadequate while attempting to preserve the equalization provisions (ad valorem taxes). All plaintiff school districts agreed the public school system could not achieve "a general diffusion of knowledge" under the Efficiency Mandate due to underfunding. During the five-week bench trial, Cantú handled the direct and cross-examination of lead witnesses, including Texas Commissioner of Education Shirley Neely. On November 30, 2004, the district court ruled in favor of the plaintiff school districts. It enjoined the state defendants from funding the school districts for ten months until October 1, 2005, giving the legislature time to cure the constitutional defects in the public-school finance system. The legislature did not reach consensus on a resolution during that regular session, or the two following special sessions called by the governor. The injunction was stayed upon appeal by the State defendants.

Six appeals, in which 329 school districts in the state participated as parties or intervenors, were consolidated before the Texas Supreme Court. In *West-Orange-Cove I.S.D. et al. v. Neeley et al.*, 176 S.W.3d 746 (Tex. 2005), the Texas Supreme Court adopted the district court's finding that the local ad valorem taxes had become a state property tax in violation of the Texas Constitution Article VIII, § 1-e (upon summarizing the holdings in the *Edgewood ISD* cases). The court agreed with the wealthy public-school districts that they lacked meaningful discretion in setting their local taxes. It also recognized the gross inequities stemming from the disparate tax bases in wealthy vs. poor school districts (MALDEF's theory of the case). "Compensation must be made for disparities in the amount of property value per student so that property owners in property-poor districts are not burdened with much heavier tax rates than property owners in property-rich districts to generate substantially the same revenue per student for public education." *West-Orange-Cove*, 176 S.W.3d at 756. The Texas Supreme Court stayed the injunction until June 1, 2006, to give the legislature additional time to address the constitutional deficiencies. It remanded the case on the issue of attorneys' fees raised by MALDEF. Prevailing at appeal on attorneys' fees, Cantú donated her portion of the fees—over $150,000—to plaintiffs' counsel for contribution to a nonprofit corporation representing low-income children.[73] By May 2006, the Texas Legislature passed a new school finance bill that injected more money into the public school system.

In his national best-selling book, *Savage Inequalities: Children in America's Schools* (1991), author Jonathan Kozol shed light on the disparate treatment of poor children in public school systems across the nation.[74] Kozol included the school districts of San Antonio, Edgewood ISD, and West-Orange-Cove, the cases litigated by MALDEF and Cantú.

Cantú was lead counsel in *U.S. and CRUCIAL v. Ector County I.S.D.* (*Ector ISD*), 722 F.2d 1182 (5th Cir. 1983). The case was first filed in 1970 to remedy Ector ISD's failure to integrate its schools between 1954 and 1982. Plaintiffs alleged violations of Title IV of the Civil Rights Act of 1964, 42 U.S.C. § 2000c-6 (1976), and the Fourteenth Amendment. Cantú represented a coalition of African American, White, and Latino parents in Odessa, Texas, in a successful bid to desegregate the district's pub-

73. Cantú's biography was compiled from various sources, including her resume, on-line summaries from UT–Austin, the U.S. government, MALDEF and organizations who honored her and newspaper articles.

74. A former public school teacher, Kozol visited schools across the country, including San Antonio (1988–1990). He advocates for free and equal public education to all economic classes. Kozol argues gross inequalities in school financial and racial segregation deprive the poorest students of productive and fulfilling futures. https://www.jonathankozol.com/savage-inequalities.

lic schools. Ector County ISD is a countywide school district that encompasses all of Ector County which includes the city of Odessa. A railroad track that divided the northern and southern parts of the city separated the Black and Hispanic communities in south Odessa from the White population. Despite SCOTUS rulings outlawing *de jure* dual school systems and ordering unitary districts starting with *Brown v. Board of Education of Topeka*, 347 U.S. 483 (1954), and *Green v. County School Board of New Kent County*, 391 U.S. 430 (1968), Ector ISD and the city of Odessa delayed integrating its schools. The federal government filed suit against *Ector ISD* in August 1970, and the parties shortly thereafter entered into a settlement agreement in which the school district agreed to desegregate its schools by affirmatively implementing changes in eight distinct areas that included faculty, students, and facilities. *Ector ISD*, 722 F.2d at 1185. In February 1981, the parent group CRUCIAL moved to intervene and the case proceeded to trial. The trial court found the district intentionally segregated assignments of faculty and staff and student transportation, resulting in an increase in the student minority population in south Odessa schools from 87.4% during the 1967–1968 academic year (AY) to 96.4% by AY 1980–1981. *Ector ISD*, 722 F.2d at 1184. The trial court noted that Ector ISD "not only continued to fail to meet its duty to dismantle its dual school system but actually increased the segregation in its schools of both Blacks and Mexican-Americans." *Ector ISD*, 722 F.2d at 1182. A desegregation plan was ordered; CRUCIAL filed its own plan. On appeal, the principal issue was whether the trial court erred in failing to conduct an evidentiary hearing on the desegregation plan. For this reason, the matter was reversed and remanded. A desegregation plan eventually was ordered and implemented. In 2005, the Western District Court (W.D. Texas) ordered the parties to address whether the district should be released from the desegregation plan. On August 15, 2006, the parties reached agreement, and the court entered a consent order, retaining jurisdiction for three years to 2009. The court severed its jurisdiction of nonfaculty staff, facilities, extracurricular activities, and education issues.

Odessa's refusal for 28 years to desegregate, from 1954 to 1982, and the integration that followed formed the backdrop of a national best-selling book and popular TV series *Friday Night Lights*. The series highlights the city's high school football teams amidst Odessa's segregated history that was based upon the 1990 non-fiction book written by H.G. Bissinger, *Friday Night Lights: A Town, a Team, and a Dream*.

Cantú served as co-counsel in other desegregation cases, including *Diaz v. San Jose Unified School District*, 633 F. Supp. 808 (N.D. Cal. 1985), wherein the district agreed to implement changes in educational programs for limited English-proficient students; *Price v. Austin Independent School District*, 834 F.2d 1711 (5th Cir. 1988), where Cantú successfully served as plaintiffs' co-counsel from transition to a unitary school system, withdrawing when appeals were pursued (contrary to her advice) that ultimately were unsuccessful; and *Keyes v. School District No. 1, Denver*, a protracted desegregation case involving language minority students. Filed in 1969, the Denver school district remained under court supervision until the late 1980s. It resulted in numerous court decisions, including two rulings by the Tenth Circuit and one by SCOTUS. Cantú served as co-counsel starting with *Keyes XIV*, 609 F. Supp. 1491 (D. Colo. 1985), and through the Tenth Circuit's second ruling in *Keyes v. School District No. 1, Denver*, 895 F.2d 659 (10th Cir. 1990). Plaintiffs proved the school district had operated a segregated school system since 1960. Memorandums and orders were issued in which the district agreed to effectuate major changes to improve the quality of services to limited English-proficient students. The second memorandum and order of February 25, 1986, addressed the district's failure to complete its transition to a unitary system, and the court adopted the plan proffered by the school district. *Keyes XVI*, 653 F. Supp. 1536 (D. Colo. 1985). Two years later, the court imposed an interim binding decree that included additional remedial steps and a plan to achieve full integration of the district's schools and retained jurisdiction over the case in *Keyes XVII*, 670 F. Supp. 153 (D. Colo.1987). On appeal, the Tenth Circuit held that a finding that part of a school district was guilty of segregation did not render the entire school district guilty of segregation and ended court jurisdiction over the case.

In *U.S. v. Texas Education Agency*, 506 F. Supp. 405 (E.D. Tex., 1981), Cantú co-counseled a partially successful suit that required a state education agency to improve the quality of services to limited English-proficient (LEP) students. The district court found the appeal was moot after the Texas Legislature responded to the trial court's decision by designating significant investments in state funds for hiring and training of teachers to instruct LEP students. The focus shifted to higher education in *League of United Latin American Citizens et al., v. Richards*, 863 S.W.2d 449 (Tex. 1993), which was a partially successful challenge to the state funding system brought by low-income residents of counties along the Texas-Mexico border which Cantú co-counseled. She challenged the state's low funding of college facilities and programs in the border region which contained one-fourth of the state's population. College faculty were teaching in high school buildings, only 3% of doctorate programs were offered in the region and no programs were offered in law or medicine. Plaintiffs won at trial, prompting the legislature to appropriate close to $600 million new dollars to support state border colleges and universities and higher education programs in engineering, medicine and research centers. New campuses started with the border initiative funds including the downtown UT-San Antonio campus and Texas A & M at Laredo. The Texas Supreme Court declined to extend their rulings from *Edgewood ISD* to higher education and reversed the trial court, but it did not disturb the funding that resulted in new campuses and graduate schools for the border region.

In *Castaneda v. Pickard*, 781 F.2d 456 (5th Cir. 1986) (*Castaneda II*), Cantú was co-counsel in this partially successful suit to require the five local school districts in Raymondville, Willacy County, Texas.[75] Cantú represented the class consisting of

75. Raymondville was the home of Edna Cisneros (1930–2013) and her sister, Diana Cisneros-Klefisch (1932–1991) who each serverd as the District Attorney for Willacy County. Edna was the first Luminaria-Latina elected district attorney in the country; Diana succeeded Edna as the second.

Mexican American children and their parents; 77% of the population in the Rio Grande Valley (where Willacy County sits) is Mexican American. One-third of Raymondville's population are migrant farm workers and three-quarters of the school children qualify for the federally funded free school lunch program. In the predecessor case, *Castaneda v. Pickard*, 648 F.2d 989 (5th Cir. 1981) (*Castaneda I*), the plaintiffs sued to hire more qualified bilingual education teachers under the Equal Education Opportunities Act of 1974 (EEOA),[76] and they also alleged statutory and constitutional violations of their educational rights. The plaintiffs challenged the districts' ability grouping—placement of students in particular groups and educational programs within their grade—which plaintiffs alleged was based on discrimination; though in *Castaneda I*, grouping was partially based on language proficiency. The EEOA provides: "No state shall deny equal educational opportunity to an individual on account of his or her race, color, sex or national origin by (f) the failure by an educational agency to take appropriate action to overcome language barriers that impede equal participation by its students in its instructional programs." In *Castaneda I*, the Fifth Circuit noted the lack of guidelines from SCOTUS/rulings to determine what constitutes appropriate remedial action in student language remediation programs under §7703(f) and adopted a new three-part test: 1) programs must be based on "sound educational theory," 2) they must be "implemented effectively" with adequate resources and personnel, and 3) after a trial period, the program must be evaluated as effective in overcoming language handicaps. *Castaneda*, 648 F. 2d at 1009–1010. Though the Fifth Circuit affirmed the district court's finding on remand of no discrimination, it held that ability grouping of students was prohibited unless shown such grouping would serve a valid educational purpose. The U.S. Department of Education adopted the legal standards from *Castaneda II* as part of its 1992 national guidance to school districts.[77] Cantú later testified before Congress on the case and its national impact.[78]

In the class action lawsuit *Gomez v. State Board of Education of Illinois*, 614 F. Supp. 342 (E. D. Ill. 1987), *rev'd.* 811 F.2d 1030 (7th Cir. 1987), co-counsel Cantú represented Spanish-speaking school children challenging the state's failure to enforce and monitor programmatic quality for LEP students. The LEP students had not been tested for English proficiency and received no bilingual or compensatory instruction in contravention of state law. Plaintiffs alleged violation of their federal rights under

---

76. EEOA, 20 U.S.C. § 1701 *et seq.*, § 1703(f). Plaintiffs introduced evidence of past discriminatory segregation which the district court failed to address in its factual findings. Notwithstanding, the Fifth Circuit found the plaintiffs could assert unconstitutional racial discrimination in the employment of teachers and administrators under 42 U.S.C. § 1983. On this basis, the case was remanded back to the district court. The district court found there was no discrimination by the district in its ability grouping and the case was appealed, resulting in *Castaneda II*.

77. *See e.g.*, OCR Memorandum Sep 27, 1991, *Developing Programs for English Language Learners*, last modified 01/16/2020: https://www2.ed.gov/about/offices/list/ocr/ell/september27.html.

78. Cantú Resume, *supra*, note 73.

the EEOA, Title VI of the Civil Rights Act of 1964,[79] and the Equal Protection Clause of the Fourteenth Amendment, seeking declaratory and injunctive relief. Relying on *Pennhurst State School and Hospital v. Halderman*, 46 U.S. 89 (1984), defendants argued the Eleventh Amendment barred suits against a state where it is not the real party in interest, thereby prohibiting declaratory relief against the Illinois state officials. Ruling the EEOA provides no particular remedy, the district court ruled that the state is free to establish its own program and to delegate the authority and responsibility to promulgate such programs to local schools. The district court further found the state had issued detailed regulations and delegated the authority and responsibility of implementing the programs, thereby relieving the state agencies of further responsibility. It concluded that the local school districts were the appropriate parties to sue to address bilingual services under EEOA and instructed plaintiffs to amend their complaint naming the proper defendants. As plaintiffs had neither alleged nor shown purposeful discrimination nor past de jure discrimination in defendants' attempts to enact transitional bilingual educational programs, the plaintiffs' claims under the Fourteenth Amendment were dismissed. On appeal, the Seventh Circuit held that *Pennhurst* was inapplicable as the plaintiffs sought remedy under federal, not state, law. Gomez was the first case to rule that a state agency could not delegate its federal legal responsibilities to a local district.

In *Adams v. Bennett*, 675 F. Supp. 667 (D. D.C. 1987), Cantú was co-counsel to plaintiffs-intervenors (one of five such organizations) in a successful lawsuit challenging the abdication by the Department of Health, Education, and Welfare (HEW) of its responsibility to process and enforce Title VII discrimination laws in colleges and secondary schools. Plaintiffs argued that HEW failed to ensure the schools were integrated. In the original *Adams* case, the court mandated HEW to commence proceedings against public educational institutions and ordered remedial measures. *Adams v. Richardson*, 351 F. Supp. 636, 641 (D.D.C. 1972), aff'd, Adams v. Richardson, 480 F.2d 1159 (D.C. Cir.1973). The parties agreed to a consent order in 1973 that was expanded in 1983 to include additional time frames for the schools to comply. By the time the case went to trial, there were forty plaintiffs in the certified class and additional plaintiffs-intervenors in numerous states. At issue was whether prolonged judicial intervention in the operations of executive branch agencies violates the separation of powers doctrine. Also, at issue was whether the matter was moot under Article III, limiting adjudication to cases and controversies. The trial court found there was inappropriate judicial intervention, based partly on the length of time the consent decree was in effect, that warranted dismissal of the consent orders. Notwithstanding, the case had regulatory impact as it prompted the U.S. Department of Education to adopt and comply with court-ordered timetables for investigating and negotiating settlements with statewide systems of higher education.

79. Title VI of the Civil Rights Act of 1964, 42 U.S.C. §2000d and regulations promulgated thereunder, 34 C.F.R. § 100.3 *et seq.*

3. Assistant Secretary Cantú, 1993–2001

Cantú's impactful litigation led to her nomination in March 1993 by President Clinton as Assistant Secretary of Civil Rights for the Department of Education (OCR), that provoked immediate reactions.

> [Lani] Guinier and Ms. Cantu are far from household names, but the duo has the litigation experience and mental firepower to profoundly alter the civil rights landscape. Both have blazed the outer frontiers in their respective areas of voting law and education.... Ms. Cantu brings to her civil rights post in the Department of Education a zeal for social engineering both old and new.... The appointment of Guinier and Ms. Cantu would place the powerful federal civil rights arsenal in the hands of idealogues.[80]

Notwithstanding the press attacks, Cantú was confirmed unanimously. As OCR assistant secretary, Cantú supervised a staff of approximately 850 employees and managed a budget of over $53 million. She advised the president and Education Secretary Richard Riley on education policy. During her tenure (May 24, 1993, to January 20, 2001), the Assistant Secretary guided the nation in significant education reform through her interpretations of existing laws and promulgation of regulations that would permanently change Americans' daily lives. A significant example is Cantú's interpretation and regulation of women and girls' athletics.

OCR is responsible for enforcing Title IX which provides that "no person in the United States shall, on the basis of sex, be excluded from participation in, be denied the benefits of, or be subjected to discrimination under any education program or activity [including athletics] receiving Federal financial assistance."[81] Cantú interpreted Title IX as requiring "proportional opportunity" for female (and male) athletes. In 1979, a policy interpretation was issued by OCR for the benefit of colleges and universities to clarify the athletics requirements of Title IX. Upon assuming office, Cantú conducted focus groups on discrimination in athletics that led to the issuance on January 16, 1996, of "Clarification of Intercollegiate Athletics Policy Guidance: The Three-Part Test" (Clarification).[82] To comply with Title IX, colleges or schools may apply any of the three approaches:

---

80. Clint Bolick, *Clinton's Quota Queens*, Wall Street Journal, April 30, 1993. Law professor Lani Guinier was the first female of color to acquire tenure at Harvard Law School. In 1993, President Clinton nominated and subsequently withdrew Guinier's nomination for Assistant Attorney General for Civil Rights. Professor Guinier had earned a national reputation as a skilled civil rights litigator and opposed quotas. *Quota Queen* was a pejorative term used to suggest that those supporting diversity played a numbers game instead of relying on qualifications.

81. *Supra* note 30. Title IX regulations were not effective until July 21, 1975.

82. OCR-00016-A, Clarification of Intercollegiate Athletics Policy Guidance: The Three Part Test (Jan. 16, 1996), Assistant Secretary Norma V. Cantú, https://www2.ed.gov/about/offices/list/ocr/docs/clarific.html.

(1) substantial proportionality between the enrollment and participation rates of the underrepresented sex;

(2) a history and continuing practice of program expansion for the underrepresented sex; or,

(3) full and effective accommodation of the interests and abilities of the underrepresented sex.[83]

OCR subsequently issued two letters in July 1998, clarifying how scholarship dollars must be awarded to men's and women's athletic programs in "substantially equal amounts, proportionate to the participation rate of male and female athletes."[84] Part of the substantiation included in the Clarification was OCR's conclusion that "more than 25 years after the passage of Title IX, women college athletes receive[d] fewer athletic opportunities and less support from their institutions than male athletes." The Clarification reported that 82% of college recruiting money, 76% of college sports' operating budgets, and approximately 72% of athletic scholarships went to men's sports, despite that male athletes comprised only 60% of all student-athletes nationwide at the time. Cantú focused on generating equal opportunity through compliance efforts yielding agreements to help increase the number of women participating in intercollegiate athletic programs and by resolving gender discrimination that resulted in hundreds of thousands of scholarship dollars directed toward women athletes, who were previously denied monetary benefits.[85]

Another important example of Cantú's work was the expansion of educational opportunities for students under Title VI for which OCR was responsible. Title VI prohibits discrimination on the basis of race, color, or national origin and has jurisdiction over access to educational opportunities for language minority LEP students.[86] The Assistant Secretary expanded opportunities for students of color through partnership agreements with states through their respective Departments of Education, including resolving compliance issues on behalf of LEP students and endorsing and formulating plans to increase certified teachers for programs where none previously existed.[87] Cantú expanded OCR's administrative efficiency, increasing the number of illegal discrimination complaints resolved by 20% within the first two years of her tenure, which, by her final year, had risen another 20%. Under her tenure, 80% of complaints were resolved by OCR within 180 days of receiving a complaint. Significantly, more than a third of the cases filed were resolved without adversarial proceedings as schools and complainants entered voluntary corrective actions.[88]

---

83. 44 Fed. Reg. at 71418.

84. *Supra* note 82.

85. *Id.*

86. *See* Congressional Testimony Statement by of Norma V. Cantú, Assistant Secretary for Civil Rights, June 22, 1999, https://www2.ed.gov/about/offices/list/ocr/docs/testm01.html.

87. OCR Congressional Testimony Statement by Norma Cantú Assistant Secretary for Civil Rights, June 22, 1999, https://www2.ed.gov/about/offices/list/ocr/docs/testm01.html.

88. *Id.*; *see also* GAO Report Resolving Discrimination Complaints Has Improved With New Processing System, Tab A of Cantu's June 1999 written statement.

In recognition of her work, Cantú was inducted into the Women's Institute on Sports and Education on September 27, 1996. She also was inducted into the San Antonio Women's Hall of Fame and received the American Bar Foundation Fellows 2023 Outstanding Service Award.[89] President Joseph Biden appointed her to the U.S. Commission on Civil Rights (2020–2022) where she served as the first Latina appointed and elected as Chair.[90] From 2001 to 2023, Cantú was a Professor of Law and Education and served as department chair at the University of Texas at Austin. She taught education and law courses at UT-Austin School of Law, creating its first disability law class.[91] In April 2024, Cantú became chair of MALDEF's Board of Directors.[92]

D. Irma Herrera

1. Herrera's Formative Years

After three years working in New Orleans as an architectural and urban planner, Irma enrolled in law school—which was no accident given her upbringing in segregated Alice, Texas, where she first experienced injustice.[93] Irma was born on March 12, 1951, the third child of Claudio and Esperanza (*nee* Martinez) Herrera. Esperanza was the daughter of Mexican-born parents. Claudio was born in Texas as were his parents. Claudio quit school at an early age to support the family and Esperanza completed elementary school. He enlisted in the army during WWII and earned a Bronze Medal for his service in the South Pacific. Claudio later owned and operated the Central Barber Shop and additionally did bookkeeping work for others. Esperanza worked as a seamstress and housekeeper, while also becoming a mother to four children.[94] Irma attended St. Joseph's Catholic School through eighth grade, skipping one grade. Of her segregated education, Irma observed:

> I sometimes say this with worry that people will take it the wrong way but one of the benefits of being in a segregated school was that everyone was from your color, everyone was from your socio-economic group, at least in my community and you stood or failed without reference to that. The smartest kid was a Mexican American kid; the least capable was a Mexican American kid. I was

89. Biography of Norma V. Cantú, https://www.palmbeachschools.org/site/default.aspx?PageType=3&DomainID=362&ModuleInstanceID=3592&ViewID=6446EE88-D30C-497E-9316-3F8874B3E108&RenderLoc=0&FlexDataID=9549&PageID=2254; https://www.americanbarfoundation.org/professor-norma-v-cantu-to-receive-the-2023-abf-fellows-outstanding-service-award/.

90. *Commissioner Norma V. Cantú Selected as Chair of the U.S. Commission on Civil Rights*, April 30, 2021, https://www.usccr.gov/news/2021/commissioner-norma-v-cantu-selected-chair-us-commission-civil-rights.

91. UT at Austin Norma Cantú Ken McIntyre Professor for Excellence in School Leadership, https://education.utexas.edu/faculty/norma_cantu/.

92. MALDEF, Norma Cantú Board Chair, https://www.maldef.org/about/board-of-directors/.

93. Rebecca Westerfield, ABA Senior Lawyers Division Women Trailblazers in the Law, *Oral History of Irma Herrera*, August 10, 17, October 26, 2007, at 4, 21–22 (Herrera ABA Oral History).

94. *Id.* Herrera ABA Oral History at 17.

among the top students. I was always either first in my class or second. I was a good student. That was something clearly my parents were very proud of... [e] specially, it meant a lot more to my father than my mother.... I went to an integrated high school; however, it was pretty much segregated by tracking.... I found myself with a most peculiar set of courses.[95]

Ninth grade was Irma's first exposure to integrated classes. She then experienced an academic education as the only Mexican American amid white students, attributable in part to taking accelerated courses. High school was the first time Irma visited a white student's home and when she became fully aware of segregation's impact.[96] She graduated from high school at age 16 with a 4.0 grade point average but had earned enough credits to graduate at age 15. Irma credits her father for serving as a role model, developing her love of reading from him.[97] Unlike most other Mexican American girls who, at the time, graduated high school and married, Irma was "a quiet, studious girl so it was out of the question that somebody like me was going to get married." She ventured further than any family members and obtained a bachelor's degree in urban studies and planning from Trinity College, though it was only "28 miles away from [her] hometown."[98] Serving as an urban planner for three years in New Orleans, Irma specialized in land use and transportation planning studies.[99] Irma was then admitted to and graduated from Notre Dame Law School in 1978. Upon graduating, she moved to, and passed the bar exam in, Washington state. Irma started her legal career with Vergreen Legal Services and devoted her career to legal and public interest nonprofit organizations. As a staff attorney at MALDEF (1980 to 1983) and at META (1991 to 1995), Irma specialized in education law. As she practiced, Irma intermittently taught at the college/university level, instructing Spanish to students at Notre Dame, political science at Colorado College, and education law classes at California State University-Sacramento. Irma's infusion of advocacy, litigation, and teaching continued throughout her career.

2. Equal Rights Advocates Executive Director, 1995–2009

For nearly 15 years, from 1995 to 2009, Irma (Herrera) was executive director of Equal Rights Advocates (ERA), a litigation and advocacy organization based in San Francisco committed to protecting and securing equal rights and economic opportunities for women. She became the first Latina/Luminaria and woman lawyer of color to lead a national women's law firm. She supervised a staff of fourteen and managed a $1.9 million budget. During her tenure, ERA litigated cases regarding

95. Herrera ABA Oral History at 6–7.

96. Herrera ABA Oral History at 21.

97. Herrera ABA Oral History at 8–9.

98. Herrera ABA Oral History at 14. During her first year of college, Irma lived at the mother's home of Luminaria Irma Rangel (J.D. 1969, St. Mary's Law School).

99. Herrera Resume, https://abawtp.law.stanford.edu/files/original/d8d365d73226ff807c111535afe1f2ca.pdf.

hour and wage laws, safety issues and overtime pay, Title VII pregnancy discrimination, promotions in nontraditional jobs, sexual harassment, and the first Title IX case regarding student-to-student harassment (*see discussion infra*). Under her leadership, ERA worked to defeat California Proposition 209, the ballot initiative to prohibit affirmative action programs.[100]

During a transitional period of ERA's then 22-year history, in May 1996, the ERA Board hired Herrera[101] who became the first Latina and woman of color to lead a national women's legal organization in the country; her goal was a return to ERA's cutting-edge litigation.[102] While the organization's focus remained on equality and economic justice for all women, its emphasis was on laws and practices disproportionately impacting women of color in traditional industries such as garment and restaurant, and female farmworkers.[103] Herrera sponsored Elia Gallardo, the legal coordinator of *Organización en California de Lideres Campesinas*, a statewide entity formed by women farmworkers, to address domestic violence and environmental protection issues. Gallardo worked with ERA for three years (1997 to 1999), funded through a green foundation fellowship and ERA.[104] ERA also sought to expand job opportunities for women in nontraditional jobs. Under Herrera's tenure, the organization created an Affirmative Action Public Education Project and award-winning video, *Keeping the Door Open: Why Women Should Support Affirmative Action* (1996), to counter misinformation and educate the public. The video featured women's success in nontraditional jobs industries, including firefighting. ERA worked with a coalition of 150+ civil rights groups to defeat Proposition 209, the 1996 state ballot initiative to prohibit affirmation action programs in state employment education and contracting.[105] In 2000, under Herrera's leadership, ERA joined a grassroots effort (including Hernández/MALDEF) to defeat Proposition 22, the statewide ballot initiative to ban recognition of same-sex marriage.[106] Simultaneously, ERA expanded the scope of its sexual harassment cases to include school peer harassment cases, returned to immigrant women's rights cases, and took on welfare issues stemming from the 1996 federal welfare reform laws.[107] ERA settled multiyear litiga-

---

100. Equal Rights Advocates, SUMMER 1996 AT 1 (ERA ARTICLE).

101. Judy Scales Trent, *Equal Rights Advocates: Addressing the Legal Issues of Women of Color* (Trent Article), 13 Berkeley Women's L.J. 34 (1998): 34–80, at 75. Herrera had served as interim director since November 1995.

102. Trent Article at 74, 76–77.

103. Trent Article at 78, fn. 281, available at: https://smith.hosted.panopto.com/Panopto/Pages/Embed.aspx?id=de435775-ed03-4720-b5ae-afa300fc1290.

104. *Id.* at 76–78.

105. *Id.* at 78–79.

106. ACLU press release, *Latino, Religious Rights Groups Oppose CA Initiative to Ban Same-Gender Marriage*, March 2, 2000, https://www.aclu.org/press-releases/latino-religious-rights-groups-oppose-ca-initiative-ban-same-gender-marriage.

107. *Supra* note 101 Trent Article at 78–79.

tion—cases initiated prior to Herrera's tenure—and filed lawsuits that significantly improved the lives of California women.

Doe v. Petaluma City School District, 830 F. Supp. 1560, 1576 (N.D. Cal. 1993) (*Petaluma I*), was the first case in the country where the court held a student could claim relief for peer-based sexual harassment under Title IX and other federal and state laws. "No court has addressed the question of whether student-to-student sexual harassment is actionable under Title IX." *Petaluma I*, 830 F. Supp. at 1574. Jane Doe, a junior high school student, sued the school district, counselor, and principal alleging they failed to stop repeated and ongoing sexual harassment by her peers that she endured. In its initial ruling on defendants' motion to dismiss, the court held that hostile environment sexual harassment claims were appropriate under Title IX on a continuing violation theory, which required proof of intentionality, not the negligence standard of "knew or should have known":

> [T]he school district must be found to have intentionally discriminated against the plaintiff student on the basis of sex. The school's failure to take appropriate action, as alleged in plaintiff's complaint, could be circumstantial evidence of intent to discriminate. Thus, a plaintiff student could proceed against a school district on the theory that its inaction (or insufficient action) in the face of complaints of student-to-student sexual harassment was a result of an actual intent to discriminate against the student on the basis of sex. *Petaluma I*, 830 F. Supp. at 1577.

The plaintiff's Title IX claim was dismissed with leave to amend the complaint to include intentional discrimination; the complaint subsequently was amended. In *Doe by and through Doe v. Petaluma City School District*, 949 F. Supp. 1415 (N.D. Cal. 1996) (*Petaluma II*), the ERA and co-counsel argued that the standard of proof in Title IX sexual harassment cases should be the same as those in Title VII cases, not intentionality. Upon a review of the cases decided post *Petaluma I*, the court agreed, concluding the standard of proof in traditional Title VII hostile environment cases was appropriate:

> Thus, the elements which Plaintiff must prove are that Plaintiff was subjected to unwelcome harassment based on her gender, that the harassment was so severe or pervasive as to create a hostile educational environment, and that the Defendants knew, or should in the exercise of their duties have known, of the hostile environment and failed to take prompt and appropriate remedial action. *Petaluma II* at 1427.

In 1997, ERA settled the case on the eve of trial for $250,000 on behalf of the plaintiff; it was settled partly because the plaintiff had graduated.

In an undocketed 1998 matter involving court reporter Keslar, the ERA successfully settled her Title VII sexual harassment case brought against a Nebraska state judge for sexual harassment. The court reporter settled for $70,000 and attorneys' fees. *See Keslar v. Bartu*, 81 F. Supp. 2d 960 (D.C. Neb. 1999) (regarding co-counsel attorneys' fees). The Nebraska judiciary also agreed to adopt a sexual harassment policy that expressly includes court reporters and provides separate and expedited procedures for handling claims of harassment by judicial officers.

Brown v. Sacramento Transit Dist., No. 2:98-cv-01719 (E.D. Cal., Sept. 4, 1998), was a sex discrimination lawsuit initially filed by private counsel on behalf of a former female employee of the Sacramento Regional Transit (SRT). The plaintiff sought monetary damages and injunctive relief for failure to promote under Title VII and California's Fair Employment and Housing Act, Cal. Gov't Code § 12900. The ERA and the Impact Fund joined as co-counsel and a class was certified to include all current or former women employees of SRT who: (1) applied for promotions but were denied or discouraged on the basis of gender discrimination; (2) sought training and/or were discouraged from seeking such training by virtue of defendant's discriminatory policies and practices; and (3) were salaried and discriminated against with regards to salary, job title, job description and/or grade level. The defendant's motion for summary judgment was denied without prejudice in July 2001. In 2002, ERA and the Impact Fund reached a landmark settlement that included extensive injunctive relief, compensatory damages of $42,857 to each of the named plaintiffs, and $900,000 in attorney's fees. SRT created an approved 15A pay grade level at which the plaintiffs were reclassified. On February 23, 2003, the order granting final approval of class settlement consent decree and final judgment was entered, and the case was dismissed. Both parties appealed the special master's various orders after the consent decree was finalized with all issues resolved by May 10, 2007, including a prima facie retaliation claim filed by one of the plaintiffs. *See, Brown v. Sacramento Regional Transit Dist.*, 2007 WL 1395349 (2007).

In 1987, 86% of San Francisco's Fire Department (SFFD) were white males. On behalf of the plaintiffs' women of color, ERA settled a multiyear challenge against the SFFD for discriminatory hiring and promotion policies with a consent decree filed on May 20, 1988.[108] *See, United States v. City and County of San Francisco*, 696 F. Supp. 1287 (N.D. Cal. 1988), *aff'd as modified by Davis v. City and County of San Francisco*, 890 F.2d 1438 (9th Cir. 1989) (consent decree adopted), *U.S. v. City and County of San Francisco*, 747 F. Supp. 1370 (N.D. Cal. 1990) (resolving outstanding backpay awards). Other plaintiffs-intervenors joined the suit, including MALDEF's CRP, which joined under Martinez's tenure as President and General Counsel and was settled under Hernandez's tenure. The consent decree contained specific goals for hiring and promotion goals, with further specified goals for women of color, to be implemented through the following decade during Herrera's ERA tenure. The consent decree required the SFFD force to reflect the San Francisco community and set hiring goals in selecting candidates: 40% minority and 10% female. During 1993–1994, "[o]f fe-

108. SFFD Racial Equity Action Plan 2021–2023, 1-52 at 4 (SFFD Plan), https://sf-fire.org/files/2021-01/Fire%20Racial%20Equity%20Action%20Plan.pdf.

male applicants, 71% or 1,465 female applicants were ethnic minorities, and 60% of 4,721 male applicants were ethnic minorities ... 23% of all applications were from women."[109] When the court's supervision ended in January 1999, minorities constituted 37.5% and women comprised 8.75% of the nearly 1,500-member force, just short of the projected goals.[110] In 2004, then San Francisco Mayor Gavin Newsom appointed the SFFD's first female fire chief, Joanne Hayes-White.[111] Herrera "hailed the appointment," stating, "[w]omen have proven we are capable of doing firefighting jobs, and today, the proof is in the pudding... [t]o have a woman as the head of the department is exciting."[112] Once court supervision ended, so too, did some of the initiatives and programs responsible for increasing recruitment and minority hiring and funding, leaving the task to individual SFFD fire fighters of color and their respective organizations. The numbers fell until 2020 when the SFFD's Racial Equity Action group propelled the SFFD to implement a Racial Equity Action Plan.[113]

By 1991, after thirteen years of litigation, the ERA and co-counsel settled a class-action discrimination lawsuit with Pacific Bell over its denial of early retirement benefits to workers who took maternity leave prior to 1978. In *Pallas v. Pacific Bell*, 940 F.2d 1324 (9th Cir. 1991), the class of nearly 10,000 women agreed to the settlement securing additional retirement benefits valued at more than $25 million. Pre-1979, Pacific Bell required pregnant employees to take personal leave while on maternity leave. After 1979, Pacific Bell changed its policy, allowing employees with pregnancy-related disabilities to take disability leave. In 1987, Pacific Bell instituted a new retirement benefit for management employees called the "Early Retirement Opportunity." An eligible employee qualified upon accruing 20 years of service. Prior to enactment of the Pregnancy Discrimination Act (PDA) in 1978,[114] Pacific Bell calculated an employee's length of service with a "net credited service" system, crediting time taken due to a temporary disability, but not for "personal leave." Employed since 1967, the plaintiff applied for the Early Retirement Opportunity benefit but was ineligible by three to four days as Pacific Bell did not credit her maternity leave taken in 1972. The Ninth Circuit found Pacific Bell discriminated against plaintiffs in violation of the PDA.

Ten years later, in *Hulteen v. AT&T*, 441 F.3d 653 (9th Cir. 2006), ERA settled an identical class action lawsuit on behalf of four female employees whose pregnancy leave were not credited for disability leave in calculating their retirement benefits. Hulteen had 210 days of uncredited pregnancy leave and the other plaintiffs had 67,

---

109. SFFD Plan at 5.

110. *Id.*

111. Ryan Kim, *Newsom Names Female Fire Chief: Historic Choice for Big-City Department*, San Francisco Chronicle, January 11, 2004, https://www.sfgate.com/politics/article/Newsom-names-female-fire-chief-Historic-choice-2813593.php.

112. *Id.*

113. *Supra* note 109, SFFD Plan at 8–18, 26–27, 30–33, 35–37.

114. Title VII, 42 U.S.C. § 2000e(k) effective October 31, 1978.

73 and 210 days of uncredited pregnancy leave. Plaintiffs sued AT&T, alleging the company's policy for calculating employee pension and retirement benefits discriminated against women who had taken leave due to pregnancy in violation of the PDA, citing *Pallas* as precedent. The AT&T policy considered temporary disability leave as service time for the purposes of calculating retirement benefits except when the leave was taken by pregnant women. Asserting as authority *Landgraf v. USI Film Products*, 511 U.S. 244 (1994), AT&T argued that *Landgraf*—not *Pallas*—was the controlling authority as it created a "sea change" in retroactivity principles such that the PDA should not apply to pregnancy leave taken before it was enacted. *Hulteen*, 441 F.3d at 658. The district court granted summary judgment in favor of the plaintiffs, predicating its ruling on *Pallas*. AT&T's admitted that its current retirement calculations excluding pre-PDA pregnancy leave violates Title VII. A panel of the Ninth Circuit initially reversed the trial court's decision adopting AT&T's argument that the lower court gave impermissible retroactive effect to the PDA, noting "[p]rospectivity remains the appropriate default rule." *Hulteen*, 441 F.3d at 658. Upon rehearing *en banc*, the Ninth Circuit reversed itself and upheld the trial court's decision. *Hulteen*, 498 F.3d 1001 (2007). Luminaria Circuit Court Judge Wardlaw authored the Ninth Circuit's opinion. Relying on *Bazemore v. Friday*, 478 U.S. 385, 106 S.Ct. 3000, 92 L.Ed.2d 315 (1986), Judge McLane Wardlaw concluded that AT&T's calculation constituted a current violation of Title VII that does not involve retroactive application of the PDA and thus rejected its "sea change" argument and AT&T's *Landgraf* authority and other caselaw. She wrote:

> Pacific Bell's decision to discriminate against Pallas in 1987 was actionable because 'liability may be imposed' for a pre-Title VII discriminatory policy to the extent it is perpetuated in post-Title VII employment decisions...In 1991, Congress amended the Civil Rights Act to make it clear if *Pallas* had not already done so, that an employer who adopts a seniority system for an intentionally discriminatory purpose commits an unlawful employment practice 'when the seniority system is adopted, when an individual becomes subject to the seniority system, or when a person aggrieved is injured by the application of the seniority system or provision of the system.'" *Hulteen*, 498 F. 3d at 1011.

AT&T appealed to the U.S. Supreme Court raising the impermissible retroactive application of the PDA in *AT&T Corp. v. Hulteen*, 556 U.S. 701, 129 S.Ct. 1962 (2009). AT&T continued to rely on *Landgraf* as authority, and this time, SCOTUS agreed. *Landgraf* held that in the absence of a clear expression of intent by Congress, no retroactive application applies. The Court refused to apply retroactive application of the PDA, concluding AT&T had not discriminated because its policy was adopted prior to the PDA's enactment. In its analysis, the Court noted the Ninth Circuit's ruling was contrary to those adopted in the Sixth and Seventh Circuits. Justice Ruth Bader Ginsburg dissented, concluding AT&T's prior policy was discriminatory because it expressly excluded pregnancy from the seniority credit system resulting in lower pension payments to women. She reasoned that because AT&T continued to use the flawed system to calculate benefits after the passage of the PDA, it engaged in ongoing impermissible discrimination. Justice Ginsburg wrote:

> In *General Elec. Co. v. Gilbert,* 429 U.S. 125, 97 S.Ct. 401, 50 L.Ed.2d 343 (1976), this Court held that a classification harmful to women based on pregnancy did not qualify as discrimination 'because of... sex' prohibited by Title VII... Exclusion of pregnancy from an employer's disability plan, the Court ruled, 'is not a gender-based discrimination at all.' [Citation omitted.]
>
> The PDA does not require redress for past discrimination. It does not oblige employers to make women whole for the compensation denied them when, prior to the Act, they were placed on pregnancy leave, often while still ready, willing, and able to work, and with no secure right to return to their jobs after childbirth. But the PDA does not protect women, from and after April 1979, when the Act became fully effective, against repetition or continuation of pregnancy-based disadvantageous treatment... Congress interred *Gilbert* more than 30 years ago, but the court today allows that wrong decision to hold sway. The plaintiffs... in this action will receive, for the rest of their lives, lower pension benefits than colleagues who worked for AT&T no longer than they did. They will experience this discrimination not simply because of the adverse action to which they were subjected pre-PDA. Rather, they are harmed today because AT&T has refused to fully heed the PDA's core command: Hereafter, for '*all* employment-related purposes,' disadvantageous treatment 'on the basis of pregnancy, childbirth, or related medical conditions must cease. I would hold that AT&T committed a current violation of Title VII when, post-PDA, it did not totally discontinue reliance upon a pension calculation premised on the notion that pregnancy-based classifications display no gender bias. *AT&T,* 556 U.S. at 719–721.

In a series of cases, ERA tackled employer practices that deprived working-class women in the garment industry of full pay, a safe work environment, and day care opportunities. *Does 1-8 v. ASC Fashion, US Boys et al.,* No. 96-6195 WJR (C.D. Cal, 1999), was the first time a clothing manufacturer agreed to pay for its contractor's violation of labor laws. Nine Thai and Latina garment workers filed the action against US Boys, a sportswear manufacturer, for minimum wage and overtime pay. Some were not paid overtime for their labor on weekends. ERA secured improved compliance with wage and hour laws and improved workplace safety regulations. US Boys also agreed to monitor its contractor to ensure compliance and to pay $200,000 to settle the case. This case triggered passage of California Assembly Bill 633 (1999) (AB 633), the first of its kind in the country, establishing joint and several liability on garment manufacturers and retailers when workers' rights are violated. AB 633 also enabled garment workers to recoup back wages.[115] AB 633 was the precursor to the

---

115. AB 633 (February 19, 1999), Cal.Lab.Code, amending §§ 2671, 2675, 2675.5, 2676, 2677, and 2680 and adding §§ 2673.1 and 2684.

California Garment Worker Protection Act (SB 62), effective January 1, 2022.[116] SB 62 intended to address deficiencies in AB 633 and increase protections to garment workers. The law prohibits paying garment workers on per piece, adds stronger measures of liability on brands if subcontractors fail to pay full wages, and grants authority to the labor commissioner to act when workers present "credible evidence." *Kamsan Mao v. Top Line Electronics, Inc. and Lite-On, Inc.*, No. C-99-21203 RMW/EAI (N.D. Cal. 2000), was the first lawsuit in California to challenge the "homework" practice. Among some electronics assembly businesses, Asian immigrant workers were paid on a piece rate basis for work completed at home after a day's work, depriving them of overtime pay. ERA entered an unprecedented and confidential monetary settlement with two Silicon Valley companies who agreed to cease the illegal "homework" practice. The companies agreed to a stipulated injunction barring them from assigning after-hours work—directory or indirectly—including from their subcontractors. Top Line and Lite-On also agreed to provide workplace safety resources to all employees.

As part of its targeted legal strategy to fight sexual harassment in the restaurant industry, ERA represented two African American women servers employed at TGI Fridays, Tiffany McIntyre and Deneane Hibbitts, No. C-99-5328 MJJ (EDL, 2000). ERA alleged the restaurant chain violated Title VII, the California Fair Employment and Housing Act, Government Code §§12940 *et seq.*, the Fair Credit and Reporting Act, 15 U.S.C. §1681, *et seq.*, and state contract law. In a discovery dispute, the court ordered the defendant "to produce all documents relating to discrimination complaints filed by other employees in all restaurants owned by defendant in the state of California since January 1, 1998." *McIntyre and Hibbitts v. Main Street and Main Street Inc. d/b/a TGI Fridays,* 2000 WL 33117274, 84 Fair Empl. Prac. Cas. BNA 1032 (2000). The defendant thereafter settled. In a 2006 case, *Donaldson v. Lori's Diner,* the ERA successfully sued the San Francisco restaurant chain on behalf of women wait staff who were subjected to sexual and racial harassment at work.[117]

Jackelyn Lundy v. University of California-Santa Cruz, American Arbitration Association No. 74-L300-197 (2000), involved a formal grievance after Lundy, a female faculty member, took parental leave to adopt and care for her first child. ERA represented Lundy in the arbitration. A confidential settlement was reached that included back pay and benefits. This case led to the 2002 passage of California's Paid Family Leave Law (CA-PFL), effective July 1, 2004. The CA-PFL was financed under the bill through an employee payroll tax added to the state's temporary disability insurance.

116. Cal.Lab.Code, Chapter 329 (passed September 27, 2021), amending section 2, §1174.1, section 3, §2670, section 5, §2673, section 6, §2673.1, and section 8, §2675.5, and adding §2673.2 to section 7.

117. This case was not retrievable on Westlaw and the ERA could not locate its archived file to provide a case citation though it is mentioned on the ERA website.

The CA-PFL provided employees six weeks partial paid leave to care for infants or family members; it was amended in 2020 from six to eight weeks leave.[118]

Filed initially in 2001 in San Francisco by ERA, *Dukes v. Wal-Mart, Inc.*, 603 F.3d 571 (9th Cir. 2010), involved the largest certified gender discrimination class action lawsuit—a potential class of 1.5 million female employees who had been working at Wal-Mart since December 26, 1998, alleging discrimination in pay and promotion. *Dukes v. Wal-Mart, Inc.*, 222 F.R.D. 137 (D.C. Cal. June 2, 2004). ERA represented Betty Dukes, an African American, who started working for Wal-Mart in 1994, earning $5.50 an hour as a Wal-Mart greeter at the Pittsburgh, Oakland store. A major discovery fight erupted over a 1995 memo written by Wal-Mart's outside counsel (Dkt. No. 840-1, Ex. 1., Memo) that was featured in the New York Times, *Lawyers Warned Wal-Mart of Risks before Bias Suit* (June 3 and 4, 2010). ERA and co-counsel argued the memo should be produced as the attorney-client privilege was waived by its publication and subsequent statements by Wal-Mart management. Quoting from the memo, the Court discussed Wal-Mart's potential liability based on work conditions at the company during 1993, as assessed by its counsel:

> While the New York Times did not publish the Memo, the newspaper did report several findings contained in the Memo, including that "women employed by Wal–Mart earned less than men in numerous job categories, with men in salaried jobs earning 19 percent more than women." (Dkt. No. 840–1, Ex. 1.) "By one measure ... men were five and a half times as likely as women to be promoted into salaried, management positions." (Id.) Further, in 1993, men employed by Wal–Mart as department managers were paid an hourly rate 5.8 percent higher than women in those positions. (Id.) Because the company "would find it difficult to fashion a persuasive explanation for disproportionate employment patterns," the Memo estimated that Wal–Mart's potential legal exposure in a class-action sex discrimination suit was $185 million to $740 million for 1993 alone. (Id.) The Memo also indicated that the overall disparities in job assignments were "statistically significant and sufficient to warrant a finding of discrimination unless the company can demonstrate at trial that the statistical disparities are caused by legitimate, nondiscriminatory factors." *Dukes v. Wal-Mart Stores, Inc.*, 2013 WL 1282892 (March 26, 2013).

Ultimately, the court found that the attorney-client privilege had not been waived and denied ERA's motion for production of the memo.

Sitting *en banc*, the Ninth Circuit substantially affirmed the district court's class certification (and the initial panel decision) on the issue of backpay. At the time, women filled 70% of all hourly jobs but only 33% of management. *Dukes*, 564 U.S. at 370. Wal-Mart appealed the Ninth Circuit's ruling. In a 5–4 decision written by

118. As of July 1, 2014, PFL benefits were expanded to cover care for a seriously ill parent-in-law, grandparent, grandchild, or sibling, http://www.edd.ca.gov/disability/Paid_Family_Leave.htm.

Justice Antonin Scalia, SCOTUS decertified the class for failure to show and meet commonality on questions of law or fact under Rule 23(a)(3) and (4) or (b)(2). *Wal-Mart Stores, Inc. v. Dukes*, 564 U.S. 338, 131 S. Ct. 2541, 180 L. Ed. 2d 374 (2011) (Ginsberg J. dissent). In June 2012, After the SCOTUS ruling, nearly 2,000 female workers filed discrimination complaints against Wal-Mart with the EEOC. While the case did not proceed as a class action, the suit settled in May 2015, achieving landmark changes and relief for female workers across the country that include ERA's subsequent partnerships that formed the Equal Pay Today! Campaign.[119] Ms. Dukes retired from the company in 2016 after 23 years of service. She passed the following year on July 10, 2017.

In 2005, ERA brought a groundbreaking class action lawsuit against a tribal gaming company. Filed in Placer, California on behalf of Corinn Medina and seven former Thunder Valley Casino female workers in the Sacramento area, the plaintiffs alleged gender and age discrimination under Title VII. Plaintiffs asserted they were sexually harassed (one claimed she was raped), subjected to a hostile work environment by customers and management, wrongfully terminated, and retaliated against for filing complaints and violations by casino management of state and federal labor codes. *Medina v. Station Casinos et al.*, No. S-CV-0019017 (May 18, 2005). Thunder Valley Casinos was owned by Station Casinos and the United Auburn Indian Community. The case was dismissed against the tribe based on sovereign immunity. The defendants invoked Indian sovereignty laws, arguing these laws precluded EEOC from investigating the complaints but did not preclude it from issuing right to sue letters. (In California, only the governor may authorize an investigation into whether Indian nations are violating the civil rights of employees.) Commissioner Margaret Wells subsequently ruled the case could move forward against the Nevada-based Station Casino which had hired the plaintiffs. Nevada requires casinos to comply with all local and state laws. The tribe established an independent arbitration procedure to address harassment complaints such as those raised by the plaintiffs.[120] Thus, the parties entered the first-of-its-kind arbitration, resulting in a multimillion-dollar settlement to the plaintiffs' favor. The case was closed on January 13, 2009.

Brust, et al. v. Regents of the University of California, No. 2:07-CV-01488-FCD-EFB (E.D. Cal., 2009), was a class action challenge to end the decades of noncompliance by the University of California system (UC) with Title IX that required schools to provide female students with equal opportunities to play sports. On behalf of its female student clients, ERA entered protracted negotiations with a mediator. In Oc-

---

119. ERA Executive Director Noreen Farrell, *How We Pay Tribute to Betty Dukes in the Fight for Fair Pay*, August 9, 2017, https://nfarrellera.medium.com/how-we-pay-tribute-to-betty-dukes-in-the-fight-for-fair-pay-67f2b3a66018.

120. *See* Peter Byrne, *Taking on a Nation*, Salon, January 13, 2006, https://www.salon.com/2006/01/13/thunder_valley/; and Gus Thomson, *New Wrinkle in Casino Lawsuit*, Gold Country Media, June 21, 2006, https://goldcountrymedia.com/news/103669/new-wrinkles-in-casino-lawsuit/.

tober 2009, the court approved the final class action settlement and stipulated judgment. The settlement added new women's sports teams, a substantial increase in the funds to support the development of UC female students' athletic abilities and included an agreement to monitor the process for the addition of teams and varsity squad sizes. Each of the representative plaintiffs were awarded $8,000, and the court approved and ordered UC to pay attorneys' fees of $460,000.

3. Herrera's Post Litigation Career

The Renaissance woman developed a passion for writing that started with appellate work at MALDEF and continued thereafter. From 1983 to 1986, Herrera was a freelance journalist with New American Media writing about social justice issues for the *New York Times*, *Washington Post*, *Newsday*, *Mexico City News*, and the *Sacramento Bee*. Upon retiring from practice in 2009, Herrera turned from formal legal writing into writing plays and became a solo performer. Her inaugural productions, "*Tell Me Your Name, one woman's journal from a small segregated South Texas town to the Bay Area's multicultural mecca*" and "*Why Would I Mispronounce My Own Name?*" have been performed in venues throughout the country.[121] Herrera characterizes her "multiple identities as indivisible ... [a]t all times ... Chicana, Latina, madre, lawyer, playwright, writer, stand-up comic, feminist, world-traveler, avid hiker." In her work, Herrera:

> explore[s] what it is to be a class migrant who benefited from expanded opportunity. I am committed to fighting the well-financed efforts presently underway to shut down these paths for marginalized communities. My +30 years as a civil rights lawyer has given me a front-row seat to the most exciting and challenging societal tectonic shifts ... I am a refugee from a racially polarized South Texas town who fell in love with big cities. I am both urbanite and anonymous small-town girl. Mexican-American by birth, world citizen by choice, and proud speaker of Spanish, the greatest gift my parents bestowed. Studying languages and discovering how words from different languages connect is something I find downright thrilling. I love comedy, mimicry, puns, and anything that gets a genuine response from people, whether laughter or even a groan.[122]

For her body of professional work, Herrera received the prestigious Margaret Brent Women Lawyers of Achievement Award from the ABA Commission on Women (2001).

---

121. Casa | Irmaherrera, https://www.irmaherrera.com/. The production ideas emanate from eighth grade when she and other students were asked to introduce themselves to their ninth grade white classmates. Irma pronounced her name properly in Spanish, causing the students to "look at her aghast" for not anglicizing her name.

122. *Id.*

E. Deborah Escobedo

1. Escobedo's Formative Years

Deborah Escobedo was born on March 8, 1954, to Albert and Mercedes (*nee* Alonzo) Escobedo, both natives of Los Angeles County who settled in Lynwood as the only Latino family on the block. There, Deborah was born as the youngest daughter of four children, and the only daughter. Mercedes was a homemaker. Albert was a factory worker at Firestone Tire & Rubber Corporation for more than 35 years until the plant closed. He then pivoted and became a janitor at the local school district. The Escobedos sent their children to Catholic elementary and high schools, expecting them to obtain a college education; all did. As their parents were punished at school for speaking Spanish, they chose not to raise their children bilingually. "Political discourse was a constant at [their] home."[123] Albert was a "union man" and treasurer of his local union at Firestone. He and other LA Latino union workers were big supporters of Cesar Chavez and took Deborah to experience her first picket line in high school. Albert's union organized a fundraiser for the United Farmworkers Union (UFW) where Deborah and her family met Cesar Chavez. During college, her brothers Eddie and Rudy and Deborah (since high school) were involved in the Chicano movement. In college, Deborah became a "MEChista" like her brothers. This background influenced Deborah to "use [her] education to give back to her community" and be an advocate. Deborah's oldest brother, Albert, graduated from Loyola University and earned his law degree at Berkeley Law. Eddie, Rudy, and Deborah graduated from the University of California-Santa Cruz. Eddie became a university administrator and Rudy a college professor. Deborah "decided to pursue a law career aligned with these values of service."[124] Like Albert, Deborah attended Berkeley Law, earning her J.D. in 1979.

2. Agricultural Labor Rights Board, 1979–1984

Upon passing the California bar exam, Deborah (Escobedo) worked for five years at the Agricultural Labor Rights Board (ALRB), a state agency that assisted farmworkers in unionizing and securing their labor rights. The following case exemplifies the nature of her work at the ALRB and the grueling circumstances of the farmworkers in the country. Escobedo is listed as co-counsel in *Maggio, Inc. v. Agricultural Labor Relations Board (Board) and United Farm Workers of America, AFL-CIO*, 154 Cal. App. 3d 40, 201 Cal. Rptr. 30 (1984). *Maggio* was a consolidation of petitions brought by employer-growers when they and the UFW failed to negotiate new collective bargaining agreements (CBAs) that stemmed the period between the start of the negotiations in January 1979 up to the appeal issued in 1984. In total, 28 owners

---

123. Escobedo notes on file with the author (Escobedo notes).

124. *Id.*

(growers) and the UFW were involved in the negotiations with two specific groups of growers involved in the disputed negotiations, the Salinas growers and the Imperial Valley growers. The UFW and growers had reached an agreement four years earlier (the "Master Contract"). In late 1978, negotiations for a new Master Contract began and continued in 1979 with Cesar Chavez attending the first session in January 1979. The parties agreed they would not release details of the negotiations to the press or the public. The UFW presented changes to "over one-half of the forty-three articles" dealing with seniority, mechanization, union security, and hiring issues characterized by the court as "noneconomic concerns." *Maggio*, 201 Cal. Rptr. at 48 and top of page 49. The UFW submitted its economic proposal:

> The proposal called for a one-year contract with substantial pay increases for all field workers... for the hourly rate for general laborers to increase from \$3.78 to \$5.25, for cutters on lettuce harvest machines from \$3.78 to \$6.00, and for tractor drivers from \$4.52 to \$8.25; for piece rate workers, there would be an increase from 57 cents to 87 cents per box of hand-packed lettuce, and from 85 cents to \$1.41 per box of celery... the reasons for the wage increases, noting the earnings of many of the workers had not kept abreast of inflation, the failure of the agricultural workers' conditions to improve at the same rate as other union members in the state and the generally prosperous year enjoyed by the vegetable industry. The UFW's proposal also provided for longer rest periods, an additional five holidays, overtime pay, improved vacation rights, cost of living adjustments, standby and reporting pay, guaranteed minimum workdays and workweeks, mileage and expense allowances, and increased contributions to medical and pension plans. Employers estimated their labor cost under the proposal would be increased by 128 to 196 percent. UFW does not contest this estimate. *Maggio*, 201 Cal. Rptr. at 48.

The growers proposed a 7% annual salary increase across the board that they contended was consistent with then U.S. President Jimmy Carter's wage and price guidelines (Guidelines).[125] Their counterproposal rejected nearly all the UFW's proposals and modified existing provisions that eliminated some of the union members' rights under the Master Contract. The Master Contract contained a no-strike provision, which had expired on January 15. After the January 18 session, the UFW printed and distributed leaflets to the farmworkers and placed an ad in the local Mexicali *La Voz* Spanish-language newspaper to inform farmworkers of the status of the negotiations. The growers objected to the UFW's ad, claiming it violated their agreement. Thereafter, a Committee for Fair Negotiations (CFN) was formed that consisted primarily of growers' employees. CFN placed an ad in *La Voz*, addressed to the farmworkers in the Imperial Valley, in which the growers relayed they wanted "to do what was right." The CFN continued to place ads. One ad depicted Cesar Chavez

---

125. Executive Order 12092, 43 Federal Register 60772 (Dec. 28, 1978), which generally limited salary increases to 7% per year.

"wielding a whip over the workers" and another depicted him overweight and "sitting atop of money bags ignoring the pleas of starving farmworkers and accused him of misdirecting funds from the union benefit plans." *Maggio*, at 36–38. The ads exacerbated the already-existing tension and impacted the negotiations.

By late February, the Imperial Valley growers declared they had reached an impasse. The UFW went on strike and began picketing. Some days involved minor violence between farmworkers and growers, which ultimately resulted in the death of a farmworker by a foreman working at one of the grower's ranches. Notwithstanding the climate, negotiations between the UFW and the Salinas Valley growers resumed, resulting in new contracts by June 1979, with all but three of the Salinas Valley growers. The Imperial Valley growers remained steadfast at a 22% annual salary increase rejecting the UFW's proposed 123–190% increase in wages. *Maggio*, at 38. After months of ongoing negotiations, by August 1979, no new master agreement was reached with the remaining growers despite that the terms in the new CBA were almost identical to the old Master Contract.

The UFW filed an unfair labor practice (refusal-to-bargain) complaint with the board pursuant to the Agricultural Labor Relations Act (ALRA), which is based on the National Labor Relations Act (Act).[126] A hearing was held in September 1979, by which time agreements had been reached with 15 of the 28 original growers. The UFW obtained a ruling from the administrative law officer (ALO) that the growers violated the ALRA, specifically, §§ 1140, 1153(a) and (e).[127] The ALO found that the growers negotiated in bad faith prior to the impasse and thereafter. The growers appealed to the Board, which decided the growers did not bargain in good faith based on their "take-it-or-leave-it-offer" from which they never deviated. The Board cited as support *N.L.R.B. v General Electric Company*, 418 F.2d 736 (1969) (holding that the take-it-or-leave-it bargaining methods combined with a *"widely publicized stance of unbending firmness"* constituted an unfair labor practice). *Maggio*, 201 Cal. Rptr. at 46. On appeal in *Maggio*, 201 Cal. Rptr. the California Supreme Court found that the record did not support the Board's decision. It determined that the growers' attitude (even if true) did not constitute a violation of the Act. *Maggio*, at 40. The court concluded the parties stalemated on the single issue of economics and the question was whether the growers acted in bad faith in adhering to the 7% annual salary increase. The court found credible the growers' claim that their proposals were within the Guidelines and their belief they would be sanctioned if they did not follow them (though they were voluntary); alternatively, the court ruled this was a legitimate bargaining chip. The growers also convinced the court that its public relations campaign (the ads placed) intended to convey the message that they were

126. Cal.Lab.Code, § 1148, *et seq.*; 29 U.S.C.A. § 151 *et seq.* (1964), specifically §§ 158(a)(I), (3), and (5).

127. 7 ALRB No. 43: *Admiral Packing Company et.al. Respondents and United Farm Workers, Charging Party.*

negotiating within the Guidelines, which the court held constituted further proof of the growers' good faith. The court held the growers did not violate the Act. The court held there was "no substantial evidence to support the Board's finding of bad faith," concluding it was the UFW that made extreme demands from the outset and was unwilling to compromise or negotiate in good faith. *Maggio*, 201 Cal. Rptr., at 41–43, 50. Finding the growers did not violate the ALRA, the court remanded the matter on employees' reinstatement rights as economic strikers. *Maggio*, 201 Cal. Rptr. at 72 (Associate Justices Howard B. Wiener and Cruz Reynoso dissented.)

Escobedo moved from El Centro to San Francisco, devoting the rest of her legal career to education advocacy, specifically on behalf of Latino children, securing access to equal education under civil rights laws, starting as a staff attorney with Legal Aid Society of Alameda County (1985–1989). Reflecting on growing up speaking English only, she observed. "Ironically, I focused on the language access rights of English learner and immigrant students, advocating they should [not] be forced to lose their language and culture in pursuing an education."[128] For 15 years, Escobedo litigated education cases at META. She also championed the rights of juveniles as a staff attorney at the Youth Law Center (2005 to 2014), causing dramatic changes in the child welfare and juvenile justice systems.

3. Litigation and Legislative Advocacy, 1989–2023

Bilingualism and bilingual education in California have a tortured history that predates Escobedo's advocacy. Dating back to 1848 when the Treaty of Guadalupe Hidalgo ended the United States' intervention in Mexico, Article IX guaranteed the civil rights of Mexicans (soon-to-be U.S. citizens). The article, interpreted to include the right to speak their native tongue, Spanish, triggered a battle over language rights in the state. Nearly a century later, California passed a law mandating English-only instruction in the classroom. California Governor Ronald Reagan signed Senate Bill 53 in 1967, which repealed the English-only law and authorized public schools to use other instructional languages. One year later, President Johnson signed the Bilingual Education Act of 1968 (BEA). AB 1329, the Chacón-Moscone Bilingual-Bicultural Education Act (BBEA), adopted in 1976,[129] created transitional bilingual education programs, mandating school districts to provide language minority students with equal educational opportunities (when necessary, in their native language) and promote cross-cultural understanding, and provide equal opportunity for students' academic achievement. The federal BBEA was strengthened in 1981 by amendments assigning additional, specific responsibilities to public school districts in educating limited English-proficient (LEP) students. In 1980, the legislature passed AB 507, the Bilingual Education Improvement and Reform Act (BEIRA), to update and strength-

128. *Supra* note 123, Escobedo Notes.

129. Education Code (hereafter Cal. Ed. Code) Article 3, Bilingual-Bicultural Education Act of 1976, §§ 52160–52178.

en the BBEA. BEIRA mandated districts to provide bilingual instruction for every LEP student enrolled at public K–12 schools in California. It strengthened the BBEA in several ways, including expanding the use of students' primary languages in classroom instruction.

In 1986, Californians overwhelmingly passed Proposition 63 (California State Constitution, Article III, Section 6), declaring English as the official language of California. Although passage of this initiative itself did not prevent non-English native language instruction, its well-timed introduction coinciding with the BBEA's reauthorization, provided the popular mandate upon which the law was allowed to sunset. Bilingual education was weakened by Governor Deukmejian who vetoed bills in 1986 and 1987 to legalize and reauthorize bilingual education.[130] In practice, California public school districts continued implementing the basic principles of the BBEA until 1998 when Proposition 227, English Language in Public Schools (Prop. 227), was passed by a margin of 61% to 39%. Prop. 227 required LEP students to be placed in sheltered English immersion programs (classes in which all instruction is taught in English). Despite its passage, the state's districts designed instructional programs for LEP students and, critically, used students' primary languages in instruction or to support their learning.

This legal landscape provided Escobedo the opportunity and challenge to strengthen laws for LEP students and disadvantaged youth. The stakes were high: the availability and quality of education gained or lost for students with immediate impact and life-lasting effects. Though not always successful, Escobedo was persistent. *Teresa P. v. Berkeley Unified School District*, 724 F. Supp. 698 (1989), exemplifies her tenacity. Escobedo served as co-counsel for the Legal Aid Society of Alameda County, representing the plaintiff class of nearly 500 LEP students who spoke 38 languages, with the majority—268—being Spanish speakers. Plaintiffs alleged the district's testing and procedures to identify and assess students' language needs were inadequate, employed inappropriate criteria to determine LEP services, and failed to allocate necessary resources and ensure teachers and staff were adequately qualified to deliver LEP instruction in violation of the EEOA and Title VI. In detailed findings of fact, the court held the district's LEP programs were implemented effectively, that the district appropriately assigned noncertified, English-speaking teachers who met the district's local criteria to teach the LEP students (noting the state's critical shortage of bilingual/bicultural credentialed teachers), and there was no violation of the law.

4. Multicultural Education, Training, and Advocacy, 1989–2004

At META, Escobedo litigated several cases challenging different California ballot propositions. Like Hernández at MALDEF, Escobedo challenged Prop. 187, which attempted to exclude undocumented children from attending California public schools. *Pedro A. v. Dawson and the State Board of Education*, No. 965089 (S.F. Sup.

130. AB 1329/76 (1986) and AB 1329/80 (1987).

Ct., 1994), was one of five court challenges to Prop. 187 in which Escobedo joined as META co-counsel. *Pedro A.* involved a petition for writ of mandamus in which plaintiffs (five families and their children) represented the class of nearly 300,000 students who were to be excluded under Prop 187. Upon passage of Prop. 187, California's Education Code Section 48215 was automatically enacted. In November 1994, plaintiffs sought to permanently enjoin implementation of Prop. 187. Escobedo and co-counsel obtained a temporary restraining order and an order to show cause for preliminary injunction on November 9, 1999. The subsequent entry of preliminary injunction and ultimate final judgment in the federal litigation mooted the state court case. *See,* Prop. 187 discussion Hernández, *supra.* Ultimately on March 13, 1998, the proposition, specifically §§ 1, 4, and 9, was ruled unconstitutional.[131] In June 1999, California Governor Gray Davis requested mediation to resolve the appeal of Prop. 187, which resulted in an agreement on July 29, 1999.[132] Escobedo's Prop. 187 experiences prepared her for future advocacy efforts some 25 years later when she discovered registration practices by hundreds of school districts that would discourage immigrant families from enrolling their children in school.[133]

While at META, Escobedo challenged provisions of Prop. 227, which dismantled bilingual programs and reverted to an English-only immersion curriculum for California's then 1.6 million LEP students. *Angel V. v. Davis* (formerly *Valeria G. et al. v. Pete Wilson*),[134] 12 F. Supp. 2d 1007 (N.D. Cal. 1998), was the federal court challenge to Proposition 227 (*see also Valeria v. Davis*, 307 F.3d 1036 (N.D. Cal. 1998). In this case, plaintiff-LEP students sought a preliminary injunction enjoining the state superintendent of public instruction (Superintendent), and the State Department of Education (SDE) and the California Department of Education (CDE) from implementing Prop. 227. Plaintiffs claimed violation of their rights under the EEOA, Title VI, the Supremacy Clause,[135] and the Equal Protection Clause of the U.S. Constitution. The proposition, § 300 (d), defined the immersion system as "an English language acquisition process for young children in which nearly all classroom instruction is in English but with the curriculum and presentation designed for children who are learning the language." Section 305 required that children "shall be taught English by being taught in English" for a transitional period not to exceed one year and then transferred to English-language mainstream classrooms. Prop. 227 required parents to apply for waivers to enroll their children into bilingual or dual

131. ACLU News, *Judges Block Anti-Immigrant Measure*, December–November 1994

132. *Id.*

133. *Supra* note 123, Escobedo Notes.

134. Co-counsel included Hernández and Luminaria Theresa Fay-Bustillos (1980 J.D., UCLA) on behalf of MALDEF and Vilma Martinez who then was a partner at Munger Tolles & Olsen, LLP.

135. U.S. Const. Art. VI, paragraph 2, "This Constitution, and the Law of the United States which shall be made in Pursuance thereof; and all Treaties made, or which shall be made, under the Authority of the United States, shall be the supreme Law of the Land; and the Judges in every State shall be bound thereby, any Thing in the Constitution of Laws of any State to the Contrary notwithstanding."

immersion programs when the student (1) already knows English; (2) is 10 years or older and the school agrees an alternative curriculum would better serve the student's English education; and/or (3) has tried the immersion program for at least 30 days and the school agrees the child has special needs such that an alternative curriculum would better serve the student.

Escobedo presented the lead argument for the plaintiffs at the preliminary injunction hearing. In the introduction, Escobedo wanted the court to know who was being impacted by this initiative:

> I'd like to talk a little bit about these children, your honor. I think that the court has to recognized that these children are some of the most vulnerable children in our state schools. They and their families generally live in poverty. They bring with them the burden of poverty into that classroom, and they begin school already at risk for failure. The parents of these children clean our houses; they clean our courtrooms; they work in the field; they tend our gardens, and they tend for our children... they are the working poor. They believe that their children can have a better life,... if they in fact get an education, something they never got. And your honor, it has to be a meaningful education. Obviously, your honor these children need to learn English. There's no dispute about that, but education has to mean more than learning English. These children should and are entitled to learn what all other children learn: algebra, biology, chemistry, world history, American history, comparative literature, social studies, art and so on.
>
> These parents have the audacity to think that their children can actually graduate from high school, and they also have the audacity to think that perhaps they might even go on to the university.[136]

The district court ruled the case was not ripe for adjudication. Citing as authority *Castaneda I, supra*, it applied the three-prong test adopted in that case to conclude that the EEOA does not mandate bilingual education. The district court concluded Prop. 227 presented a sound educational theory, that English immersion does not *per se* violate Section 1703(1) of the EEOA, and the immersion program had yet to be implemented such that it could be analyzed under the third prong of *Castaneda. Valeria G.*, 307 F.3d at 1017–1018, 1020–1021. The district court found no conflict between Prop. 227 and federal law and rejected plaintiffs' supremacy clause argument. Upon analyzing discriminatory intent versus discriminatory effect (as plaintiffs alleged), the court concluded plaintiffs could not establish an equal protection violation or irreparable harm as the proposition had yet to be implemented. Accordingly, injunctive relief was denied. *Valeria G.* at 1024–1025, 1028.

On November 8, 2016, Prop. 227 was overwhelmingly repealed by Proposition 58 (Prop. 58) securing 73.5% of the favorable vote. Effective July 1, 2017, Prop. 58, known

136. Escobedo notes on file with the author.

as the California Education for a Global Economy Initiative, allows students to learn English and academic content through multiple programs but districts must provide, at a minimum, a program of structured English immersion. Parents can ask for bilingual programs without applying for a waiver. Notices sent to parents describe the process for parents to request a specific program. Where parents of 30 students or more per school or 20 students or more in any grade request a certain program, schools are required to offer such a program to the extent possible. If a district determines it is not possible to implement the program requested, it must provide a written explanation of the reason(s) the program cannot be provided.[137]

The validity of public-school districts to charge fees for public transportation was challenged in *Arcadia Unified School District v. State Department of Education*, 229 Cal. App. 3d 913 (1991). Escobedo was co-counsel for client Francisco Salazar as intervenor and respondent.[138] (This case involved numerous procedural twists, predicated on an earlier case in which the superior court failed to issue a decision on the merits but reversed on other grounds, before reaching the appellate court.) The CDE adopted § 39087.5 that charged students for transportation fees.[139] The plaintiffs argued the transportation fees violated the state's "free school" guarantee pursuant to the California Constitution, Art. IX § 5.[140] The California Court of Appeals (Fourth Division) agreed, finding the section facially defective as it failed to exclude indigent and handicapped students, "for whom school-provided transportation is the sole link to education." *Arcadia*, 229 Cal. App. 3d at 473. Upon remand, the superior court reversed the basis of its initial ruling, adopting the appellate court's finding that the section violated the state's "free school" guarantee pursuant to the state constitution. The California Supreme Court denied the CDE's appeal but ordered the opinion to be depublished. *Salazar v. Honig*, Cal. App. No. B026629, (May 10, 1988), *review denied*, *Opn. Ordered nonpub*., (Sept. 1, 1988,). Thereafter, the CDE issued a legal advisory informing all school districts that § 39087.5 was declared unconstitutional and directed them to cease charging fees for student transportation to which some districts objected. The CDE and twenty-five school districts agreed to submit the validity of the section to the Sacramento County Superior Court, which then found the section facially unconstitutional. This appeal followed, at which time Salazar intervened and asserted collateral estoppel, to prevent another division of the appellate court from reconsidering the ruling in *Salazar*. Salazar also argued the section was unconstitutional as transportation was vital to accessing education—constituting an essential element of school activity—and that charging fees violated the rights of indigent students. Lastly, Salazar argued the alternative, apply-

137. Cal. Ed. Code § 310, 5 CCR §§ 11310, 11311.

138. Escobedo's co-counsel in this case and *Teresa P.* was Peter Roos, who later became MALDEF's litigation director during Martinez's tenure.

139. Cal. Ed. Code § 39807.5.

140. That clause provides, "The Legislature shall provide for a system of common schools by which a free school shall be kept up and supported in each district at least six months in every year, after the first year in which a school is established."

ing for a waiver of transportation fees, created a stigma for indigent children. The Court of Appeal's Third District applied the public interest exception to the collateral estoppel rule, and held the section was constitutional because transportation was not a necessary element of school activity. The California Supreme Court adopted the rationale and findings of the Third District Appellate Court.

Escobedo was co-lead counsel[141] in *Betty Pazmiño v. California Board of Education*, No. CPF-03-502554 (S.F. Sup. Ct. 2003), which was proved to be one of the successful cases brought under the No Child Left Behind Act (NCLB). On behalf of immigrant LEP children, parents, teachers, and nonprofit educational organizations, Escobedo pursued bilingual education inclusion in California's $133 million portion of the NCLB Reading First Grant Program ("Reading First"), which helped children achieve their assigned-grade–level reading by the end of third grade. The Superior Court granted a writ of mandate and preliminary injunction that prohibited the State Board of Education (SBE) and CDE from using grant criteria not promulgated pursuant to the California Administrative Procedures Act (CAPA). On January 28, 2004, the parties entered into a settlement agreement that required the SBE and CDE to "1) fund alternative bilingual programs under Reading First; 2) designate an appropriate agency to provide technical assistance and develop materials for professional development for instructional bilingual materials; and 3) appoint an expert on English Learner instruction to advise the SDE on the program's implementation."[142] AB 1485, effective January 1, 2004, was passed in response to the lawsuit and prohibits the SBE from excluding alternative bilingual classrooms from Reading First while also prioritizing $13 million of such funds for bilingual classrooms.[143]

A 25-year case, *Comité de Padres v. State Superintendent* (*Comité*), No. C042166 (2004), 2004 WL 179212, involved two enforcement actions initiated in 1979 under the BBEA by plaintiff Latino organizations. They filed the action to force the SBE and CDE to monitor and ensure LEP students were receiving instruction in a language understandable to them (i.e., receiving bilingual services). In 1985, plaintiffs were successful in obtaining a consent decree requiring the CDE to monitor bilingual services under the BBEA based upon an annual census and report. The report was to identify the LEP students, their progress, and whether they met the language reclassification criteria (i.e., achieved bilingualism). Such monitoring was to occur once every three years.[144] The consent decree provided the court could relinquish jurisdiction upon showing CDE met its obligations and had structures in place to continue compliance. Escobedo became co-counsel in 1994 when the CDE moved

141. Escobedo/META was joined in the lawsuit by CRLA, Inc., MALDEF, the Youth Law Center, and Public Interest Law Firm.

142. The Settlement Agreement is on file with the Author.

143. Youth Law Center, Pazmiño v. California Board of Education Alternatie [sic] Writ of Mandate, https://www.ylc.org/resource/pazmino-v-california-board-of-education-petition-and-complaint/.

144. Cal. Ed. Code, §§ 52161-52165, 52177.

to relinquish jurisdiction based partly on the sunsetting of the BBEA, including the monitoring provisions. In July 1995, the trial court ruled the CDE's obligations remained intact as the consent decree created a contractual obligation and denied the motion. The parties entered a stipulated amendment to the consent decree in March 1996 that modified the monitoring requirement from every three to every four years. CDE abandoned its appeal. Though the consent decree remained in effect until 2002, the CDE continued to violate it, prompting the plaintiffs to file motions in April 2001 asking for enforcement or citing the CDE for contempt. The trial court required the defendants to file a compliance plan, which was adopted on July 25, 2001. By June 2002, CDE had continued to violate the consent decree, but the court, recognizing the "degree of interference in the orderly operation of the programs," invited defendants to amend, modify, or terminate the decree. Defendants moved to terminate; plaintiffs objected, arguing additional state and federal laws were being violated. The trial court granted the defendants' motion to terminate its jurisdiction, finding the purposes of the consent decree were no longer relevant. The California Third District Court of Appeals, affirmed the trial court's ruling, but repeated part of the trial court's comments in dismissing the case:

> [T]he defendants' showing was disappointing, and even offensive, to the court. Rather than showing that the consent decree is no longer needed due to a fundamental shift in their approach to monitoring the State's bilingual programs, defendants have reached back into two decades of files, and dusted off their old, hackneyed, and ineffective arguments against a consent decree at all.... Despite defendants' abysmal performance through the years... over the last two years, they had shown some degree of commitment to the idea that the way to "get out from under the perceived burden of the consent decree" was to attempt compliance. Defendants "have, at last... been dragged kicking and screaming into substantial compliance with more of the objectives [under the amended consent decree] than under any other agreement in this sad matter's history."
>
> The trial court observed, rather than putting their resources and energy into meeting the terms of the compliance plan over the years, the defendants had engaged in game-playing, obstructive tactics, and an arrogance toward the legal system. 'If [they] were a private organization, there would be little chance of the court relieving them from the bed that they themselves made to lie in. However, we are face here with significant public assets being diverted from potentially more useful program funding.... This, then is the court's dilemma. *Supra* at 5.' Taking all of the above into consideration, the court is now ready to say, Enough. The court cannot emphasize strongly enough its displeasure with defendants, their attorneys, and their bad faith approach to their signed agreements over the years. (Those who consider making good faith agreements with the defendants in the future should be forewarned.)[145]

---

145. The Third District Court of Appeals decision in *Comité* is unpublished but on file with the author.

In affirming the trial court, the Court of Appeals noted the passage of Prop. 227 in 1998, ruling there was a "dramatic change from the BBEA" justifying termination of the consent decree. *Comité*, No. C042166 at 8. Further, it concluded the EEOA did not support, "much less mandate," bilingual education programs or their monitoring but instead affirmed that the CDE had ongoing legal obligations to monitor LEP services. *Comité*, No. C042166 at 9, 10.

5. Youth Law Center Staff Attorney, 2005–2015

Escobedo's specialty at the Youth Law Center (YLC) was advocacy in the area of education law. She led the YLC's Educational Equity for Foster Care and Juvenile Justice Project, which was created to increase awareness of the educational issues impacting children and youth in the child welfare and juvenile justice systems.[146] In *Alejo et al. v. O'Connell*, No. CPF 09-509568 (S.F. Sup. Ct. 2009), a writ of mandamus (Writ) was filed to compel the respondents to comply with California Ed. Code §52177, federal law, and the mandate to fund monitoring of juvenile court site schools and other programs.[147] The monitoring was designed to help academically at-risk students overcome educational challenges. Escobedo represented parents and community groups throughout California; the named petitioner, Luis Alejo, was mayor *pro tem* of Watsonville. State Superintendent of Public Instruction Jack O'Connell (Superintendent), canceled hundreds of scheduled monitoring visits, which he deemed "non-mandated" for the 2008–2009 school year, likely to continue into 2009–2010. Writ ¶¶ 4, 6, 18, 51, 55. Petitioners alleged that in certain districts, monitoring had not been conducted in eight years. Writ ¶¶ 52, 54. Further, monitoring at juvenile court site schools either had not occurred or occurred once or on an irregular basis, despite funding in the millions of dollars. Writ ¶¶ 55–60. Monitoring was supported with categorical funding from the NCLB Act and other state and federal monies. Writ ¶¶ 34–37. The petitioners alleged the state was unlawfully diverting these funds to other purposes and allowing districts to do the same. Writ ¶¶ 81–82. Ultimately, the trial court found § 52177 remained operative but ruled that the Superintendent exercised appropriate discretion and granted summary judgment in favor of respondents.

On appeal, respondents relied on *Comité* to support its position that their obligation to monitor the programs ended with the sunsetting of BBEA. They argued the Superintendent had exercised his discretion in discontinuing monitoring. On behalf of YLC, Escobedo asserted the matter did not involve bilingual education and distinguished this case from *Comité*. She argued both federal and state law required continued monitoring, as did the existence of the funding allocated for monitoring.[148] In the absence of statutory law and by his acceptance of the funding, Escobedo asserted the Superintendent did not have discretion to accept the funding and

146. Escobedo Resume on file with the author.

147. Petition at https://www.ylc.org/wp-content/uploads/2018/11/AlejovOConnellPetition.pdf.

148. EEOA § 52177 and NCLB § 6301, Cal.Ed.Code § 64001.

discontinue the monitoring; his discretion was limited to that granted by the legislature, which did not authorize him to discontinue monitoring.[149] The Court of Appeals ruled in favor of the respondents, clarifying under BEIRA that the Superintendent's monitoring duties sunset, citing as authority *Alejo v. Torlakson*, 212 Cal. App. 4th 768 (2013).[150]

Escobedo's YLC work included involvement with the Juvenile Detention Alternatives Initiative, an effort to reduce the number of youths detained in juvenile detention facilities, that was funded by the Annie E. Casey Foundation. Escobedo chaired the statewide Education Access Taskforce, which involved collaborative work among thirty-five legal service and public interest advocacy organizations on statewide education, policy, and legislative issues. The Fix School Discipline Policy Group, a statewide coalition focused on discipline reform, was also a part of the collaborative. Escobedo also litigated numerous education reform cases and successfully advocated for legislative change:

- SB 1088, effective January 1, 2013, prohibited a school from denying enrollment or readmission to a student because they had contact with the juvenile justice system. It defines juvenile justice contact as arrest, adjudication by a court, probation supervision, and/or detention for any length of time. Escobedo introduced testimony during hearings that established that Black and Latino youth were most impacted by the failure to ensure subsequent enrollment, comprising 80% of the total student enrollment during 2011–2012.[151]
- SB 1111, effective January 1, 2015, reformed the enrollment process for county-operated community schools by mandating that probation youth could not be transferred to such a school without parent or guardian consent or an expulsion or court order. It provided procedures (including addressing logistical needs) for such transfer and ensured that the best educational needs in the interest of the pupils were met, especially as regards special needs pupils. In the case of special needs pupils, the law required school districts to ensure students were informed and that they ensured the return of the pupils to their prior school or another appropriate school.[152]
- AB 420 amended § 48900(k) of the California Education Code. Through her involvement with the Fix School Discipline group, Escobedo focused on eliminating "willful defiance" as grounds for suspension or expulsion. Escobedo was instrumental in exposing the fact that "willful defiance" was

149. 2011 WL 3560988 (Cal.App. 1 Dist.), Appellate Brief filed July 22, 2011 at 1, 5-6, 31.

150. The Asian Pacific and African American Coalition and others filed an Amicus brief in support of YLC, 2011 WL 3560990 (Cal.App. 1 Dist.)(Appellate Brief), August 4, 2011.

151. Cal.Ed.Code § 48645.5 (a)–(b)(4).

152. EC §1981—Amended (a)–(f); EC § 1981.5—Added, EC § 1883—Amended and EC § 48918—Amended.

> identified as the most severe grounds in 42% of all California suspensions. Because § 48900(k) was so subjective, students of color and other vulnerable student groups were disproportionately suspended and expelled from California schools. After several unsuccessful legislative attempts, AB 420 amended § 48900(k) to prohibit students from being suspended or recommended for expulsion on defiance or disruption grounds for students in grades kindergarten through three. In 2019, the legislature extended this prohibition on suspension to students in grades four through eight and for expulsion for kindergarten through grade twelve through SB 419. In 2023, SB 274 expanded the prohibition to cover all of kindergarten through grade twelve for both suspension and expulsion.

6. Lawyers Committee for Civil Rights Senior Staff Attorney, 2016–2023

As senior staff attorney for the Lawyers Committee for Civil Rights (LCCR), Escobedo continued litigating cases on behalf of children. *Advocates for Justice v. Modesto City Schools* (2017–2018) was a lawsuit prepared on behalf of parents alleging the school district unfairly targeted and disciplined African Americans, Latinos, and English learners at up to 3.5 times higher than other students. Latino students comprised more than 60% of all students at the time of the lawsuit. Advocates for Justice, the LCCR led by Escobedo, and other outside counsel presented the district with the lawsuit in December 2017 but did not file the suit. A formal settlement agreement effective to June 2021 was reached to address the district's discriminatory discipline policies and practices. These efforts included hiring a national expert to review the district's discipline policies and practices and make recommendations, and a monetary award of $50,000 to claimants, plus payment of attorneys' fees.[153]

N. U. v. Bakersfield City School District, No. BCV-19-101166 (Cal. Sup. Ct., Kern County, April 29, 2019), was a state court challenge to the district's unilateral dismantling of its summer school program. The program was designed to accelerate academic achievement for specific categories of at-risk students. A writ of mandamus was filed against CDE and the school district. As the LCCR attorney, Escobedo co-counseled the case with the California Rural Legal Assistance, Inc. (CRLA) and the Greater Bakersfield Legal Assistance, Inc. Under the Local Control Funding Formula/Local Control and Accountability Plan (LCAP), restrictive funding of $1.6 million was earmarked for the summer program. Escobedo and co-counsel settled the case in October 2020. The district agreed to solicit required stakeholder input before making any substantial changes to the LCAP, provide all LCAP information

153. *Supra* note 127; *see* Ken Carlson, *Modesto School District Charged with Unfair Discipline Practices, Reaches Settlement*, Modesto Bee, May 22, 2018, https://www.modbee.com/news/article211604669.html.

in Spanish and English, and dedicate state funding to benefit educational services for low-income English learners and foster students.[154] In reaching the settlement agreement, Escobedo stated, "[d]edicated funds from the state are supposed to be used to benefit some of our highest need students, especially students who are low-income, English Learners, or foster students. This settlement helps make sure those dollars reach the student they were intended to reach."[155]

Azucena Wendz v. California Department of Education, 93 Cal. App. 5th 607 (2023), involved a challenge to the state's implementation of regulations pursuant to the Migrant Education Program (MEP) that was created to address the unique educational needs of migrant children. Migrant Regional Parent Advisory Councils were established to promote and ensure parental involvement in their children's education.[156] Escobedo, along with co-counsel CRLA and Munger Tolles and Olson, filed a writ of mandamus against the superintendent and CDE to comply with MEP, specifically as regards the composition of the Migrant Regional Parent Advisory Councils (Advisory Councils). Pursuant to state law, the Advisory Councils were to consult with districts about migrant education programs. The superintendent was charged with "ensur[ing] effective parental involvement."[157] It was the petitioner's interpretation of the law that they alone had authority to decide the composition of the Advisory Councils. In 2019, the superintendent adopted regulations concerning the formation and governance of the Advisory Councils, including regulations that could affect their size and member composition. Appellant Milagros Azucena Wendz sought to invalidate the regulations, and she appealed from the trial court's partial denial of her petition. The trial court ruled that the superintendent had the authority to adopt the regulations but failed to abide by the Administrative Procedures Act (APA) notice requirements and granted the writ to that extent. Wendz claimed the trial court should have granted her petition in its entirety because the superintendent's adoption of the regulations was outside his statutory authority and the regulations conflict with the MEP, placing an impermissible restriction on the authority of migrant parents to nominate and elect Advisory Council members. The Court of Appeals granted the writ in part, finding the superintendent's 15-day notice violated the APA's requisite 45-day notice mandate, which failed to provide adequate notice and specificity about the proposed regulations, including member alternates.

While carrying a litigation docket at the LCCR, Escobedo continued her advocacy work (as she did at YLC) that included challenging discriminatory student discipline practices. She negotiated a formal settlement with Modesto City Schools to address suspensions disproportionately impacting Black, English-limited students,

---

154. California Rural Legal Assistance (CRLA) Press Release, *Bakersfield Students Settle Lawsuit Over Summer School Cancellation and School Funding*, October 30, 2020, https://archive.crla.org/bakersfield-students-settle-lawsuit-over-summer-school-cancellation-and-school-funding.html.

155. Lawyers Committee for Civil Rights website, posted April 1, 2019, https://lccrsf.org/cases/n-u-v-california-department-of-education-education-equity/.

156. Cal. Ed. Code, §§ 54440, 54444.2 (a).

157. *Id.*

and other vulnerable student groups. Escobedo also successfully challenged exclusionary enrollment policies and procedures targeting immigrant students through separate administrative complaints filed with the California attorney general and school districts. AB 699, which LCCR co-sponsored and Escobedo advanced, was adopted by the legislature, effective January 1, 2018. The bill protected the educational rights of immigrant students by prohibiting school personnel from collecting information or documents regarding the citizenship or immigration status of students or their family members, unless it is required by state or federal law. It included other provisions requiring school personnel and the attorney general to take steps necessary to ensure that the enrollment rights of immigrant children are protected. It also instructed schools on how to protect their students and their students' private records from immigration enforcement and required schools to adopt supportive practices in response to potential concerns around immigration enforcement.[158] Prior to the enactment of AB 699, Escobedo with CRLA filed an administrative complaint with the attorney general alleging that 75 school districts were inquiring about the citizenship status and requesting Social Security numbers through their enrollment processes. After AB 699 became law, Escobedo filed several additional complaints/addendums with the attorney general's office naming over 400 districts in noncompliance with AB 699. The process proved very effective in bringing districts in compliance with the law.

After 44 years of litigating and serving disadvantaged youth in accord with her values, Escobedo retired as senior staff attorney from the Lawyers Committee in 2023. The value of her work to the Latino community was recognized with numerous awards, including the CRLA Access to Justice and Legal Excellence Award (2023), the HNBA Latina Commission *Las Primeras Abogadas* Award (2017), the California La Raza Lawyers Association Cruz Reynoso Community Service Award (1992), and many more.[159]

Conclusion

By the time Martinez left MALDEF in April 1982, she had increased the budget from less than $800,000 to over $2.6 million and "achieved the sophistication of a first-class legal firm."[160] Almost one year later, in March 1983, the Chicana Rights Project closed its doors due partly to Martinez's absence and, in other part, to a lack of funding. Under Martinez's leadership, the legal talent of the Project's attorneys established the legal presence of Latinas in the Southwest. Hernández expanded their platform, as did the fierce litigation of Cantú. As the country's first legal director of a national woman's organization, Herrera further refined the pro-

158. https://leginfo.legislature.ca.gov/faces/billTextClient.xhtml?bill_id=201720180AB699.
159. *Supra* note 127.
160. *Supra* note 9 at 87, 99–100.

file of Chicana litigants, while elevating the profile of Chicana attorneys. Remaining true to her values, Escobedo—the enigmatic and dynamic litigator—blew down the doors on behalf of disadvantaged youth, most of whom were Chicano kids left unnoticed in the vast California educational system. Combined, these Luminaria litigators expanded voting rights for language minorities that led to successful reapportionment battles, increased national funding for girls' and women's sports, broke down employment barriers for women of color in traditional jobs and nontraditional industries, successfully challenged segregation in K–12 education, and altered the funding mechanisms on behalf of children in property-poor school districts. The legal landscape would never be the same. The Luminaria activistas collectively transformed the legal landscape through their landmark litigation, commitment to civil rights, and social justice advocacy. Each of these women broke barriers, serving as powerful role models and mentors for future generations of attorneys. Their leadership not only created legal precedence but also inspired systemic change, ensuring greater inclusivity and representation within the legal profession and U.S. society. Most admirable is their success in the face of social and professional barriers over which they triumphed to fight on behalf of American women, propelled by a profound belief in egalitarianism. Their transformative legacy is one of distinctive courage.

Martinez's Departure from MALDEF and the Future of Latinas in the Law

Martinez left MALDEF in 1982, but continued breaking traditions. She was among the first Luminaria large law firm partners at Munger Tolles & Olsen, Los Angeles (1982–2009) and regent of the University of California (1976–1990, chair 1984–1986). Upon nomination by President Barack Obama, Martinez became the first Luminaria to serve as the U.S. Ambassador to Argentina (2009–2013).[161] Like a ship's wake, the wave pattern left on the water's surface by a moving ship, Martinez left Luminarias to carry on MALDEF's work. Part of that work included advocacy for a diverse judiciary. Martinez, like her predecessors, recognized the magnitude of the impact of the judiciary on its litigation and advocacy agendas. Painfully aware of the absence of Latinos on the bench—from the local level up to the highest appellate court—MALDEF began advocating for a diverse bench from its earliest days. To earn a seat at the hearings of the powerful Senate Judiciary Committee, the first MALDEF Director Mario Obledo created the first national Hispanic bar association, initially called the La Raza National Lawyers Association, now known as the His-

---

161. https://history.state.gov/departmenthistory/people/martinez-vilma-s; http://www.allgov.com/officials/mart%C3%ADnez-vilma?officialid=29164.

panic National Bar Association (HNBA).[162] The call for the first Hispanic U.S. Supreme Court Justice was the impetus for its creation.

> In November 1971 the United States Senate Committee on the Judiciary began interviewing William H. Rehnquist to be the next Associate United States Supreme Court Justice. The lawyer members of MALDEF strongly opposed... Rehnquist's appointment on various grounds of discrimination based on reported actions taken and comments made by Mr. Rehnquist against the civil rights of minorities. The MALDEF lawyers also sought the appointment of a Latino to the United States Supreme Court... While many civil rights groups opposed the confirmation of Justice Rehnquist, including the American Federation of Labor and Congress of Industrial Organizations (AFL-CIO) and the National Association for the Advancement of Colored People (NAACP), there was no national group of Hispanic attorneys on record opposing the Rehnquist nomination. Finding this fact unacceptable [and]... [k]nowing that the Committee on the Judiciary would only recognize a legitimate organization, they founded LA RAZA NATIONAL LAWYERS ASSOCIATION (LRNLA)....
>
> Mario Obledo, along with a small group of LRNLA members, wrote a telegram to the Senate Judiciary Committee opposing the Rehnquist nomination and recommending instead Federal District Court Judge Reynaldo G. Garza, a well-qualified Hispanic jurist... In 1961, Judge Garza was the first Mexican-American to serve on the federal bench, appointed by President John F. Kennedy. A Western Union Telegram on behalf of LRNLA was crafted, signed by each founder and transmitted to President Nixon and the U.S. Senate Committee on the Judiciary. LRNLA called for the withdrawal of William Rehnquist['s] nomination under allegations of racism. Rehnquist was brought to task during his Senate confirmation hearings for his attitudes and actions while in Arizona against Hispanics, Native Americans, Black and other ethnic minorities. Despite the Committee on the Judiciary questioning regarding his attitude about the civil rights of minorities, William Rehnquist was sworn in January 1972.... In due course, Judge Reynaldo Garza was nominated by President Jimmy Carter to the Fifth Circuit Court of Appeals in 1978.[163]

---

162. In June 1977, four years after Obledo created the LRNLA, Martinez wrote a proposal to the Ford Foundation to create a national Chicano Bar Association, MALDEF Archives RG #4, Box 73, Folder 8, *Chicano Bar Project* proposal. A national survey of Spanish-surnamed attorneys in California was completed by October 25, 1977, in which "[t]he overwhelming number of respondents do not believe that established bar associations serve Chicano needs." Memo by Ed Marenco/MALDEF to Martinez, Oct. 25, 1970 [sic].

163. Hon. Francisca Cota, "The Formation of the HNBA" available at https://hnba.com/what-we-do/excerpt-from-history-of-the-hnba/ https://hnba.com/wp-content/uploads/2022/10/CELEBRATING-50-YEARS.pdf. In 1984, the name was officially changed to the Hispanic National Bar Association.

Obledo's earliest advocacy effort launched the HNBA's quest for the first Hispanic Supreme Court justice that spanned nearly four decades.[164] Over those forty years, the HNBA adapted the strategic tools used by others to effectuate judicial appointments at the state and federal levels. Thus, by the 1980s, Latinas (and Latinos) were ascending to the bench as state Supreme Court Justices and Article III Judges.

164. Dolores S. Atencio, *The Making of An American Justice: The HNBA's Quest for the First Hispanic Supreme Court Justice,* HNBA Journal of Law and Policy, Vol. 1:1 (Summer 2010) (hereafter HNBA Law Journal).

Table 1 **Luminaria Litigator-Activistas**

Luminaria	Public Interest Organization & Title	Tenure	Status
Vilma Martinez 1967 LL. B Columbia	Mexican American Legal Defense & Education Fund (MALDEF), President & General Counsel NAACP	1973–82 1967–70	Retired
Antonia Hernández 1974 J.D. UCLA	MALDEF • President & General Counsel • Executive Vice President & Deputy GC • Employment Program Director • Regional Counsel • Staff Attorney, Washington, D.C. Office Los Angeles Center for Law & Justice, Staff Attorney	 1985–2004 1984–85 1983–84 1981–83 1977–79 1974–77	Retired 2023
Norma V. Cantú 1977 J.D. Harvard	U.S. Commission on Civil Rights, Chair Office of Civil Rights, U.S. Department of Education, Assistant Secretary MALDEF • Regional Counsel/Education Director: Texas, Colorado, New Mexico • Education, Litigation & Advocacy Project • Chicana Rights Project Texas Attorney General Office, Assistant Attorney General, Nursing Home Task Force	2021–23 1993–2001 1979–93 1985 1983–85 1979 1977–79	Retired Chair MALDEF Board of Directors
Irma Herrera 1978 J.D. Notre Dame	Equal Rights Advocate, Executive Director META, Staff Attorney MALDEF, Staff Attorney/Director of Education Programs WA Vergreen Legal Services, Staff Attorney	1995–2009 1991–95 1980–83 1978–80	Playwright, Solo Performer
Deborah Escobedo 1979 J.D. Berkeley	Lawyers Committee for Civil Rights, Senior Racial Justice Staff Attorney Youth Law Center, Senior Staff Attorney META, Managing Attorney	2016–23 2005–15 1989–2005	Retired 2023

Two

Reigning Supreme, 1982–2017

A. Introduction

State justices wield enormous power, issuing decisions and opinions in "over 95% of all cases filed in the country that 23,000 lower-court judges must follow,"[1] thereby impacting most in the country. Such authority was exercised by the first eight Luminaria state supreme court justices and judges on courts of last resort, who are the subject of this chapter: Dorothy Comstock Riley, Miriam Naveira Merly, Rosemary Barkett, Carmen Beauchamp Ciparick, Vanessa Ruiz, Petra Jimenez Maes, Liana Fiol Matta, and Carmen Espinosa (collectively "Justices"). As Latinas, they brought to the bench the advantage of their diverse backgrounds and perspectives.

> By their mere presence, women judges enhance the legitimacy of courts, sending a powerful signal that they are open and accessible to those who seek recourse to justice.... Adjudication is enhanced by the presence of women who bring to the fore considerations that would not have been taken into account in their absence; the scope of the discussion is hence enlarged, possibly preventing ill-considered or improper decisions. By elucidating how laws and rulings can be based on gender stereotypes, or how they might have a different impact on women and men, a gender perspective enhances the fairness of adjudication, which ultimately benefits both men and women. All judges should strive to bring a gender perspective to adjudication. Judge Vanessa Ruiz, *The Role of Women Judges and a Gender Perspective in Ensuring Judicial Independence and Integrity*, United Nations Office on Drugs and Crime, January 2019.[2]

That there were so few Luminaria justices should be questioned and is worthy of greater inquiry. The Luminarias Study confirmed there were double the number of Luminaria Article III judges (17) with one reaching the U.S. Supreme Court. This disparity strongly suggests it was more difficult for Luminarias to ascend to a state court of last resort than the federal bench. Aside from the obvious mixed racial and gender implications, the gross disproportionate number may be reflective of the

1. Dr. Jill Lynch Cruz, *Still Too Few: The Status of Latina Lawyers in the U.S.*, Chicanx-Latinx L. Rev. 7 (2025): 49–50 (hereafter Cruz Article), https://escholarship.org/content/qt67w299vn/qt67w299vn_noSplash_126ba9fd3fae80b788faeb3a6b8f51f6.pdf?t=sejzqy.

2. Available at https://www.unodc.org/dohadeclaration/en/news/2019/01/the-role-of-women-judges-and-a-gender-perspective-in-ensuring-judicial-independence-and-integrity.html.

arduous appointments process, complicated by elections in certain states.[3] "Judicial elections have rarely been a path to the supreme court bench for people of color, and they have often been a path off the bench for incumbents of color."[4] Of the eight Justices, only one reigned in the Southwest, Justice Petra Jimenez Maes in New Mexico. The state with the largest Latino population—California—only recently welcomed its first Latina justice. On March 22, 2022, 173 years after the state's founding, the Honorable Patricia Guerrero was confirmed. Ten months later, on January 2, 2023, she became the state's 29th Latina justice and first Latina Chief Justice on the California Supreme Court.[5]

> Although precise data on the number of Latina state court judges is not readily available, available information about Hispanic/Latinx State Supreme Court Justices allows us to make inferences about their representation in the judiciary. In 2023 . . . Hispanics accounted for less than 6 percent of State Supreme Court Justices nationwide. Alarmingly, 40 states and the District of Columbia did not have any Hispanic/Latinx Justices on their courts.... [There are no Latino justices in 15 out of the 26 states where the population is over 10 percent Hispanic including D.C.[6]] Given that half of all state appellate court seats are held by men, this strongly suggests Latinas represent less than 3 percent of state Supreme Court Justices, even lower than their representation in the federal judicial system (4.5 percent).[7]

Another contributing explanation may be the historically low number of women justices. By 2023, 41% of all state justices were women, however, the increase is relatively recent. Florence Ellinwood Allen was the first woman elected to the Ohio Supreme Court in 1922 and reelected in 1928. She was the sole female justice in the country until 1934 when she was elevated to the Sixth Circuit Court of Appeals.[8] In

3. For a fascinating discussion on supermajority requirements in judicial retention elections, *see Sarah Elizabeth Saucedo, Majority Rules Except in New Mexico: Constitutional and Policy Concerns Raised by New Mexico's Supermajority Requirement for Judicial Retention*, Boston Univ. L.Rev., 86 (2006): 173.

4. *State Supreme Court Diversity*, Brennan Center For Justice, July 23, 2019, at 13; updated by Amanda Powers & Alicia Bannon, May 2023, https://www.brennancenter.org/our-work/research-reports/state-supreme-court-diversity-may-2023-update.

5. Justice Guerrero was born in 1971 and raised in the Imperial Valley while the Luminaria activistas were litigating. https://supreme.courts.ca.gov/about-court/justices-court/chief-justice-patricia-guerrero; *Historic Supreme Court Nominations*, https://www.gov.ca.gov/2022/08/10/governor-newsom-announces-historic-supreme-court-nominations/. For this book, the Luminarias Study identified a minimum of 16 Latina state supreme court justices up to 2023, still one lower than Article III judges; research on file with the author.

6. *Supra* Cruz Article note 1 at 51, fn. 142, citing Brennan Center for Justice State Supreme Court Diversity 2023 Update (supra note 4); *see also* Brennan Center Update 2024, https://www.brennancenter.org/our-work/research-reports/state-supreme-court-diversity-may-2024-update.

7. *Id.*, Cruz Article note 1 at 49–50.

8. Circuit Courts of Appeals will be cited as Circuit Courts. Florence Ellinwood Allen, *The Supreme Court of Ohio & The Ohio Judicial System*, https://www.supremecourt.ohio.gov/courts /judicial-system/supreme-court-of-ohio/justices-1803-to-present/florence-allen/. Allen was Chief Judge of the Sixth Circuit from September 18, 1958, to February 5, 1959.

1959, Rhonda Valentine Lewis was *appointed* to the Hawaii Supreme Court. Nearly 30 years later the second female justice was elected in 1961 to the Arizona Supreme Court, Lorna Lockwood. In 1965, she became the state's first female chief justice.[9] By 1982 when the first Luminaria, Dorothy Comstock Riley, was appointed to the Michigan Supreme Court, there were at least 29 women serving as state supreme court justices.[10] By the early 1980s, Luminarias constituted nearly 2.5 percent of the total women lawyer population.[11]

The Luminarias Study found that twenty-two Luminarias-Latinas have served on state supreme courts or benches of last resort. *See,* Appendix A, List of Luminaria & Latina State Supreme Court Justices 1982 | 2025. In contrast over the same period, fifty-three Luminarias-Latinas have been appointed to sixty Article III judicial positions. *See,* Appendix B, List of Luminaria & Latina Article III Judges 1980 | 2025. The average tenure of the Luminaria justices is 16.3 years; the non-Luminaria justices is 7.74 years, a difference of 8.6 years. This statistic is exactly what it portends to be, a snapshot as the incumbent Supreme Court Justices have yet to complete their tenures. The leadership inherent in these Latina judges was recognized by their colleagues when chosen to serve as chief justices of their respective courts. Eight have, or are, serving as chief justices: four of the eight Luminaria justices and four of the fourteen non-Luminaria judges. This contextual lens captures the significance of the eight Luminarias who ascended to their respective courts of last resort.

B. Luminaria Justices

Luminaria Justices 1982–2004

Justice | Judge	Court	Tenure	Chief Justice
Dorothy Comstock Riley	Michigan Supreme Court	1982–1983 1985–1997	1987–1991
Miriam Naveira Merly	Puerto Rico Supreme Court	1985–2004	12/2003–2004
Rosemary Barkett	Florida Supreme Court	1985–1994	1992–1994
Carmen Beauchamp Ciparick	New York Court of Appeals	1994–2012	N/A
Vanessa Ruiz	District of Columbia Court of Appeals	1994–2011	N/A

continues

9. Arizona State Library Archives, & Public Records, Lorna Elizabeth Lockwood, https://apps.azlibrary.gov/officials/Legislators/Person/858.

10. The compilation of these 29 justices was gathered from state court websites in their respective states.

11. *Supra* Introduction, note 2 at 33.

continued

Justice | Judge	Court	Tenure	Chief Justice
Petra Jimenez Maes	New Mexico Supreme Court	1998–2018	1/2003–2005 2012–2014
Liana Fiol Matta	Puerto Rico Supreme Court	2004–2016	2014–2016
Carmen Espinosa	Connecticut Supreme Court	2013–2017	N/A

Seven of the eight Luminaria Justices were the first women and Latinas on their courts: Justices Comstock Riley, Naveira Merly, Barkett, Jimenez Maes and Espinosa and Judges Beauchamp Ciparick and Ruiz. Five were the first Hispanic justices/judges on their courts: Riley, Barkett, Beauchamp Ciparick, Ruiz, and Espinosa. Five served as chief justice: Riley was the first Latina chief justice in the country (1987–1991), followed by Barkett (1992–1994), Jimenez Maes (January 2003–2005), Naviera Merly (December 2003–2004), and Fiol Matta (2014–2016). Justice Jimenez Maes served two terms as chief justice. Five of the Luminaria Justices are or were of Puerto Rican ancestry (Naveira Merly, Beauchamp Ciparick, Ruiz, Fiol Matta and Espinosa) one was Mexican born (Barkett), and two were/are Mexican American (Comstock Riley and Jimenez Maes). At the time of appointment, the median age of the Luminaria Justices was 53.1 years.[12] Six justices were judges prior to being elevated: Comstock Riley, Barkett, Beauchamp Ciparick, Jimenez Maes, Fiol Matta, and Espinosa. *See* end of chapter, Table 2, Supreme Court Justices. Five of the Luminaria Justices served concurrently for nine years from 1985 to 1994: Comstock Riley, Naveira Merly, Barkett, Beauchamp Ciparick and Ruiz until Justice Barkett was elevated to the Eleventh Circuit. She was the only one elevated to an Article III appointment. The remaining seven retired from the bench. With the retirement of Justice Jimenez Maes on December 31, 2018, there are no first-generation Luminarias serving on a state supreme court. The successful tenures of the Luminaria justices led to the appointment of fourteen new Latina justices—four succeeding their Luminaria predecessor on the supreme courts/courts of last resort—in Florida (Barbara Lagoa), New York (Jenny Rivera) and Puerto Rico (Liana Fiol Matta and Maite Oronoz Rodríquez). Five additional states appointed Latinas to their highest courts: Arizona (Maria Elena Cruz), California (Patricia Guerrero), Colorado (Monica Márquez), Massachusetts (Dalila Argaez Wendlandt) and Texas (Eva Guzman). Of the fourteen, two have since retired and another, Barbara Lagoa, was elevated to the Eleventh Circuit, succeeding Judge Barkett (see chapter five). Ten Latinas currently serve on state supreme courts. *See,* Appendix A, List of Luminaria & Latina State Supreme Court Justices 1982 | 2025. Upon Judge Barkett's elevation, the tenures of seven Luminaria and four new Latina Justices—eleven in total—overlapped, the number of

12. Luminarias Study on file with author.

consecutive years of service varying from the date of new appointments. Ten is the highest number of Latina justices serving at one time.

The Luminaria (and most Latina) Justices were chosen primarily through gubernatorial appointment upon a merit selection process (the Missouri Plan) except Justice Ruiz.[13] The District of Columbia Judicial Nominating Commission evaluates and selects three candidates that are sent to the U.S. President for his nomination and U.S. Senate confirmation—a process identical to that of Article III judges. Nine judges are appointed to 15-year terms, subject to renewal.[14] A merit selection process with gubernatorial appointment to finite terms has been adopted in Connecticut (eight years), Florida (six years), New York (14 years), and Puerto Rico (mandatory retirement at age 70). In New Mexico, the governor initially selects justices to eight-year terms who, upon one year of service, must run in partisan elections to fulfill the remainder of that term. Michigan adopted the Michigan method, which consists of partisan gubernatorial selection followed by nonpartisan elections to eight-year terms. New Mexico and Puerto Rico have five justices; the remaining states have seven justices.[15] In the states that require state or U.S. Senate confirmation—Connecticut, Florida, New York, Florida, and D.C.—five of the eight Justices faced minimum opposition. Justices Riley, Beauchamp Ciparick and Barkett (during her retention election) faced some opposition. In the face of that opposition, their adversaries recognized the Luminaria nominees as trailblazers and highly qualified candidates for the bench.

Combined, the Luminaria Justices issued majority opinions in nearly 2,000 cases of first impression and participated in hundreds more panel decisions and orders—far exceeding the scope of this book. Indeed, individual books could be written about each one of the justices and their jurisprudence. This chapter provides a primer on their professional careers and cases. A timeline of their careers, starting with graduation from college up to their judicial appointments, precedes each biographical summary. The summaries include the justices' formative years, followed by discussion of their judicial work, which may include cases they litigated or decided while sitting on lower-level benches—a few of those cases following them to the higher court. The focus is on select cases of first impression. Included are a lesser number of cases, not of first impression, that were chosen for their facts and significance or interesting facts and legal findings. In the jurisdictions over which the justices presided—Connecticut, Florida, Michigan, New Mexico, New York, Puerto Rico, and the District of Columbia—their courts were and are the final arbiter of state civil and criminal appeals. Thus, most of their legal work required interpreta-

---

13. There are six primary types of judicial selection: gubernatorial appointment, assisted gubernatorial appointment (Missouri Plan), partisan and nonpartisan elections, the Michigan method, and legislative elections.

14. D.C. Code §§ 1-204.34(d)(1), 1-204.31.

15. In effect at time of their appointments: Conn. Const. 1982, art. V, § 2; FL. Const. 1976, art. V § 3; MI. Const. 1963, art. 6 § 2; N.M. Const. 1988, art. 6; § 4, N.Y. Const. 7, art. VI, §§ 2, 20; P.R. Const. art. V §§ 3, 8.

tion of state or territorial constitutional provisions in *pari matera* with the U.S. Constitution and other sister-state cases. For the most part, the SCOTUS and sister-state cases are not cited or discussed as the emphasis is on the Justices' legal analyses and findings. Where available, law review articles are footnoted that provide a fuller discussion about their rulings. Unfortunately, there are not many law review articles that analyze the jurisprudence shaped by the Luminaria Justices. This book provides the broader framework from which future comprehensive study may be undertaken on the importance of state supreme courts—a task assuming greater importance with the explosion of state and SCOTUS cases on issues harkening back to the 1980s: voting rights, women's reproductive rights and the rights of the LGBTQ+ community combined with new challenges on executive power (expansion thereof), the interplay between state and federal jurisdiction and power and likely in the near future, states' rights relative to managing and funding state services previously handled by the federal government.

C. Biographical Summaries

1. Justice Dorothy Comstock Riley

a. Formative Years

1946	B.A. Liberal Arts, Wayne State University, Student Council President
1949	LL.B., Wayne State University Law School[16]
1949–1954	Solo practice, Assistant Wayne County Friend of the Court
1955	Wayne County Friend of the Court
1972	Wayne County Circuit Judge
1973–1976	Partner, Riley and Roumel, Detroit
1976–1982	Michigan Court of Appeals, Appointed
1978	Won election to eight-year term[17]
1982	Ran unsuccessfully for Michigan Supreme Court
1982–1983	Appointed Associate Justice to Michigan Supreme Court
1984–1993	Elected Justice Michigan Supreme Court to term ending 1/1993
1992–1997	Reelected Michigan Supreme Court to term ending 1/2001 Chief Justice 1987–1991
1997	Retired

16. Wayne University (WU) 1946 Yearbook at 29, https://reuther.wayne.edu/files/WU_1946_Yearbook_pt1.pdf.

17. Michigan Supreme Court Historical Society, Dorothy Comstock Riley (MI Comstock Riley Article), https://www.courts.michigan.gov/courts/court-of-appeals/judges/past-judges/; MI Supreme Court Historical Society, https://www.micourthistory.org/women-and-the-law/dorothy-riley/.

The first Latina on the mainland to serve on a county circuit court bench and state supreme court, Dorothy Comstock, was born on December 6, 1924, in Detroit, Michigan. Her mother Josefina Aminta Elisa Grima was born in Tamaulipas, Mexico, to Bartolo C. Grima and Ursula Fuentes De Grima. Josefina came to the United States to study nursing and became a U.S. citizen.[18] Her Irish father Charles A. Comstock, was a Michigan native and auto factory laborer who served in WWII. Josefina was a nurse during WWII when she met Charles as an injured soldier which led to marriage. They had two daughters; Margaret was the youngest by three years. Dorothy attended Detroit Public Schools and graduated from Northwestern High School. She attended Wayne State University where she not only received her B.A. in 1946 but also was selected Homecoming Queen.

Riley was one of three women in her law school class at Wayne State University. Upon earning her law degree (LL.B.) in 1949, Riley interviewed with law firms. "Unfortunately, women lawyers were unheard of at the time and the only question... asked was how fast she could type."[19] As a result, Riley practiced on her own for six years, making a name for herself. Eventually, she was appointed Assistant/ Wayne County Friend of the Court. In 1967, she married Wallace D. Riley, 1957 president of the American Bar Association (ABA), and they had one son, Peter Comstock Riley. In 1972, Dorothy was appointed to the Wayne County Circuit Court on an interim basis. In 1976, year, she became the first woman judge on the Michigan Court of Appeals and the first Latina in the country appointed to a state appellate court. She served as an appellate judge for six years until 1982.

b. Michigan Supreme Court, 1982–1983, 1984–1997

On November 2, 1982, Judge Comstock Riley lost her election for the Michigan Supreme Court. A Democrat incumbent, Justice Blair Moody, Jr., whose current term was due to expire on January 1, 1983, won reelection to another eight-year term on the state's highest court. Weeks later before taking the "constitutionally required oath of office," Justice Moody passed. On December 9, 1982, outgoing Republican Governor William Milliken appointed Judge Riley to serve on the high court until January 1, 1985, igniting a firestorm. In *Attorney General v. Riley*, 417 Mich. 119, 332 N.W.2d 353 (1983), newly installed Democratic Governor James Blanchard filed an action for *quo warranto* asking the Michigan Supreme Court to determine the legitimacy of Judge Riley's appointment. Twenty-one hearings before the court were postponed pending the lawsuit.[20] Article 6 § 23 of the 1963 Michigan Constitution provided, in pertinent part:

---

18. https://www.courts.michigan.gov/4a5f1a/siteassets/msc-learning-center/witnessthis-justicedorothy comstockriley.pdf; WU 1949 Yearbook at 114, 192, https://reuther.wayne.edu/files/ WU_1949_ Yearbook_pt2.pdf.

19. *Supra note 17, MI Comstock Riley Article.*

20. *Appointee Agony, Michigan Lame Duck Muddle*, ABA Journal 69 (March 1983), 267.

> A vacancy shall occur in the office of judge of any court of record or in the district court by death, removal, resignation or vacating of the office, and such vacancy shall be filled by appointment of the governor. The person appointed by the governor shall hold office until 12 noon of the first day of January next succeeding the first general election held after the vacancy occurs, at which election a successor shall be elected for the *remainder of the unexpired term.* Whenever a new office of judge in a court of record, or the district court, is created by law, it shall be filled by election and served as judges to perform judicial duties for limited periods or specific assignments. [Emphasis added.]

At issue was whether "the remainder of the unexpired term" meant when the vacancy occurred or when the election occurred. The state argued the remainder of the unexpired term referred to when the vacancy occurred. Relying on legislative history emphasizing the public's desire for elections/elected judicial officers, the court ruled in favor of the state. *Attorney General v. Riley*, 417 Mich. at 138. In a case of first impression, the court distinguished the instant case from those cited by Justice Riley, noting the absence of a holdover provision, concluding:

> We find that, while there may be a slight tilt in the language favoring the interpretation that the appointment is restricted to the term in which the vacancy occurs, the language may arguably be interpreted either to limit the appointed term to the eight years in which the vacancy occurs, or to extend the appointed term into the next eight-year term. However, we are convinced that the injustice that can arise from the extended appointment term, combined with the historical preference for an elected judiciary and non-holdover Supreme Court terms, indicates the more limited appointment was the intent of the people. We would therefore in the instant case find that the appointed term should have been until noon January 1, 1983. Additionally, since the remainder of the purported appointment is void, the present Governor is authorized to make an appointment as of January 1, 1983. *Attorney General v. Riley*, 417 Mich. at 130–131.

Meanwhile, the Michigan Supreme Court itself was determining Justice Riley's fate. The court was proportionately represented by two Democrats, two Republicans, and two Independents. (Justice Riley, a Republican, did not vote.) Were the court to stalemate, the *quo warranto* could not be granted. In February 1983, the Michigan Supreme Court justices initially stalemated on the question of whether to remove Justice Riley, voting 3–3. One justice shortly thereafter reversed his vote, rendering the vote 4–2 in favor of ouster. The court issued the initial decision on February 11 and its reconsideration on February 15 upholding the ruling in favor of the state. The next day, Justice Riley left the bench. Governor Blanchard appointed U.S. District Judge Patricia Boyle to fill the vacancy.[21] The justice's "philosophy reflected her ac-

---

21. *Boyle New Michigan Justice*, ABA Journal 69 (May 1983), 580.

tions" which appeared to serve the judge well during this difficult and very public transition: "[t]he way to proceed is to always do the very best you can. Try to make yourself invaluable to the person you work for, and don't bring your problems to the office because that is not what you were hired to do. That formula worked for me, and I believe it can for anyone."[22]

On November 6, 1984, Riley ran for the court a second time and won election to a full-term ending January 1, 1993. She became the first Hispanic woman in the country elected to a state supreme court. On November 3, 1992, she was reelected to a full-term ending January 1, 2001. Justice Riley served as chief justice from 1987 until 1991.

c. Majority Opinions in Criminal Cases

The justice wrote the majority opinion in 113 cases with few involving issues of first impression and few dissents.[23] She wrote the majority opinion in 34 criminal cases addressing issues of bail, right to counsel, suppression of evidence, seizure, waiver of jury trial, impeachment, sanity as an element, insanity defense, battered woman syndrome, *ex parte* communications with jurors, double jeopardy, and sentencing. The selected cases represent a cross-section of Justice Riley's criminal decisions.

In *In re Certified Question, Duffy, Jr. v. Foltz*, 390 N.W.2d 620 (1986), the Sixth Circuit asked the Michigan Supreme Court to address whether sanity was an element of the crimes of rape and kidnapping as defined by Michigan law. In 1974, the petitioner (Duffy) entered a plea of not guilty and not guilty by reason of insanity. Duffy's plea was entered upon advice of counsel after (1) the prosecutor introduced "overwhelming proof" that Duffy abducted and raped the victim, (2) during opening statement, defense counsel stated Duffy would concede the crimes, (3) Duffy testified and conceded committing the crimes, (4) one of two psychiatrists testified Duffy was temporarily insane, and (5) the judge, upon hearing the whole of this evidence, suggested to defense counsel Duffy enter such pleas. Thereafter, a jury convicted Duffy of rape pursuant to Michigan Compiled Laws (M.C.L.) § 750.520 and Michigan Statutes Annotated (M.S.A.) § 28.788, and kidnapping, M.C.L. § 750.349. Justice Riley started by citing the statutes that neither defined nor included sanity as an element of the state's rape or kidnapping crimes and clarified that insanity was an affirmative defense raised by defendants. The justice explained Duffy misconstrued *People v. Murphy*, upon which he relied, specifically the following dicta:

> A defendant in a criminal proceeding is presumed sane. Once any evidence of insanity is introduced, however, the prosecution bears the burden of es-

22. Michigan Women's Hall of Fame, *Dorothy Comstock Riley (1924–2004)*, https://miwf.org/celebrating-women/michigan-womens-hall-of-fame/dorothy-comstock-riley/.

23. The justice participated in 103 criminal cases, seven were summary orders. Westlaw last visited April 5, 2025.

> tablishing defendant's sanity beyond a reasonable doubt.... [citations omitted]...The prosecution does not argue that defendant failed to controvert the presumption of sanity. Thus, *defendant's sanity at the time of the crime was as much an element to be proved by the prosecution beyond a reasonable doubt as the other statutory elements of the offenses charged.* (Emphasis theirs.)

Duffy, Jr. v. Foltz, 390 N.W.2d at 624. Justice Riley explained the court never intended to add sanity as an element of state crimes but rather meant to articulate the prosecutor's burden of proof beyond a reasonable doubt to establish sanity after an insanity defense has been raised. She wrote, "[B]ecause it is a burden-shifting affirmative defense, the defendant must first raise the issue and present evidence of insanity before the prosecution is required to go forward and prove the defendant's sanity beyond a reasonable doubt," thereby fulfilling the due process requirements. *Duffy, Jr. v. Foltz*, 390 N.W.2d at 625.

After multiple appeals, Duffy eventually sought relief in federal district court, which denied his writ of habeas corpus, prompting an appeal to the Sixth Circuit. Duffy argued the jury could not find him guilty beyond a reasonable doubt as the circumstances established, he was insane. Relying on an earlier Michigan Supreme Court case, *People v. Murphy*, 331 N.W.2d 152 (1982), a divided Sixth Circuit concluded sanity was an element of the state's rape and kidnapping crimes and ruled Duffy's writ of habeas corpus was reviewable. *Duffy v. Foltz*, 772 F. 2d 1271 (6th Cir. 1985), *aff'd*, 804 F.2d 50 (6th Cir. 1986).

In *People v. Wiese*, 389 N.W.2d 866 (1986), defendant was convicted of breaking and entering an occupied dwelling with intent to commit larceny and received an eight-to-fifteen-year prison term. He appealed the conviction, which was based substantially on the co-defendant's testimony. The Court of Appeals affirmed the conviction. Justice Riley concluded that the defendant was denied due process by the prosecutor's failure to correct the false preliminary testimony of the prosecution's principal witness, the co-defendant. The co-defendant was charged with the same offense and falsely testified there was no promise of consideration (dismissal of the charges) in return for his testimony. The justice concluded the prosecutor compounded the problem by bolstering the co-defendant's credibility and testimony at closing and in rebuttal by implying no consideration had been promised. Justice Riley wrote the prosecutor had an affirmative duty to correct the false testimony and the failure to do so compelled reversal of the conviction.

To reach the decision in *People v. Chapman*, 387 N.W.2d 835 (1986), Justice Riley and the court granted the prosecution's motion for leave to appeal after the Court of Appeals twice denied such leave. The defendant was charged with possession of a controlled substance procured from a stop and search for a cracked windshield.[24] Upon verifying there was an outstanding warrant, and that the defendant's license

---

24. M.C.L. § 333.7403(2)(b), M.S.A. § 14.15(7403)(2(b).

was suspended, defendant was arrested, and a pat-down search was conducted when the drugs were found. The defendant objected to the prosecutor's motion to bind him over for trial and moved for dismissal arguing the drugs were discovered upon an illegal search. Defendant asserted that arrest for a misdemeanor limited the police to a pat-down search for weapons only, enabling him to post bond under the bail statute, M.C.L. 780.581, M.S.A. 28.872(1). Alternately, defendant argued the police lacked probable cause to conduct the search as there were no exigent circumstances. The district court agreed (with the recorder's court) that the search was illegal and there were no exigent circumstances. It concluded the police had time to obtain a warrant. It suppressed the evidence and dismissed the charges. The Court of Appeals affirmed the ruling was appealed. The Michigan Supreme Court remanded the matter back to the Court of Appeals, 349 N.W.2d 512 (1984), which again affirmed the trial court's ruling. The prosecution argued the search was proper under federal law which permits a full search absent exigent circumstances, and further, that the recorder's court substituted a state reason for finding an illegal search. The prosecution distinguished *People v. Dixon*, 222 N.W.2d 749 (1974) relied upon by defendant, as inapposite because it involved an inventory search conducted at the police station when defendant was entitled to release. The court considered whether the interim bail statute "circumscribe[s] the otherwise constitutionally permissible scope of searches and seizures without warrants 'incident to a lawful arrest' to a limited pat-down search or 'protective frisk....'" *Chapman*, 387 N.W.2d at 837. Citing as authority *United States v. Robinson*, 414 U.S. 218 (1973), Justice Riley wrote the interim bail statute did not limit the "permissible scope of searches incident to a full custodial arrest" and reversed the Court of Appeals. *Chapman*, 387 N.W.2d at 838.

Justice Riley delivered the court's decision in two consolidated cases, *People v. Kirby* and *People v. McKinney*, 487 N.W.2d 404 (1992), ruling there is no constitutional right to waive a trial by jury in Michigan and reversed the Court of Appeals decision in both cases. Defendant Kirby was charged with five criminal charges and signed a form waiving the right to a jury trial. Defendant McKinney was charged with felonious assault and a firearm possession and before the same judge as Kirby, also signed a form waiving a jury trial. The prosecutor objected to the waivers in both cases. The trial court accepted both waivers, ruling the Michigan statutes implicated were unconstitutional. In *Kirby* and *McKinney*, the Court of Appeals granted the prosecutor's motions for a jury trial and reversed the trial court's rulings. At issue was whether defendants' right to waive a jury trial was preempted by Michigan statutory law that required the prosecutor's consent and court approval.[25] Defendants asserted the right to waive a jury trial was imbedded in the state's constitutional right to a jury trial[26] and was impaired by the prosecutor's ability to object. Justice

25. M.C.L. § 763.3, M.S.A. § 28.856 (amended 1988), and M.C.R. 6.401.

26. Mich. Const. 1850 art. 6, § 27 provides, "The right of trial by jury shall remain inviolate."

Riley wrote the Michigan constitution created no corresponding right to waive a jury, and therefore, no due process violation derived from the prosecutor's objection.

For the first time in Michigan, battered woman syndrome was recognized in *People v. Christel*, 537 N.W.2d 194 (1995). Justice Riley addressed the sole issue before the court, whether the expert witness testimony was properly admitted outside of a self-defense claim. Defendant was convicted of first-degree criminal sexual assault and acquitted of breaking and entering for which he was sentenced to 15–25 years in prison. He and the victim were involved in a prolonged relationship with multiple breakups. At the time of the final breakup, the victim was pregnant with defendant's child. The victim testified she was subjected to verbal and physical abuse throughout the relationship, including beatings and forced sexual intercourse upon defendant's jealous rages. A neighbor attested to defendant's rages and attempts to enter the victim's apartment. During one of the last beatings, defendant broke into the apartment and raped the victim, causing premature labor. The victim went to the hospital and was treated for premature labor. Cuts and bruises on her were visible to the doctors. At trial, defendant testified the victim was a liar, embezzler, and self-mutilator. He claimed the rape allegation was in retaliation for his threats to report the victim to her employer for embezzlement. Lastly, defendant presented witnesses who testified they saw the two together on New Year's Eve, weeks after the victim stated the relationship ended. To rebut the defendant's testimony and rehabilitate the victim, the prosecutor elicited expert witness testimony from a clinical psychologist about battered woman syndrome, explaining why a woman remains with a batterer. The psychologist had not examined or treated the victim. The Court of Appeals upheld the conviction and ruled the expert witness testimony was properly admitted assisting the jury in understanding the victim's testimony and actions. Justice Riley extended the court's earlier ruling in *People v. Berkeley*, 456 N.W.2d 391 (1990) in which it upheld the admission of expert witness testimony about rape trauma syndrome. The Justice wrote the expert witness testimony about battered woman syndrome was admissible but limited the expert's testimony to general descriptions about the syndrome and addressing only the specific behavior at trial. Justice Riley explained the expert witness could not opine about a defendant's guilt or whether a victim was a battered woman, having never examined the victim. *People v. Christel*, 537 N.W.2d at 591.

In *People v. Dumas*, 563 N.W2d 31 (1997), Justice Riley wrote defendant's conviction for felony-murder was reversable error as it was based on an instruction permitting the jury to infer intent for felony-murder from intent to commit the underlying felony. Defendant Dumas and co-defendant Smith previously committed three other robberies at which time Smith carried a gun. They attempted to rob a self-employed mechanic (Thomas) in his garage while a customer, Fultz, was present. Co-defendant Smith pushed Thomas into the garage and Fultz escaped. Upon climbing a seven-foot fence, Fultz heard Thomas state he did not have any money followed by a gunshot. When Fultz returned, he found Thomas suffered a chest wound from which he died. In closing argument, defense counsel conceded defendant attempted to rob Thomas but was unaware Smith would shoot anyone. Defendant objected to the jury instruction informing the jury it could predicate intent to commit felony-murder based on his intent to commit robbery. He was sentenced to life in prison without parole. Pivotal to the court's reversal was the evidence of malice was not overwhelming. Justice Riley concluded the issue of defendant's intent to agree with Smith's shooting was a question for the jury.

People v. Budzyn, 566 N.W.2d 229 (1997), involved the appeal by two white officers of second-degree murder convictions for killing a black suspect. Officers Larry Nevers and Walter Budzyn were tried separately for killing Malice Green. While on patrol duty in an unmarked car, the defendants noticed Green's car had gun bullets and saw him pull up to a house known for drug activity. Nevers asked Green for his driver's license, which Green ignored and proceeded to walk toward and sit in the passenger side of the car. Budzyn approached Green, shone his flashlight on him and asked for his license. Green started looking in the glove compartment and had something in his hand, later identified as rock cocaine. Budzyn sat, straddling Green and tried to retrieve items from his hand which turned out to be rolling paper and car keys. The defendants and the five civilian witnesses differed on their accounts of what next transpired. The witnesses testified they heard but did not witness Budzyn hit Green on the head. Budzyn denied hitting Green. Nevers testified he hit Green in the knees when Green tried to hit him and admitted hitting Green in the head with his flashlight. The witnesses testified Nevers hit Green repeatedly in the head when Green was not resisting. Other officers arrived at the scene, one who struck Green. The EMS arrived and Green, while handcuffed, suffered a seizure and died. The coroner testified the cause of death was blunt force trauma from at least 14 blows to the head. Occurring soon after the Rodney King incident, Green's death received great media coverage, leading to a multimillion-dollar settlement. The city attorney confirmed the settlement might avoid disruption during the defendant's trial from uproar caused by the Rodney King beating. Defendants submitted juror affidavits that they were exposed to extrinsic evidence that included the media blitz, reports that the National Guard was placed on alert, and viewing the movie *Malcolm X*, which included snippets of the Rodney King beating. The Court of Appeals confirmed the convictions. Writing for the court, Justice Riley reversed Budzyn's conviction, concluding the extrinsic evidence created a real and substantial possibility of prejudice heightened with a lack of eyewitnesses to Budzyn's battery of Green.

d. Majority Opinions in Civil Cases

Seventy-nine of the justice's majority opinions were civil cases arising primarily in contract, tort, employment/labor, medical malpractice, and workers' compensation law. *Reardon v. Department of Mental Health*, 424 N.W.2d 248 (1988), consolidated two tort cases against the state's Department of Mental Health that involved the public building exception to the state's governmental immunity.[27] One was filed

---

27. M.C.L. § 691.1407, M.S.A. § 3.996(107) establishes governmental immunity from tort liability for actions accruing while in the performance of a governmental function. The public building

by nursing student Claudette Reardon who was living at a regional health center residence while completing a training program. She was sexually assaulted by an employee, Arthur Green, who entered her room with a master key lock. Reardon argued the room was unsafe due to the number of keys in circulation (eighteen at the time), asserting Green copied one of the master keys. The guardian for Linda Kay Schafer filed the second lawsuit triggered by her pregnancy while receiving care at the state's Oakland regional medical facility. Schafer was profoundly mentally impaired with the capacity of a two-year-old; she could neither speak in sentences nor feed herself. She was being treated for a urinary tract infection when she was impregnated. Schafer gave birth to a son and her mother filed for damages and future support of her grandson. In both instances, the Court of Claims found both buildings were defective or dangerous and awarded Reardon $500,000 and Schafer $282,000. The Court of Appeals affirmed Reardon's award but reversed Schafer's award ruling the issue was ineffective supervision, not a defective building even after factoring in the poor lighting. Writing for the court, Justice Riley addressed the applicability of the public building exception to the state's governmental immunity act. The justice concluded the exception applies only when injury or damage "aris[es] out of a dangerous or defective condition of the building itself" but recognized Michigan cases extending the exception to maintain safe public places. She noted these latter cases involved structures or equipment. *Reardon*, 424 N.W.2d at 253. Accordingly, the justice found that neither case involved a defective or dangerous building. Specifically, she wrote that the excess number of keys in *Reardon* and the ineffective lighting and supervision in *Schafer* did not involve or constitute a defective or dangerous building (even after accounting for a less modern interior design that included pillars and poor lighting). She concluded in *Schafer* that adequate supervision would have offset any flaw in the building's design. Both cases were reversed. In *Velmar v. Baraga Area Schools*, 424 N.W. 2d 770 (1988), the court reached a different result. A high school student injured his hand while operating a milling machine during class. Justice Riley reasoned that a milling machine could constitute a dangerous or defective condition of a fixture without implicating the public building exception to governmental immunity. As there was a genuine issue of fact as to whether the milling machine was a fixture, the trial court and Court of Appeals erroneously granted summary judgment. In a procedurally complicated consolidation of two cases, Justice Riley held that intentional nuisance was not an exception to governmental immunity in cases involving municipalities. *Li v. Feldt*, 456 N.W.2d 55 (1990), abrogated in *Pohutski v. City of Allen Park*, 465 Mich. 675 (2002).

---

exception is codified in M.C.L. 691.1406, M.S.A. § 3.996(106), which requires state agencies to repair and maintain public buildings and creates liability for bodily injury and property damage resulting from a dangerous or defective condition where there is actual or constructive knowledge of the condition.

Teachers filed an unfair labor practices action[28] in *Smith v. Lansing School District*, 406 N.W.2d 825 (1987), challenging agency shop fees they had not previously paid for 12 years under a grandfathered clause in the preexisting collective bargaining agreement (CBA). Upon negotiation, this clause was omitted from the new CBA in exchange for recognizing the Lansing Schools Education Association (LSEA) as the teachers' exclusive bargaining representative. As a condition of their employment, the new CBA required teachers to either join the LSEA or pay service fees in amounts equaling union dues. The Michigan Employment Relations Commission (MERC) refused to grant the teachers a hearing and summarily dismissed their complaint after issuing a show cause order requiring teachers to file an amended complaint. When the teachers failed to comply, a MERC referee *sua sponte* dismissed their complaint. The Michigan Court of Appeals reversed. It held MERC was not empowered to summarily dismiss the complaint under § 72(3) of the Michigan Administrative Procedures Act (MAPA) which requires parties in a contested case to "be given an opportunity to present oral and written arguments on issues of law and policy and an opportunity to present evidence and argument on issues of fact." *Smith*, 406 N.W.2d at 256. Justice Riley analyzed MERC's procedural authority under MERC rules, the MAPA, and the Public Employment Relations Act (PERA). The justice held the commission had the procedural authority to dismiss unfair labor charges for failure to state a claim but was required to hold a full hearing allowing the teachers to present oral argument on issues of law and policy in support of their facts and/or to oppose a summary disposition. She concluded MERC did not have to conduct a full *evidentiary* hearing where, as here, all alleged facts were taken as true. *Smith*, 406 N.W.2d at 258–259.

The constitutionality of the state's homeschooling teacher certification requirements was challenged under M.C.L. § 15.1923, in *People v. DeJonge*, 501 N.W.2d 127 (1993). The parents of two school-age children were homeschooled in accordance with their religious beliefs through programs administered by the Church of Christian Liberty and Academy. They did not use certified teachers as required by the compulsory education law for children six to sixteen, M.C.L. § 380.1561(1), (3) and M.S.A. § 15.4156(1), (3). At trial, the adequacy and quality of the children's education was not challenged. The parents established their decisions, including the nonuse of certified teachers, were based on their religious beliefs. Notwithstanding, both parents were convicted and sentenced to two years' probation, fined, and ordered to implement certified instruction. The Court of Appeals affirmed the convictions. On appeal, the parents argued their right of free exercise of religion pursuant to the First Amendment[29] was violated and that the appellate court misapplied the compelling

28. M.C.L. § 423.201 *et seq.* and M.S.A. § 17.455(1) and Section 16 of PERA defining unfair labor practices, the filing of a complaint and notice of hearing. Chapter 4 of the MAPA, M.C.L. §§ 24.271–24.287 establishes the hearing procedures.

29. The First Amendment states: "Congress shall make no law respecting an establishment of religion, or prohibiting the free exercise thereof."

interest test. The Michigan Supreme Court agreed. Under a strict scrutiny analysis, Justice Riley concluded the state failed to show the certification requirements were the least restrictive means of achieving the state's interest. She wrote that "the state has failed to provide one scintilla of evidence that the... children have suffered for the want of certified teachers." *DeJonge*, 501 N.W.2d at 292.

Swickard v. Wayne County Medical Examiner, 475 N.W.2d 304 (1991), involved the court's evaluation of the privacy rights of family members and the extent of intrusion resulting from a reporter's suit under the Freedom of Information Act (FOIA). District Court Judge Longworth Quinn Jr. was found shot in his mother's home; drug paraphernalia was found in the home. The Wayne County Medical Examiner (ME) found the cause of death was a self-inflicted gunshot wound to the head. *Detroit Free Press* reporter Joe Swickland wrote an article about the judge's suicide and planned to write a second. He requested the autopsy report and toxicology results from the ME. The ME agreed to release the information upon "duly executed authorization" from the next of kin. The reporter sued under FOIA. Defendants, which included the judge's mother who intervened, requested an evidentiary hearing. The trial court refused and ordered the defendant ME to release the information as required by FOIA.[30] Defendants claimed the information was exempt under § 13(1)(a) because disclosure would constitute a "clearly unwarranted invasion of an individual's privacy." Writing for the majority, Justice Riley evaluated the right of privacy under FOIA pursuant to common law and Michigan statutory law. She wrote that the right of privacy belonged to the decedent and that no such right existed for decedents under Michigan law. Further, Judge Riley wrote that family members had to establish they had a right to privacy and that disclosure would be highly offensive. Finding neither, the court upheld the trial court's ruling.

In a series of consolidated and companion cases, Justice Riley clarified the extent to which, under a homeowners liability policy, an insurer has a duty to defend an insured for an underlying tort action for deliberate acts resulting in intended or expected injuries: *Allstate Insurance Company v. Freeman* consolidated with *Metropolitan Property & Liability Insurance Company v. DiCicco*, 443 N.W.2d 734 (1989), and *Frankenmuth Mutual Insurance Co. v. Piccard*, 489 N.W.2d 422 (1992). In *Freeman*, neighbor Mary Kelly sought relief under a homeowners insurance policy issued to Marshall and Alonda Freeman. Kelly, who lived two houses from the Freemans, was shouting at another neighbor when Alonda told her to shut her mouth. Alonda retrieved a .38 loaded gun from her home, shot in Kelly's direction, and hit her in the shoulder. Alonda claimed she did not intend to harm Kelly but was convicted of intentionally discharging a firearm. Kelly filed suit and Allstate moved for declaratory judgment, seeking relief from defending the Freemans. The Michigan

30. M.S.A. § 4.108(3)(1) grants a person to "inspect, copy, or receive copies of a public record of a public body" upon an oral or written request, unless specifically exempt under § 13(1)(a). The public body bears the burden of proving the refusal was justified, M.S.A. § 4.1801(10)(1).

Supreme Court adopted a two-part objective test to determine the applicability of an exclusionary clause. The test required a finding that the 1) insured acted either intentionally or criminally, and 1) resulting injuries occurred as the natural, foreseeable, expected and anticipated result of an insured's intentional or criminal acts. Justice Riley affirmed the Court of Appeals ruling that the exclusion clause precluded coverage for Alonda Freeman, agreeing she acted either intentionally or criminally and that Kelly's injuries were the "expected" result of Alonda's actions (i.e., both prongs of the test were met). Addressing Allstate's derivative duty to defend and indemnify Marshall, Justice Riley characterized the claim as "essentially one of negligent entrustment." She concluded as the exclusionary clause exempts coverage for a particular injury, so too it excludes coverage for negligent entrustment. *Freeman*, 443 N.W.2d at 690.

DiCicco involved a fight between two college students living in a residence dorm hall, DiCicco and Gravenmier. The fight escalated with DiCicco returning with a knife and stabbing Gravenmier in the stomach. DiCicco was insured under his father's homeowner's policy issued by Metropolitan Property & Liability Insurance Company (Metropolitan). Gravenmier filed a tort action alleging in the alternative an intentional tort and negligent, inadvertent stabbing. There was evidence that DiCicco was shocked by the stabbing and that it was not intentional, and criminal charges were dismissed against him. Metropolitan filed a lawsuit seeking a declaration that the policy did not cover a stabbing, thus relieving it from defending or indemnifying DiCiccio. The trial court ruled in favor of Metropolitan and DiCiccio appealed. The Court of Appeals reversed and remanded back to the trial court to determine DiCiccio's culpability. Justice Riley wrote the stabbing, under these facts, was an occurrence under the policy but held it fell within the exclusionary clause excluding bodily injury, which was either expected or intended. She wrote that Gravenmier's injuries were expected, even if unintended. In *Piccard*, Justice Riley applied the two-part test adopted in *Freeman*. Firefighter-defendant Thomas Deane was injured when putting out a fire at Piccard's Towne & Country Music Store. Piccard testified he left the store in frustration, intentionally leaving a soldering iron plugged in after spilling cleaning fluid on a pad. The store caught fire and Deane, on top the roof of a neighboring store, fell and suffered permanent disability to his knee. The Court of Appeals upheld the trial court ruling which denied the insured's motion for summary judgment. The Michigan Supreme Court remanded the case back to the Court of Appeals to specifically address "whether the definition of 'occurrence' in the policy... includes the unforeseen consequences of an intentional criminal act of the insured." *Piccard,* 489 N.W.2d at 541. The Court of Appeals reasoned that because Piccard did not intend Deane's injury, it constituted the accident or occurrence under Frankenmuth Mutual's commercial liability policy. The high court agreed. Justice Riley wrote that the appropriate focus was the scope of the covered risk at Piccard's business rather than the subject matter of the policy. In her opinion, she rejected the insurer's argument that arson was not intendent to the "ownership, maintenance or use" clause under the policy. *Piccard*, 489 N.W.2d at 545. The justice wrote that the Court of Appeals was correct in recognizing that the *DiCiccio* "policy-blended subjective standard" was distinguishable from a purely subjective standard which excludes coverage for an intentional act and intentional injury. Justice Riley concluded Piccard did not intend to inflict bodily harm to anyone, thus requiring Frankenmuth Mutual to defend Piccard. *Piccard*, 489 N.W.2d at 553.

In *Michales v. Morton Salt Co.*, 538 N.W.2d 11 (1995), Justice Riley applied the newly revised statutory definition of disability for the first time. She wrote the claimant did not establish his wage-earning capacity was limited by loss of hearing and was not compensable under the revised definition of disability. In a wrongful discharge case, *Corl v. Huron Castings, Inc.*, 544 N.W.2d 278 (1996), the court refused to extend the collateral source rule to an unemployment compensation claim, Justice Riley writing the liability to the employee did not arise in tort. In *Price v. General Motors Corp.*, 504 N.W.2d 648 (1993), the justice resolved a workers compensation disability matter, premised on the plaintiff's nerves and nervous disability that started in 1967. The plaintiff began drinking as a teenager and was an alcoholic (as was his father) for which he received treatment. Plaintiff asserted his condition resulted from an occupational disease predicated on repeated harassment he endured while employed for General Motors. The harassment was especially harsh over the last year of his employment which ended in 1981. The hearing referee ordered an open award based on plaintiff's nervous disability. The Workers' Compensation Appeal Board (WCAB) upheld the open award concluding that plaintiff's disability was compensable because his emotional problems could not be extracted from the disability. The Court of Appeals affirmed the award. Writing for the court, Justice Riley disagreed with the lower court's analysis, essentially concluding it did not apply the correct legal standard enunciated in *Gacioch v. Stroh Brewing Co.*, 396 N.W.2d 1 (1986) in which she wrote a concurring opinion. The justice held the plaintiff's condition stemmed from progressive alcoholism (an ordinary disease of life), neither derived from an employment injury (no nexus shown) nor aggravated or accelerated by his employment. Justice Riley remanded the case back to the WCAB to determine whether the plaintiff suffered a disabling personal injury, separate and distinct from his alcoholism. In another workers' compensation case involving General Motors, *Simkins v. General Motors, Corp.*, 556 N.W.2d 839 (1996), Justice Riley considered the compensability of injuries stemming from an automobile injury on property not leased or owned by an employer. She held such an injury is within the course of employment only if the (1) injury occurred when coming or going from work and (2) employee was traveling in a reasonably direct route between the worksite and the parking area owned, leased, or maintained by the employer. In this case, the plaintiff parked in the parking lot maintained by General Motors but thereafter traveled to a private lot with a co-employee before traveling to her worksite. As no evidence was in the record regarding plaintiff's decision to take this route, Justice Riley remanded back to the WCAB to address the alternate route and reach a decision on that additional evidence.

On balance, the rulings issued by Justice Riley reflect a thoughtful judge who issued rulings in conformity with the court's majority. A colleague on the court reflected,

> Opinions, majority, concurring, and occasionally dissenting, were always timely. Dorothy was infrequently in dissent. She was, year in and out, the most influential person at the conference table, insidiously and collegially, to craft a majority view so that as many justices as possible could join in signing. Dorothy's talents were manifest immediately upon taking her office in January 1985. Just two years later, in January 1987, she was elected Chief Justice, an accolade that is a testimonial to the respect and admiration in which she was held by her colleagues."[31]

The Justice founded the Michigan Supreme Court Historical Society in 1988 and was Honorary Chair. In 1991, Justice Riley was inducted into the Michigan Women's Hall of Fame. She retired from the Michigan Supreme Court on September 1, 1997, due to the onset of Parkinson's disease. At age 79, the justice passed on October 23, 2004, at her home at Grosse Pointe Farms. She was awarded posthumously the Distinguished Public Servant Award.[32] Report of her passing read in part, "[d]espite her small stature, Chief Justice Dorothy Comstock Riley will be remembered as a pillar of strength and conviction and as a stalwart believer in the rule of law and in the ideal of justice for all. She was a study in contrasts, both strong, and delicate, commanding and gentle."[33] "Her thirteen years as a Supreme Court justice began and ended in controversy. Her appointment to the Court in 1982 set off a partisan power struggle that at one point pushed her back off the Court until the following election. 'She was said to have handled the entire situation with dignity and grace.'"[34]

2. Justice Miriam Naveira Merly

a. Formative Years

1956	B.A., Chemistry, College of Mount Saint Vincent
1960	LL.B., University of Puerto Rico Admitted to Puerto Rico Bar
1963–1971	Law Clerk, Supreme Court of Puerto Rico,[35] Associate Justice Lino Saldaña and Chief Justice Luis Negrón Fernández

31. Michigan Supreme Court Historical Society, *Presentation of the Portrait of The Honorable Dorothy Comstock Riley*, October 7, 1997, https://www.micourthistory.org/special-sessions/presentation-of-the-portrait-of-the-honorable-dorothy-comstock-riley/.

32. Justine Hyde, *Justice Dorothy Comstock Riley Wins Honors after Retirement from the Court*, Lansing State Journal, October 8, 1997.

33. *Lansing State Journal, Deaths Funerals*, October 26, 2004.

34. *Supra note 17, Comstock Riley Article.*

35. Selma Moidel Smith, *ABA Senior Lawyers Division Meets in Puerto Rico, Women Lawyers Journal 14 (Spring 2000),* https://static1.squarespace.com/static/5c97fb8b4d546e5350d0593b/t/5cbacc4271c10b880e44d4f2/1555745871386/SMS-SLD-WLJ-86.1.pdf.

1966	Assistant Attorney General
1969	LL.M., Columbia University
1972	Postgraduate Studies, Leiden University, Holland Assistant Attorney General, Antitrust Affairs, Department of Justice
1973–1976	Solicitor General of Puerto Rico
1976–1985	Private Practice Professor, Inter-American University School of Law
1985–2004	Associate Justice on the Supreme Court of Puerto Rico Chief Justice, 2003-2004[36]

As she scaled her career, Miriam was the first Latina and female lawyer at each apex. Starting as a law clerk in service to justices of the Island's highest court, she ultimately presided over that very court as its Chief Justice. She was born on July 28, 1934, in Santurce, Puerto Rico, to Arturo (*"Papote"*) Naveira and Matilde Merly. Married in 1930, Arturo was a laborer and Matilde a homemaker. Miriam, the middle child and only daughter, was raised in San Juan. At times, her maternal widowed grandfather and extended family lived with her immediate family. In 1962, Miriam married lawyer and businessman Rodón, and while married practiced as Naveira de Rodón. Their daughter, Miriam, was born in 1963 and became a distinguished scientist. A year later their son was born, Victor Arturo, and he followed in his parents' footsteps and became a lawyer.

In 1973, Miriam became the first Latina Solicitor General of Puerto Rico and in the country. In that capacity she was the first Latina lawyer to appear before the U.S. Supreme Court representing the Commonwealth of Puerto Rico in[37] *Examining Board v. Flores de Otero*, 426 U.S. 572 (1976). This was the first case before SCOTUS in which Latino lawyers appeared on both sides.[38] Under Puerto Rico law,[39] licenses were granted only to civil engineers who were Puerto Rican citizens. Conditional licenses were granted to noncitizens to work for the Commonwealth. Maria Flores de Otero was a native Mexican and legal resident of Puerto Rico. She met all licensure requirements but was denied a license. A native Spaniard residing legally in Puerto Rico, appellant Perez Nogueiro was granted a conditional license as he worked for Carolina municipality's Public Works Department. His case was consolidated with

36. Puerto Rico Supreme Court, Biographies of Former Chief Justices, Miriam Naveira Merly, Chief Justice 2003–2004, https://poderjudicial.pr/eng/supreme-court/biographies-of-former-chief-justices/.

37. *Supra* chptr. 1 note 15, Maria G. Mendoza Article at https://ssrn.com/abstract=1802008.

38. Michael Olivas, *The First Latina & Latino Lawyers to Argue Before Supreme Court*, NewsTaco, March 31, 2011, https://newstaco.com/2011/03/31/the-first-latina-latino-lawyers-to-argue-before-supreme-court/.

39. Puerto Rico Act of May 10, 1951, No. 399, as amended, P. R. Laws Ann., Tit. 20, 681–710 (Supp. 1973), § 689.

Flores de Otero. Appellees sought declaratory and injunctive relief claiming jurisdiction under 28 U.S.C. § 1343(3) and alleged the statute's citizenship requirement violated 42 U.S.C. § 1983. Section 1343(3) establishes the jurisdiction of district courts to "redress the deprivation, under color of any State law" of federal constitutional rights, privileges, or immunities. Section 1983 provides citizens of any state or territory to avail themselves of the remedies thereunder. In separate rulings, three-judge panels ruled in favor of the plaintiffs and ordered the Commonwealth to license them. Solicitor General Naveira de Rodón argued that before appellees could proceed under Section 1983, they had to establish the $10,000 jurisdictional amount prescribed by 28 U.S.C. 1331 (a)8. The Supreme Court affirmed the district court's rulings, expressly noting that in becoming a Commonwealth in 1952 (the Foraker Act[40]), Congress did not "intend to leave the protection of federal rights exclusively to the local Puerto Rico courts and... repeal the jurisdiction of the U.S. District Court in Puerto Rico to enforce 1983." It rejected the Commonwealth's jurisdictional argument requiring federal abstention until the state-law question whether plaintiffs had to avail themselves of remedies under the Puerto Rican Constitution first had to be resolved. SCOTUS found the district court had personal jurisdiction as both federal laws were applicable to states and territories. Applying a strict scrutiny standard, the Supreme Court found the Puerto Rico law deprived appellants of their "rights, privileges and immunities within the meaning of 1983." *Flores de Otero,* 426 U.S. at 585–586.

During her three-year tenure as Solicitor General, Naveira de Rodón was involved in 163 appeals to the Puerto Rico Supreme Court, the vast majority (105) were criminal cases.[41] On appeal, the Solicitor General represented the interests of the Commonwealth on a broad range of matters from bail bonds, the lottery, felonies and multiple criminal law issues, to the administration of attorneys. The following select cases provide examples of her litigation. The Solicitor General filed disbarment cases against attorneys licensed in Puerto Rico, including *In re Ostolaza*, 103 D.P.R. 72, 1974 PR Sup. LEXIS 438, attorney was disbarred for failing to diligently protect client in a criminal appeal, *In re Ruiz*, 106 D.P.R. 257, 1977 PR Sup. LEXIS 2871 involved an indefinite suspension ofa lawyer for serving simultaneously as attorney for a bonding company and as counsel to defendants for whom the company posted bonds, and *In re Garcia*, 104 D.P.R. 604, 1976 PR Sup. LEXIS 1855, the attorney was disbarred for cashing a client's check without authorization, unlawfully retaining mortgage notes, and failing to deliver the proceeds, among other illegal actions. In *Schneider v. Colegio de Abogados de Puerto Rico* (College of Attorneys of Puerto Rico), 565 F. Supp. 963 (1983), the Solicitor General represented the Puerto Rico Supreme Court

40. Act of April 12, 1900, 31 Stat. 77 and 84, which established the federal district court system in Puerto Rico, followed by the Organic Act of 1917, 39 Stat. 951 further defined the jurisdiction of the federal district court in the Commonwealth and the Act of June 25, 1949 codifying the district courts of Puerto Rican and Hawaii as part of the U.S.C. Title 28, 62 Stat. 889; H.R. Rep. No. 308, 80th Cong., 1st Sess., 6 (1947).

41. Lexis last visited April 5, 2025.

in a 42 U.S.C. § 1983 challenge by Puerto Rican attorneys. Specifically, the attorneys alleged the Bar Association fees were used to support the political agenda of the Bar Association in violation of their First Amendment rights to be free from governmental compulsion to engage in speech or associational activities. The district court held the dues and fees supporting the Bar Association's ideological and/or political activism violated the attorneys' rights. The Income Tax Act of 1954 was at issue in *Pardavco, Inc. v. the Treasury of Puerto Rico*, 104 D.P.R. 65, 1975 PR Sup. LEXIS 2229. Plaintiff company earned interest from deposits with foreign banks conducting business in Puerto Rico and paid no taxes on the interest. The court held that interest from deposits in the local banking business or in foreign banks doing business in Puerto Rico constituted income derived from sources within Puerto Rico, computable in the gross income and therefore taxable.

In a criminal case, *Conjugal Partnership v. Commonwealth*, 103 D.P.R. 876, 1975 PR Sup. LEXIS 1960, the Solicitor General took an unusual step and asked the Puerto Rico Supreme Court to reverse the conviction of a man for killing a child. An eight-year-old boy suffered a fatal injury immediately upon leaving school while he was playing on the grounds adjacent to the school. There was no evidence that anyone or anything caused his fall or death and there were no witnesses. Predicated on the child's injuries resulting in death and an expert witnesses' testimony of a fatal blow to the head, the trial court surmised the injuries could be inflicted in one of three ways: he was thrown, he stumbled and fell, or someone inflicted the blow to the boy's head. Based upon logical conjecture, the trial court determined the injury was intentional and found the defendant guilty. The Solicitor General based her petition upon the insufficiency of the evidence, asserting there was inadequate evidence establishing a causal relationship between the defendant's actions (there was none) and the injury suffered by the child. The Puerto Rico Supreme Court granted the reversal, agreeing the trial court's finding of guilt was based upon insufficient evidence.

b. Puerto Rico Supreme Court, 1985–2004

Naveira de Rodón's litigation skills and successful tenure as Solicitor General earned her the distinction of being appointed as the first woman and Latina to the Puerto Rico Supreme Court. In making the historic appointment on June 11, 1985, Governor Rafael Hernández Colón stated he chose Naviera de Rodón because "of her deep knowledge of law and her understanding of justice."[42] Justice Naveira de Rodón made a significant contribution to both justice within the law and the judiciary. In 1993, she served as chair of the newly created Special Judicial Commission to Investigate Gender Discrimination in the Courts of Puerto Rico (Commission). The Commission issued a report on the status of women in the Puerto Rico

42. New York Daily News, June 16, 1985.

Judiciary (1995 Report).[43] (The justice's successor, Liana Fiol Matta, served as a member of the Commission.) The 1995 Report was undertaken during the period on the mainland when state courts were establishing gender task forces throughout the country. The 1995 Report (articulated by Justice Fiol Matta)[44] captured the essence of its purpose:

> The Special Judicial Commission to investigate Gender Discrimination in the Courts of Puerto Rico defines the concept of *gender perspective* as the 'set of knowledge, intuitions, wisdom and attitudes that women and men have accumulated over time as a consequence of their social location and their particular experiences resulting from their lives on a world culturally divided by reason of gender.' The Commission thus recognizes that the diversity of analysis between men and women is due, in part, to the different points of view acquired based on the roles assigned by society to their respective genders. This divergence of perspectives motivated by gender necessarily makes itself felt in judicial decisions. After all, the Law is a social and historical construction imbued with ideas and values. In this sense, the incorporation of women's perspective in the adjudication of legal cases contributes to the establishment of a diverse, more balance analysis enriched by new sensitivities.

The 1995 Report found of the 317 judges sitting in the General Court of Justice, 216 were men, constituting 68% of all judges, and 101 were women, comprising 32%. Most of the female judges were on municipal courts, 41 at 59%, followed by the District Court 22 at 27%, Superior Court 38 at 30%, Appellate Court, only 7 at 21%, and 1–14% on the Supreme Court (the justice). Through her leadership and guidance of the Commission's work, Justice Naveira de Rodón helped establish the baseline from which the judicial branch could document the progress of women in Puerto Rico's judiciary.

c. Majority Opinions in Criminal Cases

Most of her Supreme Court rulings were issued as Justice Naveira de Rodón and will be cited accordingly. In her later years she returned to her maiden name, Naveira Merly. Justice Naveira de Rodón authored 103 majority opinions, fifteen were criminal cases. The justice's cases were delivered in Spanish; the translated versions are quoted in this discussion. The translated LEXIS versions do not bear page numbers but reference discussions under Roman numerals (I, II, etc.) or by paragraphs

43. *See e.g., Puerto Rico Supreme Court Report on Gender Discrimination in the Courts of Puerto Rico, Special Judicial Commission to Investigate Gender Discrimination in the Courts of Puerto Rico*, August 1995, at 15 and 19; https://poderjudicial.pr/Documentos/SecretariadoConf/REPORT-ON-GENDER-DISCRIMINATION-AUGUST-1995.pdf.

44. Liana Fiol Matta, *Women in the Judiciary: Assessment of the Process of Award, UPR L. Rev. 79 (2010): 972, quoting in part from the 1995 Report, chptr. 1 at 21.*

in bracketed numbers, e.g., [3]. Accordingly, citations are to those Roman numerals or bracketed paragraphs.

Billposting in Puerto Rico is one of the most inexpensive and effective means to post messages to the public. It is the mass communication device typically used by minorities and dissenting groups on the Island that was at issue in *People v. Arandes de Celis*, 120 D.P.R. 530, 1988 Sup. LEXIS 147. Two groups were charged with and convicted of billposting under Act No. 4 of June 13, 1976, 1976 P.R. Laws Penal Code sec. 181, that addresses billposting by private persons for noncommercial purposes. Group 1 put up posters on the Iturregui Avenue underpass columns in Rio Piedras. Group 2 placed posters on the Domenech Avenue underpass columns in Hato Rey. The posters read, "79 Panamerican Games, Welcome, Puerto Rico Socialist Party," and depicted the U.S. flag upside down with the Puerto Rican flag flying at the top of the poles. At issue was whether the lack of consent of the custodian of public property is an element of the crime and whether underpass columns are excluded as part of the definition of utility poles under the 1976 amendment. Section 181 provides in pertinent part: "[e]very person who ... affixes ... upon any public property ... any poster[s] ... without the consent of the custodian ... shall be punishable by a minimum fine of fifth (50) dollars or a maximum fine of two hundred fifty (25) dollars." The defendants were convicted, and they appealed. Justice Naveira de Rodón wrote that consent for posting bills "was the mechanism employed by the lawmaker to harmonize and balance the exercise of the freedoms of speech and of the press of the citizenry with the State's right to protect its property." *de Celis*, 120 D.P.R. at [3]. Upon review of the legislative history and record, she concluded consent was an element of the offense. The justice wrote, however, that the prosecutor was not required to prove a negative—the lack of consent as that was evidenced by the posting itself but she concluded that the convictions of the defendants should be reversed. In deliberating, the justice weighed the protective interests of the Commonwealth against the public's freedom of speech. To guide that deliberation, she quoted from *Pacheco v. Vargas, Alcaide*, 120 D.P.R. 404, 410–411 (1988), "[w]e should never forget that 'the meaning of today is not always the meaning of tomorrow' ... [and that] [j]udicial interpretation has, by its very nature, a natural evolution for the different eras.... The law lives and develops in environments of change and evolution, and if we do not want to make [frequent] reforms we must adapt it, as its own will permits, to the new needs of the time' ... '[Laws must be construed] in the light of the specific realities of the society in which it operates.'" *de Celis*, 120 D.P.R. at [9]. While seemingly an unimportant offense, Justice Naveira de Rodón underscored the importance of free speech, especially for the minority of scare means who had no other means of communicating. By concluding columns were poles as defined by section 181, she held that columns were exempted, and no permission was necessary to billpost. She rejected the rationale of the concurring opinion to adopt a more stringent definition of poles to exclude columns and thereby omit columns the pole exception, writing:

> Nothing would disturb our judicial conscience more than to remain silent, or as mere spectators or timid guardians of the law, in the face of a violation of the essential and fundamental right of free speech. If this were the case, the law, whose ultimate purpose is to do justice, would at that tragic moment turn into an accomplice of the individual's throttling idleness and, consequently, become an oppressive tool against the social conscience of the people. We shall never allow this...
>
> The exercise of this fundamental right should be within the reach of all the members of our society, free from stifling ideological, social, political, and economic considerations. Protection should be afforded to minorities, dissidents and outcasts of society, who usually do not have access to the sophisticated and costly mediums of the press, television and radio. They must be guaranteed their right to effectively express and communicate their ideas, without unreasonable and needless restrictions. The flow of ideas, the public debate, controversies and exchange of ideas open up new options and choices and encourage human understanding. Section 181 must be construed in such a way that it stimulates and encourages the best atmosphere of understanding through the effective communication of ideas. We will thus be wiser and freer.

de Celis, 120 D.P.R. at [11].

People v. Castro Rosario, 125 D.P.R. 164, 1990 PR Sup. LEXIS 121, involved a warrantless search of a vehicle. Defendant was convicted with possession of drugs, pursuant to the Controlled Substances Act, 24 L.P.R.A. § 2404. Police officer Soler testified he stopped defendant upon observing him driving while smoking marijuana and run a red stop light. Soler followed and pulled the car over. While radioing for assistance, the defendant and his companion fled in the car, causing Soler to give chase. The defendant abandoned the vehicle. Soler waited for assistance and searched the "hotwired" car, finding marijuana and a driver's license. A check of the license plate revealed the car was stolen. Defendant offered no evidence at trial. On appeal, defendant argued Soler conducted an illegal search. While the opinion offers no new law, in this case, Justice Naveira de Rodón provides an artful primer on unreasonable searches and seizures caselaw pursuant to the Puerto Rico Constitution, art. II, Section 10.[45] She concluded the defendant's claim was meritless.

In *People v. Hernandez Torres, Barreda*, 125 D.P.R. 560, 1990 PR Sup. LEXIS, defendants Hernández Torres and Barreda were employees of the Puerto Rico Telephone Company (TELCO) who allowed the unauthorized massive replacement of black lines or downpipes and certified as correct invoices for work not done. The

45. In her overview of caselaw, the justice included an article authored by Luminaria Olga Resumil de Sanfilippo (JD 1973 UPR Law School), *En nombre del debido proceso de ley (In the name of due process of law)*, Rev. Jur. U.P.R. 58 (1989), 171 (1989). Professor Resumil was the first Luminaria tenured professor at UPR Law School in 1987 and thus, the first in the country. Source: Luminarias Study.

invoices were used by third parties to defraud TELCO. The defendants moved to dismiss on the basis that TELCO, incorporated in Delaware, was a private corporation and they were not public employees for purposes of Section 314, 33 L.P.R.A. § 4365. Section 314 creates criminal liability for public officers who willfully neglect to perform their duties or who violate any legal provision relative to those duties, punishable by imprisonment not exceeding six months or fine or both. The Superior Court agreed with defendants that TELCO was a private corporation or, alternatively, if a public-private company, the statute was vague as concerns the status of employees working for such a corporation.[46] The Solicitor General appealed the Superior Court's ruling and certiorari was granted. Justice Naveira de Rodón analyzed TELCO "as established in its organic act and applicable caselaw" and reaffirmed the ruling in *Torres Ponce v. Jiménez*, 113 D.P.R. 58 (1982), that TELCO is a public-private corporation. She concluded the manner of a company's creation is not determinative, distinguishing those that are totally or partially controlled by the government, such as TELCO. Justice Naveira de Rodón's ruling was guided by the legislature's statement of purpose in creating the Telephone Authority to which it granted the right to purchase the private stock of TELCO so that TELCO would serve as the Commonwealth's public instrumentality on the island.[47] The fact that TELCO employees were not part of Puerto Rico's personnel system did not dissuade the court from recognizing them as public employees. Accordingly, the court held the defendants were public employees and remanded the case back to the Superior Court.

At issue in *People v. Isabel Félix Avilés*, 128 D.P.R. 468, 1991 PR Sup. LEXIS 201, was the jurisdiction of a court over a defendant—more precisely, the scope of the bond posted—when the defendant did not appear on appeal of a preliminary hearing at which he was acquitted. Defendant was arrested for possession of illegal drugs and bail was set at $3,000. At the preliminary hearing, the court found no probable cause and the prosecution did not announce its intention to appeal the dismissal of charges; consequently, defendant was not then summoned. Defendant did not appear at the appeals hearing or the rescheduled appeals hearing as no summons was served. Notwithstanding, the court confiscated the posted bond. The bond company appealed, and the court ordered the Solicitor General to show cause why the judgment should not be set aside. While the court recognized an acquittal at a preliminary hearing does not preclude the state from initiating further proceedings, the failure to properly summon the defendant abrogates a court's *in personam* jurisdiction over the defendant. Justice Naveira de Rodón held the prosecutor was required to effectuate service to proceed to hearing, as "summons to the preliminary hearing on appeal is an indispensable requirement of due process."[48] Accordingly, she con-

46. Section 7(16), 33 L.P.R.A. § 3022 (16) defines public official or employee in pertinent part as any person holding office or performing a paid or gratuitous duty for the legislative, executive, or judicial branch of Puerto Rico or in any of its municipalities, agencies, or public corporations.

47. Act No. 25 of May 6, 1974.

48. Criminal Procedure Rules (C.R.P.) 24(c) and 235, 34 L.P.R.A. App. II.

cluded the trial court lacked *in personam* jurisdiction over the defendant, was barred from conducting hearings, and had no authority to confiscate the bond. Under C.R.P. 218, Bail; Conditions; Requirements, Justice Naveira de Rodón also concluded the defendant remained free on bail until convicted. The judgment was reversed.

In *People v. Marquez y Bermudez*, 122 D.P.R. 80, 1988 PR Sup. LEXIS 239, Justice Naveira de Rodón began her opinion with the following introduction:

> Today we must address again a case that sadly reflects the decay of values in the discharge of public functions. In view of the nature of the criminal acts under our consideration today, we believe it is important to pronounce ourselves by opinion. A wider promulgation of this matter will convey a lesson to some and will deter this type of antisocial conduct that undermines the People's faith in the Government, gnaws away at the interstices of the social web, and upsets the delicate balance between the individual's interests and the mechanisms of community life and coexistence.

Defendant-appellants Marquez Diaz and Bermudez Berrios were charged and convicted of offering a bribe[49] to Treasury Department employee Rojas Calderon. The defendants' scheme involved paying the outstanding $5,157.55 real property tax debt with a fraudulent check, having the check removed, and causing the production of fraudulent receipts by Treasury Department employees to prove satisfactory payment. They were sentenced to eight years of probation. On appeal, defendants alleged the trial court erred in admitting their identification by Rojas Calderon, which, if excluded, resulted in insufficient evidence to sustain their conviction. The trial was held three years after the bribery offense; the only error in the identification was Rojas Calderon's testimony that defendant Bermudez was shorter than him when both were the same height. Rojas Calderon was granted immunity for his testimony, which consisted of confirming contact by the defendants and two in-person meetings: the first where defendants offered to pay him $1,000 to remove a forthcoming check that would bounce due to insufficient funds, and the second, two to three weeks later after the $5,157.55 check arrived at his office. Defendants had paid $800, with $200 outstanding. Rojas Calderon called and met the defendants at which time he gave them the check and relayed the tax debt would be recorded as satisfied. Rojas Calderon worked with two other Treasury Department employees to effectuate removal of the check and production of the fraudulent receipts reflecting satisfactory payment of the tax debt. Rojas Calderon identified the defendants at trial, relaying he further recognized Marquez Diaz as the brother of a tax collector at another Treasury Department office. Other witnesses attested to the defendants' identities, including one who knew defendant Bermudez since birth and was the person to whom he gave the money to pay some of the taxes. Defendant Marquez Diaz denied knowing defendant Bermudez and denied Rojas Calderon's testimony, relay-

49. Section 212, 1974 Penal Code, 33 L.P.R.A. §4363, offer of bribery to a public officer or employee is punishable by imprisonment.

ing he purchased stereo equipment from Rojas Calderon for $800. The justice reviewed the factors of reliability of witness identifications, including the opportunity to observe during the commission of the crime, correctness of prior identification, degree of the witness' attention, level of certainty, the time elapsed between the crime and the identification. Justice Naveira de Rodón wrote the totality of the circumstances established the reliability of the defendants' identification and upheld their convictions.

d. Majority Opinions in Civil Cases

Justice Naveira de Rodón authored 88 majority opinions in civil cases, some unique to the Commonwealth such as the Federal Air Transport Act, the Beach and Traffic and Safety Act,[50] and federal admiralty jurisdiction. In *Iberia, Lineas Aereas de Espana, S.A. v. Secretary of the Treasury*, 135 D.P.R. 57, 1993 PR Sup. LEXIS 180, Iberia Airlines, a Spanish majority-owned company, sought refunds for taxes paid from 1976 to 1979 on three of its offices in Puerto Rico. Iberia asserted the 1973 Air Transport Agreement ("Agreement")[51] between Spain and the United States precluded Puerto Rico from taxing Iberia's personal property. The lower court ruled the taxes were valid and Iberia appealed. Construing Puerto Rico's 1952 Constitution, Justice Naveira de Rodón wrote the Commonwealth has the inherent power to levy taxes on the property of a foreign corporation where that sovereign owns a majority share of the company. The issue was whether taxes were permissible under the Agreement that included Puerto Rico, 49 U.S.C. § 1301(31). Citing cases recognizing the court's ability to construe international agreements, the justice considered article 8 of the Agreement that exempted "national duties and charges on fuel, lubricants, consumable technical supplies, spare parts including engines, regular equipment, ground equipment, stores and other items intended for use solely in connection with the operation of servicing of aircraft of the airlines...," none related to office buildings. Iberia also argued that the Commonwealth's levying of taxes on its property violated the Foreign Commerce Clause, U.S. Const, art. I, § 8, cl. 1, L.P.R.A., vol. 1 (1982) at 163, which provides that "[t]he Congress shall have [p]ower... [t]o regulate [c]ommerce with foreign [n]ations...." The justice provided an in-depth overview and analysis of the Commerce Clause and held it was inapplicable because the clause expressly granted states the ability to levy property taxes, and therefore, was inapposite to Iberia's argument that the Commerce Clause was dormant. *Iberia*, 135 D.P.R. at [12]. She also considered the Airport Development Acceleration Act of 1973, as amended in 1982, 49 U.S.C. § 1513, which did not prohibit Puerto Rico from levying taxes, including on property. The justice concluded no other applicable bilateral agreements prevented Puerto Rico from levying taxes and interpreted article 8 as exempting federal taxes, not taxes imposed by territories. Holding that neither the Agreement nor the Act prohibited Puerto Rico taxes, Justice Naveira de Rodón up-

---

50. 12 L.P.R.A. §§ 1391–1397e.
51. 24 UST 2103, effective August 3, 1973.

held the trial court's decision, writing the Commonwealth did "not violate the federal scheme devised to deal with state taxation of foreign air commerce." *Iberia*, 135 D.P.R. at [18].

Plaintiff Leon sued Transconex in a Puerto Rico court for breach of the bill of lading for wrongful delivery of over thirteen bales fabric to an unauthorized recipient in *Leon v. Transconex, Inc.*, 119 D.P.R. 102, 1987 PR Sup. LEXIS 144. The fabric was delivered to a Claudio Fuentes instead of Tomiko's Originals, Inc. (Tomiko's). Fuentes returned some but not all the fabric, and of that returned, Transconex claimed the fabric was not of the same quality as the fabric shipped. Transconex moved to dismiss the case, claiming exclusive jurisdiction over admiralty cases lay with the federal court. The trial court denied Transconex's motion, and the Superior Court affirmed. Justice Naveira de Rodón wrote that the Judiciary Act of 1879, article 9 slightly modified Article I, section 2 of the U.S. Constitution. It provided that the district courts shall have original jurisdiction of any civil case of admiralty or maritime jurisdiction, "saving to suitors in all cases all other remedies to which they are otherwise entitled" ("saving to suitors clause").[52] She held that state courts, including Puerto Rico, had concurrent jurisdiction to enforce federal maritime law under the savings to suitors clause, provided the state law was consistent with federal law. The justice explained the saving clause grants plaintiffs their choice of a state court in the pursuit of state or common-law remedies, rather than admiralty remedies. The decision was affirmed and remanded.

In *Monllor Arzola v. Conjugal P'ship Constituted by Luis González Ortiz*, 138 D.P.R. 600, 1995 PR Sup. LEXIS 285, the court was asked to interpret whether Section 2 § 1391(h) of the Beach Traffic and Safety Act (Act) covered ski jets. The Act defined "[b]oat or ships" as "any vessel propelled by machinery as its main source of power" and "[n]avigation vessel" as "canoes, sailboats, rowboats, water skis, surfboards ... watercycles and any apparatus that moves on the surface of the water and serves to transport persons or is used for recreation." *Monllor*, 138 D.P.R. at III. The 13-year-old defendant was operating a ski jet west–east and had 180° field of visibility when she hit the 22-year-old plaintiff who was windsurfing north–south who lacked visibility to the west. The plaintiff suffered three femur fractures, leaving him unable to windsurf without back pain. Suing the defendant's parents, plaintiff claimed the defendant failed to yield right of way and that the parents were negligent in permitting their underaged daughter to operate the ski jet. The trial court ruled in favor of the plaintiff, awarding him over $30,000. On appeal, the defendant sought a ruling that the trial court also erred by applying the Act and Regulation No. 3589, § 26(2), Department of Natural Resources for the Registration of Motor Vessels and General Safety Rules (Regulation) that a minor under fourteen cannot operate a motor vessel. Subsection 10 further provides "[a]ny motor-propelled boat or vessel shall yield the right of way to any other vessel propelled by sails or oars." *Monllor*, 138 D.P.R. at

52. 28 U.S.C. § 1333.

III. The defendant argued ski jets were not included or covered by the Regulation, notwithstanding it specifically prohibits any person under fourteen—and specifically bars any adult from allowing such persons—to operate a motor vessel. (Parents admitted at trial they were ignorant of the maritime laws.) Justice Naveira de Rodón concluded the plaintiff proved the three elements necessary to recover under Puerto Rico civil law: harm, nexus between harm and act of the other person, and that the act was tortious or negligent. Relying on the legislative intent and purpose of the Act and regulation to ensure public safety on the waters, Justice Naveira de Rodón affirmed the trial court's award.

Writing for the court, Justice Naveira de Rodón addressed issues of first impression in the following cases. The precedential nature of the court's published vs. unpublished decisions arose in *Rivera Maldonado v. Commonwealth of Puerto Rico, Department of Sports and Recreation*, 119 D.P.R. 74, 1987 PR Sup. LEXIS 141. The facts giving rise to the appeal involved a suit filed by the plaintiffs against the Puerto Rico police department and the Commonwealth's Department of Sports and Recreation (Department). The court *sua sponte* issued a show cause order why the lawsuit should not be dismissed for lack of standing. The plaintiffs agreed to dismiss the Puerto Rico Police but not the Department. They relied on a prior unrelated judgment and unpublished concurring opinion expressing the Department had standing to sue and be sued ("Judgment"). The trial court ruled the Judgment did not set precedent and dismissed plaintiff's lawsuit, which they appealed. Justice Naveira de Rodón concluded that the Judgment was not issued with a court opinion and therefore had no precedential value. The justice recognized the Department was an exception to the general rule that executive departments do not have standing through legislative mandate in accord with 15 L.P.R.A. § 2 (the power to sue and be sued). The trial court's decision was reversed.

In *Pacheco v. National Western Life Ins. Co.*, 122 D.P.R. 55, 1988 PR Sup. LEXIS, the U.S. District Court for Puerto Rico certified the question to the court, which tolling provision applies to extrajudicial claims under Puerto Rico Dealer's Contract Act (Law 75 of June 24, 1964, as amended): the Commerce Code's one-year limitation or the Civil Code, which has a three-year statute of limitation.[53] Puerto Rican representative Pacheco was terminated by National Western in 1979 but did not file an extrajudicial claim until 1983, four years later, seeking monies and benefits owed under the Dealer's Act (which regulates the termination of contracts). National Western moved the suit to federal district court and filed a motion to dismiss asserting the one-year filing limitation under the Dealer's Act barred Pacheco's lawsuit. Though not specifically delineated in the Commerce Code, Justice de Rodón took judicial notice of Puerto Rico caselaw holding dealers' contracts, because of their mercantile-commercial nature, are controlled by the Commerce Code and subject to the three-year limitation. Not addressed in the Commerce

53. Dealer's Act, 10 L.P.R.A. § 278 *et seq.*, Art. 10 of the Commerce Code, 10 L.P.R.A. § 1903 or art. 1873 of the Civil Code, 31 L.P.R.A. § 5303.

Code is the manner of tolling or extrajudicial claims. The Civil Code recognizes that extrajudicial claims toll the statute of limitations. Describing the gap in the Dealer's Act as failing to provide adequate redress, Justice Naveira de Rodón concluded the tolling prescriptive periods in the Commerce Code fix the gap as a supplemental remedy. Notwithstanding, the justice held that extrajudicial claims do not toll the three-year statute of limitations.

Pagan Caraballo v. Silva Delgado, Insular De Seguros, Inc., 122 D.P.R. 105, 1988 PR Sup. LEXIS 240, addressed the scope of an insurance company (Seguros) to provide legal representation to Dr. Silva Delgado, and codefendant Dr. Ortiz Perez for malpractice stemming from Dr. Ortiz Perez's abortion on a fourteen-year-old minor. The parents alleged their daughter was induced into lying about her age and marital status and sued for damages, not specifying medical malpractice. Seguros refused to provide legal representation because the complaint alleged a criminal and illegal abortion, outside the scope of coverage. Approximately two years later, the plaintiffs amended their complaint to include negligence at which time Seguros agreed to provide legal representation for Dr. Ortiz Perez; soon thereafter, the plaintiffs dismissed the suit against the doctor but the action for attorneys' fees continued. Liberally construing the complaints and insurance policy, Justice Naveira de Rodón and the majority determined that a reasonable interpretation of the pleadings was a cause of action for medical malpractice. The justice found Seguros was responsible for Dr. Ortiz Perez's legal fees. Three of the justices dissented, concluding Seguros could not be held responsible before the complaint was amended.

In a divorce case, *Rivera v. Algarin*, 159 D.P.R. 482, 2003 PR Supp LEXIS 81, Justice Naveira de Rodón addressed the finality of a divorce when a spouse passes before the judgment is notified and a copy is filed in the record. Married in 1990, the spouses obtained a stipulated divorce on August 18, 2000, but the next day, the husband passed away in a car accident. The judgment was entered but not yet notified until over a month later, on September 22. The widow timely moved under C.P.R. 49.2 (motion for relief) to nullify the judgment, asserting it could not become final because her husband was dead by the time the notice was filed in the case record. The circuit court upheld the trial court's denial of the motion, concluding jurisdiction had lapsed as the divorce was final and unappealable under Guideline 6 of the Uniform Procedure for Divorce by Mutual Consent. Guideline 6 provides that where an action for dismissal has not been filed within thirty days after the divorce judgment, the divorce is final and unappealable. Justice Naveira de Rodón wrote,

> Neither Guideline 6 nor the rule laid down in *Figueroa Ferrer* could breathe life into a marriage bond that had been dissolved by the death of one of the spouses. In the specific circumstances of this case, we have no doubt that the procedural mechanism of the Rule 49.2 motion for relief was adequate. It was not Mrs. Algarín Cruz's intention to seek review of the trial court judgment because she believed that it had erred when rendering said judgment. Neither did she intend to have an appellate court review and correct any error committed by the trial court. It was the death of Mr. Rivera Meléndez, a subsequent

> event, that made the previously rendered judgment of divorce by mutual consent ineffective, null, and completely devoid of justification.

Rivera, 159 D.P.R. at III. The circuit court's ruling was reversed, and the divorce nullified. In another 1988 divorce case, Justice Naveira de Rodón addressed the issue of whether the absence of sexual relations constitutes a separation and grounds for divorce, *Cosme v. Marchand*, 121 D.P.R. 98, 1988 PR Sup. LEXIS 182. The spouses had no relations for more than three years but continued living with one another when the husband sought a divorce; there were no children. The trial court granted a divorce on the grounds of separation and awarded wife Marchand $1,000 in alimony *pendente lite* and ordered her to pay $1,500 in attorneys' fees for obstinacy. Marchand appealed. Justice Naveira de Rodón wrote that marriage could only be dissolved in the manner provided by statute that includes separation, established by showing uninterrupted separation of more than two years.[54] The justice focused on the legal aspect of marriage and concluded separation had not been proven in this case: "Granting the divorce in these circumstances would impair and corrupt the ground of separation invoked by plaintiff." *Cosme*, 121 D.P.R. at [18]. She further wrote, "... the mere absence of sexual relations in a marriage, when the parties continue living together and functioning as a married couple in other aspects, cannot be solely invoked to allege the ground of separation for a divorce." *Cosme*, 121 D.P.R. at [18].

The interplay between federal Social Security benefits and retirement benefits was at issue in *De Cortes v. Admin. of the Employees Ret. Sys. of the Gov't & the Judiciary*, 123 D.P.R. 589, 1989 PR Sup. LEXIS 113. De Cortes was pensioned by Puerto Rico's Employees Retirement System upon which he, his wife, and his daughter were dependent ("pension benefits"). When De Cortes died at age fifty-five, the pension benefits ceased, and the widow and daughter received Social Security benefits until the daughter turned eighteen. The widow had no income. The court considered the scope of Puerto Rico law,[55] Act No. 105, which states, "[i]f the pensioned participant is, at the time of his death, covered by Title II of the Federal Social Security Act, [the surviving spouse] shall not be entitled to the pension." Citing *Figueroa v. Diaz*, 75 P.R.R. 152, 160 (1953), Justice Naveira de Rodón quoted, "[l]aws must be construed and applied in keeping with the social purpose that inspired them. We must not estrange them from the human problem whose solution they seek... [i]n construing them, the reality of human life must predominate, and not the dogmatic abstraction of eternal and invariable rules." *De Cortes*, 123 D.P.R. at [4]. Concluding that De Cortes was not receiving Social Security benefits at the time of his death, Justice Naveira de Rodón held he was not covered under the federal law "for the purposes

54. Civil Code sec. 96(9) and Civil Code sec. 95, 31 L.P.R.A. § 301.

55. Section 1 of Act No. 105 of June 28, 1969, 3 L.P.R.A. § 788a(a) (hereafter Act No. 105). *See also* Guillermo García Valdecasas, parte general del derecho civil español, 111 Madrid, Ed. Civitas (1983) from which the justice borrowed. Valdecasas (1940–2020) was a practicing lawyer (1962 Complutense University, Madrid) and a Professor of Philosophy of Law and author renowned for his historical, philosophical, aesthetic and literary works.

of excluding his surviving spouse and minor children from the Retirement System benefits under Act No. 105." The widow was entitled nevertheless to De Cortes's pension benefits, for to rule otherwise, the justice wrote, would be an untenable result. The justice determined Act No. 105 was a supplementary protection to cover cases where the Social Security does not cover the beneficiaries. Borrowing from the 37-year rector of the Collegio di Spagna in Bologna Guillermo Garcia Valdecasas, the justice conveyed his interpretation of the law:

> We must bear in mind that laws are 'part of a coherent and harmonic whole—the legal system—within which they perform a function that is coordinated with, or subordinated, as the case may be, to the other legal standards.' Laws must be seen 'as the product of social conditions, and the need to relate to the rule to others forming a juridical institution, and each institution with the others, until we get to the basic principles of the juridical system as a whole.' *Rocafort v. Álvarez,* 112 D.P.R. 563, [12 P.R. Offic. Trans. 706] (1982).

The extent of responsibility by schools and shopping malls were the focus of Justice Naveira de Rodón's majority opinions in *Elba A.B.M. v. U.P.R.*, 125 D.R.P. 294, 1990 PR Sup. LEXIS 127, and *Et Ah v. Plaza Carolina Shopping Mall*, 132 D.P.R. 785, 1993 PR Sup. LEXIS 177. In *Elba*, a female student was raped by an unknown assailant on the UPR campus that was poorly lit with overgrown vegetation and no security. UPR knew that campus area was high risk but took no preventative or corrective measures. The student suffered severe emotional trauma from the multiple assaults perpetrated by the assailant with threats to use a knife. The student freed herself by stabbing and fatally wounding the assailant. Other students came to her assistance and police were called. Campus security arrived within ten minutes driving an ambulance, after the assisting students sought help. They picked up the wounded assailant and placed him in the ambulance with the victim, despite her refusals to ride in the same ambulance. Consequently, she left the ambulance. Another student drove her to the hospital. A year prior, students presented to the chancellor a study on sexual assaults on the campus to prevent assaults in high-risk areas that included the area where plaintiff was assaulted. The justice examined whether there is a causal nexus between the criminal acts of a third person and the omission to take preventative measures, including previous similar occurrences known to the institution, lack of adequate investigation or follow-up from such knowledge, absence of a plan to address the problem to eliminate the dangerous conditions, and adequacy of trained security. Pursuant to Civil Code art. 1802 (tort Liability), Justice Naveira de Rodón concluded UPR had a duty to provide heightened security. She ruled UPR was liable for negligence that resulted in the student's injuries. Damages assessed at $450,000 were upheld. In *Et Ah*, a sixteen-year-old co-plaintiff and her friend went to a shopping mall and, when done, waited in front of J.C. Penney looking for transportation home. The assailant approached them with a knife and forced them to walk away from the Plaza Carolina Shopping Mall and parking lot to a brush patch under a bridge. They both were sexually assaulted for hours. The teens and their parents filed suit against the mall, which filed a motion for summary judgment, asserting they could not be held liable for the criminal acts of a third person. Plaintiffs countered the mall was aware of the high crime rate, submitting crime statistics and newspaper articles documenting the crime rate. The mall's motion for summary judgment was supplemented with citation to two prior superior court judgments finding no liability. The trial court ruled, even if the assaults were foreseeable, the mall could not stop the assaults. Justice Naveira de Rodón held the foreseeability factor did not require precise foreseeability of the intended harm, rather the duty to foresee was more general, especially where a causal nexus could be established. Upon reviewing relevant caselaw, she concluded that for liability to be imposed on a regional mall, proof of a breach of duty to provide adequate and reasonable security must be established. Such a finding must be based on three factors: 1) nature of the shopping center and activities conducted, 2) nature of the criminal activity, and 3) whether security measures adopted were reasonable and sought to reduce damage to patrons. Justice Naveira de Rodón held defendants submitted insufficient evidence to sustain summary judgment and reversed.

In *Velez Rodriguez v. Pueblo Int'l, Inc.*, 135 D.P.R. 500, 1994 PR Sup. LEXIS 201, Justice Naveira de Rodón applied the three-year statute of limitations in the Wage Claims Act in a worker's compensation case. The Workmen's Accident Compensation Act[56] requires employees to file claims within one year from the date of injury. To address the unjust/retaliatory dismissal of an employee for filing a worker's compensation claim, Justice Naveira de Rodón adopted the three-year statute of limitations in the Wage Claims Act. She reasoned that the worker's awareness of his/her claim starts upon seeking and being denied reinstatement. Justice Naveira de Rodón analyzed the interplay and impact of the Americans with Disabilities Act (ADA) and the Puerto Rico disability discrimination law[57] in *Rivera Flores v. Compañia ABC*, 138 D.P.R. 1, 1995 PR Sup. LEXIS 211. Plaintiff alleged McGaw failed to accommodate his back condition and filed a lawsuit without exhausting administrative remedies with the Department of Labor. McGaw moved to dismiss plaintiff's lawsuit on this basis, which the trial court denied. On behalf of the court, Justice Naveira de Rodón held that Act No. 44 does not require exhaustion of administrative remedies and plaintiff's lawsuit was properly filed. Similarly in a Title VII sex discrimination case involving plaintiff's demotion, *Matos Molero v. Roche Products, Inc.*, 132 D.P.R. 470, 1993 PR Sup. LEXIS 139, the justice held that the processing of a case by EEOC effectively replaced processing by the Puerto Rico agency, tolling the one-year period of limitations for filing under Act No. 100.[58] The plaintiff in *Rivera Aguila v. K-Mart de*

56. Act No. 80 of May 30, 1976, as amended, 29 L.P.R.A. §§ 185a–185i establishing cause of action for unjust or retaliatory discharge; Minimum Wage Act, Section 32, 29 L.P.R.A. § 246d(a), sets three-year statute of limitations for action to recover wages from the date employee learns of the termination.

57. 42, U.S.C. § 1981 *et seq.*, Section 13 of the Act of No. 44, § 149, 29 L.P.R.A. 149.

58. Act No. 100 of June 30, 1959, of Puerto Rico, 29 L.P.R.A. §§ 146–151.

Puerto Rico, 123 D.P.R. 599, 1989 Sup. LEXIS 114, sued K-Mart for terminating her employment because she was pregnant. Justice Naveira de Rodón applied Puerto Rico's Working Mothers Protection Act ("Act No. 3"),[59] ruling it creates a presumption that the discharge was unjustified, which the employer is required to rebut by a preponderance of the evidence. The plaintiff was employed as a head/cashier and promoted to full-time head clerk. In January 1985, K-Mart discharged plaintiff two months into her probationary promotion because, plaintiff claims, of her pregnancy. K-Mart asserted plaintiff was terminated due to unsatisfactory performance based on its written standards. The trial court dismissed plaintiff's lawsuit based on K-Mart's proffered evidence of copies of three documents. One document signed by the plaintiff was notice that she was promoted and had to undergo a probationary period, a second contained general customer dissatisfaction of long lines and another informed plaintiff she was not performing satisfactorily that was signed by K-Mart but not the plaintiff. K-Mart did not submit its employee handbook setting forth employee performance standards. Plaintiff appealed, arguing the trial court erred in admitting copies that were unsigned and further by failing to permit her counsel to examine the originals. Establishing Act No. 3 affords pregnant employees (including those on probation) even greater protections, Justice Naveira de Rodón concluded K-Mart failed to overcome the presumption that its discharge was unjustified. It failed to prove it supplied plaintiff with a copy of the standards or afforded her any due process, including legitimate, written unsatisfactory performance warnings. The justice again addressed the Working Mother's Act in *Santiago v. Oriental Bank and Trust*, 125 D.P.R. 560, 2002 PR Sup. LEXIS 79. Though the parties stipulated Oriental did not know about the pregnancy at the time of plaintiff's discharge, the trial court denied Oriental's motion to dismiss, ruling unawareness was not an affirmative defense. In this case, the justice held the employer's lack of knowledge of plaintiff's pregnancy at the time of dismissal constitutes an affirmative defense, however, the burden remains on the employer to prove it was unaware. Furthermore, such a stipulation enables an employer to escape the harsher damages provisions of the Working Mother's Act, leaving for resolution damages from wrongful discharge. As Oriental paid plaintiff the monthly wages due, Justice Naveira de Rodón reversed the trial court's ruling and dismissed the case.

The issue, whether service on the operational manager of a store operated by a foreign corporation was sufficient, arose for the first time in *Quiñones Román v. CIA ABC*, 152 D.P.R. 367, 2000 PR Sup. LEXIS 169. Justice Naveira de Rodón wrote that the operational manager for a supermarket chain authorized to do business throughout Puerto Rico with its corporate headquarters in Puerto Rico may be summoned through an operational manager as the managing agent under C.P.R. 4.4(e), 32 L.P.R.A. App. III. In this case, the plaintiff fell in a supermarket in Yauco and suffered

---

59. Act No. 3, section 4 of March 13, 1942, as amended, 29 L.P.R.A. § 469, which specifically prohibits discrimination based on pregnancy.

injuries. He served the summons and complaint on the manager of the Yauco store. The store never answered the complaint and default judgment for $30,000 was entered. After plaintiff tried to satisfy the judgment, the store filed a motion to set aside the judgment alleging the Yauco manager was not authorized to accept service. The trial court agreed and voided the service. The Court of Appeals reversed the trial court's decision. Justice Naveira de Rodón analyzed the issue pursuant to the Judicial Act of 1994, the General Corporation Act of 1995, and C.P.R. 4.4(e). She wrote, "[i] n the field of civil procedural law, when construing the rules that will govern and guide proceedings, we must bear in mind, as a guiding principle of hermeneutics, that procedural rules have no life of their own, but exist in order to facilitate proceedings and to guarantee that they will be expeditiously conducted in a just, speedy, and inexpensive manner." *Quiñones* 152 D.P.R., [7]. Justice Naveira de Rodón concluded that service may be made through a resident, managing, or general agent designated by the corporation—in this case the manager of the local supermarket, fulfilling the purpose of the judicial reform to offer court venues close to home.

In an earlier jurisdictional case, *Unisys Puerto Rico, Inc. v. Ramallo Bros. Printing, Inc.*, 128 D.P.R. 842, 1991 PR Sup. LEXIS, afforded Justice Naveira de Rodón the opportunity to analyze and determine the validity of forum selection clauses, an issue left unresolved in *Walborg Corp. v. Tribunal Superior*, 104 D.P.R. 184 (1975). At controversy was the forum selection contractual provision between Ramallo and Unisys. Ramallo purchased computer equipment from Unisys and software from MIC upon their joint proposal. Ramallo entered into separate contracts with both. When the installed system did not work, Unisys sued Ramallo who countersued (seeking recission of both contracts) and joined MIC as a third-party defendant. MIC moved to dismiss based on the forum selection provision that contractual disputes would be decided in Michigan courts and demanded specific performance. The trial court denied the motion and the Supreme Court agreed to review the case. The justice reviewed federal caselaw favoring forum selection clauses but concluded the facts compelled its nonapplicability. Justice Naveira de Rodón concluded Ramellos's purchases constituted a single business transaction. The justice concluded that MIC was an indispensable party and dismissing MIC by granting specific performance would result in a "clear and patent injustices for all of the parties concerned." *Unisys*, 128 D.P.R. at IV.

Justice Naveira de Rodón authored the extensive opinion on the constitutionality of Section 1 of Act No. 324 of November 6, 1999, in *Colón v. Pesquera*, 150 D.P.R. 724, 2000 PR Sup. LEXIS 56, including on the separation of powers in the Puerto Rico Constitution, art. I, Sec. 2. This case was the sequel to the court's decision in *Colón y otros v. J.C.A. (Colón I)*, 148 D.P.R. __ (1999). At issue was the failure of the Highway and Transportation Authority (HTA) to produce an adequate final Environmental Impact Statement (EIS) concerning its plan to construct an expressway, connecting the towns of eastern Puerto Rico with the San Juan metropolitan area, known as Routt 66. The complex fact pattern ultimately triggered the instant controversy when HTA segmented Routt 66 to avoid fully assessing the project's environmental impact. The Environmental Quality Board (EQB) held hearings and received comments on the preliminary EIS (PEIS), concluding vital information was missing to enable it to make an adequate assessment of the project. Notwithstanding, the EQB approved the report, requiring HTA to supplement the PEIS with an addendum addressing multiple items. Three years later in 1996, the HTA submitted an addendum that failed to address the items requested and, further, eliminated the most controversial parts of the Routt 66 project while retaining the original project description. Colón and local communities (Communities) objected and filed a motion for a new EIS to which HTA filed a motion in opposition. EQB determined that by shortening the project, the HTA met the requirements of the Environmental Public Policy Act (Act).[60] Colón and the Communities filed a petition for certiorari, which the court denied. In *Colón I*, the court held the addendum filed by HTA failed to correct the deficiencies in the PEIS. Shortly after *Colón I* was issued, the EQB (upon HTA's request) denied the Communities' motion for a new EIS and declared the process hearing process completed. After a series of filings and rulings in the trial and Circuit Court (that suspended and restarted the project), the Communities filed a petition of certiorari with the court. The court issued show cause orders to both parties to "discuss the tenability of the writ of mandamus to compel HTA to issue a Final EIS for the totality of the Route's segments"; it also halted the construction through a resolution. The legislature passed two acts a month after the court's resolution, one that amended the Uniform Administrative Procedures Act and the second that amended the Environmental Public Policy Act (EPPA), adding a third paragraph to section 4(c) that directly impacted the case pending before the court. Specifically, the third paragraph 1) eliminated the adjudicative element of the EIS approval process and stripped it down to an informal and informative character, 2) eliminated mandamus to challenge an EQB determination, leaving court action as the sole remedy, 3) exempted some administrative agencies, including EQB, from having to justify informal determinations, and 4) allowed project segmentation for environmental assessment purposes. In short, the legislation was passed to circumvent the court's case. HTA accordingly moved to dismiss the action before the court. Justice Naveira de Rodón assessed the court's duty:

> The task that lies ahead of us is very delicate. This case is very special. On the one hand, it involves a controversy that results from the obstinate noncompliance of an administrative agency with the parameters of a previous Opinion of this Court. On the other hand, we are faced with legislation that seeks to upset the checks-and-balances system established in our Constitution to prevent the so-called "tyranny of the majority." *Colon*, 150 D.P.R. at I.

The justice held that the amendment to 4(c) allows government agencies to submit piecemeal EISs of public infrastructure projects, enabling HTA to circumvent the court's orders and opinions. The justice wrote,

---

60. Act No. 9 of June 18, 1970, as amended, 12 L.P.R.A. § 1121 *et seq.*

> The consequence of the legislation under our consideration is to relieve the HTA from the ministerial duties that, as we held in *Colón I*, it had not discharged yet. We cannot be so naive as to ignore the true purpose and intent of a given action and be blinded by what is conveniently presented to us in legal pleadings as the "legislative intent." This Court will not lend itself to such contradiction or to play on words that, in the long run, does not correspond to reality. This Court, as custodian and ultimate interpreter of our Constitution, will protect the Constitution and will now allow actions such as that under our consideration to overshadow or diminish its value by endorsing the enactment of tailor-made legislation passed at the request of a losing party to a legal proceedings for the purpose of allowing said party to engage in an action that was declared illegal by the Judicial Branch. In other words, we cannot allow the Legislature to become with the consent of the Governor, a *de facto* Supreme Court, and to reverse actions taken by this Court.

Colon, 150 D.P.R. at II. Justice Naveira de Rodón ruled the amendment was unconstitutional as it contravened the separation of powers under the Puerto Rico Constitution.[61] She concluded the HTA ignored the court's ruling in *Colón I*, having failed to carry out its ministerial duties to produce a final EIS. The justice, on behalf of the court, rejected HTA's segmentation of Routt 66 as a legitimate new project. She ruled that mandamus is invoked under sec. 30 of the EPPA as the exclusive remedy available to private citizens to compel specific compliance of the EPPA. The permanent injunction against HTA was affirmed.

e. Conclusion

Governor Sila Calderón appointed Naveira de Rodón as the first female chief justice in December 2003. (The Chief Justice's children and two granddaughters were present at the swearing-in ceremony.) She presided only seven months but long enough to make history once again. Due to the mandatory retirement age of 70 codified in the Puerto Rico Constitution, the justice had to retire. After sitting as the sole female on the Puerto Rico Supreme Court for nineteen years, on July 21, 2004, Justice Naveira de Rodón retired from the bench. She earned a reputation as a pragmatic and moderate jurist dedicated to women's equal rights. In 2008, her university alma mater bestowed upon Justice Naveira de Rodón the *Ad Laudem Dei*, presented to alumni whose careers were of historical significance.[62] Speaking of her Supreme Court experience at a lecture titled, "Women in Puerto Rico in the Face of a Global Era," the justice expressed:

> I brought to the Court [Tribunal] a wealth of new experiences, a way of seeing things different from those of my colleagues. A way that they had not had the opportunity to hear since they had never shared with a female colleague on

61. The justice and the court relied on P.R. Const., art. V, § 4 (L.P.R.A. vol. 1), as providing the specific manner in which the court declares acts unconstitutional.

62. Mt.SaintVincent,https://mountsaintvincent.edu/alumnaei/alumnaei-association/ad-laudem-dei/.

equal terms and conditions, that is, with equal power. Not only was I a woman, but both my education and my experiences were different from those of my colleagues. I understand that all this was very positive and healthy for the Court.[63]

On April 15, 2018 at the age of 83, the justice passed. Upon her death, Chief Justice Maite Oronoz Rodriguez ordered flags on all judicial buildings be lowered to half-mast for five days, expressing:

> The Judicial Branch is moved by the death of Miriam Naveira Merly, who was an avant-garde and brave woman, who opened gaps that still resonate. Her fight to achieve equality and empowerment of women is the essence of her legacy. Today I signify my admiration and gratitude for her service to our Country and, above all, for overcoming the barriers that, to a large extent, today, allow me to continue her legacy.[64]

3. Justice Rosemary Barkett

a. Formative Years

1959	A.A., St. Joseph College, Jensen Beach, FL
1960–1968	Elementary/Junior High Teacher, Sisters of St. Joseph of St. Augustine, FL
1967	B.S., English Literature and Education, *summa cum laude* Spring Hill College
1970	J.D., University of Florida Law Miller Memorial Outstanding Student Award Admitted to Florida Bar
1971–1978	Associate/Partner, Farish & Farish Law Firm, West Palm Beach, FL
1979	Solo Practitioner, West Palm Beach, FL
1979–1985	Trial Judge, Florida Fifteenth Judicial Circuit Chief Judge (1983–1984)
1984–1985	Judge/Chief Judge, Florida Fourth District Court of Appeal (to October 14, 1985)
1985–1994	Justice, Florida Supreme Court Retained in 1986 and 1992 Chief Justice 1992–1994[65]

63. Master Class by the Honorable Miriam Naveira, Revista de Ciencias Sociales Homines 467, 473–74 (2003–2004); Microjuris al Día, *Requiem for a pioneer: Hon. Miriam Naveira Merly*, April 27, 2018, https://aldia.microjuris.com/2018/04/27/requiem-para-una-pionera-hon-miriam-naveira-merly/. These remarks also appeared as her testimony in the 1995 Report.

64. *Primera Hora, Muere la primera mujer que fue president del Tribunal Supremo de Puerto Rico,* Noticias, https://poderjudicial.pr/la-jueza-presidenta-oronoz-rodriguez-expresa-su-pesar-ante-el-fallecimiento-de-la-ex-jueza-presidenta-miriam-naveira-merly/.

65. Nominee Rosemary Barkett, Senate Judiciary Committee Hearings, One Hundred Third Congress, Second Session, Part 2, Serial No. J-103-28, Feb. 3, 1994:359–522, 429–438 includes Judicial Questionnaire.

The second youngest of sixteen children, Rosemary was born on August 19, 1939, in Ciudad Victoria, Tamaulipas, Mexico, to Mariam and Assad Barakat, Syrian immigrants to Mexico *via* Marseilles. At age six, the family migrated to Miami, and Rosemary arrived speaking her native tongue of Spanish and no English (except New York Yankees and Notre Dame, thus becoming lifelong fans of both).[66] The family's last name was changed to Barkett,[67] and they opened Barkett Market. Rosemary attended Catholic schools, played basketball, and worked in her family's market. She enjoyed a rich, trilingual environment and culture of Syrian, Mexican, and American influences, languages, and music, considering herself to be 100 percent of all three. Rosemary planned to study theatre at Catholic University in Washington but instead became a novitiate of the Sisters of St. Joseph as Sister St. Michael at age seventeen.[68] Upon entering, Sister St. Michael embarked on her higher education, as all were required to do. She became a naturalized citizen in 1958 and completed her A.A. degree in 1959. Sister St. Michael chose Spring Hill in Mobile, Alabama, over Barry College, where she began her elementary and junior high school teaching career. There, she developed her confidence and independence, indulging her love of music by becoming the choir leader. In the ensuing years, she became ordained. Aware of the country's turmoil over the Vietnam War and influenced by philosophers Pierre Teilhard de Chardin and Hans Küng, she left the Order in 1967 at age twenty-six. Rosemary continued to teach in secular schools but sought greater intellectual challenges and independence than teaching afforded. She chose to study law at the University of Florida College of Law as one of the few women admitted.[69] The tradition of being known as the first, "*la primera*," started. She was the first female student on moot court and recipient of the Miller Memorial Outstanding Student Award, the first female lawyer and Hispanic on the Florida Supreme Court, and the first Latina appointed to the Eleventh Circuit upon the submission of her name by "[s]everal individuals and groups."[70] The Justice has never married. When asked why, "...she respond[ed] with a joke—the last guy who asked me I didn't think was going to be the last guy—then more seriously, '[d]eveloping a relationship takes an enormous amount of effort and time. Do you want to see my calendar?'"[71] The judge

66. New York University Law—Institute of Judicial Administration (IJA) Oral History of Distinguished American Hon. Rosemary Barkett (Nov. 2, 2022) by Sarah E. Harrington, 01:25–03:13, 2:03:35 (hereafter *Barkett Interview).*

67. *Supra*, note 65, Judicial Questionnaire at 429: "name changed by order of the circuit court of Dade County in approximately 1967 to correspond to [their] Miami relatives' name and to our commonly used name."

68. Thomas J. Billitteri, *Chief Justice Fights for Her Life on Bench*, Tampa Bay Times, October 12, 1992, updated October 11, 2005, https://www.tampabay.com/archive/1992/10/12/chief-justice-fights-for-her-life-on-bench/

69. *Supra* note 66 *Barkett Interview* at 9:35–13:06, 17:53, 20:04.

70. *Id.*, *Barkett Interview* at 19:36, 20:48, 35:08, 51:47–52:07; supra, note 62 Judicial Questionnaire at 451.

71. Thomas J. Billitteri, *Chief Justice fights for her life on the bench*, Tampa Bay Times (Oct. 12, 1992).

is known for her humor, energy and dedication to her job and was quite popular in Florida, notwithstanding opposition during her retention election.

On November 15, 1985, Rosemary became the seventy-first justice of the Florida Supreme Court. She was appointed by Governor Bob Graham to an initial six-year term ending in 1991. The new justice asked one of the nuns from the "motherhouse" to give the inaugural prayers at the swearing-in ceremony.[72] Two logistical traditions were immediately impacted when Rosemary became Justice Barkett, from the practical (*toilettes*) to the laudatory. The justices then were called "Mr. Justice." As the new justice was unmarried, she refused to be called "Madam Barkett" and instead chose "Justice Barkett." The remaining all-male court, thereafter, adopted her moniker. There were two bathrooms—one for the justices and one for women. The court added a bathroom in the judge's chambers, the justice recalling, "And I did say if you don't want me to follow you in there, you better do something about that or something along that line."[73] Justice Barkett faced minority opposition during her 1992 retention election[74] that was mimicked during her 1994 confirmation to the bench and transported to the federal arena with her nomination to the Eleven Circuit (*see Circuit Court discussion infra*). During her 1992 retention election, three other male justices were also up for retention who joined her majority opinions and/or issued majority opinions in which she joined—none of the three experienced the same intense opposition. Two examples are *In Re TW*, 551 So. 2d 1186 (1989), issued by Justice Shaw. In this case, Justice Barkett and six other justices joined in whole or part in the majority opinion that struck down Florida's parental-consent law on abortions for minors. A second case written by Justice Barkett held that permanently incapacitated people should not be forced fed where a living will exists or such prior wishes were expressed, *In re the Guardianship of Browning*, 568 So. 2d 4 (1990) (upon certification of the question). She was elected to a second term with 61% of the vote.

b. Florida Supreme Court, 1985–1994

During her tenure, the justice issued 3,000 opinions and participated in 12,000 cases. The justice's responsibilities involved administrative tasks, such as certifying the need for additional judges that required analysis of case filings and dispositions in the state court system. *See, In re Certification of Judgeships*, 611 So. 2d 1244 (1993), and *In re Certification of Need for Additional Judges*, 631 So. 2d 1088 (1994). The justice and court created family court divisions within the state circuit courts in 1991, *In re Report of Commission on Family Courts*, 633 So. 2d 14 (1994). The state circuit courts required additional time to implement the new rules and asked the Supreme

---

72. *Id., Barkett Interview* at 14:29, ABA Women Trailblazers Project, Biography Rosemary Barkett, https://abawtp.law.stanford.edu/exhibits/show/rosemary-barkett/biography.

73. Florida Supreme Court, https://supremecourt.flcourts.gov/Justices/Former-Justices/Justice-Rosemary-Barkett; *supra* note 66 *Barkett Interview* at 37:04.

74. *Supra*, note 66 *Barkett Interview* at 38:44–51:47.

Court for clarification. Accordingly, the Supreme Court held a Family Court Workshop in April 1993 where additional guidance was provided. The Supreme Court ultimately sought funding from the legislature to assist with implementing the family court divisions within the guidelines and goals it adopted. The justice also resolved matters involving the legislature. For example, in a matter involving a governor's veto, *Florida Society of Ophthalmology v. Florida Optometric Association*, 489 So. 2d 1118 (1986), the justice held that after the legislature has adjourned *sine die* (without a fixed day or indefinitely), the governor had fifteen days, rather than seven, to veto bills under the state constitution.[75] At issue was a bill passed by both houses that gave ophthalmologists the ability to prescribe medication. The petitioners filed a writ of mandamus to compel the secretary of state to publish the bill as a new law because the governor had not vetoed the bill within the normal seven days attaching when the legislature was in session. The administration and practices of the courts also was within the high court's purview. Justice Barkett issued substantive opinions that established rules for judges in cases such as *Ciccarelli v. State*, 531 So.2 d 129 (1988), in which she held that each appellate judge (not lawyers or law clerks) evaluating harmless error in criminal appeals must independently read the record, and in *Pope v. State*, 561 So. 2d 554 (1990), where the justice instructed appellate courts that upon reversing a departure sentence because there were no written reasons, the court must remand for resentencing with no possibility of departure from the guidelines. Lastly, the justice was required to review attorney disciplinary matters in which disbarment, suspensions, or public censure were administered.

c. Majority Opinions in Criminal Cases

Justice Barkett issued the majority opinion in 265 cases, many which involved criminal convictions. Over eight years, Justice Barkett joined the majority in affirming the death penalty in 276 cases. The justice wrote the majority opinion in thirty-eight first-degree murder cases where the death penalty was imposed. A few of these death penalty sentences were reversed that later formed the basis of the opposition against Justice Barkett during the 1992 retention election, including the following cases: *Fead v. State*, 512 So. 2d 176 (1987), *Brown v. State*, 526 So. 2d 903 (1988), *Cherry v. State*, 544 So. 2d 184 (1989), and *Rose v. State*, 601 So. 2d 1181 (1992). In *Fead v. State*, the defendant shot and killed his girlfriend that was witnessed by her sister and brother-in-law. There was testimony that defendant had been drinking the entire day of the murder with a resulting .25 blood alcohol level. Defendant argued his intoxication prevented him from forming a specific intent to commit first-degree murder of which he was convicted. Fead's former girlfriend and mother of his eight children testified that in 1973, she had witnessed defendant killing another woman. Defendant's prior conviction for that murder was stipulated to at trial. The jury agreed and recommended a life sentence, which was set aside by the trial court. On

75. Fla. Const., Article III, section 8(a) that sets the deadline of seven days during the legislative session but fifteen days after the legislature has adjourned sine die.

appeal, the defendant argued that the intoxication warranted a proportional review that would result in a life sentence. Justice Barkett held that there was sufficient evidence for a jury to find mitigating factors, such that the trial court's override of the jury's recommendation was improper, and that the imposition of the death penalty was not proportional. In *Brown v. State*, the eighteen-year-old defendant and co-defendant robbed a convenience store and fled. They were chased by a county sheriff who pulled their car over. The defendant wrestled with the sheriff, grabbed his gun, and shot him twice in the head. Either shot would have caused the sheriff's death. The jury recommended a life sentence but the trial court, relying on the sheriff's status as a law enforcement officer, imposed the death penalty. Justice Barkett concluded that law enforcement status was an inadequate basis on which to impose the death penalty and, further, that the facts did not constitute a heinous and cruel crime. In *Cherry v. State*, Justice Barkett concluded the death penalty was not an appropriate penalty imposed on the defendant for the death of one of two victims who died during his burglary of their home. Defendant was convicted of two counts of first-degree murder, burglary, and other crimes for burglarizing the home of an elderly married couple. The wife died of wounds from a severe beating; the husband died of a heart attack. Death penalties were imposed on the defendant for both deaths. The justice concluded the death penalty imposed for the husband's death was too severe. In *Rose v. State*, the defendant was convicted of the first-degree murder of eight-year-old Lisa Berry, who was the daughter of Rose's girlfriend. While at a bowling alley with the mother, Lisa and other friends, the defendant took Lisa from the bowling alley and murdered her. The trial court imposed a death sentence for the murder and a life sentence for Lisa's kidnapping. The Florida Supreme Court affirmed the convictions but vacated the death sentence and remanded for resentencing. On remand, the jury recommended the death penalty. The trial court found no mitigating circumstances but found aggravating factors. The Florida Supreme Court again affirmed the decision, which prompted defendant's filing of a motion for post-conviction relief. Defendant relied on the trial court's *ex parte* directive to the state to prepare the proposed order, the court's approval of that order without a hearing, and the state's concession that there were factors that could have been introduced as mitigating circumstances.

In another first-degree murder case involving the death penalty, *Castro v. State*, 597 So. 2d 259 (1992), the defendant argued the state should have been disqualified from prosecuting him. Defendant was convicted for stabbing his roommate to death. The jury recommended a life sentence, but the trial court imposed the death penalty. At trial, defendant was represented by Public Defender (PD) Anthony Tatti who thereafter joined the state prosecutor's office. On the first appeal, the Florida Supreme Court vacated the death sentence and remanded for resentencing. During the new penalty phase, the prosecutor conferred with (now) state Prosecutor Tatti about how to best respond to defendant's motion to disqualify the state's office. The trial court denied the motion. Justice Barkett ruled that these facts dispositively established the conflict to grant defendant's motion to disqualify the entire office. She concluded Florida law prohibited the disqualified attorney from providing prejudicial information or personally assisting in the prosecution on the criminal charge. The justice also wrote that the trial court erred in considering duplicative aggravating circumstances. A new penalty hearing was ordered.

Conversely, the justice and the majority court vacated a stay of execution and upheld the imposition of death in *Tompkins v. Dugger*, 549 So. 2d 1370 (1989), as they did in numerous other cases. In all but a few instances in which Justice Barkett wrote the majority opinions, the murder convictions in death penalty cases were upheld but the sentences were vacated and remanded for new sentencing.

In a series of cases, Justice Barkett wrote the majority opinions reversing serious criminal convictions on procedural errors. *Lavado v. State*, 492 So. 2d 1322 (1986), was reversed for failure of the trial court to permit defense counsel to ask prospective jurors during *voir dire* about their willingness to accept the defense of voluntary intoxication. Defendant was convicted of armed robbery, which contained the element of specific intent. During deliberations, jurors asked about the rule on voluntary intoxication and defendant's intoxication during the robbery. Defendant's conviction was upheld by the Third District Court of Appeals. Justice Barkett adopted the appellate judge's dissent that "[i]f he knew nothing else about the prospective jurors, the single thing that defense counsel needed to know was whether the prospective jurors could fairly and impartially consider the defense of voluntary intoxication." *Lavado*, at 1324. Justice Barkett ordered a new trial.

State v. Tyner, 506 So. 2d 405 (1987), involved defendant's conviction for armed burglary, but it was the dismissal of two murder charges that generated the controversy and prompted the issuance of a certified question in the case. Defendant and co-defendant decided to rob a home. Defendant was informed no one would be at home, but defendant was present when the co-defendant borrowed a gun. The defendant drove co-defendant to a home and left, driving half a mile away to await the co-defendant. The co-defendant entered the home alone and killed the two persons inside. These facts were stipulated to but were not admitted at trial and formed the basis of the motion to dismiss the charges. At trial, the court relied on the stipulated facts to impose a departure sentence on defendant for the murders. The district court reversed the trial court's sentencing based on the Florida Rule of Criminal Procedure, § 3.701(d)(11), which prevents departure sentencing that include facts relating to prior arrest without conviction. The state appealed. Justice Barkett concluded that a judge under Florida law is able only to consider facts that support a conviction. She wrote that to impose a departure sentence would constitute "an egregious violation of due process." *Tyner*, 506 So. 2d at 406. As authority, the justice cited caselaw holding that where there are insufficient facts to establish a prima face case of guilt. She wrote that a determination and departure sentence that the defendant is guilty beyond a reasonable doubt based on those facts impermissibly denies the defendant his right to a jury trial.

Justice Barkett upheld the district court's reversal in *State v. Brown*, 530 So. 2d 51 (1988), of a life sentence imposed on the defendant for armed robbery when the recommended sentence was seven to nine years. The trial court first determined the defendant was a habitual offender that fell under a mandatory life sentence.[76] It issued a second order imposing a life sentence as a departure under the sentencing guidelines. The district court held the life sentence was an improper departure from the sentencing guidelines of seven to nine years. At issue were the state's sentencing guidelines pertaining to mandatory life sentences and habitualizing a defendant. Upon researching the mandatory life sentence in § 775.084 relied on by the trial court, Justice Barkett discovered that the word "shall" (be sentenced to a life sentence) was erroneously inserted and published. "Both chapters 75-116 and 75-298, Laws of Florida, the only two laws amending section 775.084 during the 1975 session, clearly use the word 'may.' This expresses an unequivocal legislative intent that the life sentence should be permissive, not mandatory." *Brown*, 530 So. 2d at 53. She held that the imposition of a life sentence was permissive under the statute, not mandatory and affirmed the district court's order.

In *State v. Garcia*, 547 So. 2d 628, 629 (1989), Justice Barkett addressed the following certified question from the district court: "should the good faith exception to the exclusionary rule authorized by *United States v. Leon*, 468 U.S. 897 (1984) be applied to the exclusionary provisions of the Florida wiretap law in chapter 934, Florida Statutes (1985)." Two cases were consolidated on appeal, *Garcia v. State*, 536 So. 2d 1048 (Fla. 4th DCA 1988) and *Davis v. State*, 529 So. 2d 732 (Fla. 4th DCA 1988). Defendants were charged with RICO charges and cocaine offenses that were filed based on wiretap surveillance of Davis's home pursuant to a court order. Defendants moved to suppress, alleging the application and affidavit were facially defective. In denying their motion, the state circuit court judge invoked the exclusionary rule. The district court reversed. Justice Barkett conveyed the court's opinion that any wire or oral communication that violates § 934.06, Fla. Stat., prohibits the admission of contents derived from any wire or oral communication that violates the chapter.

In a consolidated case that involved six minor children, *A.A. et al v. Rolle*, 604 So. 2d 813 (1992), Justice Barkett wrote for the majority that the children could not be incarcerated for contempt of court by being placed in a secure detention facility. Some of the children had run away from such placements. The district courts denied the children's writs of habeas corpus and upheld their sentences. At issue was whether the Florida legislature permitted placement in secure detention facilities pursuant to the Juvenile Justice Act, 1988 amendment that prohibited secure detention facilities. The State argued that the 1990 amendment, permitted such detention.[77] Justice Barkett analyzed the statutory authority and caselaw interpreting punishment and

---

76. Fla. Stat. § 775.084(4)(a)1, which provided in pertinent part, "The court... shall sentence the habitual felony offender... in the case of a felony of the first degree, for life."

77. Fla. Stat., chapter 39 (as amended, 1988), § 39.0321, prohibited use of secure detention on children; and § 39.043 (Supp. 1990).

imposable sanctions following a finding of contempt of court. She noted the legislature's purpose in prohibiting juvenile placement in secure detention facilities, namely that the juveniles would be exposed to negative adult inmates that would place them in possible jeopardy. The justice rejected the state's proffered interpretation that the prohibition was directed only at pre-adjudicated, not post-adjudicated youth. She distinguished the instant case from conflicting cases issued before enactment of the amendments.

In 1987, the justice addressed the state's challenge to the constitutionality of the Jail Time Credit Act (Act)[78] in *Tal-Mason v. State*, 515 So. 2d 738 (1987). Tal-Mason was arrested for first-degree murder, found incompetent to stand trial, and was committed to the state mental hospital where he remained for slightly over five years. When declared competent to stand trial, Tal-Mason pled guilty to second-degree murder and was given a life sentence. He filed a motion requesting credit for time served in the state mental hospital. The trial court eventually granted Tal-Mason's motion and declared the Act unconstitutional, which was reversed by the appellate court. The appellate court relied upon the Florida Supreme Court case of *Pennington v. State*, 398 So. 2d 815 (Fla. 1981), in which Pennington was denied credit for time spent in a live-in drug rehabilitation program. Justice Barkett distinguished *Pennington* from Tal-Mason based on Tal-Mason's incompetency and coercive incarceration. Taking judicial notice of the facilities for enforced confinement in Florida, the justice wrote there was no meaningful distinction between granting jail-time credit for preconviction confinement in a hospital for physical injuries or credit for incarceration for mental incompetence. The court credited Tal-Mason for the time served in the state mental hospital.

Justice Barkett held § 24-61 of the City of Tampa Code (1987) was unconstitutionally vague and relied on the subjective observations and discretion of law enforcement officers. *In re Guardianship of Estelle Browning,* 568 So. 2d 4 (1990), involved the constitutional right of privacy of one who is incompetent. The justice recognized that a surrogate or proxy of one who is incompetent may exercise their right of privacy. In this case, the guardian petitioned the state circuit court to remove Estelle from life support, which she had been on for two years. The guardian, Estelle's second cousin, submitted as evidence Estelle's signed declaration directing life-prolonging procedures to be withheld in exactly the circumstances that existed. Witness testimony about Estelle's wishes also was tendered. The state circuit court denied the petition, but the court through Justice Barkett held that self-determination cannot be qualified by the patient's condition.

The justice remanded four cases back for new trials where the state excluded black prospective jurors from serving on the jury through peremptory challenges. She concluded that in each case, the proffered explanations given to exclude the poten-

78. Fla. Stat. § 921.161(1), Fla. Stat. (1985), which states, "the court imposing a sentence shall allow a defendant credit for all of the time he spent in the *county jail before sentence.*"

tial jurors were insufficient to rebut the presumption of discrimination. *See, State v. Slappy*, 522 So. 2d 18 (1988) (four blacks were excluded from the panel, discussed *infra* in Chapter 5), *Blackshear v. State*, 521 So. 2d 1083 (1988) (eight of ten peremptory challenges used to exclude blacks from jury), *Wright v. State*, 586 So. 2d 1024 (1991) (prosecutor excluded black juror, stating since they were both black men, juror would identify more with defendant than the state), and *Hall v. Daee*, 602 So. 2d 512 (1992) (medical malpractice suit against doctors and hospital where state excluded four out of five jurors without reason). The justice affirmed the trial court's suppression of evidence in *State v. Johnson*, 561 So. 2d 1139 (1990). Trooper Vogel, the arresting officer in this case, was involved in three other profiling cases considered by other Florida courts and the Eleventh Circuit in yet another case. Trooper Vogel testified he stopped the defendant based on his own profile: single man, thirty years of age in a large model car driving at the speed limit with out-of-state tags on a known drug corridor. Trooper Vogel made an investigatory stop based on these factors and found marijuana in the car. Justice Barkett held that Trooper Vogel's profile—that includes innocent activity—prohibits the police from engaging in such conduct pursuant to article I, § 12 of the Florida Constitution prohibiting unlawful searches and seizures.

d. Majority Opinions in Civil Cases

The constitutionality of Florida's laws was the subject of Justice Barkett's majority opinions, the following cases exemplifying the breath of the issues considered. The justice held in *DeAyala v. Florida Farm Bureau Casualty Insurance Company*, 543 So. 2d 204 (1989), that the workers' compensation death benefits for nonresident aliens limited to $1,000 violated the due process and equal protection clauses of the Florida Constitution, article I, §§ 2 and 21. DeAyala, a Mexican citizen, was killed during a motor vehicle accident while working for Steve's Harvesting, Inc. He had worked in the country for twenty-five years. The widow and family requested $100,000 under the state's workers' compensation system, which the insurance company rejected and issued a check for $1,000 pursuant to § 440.16(7), Fla. Stat. (1983). That section limits awards to $1,000 for surviving spouses and children of nonresident alien workers, except for Canadians. The trial court found the section arbitrarily discriminated against nonresident aliens and declared the statute unconstitutional. The appellate court reversed, concluding that the right to compensation is a statutory, not a fundamental, right. The insurance company urged the court to find that the nonresident alien survivors were not entitled to constitutional principles forming the basis of the lawsuit. This latter assertion was summarily rejected by Justice Barkett, ruling the statute facially violated the Florida Constitution. She held that the rights were those of the deceased worker and that the section could not pass a rational basis test.

In *Department of Law Enforcement v. Real Property*, 588 So. 2d 957 (1991), the constitutionality of the state's Contraband Forfeiture Act was upheld, specifically, §§ 932.701–704 (1989) (the Act). Upon Charles DeCarlo's arrest for drug trafficking, the state initiated forfeiture proceedings against his property. The property included an RV mobile home, a 280-acre subdivision, and a 100-acre platted subdivision plus personal property. The show cause order was opposed by DeCarlo and others with an interest in the land. They asserted the Act was unconstitutional and violated their due process rights. Justice Barkett acknowledged the Act failed to establish requirements for filing petitions or procedures in partitioning the land, concluding the forfeiture practice has been established by caselaw, with the ultimate forfeiture determination resolved by a jury. Accordingly, the justice ruled the Act was constitutional but held in the instant case that the state did not comply with due process requirements.

Tampa's loitering code was ruled unconstitutional in *Wyche v. State*, 619 So. 2d 231 (1993). Renetha Wyche was convicted of loitering for the purpose of prostitution based on a policeman's observation of her wearing a skimpy outfit, waiving to passersby, and entering a car that had stopped. Justice Barkett also found another city loitering ordinance unconstitutionally vague in *E.L. v. State*, 619 So. 2d 252 (1993), as applied to juveniles.

Foster children sought a ruling from the court that the statutory scheme establishing the state's budget reduction procedures were unconstitutional in *Chiles v. Children A, B, C, D, E, and F*, 589 So. 2d 260 (1991).[79] The state experienced a $621 million shortfall, and the governor directed all state agencies, including the judiciary, to reduce their operating budgets through revised financial plans. The Administration Commission adopted the governor's recommendations reducing the budgets established by the Appropriations Act. Justice Barkett addressed the core issue in the case, whether the legislature in passing § 216.221(2) violated the separation of powers by assigning the authority to reapportion the budget to the executive branch. Justice Barkett wrote the section was an impermissible legislative attempt to abdicate its responsibility by transferring it to the executive branch.

In *The Florida Star v. B. J. F.*, 530 So. 2d 286 (1988), the U.S. Supreme Court certified a question to the court: whether the Florida Supreme Court had jurisdiction, to hear the newspaper's petition for review pursuant to Article VI, § 3(b)(3) of the Florida Constitution. *The Florida Star v. B. J. F.*, ___ U.S. ___, 108 S. Ct 499, 98 L. Ed. 2d 498 (1987). The *Florida Star* published the name of a rape victim B. J. F. which it received from material released by the police to press before trial. The publication of a rape victim's name was a criminal violation under § 794.03, Fla. Stat. (1985). B. J. F. filed suit premised on a statutory duty arising under § 794.03. The *Florida Star* moved for dismissal based on the theory of recovery, which it claimed violated the First and Fourteenth Amendments. The trial court ruled that no such violation would occur and upheld the constitutionality of § 794.03 and denied the motion to

---

79. Fla. Stat. §§ 216.011(1)(II) and 216.221 (1989), the latter section providing, "If, in the opinion of the Governor... a deficit will occur in the General Revenue Fund, he shall so certify to the [Administration] commission. The commission may, by affirmative action, reduce all approved state agency budgets and releases by a sufficient amount to prevent a deficit in any fund."

the victim's favor. On appeal, the *Florida Star* again challenged the constitutionality of the statute. The First District Court Appeal affirmed the trial court's decision but did not address the constitutional challenge. The *Florida Star* sought discretionary review with the court that was summarily denied, prompting it to seek review in the U.S. Supreme Court. Appellee filed a motion to dismiss asserting the appeal was untimely filed. SCOTUS certified the question to the Florida Supreme Court. Justice Barkett wrote, "[w]e do not read the question presented by the Supreme Court as a request to explain the internal mechanism of the court or to attempt the impossible task of second-guessing the original panel's decision on jurisdiction. Nor do we believe, as appellee suggests, that the present court should reexamine the question and decide anew whether conflict existed." *The Florida Star* at 287. She concluded that Article V, § 3(b)(3) dictates the scope of the court's discretion whose authority is limited but includes review of any decision of a district court of appeal that expressly and directly "conflict with opinions of another district court of appeal or of [the supreme court]" on the same question of law. *The Florida Star,* 530 So. 2d at 288. Accordingly, Justice Barkett ruled that the court had subject-matter jurisdiction to hear the *Florida Star*'s petition, which was denied.

Justice Barkett found the state's forfeiture statute was unconstitutional, *In re Forfeiture of 1969 Piper Navajo*, 592 So. 2d 233 (1992). The owner of a Piper Navajo aircraft appealed its seizure pursuant to forfeiture under § 330.40, Fla. Stat. (1987), asserting it violated due process of law. The aircraft was seized by Broward County sheriffs at a private airfield because it was equipped with extra fuel tanks that were not in conformity with the Federal Aviation Administration (FAA) regulations. The sheriffs concluded the plane was used for smuggling. The statute makes it unlawful for any person to possess any aircraft equipped with fuel containers that do not conform to FAA regulations, which are conclusively considered contraband and subject to forfeiture. The trial court dismissed the forfeiture petition, finding the section unconstitutional because it brought within its ambit innocent activity. Justice Barkett and the court's majority upheld the trial court's determination, finding the statute unconstitutional under article I, section 9 of the Florida Constitution.

In re Matter of Patricia Dubreuil, 629 So. 2d 819 (1993), raised the issue whether a hospital and physicians may override the patient's constitutional right to refuse treatment. In this case Dubreuil refused life-saving blood transfusions that were administered to save her life. Dubreuil was in the latter stages of pregnancy and, upon being admitted to the hospital, it was determined a caesarian operation was necessary. Dubreuil initially signed her consent to blood transfusions but before the operation, she refused the blood transfusion because of her Jehovah Witness religious beliefs. Her estranged husband was called to the hospital, and he consented to the blood transfusions. The hospital petitioned the state circuit court, which conducted a hearing and authorized ongoing transfusion. Dubreuil recovered. Though the matter was moot, the Supreme Court granted discretionary review. Justice Barkett held Dubreuil's constitutional rights were violated under the Florida Constitution, Article I, section 23 that gives citizens the constitutional right to refuse medical treatment. Justice Barkett rejected the trial court's finding that the state's interest in the protection of third parties (Dubreuil's children) overrode her constitutional right to refuse treatment.

A question of first impression arose in *Dorse v. Armstrong World Industries, Inc.*, 513 So. 2d 1265 (1987), regarding Florida's products liability law. The Eleventh Circuit certified a question to the Supreme Court that was addressed by Justice Barkett. Plaintiff Alfred Dorse filed a federal lawsuit in 1982 against ten corporations that manufactured or distributed asbestos-containing material. While constructing naval vessels in Brooklyn, New York, during and after WW II, Dorse was exposed to the asbestos while working as a coppersmith. Dorse died from asbestos-related disease after the complaint was filed. His widow Josephine Dorse filed an amended complaint for wrongful death and, under the survival statutes, alleged negligence, strict liability and breach of implied warranty. One of the defendants, Eagle-Picher Industries Inc., asserted the government specification defense not previously recognized under Florida law. Eagle-Picher manufactured and sold asbestos-containing materials to the Navy pursuant to federal contracts which required strict compliance with certain contract specifications. Eagle-Picher also asserted that the government's knowledge of asbestos hazards was equal to or greater than its own knowledge. Plaintiff disputed Eagle-Picher's allegations, asserting it manufactured asbestos prior to the government contract, provided the specifications to the Navy, and failed to provide warnings of the dangers associated with asbestos exposure. The district court denied Eagle-Picher's motion for summary judgment, which was based on the affirmative defense and granted plaintiff's motion to strike the defense from Eagle-Picher's answer. Eagle-Picher appealed to the Eleventh Circuit. As the Eleven Circuit found no Florida authority on the affirmative defense, it certified the question whether the military contractor defense exists in Florida and whether a manufacturer may avoid liability by asserting the defense. Justice Barkett defined Eagle-Picher as an independent contractor. Agreeing with Eleventh Circuit precedent, she wrote that the defense fell under the federal war-making and defense power and rejected other authority holding the military contractor defense falls under sovereign immunity that extends to the agent. Affirmatively recognizing the military contractor defense in Florida, the Florida Supreme Court adopted the Eleventh Circuit's test in *Shaw v. Grumman Aerospace Corp.*, 778 F.2d 736 (11th Cir. 1985), to determine product liability involving a military contractor's defense.[80]

In a wrongful discharge case, *Tedder v. Video Electronics, Inc.*, 491 So. 2d 533 (1986), the trial court's change in the juror selection procedure prompted the defendant's appeal. The appellate court certified the question to the Florida Supreme Court: whether in the absence of exceptional circumstances, it constitutes an abuse

80. A contractor may escape liability only if it affirmatively proves: (1) that it did not participate, or participated only minimally, in the design of those products or parts of products shown to be defective; *or* (2) that it timely warned the military of the risks of the design and notified it of alternative designs reasonably known by the contractor, and that the military, although forewarned, clearly authorized the contractor to proceed with the dangerous design. Shaw, 778 F.2d at 746.

of discretion for a trial court to swear in some but not all prospective jurors for the purpose of prohibiting peremptory challenges to backstrike such jurors. Here, the trial court swore in four prospective jurors prior to the completion of *voir dire* and prohibited defense counsel from backstriking a sworn juror. Plaintiff-respondent lost at trial but preserved the issue for appeal. The appellate court reversed the judgment and employer appealed. Justice Barkett wrote that the altered juror selection violated the plaintiff's right to peremptory challenges, which may be exercised under Florida law only until the jurors are sworn in by the trial court. She concluded that the trial court abused its discretion by employing the altered practice that deprived the plaintiff of his rights.

The validity of the presumption of abandonment in a wrongful termination case by a state employee was the subject of a certified question in *Machules v. Department of Administration*, 523 So. 2d 1132 (1988) (DOA). Machules was terminated from his job as a special investigator for the Department of Insurance (Department) for abandonment of his job upon missing three days due to alcoholism. The employee's union erroneously filed a grievance complaint with the Department instead of with DOA. The Department set a hearing date one day after the twenty-day limitation expired but proceeded to hearing at which Machules's grievance was dismissed. Machules appealed to DOA. DOA concluded the appeal was untimely and outside the twenty-day limitation. He then filed an appeal with the district court asking for equitable tolling. Because there was no Florida authority on the issue, the question was certified by the district court to the Florida Supreme Court. Justice Barkett wrote, "[w]e find the doctrine of equitable tolling applicable under the facts of this case for two reasons: petitioner was misled or lulled into inaction by his Employer, and his appeal to DOA raised the identical issue raised in the original timely claim filed in the wrong forum." *Machules*, 523 So. 2d 1132 at 1134.

In *Byrd v. Richardson-Greenshields Securities, Inc.*, 552 So. 2d 1099 (1989), the justice held that the state's Workers Compensation Statute (Act) was not the exclusive remedy for women employees seeking remedy against employers on various claims. Those claims included sexual harassment, assault, and battery, negligent hiring and retention of employees who committed the acts, and intentional infliction of emotional distress. The question certified by the appellate court stemmed from the female employees' complaint that they were repeatedly touched and subjected to sexual advances by male employees. The trial court dismissed their complaint, concluding the Act, §440.01(14), Fla. Stat. (1987), provided the exclusive remedy. The appellate court agreed but certified the question to the Florida Supreme Court. Section 440.01(14) defines injury as a "personal injury by accident arising out of and in the course of employment" and accident as an "unexpected and unusual event or result, suddenly happening." Interpreting the term, "arising out of and in the course of employment," the justice recognized that the term already had been construed as extending beyond the statutory language to include injuries that were not accidental. She wrote, "[a]pplying the exclusivity rule of workers' compensation to preclude any and all tort liability effectively would abrogate [the public] policy [against sexual harassment], undermine the Florida Human Rights Act, and flout

Title VII of the Civil Rights Act of 1964." *Byrd*, 552 So. 2d at 1104. The district court's decision was quashed and the matter remanded.

In a case exemplifying the state's marine life, *State v. Davis*, 556 So. 2d 1104 (1990), the following was certified to the Florida Supreme Court: does the Marine Fisheries Commission (Commission) have the statutory authority to promulgate rules requiring the use of turtle excluder devices (TEDs) in shrimp nets to protect endangered and threatened Florida sea turtles?" David Davis, a shrimper, was cited by a marine patrol for possessing a trawl rigged for fishing that did not have a TED installed. The Commission had passed an emergency rule requiring TEDs, rule 46ER89-3(2), to protect endangered turtles. The rule provided: "No person shall possess, aboard any vessel 25 feet or greater in length in offshore waters of the state, any trawl rigged for fishing that does not have a qualified turtle excluder device (TED) installed therein." It was adopted pursuant to Florida Statutes §§ 370.025 and 370.027 (1987). The county court found the Commission exceeded its statutory authority, prompting the State's appeal. The appeals court certified the issue to the court. Justice Barkett wrote that the Commission had the statutory authority to promulgate emergency rules to protect endangered and threatened Florida sea turtles.

In *Blanchard v. State Farm Mul. Auto Ins. Co.*, 575 So. 2d 1289 (1991), Justice Barkett wrote the opinion answering the question certified by the Eleventh Circuit Court. The Blanchards were injured in a car accident in which State Farm refused to provide coverage up to $200,000 for uninsured motorist that was included in their policy. They proceeded against State Farm seeking specific performance for $200,000 and against the uninsured motorist for damages. The Blanchards obtained a verdict for $396,990 and judgment was entered against State Farm for $200,000 and for full damages against the uninsured motorist. Pursuant to Florida's civil remedy statute for first-party insurer bad faith, the Blanchards thereafter sued State Farm.[81] State Farm moved to dismiss, arguing that the bad faith claim had to be asserted in the initial state lawsuit. The Eleventh Circuit certified the question whether an insured's claim of bad faith accrues before the conclusion of the underlying litigation. Justice Barkett summarized the split among the Florida appellate courts on the question. She concluded that if an uninsured motorist is not liable to the insured for damages arising from an accident, then the insurer has not acted in bad faith in refusing to settle the claim. The justice reasoned that a cause of action cannot exist for a bad faith failure to settle, absent a determination of liability on the part of the uninsured tortfeasor. Under this analysis, Justice Barkett held that an insured's claim does not accrue before the conclusion of the underlying litigation.

e. Conclusion

A review of Justice Barkett's majority opinions reflect a compassionate justice who thoroughly researched issues and interpreted Florida's laws, statutes, and Constitution with the public's best interest at the forefront of her analysis. Her writings

81. Fla. Stat. § 624.155 (1987).

evince a justice unafraid to consider and infuse the human experience into her rulings. As she noted, "I think we are the sum of all of our experiences, and I don't know that you can separate out threads and attribute some view…to a particular thread…all of the experiences: my family experience and my being an immigrant has…made me; it's made me care about people."[82] For her prestigious career, the judge has received seven honorary doctorates, numerous state awards, induction into the Florida Women's Hall of Fame (1986), and the 1996 ABA Margaret Brent Women Lawyers of Achievement Award; she also is the namesake of two awards. Annually, two awards are given in her honor, the Rosemary Barkett Award (1992) presented by the Academy of Florida Trial Lawyers to a person who has demonstrated outstanding commitment to equal justice under law, and the Rosemary Barkett Outstanding Achievement Award (2015) bestowed upon an outstanding lawyer by the Florida Association of Women Lawyers. What many regard as the pinnacle of a legal career—to serve on the state's highest court—was not the end of the justice's judicial career. Justice Barkett's appellate experience translated onto a federal and then international bench.

4. Judge Carmen Beauchamp Ciparick

a. Formative Years

1963	B.A., History, Political Science, Hunter College
1963–1967	Teacher, 136 Central Harlem, New York Public Schools
1967	J.D. St. John's University School of Law (night classes) Admitted to New York Bar Staff Attorney, Legal Aid Society, South Bronx
1969–1972	Assistant Counsel, New York State Judicial Conference
1972–1978	Chief Law Assistant, New York City Criminal Court
1978–1982	Judge, New York City Criminal Court and Supreme Court Criminal Branch
1982–1993	Elected Justice, New York Supreme Court
1994–2012	Associate Judge, New York Court of Appeals[83]
2012	Retired
2015	Of Counsel, Greenberg Traurig, New York Office

---

82. *Supra*, note 66, *Barkett Interview* at 1:56:14–52.

83. Antonio E. Galvao wrote a beautiful tribute to the judge, *see Carmen Beauchamp Ciparick—Historical Society of the New York Courts,* 1–13 (Galvao Article), https://history.nycourts.gov/biography/carmen-beauchamp-ciparick/; Latino Judges Association, Hon. Carmen Beauchamp Ciparick (Ret) biography (Ciparick Bio), https://latinojudgesassociation.org/hon-carmen-beauchamp-ciparick-ret/.

The youngest of two daughters, Carmen was born on January 1, 1942, in Washington Heights to Patria Comas, "the daughter of a local poet of some renown," and Eduardo Beauchamp, a civil servant in the U.S. Army Corps of Engineers.[84] Patria and Eduardo moved to New York City in 1929 from Mayaguez, Puerto Rico, providing their daughters a "normal, happy childhood" filled with music and dancing. Carmen took ballet lessons throughout grade school. Upon graduating from George Washington High School, Carmen attended the all-female Hunter College and, as a political science major, became interested in law school. Eduardo, wanting his daughter to marry, initially opposed the idea but soon embraced her career choice. At St. John's University Law School, she was one of eight females enrolled in the day division, there were three in the night division. Carmen endured the gender bias of the times. A torts professor once "grilled" her on whether "a lady's evening gown was an inherently dangerous instrument."[85] To support herself through law school, Carmen taught junior high school at 136 in Central Harlem. Upon graduating, Carmen applied only to the Legal Aid Society in the South Bronx. As a newly minted legal aid attorney, she carried the typical caseload. Carmen experienced the stereotyping of women lawyers at the time, often being mistook for the secretary or interpreter. After five years of practice, Carmen married Damian Ciparick, a former priest turned high school science teacher. Two years later they had their daughter, Roseanne, who became a professional singer. Carmen also enjoyed singing as a member of the Village Light Opera Group and the New York Bar Association's Entertainment Committee, performing at numerous bar association events. From 1972 on, Carmen devoted her career to New York's judicial department, starting as the chief law assistant and ending as a judge on the state's highest court.

Carmen's experience supervising lawyers in researching and preparing memorandums for the criminal court judges proved invaluable to her judicial career. In 1978, Mayor Edward Koch appointed Carmen (Judge Beauchamp Ciparick) to the New York City Criminal Court as the first Puerto Rican/female judge to serve. Judge Beauchamp Ciparick's work on the criminal court earned her the Democratic Party's nomination to the New York Supreme Court. As the party missed the filing deadline, the judge ran as the Liberal Party's nominee and won.[86] In 1982, Judge Beauchamp Ciparick was elected to the New York Supreme Court, the state's intermediate appellate court (judges are called justices). Once on the court, Justice Beauchamp Ciparick generated public attention, partly for her rulings in two cases; the latter would take front seat at her Court of Appeals confirmation hearing.

The first case, *Mercury Bay Boating Club, Inc. v. San Diego Yacht Club, Inc.*, Supreme Court, IAS Part 15, 18 (Unreported November 25, 1987) (*Mercury Bay Boating I*), was a trilogy of unreported decisions that, according to Galveo, brought Judge

84. *Id.*, Galvao Article at 1.

85. *Supra* note 83, Galvao Article at 2.

86. *Id.* Galvao Article at 4.

Ciparick international fame as the "dispute captured the public's imagination and stirred passions all around the world."[87] The America's Cup was donated on July 8, 1857, to the New York Yacht Club by America's six owners. The final conveyance was made in 1887 by the final donor George Schuyler pursuant to a deed of gift (Deed). The Deed established the race parameters and vessel dimensions and mandated the vessels race under the rules of the club holding the Cup.[88] On July 27, 1987, a letter of challenge for the America's Cup was issued by Mercury Bay Boating Club (Mercury Bay) to the San Diego Yacht Club (San Diego) for two races in September 1988. The challenge deviated from the traditional races in three to four intervals. Mercury Bay advised it would race a larger yacht. San Diego ignored the challenge and called a press conference to announce 1991 racing dates for a multinational "Twelves regatta." Mercury Bay sought relief in the New York Supreme Court asking Justice Beauchamp Ciparick to enjoin San Diego from considering other challenges. San Diego responded with an action in *cy pres* (as near as possible to the donor's intent) requesting retroactive relief dating back to the Deed, which it claimed Mercury Bay violated. Justice Beauchamp Ciparick denied San Diego's request for relief and granted the injunction. *Mercury Bay Boating I.* Mercury Bay filed a second action challenging the use of a multihull defender, asserting San Diego was in contempt of Judge Ciparick's initial ruling. *Mercury Bay Boating Club, Inc. v. San Diego Yacht Club*, Supreme Court IAS, Part 15, 2 (Unreported July 25, 1988) (*Mercury Bay Boating II*). As the type of vessel was not previously raised, Justice Beauchamp Ciparick refused to hold San Diego in contempt. The first two races were held before the next disputed issue arose—the type of vessel that could be raced. San Diego successfully defended the America's Cup by "racing a 60-foot wing-sailed catamaran *Stars & Stripes* against Mercury Bay's 133-foot monohull yacht, the *New Zealand.* It was a mismatch on the water as *Stars & Stripes* easily defeated the challenger *New Zealand* in two matches."[89] Justice Beauchamp Ciparick disqualified San Diego's catamaran on the basis that its multihulled vessel design violated the original Deed. *Mercury Bay Boating Club v. San Diego Yacht Club*, Supreme Court IAS, Part 15 (Unreported Mar. 28, 1989) (*Mercury Bay Boating III*). She wrote that San Diego was aware of the risk when choosing to follow the unprecedented course of defending in a catamaran with a clear goal to retain the America's Cup. Justice Beauchamp Ciparick ruled in favor of Australia's *New Zealand* catamaran, stripping *Stars & Stripes* of the America's Cup. "The *London Times* deemed the justice a 'heroine' and she was deluged with congratulatory mail from homemakers in New Zealand and farmers in Australia... [and] less flattering mail from many unhappy Americans, including a passion-

87. *Id.* Galvao Article at 5.

88. These facts are summarized from the trilogy of cases cited. The factual and procedural history is far more complex and interesting than those provided here.

89. *Supra* note 83 *Galvao Article* at 5; *see* Peter Grainger German, *The America's Cup and the Law of Trusts: Mercury Bay Boating Club's 1988 K-Boat Challenge*, VUW Law Review 211 (1993), for an in-depth discussion of the complex legal maneuverings.

ate sailor from California who went so far as to prophesy that the name of Ciparick would live on, 'synonymous with Benedict Arnold in drag.'"[90] In a split decision, the appeals court restored the America's Cup to San Diego, finding the Deed did not prohibit multihull vessels. *Boating Club v. Yacht Club*, 545 N.Y.S.2d 693 (1989) (*Boating Club*). The New York Court of Appeals affirmed the decision because the Deed did not expressly prohibit multihull vessels but permitted any one yacht or vessel. *Mercury Bay Boating Club v. San Diego Yacht Club*, 76 N.Y.2d 256, 267 (N.Y. 1990). It noted the matter was not suitable for judicial resolution but rather should have been resolved by the International Yacht Racing Union. The dissent agreed with Justice Beauchamp Ciparick's ruling.

In the class action case of *Hope v. Perales*, 571 N.Y.S.2d 972 (Sup. Ct. 1991), *aff'd.* 595 N.Y.S.2d 972 (App. Div. 1993), Justice Ciparick addressed the New York Senate's decision to exclude funding for abortions when it created in 1989 the new Prenatal Care Assistant Program (PCAP) for poor women.[91] Plaintiffs sought injunctive relief to prohibit the law from taking effect asserting it was "underinclusive in its blanket exclusion of funds for all abortions without exception," including to preserve the life of the mother. *Hope*, 571 N.Y.S.2d at 989. They claimed chapter 584 violated numerous constitutional rights, including their free exercise of religion, due process, and equal protection, the state's pledge to provide aid, care, and support of the needy, and the protection and promotion of the health of New York citizens.[92] Under a strict scrutiny analysis, Justice Beauchamp Ciparick held PCAP was unconstitutional because it violated plaintiffs' right to privacy. She wrote,

> A full three years before the United States Supreme Court decision in *Roe v. Wade* (410 U.S. 113), New York amended its law to recognize that the State had no right to interfere in the most personal and important decision a woman can make regarding her body and her life. In 1970, New York State repealed the criminal sanctions against abortions performed during the first two trimesters of pregnancy (Penal Law § 125.05). This dramatic change in the law is the cornerstone principle of what has come to be recognized as a woman's constitutional right to abortion. *Hope v. Perales* at 991. Historically, the New York Court of Appeals has read our State Constitution expansively, broadening the scope of individual rights and liberties accorded by the Federal Constitution, finding the basis for such rights in our State Constitution.... The Due Process Clause of the New York State Constitution has "'long safeguarded any threat to individual liberties, irrespective of from what quarter that peril arose"'.... *Hope*, 571 N.Y.S.2d at 994–994. The right of a pregnant woman to choose an

90. *Id., Galvao Article* at 5.

91. Laws of 1989, chapter 584, amending Public Health Law §§ 2521, 2522, 2529, eff. January 1, 1990.

92. New York Constitution (N.Y. Const.), Article I, §§ 3 (religious freedom), 6 (due process) and 11 (equal protection, N.Y. Const. art XVII, § 1 (support of the needy), NY Const. art XVII, § 3 (support of citizens' health).

> abortion in circumstances where it is medically indicated is one component of the right of privacy rooted in the due process clause of the New York Constitution. *Hope,* 571 N.Y.S.2d at 994.

The justice cited the compelling story of Hope, one among many instances of hardship the Plaintiffs' proffered:

> Hope, a carrier of sickle cell anemia, is 19 years old, works 44 hours per week and attends college at night. After noticing a marked weight loss and feelings of nausea and dizziness in the mornings, Hope visited a clinic for a pregnancy test. The test came back positive. At this point, Hope visited a clinic for pregnancy test. The test came back positive. At this point, Hope was advised that an abortion would cost $900. Hope left school to save money for the abortion. Four weeks later, Hope again visited the clinic. At this point she was 21 weeks pregnant and...was advised that the abortion would now cost between $1,000 and $1,500. Further the attending physician informed her that under the Medicaid standard, an abortion was medically necessary in her circumstance. Hope, however, is ineligible for all Medicaid because her income falls between 100 and 185% of the Federal poverty line, despite the fact that after her rent and daily living expenses are satisfied, she lacks the resources to maintain medical insurance. After saving for four weeks and borrowing money from friends, Hope still lacked the money for an abortion. *Hope,* 571 N.Y.S.2d at 995.

Justice Beauchamp Ciparick concluded the PCAP violated the due process, equal protection, and public health clauses of the New York state constitution by affirmatively and impermissibly pressuring women to choose childbirth over abortion. "By funding all of the expenses associated with childbirth and none of the expenses incurred in terminating pregnancy, the Government literally makes an offer that the indigent woman cannot afford to refuse."[93] *Hope,* 571 N.Y.S.2d at 995. She ordered the PCAP to pay for abortions for poor women. The appeals court agreed with Justice Ciparick's finding that the PCAP pressures women to choose childbirth over abortion and affirmed her decision because the PCAP "coerced, steered or forced low-income women to bear children in contravention of their fundamental right to choose." *Hope v. Perales, aff'd,* 595 N.Y.S.2d 948 (App. Div. 1993) (per curiam). It clarified,

> The State's interest in advancing the cause of healthy mothers bearing healthy babies has no reasonable relationship to the statutory abortion exclusion. The promotion of healthy births is certainly not enhanced by requiring poor women to give birth regardless of the medical implications. Notwithstanding that PCAP purports to be strictly concerned with the health of the child and

93. Citing Justice Brennan's dissent in *Harris v. McRae,* 448 U.S. 297, 333–334.

> the mother, it has the effect of forcing needy women to give birth even when this is not medically indicated and is detrimental to their physical and mental well-being. Yet, notwithstanding the dissent's view that PCAP in no way interferes with a woman's exercise of her right of reproductive choice, the fact is that, as a practical matter, low-income women who are unable to obtain aid for therapeutic abortions under PCAP may be compelled to delay or forego altogether medically indicated procedures or to continue pregnancies that undermine their health. It is, therefore, extremely facile for defendants to take the position that no one is illegally prohibited from procuring an abortion, an argument deemed persuasive by the dissent, when poor women frequently lack the means to pay for an abortion on their own. Since these women usually cannot afford abortions, even ones that are medically necessary, PCAP, by excluding funding for therapeutic abortions, has the practical effect of being a measure that supports childbirth, sometimes at the expense of the mother's health. *Hope,* 595 N.Y.S.2d at 293–294, 296.

The Appeals Division noted its approval of Justice Ciparick's analysis under the New York Constitution, writing that "[t]he Court of Appeals, which clearly has not hesitated to diverge from the more restrictive constitutional law interpretative track pursued by the United States Supreme Court, especially in recent years, has an enduring commitment to an independent and expansion construction of the State Constitution. Therefore, irrespective of how the Federal courts would approach the instant challenge to PCAP, its evaluation under the State Constitution is certainly appropriate." *Hope*, 595 N.Y.S.2d at 295.

The state appealed to the New York Court of Appeals to which, by that time, Judge Ciparick had been elevated. *See discussion infra.* Justice Beauchamp Ciparick's ruling realized the vision and position of Martinez and the Chicana Rights Project—which they advocated as early as 1975 through 1982—to constitutionally protect a woman's right to choose.[94]

b. New York Court of Appeals, 1994–2012

On December 1, 1993, Governor Mario Cuomo nominated Justice Beauchamp Ciparick to the New York Court of Appeals, the state's court of last resort.[95] (She had been rejected by the governor's selection panel.) Beauchamp Ciparick was rated "qualified" by the New York State Bar Association. At the press conference announcing his selection, Governor Cuomo stated, "Now, after 200 years, we know at least

94. For an analysis of the impact on other rulings, see Marni Brown, *Hope v. Perales*, 571 N.Y.S. 972 (Sup.Ct. 1991), aff'd 595 N.Y.S.2d 948 (App.Div. 1993): *Expanding Medically Necessary Abortion Rights of Pregnant Indigent Women under New York and Nebraska State Constitutional Due Process Clause*, Neb. L. Rev. 72 (1993), https://digitalcommons.unl.edu/cgi/viewcontent.cgi?article=1640&context=nlr.

95. N.Y. Const. 7, art. VI, §§ 2(a)–(e).

the following: that you will not be disqualified from the Court of Appeals because you're a woman..., you won't be disqualified from the Court because you're black, you won't be disqualified from the Court because you're Hispanic.... [What] makes you a judge of the Court of Appeals is your competence.[96] The Republican-controlled New York Senate had thirty days to confirm Governor Cuomo's nomination. Justice Beauchamp Ciparick's ruling in *Hope v. Perales* became a focal point at her confirmation hearing:

> Anti-abortion groups called on the New York State Senate to reject the nomination of Carmen Beauchamp Ciparick to the Court of Appeals today because of her landmark ruling that said the State Constitution protects the right to have an abortion...the testimony from Justice Ciparick's critics, combined with some sharp questioning from Republican senators, gave today's hearings a more contentious air than is typical for a Court of Appeals nomination.... The focus of today's testimony was Justice Ciparick's decision ... in *Hope v. Perales*...The Appellate Division of State Supreme Court upheld Justice Ciparick's decision in the case...The state has appealed the decision, and the Court of Appeals will hear arguments next month...Today several Republican senators questioned her ruling in the abortion case, sending the clear message that they thought Justice Ciparick had overstepped her powers and infringed on their right to make law. "If you felt the Legislature's intent was clear, do you feel it would be appropriate for a judge to question the motivations of the Legislature?" asked Senator Michael J. Tully, a Republican from Roslyn Heights, L. I. Justice Ciparick replied, "Certainly if the court feels it is a bad law, it has a right to correct the wrong, it certainly has the right to correct the excesses of government." However, she repeatedly deflected specific questions about the case, saying her statements might prejudice the Court of Appeals when it reviews the decision. But she emphasized that her ruling was not based on personal beliefs. "I thought it was the right interpretation of the law," she said.[97]

The New York Senate confirmed her appointment upon a 59–25 vote.[98] Judge Beauchamp Ciparick became the court's first Hispanic and second woman judge, joining Chief Judge Judith S. Kaye. Judge Beauchamp Ciparick was joining one of the most powerful state appellate courts in the country. The court is considered the preeminent state court in the country, particularly in cases involving tort law, con-

---

96. Gary Spencer, *Ciparick Named to Court of Appeals*, New York Law Publishing Co., December 2, 1993, https://www.judgewatch.org/judicial-selection/ciparick/134-nylj-12-2-93.pdf.

97. James Dao, *Nominee Questioned on Abortion Case*, New York Times, December 16, 1993, https://www.nytimes.com/1993/12/16/nyregion/court-nominee-questioned-on-abortion-case.html.

98. Michael Hutter, Vincent Bonventre, and Luke Bierman, *State Constitutional Jurisprudence: Decision Making at the Court of Appeals*, Touro L. Rev. 13, no. 1 (1996): 3, 47 (Touro Article), https://digitalcommons.tourolaw.edu/cgi/viewcontent.cgi?article=1630&context=lawreview.

tracts, and the interpretation of state statutes. The New York Constitution was adopted on April 20, 1777,[99] and predates the U.S. Constitution (1788) by eleven years; a fact that filters into the court's power, powerful image, and work.

> ... this Court decides cases of federal law—or it is perceived to be—as uniquely New York without relying on outside sources. The result is findings of unconstitutionality based upon the state constitution that are constitutional under federal law.... They [judges] treat the State Constitution as an independent source not subject to influence, even though this is an issue that has been dealt with in many courts across the country. They treat the issue as their own.[100]

Judge Beauchamp Ciparick had already been accused of doing so in *Hope v. Perales*. The judge was to sit with simpatico fellow jurists, Judge Kaye among them with whom she served until Judge Kaye's departure in December 2008. Judge Kaye's observation about state courts seemingly aligned with Judge Ciparick's rulings: "state court dockets comprise the battlefields of first resort in social revolutions ... state courts have openly and explicitly balanced considerations of social welfare and have fashioned new causes and action where common sense justice required."

c. Majority Opinions in Criminal Cases

Judge Beauchamp Ciparick wrote the majority opinion in 322 cases, 62 dissents (among the lowest), and seven concurring opinions. The judge authored majority opinions in some of the court's most significant decisions on education, civil rights, and civil and criminal law. She was described as "perhaps the most liberal judge on the bench," with a "strong commitment to the constitution, as a protector of individual rights."[101]

At issue in *People v. David W.*, 95 N.Y.2d 130 (2000), was whether a person convicted of a sex offense has a constitutional right to due process, notice, and hearing before being classified as a sexually violent predator under the state's Sex Offender Registration Act (SORA, i.e., Megan's Law), Correction Law §§ 168-g [2] and 168-t. The defendant was convicted of sodomy in the second degree and sexual abuse in the first degree of two underage victims and served concurrent ninety-day sentences. As defendant failed to register under SORA, his probation officer sent a letter and registration form, advising him of the requirement to register at the highest level three designation ("sexually violent predator"). He moved to dismiss the information alleging SORA violated the equal protection and due process guarantees of the New York and U.S. Constitutions as he was never notified the determination of sex-

---

99. N.Y. Const., as amended, https://dos.ny.gov, https://dos.ny.gov/system/files/documents/2024/05/constitution-5-8-24.pdf.

100. *Supra* note 98, Touro Article at 27, 33–34.

101. Jillian Kasow, *Judge Carmen Beauchamp Ciparick: A Glimpse into the Senior Associate Judge's Judicial Philosophy through Her Dissents, Albany L. Rev.* 73, no. 3 (2010): 953, 960–962, tables on number of dissents (Kasow Article); Antonio E. Galvao, Judge Carmen Beauchamp Ciparick: An Extraordinary Judge and Public Servant, Albany L. Rev. 76, no. 2 (April 9, 2013).

ually violent predator was being made. The Department of Probation and Correctional Alternatives (DCPA) was responsible for the assessments, including Defendant's level three rating. Upon advice of counsel, Defendant refused to return the sex offender registration form and was thereafter charged and convicted with failure to register. That conviction caused Defendant to violate the terms of his probation. SORA had been in effect for nearly one year and ten months by the date of conviction. Judge Beauchamp Ciparick, writing for the court, found SORA's notice and review procedures constitutionally inadequate. She held the privacy and liberty interests were substantial, as SORA classified and stigmatized one as a sexually violent predator that imposed significant burdens. Characterizing the DCPA's risk level determination process as streamlined, the judge found there was no opportunity to challenge the process or assessment and thus, no record for judicial review. Concluding the Defendant was entitled to procedural due process, the defendant's motion to dismiss the information was granted.

In a case of first impression, *People v. Arnold*, 98 N.Y.2d 63 (2002), Judge Beauchamp Ciparick addressed whether the judge presiding over a criminal trial could *sua sponte* call a witness to testify. Concluding it was error for the judge to call a witness absent an explanation or opportunity for the parties to address any prejudice and create a record for appellate review, she wrote the trial court's fundamental function is to protect, rather than make, the record at trial. At issue in *People v. McDonald*, 1 N.Y.3d 109 (2003), was whether defense counsel's incorrect advice about deportation consequences could constitute ineffective assistance of counsel under the U.S. Constitution, Sixth Amendment. The defendant was a Jamaican immigrant and lawful resident of the United States for twenty years and had three children born in the country. He was charged with an eight-count indictment for selling marijuana to undercover police, whereupon Defendant pleaded guilty to one count of criminal sale of marijuana in the third degree and criminal possession of a controlled substance. Defendant was sentenced to concurrent terms of one to three years. The INS served Defendant the following day with notice of deportation. Weeks later, defense counsel filed a motion to vacate the judgment on the ground of ineffective assistance of counsel, averring he incorrectly advised the Defendant he would not be deported (as did the district attorney), and admitted it was plain error. *McDonald*, 1 N.Y.3d at 111–112. The trial and appellate courts denied Defendant's motion. Applying the two-prong test of *Strickland v. Washington*, 466 U.S. 668 (1984), Judge Ciparick wrote defense counsel's representation, as interpreted by New York law, fell below the objective standard of reasonableness, concluding defendant failed to show the requisite prejudice in his pleadings. *McDonald*, 1 N.Y.3d at 114–115.

d. Majority Opinions in Civil Cases

Judge Beauchamp Ciparick wrote majority opinions on a broad array of issues in diverse areas of civil law. One of the first cases before the newly confirmed judge was her decision in *Hope v. Perales, rev'd*, 83 N.Y.2d 563 (1994), finding the PCAP program unconstitutionally infringed on women's right to reproductive freedom and their right to privacy. Judge Beauchamp Ciparick recused herself from the appeal. The New York Court of Appeals reversed Justice Ciparick's finding that the state's constitution protects a woman's right to an abortion. It held there was no evidence that PCAP infringed on the rights of PCAP-eligible women, who "presumptively ha[ve] the financial means to exercise [their] fundamental right of choice." *Hope v. Perales*, 83 N.Y.2d at 577. Thereafter, in 2019, the New York legislature passed S240, the Reproductive Health Act, to ensure women's reproductive rights. In 2022, the New York City Council announced $1 million in funding for poor women to access abortion care, the funds to be distributed through two New York nonprofit organizations. This funding supplemented that committed in 2019. During the 2023–2024 legislative session, S348C, Reproductive Freedom and Equity Grant Program, was introduced on January 4, 2023, to provide funding to poor women for abortion health care.

In a significant school financing case, Judge Ciparick wrote the majority opinion (5–2) in *Campaign for Fiscal Equity v. State of New York*, 86 N.Y.2d 307 (1995). Fourteen of New York's thirty-two school districts and students joined with the nonprofit organization *Campaign for Fiscal Equity, Inc (CFE)* to file suit against the state. CFE's members were community school boards, citizens, and parent advocacy organizations. The plaintiffs challenged public school funding under numerous theories, including the State Constitution's Education Clause, N.Y. Const. art. XI § 1. The Education Clause required the legislature "to provide for the maintenance and support of a system of free common schools, wherein all the children of this state may be educated." At issue was whether Plaintiffs pled sustainable claims under the Education Clause and the State's Equal Protection Clause, Const. art. 1 § 11, and federal law, Title VI, and anti-discrimination regulations. The Plaintiffs relied on *Plyler v. Doe* and *San Antonio School Dist. v. Rodriguez, supra*, as support for its state and federal equal protection claims, advancing arguments raised in 1982 by Martinez and MALDEF. Defendants, New York's Senate Majority Leader, and Assembly Minority Leader moved to dismiss. Defendants relied on *Board of Educ., Levittown Union Free School Dist. V. Nyquist (Levittown)*, 57 N.Y.2d 27 (1995), as dispositive of their position. The plaintiffs in *Levittown* were twenty-seven property-poor plaintiff school districts. The *Levittown* court rejected the plaintiffs' equal protection claims based on *San Antonio School Dist. V. Rodriguez, supra*, finding plaintiffs advanced no claim of minimal acceptable facilities or services under the Education Clause or proved that the state's lump sum financing of public education discriminated in funding poverty-poor schools. The appellate court, however, found *Levittown* "manifestly left room" for plaintiffs' Education Clause claim. Of that authority, Judge Beauchamp Ciparick wrote:

> We recognized in *Levittown* that the Education Article imposes a duty on the Legislature to ensure the availability of a sound basic education to all the children of the State. Contrary to the dissenting expression of Judge Simons, we are unable to adopt the view that the constitutional language at issue is, in effect, hortatory. Indeed, we should not do so in the face of *Levittown's* unam-

> biguous acknowledgment of a constitutional floor with respect to educational adequacy. We conclude that a duty exists and that we are responsible for adjudicating the nature of that duty....
>
> The State must assure that some essentials are provided. Children are entitled to minimally adequate physical facilities and classrooms which provide enough light, space, heat, and air to permit children to learn. Children should have access to minimally adequate instrumentalities of learning such as desks, chairs, pencils, and reasonably current textbooks. Children are also entitled to minimally adequate teaching of reasonably up-to-date basic curricula such as reading, writing, mathematics, science, and social studies, by sufficient personnel adequately trained to teach those subject areas. *Campaign for Fiscal Equity*, 86 N.Y.2d at 316, 318; Judge Smith's *partial concurring opinion* at 356.

Judge Beauchamp Ciparick concluded, on behalf of the majority, that plaintiffs properly pled a cause of action that New York's school financing scheme violated the state's Education Clause to survive a motion to dismiss. The court also reinstated plaintiffs' Title VI regulations claim, finding they adequately pled discrimination (buttressed by statistical evidence) based on the state's lump sum benefit distribution practice. On that issue, Judge Beauchamp Ciparick wrote,

> The Appellate Division's reasoning fails to account for the fact that the City can only suballocate what the State allocates to it. If, as alleged, the State allocates only 34% of all State education aid to a school district containing 37% of the State's students (81% of whom are minorities comprising 74% of the State's minority student population), then those minority students will receive less aid as a group and per pupil than their nonminority peers who attend public schools elsewhere in the State, irrespective of how the City suballocates the education aid it receives.

Campaign for Fiscal Equity, 86 N.Y.2d 307, at 325.

In *Dawson v. White & Case*, 88 N.Y.2d 666 (1996), while the court recognized goodwill as a distributable asset upon a firm's dissolution, it found goodwill was not compensable here. For almost twenty years, Plaintiff Evan R. Dawson was a partner at the firm of White & Case. Before 1988, the firm tried persuading Dawson to withdraw as a partner, and upon his refusal, the firm dissolved and reformed without him. At issue was Dawson's interest in the accounting of goodwill that a special referee valuated but for which Dawson was not paid. The recognition and distribution of goodwill was affirmed by the appellate court. Judge Ciparick concluded goodwill was not compensable in this case. The judge based the court's ruling on two facts: one, incoming firm members (including Dawson) were never asked to contribute to the firm's goodwill and had not paid into the firm's goodwill when leaving; and two, goodwill was not accounted for in the firm's accounting books.

Grumet v. Cuomo, 90 N.Y.2d 57 (1997), centered on the issue of separation of church and state, specifically the prolonged litigious efforts of the Satmar Hasidic sect to secure and continue state funding for a religious school district. The Village of Kiryas Joel (Village) was comprised of members of the Satmar Hasidic sect, located in the Town of Monroe, Orange County. The Village operated private religious schools within the Monroe-Woodbury Central School District (MW-CSD) but lacked resources to provide educational services to disabled children, which the district funded through state subsidies. The state legislature eventually created a Kiryas Joel School District coterminous with the Village (Village District) that was authorized to provide education for all school children. In practice, the Village District operated a special education only for its disabled children pursuant to the Laws of 1989, chapter 748 (Chapter 748). (In *Grumet v. Board of Educ.*, 81 N.Y.2d 518, 528–239 (1993), the court held that Chapter 748 violated the Establishment Clause.) The U.S. Supreme Court granted the Village's petition for certiorari and upheld the lower court's decision. *Board of Educ. of Kiryas Joel Vil. School Dist. V. Grumet (Kiryas Joel I)*, 512 U.S. 687 (1994). In a case already factually complicated, the legislature then passed the Laws of 1994, chapters 241 and 279. Chapter 279 repealed Chapter 748 and abolished the Village District but permitted it to operate within MW-CSD until it merged with or was replaced by another school district. MW-CSD created a new Village school district under Chapter 241 (permitting the creation of new school district within parameters) of which the residents of Kiryas Joel approved. Plaintiffs (tax-paying citizens) filed suit and both parties moved for summary judgment on the constitutionality of the new law. Applying the tripartite test in *Lemon v. Kurtzman*, 403 U.S. 602 (1971), to determine whether the requirements of the Establishment Clause were met, the New York Supreme Court granted defendants' cross motion for summary judgment and dismissed plaintiff's complaint, ruling the new law met the test. Accord, *Grumet v. Cuomo*, 625 N.Y.S.2d 1000 (1995). The plaintiffs appealed. Declaring Chapter 241 unconstitutional, the Appellate Division reversed and granted summary judgment to the plaintiffs in *Grumet v. Cuomo*, 647 N.Y.S.2d 565 (1996). Writing for the majority in *Grumet v. Cuomo*, 90 N.Y.2d 57, 69–70 (1997), Judge Beauchamp Ciparick upheld the Appellate Division's decision, ruling Chapter 241 "transgresses *Lemon's* second prong" as it conferred a special religious benefit on the Village. She wrote, "The provision of a governmental benefit to a restricted class, when that class is formed along religious lines, is a telling index of nonneutral sectarian effect." *Grumet*, 90 N.Y.2d at 74. Judge Beauchamp Ciparick concluded Chapter 241 was enacted days after the U.S. Supreme Court's decision, for the sole benefit of the community of Kiryas Joel. The judge noted that the Village District was the only district out of the 1,546 in the state to be organized under Chapter 241 and further observed it was doubtful any other school district could meet the requirements of the chapter.

In *Engel v. CBS, Inc.*, 93 N.Y.2d 195 (1999), attorney Engle sued CBS (an adverse client) for malicious prosecution after CBS filed suit against him, charging the action was filed to undermine his representation of his client. Engle asserted these circumstances constituted a special injury. The Second Circuit certified the question to the New York Court of Appeals, whether under New York law, special injury, or concrete harm is required to satisfy the elements of a common law action for malicious prosecution, beyond the physical, psychological, or financial demands of defending a lawsuit. Upon a review of New York cases requiring proof of special injury, Judge Beauchamp Ciparick outlined the majority's rationale for declining to overrule these cases, finding Engle neither pled nor proved special injury. As substantiation for the court's answer, the judge recounted the convoluted proceedings involving Engle's representation of the band Boston and its leader Donald Scholz for whom he ultimately obtained a $6.5 million verdict in New York that included Engle's successful negotiation of an MCA contract, CBS's breach of contract and copyright infringement lawsuit based on the MCA contract (in which CBS admitted this lawsuit was brought partly to dissuade Engle from representing Scholtz), and Engle's subsequently filed malicious prosecution lawsuit in California. Engle's California suit was dismissed against CBS by summary judgment but was reinstated by the Ninth Circuit, which ruled New York was the proper venue.

Judge Beauchamp Ciparick wrote the majority opinion in two cases and dissent in one involving the gay and lesbian community. In *Levin v. Yeshiva University*, 96 N.Y.2d 484 (2001), lesbian medical students brought an action under the state and New York City Human Rights Law challenging the university's housing policy which gave married couples preference in residential university-owned housing. Plaintiffs alleged that the policy discriminated based on one's marital status and had a disparate impact on lesbians and gay men. Judge Ciparick concluded plaintiffs pled a prima facie case of disparate impact under the city's Human Rights Law, which prohibited housing polices or practices that have a disparate impact based on sexual orientation. The plaintiffs' lawsuit was reinstated. *In the Matter of H.M. v. E.T.*, 14 N.Y.3d 524 (2010), raised a subject matter jurisdictional issue, whether the court had subject matter jurisdiction over a lawsuit filed by a biological parent living in Montreal, Canada. The biological parent, H.M. sought a declaration of parentage and child support from a former same-sex partner, E.T., under the Uniform Interstate Family Support Act (UIFSA).[102] The former partners resided in New York from 1989 to 1995 and discussed parenting issues, including whether the child would be raised as a sibling to E. T.'s children. Four months after the son was born, the relationship ended. E. T. gave H. M. gifts and money for the child's care and H. M. sought judgment of parentage retroactive to the child's birth. E. T. successfully moved to dismiss the petition in New York's Family Court where a magistrate judge agreed the Family Court had no legal jurisdiction. The Family Court reversed this decision and scheduled a hearing to determine whether E. T. should be equitably estopped from denying parentage. E.T. appealed and a split appellate court reinstated the Family Court's original dismissal. *In the Matter of H.M. v. E.T.*, 65 AD3d 119 (2d Dept 2009). Writing for the majority, Judge Ciparick held the New York Constitution, art. VI, § 13(b)(4), "indisputably" gave the Family Court jurisdiction to determine child support "re-

102. 25 U.S.C. §§ 2701–2721, 18 U.S.C. §§ 1166–1168.

gardless of gender." *In the Matter of H.M.*, 14 N.Y.3d at 526. She wrote that "because Family Court unquestionably has the subject matter jurisdiction to ascertain the support obligations of a female parent, Family Court also has the inherent authority to ascertain in certain cases whether a female respondent is, in fact, a child's parent." *In the Matter of H.M.*, 14 N.Y.3d at 527. Judge Ciparick rejected the dissent's objection that the Supreme Court had original trial jurisdiction by noting the Family Court and the Supreme Court shared concurrent jurisdiction over child support matters. In another case involving the Family Court, Judge Ciparick presented the majority's ruling that a deceased child could be the subject of a Family Court Act article 10 abuse petition where the act is silent. *Matter of Alija C.*, 1 N.Y.3d 375 (2004).

Casino gaming on Indian reservations was at issue in *Dalton v. Pataki*, 5 N.Y.3d 243 (2005). Judge Beauchamp Ciparick issued a lengthy and detailed opinion on Class III gaming, including the state's authority to regulate *vis a vis* tribal compacts. The New York Court of Appeals was asked to determine whether 1) casino gaming permitted by tribal-state compacts (entered into in 2003) violated the state constitution, art. 1, § 9, 2) the Indian Gaming Regulatory Act of 1998 (IGRA) preempted state law, and 3) the constitutionality of video lottery gaming, the state's participation in the multistate Mega Millions lottery, and the allocation of net proceeds to education. At controversy were the Laws of 2001, chapter 383 (Chapter 383), parts B-tribal state compacts, C-video lottery terminals, and D-multistate lottery. The plaintiffs were taxpayers, state legislators, and nonprofit organizations; the Seneca Nation of Indians was party to a 2002 compact. The state supreme court granted the defendants-intervenors cross-motions for summary judgment, declaring Chapter 383 constitutional. The appellate division modified by ruling part C of Chapter 383, video lottery terminals, was unconstitutional. The court upheld the constitutionality of Chapter 383, parts B, C, and D. It ruled that IGRA permitted gambling on Indian reservations in New York, allowing the state to play an important and essential role in regulating gambling on Indian lands. The court further held that the installation of video lottery terminals in racetracks and the Mega Millions "promotes the State's public policy to increase funding for education via state-sponsored lotteries." Judge Beauchamp Ciparick noted, "We find no constitutional infirmity in the legislation ... [a] lthough some may argue the wisdom of the policy choice, the Legislature has made a valid legislative judgment." *Dalton*, 5 N.Y.3d at 272.

EBC I, Inc. v. Goldman Sachs & Co., 5 N.Y.3d 11 (2005), was a securities lawsuit regarding the underwriting process involving investment banks. Internet retailers eToys, Inc. sued Goldman Sachs as lead managing underwriter, alleging breach of a fiduciary duty and four other claims, by underpricing initial public offerings (IPOs) resulting in higher profits to Goldman's favored customers from which Goldman ultimately benefitted. Goldman Sachs advised plaintiff on the IPO pricing without disclosing the conflict of interest arising from its arrangements with other clients in which a lower resale IPO price resulted in higher payments to Goldman Sachs, 20 to 40 percent of the clients' profits, from trading eToys securities. The New York Court of Appeals was asked to address the procedural question certified by the appellant division: whether the court's unanimous reversal of the state supreme court's decision granting defendant's motion to dismiss the breach of contract fraud with leave to replead professional malpractice and unjust enrichment was proper. The appellate division agreed with the supreme court sustaining the breach of fiduciary duty claim and dismissal of the fraud claim but reinstated the remaining three claims. With leave of the appellate division, Goldman Sachs appealed the certified question. The court modified the appellate division's order by dismissing the breach of contract, professional malpractice, and unjust enrichment claims. It allowed the fiduciary duty cause of action to proceed and agreed plaintiff could replead the fraud claim. The New York Court of Appeals determined that Goldman Sachs had a duty to disclose its compensation arrangements with its customers especially because, as alleged, it derived a percentage of profits generated in post-offering resales.

Judge Beauchamp Ciparick joined the dissent in the seminal case of *Hernandez v. Robles*, 7 N.Y.3d 338 (2005). Four lawsuits were consolidated involving forty-four gay and lesbian couples residing throughout New York state. The majority held upon a 4–2 vote that the state's constitution did not require the recognition of same-sex marriage or violate the due process and equal protection clauses of the state or the U.S. Constitution. Applying a rational basis test, Judge Robert S. Smith recognized the state's definition of marriage as a union between a man and woman and that limiting marriage to opposite-sex couples could be based on rational social goals, primarily the protection and welfare of children. He wrote,

> The Legislature could rationally proceed on the commonsense premise that children will be best with a mother and father in the home.... Plaintiffs have not persuaded us that this long-accepted restriction is a wholly irrational one, based solely on ignorance and prejudice against homosexuals. *Hernandez, 7 N.Y.3d* at 361.

Judge Smith reasoned that same-sex marriage was distinguishable from anti-miscegenation laws because it was not "deeply rooted in this Nation's history and tradition," therefore barring it was not a violation of fundamental rights and liberties. *Hernandez*, 7 N.Y.3d at 363. Chief Judge Judith Kaye authored the dissent, which Judge Ciparick joined, finding plaintiffs' fundamental rights to marry were violated under the due process guarantee. Judge Kaye "warned that future generations would look back at yesterday's decision as an unfortunate misstep" and would consider barring of gay marriage as an injustice akin to the laws that once barred interracial marriage. *Hernandez*, 7 N.Y.3d at 381–397. Following the court's decision, the New York Assembly passed same-sex marriage legislation in 2007 and 2009, both were rejected by the state Senate. In 2011, same-sex marriage legislation embodied in New York's Marriage Equality Act passed the Senate and was signed by Governor Andrew Cuomo on June 24 (effective July 24, 2011). New York became the sixth U.S. state and the seventh U.S. jurisdiction to license same-sex marriage. The Act does not have a residency restriction, as some similar state laws do, and it also allows religious organizations to decline to officiate at same-sex wedding ceremonies. In 2015 upon a 5–4 split decision, the U.S. Supreme Court sanctioned same-sex marriage, recognizing the right to marry as a fundamental liberty as guaranteed by the due process clause of the Fourteenth Amendment in *Obergefell v. Hodges*, 576 U.S. 644 (2015). Justices Kennedy, Ginsburg, Breyer, Sotomayor, and Kagan joined in the majority opinion; Chief Justice Roberts and Justices Scalia, Thomas, and Alito dissented.

Writing for the court, Judge Beauchamp Ciparick addressed an issue in *American Building Supply Corp. v. Petrocelli Group, Inc.*, 19 N.Y.3d 730 (2012), left unresolved in *Hoffend & Sons, Inc. v. Rose & Kiernan, Inc.*, 7 N.Y.3d 152 (2006). In *Hoffend*, the court held that the failure to read a policy should not bar an action against the broker and may give rise to a defense of comparative negligence. At issue in *Petrocelli* was whether a policyholder is barred from suing the broker who had an opportunity to read the insurance policy. The plaintiff was a business that sells and furnishes building materials to general contractors that subleased a building from DRK. DRK entered into a lease agreement with a New York city agency that required a minimum coverage of $5 million for bodily injury and property damage. The initial insurance coverage with Burlington was procured by former broker (Pollack Associates), and the renewed policy procured by plaintiff's new broker (Petrocelli) did not comply with the city's requirements. In fact, the new policy specifically excluded coverage of bodily injury and property damage. Subsequently, an employee was injured. Plaintiff sued its insurance broker for failing to obtain adequate insurance coverage; averring that it specifically requested general liability coverage. Petrocelli visited the building and conveyed to the city agency that the insurance deficiency in the old policy would be cured in the new policy. Plaintiff did not read the renewed insurance policy. The state Supreme Court ruled in favor of the plaintiff concluding an issue of fact existed for a jury to decide whether plaintiff made a specific insurance coverage request of Defendant. The appellate division reversed based on plaintiff's failure to read the policy. Judge Beauchamp Ciparick wrote that plaintiff's failure to read the policy did not preclude the lawsuit against the broker. She concluded issues of fact existed on claims of negligence or breach of contract as to whether the company requested specific coverage which was supported by deposition testimony and the plaintiff's practices.

e. Conclusion

Through her opinions and dissents, Judge Beauchamp Ciparick cemented her reputation as a defender of individual rights—whether the litigants were workers, women, or criminal defendants.[103] The judge authored some of the state's most important opinions on school financing, reproductive rights, the separation of church and state and LGBTQ rights. She demonstrated her intellectual dexterity through the issuance of understandable and well-organized opinions that involved complex

103. *Supra note 101, Kasow Article at 961, 963–968; see also* Vincent Martin Bonventre, *Streams of Tendency on the New York Court: Ideological and Jurisprudential Patterns in the Judges' Voting and Opinions* (William S. Hein, 2013), 889, 897, 914–915.

procedural maneuvering, and difficult issues with convoluted facts to match. Notwithstanding, her opinions reveal a straight-forward decision-maker unafraid to reach the result warranted by the law. Only mandatory retirement rules caused the Judge in 2012 to retire at age seventy from the bench.[104] In 2015, she became of counsel with a New York law firm, advising on appellate and litigation matters while mentoring younger attorneys.[105] In August 2023, Judge Ciparick was appointed independent monitor on racial bias for the New York Court system, continuing her special brand of intellectual advocacy.[106]

5. Judge Vanessa Ruiz

a. Formative Years

1972	B.A., Philosophy, Wellesley College
1975	J.D., Georgetown University Law Center Admitted to District of Columbia Bar
1975–1983	Fried, Frank, Harris, Shriver & Jacobson, Washington, D.C.
1983–1986	Senior Counsel, Sears World Trade, Inc.
1986–1991	Founding Member, Sloan, Lehner & Ruiz (merged with Pepper, Hamilton & Scheetz)
1990	Adjunct Law Professor, Georgetown
1991	Nominated District of Columbia Court of Appeals
1991	Office of Corporation Counsel (now D.C. Attorney General's Office) 1991: Deputy Counsel, Legal Counsel Division 1993: Principal Deputy, 1994: Corporation Counsel
1994–2011	Judge, D.C. Court of Appeals[107]
2011	Retired[108]

104. CUNY Law Professor Jenny Rivera was nominated by Governor Cuomo to fill Judge Ciparick's seat, which she assumed on February 11, 2013, *see Cuomo Nominates CUNY Law Prof Rivera to High Court, Democrat & Chronicle, May 16, 2013,* https://www.democratandchronicle.com/story/news/politics/blogs/vote-up/2013/01/15/cuomo-nominates-cuny-law-prof-rivera-to-high-court/2190631/; New York Court of Appeals, Honorable Jenny Rivera, https://www.nycourts.gov/ctapps/jrivera.htm.

105. Greenberg Traurig, https://www.gtlaw.com/en/professionals/c/ciparick-carmen-beauchamp.

106. *New York State Bar Association Applauds Appointment of Judge Carmen Beauchamp Ciparick as Independent Monitor,* NYSBA, August 10, 2003, https://nysba.org/new-york-state-bar-association-applauds-appointment-of-judge-carmen-beauchamp-ciparick-as-independent-monitor/.

107. The Honorable Vanessa Ruiz Associate Judge District of Columbia Court of Appeals, https://www.dccourts.gov/sites/default/files/2017-03/DCCA_Bio_Ruiz.pdf.;

108. D.C. vacancy announcement for the retiring Judge Ruiz, https://jnc.dc.gov/sites/default/files/dc/sites/jnc/release_content/attachments/Vacancy_Announcement_for_Ruiz.pdf.

A second-generation attorney, Vanessa was born in San Juan, Puerto Rico, on March 22, 1950, to Irma Bosch de Ruiz and Fernando Ruiz-Suria. Their four children, including Vanessa, were raised speaking Spanish. Irma was a teacher and homemaker, and Fernando an accomplished litigator and Shell Oil corporate counsel. On behalf of the company in 1963, Fernando Ruiz presented oral argument to the U.S. Supreme Court.[109] Vanessa would follow suit (literally) as the fourth Luminaria to present oral argument before SCOTUS. She is the only one of the eight Luminarias who is a second-generation lawyer. Though Vanessa recalled listening to her father's discussion of cases at home, he was not the impetus for choosing law school. She majored in philosophy at Wellesley College at a time of domestic turbulence in the country. The opportunity to engage meaningfully and contribute to society drove her choice of the law.[110] Upon graduating law school and admission to the bar in 1975 in the District of Columbia (D.C. or District), Vanessa entered private practice, specializing in international commercial and intellectual property transactions.

Vanessa litigated a significant *pro bono* case representing an African American tenant and a housing nonprofit that used individual testers to identify discriminatory housing practices. She presented oral argument to the U.S. Supreme Court[111] in *Havens Realty Corp. v. Coleman*, 455 U.S. 363 (1982). Ruiz advanced the theory of racial steering against the owner of two apartment complexes in Richmond, Virginia. The seminal housing tester suit was brought under §§ 804 and 812[112] of the Fair Housing Act of 1968, which prohibits housing discrimination. Plaintiffs were three individual testers, two white and one black, Sylvia Coleman, and the nonprofit organization HOME, Housing Opportunities Made Equal. HOME sent testers to Havens inquiring about vacancies. Havens informed the African American tester there were no vacancies and the white tester that there were two apartments available. The white tester was dismissed as a plaintiff on the basis he suffered no harm. The district court entered a consent decree awarding damages and injunctive relief but did not order any other relief. Upon filing a lawsuit, the district court granted Havens' motion to dismiss ruling plaintiffs had no standing and were barred by the 180-day statute of limitations.[113] The D.C. Court of Appeals reinstated the case, ruling the allegations of harm were sufficient to withstand a motion to dismiss and, as there

---

109. Fernando Ruiz-Suria, *The Shell Company (Puerto Rico), Ltd. Petitioner v. Secretary of the Treasury of the Commonwealth of Puerto Rico*, 375 U.S. 930 (September 6, 1963).

110. Amita Parashar Kelly, *A Legal Trailblazer's Journey: Vanessa Ruiz '71*, Wellesley Magazine, Summer 2023 (Wellesley Article), https://magazine.wellesley.edu/summer-2023/legal-trailblazer%E2%80%99s-journey.

111. *Supra* note 37, Maria G. Mendoza Article.

112. Section 804(d) makes it unlawful to "represent to any person because of race, color, religion, sex, or national origin that any dwelling is not available to inspection, sale, or rental when such dwelling is in fact so available." Section 812(a) creates the enforceable cause of action for § 804(d) violations. 42 U.S.C. §§ 3604(d), 3612(a).

113. 42 U.S.C. § 3612(a).

was an ongoing violation, the claims fell within the 180-day period of § 812(a). The U.S. Supreme Court found in favor of the plaintiffs, ruling that the organization and testers had standing to sue and further defined "neighborhood standing" as producing indirect harm, in contrast to "tester standing" that resulted in direct injury. Interpreting § 804(d), SCOTUS found, "Congress has thus conferred on all 'persons' a legal right to truthful information about available housing." *Havens*, 455 U.S. at 375. The case continued and was appealed to the D.C. Court of Appeals when Vanessa was on the court (*see discussion infra*). She is married to fellow lawyer-ambassador David Birenbaum who together have a blended family that includes four children. Vanessa co-authored a book, *Europe Without Frontiers: A Lawyers Guide* (BNA 1989), and began teaching in 1990 as an adjunct professor at Georgetown.

In July 1991, Vanessa was nominated to the D.C. Court of Appeals pursuant to the D.C. Judicial Nominations Commission (Commission) process.[114] Vanessa submitted a judicial application after calling,

> only one of the women judges she knew—Ruth Bader Ginsburg, who at the time was serving on the U.S. Court of Appeals for the District of Columbia Circuit.... At the end of the conversation, Ruiz thanked Ginsburg for her time and said she'd continue to think about whether to apply. "No, stop thinking about it," Ginsburg said. "Just do it. You're going to be great at this. Just put your name in, and don't look back."[115]

President G. H. W. Bush had sixty days to make the appointment upon referral of the names by the Commission but did not choose Vanessa; she did not give up. Among others, Ruiz turned to the HNBA for its support and endorsement. Years later on July 12, 1994, she was nominated by President Clinton. The Senate held her confirmation hearing on October 4, 1994, that consisted of few *pro forma* questions. On October 7, 1994, the U.S. Senate confirmed Vanessa to a fifteen-year term, expiring October 10, 2009.[116] She was the first Luminaria-Latina to serve on the court. "After [Vanessa's] appointment to the bench, Justice Ginsburg, who had since taken her seat on the U.S. Supreme Court, administered Ruiz's oath."[117] In April 2009, Judge Ruiz "declared her candidacy for reappointment," triggering evaluation by the D.C. Tenure Commission. Of Judge Ruiz, the Tenure Commission wrote, "it is clear that her scholarship, her analytical abilities, the clarity of her writing, and her thoroughness are outstanding. Members of the Bar have made clear to the Commission that during oral argument she is deeply engaged, asks challenging questions, and is always prepared, and is deeply respectful to counsel and the position they are argu-

114. D.C. Code § 1-204.34; *see* Alison Howard, *Former Judge Nominated to D.C. Superior Court,* Washington Post, July 31, 1991.

115. *Supra* note 110, Wellesley Article.

116. CRS Report for Congress, Judicial Nominations by President Clinton During the 103rd and 104th Congresses, https://sgp.fas.org/crs/misc/96-567.pdf.

117. *Supra* note 110, Wellesley Article.

ing on behalf of their clients."[118] They concluded that through her extrajudicial activity, Judge Ruiz "played a very significant role in improving the administration of justice." The Tenure Commission issued a "Well Qualified" rating, resulting in an automatic extension for a second full term.[119] Judge Ruiz remained on the bench for two additional years, retiring on August 31, 2011.

b. District of Columbia Court of Appeals, 1994–2011

Pursuant to D.C. Code, § 11-721, Pub.L. 115-334 (2018), the D.C. Court of Appeals has jurisdiction of appeals from all interlocutory orders, final orders and judgments of the D.C. Superior Court, orders or rulings of the D.C. Superior Court appealed by the U.S. or the District pursuant to section 23-104 or 23-111(d)(2). Judge Ruiz wrote the majority opinion in 392 cases and participated in 2,000 cases appealed from the D.C. Superior Court, which covered a broad array of legal issues from criminal law to matters unique to the District. The following criminal and civil cases present issues of first impression in which Judge Ruiz wrote the majority opinions.

c. Majority Opinions in Criminal Cases

Timberlake v. U.S., 758 A.2d 978 (2000), involved tampering with evidence under D.C. Code § 22-723(a). The section establishes the elements of tampering as altering, destroying, mutilating, concealing, or removing a record, document, or other object, with the intent to impair its integrity or availability to use in an official proceeding. The crux of the case was the element of knowing or having reason to believe that an official proceeding has begun or likely to be instituted. Plain-clothed police officers arrived at a known drug trafficking area, 16th and D Streets in southeast D.C., whereupon a woman shouted, "Five-o." Immediately thereafter, the officer saw Timberlake conceal a packet of drugs in his mouth. The officer approached Timberlake, identified himself, and a struggle ensued. The defendant spit out two bags of heroin and cocaine which the officer recovered. The prosecution asserted these facts were adequate to establish the defendant's prior knowledge that an official proceeding (police investigation) had begun or was to be instituted. The prosecution also relied on a prior drug investigation of the defendant to establish his general knowledge of criminal investigations and proceedings. Defendant countered that these facts were insufficient to sustain his conviction because an official proceeding had not started at the time he placed the drugs in his mouth. On behalf of the court, Judge Ruiz interpreted and applied the "knowing" element as including an individual who is not the

---

118. D.C. Commission on Judicial Disabilities and Tenure, August 10, 2009, Letter to President Barack Obama, Re: Evaluation of the Honorable Vanessa Ruiz, 7–8.

119. *Id.* at 1–2, 8; one commissioner filed a separate objection to the "Well Qualified" rating and automatic extension based on Judge Ruiz's considerable backlog. *See* § 433(c), D.C. Self-Government and Governmental Regulations Act, P.L. 93-198, 87 Stat. 774, as amended by the Judicial Efficiency and Improvement Act of 1986, P.L. 99-573, 100 Stat. 3228.

subject of an official proceeding but knew or had reason to believe that such proceeding has begun or was likely to be instituted against him. Judge Ruiz wrote that "the tampering occurred at a time when Timberlake knew the police officers were investigating his illegal activity and thereby knew an official proceeding was imminent.... On the[se] facts..., a reasonable jury could find that once Officer Neill had identified himself and the struggle ensued. Timberlake knew an official proceeding was likely to be instituted against him and thus possessed the requisite state of mind as he attempted to destroy (*i.e.*, swallow) the evidence." *Timberlake*, 758 A.2d at 983. Judge Ruiz's analysis was predicated on precedent from six other jurisdictions reaching the same result with substantially similar facts. The court upheld the trial court's denial of defendant's motion for judgment of acquittal.

Morgan v. U.S., 47 A.3d 532 (2012), was a due process challenge raised by a single defendant based on inconsistent theories. Upon pleading guilty to one count of unarmed manslaughter, a sentence of no less than six years was imposed but suspended. Defendant was then acquitted of possession of marijuana. At the show cause hearing to provoke defendant's probation for the manslaughter conviction, inconsistent testimony was given by police officers from that offered at trial. A police officer testified at the show cause hearing that he found one bag of marijuana in a closed container but at the subsequent revocation hearing, testified the marijuana was in plain sight. The defendant admitted he had ten other bags; a total of 104 bags with marijuana were found. The trial court found the testimony was sufficient to revoke probation on the original manslaughter sentence. Appellant-defendant argued his due process rights were violated because the government switched theories from trial to the revocation hearing. Judge Ruiz acknowledged inconsistent theories could result in a violation of due process rights under certain circumstances, but noted such violations arose where there were two or more defendants and factual inconsistencies were "core" to the prosecution's case. "We have not had occasion to consider a due process challenge in the context of a single defendant whose probation is revoked following acquittal where, as alleged here, the government has changed its position between trial and the revocation hearing." *Morgan*, 47 A.3d at 538. Judge Ruiz concluded the factual inconsistencies between the police officer's testimony at trial and the officer's testimony at the revocation hearing did not violate the defendant's due process rights. Judge Ruiz ruled minimum due process is afforded at revocation probation hearings that are not part of criminal prosecution, relying on precedent.

Johnson v. U.S., 40 A.3d 1 (2012), involved a misdemeanor conviction of possession of marijuana with intent to distribute, a "controlled delivery" via the U.S. Postal Service. A post office analyst was profiling parcels in a facility near the Los Angeles airport that was addressed to the defendant's address in Washington, D.C., with the name "Corey Johnson." It contained 3,000 grams of marijuana. A second parcel with defendant's address but same fictitious name also was discovered, which received a "positive hit" by a police dog. Upon obtaining a warrant, the officers found two individually wrapped packages containing marijuana. The eleven-pound package was shipped to the defendant at the address on the two packages. Postal inspectors informed the D.C. police of the shipped parcel, conveying the defendant's name and address. An inspector, disguised as a postal carrier, delivered the package to the defendant in person. Defendant answered and agreed his name was Courtney (not Corey) Johnson. Upon the inspector's request, defendant signed and accepted the package. He was thereafter arrested. Defendant was acquitted twice of felony charges but convicted on a misdemeanor charge, which was the subject of this appeal. Defendant appealed the trial court's refusal to suppress the evidence and his statements, arguing the officers could not arrest him because they had no probable cause he knew what was in the package. Judge Ruiz wrote, "The question whether acceptance of a controlled delivery by the addressee is sufficient to establish probable cause to arrest the recipient is an issue of first impression for us and one that appears to have received scant attention by other courts." *Johnson*, 40 A.3d at 8-9. In affirming the conviction, Judge Ruiz relied on *Illinois v. Andreas*, 463 U.S. 765 (1983), careful to distinguish that acceptance of a contained delivery, alone, may not be sufficient to establish probable cause that s/he is engaged in unlawful activity (i.e., an inference may be inadequate). Upon assessing the totality of the circumstances in this case, including the facts known to the officers "with knowledge of the drug trade" before the arrest, Judge Ruiz concluded there was probable cause to arrest the defendant. *Johnson*, 40 A.3d at 9. She found no Fourth Amendment violation.

In *Mason v. U.S.*, 53 A.3d 1084 (2012), the defendant appealed his conviction after a second trial for weapons offenses and second-degree murder while armed. Defendant challenged the admission of a witness's prior consistent statement to rebut a charge. Defendant was charged with shooting Delonte Borum in the back of the head while Borum played dice in an alley. Borum's female friend testified she was sitting outside drinking and smoking marijuana when the defendant approached and told her to get inside the house because "he did not need no witnesses." She further testified she heard gunshots and later saw Borum lying in the alley and called 911. *Mason,* 53 A.3d at 1087. Judge Ruiz wrote, "The legal issue before [the court was]... whether and, if so, under what circumstances, a prior consistent statement, made when the witness had a motive to lie, may be admitted to rebut a charge of fabrication alleged to have been motivated by a more recent, and different, motive." *Mason,* 53 A.3d at 1091. After the shooting, defendant went to an apartment adjacent to the shooting in which two Crouch brothers, Miguel and Kevin, lived. Police found ammunition and the gun that killed Borum in the Crouch apartment under Miguel's bed but did not find defendant's fingerprints on the gun. Miguel was arrested for the shooting but later was released. The police found defendant's fingerprints on a paper cup in the alley where the shooting occurred. Kevin Crouch initially told a grand jury he saw defendant leaving his brother's room four minutes after the shooting. Thereafter, he changed his story to seeing "DJ" in the apartment but subsequently reverted to his initial story. By the third statement Crouch was facing weapons charges for an unrelated incident while his brother was facing murder charges for Borum's death. Defendant admitted he was in the alley and his prints were found on a cup near Borum's body. At trial, Crouch was impeached, but his credibility was rehabilitated by his police statement and grand jury testimony two years earlier. Defendant objected on well-settled law that prior inconsistent statements may not be used to bolster an unimpeached witness. Crouch explained he changed his story out of fear of defendant, the outstanding weapons charges (to which he entered a plea deal), and concern about his brother's implication in Borum's murder. Judge Ruiz concluded that the prior consistent statement was not inadmissible hearsay and constituted admissible testimony to "rebut a charge of a very recent and different reason to fabricate." She wrote, "Where the relevant ground of impeachment involves an independent criminal action arising in a different jurisdiction, which has had a significant fabrication-inducing development just two weeks prior to trial (in this case, the filing of a motion for resentencing), it is accurate to label the new motive to fabricate as 'different.' Accordingly, [Couch]'s prior consistent statement made to the police shortly after the shooting was admissible to rebut defense counsel's charge that he had a current reason to curry favor with the government notwithstanding that the witness also had other, unrelated motives to lie at the time the statement was made." *Mason,* 53 A.3d at 1092. For this reason, Judge Ruiz distinguished the instant case from *United States v. Awon*, 135 F.3d 96 (1st Circuit 1998). The jury's knowledge of the other motives coupled with accurate jury instructions weighed into the court's decision to allow the prior consistent statement. *Mason*, 53 A.3d at 1092–1093.

Judge Ruiz considered an issue of first impression in *Snowden v. U.S.*, 52 A.3d 858 (2012), whether a shooting that occurs after a co-conspirator flees is in furtherance of the conspiracy for purposes of liability. Defendant was convicted of numerous counts of conspiracy, armed robbery, and aggravated assault based on the co-conspirator's shooting. The defendant was with four others who decided to rob a group of male family members celebrating the release of a relative from prison, in a parking lot near one of their apartments. Lorenzo Ross, a victim, saw a girl he knew from the complex and went to talk with her. From that point, Lorenzo could see his family members and the defendant's group, but the two groups could not see one another. Lorenzo recognized the defendant from the school bus they both used to take. He saw defendant don a ski mask and head toward his family members with a gun. With a bandana covering his face, the second gunman walked toward the family members with a gun resembling an Uzi. Defendant robbed one of the victims. Lorenzo's cousin, Scales, tried to grab the gun from the defendant and they wrestled while the co-conspirator watched. Defendant eventually broke away and ran from Scales. Scales saw the co-conspirator and raised his arms, whereupon the co-conspirator shot him three times. Lorenzo identified the Defendant prior to and during trial. Defendant argued there was no evidence that the shooting of Scales was necessary to accomplish the conspiracy—robbery. By the time the shooting occurred, Defendant had already committed the robbery and ran away. Writing for the court, Judge Ruiz concluded under the theory of co-conspirator liability, this evidence was sufficient to support a verdict for aggravated assault because the shooting was a naturally foreseeable consequence of armed robbery, citing *Pinkerton v. United States*, 328 U.S. 640 (1946), as authority and other cases discussing when a conspiracy ends. The court accepted the government's theory of the case that the shooting was in furtherance of the conspiracy because it occurred before all the culprits had escaped and advanced the conspiracy's goals by assisting the escape and asportation of proceeds. *See especially Carter v. United States*, 223 F.2d 332, 334 (D.C. Cir. 1955) ("[S]o long as the essential ingredient of asportation continues, the crime of robbery is still in progress...."), citing *Snowden*, 52 A.3d at 866.

At issue was the scope of the superior court's authority to terminate and dismiss a juvenile proceeding, *In re D. M.*, 47 A.3d 539 (2012). The juvenile, D.M., pled to one count of misdemeanor theft of a police officer's cell phone. At a dispositional proceeding, the trial court declared D.M. delinquent and in need of care or rehabilitation and imposed six months' probation. A week before his probation expired, D.M. filed a motion to dismiss the proceeding which the trial court granted, finding D.M. behaved well during probation and was no longer in need of care or rehabilitation. The District appealed, arguing that once the trial court adjudicated D.M. delinquent, it did not have authority to dismiss the proceeding, and even if it did, the dismissal of the proceeding did not have the effect of vacating D.M.'s original delinquency adjudication. Pursuant to D.C. Code §§ 16-2335 and 16-2324 (2001), Judge Ruiz held the trial court lacked statutory authority to dismiss because the appropriate proceeding upon automatic termination of probation was expungement and sealing of the delinquency decree.

d. Majority Opinions in Civil Cases

Esteños v. PAHO/WHO Federal Credit Union, 952 A.2d 878 (2008), was a national origin discrimination and language proficiency case involving Peruvian Juan Esteños, an auditor and accountant. Esteños completed a basic English class but had a rudimentary command of English. Unsuccessful in procuring work as an accountant/auditor, he became an office clerk at Pan-American Health Organization/World Health Organization after an interview conducted entirely in Spanish. Esteños asserted English was not a bona fide job requirement because he communicated in Spanish with his co-workers and only two tasks required minimal English. A new manager terminated plaintiff on the basis that Esteños' job required proficiency in both English and Spanish. The new manager and one other Hispanic employee spoke only English when the job required proficiency in both languages. EEOC found reasonable cause of national origin discrimination due to Esteños' inability to speak English. The trial court initially denied appellee's motion to dismiss the action as time-barred by the one-year statute of limitations, reasoning the EEOC's cross-filing with the D.C. Office of Human Rights satisfied the statute of limitations contained in D.C.'s Human Rights Act (Act).[120] After discovery, the trial court granted employer's summary judgment motion. The issue of first impression was whether evidence of an English proficiency requirement sustains a national origin discrimination claim under D.C. law. In concluding affirmatively, Judge Ruiz relied on EEOC's regulations defining national origin discrimination "as including, but not limited to, the denial of equal employment opportunity because of an individual's, or his or her ancestor's, place of origin; or because an individual has the physical, cultural or linguistic characteristics of a national origin group." 29 C.F.R. §1606.1 (2008). Judge Ruiz's analysis included EEOC regulations defining "fluency-in-English" and "English-only" requirements as potentially discriminatory and problematic. C.F.R. §§1606.6(b)(1) and 1606.7 (English as a business necessity). She provided a summary of federal and D.C. law, noting that the District specifically adopted the EEOC definition defining national origin discrimination and furthermore, had incorporated the EEOC regulations into D.C. law.[121] The judge ruled a timely filing with EEOC within the one-year statute of limitations, which cross-files with the Act—tolls the time for filing a private action—noting a personal filing is not required. Judge Ruiz rejected the trial court's finding that Esteños' claim based on lack of English proficiency had no support in the Act. The judge summarized the law on English language proficiency cases, including English-only cases, and concluded that Esteños' language proficiency fell under the Act. With the conflicting evidence submitted, Judge Ruiz wrote that what was clearly disputed was whether English proficiency was, in fact, a necessary job requirement, preluding summary judgment. *Esteños*, 952 A.2d at 893. The trial court's grant of summary judgment was vacated and the matter remanded.

Doe v. Medlantic Health Care Group, Inc., 814 A.2d 939 (2003), involved discrimination based on apparent disability. Plaintiff's primary employment was the U.S. State Department, and, at night, he worked as a janitor at the Washington Hospital Center. The plaintiff suffered from AIDS and had not disclosed his illness. A co-worker, who worked temporarily at the State Department and worked at Washington Hospital Center, learned of plaintiff's AIDS diagnosis and disclosed it to other workers. They teased, ridiculed, and scorned the plaintiff, prompting his lawsuit for breach of confidential relationship. A jury awarded a $250,000 verdict to Doe against Medlantic Health Care Group, Inc. ("Medlantic"). The trial court granted Medlantic's motion for judgment notwithstanding the verdict (JNOV) on the grounds that Doe's action was filed outside the one-year statute of limitations. Plain-

120. D.C. Code §§2-1401.01, 1403.03 (2001).

121. DCMR §500.2 and D.C. Code §2-1403.04(a), stating in pertinent part: "A private cause of action pursuant to this chapter shall be filed in a court of competent jurisdiction within *one year* of the unlawful discriminatory act, or the discovery thereof.... The timely filing of a complaint with the Office, or under the administrative procedures established by the Mayor pursuant to §2-1403.03, shall toll the running of the statute of limitations while the complaint is pending."

tiff appealed claiming the trial court substituted its own view for that of the jury when the cause of action accrued and erroneously applied a one-year instead of the three-year statute of limitations. Medlantic cross-appealed on various grounds, all found meritless by Judge Ruiz. Applying the inquiry notice theory—that notice which a plaintiff would have possessed after due investigation—the judge concluded whether plaintiff conducted a reasonable investigation was a disputed question of fact found to his favor by the jury. Judge Ruiz reversed the trial court's JNOV and remanded with instructions to reinstate the jury's verdict.

In *Cerovic v. Stojkov*, 134 A.3d 766 (2016), the court adopted the preponderance of the evidence standard to determinate marital assets where a common law marriage precedes a ceremonial marriage between the same persons. Stojkov was a naturalized U.S. citizen employed as an attorney. Cerovic's citizenship application, based on her marriage to Stojkov, was pending. At issue was whether the Serbian couple who cohabitated in Serbia formed a common law marriage since 2003. In 2010, they had a ceremonial marriage in the United States. Stojkov denied the common law marriage while Cerovic asserted one existed. At trial, the parties presented conflicting testimonial and documentary evidence. Pursuant to D.C. Code § 16-910 (2012 Repl.), the trial court ruled that Cerovic failed to establish by clear and convincing evidence that the Serbian cohabitation constituted a common law marriage under either Serbian or D.C. law. Applying a clear and convincing standard, the trial court held there were no marital assets from the cohabitation (as there was no dissolution per the Code) and distributed property acquired from the April 2010 wedding. The D.C. Court of Appeals concluded that the lower standard of preponderance of the evidence should be applied to prove a common law marriage when it precedes a ceremonial marriage between the same persons. The judge distinguished D.C. precedent that required proof by clear and convincing because those cases involved common law/marriages between different persons. Judge Ruiz wrote, "[i]t is not necessary, however, to apply that heightened evidentiary burden in every case where a prior common law marriage is asserted... the requirement that the proponent of the first marriage must meet a clear and convincing evidence standard applies only in situations in which the proponent is attempting to prove that the common law marriage with one spouse precedes marriage with a *different* spouse, *i.e.*, situations in which the parties to the asserted successive marriages are not the same." *Cerovic*, 134 A.3d at 775.

In a real estate case of first impression, *1305 Rhode Island Avenue NW, LLC v. Mussells*, 292 A.3d 212 (2022), prospective purchasers and residents of a four-unit residential building sued the vendor-assignee of tenants' rights. They proceeded under the D.C. Tenant Opportunity to Purchase Act (TOPA). Plaintiffs John and Premila Mussells sought specific performance of their purchase agreement plus a declaratory judgment that the subsequent sale agreement between vendor and assignee was null and void. The vendor counter and cross-claimed, seeking a trial court declaration of which contract to honor. The Superior Court granted judgment to the Mussells and vendor. Assignee appealed the issue and trial court's decision. Judge Ruiz held the tenant's letter asserting her individual interest in exercising her right under TOPA was proper and that the trial court failed to properly prioritize the right of first refusal "due to perceived deficiencies in the tenants' assignment of their TOPA rights. Giving effect to the assertion and assignment of TOPA rights, we reverse the judgment for appellees and remand the case to the trial court for entry of judgment for appellant, an order granting specific performance of the sales contract between appellant and the Trust and for further proceedings consistent with this opinion."

Woodland Ltd. Partnership v. Wulff, 868 A.2d 860 (2005), involved a derivative action against a limited partnership filed by a law firm partner and others, asserting interest in the limited partnership. Defendants counterclaimed for declaratory judgment, asserting that the law partner was not an owner. They demanded arbitration as assignees of the firm's interest in the partnership to arbitrate the ownership dispute. The Superior Court granted plaintiffs' motion to stay the arbitration. Defendants appealed. The court reversed the trial court, Judge Ruiz holding that, as a matter of first impression, the arbitrator was the appropriate one to determine whether the right to arbitration was waived, due to the law partner's participation in the underlying litigation.

e. Conclusion

Judge Ruiz was actively involved in bar association work throughout her career. While on the bench, she was president of the National Association of Women Judges (NAWJ) and developed a flagship educational program, *Removing Obstacles to Justice for Immigrants*. She spearheaded the ABA's adoption of national standards for interpretation and translation in court and worked on updating those standards. As an active member of the International Association of Women Judges, Judge Ruiz was among those who assisted Afghan women judges to leave the country when war erupted and two of their colleagues were assassinated in 2021.[122] Judge Ruiz is a trustee of the Carnegie Endowment for International Peace and member of the American Law Institute. She is the recipient of many awards, including the 2001 HNBA Judge of the Year, 2006 Latina Leader in Law Award/Congressional Hispanic Caucus, NAWJ's first Vaino Spencer Leadership Award 2008, and the 2009 ABA Margaret Brent Women Lawyers of Achievement Award.[123]

---

122. *Supra* note 108, Judge Ruiz bio; *see also*, *The Honorable Vanessa Ruiz, 2013 Woman Lawyer of the Year*, WBA Foundation, March–April 2013 Issue, https://wbadc.org/wp-content/uploads/2021/02/WBA_RTB_2012-2013_Issue6_MarApr.pdf.

123. *See*, ABA Commission on Women, Margaret Brent Women Lawyers of Achievement Award, Past Honorees, https://www.americanbar.org/groups/diversity/women/margaret-brent-awards/pasthonorees/?login.

6. Justice Petra Jimenez Maes

a. Formative Years

1970	B.A., Arts and Sciences, University of New Mexico
1973	J.D., University of New Mexico Law (UNM Law) Private practice
1975–1981	Legal Aid Attorney, North New Mexico Legal Services
1981–1998	Judge, First Judicial District, Santa Fe
1998–2018	Elected Justice, New Mexico Supreme Court Chief Justice, 1/2003–2004, 2012–2014[124]
2018	Retired
2022	Of Counsel, Engel Law Firm, P.C.

Petra was born on October 5, 1947, in Albuquerque to Santiago and Reyna Jimenez, the oldest of five children. Her maternal grandparents were born in Mexico. Petra chose law school because she wanted to help people. She recalled that upon sharing she wanted to be a lawyer with others, the common response was, "[y]ou're too short." Petra interpreted that as accurate statement since at the time, most lawyers were white, tall men and she was "short, brown and a female."[125] At the time she entered UNM Law in 1970, few Hispanics and women had been admitted to the law school. Consequently, some New Mexican Hispanics applied to schools out of state.[126] That optical began changing with her first year entering class. "There were 100 students, 12 Hispanics, eight women and eight Native Americans but no women or Hispanic law professors."[127] After meeting with women and Hispanic students (that included Petra), the dean hired Hispanic and female law professors: Anne Bingaman, Cruz Reynoso, who became California's first Latino Supreme Court Justice (1981–1986), and Leo Romero, who later became dean of UNM Law (1991–1997).[128] The pattern of breaking established norms became part of the justice's legal career.

At the age of thirty-three, Petra was appointed by Governor Bruce King to the district court in Santa Fe where she presided for seventeen years, from 1981 to 1998.

---

124. New Mexico Supreme Court Biographical Profile: Honorable Petra Jimenez Maes, https://web.archive.org/web/20110807092012/http://nmsupremecourt.nmcourts.gov/bios/maes.htm.

125. Judge Petra Maes, ABA 2012 Spirit of Excellence Award (ABA video), available at https://www.youtube.com/watch?app=desktop&v=kzWGB75RBCY.

126. The Luminarias Study found UNM Law graduated only eighteen Latinas over the hundred-year period of 1880–1980, *Luminarias Article, see* Appendix A.

127. *Supra* note 125 ABA video.

128. *A Conversation with Anne Bingaman*, March 2, 2021, UNLV Law School, https://law.unlv.edu/events/conversation-anne-bingaman; California Courts, Cruz Reynoso, https://www.courts.ca.gov/2916.htm; and *Civil Rights Leader Cruz Reynoso receives MALSA's Fighting for Justice Award,* April 27, 2016, https://lawschool.unm.edu/news/2016/04/malsa.html; Leo M. Romero CV, UNM School of Law, https://lawschool.unm.edu/faculty/romero/index.html.

Judge Jimenez Maes rotated assignments on the criminal, civil, and family divisions. For twelve of the seventeen years, she was a children's court judge. Early in her tenure in 1983, Judge Jimenez Maes's husband passed, leaving her to raise four children as a single parent.[129]

In June 1998 Judge Jimenez Maes won the Democratic election for the New Mexico Supreme Court seat, defeating incumbent Justice McKinnon III.[130] She prevailed in the November 1998 fall election and began her tenure on December 3, 1998. She was the first Latina justice and second woman on the bench, joining Justice Pamela Minzner. Justice Jimenez Maes joined two Hispanic justices, Joseph Baca and Patricio Serna, the three Latinos becoming the majority among the five justices. In 2002, Justice Maes was retained with 75% of the vote.[131] In 2010, she was retained to an eight-year term. On January 8, 2003, Justice Jimenez Maes was selected unanimously as the first Latina chief justice and served until 2005. Chief Justice Jimenez Maes served a second term from 2012 to 2014. From 2015 to 2018, Justice Maes served with Barbara J. Vigil (2012–2021) and Judith K. Nakamura (2015–2020), forming for the first time a female majority on the court.[132] During her second tenure as chief justice (2012–2014), the court developed major revisions to the procedural rules governing petitions for habeas corpus and post-conviction relief. In January 2015, the court adopted Rule 5-802 and implemented major revisions designed to (1) clarify the limits on post-conviction relief, (2) expand case processing options for district court judges and alter the process, including discovery, for petitioners seeking to vacate their convictions, and (3) adopt a new rule to clarify the relief available such as time limitations and the preclusion doctrines for such petitions.[133]

b. New Mexico Supreme Court, 1998–2018

During her tenure, Justice Jimenez Maes wrote the majority opinions in 151 cases (18 unreported), earning a reputation as the court's moderate justice. She often cast the dispositive vote between the reputed conservative and liberal justices. Reportedly, the justice voted 67% in favor of the state in criminal cases, and in civil cases, she ruled 69% in favor of individual rights.[134]

---

129. Of Counsel Petra Jimenez Maes, http://engellawsf.com/.

130. *Santa Fe Judge Gets Dem Nod to High Court*, Santa Fe New Mexican, June 3, 1998, https://www.newspapers.com/article/the-santa-fe-new-mexican-santa-fe-judge/135298973/.

131. New Mexico Official 2002 General Election Results by Office, https://web.archive.org/web/20081130191837/; http://www.sos.state.nm.us//Main/Elections/2002/02General/rsult019.HTM.

132. *Supreme Court Unveils Portraits of Chief Justices Barbara Vigil and Judith Nakamura*, Cibola Citizen, September 6, 2023, https://www.cibolacitizen.com/news/supreme-court-unveils-portraits-chief-justices-barbara-vigil-and-judith-nakamura; Supreme Court Justices of the State of New Mexico Since Statehood, https://supremecourt.nmcourts.gov/wp-content/uploads/sites/2/2024/01/Justices-since-statehood-for-new-webpage.pdf.

133. Max Minzner, *Habeas Corpus in New Mexico*, N.M. L.Rev. 43 (Winter 2016) at 45–48.

134. Ilana A. Eck, *Liberal behind The Label?: A Comparative High Court Case Study of the New Mexico Supreme Court from 1997–2002*, Alb. L. Rev. 66 (2003).

c. Majority Opinions in Criminal Cases

In criminal cases, Justice Jimenez Maes addressed issues of ineffective assistance of counsel, statute of limitations, expert witness fees, the new crime exception to the exclusionary rule, and the rule of lenity. In *Morales v. Bridgforth*, 100 P.3d 668 (2004), a conflict-of-interest issue arose from representation by different sections within the public defender office—the trial Public Defenders (PD) and the Post-Conviction Conflict Division (Division). The court rejected a *per se* disqualification rule based on a conflict of interest where the Division represents habeas petitioners who allege ineffective counsel by the PD's trial division, even if in the same office. Justice Jimenez Maes concluded such cases require a case-by-case analysis. In *State v. Brown*, 139 N.M. 466 (2006), the justice held that an indigent defendant represented by pro bono counsel is entitled to funding for expert witness fees from the state's PD in the same amount as if represented by that office. In *State v. Grogan*, 142 N.M. 107 (2007), Justice Jimenez Maes granted defendant's petition for writ of certiorari, on an issue of first impression. She held that the trial court did not abuse its discretion by finding ineffective assistance of counsel without holding an evidentiary hearing to allow the state to rebut allegations of ineffective assistance.

The novel suppression issue involving defendant Julian Ochoa underwent several court iterations before being resolved. Defendant Ochoa moved to suppress evidence retrieved from a stop for a seatbelt violation resulting in his arrest on outstanding warrants and drug trafficking investigations. Ochoa argued to the trial court that the stop was pretextual and moved to suppress the evidence. The trial court denied his motion to suppress, whereupon Ochoa entered a conditional guilty plea of possession of methamphetamine and drug paraphernalia (a pipe) and a handgun. The drug task force agent was the officer who testified Ochoa was not wearing a seatbelt, but the Artesia Police Officer had followed Ochoa for blocks and could not tell if Ochoa was wearing a seatbelt. He appealed the conviction. The New Mexico Court of Appeals reversed the trial court's denial of Ochoa's motion to suppress in *State v. Ochoa*, 140 N.M. 573, 144 P.3d 132 (2008) based upon the misdemeanor arrest rule but did not address the issue whether pretextual stops were prohibited by the state constitution. The State filed, and the New Mexico Supreme Court granted, the writ of certiorari. In *State v. Ochoa*, 143 N.M. 749, 182 P.3d 130 (2008), the New Mexico Supreme Court reversed and remanded. Justice Jimenez Maes relayed the court's ruling that the misdemeanor arrest rule requiring an offense be committed in a police officer's presence did not apply to officers making traffic or investigatory stops.[135] The high court certified to the New Mexico Court of Appeals the question whether the stop was pretextual and, if so, does the New Mexico Constitution, Article II, section 10 prohibit pretextual stops. In *State v. Ochoa*, 146 N.M.

135. For an in-depth analysis of the law on pretextual stops in New Mexico, *see Michael Sievers, State v. Ochoa: The End of Pretextual Stops in New Mexico?*, 42 N.M. L.Rev. 595 (2012). Sievers cites an interesting law review article penned by former SCOTUS Justice William Brennan urging state supreme courts to more closely evaluate such issues under their state constitutions, at 596, note 6.

32, 206 P.3d 143 (2008), the Court of Appeals (Judge Barbara Vigil writing for the majority), departed from federal law, rejecting the ruling in *Whren v. United States*, 517 U.S. 806 (1996) holding that if a police officer has probable cause to believe a traffic violation occurred, the stop is reasonable. The appellate court agreed with Ochoa that the state constitution provides greater (an extra layer of) protection than the Fourth Amendment and prohibits pretextual stops for traffic violations. The Court of Appeals reversed the district court's denial of defendant Ochoa's motion to suppress. The Supreme Court issued a second writ that eventually (after nearly a year) was quashed. Ochoa's case was over.

In *City of Las Cruces v. Sanchez*, 210 P. 3d 212 (2009), the district court granted defendant's motion to suppress evidence from a warrantless arrest for aggravated driving while under the influence of intoxicating liquor (DWI) because officers were not present at the time of the offense. Defendant and passenger had fled the scene by the time officers arrived within 5 to 10 minutes later. Officers found the passenger hiding who identified defendant as the driver. The officers verified the defendant-driver through his license/plates. Thereafter, the officers found the defendant with injuries consistent with a car bag deployment and obtained a breath test establishing intoxication. Based on these facts, Justice Jimenez Maes wrote the warrantless arrest was made with "reasonable promptness," and concluded the officers' presence at the time of the offense was not necessary for a warrantless arrest. The retroactive application of a statute of limitations was adopted in *State v. Morales*, 148 N.M. 305 (2010), a case involving defendant's aggravated sexual penetration of a child. At controversy was whether the abolishment of a fifteen-year statute of limitations for capital felonies and first-degree violent felonies prevented the prosecution of cases committed before the effective date of July 1, 1997. Justice Jimenez Maes wrote that the statute of limitations could be extended to unexpired limitation periods, reasoning that the extension does not impair any vested rights, require or impose new duties. The decision of the Court of Appeals was reversed, and the matter remanded back to the district court.

State v. Olsson, 324 P.3d 1230 (2014), involved the issue of units of prosecution in charging pornography. Defendant was convicted of six counts of possession of child pornography pursuant to NMSA 1978 § 30-6A-3 (2007). That section provides:

> It is unlawful for a person to intentionally possess any obscene visual or print medium depicting any prohibited sexual act or simulation of such an act if that person knows or has reason to know that the obscene medium depicts any prohibited sexual act or simulation of such act and if that person knows or has reason to know that one or more of the participants in that act is a child under eighteen years of age. A person who violates the provisions of this subsection is guilty of a fourth degree felony.

To determine the correct unit of prosecution, the court consolidated *State v. Ballard*, 276 P.3d 976 (2012), with *Olsson*, which also involved multiple counts of possession of pornography predicated on multiple documents and computer files. On appeal, both defendants argued they should be charged with only one unitary act of possession. The court agreed. Justice Jimenz Maes wrote that neither the statute nor the legislative history clearly defined the unit of prosecution, requiring application of the rule of lenity. "If there is no distinctness to the acts charged, then the rule of lenity applies, meaning 'doubt will be resolved against turning a single transaction into multiple offenses.'" *Olsson*, 324 P.3d at 1234. Concluding the "statutory language is insurmountably ambiguous," the court decided both defendants should be charged with only one count of possession. *Olsson*, 324 P.3d at 1239. The justice was consistent in her application of the lenity rule when she joined the majority in *State v. Montoya*, 306 P.3d 426 (2013). The court held double jeopardy protected the defendant against being punished for both voluntary manslaughter and causing great bodily harm by shooting at a motor vehicle when both charges were predicated on a unitary act of shooting the same victim. In reaching this conclusion, the court overruled other precedent and held the double jeopardy clause barred defendant's retrial on the first-degree felony murder charge.

The new crime exception to the exclusionary rule presented an issue of first impression in *State v. Tapia*, 414 P.3d 332 (2018). Defendant was a passenger in the back seat when the car was pulled over for driving forty miles per hour in a fifty-five-mile-per-hour zone and for unreadable plates. Determining defendant was not wearing a seat belt, the officer asked for his identity and defendant gave his brother's name and birthdate. A second passenger revealed the defendant's identity to another officer, whereupon defendant was arrested and charged with concealing identity, among other charges. Tapia entered a conditional plea of guilty to one count of forgery and was sentenced to eighteen months (mostly suspended). The Court of Appeals reversed Tapia's conviction, finding the subsequent charges were not sufficiently attenuated from the taint of the illegal stop and violated the Fourth Amendment of the New Mexico Constitution, Article II, § 10. The State petitioned for a writ of certiorari. Before the New Mexico Supreme Court, defendant asked the court to limit the exclusionary rule to cases where individuals endanger the safety of the police or the public, citing such holdings in other states, which the court distinguished.[136] Upon considering the factors enunciated in *Brown v. Illinois*, 422 U.S. 590, 603–604 (1975), Justice Jimenez Maes wrote that the exclusionary rule did not apply as a matter of federal and state constitutional law to the defendant's concealment of his identity. She wrote that the defendant's conduct was sufficiently attenuated between the initial stop and his false identification to render the exclusionary rule inapplicable to the newly acquired evidence and thus, was free of the taint of the unlawful seizure. The court upheld the suppression of the seat belt evidence but reversed the Court of Appeals, reinstating the forgery conviction.

---

136. *People v. Brown*, 345 Ill.App.3d 363, 280 Ill. Dec. 431, 802 N.E.2d 356 (2003), *State v. Badessa*, 185 N.J. 303, 885 A.2d 430 (2005), and *State v. Suppah*, 264 Or. App. 510, 334 P.3d 463 (2014).

The justice authored numerous opinions involving juveniles, including three issues of first impression. At issue in *State of New Mexico In the Matter of Damion M.C., v. Kathleen D.C.*, 157 P.3d 714 (2007), was the right to the appointment of an expert in an abuse and neglect adjudicatory proceeding. The mother was charged with the manual strangulation of her four-month-old son that resulted in severe brain damage, which she denied causing. The infant was in the mother's home and in the exclusive care of the mother's friend during most of the time that the child suffered the injuries. The state elicited expert witness testimony from a pediatrician at trial. The mother's *pro se* motions for a specialist were never addressed during representation by three successive court-appointed attorneys. The trial court found clear and convincing evidence that mother abused the infant. The mother argued on appeal that she was denied due process because the trial court failed to appoint a specialist. The Court of Appeals found the trial court "implicitly" denied the mother's motion for a specialist and held there was no due process violation because the mother presented no legal authority to support her right to a specialist. Justice Maes recognized the constitutional due process inherent in the fundamental liberty interest in the "care, custody and control of their children" and wrote that an indigent parent was entitled to the appointment of an expert at the state's expense, especially "where there is increased risk of deprivation of the parents' interest." *Damion M.C.*, 157 P.3d at 539–540. She concluded that the mother's right to an expert witness to present alternative causes of her son's death was impaired.

The use of a juvenile's fingerprints was at issue in *State v. Jade G.*, 154 P.3d 659 (2007), the second of two cases. Jade G. claimed she accidentally shot her father, but upon police belief that the shooting was intentional, charges of first-degree murder were filed. During the investigation a warrant was issued for Jade G.'s fingerprints, which matched the fingerprints on the gun. The State obtained inconsistent statements made by Jade G. to relatives and friends, before and after the shooting. At the delinquency hearing, her statements and fingerprints were suppressed pursuant to the Children's Code Basic Rights Act ("Act").[137] Jade G. argued her fingerprints should remain suppressed as they were obtained through a search warrant and not an explicit court order as required by the Act.[138] The Court of Appeals affirmed suppression of Jade G.'s statements, prompting the State to file an interlocutory appeal. On the issue of the fingerprint suppression, it remanded, *sua sponte*, the matter back to the Children's Court to ascertain the meaning of "alleged... to be a delinquent child."

---

137. NMSA 1978, § 32A-2-14(F) provides: "Notwithstanding any other provision to the contrary, no confessions, statements or admissions may be introduced against a child under the age of thirteen years on the allegations of the petition. There is a rebuttable presumption that any confessions, statements or admissions made by a child thirteen or fourteen years old to a person in a position of authority are inadmissible."

138. NMSA 1978, § 32A-2-14(I) states, "A child under the age of thirteen alleged or adjudicated to be a delinquent child shall not be fingerprinted or photographed for identification purposes without obtaining a court order."

The Court of Appeals reasoned that if Jade G. was not considered to be a delinquent child, the protections of the Act were inapplicable. The Supreme Court consolidated both appeals. Justice Jimenez Maes first addressed the issue raised by Jade G., concluding that the interlocutory appeal was properly before the court. By applying the plain language of the Act, the justice upheld the suppression of Jade G.'s statements. To resolve the fingerprint suppression, Justice Jimenez Maes addressed the propriety of the Court of Appeals' *sua sponte* question. As a matter of first impression, Justice Jimenez Maes wrote that the issue involved a matter of public interest such that would substantially impact investigatory procedures in future juvenile proceedings and thus was properly raised by the Court of Appeals. The justice agreed the question was pertinent. *Jade G.*, 154 P.3d at 667. She reasoned that the fingerprints were not properly suppressed because Jade G. was not alleged to be a delinquent child at the time her prints were taken, thus they were not subject to the Act's protections; stated otherwise, she ruled the Act applies only to those alleged to be delinquent, not merely suspected of being delinquent. Justice Maes concluded on behalf of the court that the Court of Appeals' remand on the fingerprint issue was in error.

To resolve whether the juveniles were properly charged in *State v. Steven B.*, 352 P.3d 1181 (2015), the justice was required to first determine whether the use of the land involved (on which the acts were committed) was used for a dependent Indian community. Two juvenile defendants were enrolled members of the Navajo Nation, and their cases were consolidated in this case of first impression. One juvenile was charged with battery on a school employee at Wingate High School and the second was charged with multiple counts of first-degree criminal penetration of a minor under thirteen years at the staff housing area of the Wingate school campus. The crimes were committed on Parcel Three of Fort Wingate ("Parcel Three"), land transferred by Congress to the U.S. Department of the Interior for use by the Bureau of Indian Affairs (BIA). Citing lack of subject matter jurisdiction based on a determination that Parcel Three was Indian land, the cases were dismissed by the trial courts and thereafter affirmed by the Court of Appeals. At issue before the court was whether Parcel Three constituted a dependent Indian community within the United States as so defined by 18 U.S. C. § 1151(b) (2012).[139] If so, the state courts lacked jurisdiction over crimes committed by Indians, including the defendants in Indian country. *State v. Steven B.*, at 1182. Parcel Three was found to be an independent Indian community in *State v. Dick*, 4 P.3d 36 (2000), and that it was not such a community in *United States v. M.C.*, 311 F. Supp. 2d 1281 (D.N.M. 2004). The State argued *Dick* should be overruled considering the federal district court's ruling in *United States v. M.C.* The court agreed *Dick* was wrongly decided and overturned it, holding Parcel Three was not Indian country. To determine what constitutes Indian land, Justice Jimenez Maes evaluated the facts under the two-part test enunciated in *Alaska v. Native Village of Venetie Tribe*, 522 U.S. 520 (1998): one the land was set aside by the

139. June 25, 1948, ch. 645, 62 Stat. 757; May 24, 1949, ch. 139, § 25, 63 Stat. 94.

federal government for the use of Indians as Indian land and two, the land must be under federal supervision. Conveying the court's rationale, Justice Jimenez Maes wrote that Parcel Three met the first prong of the test, that it was set aside by the federal government for the use of Indians as Indian land. *Steven B.*, 352 P.3d at 1184–1185. Upon an analysis of cases addressing the types of Indian lands and uses and drawing from legislative intent, Justice Jimenez Maes interpreted "'use' as occupancy associated with long-term settlement by an Indian community as envisioned by Congress when it enacted § 1151(b)..." *Steven B.*, 352 P.3d at 1191–1192. The justice wrote Parcel Three was used for the education of Indian children but that the housing on the parcel was used by Wingate School's staff and administrators. She concluded this latter use was not one of the three uses defined as Indian country—Indian reservations, dependent Indian communities, or Indian allotments—a conclusion supported by congressional legislative intent. *Steven B.*, 352 P.3d at 1193. The court reversed the dismissal of the charges against the juveniles, holding that the criminal acts were not committed on Indian land that was used for the long-term settlement of Indians.

In 2002, Justice Jimenez Maes wrote a separate dissent in a criminal case revealing a nuanced understanding of the law.[140] In *State v. Carbajal*, 48 P.3d 64 (2002), the state appealed the trial court's dismissal of two charges against defendant for forgery and receiving stolen property. The Court of Appeals reinstated the forgery count and defendant appealed. The majority on the high court reversed concluding the stipulated facts did not constitute forgery. Relying heavily on an interpretation of commercial paper, the court ruled that the *legal effect* of the traveler's check was not changed and, thus, no forgery was committed. In her dissent, Justice Jimenez Maes undertook a sophisticated evaluation of the "interface between commercial paper and criminal law." She concluded this perspective required contextualizing the "effect" of the act under the Uniform Jury Instruction 14-1643 NMRA 2002, with the criminal element and intent of falsely altering a document under NMSA 1978, § 30-16-10(A) (1963). Reconciling the two, she wrote, would sustain a forgery conviction. *Carbajal*, 48 P.3d at 69. The justice agreed with the Court of Appeals reinstatement of the forgery count.

d. Majority Opinions in Civil Cases

During the justice's tenure, the court addressed diverse issues of first impression arising in civil matters, including matters between the New Mexico Legislature and the governor. In *Smith ex rel. v. Martinez*, 265 P.3d 1276 (2011), the state legislature filed a writ of mandamus against Governor Susanna Martinez for a partial veto of the general appropriation line item for the mortgage finance authority, specifically scaling back the appropriation by striking $100,000 because she deemed it excessive.

---

140. In both cases, the first Luminaria attorney general in the country, Patricia Madrid (J.D. 1973 UNM Law), represented the state (1999–2007) before Justice Maes.

While acknowledging an exception to the separation of powers, namely the item-veto provision granted to New Mexican governors, Justice Jimenez Maes wrote the single partial veto was unconstitutional as the quasi-legislative function did not include partial vetoes of appropriation items. Soon thereafter, the court invalidated another partial appropriation in *State ex rel. Stewart v. Martinez*, 270 P.3d 96 (2011). The bill sought to address impending insolvency in the unemployment compensation fund by reducing benefits to the unemployed and increasing employer contributions beyond the contribution amount paid in 2011. Governor Martinez exercised a partial veto and struck one of the variables that was necessary to calculate employer contributions beginning in January 2012. Justice Jimenez Maes concurred with the majority that the governor's partial veto was an invalid exercise of authority. In *State ex rel. Cisneros v. Martinez*, 340 P.3d 597 (2014) (per curiam), the court next addressed whether two similar items of appropriation in a single general appropriation act required the veto of both items to accomplish an appropriate item veto, pursuant to the Appropriations Act, 2014 N.M. Laws, Chapter 63, §§1–14. At issue were two separate judicial pay increases passed by the New Mexico Legislature in two separate sections: a 5% increase for justices that included state judges but did not specify the increase as a pay raise in Section 4(B), and a 3% increase specifically for state judges in Section 8(A)(2). Governor Martinez vetoed both increases but left intact the appropriations language and the actual funding for the 5% increase that included the state judges. Governor Martinez challenged the legislature's method of funding salary increases for justices and judges without specifying it as such in the Appropriations Act, Section 4B. To avoid an appearance of conflict, Chief Justice Jimenez Maes and several justices recused themselves from the case resulting in the appointment, *pro tempore*, of four district court judges. So constituted, the court upheld the governor's veto of the 3% increase and concluded her veto of the 5% increase had no effect as the appropriations language and funding was left intact. Upon reviewing relevant state statutes and cases interpreting judicial pay, the court held that there was no law prohibiting the legislature from appropriating a judicial salary increase under these circumstances.

Justice Jimenez Maes wrote the majority opinion in three cases of first impression involving elections and appointments. In *Gunaji v. Macias*, 31 P.3d 1008 (2001), 66 votes on incorrect ballots plus 112 extra votes (that exceeded the total registered to vote) were cast in state and county elections. Unsuccessful state senate and county commissioner candidates sought declaratory judgment to overturn the election results. The district court granted summary judgment in favor of the successful candidates on the contested election claim. By the time the state Supreme Court ruled, the case was moot as the terms for the offices at issue—senate and county commissioner—had expired. Notwithstanding, the court held that the unsuccessful candidates had standing to raise the rights of third-party voters. The court deemed valid the claim that the election was not "free and open" and raised issues of substantial public interest capable of repetition such that judicial review was necessary. The court held a reelection was not appropriate. Justice Jimenez Maes wrote, "[t]o hold a new election would not be to capture the will of the electorate as it existed at the time of the contested election but would rather reflect an entirely different set of circumstances in terms of the composition of the electorate and the attractiveness of the candidates, making it an exercise in futility to try to replicate the election." *Gunaji*, 31 P.3d at 1016–1017. While the Election Code established the exclusive *procedure* for contesting election results, Justice Jimenez Maes wrote that the challenges and remedies are not exclusively within the Election Code, especially where there are gaps addressing constitutional infirmities. She concluded a declaratory action was proper to determine whether an election was free and open. *Gunaji*, 31 P.3d at 1018. The court held the proper remedy was rejecting the votes in the precinct with the irregular ballots, rather than holding a new election.

In *State ex re. New Mexico Judicial Standards Commission v. Espinosa*, 73 P.3d 197 (2003), members of the Judicial Standards Commission (Commission) filed an action in *quo warranto* seeking to stop newly installed Governor Bill Richardson from replacing six lay members with new appointees. Under New Mexico's Constitution, Article V, Section 5, the governor appoints and removes officers "unless otherwise provided by law." The governor appoints six of the eleven Commission members to stagnated five-year terms, one term expiring each year under Article VI, Section 32. At the time of the former governor's departure, none of the Commissioners' terms had expired.[141] No other governor had removed commission members in this manner.[142] The Supreme Court granted the Petitioners' stay, halting Commission business until the matter was decided. Petitioners argued that Article VI, Section 32 prohibited a Commissioner's removal before a term expired and that the governor's removal violated the separation of powers.[143] Justice Jimenez Maes conveyed the majority's agreement with Petitioners that Article VI, Section 32 did not create a mechanism by which the governor could remove Commissioners i.e., create vacancies through removals to appoint new members. The court rejected the governor's argument that he could remove officials "at will" creating involuntary vacancies, and case authority rejecting an implied right to remove appointees holding fixed terms where vacancies are defined. The court, nonetheless, upheld the Commissioners' removals. Justice Jimenez Maes and the majority defaulted and relied upon the generic authority of a governor to remove officials under Article V, Section 5. The

141. NMSA 1978 § 34-10-1(A); the remaining five are judges § 34-10-1(B) and lawyers subsection (C).

142. For a fuller discussion, *see* Kimberly Parmer-Bannerman, *State Ex Rel. New Mexico Judicial Standards Commission v. Espinosa*: Can Judicial Integrity Survive Executive Control, N.M. L. Rev. 34 (2004).

143. N.M. Const., Article III provides, "The powers of the government of this state are divided into three distinct departments, the legislative, executive and judicial, and no person or collection of persons charged with the exercise of powers properly belonging to one of these departments, shall exercise any powers properly belonging to either of the others, except as this constitution otherwise expressly directed or permitted."

constitutional genesis of the governor's power to appoint and remove state officers, the justice wrote, did not constitute a violation of the separation of powers.

Clark v. Mitchell, 363 P.3d 1213 (2015), was an action filed by a private citizen in *quo warranto* to remove Judge Albert Mitchell from the Tenth Judicial District. In 2008, Judge Mitchell won the contested election to the Tenth Judicial District, prevailing over Judge Donald Schutte. Though the Judicial Performance Evaluation Commission recommended Judge Mitchell's retention, he lost the 2014 retention election receiving a majority of the votes but not the requisite 57% of the vote. Judges Schutte and Mitchell applied for Judge Mitchell's vacancy. Governor Martinez appointed Judge Mitchell. Petitioner argued Judge Mitchell's appointment resulted in a retention of his office, which was prohibited by the constitution. Interpreting the New Mexico Constitution, Article VI, section 33, Justice Jimenez Maes distinguished between judicial retention (holding onto office without disruption) and judicial succession. She concluded the state constitution did not prohibit the governor from appointing a judicial candidate who lost his retention election as he was otherwise qualified to serve or succeed in office. *Clark*, 363 P. 3d at 1217–1218.

The court in *Faber v. King*, 348 P.3d 173 (2015), had to determine the type of damages awardable for violating the state's Inspection of Public Records Act (IPRA).[144] Attorney Daniel Faber represented three female assistant attorney generals in a federal gender pay equity discrimination lawsuit. The state Attorney General (AG) successfully moved to stay litigation, including discovery, pending resolution of his motion to dismiss. In his own name, Faber made an IPRA request of the AG's office for employment data on all attorneys employed since 1987. The AG refused (a fact not disputed), asserting the request circumvented the stay of discovery. The district court issued a writ of mandamus ordering the AG to comply. The attorney sought damages, which were awarded at $10 per day from the date of denial to the date the federal court stay was lifted and $100 per day until the records were provided plus costs. The AG appealed to the Court of Appeals, which held the damages award was governed by § 14-2-12(D),[145] which did not support an award and remanded the matter back to the district court to specify and measure the damages (punitive or compensable). Both parties appealed and the cases were consolidated. Justice Jimenez Maes decided, as a matter of first impression, that a determination of damages was proper under § 14-2-12(D). She wrote that the IPRA does not authorize an award of punitive damages, only compensatory damages, costs, and attorneys' fees associated with litigation to enforce a wrongfully denied IPRA request. The Court of Appeals was reversed.

---

144. NMSA 1978, §14-2-1(A) provides, "Every person has a right to inspect public records of this state." Sections 14-2-8 to -12 establish the timelines for responding to IPRA requests.

145. Section 14-2-12(D) provides the court "shall award damages, costs and reasonable attorneys' fees to any person whose written request has been denied and is successful in a court action to enforce the provisions of the" IPRA.

In *New Mexico Building and Construction Trades Council v. Dean*, 353 P.3d 1212 (2015), the court exercised original jurisdiction pursuant to the state constitution,[146] to resolve the "purely legal issue" whether the labor director violated the state's Public Works Minimum Wage Act (Act).[147] The court found the Act was violated by the labor director of New Mexico's Department of Workforce Solutions for failing to set prevailing wage and fringe benefit rates for public works projects as required by the collective bargaining agreements (CBAs). A writ of mandamus, necessitated by the director's failure to adjust rates since 2009, was issued by Justice Jimenez Maes, ordering the director to comply with the Act and set rates in accordance with CBAs within thirty days of the issuance of the writ.

Justice Jimenez Maes joined the unanimous ruling in *Griego v. Oliver*, 316 P.3d 865 (2013), legally recognizing same-sex marriage in New Mexico under the equal protection clause of the New Mexico Constitution, Article II, § 18.[148] On March 21, 2013, Rose Griego, her partner, and another lesbian couple filed a lawsuit in Albuquerque challenging the Bernalillo County clerk's refusal to issue them marriage licenses. The district court found the clerk's refusal unconstitutional and ordered Bernalillo and Santa Fe County clerks to issue marriage licenses to all same-sex couples; both complied. Later in August, New Mexico's thirty-three county clerks asked the state Supreme Court to rule on the legality of same-sex marriage. (The Supreme Court rejected an earlier request to consolidate and hear the lower court cases.) On behalf of the clerks, the New Mexico Association of Counties moved to intervene in *Griego* and filed a writ of superintending control requesting a uniform decision for all clerks to follow instead of waiting for adjudication of the cases and protracted appeals. In December, the Supreme Court held the equal protection clause guaranteed marriage rights to same-sex couples, becoming the seventeenth state in the country to recognize same-sex marriage. The ramifications were swift. The Roosevelt County clerk and chief deputy clerk resigned, asserting they were unable to comply with the court's ruling. A state senator proposed a joint resolution supporting a constitutional amendment defining marriage as "a union of one man and one woman." Governor Martinez publicly announced she would not support efforts to reverse the Supreme Court's decision. On March 1, 2019, the state Senate passed a bill (39–0) replacing all references to "husband and wife" in state statutes with the gender-neutral term "spouses." The House approved the legislation 62–0, and the bill was signed into law by Governor Michelle Lujan Grisham, effective July 1, 2019.

For the first time, Justice Jimenez Maes addressed New Mexico's statute of limitations under the Tort Claims Act and Wrongful Death Act. *Sam v. Sam*, 134 P.3d 761 (2006), required the court to determine whether, under the rule of comity, to apply

---

146. N.M. Const., Article VI § 3.

147. NMSA 1978 §§ 13-4-10 to -17 (1937, as amended through 2011).

148. The article states: "All rights, protections, and responsibilities that result from the marital relationship shall apply equally to both same-gender and opposite-gender married couples."

the sovereign immunity of another state pursuant to the Tort Claims Act of New Mexico and Arizona. Benny Sam, Jr. worked for Arizona's Window Rock Unified School District. While backing out of his driveway in Gallup, New Mexico, Sam ran over and killed his four-year-old son. The parties assumed Sam was acting in the course and scope of his employment as Sam was authorized to drive the School District's truck home for the weekend. Sam passed away and his widow sued on behalf of her son against Sam's estate and the Arizona School Retention Trust. Her suit was filed one day prior to expiration of New Mexico's three-year statute of limitations for general torts actions under NMSA 1978 § 37-1-8 (1976). New Mexico's two-year statute of limitations for actions against governmental entities barred the widow's suit. Arizona required notice of claim within 180 days after the cause of action under its one-year statute of limitations. Ariz. Rev. Stat. Ann. § 12-821.01(A). The district court granted summary judgment to the defendants ruling the widow's action was barred by the New Mexico and Arizona Tort Claims Acts. The Court of Appeals reversed holding New Mexico's three-year statute of limitation was the applicable statute because, 1) the law of the place where the tort occurred was controlling, 2) Sam was not employed by New Mexico, and 3) New Mexico was not required to recognize Arizona's Tort Claims Act. Petitioner-defendants argued a comity analysis was warranted under the facts. The court agreed and extended a limited grant of immunity to Arizona. Justice Jimenez Maes wrote that New Mexico's statute of limitations did not violate public policy, and the ruling would prevent some forum shopping.

In *Estate of Brice v. Toyota Motor Corporation*, 373 P.3d 977 (2016), Justice Jimenez Maes and the court evaluated the impact of defendant's fraudulent concealment under the three-year statute of limitations in the Wrongful Death Act (WDA).[149] In 2006, Alice Brice's Toyota Camry accelerated onto a highway and collided with a tractor-trailer, causing her death when the car erupted into flames. Eleven months past the statute of limitations, her estate filed suit against the car manufacturer, the dealer, and others. Defendants moved for dismissal. The estate argued the limitations period was equitably tolled by defendants' fraudulent concealment of the acceleration problem in its vehicles for the decade preceding 2010 and before Alice's death that led to congressional hearings. The estate claimed it filed its lawsuit after learning of the defect. The district court dismissed the action, and upon the estate's filing of an appeal, the Court of Appeals certified the question to the court. Noting New Mexico's adoption of the common law doctrine of fraudulent concealment (involving a defendant's willful, deceitful conduct), Justice Jimenez Maes clarified the

149. NMSA 1978, §§ 41-2-1 (1882, as amended through 2001), provides: "Whenever the death of a person shall be caused by the wrongful act, neglect or default of another, although such death shall have been caused under such circumstances as amount in law to a felony, and the act, or neglect, or default, is such as would, if death had not ensued, have entitled the party injured to maintain an action and recover damages in respect thereof, then, and in every such case, the person who, or the corporation which, would have been liable, if death had not ensued, shall be liable to an action for damages, notwithstanding the death of the person injured."

interplay with equitable estoppel and concluded it also tolled the statute of limitations. The justice rejected defendants' argument that the court rely on the "historically strict application" of the WDA's statute of limitations and distinguished the court's cases on which they relied. She wrote, "It is consistent with the purpose of the WDA to toll the statutory limitations period where a defendant has fraudulently concealed the cause of action. Put another way, allowing a defendant to conceal a cause of action and then assert the statute of limitations as a defense would be contrary to the intent behind the WDA.... Indeed, we will neither sanction fraud nor presume the Legislature intended to do so by allowing a party to conceal a wrong until the statute of limitations has run and then benefit from the deception." *Brice*, 373 P.2d at 985. Justice Jimenez Maes concluded the doctrine of fraudulent concealment applies to the WDA's statute of limitations.

e. Conclusion

Justice Jimenez Maes retired on December 31, 2018, when her term expired. For her groundbreaking career, the justice received numerous honors, including from her alma mater, the University of New Mexico Law School (2003), and the ABA's Commission on Racial and Ethnic Diversity Spirit of Excellence Award (2012).[150] She became of counsel with a local law firm where she practices appellate law. The former justice is a member of the American Law Institute and other bar-related committees and associations.

7. Justice Liana Fiol Matta

a. Formative Years

1967	B.A., English Literature, Trinity Washington University
1970	J.D., *magna cum laude*, University of Puerto Rico (UPR) Law, Law Review Editor
1970–1972	Legal Advisor, Institute for Consumer Problems Research, UPR
1973	Special Assistant to the Puerto Rican Governor
1973–1975	Associate Commissioner, Public Service Commission
1975–1977	Legal Adviser and Assistant Secretary, Department of Consumer Affairs
1978–1987	Associate Law Professor: Inter American University School of Law (1978–1981) Pontifical Catholic University School of Law (1982–1987)
1988	LL.M., Columbia University
1988–1990	Advisor to Governor of Puerto Rico, Planning and Natural Resources, Women's Rights

150. *Supra* note 125 ABA video; 2003 UNM Zia Award, 2020 induction into Chief Justices Hall of Fame.

1992–2004	Judge, Court of Appeals of Puerto Rico
1996	Doctor of Science in Law, Columbia University
1996–2003	Lecturer Professor, UPR Law
1996–2002	Administrative Judge, Circuit Court of Appeals of Puerto Rico
2004	Associate Justice, Puerto Rico Supreme Court: Liana Fiol Matta
2004–2016	Associate Justice, Puerto Rico Supreme Court Chief Justice 2014–2016[151]

Liana was born on October 20, 1946, in Rio Piedras, Puerto Rico, to Juan Fiol Bigas and Emma Matta De Fiol. Juan was a laborer. Emma received a university education and worked as an administrator at the University of Puerto Rico. Liana spent a part of her childhood where her father was stationed in Arkansas and in El Paso where she experienced and witnessed discrimination. In giving life to Liana, Juan and Emma birthed *"a woman hungry for reasons"* which she searched for and explored throughout her legal career. On September 15, 2021, Liana was presented with the Nilita Vientós Gastón Medal by the Puerto Rico Bar Association. (A distinguished *Luminaria,* Nilita was the first woman hired in 1945 by the Department of Justice in Puerto Rico as an Assistant Attorney General and, therefore, the country). In that acceptance speech, Liana gave us a glimpse of her essence that was reflected in her impressive literary legal work. She wrote,

> I have always perceived many coincidences between Nilita's thinking and my own, therefore, I am honored that this medal bears the name of this peerless intellectual, lover and defender of our culture, brave lawyer and fighter against everything that offended human dignity, whom Dr. Carmen Centeno Añeses called the *Thinker of the Nation.* I first learned about Nilita in my teenage years. I lived with my grandmother at the time and with her I went to places that were of no interest to my friends or cousins my age; one of those places was the theater. One day, while I was waiting for the curtain to go up on some play at the Tapia Theater, I saw a woman dressed all in white. I don't know if she waited until the last moment to enter on purpose, but suddenly, as if the curtain had gone up, she made her triumphant entrance down the central aisle, to the rhythm of the audience's whispers. I then sensed that this was someone important, someone who didn't need an introduction. That's why my grandmother thought it was enough to tell me, "It's Nilita Vientós," without further ado, when I asked who she was. I got to know her better years later, although not personally, rather I got to know the character she had decided to play in the play of her life. But let's not be mistaken, the great thing about the work

151. The biographical summary is derived from multiple sources, including the justice's resume, the Puerto Rico Supreme Court (https://poderjudicial.pr/eng/supreme-court/biographies-of-former-chief-justices/#fiol), and Trinity Washington University (https://discover.trinitydc.edu/media/2014/11/13/hon-liana-fiol-matta-chief-justice-supreme-court-puerto-rico-trinity/).

of art that was Nilita is that she never stopped being the character she played. She was not an actress who, at the end of the play, takes off her makeup and puts on her costume to leave the dressing room and be someone else. Nilita's art was being Nilita. And who was Nilita? Why did I find her so intriguing? In an article I published in 1992, I summed it up like this: Nilita Vientós Gastón was a true intellectual. She questioned everything, nothing was obvious to her. She was, as a journalist said on the occasion of her death, a woman hungry for reasons.[152]

Like Article III Judge Christine Arguello, Liana is one of few Luminarias who was a law professor before ascending to the bench. For nine years, from 1978 to 1987, Associate Professor Fiol Matta taught at two of the island's law schools. She focused on environmental conservation and women's rights which led to the enactment of legislation for which she was honored in 1975 by the Puerto Rico Bar Association. The professor became a jurist when she was appointed to serve on the Puerto Rico Court of Appeals. During her twelve-year tenure (1992–2004), Judge Fiol Matta served on the Supreme Court's Commission on Gender Discrimination in the Courts (1993–1995), presided over by Justice Naveira de Rodón. In 2002, she chaired a judicial committee that published the report, "Judicial Education for the 21st Century." The report led to the creation of the Puerto Rico Judicial Academy in 2003. Judge Fiol Matta became the first dean of the academy and chair of its academic board. Since 2002, she has been a member of the Puerto Rican Academy of Jurisprudence and Legislation.

Judge Fiol Matta is a prolific writer, authoring at least thirty-one law review articles on topics as diverse as environmental law, gender discrimination in the courts, credit law guarantees, the moral basis of contracts, divorce, legal method and transculturation, and administrative regulation, as well as on individual lawyers. The justice has focused some of her writings on women, such as *On Teaching Feminist Jurisprudence*, 57 Rev. Jur. UPR 253 (1988), *Gender Discrimination in the Courts: Theoretical Framework and Fundamental Concepts*, 61 Rev. Col. Abog. 78 (July–September 2002), *Women in the Judiciary: Assessment of the Process of Award*, 79 Rev. Jur. UPR 957 (2010), and *Nilita Vientós Gastón: Passionate about Truth and Justice*, 61 Rev. Jur. UPR 201 (1992).[153] She also is a singer, poet and opera lover.

b. Puerto Rico Supreme Court, 2004–2016

Governor Sila Calderón appointed Judge Fiol Matta to the Supreme Court on February 19, 2004, as the second woman justice, effectively succeeding Naveira de Rodón. Fourteen years later, on April 11, 2014, Governor Alejandro García Padilla

152. Liana Fiol Matta Acceptance Speech, NILITA VIENTÓS GASTÓN: MUJER PARADIGMÁTICA, September 15, 2021. The Luminarias Study ascertained Nilita was the first Latina Assistant Attorney General in the country.

153. Justice Fiol Matta Resume, https://www-academiajurisprudenciapr-org.translate.goog/academicos-de-numero/liana-fiol-matta/?_x_tr_sl=es&_x_tr_tl=en&_x_tr_hl=en&_x_tr_pto=sc.

nominated her as the sixteenth chief justice of the Puerto Rico Supreme Court. She was unanimously approved by the Puerto Rican Senate on May 22, 2014, and served as chief justice until 2016.[154] That year, she was elected to the Standing Commission on Gender and Access of the Ibero-American Judicial Summit that develops projects and proposals to promote gender perspective within the various judicial branches. As was the situation with Justice Naveira de Rodón, Justice Fiol Matta's cases were issued in Spanish. The discussion is from the English translations of her cases.

c. Majority Opinions

Justice Fiol Matta, who participated in over 100 cases during her tenure, became known as one of the leading liberal voices on the court—as much (if not more) for her dissents as majority opinions. Whether majority opinion or dissents, the justice's writings constitute colorful, oftentimes passionate, discourses on the subject at hand. Justice Fiol Matta's decisions—while thorough, articulate and well-reasoned—are profound and present the opportunity to observe juridical analysis through the lens of a unique Latina-Americana scholar. The justice succeeded Federico Hernández Denton as Chief Justice (Chief Justice 2003–2014, tenure 1985–2014) who also was a law professor. Though they did not agree on every case, they joined in a number of each other's dissents, together providing dynamic dissections of the law with universal morality and principles embraced and embedded into their decisions. *See e.g.* the employment layoff cases of *Dominguez Castro v. E.L.A.*, 178 D.P.R. 1, 2010 PR Sup. LEXIS 3 (February 2, 2010) and 178 D.P.R. 375, 2010 PR Sup. LEXIS 19 (February 19, 2010).

In *Colón Perez v. Televicentro de P.R.*, 175 D.P.R. 690, 2009 PR Sup. LEXIS 74, the justice on behalf of the majority was required to "weigh the right to freedom of expression, a fundamental democratic principle, against the personal and non-transferable right to honor" to determine the bases of action for defamation. *Colón Perez,* 175 D.P.R. at 696–697. The plaintiff's image was used by Televicentro while airing information about bank fraud, not committed by the plaintiff. The Court of First Instance partially granted plaintiffs' motion for summary judgement, ruling the plaintiff's image was published without authorization or consent (libel by association) and did not constitute negligence; damages were left to be decided. The Court of Appeals upheld the lower court's ruling except the use of image claim as plaintiff failed to plead this cause of action. Televicentro appealed. Justice Fiol Matta reviewed the development of the right to honor or reputation relative to the freedom of expression dating back to Roman civil laws and the "action of boasting of the Partidas law of Alfonso X the Wise." *Colón Perez,* 175 D.P.R. at 702. She took judicial notice that sovereignty over Puerto Rico was transferred in 1898 from Spain to the United States and wrote, "[s]ince then our law has been subject to a process of adaptation to Anglo-American law known as 'Americanization.' It is in this context that the Legislative

154. *Supra* note 151, Justice Fiol Matta's biography.

Assembly of Puerto Rico adopted, in 1902, the Libel and Slander Law (1902 Law), in which the basic features of the Anglo-Saxon common law that governed defamation claims at that time were codified. Law of February 19, 1902, 32 LPRA sec., 3141–3149." *Colón Perez,* 175 D.P.R. at 702. Libel actions required a showing of malicious intent which *Romany v. El Mundo*, 89 D.P.R. 604 (1963) changed by recognizing a libel action for private persons under article 1802 of the 1930 Puerto Rico Civil Code (Civil Code) that required showing a lesser degree of fault than that required of a public figure plaintiff. The justice concluded that the 1902 Law was not applicable to the instant case in accordance with the ruling in *Cortés Portalatín v. Hau Colón*, 103 D.P.R. 734 (1975) and its progeny. The justice noted that under the tenure of Justice Trías Monge in the 1970s, the Puerto Rico Supreme Court "made efforts to revitalize [its] civil law tradition and other indigenous sources of the Puerto Rican legal system." *Colón Perez*, 175 D.P.R. at 705. Quoting Trías Monge she wrote,

> It was recognized that the action for defamation arises from the right to honor or reputation contained in our Constitution, which in turn comes from the American Declaration of the Rights and Duties of Man and the Universal Declaration of the Rights of Man: [Being a right with] aspirations of universality, distilled from very diverse legal systems, the world that is offered to us for its fair interpretation is wide. One is not bound by specific sets of historical rules. The obligation is to abide by the constitutional mandate, in consonance with other provisions of our primary law and the realities of the country. *Colón Perez* 175 D.P.R. at 706, citing *Cortés Portalatín*, 103 D.P.R. at 738–39.

As a practical matter, this legal-theoretical construct included rejecting multiple causes of action recognizing instead, only one cause of action per issue or publication. The Puerto Rico Supreme Court thus adopted the native law on forums which requires a libel case to "be heard in the district corresponding to the domicile of the plaintiff, since it was there that the cause of the litigation had the greatest scope." *Colón Perez* 175 D.P.R. at 706. Recognizing the precedential importance of the "federal Supreme Court," the justice wrote that the Puerto Rico Supreme Court's caselaw evolution included an integration of American law adopted in *New York Times Co. v. Sullivan*, 374 U.S. 254 (1964) and *Gertz v. Robert Welch*, 418 U.S. 323 (1941) and progeny with a caveat: such jurisprudence "only has persuasive value." *Colón Perez*, 175 D.P.R. 114. Against this backdrop, the justice affirmed that the Civil Code was controlling in libel cases. She concluded there was insufficient causality, however, between Televicentro's actions (the telecast of plaintiff's face was momentary with no name associated thereto) and alleged damages to the plaintiffs. The case was dismissed.

At issue in the case of first impression, *Ramirez Sainz v. Cabanillas*, 177 D.P.R. 1, 2009 PR Sup. LEXIS 152, was whether to adopt the common law doctrine of forum non conveniens, there being no legislation or jurisprudence in Puerto Rico on the doctrine. Under this doctrine, a court may dismiss a case, even where it has jurisdiction, where another court is more convenient for the parties and the litigation. The case involved the collection of attorney's fees for professional services on a fee-sharing basis between parties who were domiciled in the Dominican Republic and Ramirez Sainz, a Puerto Rican lawyer. The agreement transpired in the Dominican Republic and the property used to guarantee the debt also was in the Dominican Republic. As liquid assets were not available, Ramirez Sainz executed and obtained certificate of title on the property in the Dominican Republic through a management company. When a controversy arose over the title, Ramirez Sainz filed suit to recover unpaid fees and eventually two motions for summary judgment. The second motion for summary judgment was filed after the Dominican Republic Land Court resolved the registration in favor of the defendant thus enabling Ramirez Sainz to pursue collection from the foreclosed property. Defendant appealed to the Court of Appeals asserting the doctrine of forum non conveniens. The Court of Appeals reversed the summary judgement and remanded it back to the Court of First Instance to determine the most convenient forum. Defendant appealed. In harmonizing private international law with comparative law that includes long-arm statutes and after reviewing the common laws of Scotland, England, Australia, Canada the U.S., the law of Louisiana, the Hague Convention and Romano-Germanic traditions, the justice articulated rules for incorporating and applying the doctrine. She concluded the Court of First Instance has the discretion to determine whether a lawsuit may be suspended and that such decisions are reviewable by the appellate courts under the standard of abuse of discretion. Applying the newly adopted ruling, Justice Fiol Matta wrote that jurisdiction in Puerto Rico was proper, that the Court of Appeals correctly reviewed the trial court's decision and that the matter should proceed to trial.

Rentas Santiago v. Autogermana, Inc., 182 D.P.R. 759, 2011 PR Sup. LEXIS 132, involved a retaliation claim filed by the petitioner pursuant to the Employer Retaliation Action Act, 29 LPRA sec. 194(a) *et seq.*[155] Petitioner was terminated after she visited the State Insurance Fund Corporation ("Fund") to obtain workers' compensation benefits. The Court of Appeals dismissed her case, and Justice Fiol Matta wrote the opinion finding the dismissal was in error. The justice concluded the petitioner presented a prima facie case that she was dismissed only after she filed her claim for benefits but that the employer failed to overcome her evidence. That same year in another employment case of constructive discharge, the justice wrote the majority opinion addressing the shifting burden of proof in cases involving the Unjustified Dismissal Law, Law No. 80 (May 30, 1976), commonly known as the Wrongful Dismissal Act (Act). In *A. Rivera Figueroa v. The Fuller Brush*, 180 D.P.R. 894, 2011 PR Sup. LEXIS 23, the employee claimed he was pressured to become an independent contractor and endured a hostile environment before being constructively discharged. The Act created a presumption that dismissals are unjustified, placing the burden of proof on employers. Before the Court of First Instance, the employer filed and was granted its motion to dismiss on the grounds that the employee failed to

155. Law No. 115 of September 20, 1991 (as amended).

establish constructive discharge. The Court of Appeals affirmed the lower court's decision, emphasizing the employee's duty to first establish constructive discharge. The justice started by defining the importance of work as contributing to the "common good and self-actualiz[ation]" of people that, thereby, has a "transcendental social function both at the individual and the professional level." She next discussed the imbalance between employer and employee which gave rise to the Act. The justice confirmed that the burden of proof initially was on the employer, not the employee. *Rivera Figueroa*, 180 D.P.R. 902, 904 (citations omitted). Notwithstanding, Justice Fiol Matta recognized the threshold requirement of establishing an adverse action, a discharge—constructive or otherwise—that needed to be shown by the employee which she concluded was not met here. The justice rejected employee's claim that the mere assertion of constructive discharge met the statutory requirements and further, found the employee failed to produce sufficient evidence of constructive discharge.

Díaz Lizardi v. Aguayo Leal, 162 D.P.R. 801, 2004 PR Sup. LEXIS 142, involved a case of unjust enrichment stemming from a division of community property owned by an unmarried couple. The parties dated for years and purchased the residence in 1996 with the relationship ending in 1998. From December 1998 to August 2003, Aguayo Leal paid the entire monthly mortgage, totaling $33,656. The trial court credited Aguayo the entire amount. He eventually moved into the residence in 1999 with his wife. Mrs. Díaz Lizardi appealed asserting Aguayo should not have received credit for full mortgage payments during the time she was prohibited from using the residence. The Court of Appeals denied Díaz Lizardi's appeal, concluding she had not been deprived of her participation in the residence, and emphasized Aguayo's payments on the mortgage. Justice Fiol Matta wrote the facts triggered the issue of unjust enrichment, "namely whether one community member must compensate the other for the exclusive use of assets that they acquired in common pro indiviso, once the courtship relationship that gave rise to the acquisition ha[d] been dissolved." *Díaz Lizardi*, 162 D.P.R. at 17. The high court ruled that because Mr. Aguayo possessed the communal property and used it for his exclusive benefit without the consent of Mrs. Díaz,, she deserved compensation for the period of December 1999 to August 2003. She further wrote that Díaz Lizardi was due credit for furniture she purchased, and that Aguayo used during the same period. The matter was remanded to the trial court to determine the value of the exclusive use of the residence and furniture by Aguayo and the corresponding compensation owed to Díaz Lizardi.

d. Dissents

Justice Fiol Matta wrote no less than forty-six dissenting opinions on issues as diverse as legislative amendments, commerce, employee rights and student protests. She also penned six additional dissents and concurring opinions and joined several dissents issued by Justice Hernández Denton and others. The justice's dissents reveal a skillful sculptress who eloquently defines the legal issues with such precision, authority and persuasiveness that the majority seemingly is provoked into reflexive commentary —at times ascribing extreme interpretations that exceed the express words and objections of Justice Fiol Matta.

This pattern is probably best encapsulated by a case of first impression involving the doctrine of academicity and the exception of voluntary cessation within the context of the First Amendment, *UPR v. Laborde Torres*, 180 DPR 438, 2010 PR Sup. LEXIS 230. This case involved student protests at the University of Puerto Rico (University) involving tuition and special fees that resulted in disruption on campus and minor violence by a small group of student protestors, a fact conceded by the court's majority. Through an intrajurisdictional certification request the University asked the Supreme Court to review a ruling by the Court of First Instance (the Superior Chamber of San Juan). The students caused a 48-hour strike and chained the gates to the Rio Piedras Campus. "Hooded individuals" struggled with University security guards and chained the gates and incidents of violence were reported on and off campus. The University Rector declared an indefinite academic recess believing the University had lost control of access to the campus. The lower court initially granted a preliminary injunction and ordered the parties to mediation that resulted in an agreement, certified and signed by the University's Board of Trustees which it approved. The Court of First Instance determined the claim had become academic. A controversy may become academic when its live condition ceases due to the passage of time. Under this circumstance, the students are released from all judicial action. The University believed the dispute remained alive, since the students approved a preventive strike vote at an assembly, i.e., their behavior had not changed. The University filed a motion for a permanent injunction, a possessory injunction, and a cease-and-desist order pursuant to Article 277 of the Code of Civil Procedure, 32 LPRA sec. 2761, against several student leaders, including Gabriel Laborde Torres, President of the General Student Council. Essentially, the University asked for an order directing the cessation of all actions by students that impeded free access to the campus. The students argued that this remedy was a severe impairment of their right to free expression pursuant to Section 4 of Article II of the Constitution of Puerto Rico. Some of the students' counterclaimed the University's publication of their confidential documents and alleged abuse of judicial procedures. The students asserted that the dispute at issue was resolved through the mediation process, culminating in the agreement. They argued all causes of action were academic, "patently speculative," except for the damages which remain before the Court of First Instance.

First noting the frequency and long history of student protests at the University, the majority discussed the doctrine of academicity that seeks to: (1) avoid unnecessary use of judicial resources; (2) ensure that there is sufficient adversity for disputes to be brought and defended competently and vigorously; and (3) avoid unnecessary precedents. An academic case is one that seeks "to obtain a ruling on a disguised controversy, which does not in fact exist, or a determination of a right before it has been asserted, or a judgment on a matter which, when rendered, for some reason cannot have practical effect on an existing controversy." *Laborde Torres*, 180 D.P.R. at

281. Exceptions are: (1) a recurring or reoccurring issue; (2) when the factual situation has been changed by the defendant but is not likely to be permanent; or (3) when collateral consequences remain that are still current and relevant. The majority concluded the students' behavior had not changed citing the strike vote, a peaceful assembly and the remaining special fee issue while simultaneously acknowledging the University's position that it was operating normally, the mediation and the agreement. The Court characterized the students' arguments as a "subterfuge to evade judicial review." *Laborde Torres,* 180 D.P.R. at 265. Stated otherwise, the Court concluded the case was not academic because it projected the students' behavior would persist, was not temporary with the threat remaining and, therefore, did not fall into the exception of voluntary cessation. The Supreme Court held the University may regulate the time, place, and manner in which students engage in protected expression activities on campus, provided that such regulations: (1) are neutral as to the content of the expression and do not absolutely prohibit protesters from expressing their views; (2) are narrowly tailored so as not to substantially disrupt or impair university activities or violate the rights of all members of the university community; and (3) do not impede alternative means of communication. *Laborde Torres,* 180 D.P.R. at 320. The Court of First Instance was reversed.

Justice Fiol Matta profoundly disagreed with the majority opinion approving a broad injunction against all students without limitation to student protestors at the University who engaged in disruptive behavior and violence. The majority opinion began with the following:

> The constitutional guarantee of liberty implies the existence of an organized society maintaining order, without which liberty itself would be lost in the excesses of anarchy.... The dissenting opinion of my esteemed and distinguished colleague Fiol Matta seems to ignore such a notorious reality. That is why I now express my fundamental concerns regarding the practical implications that her presentation could have on our democratic society of law and order. Specifically, I will examine two basic elements of her opinion, namely: (1) the use of a discourse that does not recognize any border or limit to the right to freedom of expression of students, which tacitly legitimizes the violent acts of a minority group of university students under the pretext of exercising a demonstration that materializes 'the social discontent' that they experience due to "the tensions arising from the economic-social context of the country"; and (2) the confusion of the main mission of the University—to be a house of study—with one of its many accessory missions—to provide spaces for student participation that promote the development of the moral personality of the student body—thus justifying that, in order to achieve the accessory missions of the University, the attainment of its main objective is harmed.... [Fiol Matta's dissent is] an unrestricted recognition of the right to freedom of expression that tacitly endorses the violence of a small group of students and destroys the rights of those who wish to study. *Laborde Torres,* 180 D.P.R. at 466–467.

Due to the time constraints adopted by the majority, Justice Fiol Matta issued a second detailed dissent at *Laborde Torres*, 180 D.P.R. 438 (2010). Her primary objection to the injunction issued by the majority was its sweeping language encompassing all students that was devoid of any restrictions, i.e., it was not narrowly proscribed to address the problem. She wrote, "[t]he danger presented by the inclusive language used by the majority in the case before us is evident. This language encompasses 'students' in a general way and without any criteria. In this way, it opens the door for any student of the university community to become a violator of the injunction, if it is granted, by the mere fact of exercising his right to demonstrate." *Laborde Torres*, 180 D.P.R. at 441. She further wrote:

> The decision from which I dissent is historic, primarily because of the lack of consistency between the dispute raised by the appeal and the Court's statements. The result has been an opinion that, in its eagerness to control the outcome of the proceedings that will take place at the first instance level, has imposed guidelines on that forum that are both inappropriate and ambiguous. That same objective has turned the majority of the Opinion into an unprecedented *dictum*. (Emphasis hers.)
>
> The majority opinion is based on the classic view of the University as a "house of learning." However, a true "house of learning" does not store ideas on shelves or recognize only those in its catalog. Therefore, although I agree that the primary mission of the University is to be a "house of learning," I am surprised that this serves as justification for the authoritarian and repressive tone with which the Opinion analyzes student rights and the prerogatives of the Administration. We do not agree with the expressions of the majority regarding the negative effect of student demonstrations. For the majority, university protests create controversies among the ranks of our first educational center and generate great tension in Puerto Rico. This analysis ignores the possibility that the demonstrations, rather than causing unrest, are the result of social discontent. More importantly, it ignores the nature of the University as a center for the exchange of ideas that, by its very function, fosters dynamic relationships among its members that often transcend the verbal and even the physical plane of our first educational center. This is testament to the University as a 'center of ebullition, of irradiation of values and of circulation of crucial claims in our life as a people.' [cite omitted] Therefore, to say that acts of student expression trigger sui generis the general unrest of our People is irresponsible...Nor is the restrictive educational vision that subjects students to a position of passivity correct. *Laborde Torres*, 180 D.P.R. at 440, 452.

Though Justice Fiol Matta's dissent was issued twenty-five years ago, it remains instructive and relevant, resonating perhaps because of the upheaval caused to universities throughout the country by the current administration's pressure and attempt to quell student protests. The juxtaposition of the freedom of speech and association and government restraints on these constitutional rights will, no doubt, generate future interesting expressions of law on the mainland and on the Island.

Invoking Plato ("freedom is being the owner of one's own life") and the renowned writer Octavio Paz ("[w]ithout freedom there is no such thing as a person," from The Double Flame), Justice Fiol Matta objected to the majority's decision in *Salva Santiago v. Torres Padro,* 171 D.P.R. 332, 2007 PR Sup. LEXIS 91. The majority refused to recognize "irreparable breakdown" (irreconcilable differences) as a ground for divorce unless the divorce petition was jointly filed. As authority, the majority cited *Figueroa Ferrer v. Commonwealth of Puerto Rico*, 107 D.P.R. 250 (1978). *Figueroa Ferrer* allowed citizens to divorce without expressing reasons only by mutual consent in a sworn petition. The majority found no other basis in law permitting irreconcilable differences as a ground for divorce when filed by one spouse. The justice rejected the majority's rationale that a non-contentious proceeding was required because the ground was not properly adopted in jurisprudence or recognized in legislation in accordance with the right of privacy. In his concurring option, Justice Fuster Berlinger wrote:

> Personal autonomy is ordinarily exercised in the most complete way precisely when a human being decides to bind himself to another in marriage, with the privileges and responsibilities that this entails. The authentic marital bond supposes a decision by each of the spouses to live **a life together,** seeking in this endeavor the fullness of their own life. But then integral personal development becomes a common search in which each of the spouses commits his or her personal autonomy to achieving the integral development of the other. Therefore, the essence of the marriage bond is reciprocity. Of course, the project of a common life is not easy to implement, and often results in failure. At that moment, however, when what seems to be an irreparable break-up occurs, the essential vow of reciprocity, taken at the time of marriage, still persists morally and legally. Therefore, the decision to dissolve the marriage bond **must necessarily be made by both spouses,** if it is to have any appearance of success. [Emphasis his.]

Justice Fiol Matta wrote:

> In declaring my dissent, I am guided by the continuing and manifest need to calibrate our private rights to the transformations of contemporary society. The controversy that we must resolve today involves one of the fundamental rights of the human being within a liberal and democratic society. We are talking about the right to not have the state interfere in the making of certain types of decisions pertaining to marital and family intimacy, whether by imposing a[n] undue burden on those who wish to exercise their rights, or eliminating the appropriate means for the realization of personal will. We refer to the right of every human being to develop freely within the family environment and to make the decision to dissolve a voluntary bond or association

> such as marriage. Finally, today we have to express ourselves on the recognized freedom that every person enjoys in a democratic society to develop existentially. *Salva Santiago,* 171 D.P.R. at 349.

The justice declared the opinion of the majority both "incomplete" and "outdated." Typical of her decisions, the justice presented a detailed historical discussion of family law dating back to Constantine and the "institutionalized religion within the Roman Empire," the Civil Code (dating to the nineteenth century), as well as a dissertation on the right of privacy and the Bill of Rights contained in the Puerto Rico Constitution, specifically, Section 19 of Article III. She concluded the Bill of Rights "imposed and required a "liberal interpretation of human rights" that mandated a conclusion contrary to that reached by the majority. *Salva Santiago,* 171 D.P.R. at 350, 357. At the most basic level, Justice Fiol Matta rejected the majority's assertion that permitting a unilateral claim would deprive the respondent-husband of his right to hearing on his claims. In conclusion, the justice emphasized the most critical (and seemingly obvious) fact in the case—that the petitioner-wife could not agree to the grounds demanded by the respondent-husband for inclusion in the petition—ironically proving, the depth of the irreconcilable differences.

Suárez Cáceres v. CEE, 176 D.P.R. 31, 2009 LEXIS, involved a senatorial race in November 2008 in which two candidates were vying for the last seat of the minority party, the Popular Democratic Party (PPD) which was won by less than 1% of the votes cast. In this case of first impression, the Supreme Court was asked to interpret the meaning of "total votes cast for th[e] position" as defined by the Puerto Rico Constitution, Article III, Section 7 and the appropriate formula for determining a winner. The vote was 22.8481 for the candidate Suárez Cáceres and 22.8526 for the contender Rodríguez Otero. (These summary facts do not include the dispute and discussion relative to the minority law issue, the complexity of a recount vote or the interesting, procedural hoops leading to the administrative hearing and appeals of the issues.) The State Elections Commission (CEE) interpreted "total votes cast for the position" as votes cast for the candidates and discounted blank, spoiled and votes cast for fictitious characters (struck ballots). It then set aside the fractional percentages under the Electoral Law, § (2) of Art. 6.012, and determined the race was a tie. CEE ordered a drawing to be held. As the CEE deadlocked on the appropriate remedy, the CEE president made the decisions. The contender appealed asserting the CEE made an incorrect mathematical equation in concluding there was a tie. The lower court upheld the CEE's decision, and the Court of Appeals reversed that decision. The Supreme Court was asked whether and how to treat "the expression of voters" who cast the struck ballots in light of *Sanchez and Colón v. ELA,* 134 D.P.R. 445 (1993) which counted blank ballots as part of the "total votes cast" in that race. The majority opinion in *Sanchez and Colón* was written by Justice Naveira de Rodón. The Supreme Court held there was no authority to set aside the fractional percentages, Art. 6.012 permitting such set-aside only where less than .50% is cast. It upheld the CEE's handling of the struck ballots, declaring such ballots dilutes effects other votes cast and thus, addressed Justice Naveira de Rodón's inapposite opinion as follows. "It is necessary to conclude, by pure legal syllogism, that the intention of a voter who casts a blank ballot is to express his or her disagreement with the candidates on the ballot; in other words, the voter's intention is **not** to favor any candidate." *Suárez Cáceres*, 176 D.P.R. at 68 [emphasis theirs]. The court decided the race in favor of the contender and overturned *Sanchez and Colón*.

Justice Fiol Matta started her dissent by quoting respectively Octavio Paz and former Spanish Senator and philosopher Victoria Camp, "*Sin democracia la libertad es una quimera. [Without democracy, freedom is a chimera.]* and "*La democracia necesita una virtud: la confianza. Sin su construcción no puede haber una auténtica democracia.* [Democracy requires one virtue: trust. Without its construction, there can be no authentic democracy."] *Suárez*, 176 D.P.R. at 132. The justice took issue with the majority's deviation from *Sanchez and Colón*. Characterizing the case as a protection of the right to vote, she wrote, "[i]f democracy is the way in which the freedom of a country is preserved and protected, we need a justification of great magnitude to annul, by judicial fiat, the discordant and protest expressions in the electoral processes. We need the people to trust in the work that this Court does and in the certainty and stability of the highest-ranking rights that we have recognized in our Constitution. To proceed otherwise is to confiscate the will of the people and make the Constitution a straitjacket, not to limit the State, but to restrict citizens." *Suárez*, 176 D.P.R. at 135. Justices Hernández Denton and Rodríguez also filed dissenting opinions.

In *Puerto Rican Independence Party v. Free State of Puerto Rico Associates et al*, 186 D.P.R. 1, 2012 PR Sup. LEXIS, the court was asked to resolve the constitutionality of proposed amendments to the Puerto Rico Constitution, effective after the 2016 general election. These amendments included a reduction of Senate and House seats, House districts, the number of Senators from two to one in each district and House representatives from five to three, an increase of senatorial districts from eight to eleven and a formula for reducing seats in future reductions. The amendments authorized the Puerto Rican Governor to convene a Constitutional Review Board to reconfigure the new districts. These amendments were approved by both the Senate and House and signed by the Governor. The lawsuits were filed past the limitation periods, asserting the amendments were passed without the requisite two-thirds majority and exceeded the single subject requirement. After resolving jurisdictional and standing issues, the court found the case justiciable and proceeded to the merits. The court found no irregularity in the voting or publication of the amendments and no violation of the principle of separability (single subject amendments) by the submission of more than three proposed amendments—characterizing the purpose of the amendments as reducing legislative seats. The court further held that the senate alone established and applied the rules by which such resolutions are to be adopted and concluded that the amendments were subject to the public's vote and thus, dismissed the case. In her dissent (joined by two other justices), Justice Fiol Mata concluded the amendments were *null ab initio* as they were not approved by the requisite two-thirds majority and did not constitute single subject resolutions. In reaching her conclusion, the justice presented an in-depth historical review and persuasive analysis of the senate rules and caselaw interpretation of single subject amendments. The justice reflected, "[o]ur Constitution is not an exact map. On the contrary, it offers coordinates." *Puerto Rican Independence Party*, 186 DPR 79. The majority opinion asserted Justice Fiol Matta's dissent was "based upon elegant prose, but [wa] s lacking in pertinent constitutional law citations." *Puerto Rican Independence Party*, 186 D.P.R. at 69.

A presumably unemotive tax case involving the imposition of excise taxes, *Yiyi Motors, Inc. v. E.L.A.*, 177 D.P.R. 230, 2009 PR Sup. LEXIS 158, triggered a passionate discourse on the interpretative roles of the legislator vs. the judge over the tax code. Justice Fiol Matta eloquently discussed the role of the legislature and that of judges, writing,

> [o]ne may disagree as to the limits and the appropriate methods for the exercise of statutory interpretation. And certainly, one may fail to distinguish between "interpretation" and "creation" of the applicable basic norm. This would result in a usurpation of legislative prerogatives and undermine the purpose of the law. Despite the above, literality does not always result in a valid interpretation and full compliance with our interpretive function cannot mean that every time we judges use recognized interpretation methods, we legislate from the bench. Even the adjudicator will always have to use his interpretive function to decide whether the language of a statute is clear or whether there are doubts, according to his professional assessments.

That a tax issue would generate such passionate discussion was underscored by her colleague, Justice Hernández Denton who, in his dissent, quoted Miguel de Cervantes: "*[a]unque pusieron silencio a las lenguas, no le pudieron poner a las plumas, las cuáles, con más libertad que las lenguas, suelen dar a entender [al pueblo] lo que en el alma está encerrado.*" ("Although they silenced the tongues, they could not silence the pens, which, with more freedom than tongues, usually make [the people] understand what is locked in the soul.") *Don Quijote de la Mancha,* Parte I, Cap. XXIV. *Yiyi Motors, Inc.*, 177 D.P.R. 230 at 294.

In an interesting case involving the appeal by a same-sex partner prohibiting her from adopting her partner's child, *AAR, ex parte,* 187 DPR 835 (2013), Justice Fiol Matta joined the dissent (5–4). The appeal challenged the constitutionality of a statute that limited adoptions to same sex, married couples. The question on appeal was whether gender and sexual orientation were protected under the sex discrimination prohibition provision in the Bill of Rights with the analysis involving a discussion about the difference between sex and gender. The majority invoked the separation of powers doctrine, writing that such expanded protection and change was within the province of the legislature. Justice Fiol Matta objected to the majority's interpretation of the Puerto Rico Constitution, namely that it prohibited discrimination based only on sex and not sexual orientation. Justice Fiol Matta found, as a practical matter and from historical application and interpretation of discrimination law, that sex and gender were inextricably linked such as to prohibit an intellectually hollow separation.

e. Conclusion

On January 31, 2016, Justice Fiol Matta retired from the bench after fulfilling her tenure as chief justice. Upon her departure, the Puerto Rican Supreme Court adopted a resolution recognizing her contributions which stated in part:

> After twenty-three years of service in the Judicial Branch of Puerto Rico, the Honorable Liana Fiol Matta retires from her position. For this reason, and by agreement of the Associate Justices and the Associate Justices, we adopt this Resolution.... As an Associate Judge of this Court, she promoted jurisprudence in favor of human rights, the environment, women and the equal treatment of all people, without distinction of race, gender, origin or social condition. Her legal legacy reflects her commitment to justice and to sensitivity and empathy as essential elements of any adjudicative methodology.... In leaving, Judge Fiol Matta leaves a great legal legacy to our country. With her experience as an administrator and her human sensitivity, Judge Fiol Matta imprinted a character of true justice in Puerto Rican legal practice that will not be easy to replace. On behalf of the Associate Justices of the Supreme Court and the other officials of the Judicial Branch, we extend to Judge Fiol Matta our gratitude for the good service provided to her profession and her country. Tribunal Supremo De Puerto Rico, January 29, 2016, 2016 TSPR 14, Puerto Rico.

The justice returned to teaching as a distinguished professor at the Pontifical Catholic University of Puerto Rico where she currently teaches. She continued as a lecturer professor at the Interamerican University of Puerto Rico School of Law (2010–present) and at UPR School of Law (2012–present). The justice received the Balance of the Process of Award from Women in the Judicature and was honored by her alma mater, Columbia Law School in 2005.

8. Justice Carmen Espinosa

a. Formative Years

1971	B.S. with honors, Secondary Education, Central Connecticut State University
1973	M.A., Hispanic Studies, Brown University
1973–1976	7th Grade Teacher, French & Spanish, Southington Public Schools
1976	J.D., George Washington Law School
1976–1980	Special Agent, Federal Bureau of Investigation

1980–1992	Assistant U.S. Attorney, DOJ District of Connecticut
1992–2011	Judge, New Britain District Superior Court
2011–2013	Judge, Connecticut Court of Appeals
2013–2017	Justice, Connecticut Supreme Court[156]

Judge Espinosa is the first Hispanic person to serve on all three Connecticut courts, state district, Court of Appeals and the Connecticut Supreme Court. She was born February 27, 1949, in Yabucoa, Puerto Rico, to Amada and Alberto Espinosa. Both parents were laborers, her mother a factory worker. In 1952 when Carmen was three and a monolingual Spanish speaker, the family moved to New Britain, Connecticut.[157] Carmen attended New Britain public schools, graduating from high school in 1967. She is a first-generation college graduate in her extended family.[158] Carmen received a fellowship to attend Brown University where she obtained her master's degree and had been admitted to its Ph.D. program. She intended to become a college professor. Instead, she took a leave of absence and taught Spanish and French in high school.[159] Inspired by a friend, Carmen changed her professional interest and entered George Washington Law School in 1973, during the time of the Watergate scandal. According to Carmen, as she was nearing graduation, she placed her "resume indiscriminately in a basket in a law school placement office that took [her] to a stint with the Federal Bureau of Investigations" (FBI).[160] Women were not accepted by the FBI's training program until 1972.[161] The FBI recruited her and in 1976, she became the FBI's sixty-eighth female special agent.[162] Agent Espinosa worked initially in Newark, New Jersey and then New York City. She investigated terrorism, counterintelligence, and white-collar crime. She "worked on the notorious Lufthansa heist at Kennedy Airport, which became a central plot element in the movie 'Goodfellas.'"[163] Intending to apply to

156. State of Connecticut Judicial Branch, Biographies of Supreme Court Justices, Senior Justice Carmen Elisa Espinosa, https://www.jud.ct.gov/external/supapp/justice_espinosa.html; Mark Pazniokas, *Malloy Names First Hispanic to High Court*, Connecticut Mirror, January 7, 2013, https://ctmirror.org/2013/01/07/malloy-names-first-hispanic-high-court/.

157. Connecticut Bar Foundation, James W. Cooper Fellows, *History of Women in the Legal Profession Project, Hon. Carmen Espinosa*, interviewed by Hon. Peter Zarella, https://www.youtube.com/watch?v=bPqZmT17DU0, (Espinosa Interview).

158. Mary Ellen Godin, *Local Woman Adjusts to Supreme Court Bench*, Southington Citizen 9, no. 38 (September 20, 2013) (Godin Article), https://issuu.com/southingtoncitizen/docs/southington9.20.

159. *Supra* note 157, Espinosa Interview at 0:53–1:15.

160. Bill Sarno, *CT Supreme Court Justice Carmen Espinosa*, CT LatinoNews.com, October 13, 2017, https://ctlatinonews.com/ct-supreme-court-justice-carmen-espinosa/.

161. History: https://www.fbi.gov/history/artifacts/female-special-agent-briefcase.

162. Arielle Levin Becker, *Espinosa Sworn in as First Hispanic Justice, Connecticut Mirror*, March 28, 2013, https://ctmirror.org/2013/03/28/espinosa-sworn-first-hispanic-justice/; https://www.fbi.gov/history/artifacts/female-special-agent-briefcase.

163. *Supra* note 160.

Connecticut's state's attorney office, she mistakenly called the U.S. Attorney's district office, which also had an opening to which she applied. Carmen was hired by then U.S. Attorney Richard Blumenthal as an Assistant U.S. Attorney (AUSA) from 1977–1981.[164] From 1980 to 1992, Carmen was among the first Latina AUSAs in the country handling criminal cases,[165] along with Judge Lourdes Baird (see discussion in chapter three). In 1983, she married fellow lawyer Jeffry Van Kirk. While married, she was known as Espinosa Van Kirk. AUSA Espinosa Van Kirk successfully co-prosecuted *Los Macheteros*, a terrorist group that stole $7.1 million from Wells Fargo in Hartford. It was the second largest cash robbery in the country for which she received a distinguished service award in 1990. The couple had three children, two daughters and a son. One of her daughters was an all-state softball player and coach. Carmen is an avid New York Yankees fan.[166]

Then U.S. Attorney Stanley Twardy (1985–1991) recommended Carmen for a judgeship to Connecticut Governor Lowell Weicker. In 1992, Governor Weicker appointed Carmen as Connecticut's first Hispanic District Court judge.[167] Assigned to GA-14 in west Hartford, one of her earliest cases involved the criminal trial of anti-abortion protesters who had chained themselves inside a gynecologist's office. It was an "intimidating situation" as she received mail and photos from throughout the country depicting fetuses and other such images.[168] Judge Espinosa also presided over criminal dockets in New Britain, Bristol, Waterbury, and Hartford (Part A) for nineteen years, the sole judge handling criminal cases.[169] On March 16, 2011, Judge Espinosa was elevated to the Connecticut Court of Appeals,[170] achieving another historical milestone in the state.[171] Two years later on January 7, 2013, Governor Dannel Malloy nominated Judge Espinosa to the Connecticut Supreme Court for an eight-year term. Judge Espinosa captured the historical moment:

> I would like to especially thank Governor Malloy for his continued commitment to diversity in our judiciary. Not only does he honor me with this nomination, but he has honored the Hispanic community as well. I fully understand the responsibility that will fall upon my shoulders if confirmed as the first Hispanic to sit as a Supreme Court Justice in our great state. It is a responsibility

---

164. *Id.*, note 157 Espinosa Interview at 2:15–2:50; U.S. Senator Richard Blumenthal website, https://www.blumenthal.senate.gov/about/biography.

165. Luminarias Study, *results on file with the author.*

166. *Supra* note 157, Espinosa Interview at 6:43–6:50.

167. *Supra* note 157, Espinosa Interview at 3:08–3:27.

168. *Supra* note 157, Espinosa Interview at 3:40, 4:00–4:39.

169. *Id.*, note 157, Espinosa Interview at 4:38–5:18.

170. Testimony of LPRAC in Support of Judge Carmen Espinosa to Serve on the Connecticut Supreme Court, February 1, 2013.

171. Susan Haigh, *Espinosa Appointed to Conn. Appellate Court*, Victoria Advocate, March 2, 2011, https://www.victoriaadvocate.com/news/highereducation/espinosa-appointed-to-conn-appellate-court/article_3117ed3d-dc93-5669-95ce-3a4dfd885a19.html; supra note 157 at 5:43–6:14.

> which I will gladly accept and one that I would fulfill with diligence and dedication. I hope that my nomination to the Supreme Court serves as an example to young Hispanic children that anything is possible if they stay in school and use education as the bridge to success.[172]

The Connecticut General Assembly unanimously approved her nomination on March 6, 2013 (35–0 vote). The justice described her tenure on the Supreme Court as the most difficult job she held as it required gaining the vote of four other justices to agree to a majority opinion.[173] This was and is a recurrent sentiment among the Luminaria Supreme Court Justices and Article III Judges.

b. Connecticut Supreme Court, 2013–2017

Justice Espinosa wrote the majority opinion in fifty-two cases. Twenty-four or 46% were criminal cases, the remaining twenty-eight cases covered diverse legal issues from discovery matters to complex criminal issues and state constitutional challenges. Like other state supreme courts, the justice and the court instructed Connecticut attorneys on jurisdictional and other matters. For example, in *Blumberg Associates Worldwide, Inc. v. Brown & Brown of Connecticut, Inc.*, 311 Conn. 123, 84 A.3d 840 (2014), in a lengthy opinion the court articulated the circumstances under which it is appropriate to exercise its supervisory authority to review unpreserved claims. *McConnell v. McConnell et al.*, 316 Conn. 504, 113 A.3d 64 (2015), revolved around the writ of error filed by attorneys objecting to the Superior Court's order directing them to appear to give testimony and produce client files. The Superior Court issued the show cause order upon finding the attorneys induced the probate court to commit reversible error. James McConnell, one of the three siblings who were beneficiaries of their father's living trust, filed suit alleging he did not receive notice of the hearing at which his siblings each received $600,000 and $575,000, and he $35,000. The attorneys appeared and subjected themselves to the court's examination and, thereafter, filed the writ of error alleging, *inter alia*, that the court's order implicated the attorney-client privilege. (The two other siblings invoked their Fifth Amendment right not to testify.) The Superior Court found the attorneys failed to comply with the Rules of Professional Conduct, Rule 3.3, governing candor. The trial court submitted to the Connecticut Supreme Court that its order was not an appealable final order. Justice Espinosa delivered the court's opinion holding that a writ of error did not constitute a final judgment for appeal. She rejected the attorneys' argument that a writ of error (if not a final order) evinced important policy considerations.

---

172. *Supra* note 157, Espinosa Interview at 6:15–6:28; *New Judges Join Conn. Supreme, Appeals Court, Connecticut Post*, April 10, 2011, https://www.ctpost.com/news/article/new-judges-join-conn-supreme-appeals-courts-1330539.php?utm_source=feedburner&utm_medium=feed&utm_campaign=Feed%3A%20StatelineorgRss-CrimeCourts%20(Stateline.org%20RSS%20-%20Crime%20%26%20Courts).

173. *Supra* note 157, Espinosa Interview at 6:28–643.

c. Majority Opinions in Criminal Cases

State v. Kevalis, 313 Conn. 590 (2014), presented an issue of first impression involving postconviction probation of a defendant convicted for interfering with an officer. Justice Espinosa addressed whether a trial court has the discretion to find the defendant satisfactorily completed the accelerated rehabilitation program[174] when defendant was convicted of a crime during his participation in the program based on criminal conduct committed prior to starting the program. Justice Espinosa ruled the trial court was obligated to find the defendant did not satisfactorily complete the program based on his conviction. To rule otherwise, Justice Espinosa concluded, would defeat the purpose of the acceleration program, which envisioned the participants maintain a clean record. In *State v. Wright*, 319 Conn. 684 (2015), the defendant asked the court to set aside his jury convictions for aggravated assault on a child, risk of injury to a child, attempt to commit sexual assault in the first degree, and unlawful restraint in the first degree.[175] The trial court sentenced the defendant to 120 years for luring a ten-year-old boy up a hill, and hugging and fondling him before the boy escaped. On appeal, the defendant argued the crimes were not separately punishable offenses but rather imposed multiple punishments, allowing the state to seek enhanced sentencing for the predicate offense. He asserted this resulted in double jeopardy. The justice analyzed the offenses pursuant to *Blockburger v. United States*, 284 U.S. 299 (1932), and agreed with the state that the crimes constituted separate crimes not multiple offenses for the same predicate crime, because they required proof of different elements. Justice Espinosa held the offenses did not run afoul of the state's double jeopardy clause for multiple convictions under § 53a–70c (aggravated assault) for the same transaction. Defendant's convictions were affirmed.

Justice Espinosa resolved another double jeopardy claim as an issue of first impression in *State v. Johnson*, 316 Conn. 34 (2015). This case involved the aggregate package theory of sentencing. Under the theory, a trial court is free to reconstruct sentencing within applicable limits to ensure the punishment fits the crime. Here, the defendant was convicted by a jury of conspiracy to possess narcotics with intent to sell, possession of narcotics, conspiracy to possess narcotics, possession of less than four ounces of marijuana, and possession of drug paraphernalia. The defendant argued her separate convictions of conspiracy to possess narcotics and conspiracy to possess narcotics with intent to sell violated the double jeopardy clause because the conspiracy represented one agreement. The trial court sentenced the defendant to a total of five years of incarceration, execution suspended after eighteen months, and three years of probation. The trial court's conviction was reversed on the conspiracy to possess narcotics because the appellate court held it was a lesser included offense of conspiracy to possess narcotics with intent to sell. It also vacated the de-

174. General Statutes (Gen. Stat.) (Supp.2014) § 54-56(e).

175. Gen. Stat. §§ 53a–70c (a)(1) and (6) (aggravated assault), 53–21(a)(2) (risk of injury), 53a–49 and 53a–70 (a)(2) (attempted sexual assault on a child), and 53a–95 (unlawful restraint).

fendant's sentence for the greater offense of conspiracy to possess narcotics with intent to sell, in accordance with the aggregate package theory of sentencing. Justice Espinosa conveyed the court's decision that the appellate court improperly ordered the trial court to resentence on the conspiracy to possess narcotics with intent to sell count because there was no evidence in the record to support the trial court's original sentencing was effectuated under the aggregate package theory. The justice explained that the appellate court's remand to resentence was not necessary and had no effect on the trial court's sentence.

State v. Jones, 320 Conn. 22, 128 A.3d 431 (2015), presented the novel issue whether the Fourth Amendment permits a warrantless seizure of an item. Defendant was drunk, and before providing him a ride, the police conducted a pat down and found a knife. The police kept the knife for safekeeping, legally seized for a non-investigatory purpose. Thereafter, police realized the man was sought in connection with an assault with the knife. Defendant sought to suppress the knife contending the safekeeping reason did not justify its continued, warrantless retention by the police for use as evidence against him in his criminal case. The court disagreed with the defendant. Justice Espinosa wrote that if police have lawful access (non-investigatory purpose) to an item they reasonably believe constitutes evidence of criminal activity, defendant has no reasonable expectation of privacy in the item and police may seize it without obtaining a warrant.

In a case of first impression, *Anthony v. Commissioner of Corrections*, 326 Conn. 668 (2017), Justice Espinosa relayed the court's adoption of the stigma plus test to resolve whether an inmate's classification as a sexual offender implicates a protected liberty interest. The petitioner's request for habeas corpus relief was denied by the trial court for lack of subject matter. The appellate court reversed, ruling defendant had a protected liberty interest under the federal stigma test. Anthony was convicted upon a guilty plea to unlawful restraint in the first degree and violation of probation. His wife alleged sexual assault and later recanted. The state entered a nolle prosequi on the charge of sexual assault in a spousal relationship. The Department of Corrections thereafter classified Anthony as a sex offender and offered treatment which he refused. Anthony claimed the classification resulted in an increased security status and adverse impact on good time credits due to his refusal to enter treatment and, further that he suffered harassment because of the classification. Writing for the court, Justice Espinosa applied the stigma test in *Vitek v. Jones*, 445 U.S. 480 (1980), that requires establishing a protected liberty interest plus proving that the classification was false. *Anthony*, 326 Conn. at 680. She held Anthony also had to show that the consequences suffered were "qualitatively different from the punishments usually suffered by prisoners, so that they constituted a major change in the conditions of confinement amounting to a grievous loss" or stigma plus elements. *Anthony*, 326 Conn. at 682. Upon review of federal law interpreting what conditions meet the stigma plus test, Justice Espinosa concluded the court's decisions in *Baker v. Commissioner of Corrections*, 281 Conn. 241 (2007), and *Wheway v. Warden*, 215 Conn.

418 (1990), were not controlling. The justice concluded Anthony sufficiently alleged a protected liberty interest such to invoke the jurisdiction of the habeas court.

The justice joined the majority in decisions involving various aspects of a criminal trial. In *State v. Devon*, 321 Conn. 656 (2016), the court permitted a service dog to accompany a witness while testifying if it aided the witness in testifying truthfully. *State v. Dixon*, 322 Conn. 410 (2016) adopted a new rule permitting, for the first time, a nonsuggestive in-court identification and adopted a procedure for its admissibility, rejecting the defendant's argument that such identifications were so unnecessarily suggestive as to trigger due process protections. The sole exception was prior identification procedures where a witness was unable to identify the defendant. And, in a case of first impression, *State v. Edwards*, 325 Conn. 97 (2017), the court ruled that a police officer needed to be qualified as an expert witness before testifying about cell phone data and, further, required a *Daubert* hearing[176] to establish his expertise. The court found in this case that the testimony was harmless error.

The justice's legal philosophy was revealed in her rulings, including foremost in *State v. Santiago*, 319 Conn. 1 (2015). In 2012, the Connecticut legislature passed Public Acts 2012, No. 12-5 (P.A. 12-5) abolishing the death penalty but left intact death sentences for eleven inmates already on death row. In a split decision (5–3), the Supreme Court affirmed the abolishment of the death penalty, including to those sentences already imposed finding the Connecticut death penalty "no longer comported with contemporary standards of decency." The court also found the death penalty violated the state's ban on excessive and disproportionate punishment in capital cases, including those where defendants had already been sentenced. The Supreme Court denied the state's motion for argument and reconsideration, prompting an extensive dissent by one justice which was joined by Justice Espinosa. *State v. Santiago*, SC17413 (August 8, 2015).[177] The dissent disagreed with the court's majority that the death penalty no longer comports with contemporary standards of decency in the state and asserted the traditional test in *State v. Geisler*, 222 Conn. 672 (1992), was the appropriate standard to apply. The two justices argued that the "hybrid" claim adopted by the majority, "falling somewhere between a *per se* challenge and a statutory challenge," was done to avoid the *Geisler* standard of review. The justices conveyed there was support in the state for the death penalty.

d. Majority Opinions in Civil Cases

In *Sarrazin v. Coastal, Inc.*, 311 Conn. 581 (2014), Justice Espinosa penned the opinion for the court which decided when an employee's travel time between home and work constitutes compensable work time under the FLSA. Plaintiff worked for defendant plumbing subcontractor which performed work for the state, requiring interstate travel. Plaintiff traveled between his job and the work sites approximately

176. *Daubert v. Merrell Dow Pharmaceuticals, Inc.*, 509 U.S. 579 (1993).

177. For the full dissent, *see* https://casetext.com/case/state-v-santiago-207.

one hour each day. Evaluating the claim under the Portal-to-Portal Act,[178] Justice Espinosa wrote that a plumber who carried company tools in a company vehicle during his daily commute to his jobsite and home was within the normal commute and not compensable. She ruled plaintiff was entitled to overtime compensation for the after-hours time he spent picking up tools or equipment from the company's warehouse under both the FLSA, § 207(a)(1) and state law, § 31-76c), which were substantively the same. On that basis, rejected plaintiff's argument that the federal law preempted Connecticut's law.

The justice wrote majority opinions in matters concerning breach of contract and the state's Unfair Trade Practices Act. In *RBC Nice Bearings, Inc. v. SKF USA, Inc.*, 318 Conn. 737 (2015), the court was asked to resolve a dispute over the sale of goods pursuant to a contractual provision to purchase a minimum dollar amount of ball bearings (minimum purchase requirement). The trial court held that the plaintiff had annually waived the minimum purchase requirement. The appellate court reversed, ruling that even if such a waiver occurred, the trial court erred by finding the waiver continued into subsequent years of the contract. Justice Espinosa wrote that the issue before them was whether the appellate court could reverse the trial court by substituting its opinion about the trial court's findings and whether its basis for reversal was correct. Based on the parties' concession that plaintiffs essentially waived the minimum purchase requirement, the justice found the record supported a waiver had occurred for six of the eight years of the contract. (The parties also had eliminated the minimum purchase requirement and replaced it with an annual requirement to negotiate the minimum purchase.) She noted the absence of Connecticut caselaw on the applicability of the continuing waiver of contractual rights where an obligee has acquiesced in between the years of waiver. *RBC*, 318 Conn. at 757. She applied the theory of continuing waiver to conclude the trial court properly found an ongoing waiver. *RBC*, 318 Conn. at 758. Justice Espinosa concluded that the appellate court's finding that plaintiffs could not waive the minimum purchase requirement was an erroneous interpretation of the law.

In a commercial breach of contract case, *Howard-Arnold, Inc. v. T.N.T. Realty, Inc.*, 316 Conn. 596 (2015), Justice Espinosa affirmed the appellate court's partial reversal. Here, the controversy was over the option to purchase certain real property which was the subject of a lease agreement between the parties. The plaintiff objected to the trial court's refusal to order specific performance because plaintiff had not exercised its option. Plaintiff did not exercise the option because the defendant had yet to undertake the environmental remediation on the property. On the certified question before the court, Justice Espinosa wrote both the trial and appellate courts properly concluded the plaintiff had not exercised the option to purchase pursuant to the contract's express language and rejected plaintiff's argument to apply the doctrine of frustration of purpose. She noted the inapplicability of the doctrine

178. 29 U.S.C. chptr. 9 of 1947.

where, here, the failure to remediate did not interfere with the contract purpose to lease the land and the option to deposit the money in an escrow account. *Howard-Arnold*, 316 Conn. at 605–606.

Upon default of six promissory notes, lender sued the borrower in *Channing Real Estate, LLC. V. Gates*, 326 Conn. 123 (2017). Defendant asserted a counterclaim under the Connecticut Unfair Trade Practices Act (CUTPA). The trial court ruled in favor of the defendant, but on appeal, the court reversed the decision and ordered a new hearing. The plaintiff sought to have the Court of Appeal's decision overturned only on the scope of the remand—to limit a new trial to a hearing on damages. Plaintiff asserted a new trial was unnecessary because the appellate court properly applied the parol evidence rule that resolved the issue of liability and because defendant lacked standing to raise a CUTPA claim. The justice wrote that the appellate court properly applied New York contract law as defendant was required to make payment by mail to the plaintiff in New York. Accordingly, she held the Court of Appeals properly ruled that New York's parol evidence rule precluded the trial court from admitting and considering extrinsic evidence that varied the terms of the promissory notes. She wrote that a new trial was not warranted as the note established there was no question about defendant's liability. *Channing*, 326 Conn. at 132–133. Justice Espinosa rejected the defendant's defense of equitable estoppel due to post contractual modifications, distinguishing it from defendant's claim of precontractual representations about the notes. Finally, the justice addressed an issue of first impression, whether a member of a limited liability company has standing to assert a CUPTA claim. She concluded that a limited liability company—which owned the land in dispute—did not having standing to raise a CUPTA claim and, therefore, the defendant lacked standing as well. *Channing*, 326 Conn. at 139.

The construction of roads on wetlands and the jurisdiction of municipal inland wetlands agencies was at issue in *Indian Spring Land Co. v. Wetlands*, 322 Conn. 1 (2016). The plaintiff, the Indian Spring Land Company appealed the trial court's dismissal of its challenge to the decision by the Greenwich Inland Wetlands and Watercourses Agency (Agency) which the trial court approved. At issue was whether the construction of roads is a permitted activity under § 22(a)-40(a)(1) and not subject to the jurisdiction of municipal inland wetlands agencies. The Agency approved the construction of a road with conditions on wetlands owned by the plaintiff. The land in question was an unimproved land consisting of 121.5 acres, maintained as forest lands; the northeast portion of the land was to be used for the gravel road to aid in the forestry/maintenance that was also related to plaintiff's farming operations. The definition of farming under the statute includes forestry. Plaintiff alleged two errors, one that the right to construct roads was not permissible under the Wetlands and Watercourses Act (Act)[179] and two, the Agency lacked the jurisdiction to regulate the

179. Gen. Stat. § 22a-36 *et seq.*

construction. Justice Espinosa ruled that under the Act, § 22(a)-40(a)(1), the road construction directly related to farming operations was permitted as of right. She further wrote that the Agency did not have the jurisdiction to grant that right and attach conditions to roads that were significantly different from what the owner planned. The decision was reversed to the Plaintiff's favor.

In *Martinez v. Empire Fire and Marine Ins. Co.*, 322 Conn. 47 (2016), Justice Espinosa resolved an MCS-90 endorsement liability and coverage issue applying the trip-specific approach. Plaintiff's car was struck by a truck driven (to pick up repairs) by an employee of the defendant's insured, Tony's Long Wharf Transport, LLC (Tony's), causing his injuries. The plaintiff obtained a judgment against Tony's for negligence, which was unpaid at the time of the appeal. Plaintiff sought to collect from the defendant-insurer, but the defendant denied responsibility. Defendant's policy contained a federally mandated insurance endorsement known as an MCS-90 endorsement that applied to accidents during *interstate* transportation.[180] Federal law, specifically 49 U.S.C. § 31139, requires motor carriers that transport goods by motor vehicles to cover liability arising from the carrier's transportation of property in interstate commerce. Compliance is shown through MCS-90 endorsement, a surety obligation that compels an insurer to pay certain judgments against the insured, even where the policy otherwise excludes coverage. *Martinez*, 322 Conn. at 51. Defendant argued that because the accident occurred during an *intrastate* trip, it was not liable under the MCS-90 endorsement or, stated otherwise, defendant asserted the trip-specific defense in its motion for summary judgment, which the trial court granted. The Court of Appeals upheld the trial court's dismissal. Noting the court was required in this case to follow federal, not state law, Justice Espinosa adopted the trip-specific interpretation applied in *Lyons v. Lancer Ins. Co.*, 681 F.3d 50 (2d Cir.2012). She wrote the defendant was not liable for the intrastate accident that caused plaintiff's injuries. *Martinez*, 322 Conn. at 60.

Velecela v. All Habitat Services, LLC., 322 Conn. 335 (2016), centered on the exclusivity of the Workers' Compensation Act (Act), Gen. Stat. § 31–284(a), which barred a claim for a bystander's emotional distress. The plaintiff's husband was employed by the defendant. While repairing an all-terrain vehicle elevated on a lift, the vehicle slipped and killed him. Plaintiff took her husband lunch and, upon arriving at the work site, found his body crushed beneath the vehicle. Under the Act's benefits, the plaintiff received compensation for her husband's funeral expenses and received $300,000 in benefits pursuant to a stipulated agreement. Before entering the stipulation, plaintiff had filed an action for bystanders' emotional distress, alleging she suffered extreme emotional distress from finding her husband's body. Asserting the

---

180. 49 U.S.C. § 31139 requires certain motor carriers, those that transport goods by motor vehicles, to cover liability arising from the carrier's transportation or property in interstate commerce. Compliance is shown through MCS-90 endorsement, a surety obligation that compels and insurer to pay certain judgments against the insured, even where the policy otherwise excludes coverage.

Act was the exclusive remedy, the defendant filed, and the trial court granted the motion to dismiss. Justice Espinosa wrote the court had not previously interpreted the phrase "arising out of personal injury or death in § 31–284(a)" and looked to cases interpreting "arising out of" as instructive guidance. *Velecela*, 322 Conn. at 340. The plaintiff's proffered claim for negligent bystanders' emotional distress claim was rejected as was her principal claim. In another case involving the Act, *Ferraro v. Ridgeland European Motors, Inc.*, 313 Conn. 735 (2014), Justice Espinosa addressed the assessability of interest on the insurer's liability after formal proceedings were completed but before the commissioner had issued his findings and order. One of the insurers, Republic-Franklin, which agreed to liability, objected to the interest assessment objecting that the commissioner's finding on interest was not completed within a reasonable period of time as required by § 31-299b. Notwithstanding, the justice detailed the genesis and sequence of hearings and objections filed by Republic-Franklin, including a waiver of the interest assessment by its attorney at the last hearing among the insurers. Justice Espinosa concluded the essence of the issue was the commissioner's authority to impose and apportion interest, when the insurers entered into an agreement on the apportionment of liability. As Republic-Franklin failed to preserve this claim, the justice summarily denied the objection.

Justice Espinosa upheld the trial court rulings on two cases involving the termination of the mother's parental rights, *In re Jace O.*, 323 Conn. 690 (2016) and *In re Gabriella*, 319 Conn. 775 (2015). In *Jace*, the mother had her parental rights of another child terminated that was considered by the trial court. Jace's mother became pregnant at the age of fourteen and gave birth on her fifteenth birthday. At the time, Jace's mother was involved in a same-sex relationship and the partners decided to have a child. Jace's mother had sex with Jace's father to become pregnant. Upon giving birth, Jace's mother, who was placed in a home with wraparound services, ran away. The relationship ended and the mother had trouble supporting herself and began regularly smoking marijuana and taking other drugs. Jace was eventually placed in foster care and proceedings to terminate her parental rights ensued. The teen mother consented to the termination of her parental rights. The newborn Jace thereafter was adjudicated neglected and adopted by the paternal grandmother. Justice Espinosa wrote that the trial court properly took into consideration the mother's prior termination of rights. Given her current debilitated circumstances, the justice concluded there was no violation of § 17a-112(j)(3)[181] or her due process rights under

181. The provision requires a petitioner to prove by clear and convincing evidence that: (1) the department has made reasonable efforts toward reunification, or the parent is unwilling or unable to benefit from such efforts; (2) termination is in the best interest of the child; and (3) the child is under the age of seven years and is neglected or uncared for, and the parent has failed, or is unable or unwilling to achieve such degree of personal rehabilitation as would encourage the belief that within a reasonable period of time, considering the age and needs of the child, the parent could assume a responsible position in the life of the child, and the parent's parental rights with respect to another child were previously terminated.

the analysis of *Mathews v. Eldridge*, 424 U.S. 319 (1976). She also recognized that a prior termination of rights is insufficient to deprive one of their parental rights and detailed the additional procedural safeguards afforded the mother and considered by the trial court prior to Jace's removal. *Jace*, 323 Conn. at 649–650. That the mother was a minor during the first termination proceeding did not persuade the justice to reverse the trial court as all the procedural due process safeguards were given to mother. *Jace*, 323 Conn. at 652–653. Similarly in *Gabriella*, the mother had her parental rights of another ten-year-old daughter, Erica M., terminated prior to termination of her parental rights of Gabriella. The mother had five other children living in Jamaica when she traveled to the country to attend the funeral of her brother when she gave birth to Gabriella. The mother left Erica and six-week-old Gabriella with Nicolette R., who was not a biological relative. Upon learning of horrific conditions of Nicolette R.'s home that included sexual abuse, the two children were removed. Separately, both were adjudicated neglected; Gabriella was two years old. At the hearing, substantial evidence was presented detailing the rehabilitative opportunities afforded to the mother, including therapy, that did not produce any significant improvement in the mother. The court agreed that reasonable efforts had been made to reunify the mother with Gabriella and upheld the trial court's termination of parental rights as did the justice.

In a perceived disability case, *Desrosiers v. Diageo North America, Inc., et al.*, 314 Conn. 772 (2014), Justice Espinosa wrote that the Connecticut Fair Employment Practices Act (Act), § 46a-60(a)(1),[182] protects individuals who are perceived by their employers as having a physical disability. To reach this result, the justice was required to evaluate the plain meaning of the Act and stretch beyond the plain meaning. She wrote, "[t]he meaning of a statute shall, in the first instance, be ascertained from the text of the statute itself and its relationship to other statutes. If, after examining such text and considering such relationship, the meaning of such text is plain and unambiguous and does not yield absurd or unworkable results, extratextual evidence of the meaning of the statute shall not be considered. When a statute is not plain and unambiguous or would yield absurd or unworkable results, however, we also look for interpretive guidance." *Desrosiers*, 314 Conn. at 455–456. Her opinion noted that the Act was clear and unambiguous and did not cover those who were perceived to be disabled but she and the court did not end the inquiry there. Recognizing the Act was silent as to whether its protections extended to individuals who are regarded as physically disabled, the justice found instructive the definitions of

182. The statute provides in relevant part: "(a) It shall be a discriminatory practice in violation of this section: (1) For an employer... except in the case of a bona fide occupational qualification or need, to refuse to hire or employ or to bar or to discharge from employment any individual or to discriminate against such individual in compensation or in terms, conditions or privileges of employment because of the individual's race, color, religious creed, age, sex, gender identity or expression, marital status, national origin, ancestry, present or past history of mental disability, intellectual disability, learning disability or physical disability, including, but not limited to, blindness."

"physically disabled" under § 46a-51(15) and "mentally disabled" in § 46a-51(20). As defined by these sections, "[m]ental disability" includes those who are "regarded as having one or more mental disorders," but "[p]hysically disabled" includes "any individual who has any chronic physical handicap, infirmity or impairment." Justice Espinosa conveyed that while plaintiff did not meet the definition of physically disabled under the Act, she introduced convincing evidence that she was perceived to be disabled and discriminated against because of that perceived disability. Thus, the majority declined to follow the literal meaning of the statute, holding "although the language of § 46a–60 (a)(1) is plain and unambiguous, a literal application of the statutory language would lead to a bizarre result" and leave employees unprotected. *Desrosiers,* 314 Conn. at 786. The justice observed that the Commission on Human Rights and Opportunities had historically interpreted the statute to apply to those perceived to have a disability, which the legislature made no effort to correct. *Desrosiers,* 314 Conn. at 453.

e. Conclusion

In July 2017, Justice Espinosa assumed senior status after devoting forty-one years to public service. The justice was recognized and honored for her trailblazing career. Governor Malloy presented Justice Espinosa with the 2014 Lupian of the Year Award, given by the Connecticut Latinos United for Professional Achievement. She also has been honored by the Connecticut Latino and Puerto Rican Affairs Commission. In 2011, she was named to *Hispanic Business Magazine*'s "100 Influentials" list. The Central Connecticut State University bestowed on her the Women of Influence Award, and in 2023, she was named one of ten to the University's Title IX Trailblazers list.[183]

---

183. *See Governor Malloy Presents LUPA Award,* https://archives.lib.uconn.edu/node/1099518; *University Honors Justice Espinosa with Title IX Trailblazers,* https://ccsubluedevils.com/general/2022-23/releases/20230222lpdhjr.

Table 2 **Supreme Court Justices—Eight Luminarias**

Justice/ Judge	Appointing Authority	Court	Tenure	Status
Dorothy Comstock Riley 1982–1983 1987–1991	Gov. William Milliken	Michigan Supreme Court Appointed, Removed Elected, Reelected Chief Justice	1982–1983, 1984–1992 11/6/1982–2/15/1983 11/6/1984, 11/3/1992	Deceased
Miriam Naveira Merly 1985–2004	Gov. Rafael Hernández-Colón	Puerto Rico Supreme Court Appointed Chief Justice	6/11/1985–7/28/2004 12/30/2003–7/28/2004	Deceased
Rosemary Barkett 1985–1994	Gob. Bob Graham	Florida Supreme Court Appointed Elected, Retained Chief Justice Judge 15th Judicial Circuit Chief Judge	10/14/1985 1986, 1992 1992–7/1/1994 1979–10/14/1985 1983–1984	Elevated 7/1/1994
Carmen Beauchamp Ciparick 1994–2012	Gov. Mario Cuomo Gov. Eliot Spitzer Elected	New York Court of Appeals New York Supreme Court New York Trial Judge	1/4/1994–12/31/2012 11/2/1982–12/1993 1978–1982	Mandatory Retirement
Vanessa Ruiz 1994–2011	President Bill Clinton	D.C. Court of Appeals Senior Judge	7/12/1994–8/31/2011	Retired
Petra Jimenez Maes 1998–2018	Gov. Gary Johnson Elected	New Mexico Supreme Court Chief Justice Judge, First Judicial District, Santa Fe	12/3/1998–12/31/2018 1/8/2003–2005 & 2012–2014 1981–1998	Retired

Justice/ Judge	Appointing Authority	Court	Tenure	Status
Liana Fiol Matta 2004–2016	Gov. Sila Calderón Gov. Alejandro García Padilla	Puerto Rico Supreme Court Chief Justice Puerto Rico Court of Appeals Administrative Judge	2/19/2004–1/31/2016 4/11/2014–1/31/2016 1996–2002	Retired
Carmen Espinosa 2013–2017	Gov. Daniel Malloy Gov. Lowell P. Weicker	Connecticut Supreme Court Connecticut Court of Appeals New Britain District Superior Court	3/6/2013–7/16/2017 3/16/2011–3/5/2013 1/10/1992–3/15/2011	Retired

D. Lessons from the Supreme Luminarias

As noted at the start of this chapter, a comparison of the total number of justices to Article III judges, suggests it is more difficult for Latinas to secure the highest juridical apex in their state than in the nation. Nevertheless, the few Luminarias who served have made lasting contributions to U.S. jurisprudence on complex cases of first impression involving education/financing, women's reproductive rights, transgender rights, the environment, criminal law, employment and civil rights—some still resonating today. They illuminated the way for fourteen others, the second generation, to follow in their footsteps. From their majority opinions, we have documentation of how these trailblazers interpreted and implemented the law. Core to that study is an understanding of childhood influences, education and pre-judicial career on their world outlook that shaped their respective judicial philosophies. This chapter provides a skeletal outline from which a deeper sociological examination and legal study may be launched.

The Luminaria Justices were the first to unhesitatingly emboss their juridical appellate mark on behalf of citizens in their respective states, territory and jurisdiction. Of particular interest to the author was their rulings and views on issues involving gender and race. Two concepts emerged from this study of the Luminaria Justices. One, was that their judicial philosophy was not steeped in liberal or conservative ideology but rather based upon the moral values by which they were raised. These values were rooted in Hispanic, Latino culture and traditions that exposed them early in life to racial discrimination and gender inequality. Thus, their writings reveal a fundamental morality that embodied gender and racial equality, formed by their respective upbringings—even when that upbringing involved gender bias within their families. This was the predicate of their judicial philosophy, influenced by the era in which they became educated that was further refined by their chosen paths in the law. Most of the Luminaria Justices have shared in various forums, speeches and articles the significance of gender bias and discrimination on their lives and on their roles as justices.[184] Justice Fiol Matta shared her expansive view on adjudication from the gender lens:

> It must be kept in mind that the diversity of perspectives enriches the adjudication process. Therefore, when dealing with a case, the person who adjudicates, whether male or female, must adopt an attitude of openness to the pluralism of thought, so that she can accept, with humility, 'that there is more than one way of manner of seeing things and analyzing problems and that this is not necessarily the most correct, but different and must be taken into account.' In short, the judge cannot be measured by his or her sex... but rather by the richness and breadth of his or her life perspectives and how these contribute, together with his or her knowledge of the Law, to the difficult task of adjudicating and resolving disputes.[185]

Two, the interpretations of law and opinions issued by the Luminaria Justices were infused with these moral values, subtly or outright. This is the common thread that underlies their decisions. Some broadened their analyses beyond English common law, to embrace the philosophy of ethicists and writers to facilitate their deliberations and aid in explaining (perhaps first to themselves), how and why laws should be interpreted within this paradigm. As we see from their opinions on diverse areas of the law, their moral compass extended beyond gender and race. But few explicitly discussed the implications of race on their jurisprudence or the influence of Spanish and Mexican law on English common law. Unexpectedly, this study expanded the author's curiosity on the subject prompting the same question raised by Justice Fiol Matta. To what extent has legal transculturation caused the suppression of our own Hispano-Latino roots.[186]

184. Current Latina Justices continue to do the same. *See for example*, the 26th *William J. Brennan Lecture on State Courts and Social Justice* delivered by Puerto Rico Chief Justice Maite Oronez Rodríguez about gender equality and the rule of law. New York University School of Law, February 25, 2020, 95 N.Y. Law Rev. 1599.

185. Liana Fiol Matta, *Knowing the Communities We Serve, Court Review* (2013), The Journal of the American Judges Association, Vol. 49, 14 at 19–20, *see also Women in the Judiciary: Assessment of the Process of Award*, 79 Rev. Jur. UPR 957 (2010).

186. Liana Fiol Matta, *Civil Law and Common Law in the Legal Method of Puerto Rico*, Am. Jrnl. of Comp. Law, Vol. 40, No. 4 (Autumn 1992), 783–815 at 783–784.

Three, the places in which the Luminaria Justices presided heavily influenced their judicial perspectives and accordingly dictated which law was to be applied. No where is this clearer than in Puerto Rico. For example by 1897, "Puerto Rico was totally integrated into the Spanish legal system" with Spanish law still found in some Puerto Rico statutes.[187] Justice Fiol Matta's article was aimed at determining how much of that Hispanic element [was] still present in Puerto Rico's legal system . . . and how it fare[d] in the confrontation with American-influenced elements of [its] law."[188] In their opinions, Justices Naveira Merly and Fiol Matta appraised and integrated Spanish law and, interestingly, borrowed from world philosophers and writers to frame legal issues within philosophical constructs as *foundational* to their juridical deliberations. A study of Justice Barkett's opinions, reveals an honest stylistic prose with the same powerful depth of morality imbedded throughout her decisions. This is perhaps unsurprising, given the philosophical influence in her college days of Pierre Teilhard de Chardin and Hans Küng and her spiritual background. Justice Beauchamp Ciparick sitting in one of the country's most powerful courts, forthrightly exercised that moral power as did Justices Jimenez Maes and Espinosa to directly carve niches into the law. Justice Ruiz infused her sophistication into the nation's District's appellate court that was reflective of her childhood and precocious first years of practice that caused her to litigate social-economic justice issues. The bravado they exhibited in interpreting the meaning of life, love, marriage, gender equality, reproductive rights and personal freedoms is fascinating, instructive and refreshing. Above all else, law addresses citizens at profound moments of vulnerability to resolve their most basic needs and fundamental legal rights. Surely these circumstances warrant a profound, holistic analysis.

As future arbiters of the law, the Luminaria Justices have shown us how to employ the insightful poetry of philosophers, ethicists and jurists who studied and interpreted the purpose and morality of law to achieve justice. They stretched beyond English common law, not to replace it but rather to refine and enhance its applicability to our lives. Whether delivered in prosaic language or poetic verse, the Luminaria Justices brought forth the values of their Hispano-Latino experience in their collective jurisprudence, fulfilling the purpose of a diverse bench.[189] The timing of women's ascendancy to the bench coupled with advocacy by Latino organizations, clearly is relevant towards understanding how these Luminarias ascended to the bench. But this historical context provides only a partial answer to the query, how did these Luminaria jurists succeed in a de facto segregated profession. Their intellectual capabilities and drive are another part of the answer. That they were the chosen beneficiaries perhaps ultimately rested in the hands of destiny—the explicable, connective tissue that binds the supreme Luminarias.

---

187. *Id.*, at 790.

188. *Id.*, at 784.

189. The author defines diversity not only in terms of gender, race and ethnicity but also encompasses liberals and conservatives (not ideologues), believing that such wholesome diversity triggers the best deliberative processes and produces the finest decisions. A court wholly liberal or conservative does not accomplish this same diversity.

Three

The First Generation of Luminaria Article III Judges

A. Overview of the Federal Judicial Nominating Process

In 1789, the federal judicial system was created during the Constitutional Convention. One hundred and forty-five years later, women began shaping law with the appointment of Florence Allen in 1934 to the Sixth Circuit Court of Appeals. It would take another forty-six years for Latinas to emboss their juridical mark. "By the fall of 1971, there were only five male Hispanics on the nation's federal district court and none on the country's appellate courts."[1] Recognized as the first U.S. president committed to diversifying the bench,[2] President Jimmy Carter understood the historical significance of one particular appointment which remains relevant and instructive into the twenty-first century:

> I have already quadrupled the number of Federal Hispanic Judges, including the first Hispanic woman federal judge Carmen Consuelo Cerezo. And this, as you know, will have a major impact on the attitude and tone, not only in the court itself but in the entire communities where they serve, not just during my term of office, not matter whether it's 4 or 8 years, but for a long time, for a generation." Public Papers of the Presidents of the United States, Administration of Jimmy Carter 1980–1981 (September 26, 1942).

True to President Carter's vision, the number of Article III Latina judges has doubled from the first seventeen Luminarias to the thirty-nine (new) Latina federal judges in 2025—expanding the juridical reach of Latinas jurists into new federal districts.[3]

---

1. *Supra* Chptr. 1, fn. 164, 1 HNBA Law Journal at 1–2.

2. Mary L. Clark, *Carter's Groundbreaking Appointment of Women to the Federal Bench: His Other 'Human Rights' Record*, Journal of Gender, Social Policy & the Law, 11, no. 3 (2003), 1132–1163; *see also* Linda Marie Wayner, *The Affirmatively Hispanic Judge: Modern Opportunities for Increasing Hispanic Representation on the Federal Bench*, Tex. Wesleyan L. Rev. 16 (2010), 535–560, 543.

3. *Supra* Ch. 2 note 1, Cruz Article, Introduction at 45–46 in which Dr. Cruz reported thirty-seven Latina Article III judges. The author and Dr. Cruz collaborate regularly to update the number of Latina Article III judges, which increased to thirty-nine since her article was published in 2024. This number does not include the Latina Article III nominees (if any) at time of publication.

See, Appendix B, List of Luminaria & Latina Article III Judges 1980 | 2025. The overall percentage of Latina Article III judges has increased slightly from the three percent Luminaria judges to 4.3 percent of Latina federal judges today, clearly not keeping pace with the growth of the Latino community that comprises 19 percent of the country's total population. As their biographical summaries establish, the journey of the Luminaria judges reveals an independence of spirit and tenacity to succeed amid societal and professional obstacles. The current generation of Latina judges have benefitted from the path forged by the Luminarias, but they carry on the same tradition of excellence.

1. The Federal Judicial System and U.S. Senate Judiciary Committee

Articles II and III of the U.S. Constitution, which created the federal judiciary, empower the president with the "Advice and Consent" of the Senate to appoint judges to the U.S. Supreme Court and federal appellate and trial courts. The Appointments Clause states:

> He [the president] shall have Power, by and with the Advice and Consent of the Senate... shall nominate, and by and with the Advice and Consent of the Senate, shall appoint Ambassadors, other public Ministers and Consuls, Judges of the Supreme Court, and all other Officers of the United States, whose Appointments are not herein otherwise provided for, and which shall be established by Law: but the Congress may by Law vest the Appointment of such inferior Officers, as they think proper, in the President alone, in the Courts of Law, or in the Heads of Departments. U.S. Const. art. II, § 2, cl. 2.

Article III created the federal judiciary and defined its jurisdiction. Judges appointed to the U.S. Supreme Court, federal courts of appeals ("Circuit Courts"), and federal trial courts ("District Courts") are known as Article III judges. Presidents nominate only in those instances when a vacancy occurs, which includes Article III judges who transition to "senior status."[4] While the privilege of nominating a judicial candidate ultimately rests with the president, U.S. senators are deeply embedded in the judicial selection process. As part of the *advice and consent* requirement of Article II, the president's consultation with home-state senators has morphed over the centuries, from informal senatorial courtesy to present-day formalized processes, cementing senatorial privilege.

Senators, whether chosen by state legislatures, as they were at the earlier time, or by the voters of the state, must continuously nurture their political support back home; that is, if they hope for additional terms in office—and it is a rare senator who

4. Title 28 of the US. Code, Section 371(c) establishes retirement rules for Article III judges, the "Rule of 80." At age 65, a judge may retire at current salary or take senior status after performing 15 years of active judicial service (65+15 = 80). A senior judge handles about 15 percent of the court's annual workload.

does not. In this connection, senators from the First Congress on have recognized that one or two senators have a much greater stake in a particular appointment than others. It is, of course, exceedingly helpful to a senator to be able to reward supporters with good posts in the federal government. Conversely, it is enormously damaging to a senator's prestige if a president of his own party ignores him when it comes to making an appointment from or to the senator's own state. What is even more damaging to a senator's prestige and political power is for the president to appoint to high federal office someone who is known back home as a political opponent to the senator. It was easy for senators to see that if they joined together against the president to protect their individual interests in appointments, they could to a large degree assure that the president could only make such appointments as would be palatable to them as individuals. Out of such considerations grew the custom of senatorial courtesy (Chase 1972, 6).[5]

Whether formal or informal, the nomination of a federal judge is a long-standing, prestigious gift by a senator to her or his constituency.

The U.S. Senate Committee on the Judiciary (Senate Judiciary Committee) was established by resolution on December 10, 1816, "charged with [*inter alia*] the consideration of all Article III judicial nominations," which includes nominations to the U.S. Supreme Court, Circuit Courts, and District Courts.[6] Prior to the 1860s through the early part of the twentieth century, the nominations process was informal— consisting primarily of presidents and senators conferring on nominees. Senate rules were adopted in 1868 to provide more "routine referral of nominations to appropriate committees," but the process remained informal except for nominees against whom credible allegations of wrongdoing were lodged. In 1916, the first formal confirmation hearing was held as was the first public debate on the floor. Previously, debates and votes were held in secret and remained so unless the Senate voted to publicly disclose the proceedings.[7] In the 1920s and 1930s, hearings were infrequent, until 1955 when hearings started being routinely held. By the 1990s, federal confirmation hearings had become highly publicized affairs. The literature on the nomination and confirmation process that discuss presidential selections, Senate Judiciary proceedings, and Senate floor debates and votes is replete.[8] This section provides a simplified summary about relevant stages in the confirmation process where Luminaria nominees encountered obstacles.

---

5. Michael A. Sollenberger, *Must the Senate Take a Floor Vote?,* Wiley and Center for the Study of the Presidency and Congress, Presidential Studies Quarterly 34 (June 2004), 420–436, at 423.

6. Senate Judiciary Committee, The Judicial Nomination and Confirmation Process, https://www.judiciary.senate.gov/about/committee.

7. Senate Judiciary Committee, *About Judicial Nominations | Historical Overview,* https://www.senate.gov/about/ powers-procedures/nominations/judicial-nominations-overview.htm.

8. *See e.g.* Congressional Research Service (CRS), *The Appointment Process for U.S. Circuit and District Court Nominations: An Overview (Appointments Process),* updated June 17, 2016, https://crsreports.congress.gov.

2. Securing the Home-State Senators' Nomination, Interplay with the White House

By tradition, senators are consulted about in-state judicial nominees. The senior senator from the same political party controlling the White House defines and initiates the internal state nomination process.[9] Typically, that process consists of statewide committees appointed by the senator(s) and comprised of distinguished attorneys and citizens who solicit the applications, conduct interviews, and forward candidates (usually three) to the senior senator. Per protocol, where there are no senators from the president's party, the task of the state selection process defaults to the ranking congressional representative from the same party.[10] The senator (or senior representative) tenders to the White House the candidates, indicting their preferred candidate, usually resulting in a presidential nomination. "Referred" is the date the nomination is received by the Senate Judiciary Committee after being sent by the White House, which usually is the same as the date of the nomination.

3. American Bar Association (ABA) Ratings of Article III Judges

Since 1952 under President Dwight D. Eisenhower's administration,[11] the ABA Standing Committee on the Federal Judiciary (ABA Standing Committee) evaluates prospective nominees to the U.S. Supreme Court, Circuit and District Courts, the Court of International Trade, and certain territorial courts. The focus "strictly is on professional qualifications: integrity, professional competence and judicial temperament."[12] The "starting point of an [ABA Standing Committee] investigation is the receipt of the candidate's response to the public portion of the Senate Judiciary Committee questionnaire."[13] Confidential interviews of judges, practicing lawyers, and professional legal organizations are conducted. Where adverse or conflicting information arises or where a clear pattern of concerning behavior emerges, additional steps are taken to "reach a fair and accurate assessment of the nominee," including

---

9. Once nominations are referred to the Senate Judiciary Committee, nominees are required to complete Senate Judiciary Questionnaires and Financial Disclosure Reports that are entered in the official record and considered during the confirmation process (started under President Nixon). Where discrepancies arise, supplemental FBI checks may be undertaken. The FBI process is voluntary, but it is a crime to "knowingly and willfully" provide materially false information or statements. False Statements Act, 18 U.S.C. § 1001.

10. *Supra* note 8, Appointments Process at 10.

11. Laura E. Little, *The ABA's Role in Prescreening Federal Judicial Candidates: Are We Ready to Give Up on the Lawyers?*, Wm. & Mary Bill Rts. J. 10 (2001), 39–40, fn. 10, https://scholarship.law.wm.edu/wmborj/vol10 /iss1/4.

12. ABA, *The ABA Standing Committee on Federal Judiciary: What It Is and How It Works*, 1–31, https://www. americanbar.org/content/dam/aba/administrative/government_affairs_office/fjc-backgrounder.pdf.

13. *Id.*

providing the nominees with a full opportunity to rebut during their hearings or interviews.[14] The ABA Standing Committee provides one of the following ratings based on a majority vote: "Well Qualified," "Qualified," "Not Qualified." These ratings are provided to the White House, Senate Judiciary Committee, and the Department of Justice (DOJ).[15]

On March 22, 2001, March 17, 2017, and May 29, 2025, three Republican administrations informed the ABA that the White House would no longer provide "special access" to a nominee's record (i.e., stopped the practice of soliciting and considering ABA ratings).[16] Both administrations stopped the practice initiated by President Eisenhower's attorney general who sought an independent body to examine the qualifications of potential judicial nominees. President Obama reinstituted the practice, continued by President Joe Biden.[17] Over the decades, the ABA ratings/process has become increasingly controversial, garnering scrutiny and criticism from both sides of the political spectrum.[18] All Luminaria Article III judges were rated by the ABA Standing Committee.

4. Senatorial Holds and Blue Slips

A hold on a nomination means a senator objects to approving a nomination by unanimous consent, which, as that term implies, is unanimous agreement to approving a nominee or proceeding that moves the nomination forward, including to a vote.[19] Holds, especially secret or confidential holds, complicate a nominee's confirmation process, adding at least five additional steps to a Senate floor vote.

In 1917, the Senate adopted the "blue slip" process, not required by rules but imbedded by tradition. Named "blue slips" after the paper color on which the Chair of the Senate Judiciary Committee writes home-state Senators to solicit

14. *Id.*

15. *Id.*

16. March 22, 2001, letter to ABA President Martha Barnett from Counsel to the President Alberto Gonzales, http://www.whitehouse.gov /news/releases/2001/03/20010322-5.html; March 17, 2017, letter to ABA President Linda Klein from White House Counsel Donald F. McGahn II; May 29, 2025 letter to ABA President William R. Bay from Attorney General Pamela Bondi, https://www .justice.gov/ag/media/1402156/dl?inline.

17. *See Terry Carter, Do-Over After an 8-Year Pause, the ABA Is Again Vetting Possible Federal Bench Nominees, ABA J.*, May 2009, 62, 62–63.

18. E.g., Maya Sen, *How Judicial Qualification Ratings May Disadvantage Minority and Female Candidates*, Journal of Law and Courts (Spring 2014), 33–65; Susan Navarro Smelcer, Amy Steigerwalt, and Richard L. Vining, Jr., *Bias and the Bar: Evaluating the ABA Ratings of Federal Judicial Nominees*, Political Research Quarterly 65, no. 4 (December 2012): 827–840; Susan Brodie Haire, *Rating the Ratings of the American Bar Association Standing Committee on Federal Judiciary*, The Justice System Journal 22, no. 1 (2001), 1; and James Lindgren, *Examining the American Bar Association's Ratings of Nominees to the U.S. Courts of Appeals for Political Bias, 1989–2000*, J.L. & Pol. 17 (2001).

19. CRS Holds on Nominations, July 13, 2023, and sources cited therein, https://crsreports .congress.gov.

their opinions about judicial nominees. A return of a blue slip signifies a Senator's approval of a nominee. A Senator's refusal to return a blue slip ("missing blue slip") or return of a negative blue slip, communicates that Senator's disapproval of a potential nominee. The consequence of a missing or negative blue slip is determined by the Chair of the Senate Judiciary Committee, ranging from refusal to hold hearings to no impact with hearings proceeding.[20]

On September 14, 2007, the Honest Leadership and Open Government Act of 2007 was enacted, which requires public notice of holds within six session days. The Senate passed a resolution on January 27, 2011 (92–4), that requires holds to be entered into the Congressional Record two days after it is passed unless the hold is lifted within the two-day period.[21] If the senator placing the hold fails to come forward, the hold is attributed to the party leader or the senator placing the hold on behalf of the "secret" senator. A "tag-team" hold is used, however, to circumvent the rule whereby one senator places an anonymous hold but releases it before the two-day period while a second takes over the hold, *ad infinitum*.

5. Hearings, Senate Debates, and Voting to Confirm

At hearings before the Senate Judiciary Committee, senators introduce home-state/circuit nominees and provide nominees the opportunity to present their credentials and address concerns or questions, specific to their background. The Senate Judicial Questionnaires completed by nominees are entered into the hearing record, along with letters of support/opposition and other such documents as requested by senators. Typically, multiple nominees participate in a single-day hearing that consists primarily of *pro forma* questioning. Instances where a controversy arises may result in prolonged hearings for and greater scrutiny of a nominee. Public witnesses and organizations may offer testimony. Post-hearing, nominees may be asked to submit additional written responses.[22]

Upon approval by the Senate Judiciary Committee (nominee passes through committee), the nominee is placed on the Senate's Executive Calendar for debate and vote by the entire Senate.[23] A Senate vote may be delayed but ultimately debate and voting by the Senate occurs and results, most of the time, in a confirmation. Senate votes on judicial nominations may take one of three forms: by unanimous consent or *en bloc* (UC), a recorded or roll call vote (RV), or voice vote (VV) in which a

20. Camille Peeples, *Advice and Consent' Inside the Judicial Nominations Process*, Stanford Lawyer Magazine, June 14, 2008, https://law.stanford.edu/stanford-lawyer/articles/advice-and-consent-inside-the-judicial-nominations-process/.

21. S.1.ENR (110th Cong. 2007–2008), S.RES.28.ATS (112th Cong. 2011–2012); *see* John Bresnahan, *Senate Leaders End Secrecy of 'Holds'*, Roll Call, March 8, 1999, 1; Editorial, *No More Secret Holds*, Washington Post, March 10, 1999, A22, announcing agreement by Senate Majority and Minority Leaders Trent Lott (R-MS) and Tom Daschle (D-SD) to lift secret holds on legislation.

22. *Supra* note 8, Appointments Process at 22–25.

23. *Id.* at 26–28.

majority of those present approve the nomination. During a voice vote, the individual vote of each senator is not recorded, only the majority vote is entered into the official record.[24] Upon confirmation, the judge's commission (the start date of judicial service) is captured in an official document authorizing the nominee to assume judicial office. The Oath of Office is, thereafter, administered, followed by investiture, which occurs when the new judge is sworn in, typically at the courthouse. This process encapsulates the Advice and Consent requirement of Article 2, § 2.[25]

A judicial nomination may be returned when no hearing is scheduled, held, or rejected because the nominee fails to garner approval of the Senate Judiciary Committee or the full Senate. The nominee whose nomination has lapsed may be reconsidered by the Senate, but Senate Rule XXXI, ¶ 6 requires renomination by the president.[26]

B. Luminaria Article III Judges

Nineteen years separate the first Latino appointed to the federal bench in 1961, Reynaldo Garza, and the first Latina Article III judge in 1980. Since Judge Cerezo was appointed, seventeen Luminarias have been confirmed as Article III judges to nineteen federal benches: twelve as the first Latina federal judges in their respective districts, circuits, and the U.S. Supreme Court, and five as the second in the District of California (Central), New Mexico, Puerto Rico, and the Ninth Circuit Court of Appeals (Ninth Circuit). All Luminaria Article III judges were appointed to districts with large or significant Latino populations. U.S. presidents from President Carter to President Barack Obama who appointed Luminaria Article III judges include:

- George W. Bush: seven
- Bill Clinton: five
- George H.W. Bush: three
- Jimmy Carter: one
- Ronald Reagan: one
- Barack Obama: one

President Joe Biden has appointed the most Latina (non-Luminaria) judges, twenty-two jurists to twenty-four judicial posts, followed by Presidents Obama

24. *Id.* at 29–32, 40.

25. The meaning of "Advice and Consent" has been evaluated including in 2001 by the Senate Judiciary Committee. Under consideration was whether judicial philosophy should be part of the inquiry. *See* Committee on the Judiciary United States Senate, Hearings before the Subcommittee on Administrative Oversight and the Courts, One Hundred Seventh Congress, First Session, June 26 and September 4, 2001, Serial No. J-07-28, 1-276.

26. *Supra* note 8, Appointments Process at 42–44.

and George W. Bush at eleven each, and President Clinton, six.[27] *See* Appendix B, List of Luminaria & Latina Article III Judges 1980–2024. Factors contributing to the notable increase in the number of Latina federal judges may include the passage of time with Luminarias aging past what may considered prime age for appointment to the federal bench, an increase in the number of experienced Latina attorneys, an awareness of the importance of a diverse bench towards building a more perfect union, and willingness by U.S. Presidents to achieve diversity as reflected by their respective appointments. The increase of the Latino U.S. population may be one of the more critical factors, i.e., growing number of registered Latino voters. Sophisticated advocacy by the HNBA, state Latino bar associations and other Latino organizations—importantly MALDEF and the Puerto Rican Legal Defense and Education Fund (PRLDEF)—is invaluable. The ever-increasing Latino population has been emphasized consistently during HNBA testimony provided at Senate Judiciary Committee confirmation hearings for Latino and non-Latino candidates over the decades. At present, the number of Latina Article III judges is not proportionate to their U.S. population of nearly 10% (9.9%).

27. CRS, *The Appointment of Hispanic and U.S. Circuit and District Court Judges: Historical Overview and Analysis, September 29, 2023, https://crsreports.congress.gov.*

Table 3 **Luminaria Article III Judges**

District Court: 15	President	District	Tenure	Status
Carmen Consuelo Cerezo	Jimmy Carter	District of Puerto Rico (new seat[28]) Chief Judge	6/30/1980–2/28/2021 1993–1999	Retired
Lenore Carrero Nesbitt	Ronald Reagan	Southern District of Florida, Miami	11/6/1983–10/6/2001 Senior Status 7/19/1998	Deceased
Sonia Sotomayor	George H.W. Bush	Southern District of New York	8/12/1992–10/7/1998	Elevated
Lourdes Baird	George H.W. Bush	Central District of California, Los Angeles (new seat[29])	8/12/1992–4/15/2005 Senior Status 5/12/2004	Retired
Irma Gonzalez	George H.W. Bush	Southern District of California, San Diego Chief Judge	8/12/1992–10/25/2013 Senior Status 3/29/2013 2005–2012	Retired
Martha Vázquez	Bill Clinton	District of New Mexico Chief Judge	10/1/1993–12/31/2023 2003–2010	Senior Status
Kim McLane Wardlaw	Bill Clinton	Central District of California Ninth Circuit Court of Appeals	12/26/1995–8/3/1998 8/3/1998	Elevated Incumbent
Hilda Tagle	Bill Clinton	Southern District of Texas, Brownsville	4/17/1998–12/31/2021 Senior Status 12/21/2018	Inactive Status
M. Christina Armijo	George W. Bush	District of New Mexico Chief Judge	11/12/2001–2/7/2018 2/7/2018 Senior Status 2012–2018	Inactive Senior Status

continues

28. 92 Stat. 1629 (Oct. 20, 1978).
29. 104 Stat. 5089.

continued

Judith Herrera	George W. Bush	District of New Mexico	6/13/2004–7/1/2019	Senior Status
Dora Irizarry	George W. Bush	Eastern District of New York Chief Judge	7/8/2004–1/26/2020 2016–2020	Senior Status
Virginia Hernandez Covington	George W. Bush	Middle District of Florida, Tampa	9/10/2004–7/12/2020	Senior Status
Aida Delgado-Colón	George W. Bush	District of Puerto Rico Chief Judge	3/17/2006 2011–2018	Incumbent
Christine Arguello	George W. Bush	Tenth Circuit Court of Appeals District of Colorado	2000, Returned 2002 10/21/2008–7/15/2022	Retired
Nitza Quiñones Alejandro	Barack Obama	Eastern District of Pennsylvania	6/19/2013	Incumbent
CIRCUIT COURT: 4				
Sonia Sotomayor	Bill Clinton Barack Obama	Second Circuit Court of Appeals	10/7/1998–8/8/2009	Elevated
Rosemary Barkett	Bill Clinton U.S. Dept. of State	Eleventh Circuit Court of Appeals The Hague, Iran–U.S. Tribunal (non-Article III post)	4/15/1994–9/30/2013 10/1/2013	Elevated Incumbent
Kim McLane Wardlaw	Bill Clinton	Ninth Circuit Court of Appeals	8/3/1998	Incumbent
Consuelo Maria Callahan	George W. Bush	Ninth Circuit Court of Appeals	5/28/2003–7/1/2019	Incumbent
SUPREME COURT: 1				
Sonia Sotomayor	Barack Obama	111th Associate Justice	8/8/2009	Incumbent

Of the seventeen, eleven were judges prior to elevation to the District Court; five had no prior judicial experience: Judges Sotomayor, Vázquez, McLane Wardlaw, Herrera, and Arguello. Two Luminaria Judges Sotomayor and McLane Wardlaw were elevated from the District to the Circuit Court. Judge Sotomayor was nominated by three U.S. presidents: H.W. Bush in 1992 to the Southern District of New York (SDNY), Clinton in 1998 to the Second Circuit Court of Appeals (Second Circuit), and Obama in 2009 to the U.S. Supreme Court. Judge McLane Wardlaw was appointed as the second Latina in 1995 to the Central District of California in Los Angeles (C.D. CA), following the first, Lourdes Baird in 1992, and in 1998 as the first Latina on the Ninth Circuit. In the District of New Mexico, the tenures of three Luminaria judges overlapped: Vázquez (1993–2021), Herrera (2004–2019), and Armijo (2001–2008). Judges Baird and McLane Wardlaw served concurrently on the Central District of California for three years (1995–1998) until McLane Wardlaw was elevated to the Ninth Circuit. Judges McLane Wardlaw and Callahan have served concurrently on the Ninth Circuit since 2003. Judge Barkett was the first woman and first Latina appointed to the Florida Supreme Court in 1985 and in 1994, to the Eleventh Circuit Court of Appeals (Eleventh Circuit). In another historic first, she was selected to serve on the Iran–U.S. Tribunal at The Hague in 2013 by the U.S. State Department and International Court of Justice (World Court), a non-Article III judicial post.[30]

Six of the Luminarias served as chief judges of their respective courts with Judge Cerezo serving as the first Latina chief judge in the country. The tenures of the Luminaria chief judges overlapped as follows:

Judge Cerezo	1993–1999	
Judge Vazquez	2003–2010	5 years concurrent with Judge Gonzalez
Judge Gonzalez	2005–2012	5 years concurrent with Judge Vázquez
Judge Delgado-Colón	2011–2018	1 year concurrent with Judge Gonzalez
Judge Armijo	2012–2018	6 years concurrent with Delgado-Colón
Judge Irizarry	2016–2020	2 years concurrent with Delgado-Colón and Armijo

All but two of the Luminaria judges were first-generation lawyers. Ten Luminarias attended public schools and seven received Catholic educations. The Luminarias graduated from colleges and universities that range from local to Ivy League, includ-

30. U.S. Department of State, Iran-U.S. Claims Tribunal, https://www.state.gov/iran-u-s-claims-tribunal/#:~:text=The%20Tribunal%20sits%20in%20%20by%20an%20appointing%20authority. The Iran–U.S. Tribunal was created by the Algiers Accord of January 19, 1981, to address the Tehran hostage situation in Iran and address resulting grievances. http://www.iusct.net/General%20Documents/2-Claims%20Settlement%20Declaration.pdf. It is a non-Article III judicial post.

ing Notre Dame, Princeton, Stanford, UCLA, Yale, East Texas State University (A&M-Commerce), and the Universities of Florida, New Mexico, Colorado at Boulder, Puerto Rico, and Tampa. Nine graduated with honors, four *summa cum laude*, and five *cum laude.* Nine judges graduated from Tier 1 law schools,[31] including Columbia, Georgetown, Harvard, Notre Dame, Texas, UCLA, and Yale. Two matriculated at Puerto Rican law schools—Escuela de Derecho de Puerto Rico (UPR) and Pontifical Catholic University of Puerto Rico (Pontifical Catholic)—two from the University of Florida Law School, and one each from the University Law Schools of Arizona, Colorado, New Mexico, and Pacific McGeorge. Five Luminarias served on law journals: Judges Sotomayor (Yale Law Journal), McLane Wardlaw (UCLA Law Journal as articles editor), Hernandez Covington (Georgetown Law Review and Tax Lawyer as editor), Delgado-Colón (as editor of the Pontifical Catholic Law Review) and Arguello (Harvard Civil Rights Civil Liberties Law Review as articles editor). Four judges were law clerks: Cerezo (District of Puerto Rico and Puerto Rico Supreme Court), Carrero Nesbitt (Hon. Wallace Sturgis, Florida District Court of Appeal), Gonzalez (Hon. William Frey, District of Arizona), McLane Wardlaw (Hon. William P. Gray, C.A. CA.).

The seventeen judges were licensed in nine jurisdictions: Arizona (1), California (5), Colorado (1), Florida (4), Iowa (1), New Mexico (3), New York (2), Puerto Rico (2), and Texas (1), with two licensed in more than one state, Judges Gonzalez (Arizona and California) and Arguello (Colorado, Florida, and Iowa). Fourteen were in private practice, and three were solo practitioners. Seven were prosecutors, two were public defenders, and one was a legal aid attorney. One Luminaria was elected to political office, another to a public-school board, and one ran but lost election for state attorney general. None served in the military. Eleven Luminarias were state or county judges and two served as federal magistrate judges, Gonzalez and Delgado-Colón, before their elevation to the District Court.

On the date of confirmation, the median age of the seventeen Luminarias appointed to the District Court was 47.35 years. Judge Sotomayor was the youngest at age 38, followed by Judge Cerezo at age 39. The others were in their 40s or 50s on their respective dates of confirmation. The District Court judges served for a combined 235.3 years. Judge Cerezo, at 40.8 years of service, had the longest tenure—20 years over most others, including non-Latina judges. Judge Vázquez followed at 28.3 years and Judge Gonzalez at 21.2 years. Judge Delgado-Colón, an active incumbent judge, has served for 18 years. Judge McLane Wardlaw had the shortest tenure at 2 years and 8 months, having been elevated to the Ninth Circuit where she is an incumbent. The median judicial tenure of the Luminarias is 16.80 years. The median

31. The top fourteen law schools in the country—Tier 1 law schools—changed over the decades. *See e.g. Ranking the Law Schools: The Reality of Illusion?, American Bar Foundation Research Journal 7, no. 3 (Summer 1982): 649–684. By 2023 standards, the seven law schools at which the Luminarias matriculated were Tier 1 schools.*

age of the four Circuit Court judges on their respective dates of confirmation was 53 years. Circuit Court Judges Sotomayor and McLane Wardlaw were the youngest at 44 years of age. Judge Barkett and Callahan were 55 and 53, respectively. Combined the four Circuit Court judges have served 79 years plus with Judges McLane Wardlaw and Callahan, as of 2025, serving as incumbent judges.

The biographical summary section for each Luminaria judge starts with a career timeline, starting with the year of their undergraduate degrees through retirement and/or current position. The biographical summaries capture their formative years and family background, including what motivated them to become lawyers. This information was compiled from various sources, including resumes, court biographies, and articles. Where available, the judges' insights and explanations are presented from personal interviews conducted by others.

1. Carmen Consuelo Cerezo, District of Puerto Rico, 1980–2021

1963	Bachelor of Arts (B.A.), Philosophy, *summa cum laude*, University of Puerto Rico (UPR)
1966	LL.B., UPR Law School
1966–1967	Private practice, Benny Frankie Cerezo, Esq.
1967	Admitted to the Puerto Rico Bar
1968	Law Clerk, Chief Justice Puerto Rico Supreme Court Luis Negrón-Fernández
1967–1972	Law Clerk, District Court of Puerto Rico (D.P.R.)
1972–1976	Judge, Superior Court Bayamón, appointed by Governor Luis A. Ferré
1976–1980	Judge, Court of Intermediate Appeals, appointed by the Chief Judge
1980	Article III Judge, District of Puerto Rico (new seat)
1988	Masters of Law (LL.M.) in judicial process from the University of Virginia[32]
1993–1999	Chief Judge, first Latina Chief Judge of Article III bench[33]
2021	Retired February 28, 2021

32. Hearings before the Committee on the Judiciary, United States Senate (Senate Judiciary Committee Hearings), Ninety Sixth Congress 1979–1981, Second Session, Part 7, Serial No. 96-21, June 10, 1980:464-488, 475; Federal Bar Association, Hon. Raymond L. Acosta Puerto Rican Chapter, *From the Bar, 1st Issue on Judicial Profiles* 59 (Summer 2018): 13–14, https://www.fedbar.org/hon-raymond-l-acosta-puerto-rico-chapter//wp-content/uploads/sites/36/2019/10/PR-FTB-First-Issue-on-Judicial-Profiles-pdf.pdf.

33. To qualify for chief judge of a circuit or district court, a judge must be in active service for one or more years, hold seniority over the commissioned judges who are sixty-four years of age or under, have not previously served as chief judge, and be under seventy years of age (unless there are no other eligible judges). The term is seven years. No vacancy is created by promotion to chief judge. Upon completing the term, a chief judge returns to active service.

Carmen Consuelo Vargas was born on August 22, 1940, in San Juan, Puerto Rico to Consuelo Martinez-Cuebas and Pablo Vargas-Badillo, the fourth of five children. Though dancing was her avocation growing up, she was destined for the judiciary. "Perhaps Judge Cerezo's training in classical ballet as a young woman—a discipline characterized by inspiration, focus and strength—is the best symbol, a premonition of the jurists that she would become."[34] During law school she met and married fellow law student Benny Frank Cerezo in 1964, taking his name.[35] Benny Cerezo served in the Puerto Rico House of Representatives (1969–1973) and was a founder of the Puerto Rico Partido Nuevo Progresista (New Progressive Party). They had two children, Francisco Javier (an attorney) and daughter Rossana; she is grandmother to Sara Gabriela. Mrs. Cerezo was recruited eight months out of law school by the chief justice of the Puerto Rico Supreme Court to serve as its law clerk. From that point, she dedicated her career to the judicial branch, starting as a law clerk and later becoming a federal judge. In 2020, Judge Cerezo achieved the milestone of serving on the bench for forty years. She is recognized as an exceptional and principled jurist who left an endearing mark on the Island and U.S. jurisprudence. At age eighty, Judge Cerezo retired on February 21, 2021, as the longest tenured Luminaria Article III judge. Chief Justice Gelpi wrote,

> Judge Cerezo's understanding of the essence of the fundamental right to equal treatment under the law is her lifeblood—the respect with which she approaches all cases no matter their degree of difficulty or their high publicity—all litigants not only demand but deserve equal protection. Social upbringing or disadvantage, a privileged or poverty-stricken background, religious beliefs, political class, race, gender, any and all other labels to be thought of—none have ever mattered in Judge Cerezo's classroom.[36]

2. Lenore Carrero Nesbitt, Southern District of Florida, 1983–2001

1949	Study at University of Havana
1952	Associate of Arts Degree (A.A.), Stephens College
1954	Bachelor of Sciences (B.S.), Communications, Northwestern University
1957	LL.B., University of Miami (Miami Law)
1957–1959	Research Assistant to Chief Judge, Florida First District Court of Appeal

34. U.S. District Court Chief Judge Gustavo A. Gelpi Press Release, *Retirement of the Honorable Carmen Consuelo Cerezo,* February 16, 2021.

35. Federal Bar Association, Hon. Raymond L. Acosta Puerto Rico Chapter, *The Bar*, Issue No. 59 (Summer 2018).

36. *Id.*

1958	Admitted to Florida Bar
1960–1963	Partner, Nesbitt & Nesbitt
1962–1963	Special Assistant to Florida Attorney General Richard W. Ervin
1963–1965	Legal Research Assistant, Dade County Circuit Court Judges
1965–1969	Homemaker
1969–1973	Associate, Law Office of John Robert Terry
1973–1975	Associate, Petersen McGowan & Feder
1975	Associate, Norman Somberg
1975–1983	Judge, Circuit Court of Florida, Eleventh Judicial Circuit
1983–2001	Article III Judge, Southern District of Florida[37] (Miami)
1998–2001	Senior Status July 19, 1998–October 6, 2001
2001	Deceased October 6, 2001

Lenore was born in Key West, Florida, on July 19, 1932, to Tildo Sanchez and Katherine "Kitty" (*nee* Hodge) Carrero, the oldest of two daughters.[38] Kitty was born in New York, Tildo in Florida. Tildo's parents, Amado and Leonora Carrero, were born in Cuba. Amado, whose father was born in Spain, was a cigarmaker; he migrated to the U.S. in 1882 and was naturalized. Tildo worked at Pan American Airlines for twenty-five years and later owned Holiday Tours Travel Agency.[39] Recognizing Lenore's "leadership abilities and pragmatic style," her parents encouraged Lenore to pursue a career in the legal profession.[40] During registration on the first day of school, Lenore met her future husband, Joseph Nesbitt. The sole female law student, Lenore graduated at the top of her class. In 1958, Lenore and Joseph Nesbitt married; they had two children.[41] For three years, they practiced together as Nesbitt & Nesbitt in Miami before pursuing individual careers that resulted in judicial service. Joseph preceded Lenore as a judge on the 11th Judicial Circuit Court; she was appointed to the same bench in 1975.[42] Judge Carrero Nesbitt became the first woman appointed

37. Nominee Lenore Carrero Nesbitt, Senate Judiciary Committee Hearings, Ninety Eighth Congress 1983–1984, First Session, Part 2, Serial No. J-98-6, November 7, 1983:71, 80; PN55—Lenore Carrero Nesbitt—The Judiciary, https://www.congress.gov/nomination/98th-congress/551?x=5&r=79 (PN).

38. Sarah Nesbitt Arcona, *Benchstories, Judge Lenore Carrero Nesbitt*, Gables Foundation 1 (2018): 3, https://gablesfoundation.org/wp-content/uploads/2018/04/Benchstories-Volume-1.pdf.

39. Obituary of Tildo Sanchez Carrero, *Miami Herald*, November 1987.

40. *Id.*

41. Obituary of Joseph Nesbitt, 76, *Longtime Appeals Judge Is Called 'Very Cool, Fair'*, Miami Herald, March 12, 2006, https://www.newspapers.com/article/the-miami-herald-obituary-for-joseph-nes/133998528/SarahNesbittArtecona; All About the U, https://miami.giftlegacy.com/?pageID=3&storyNum=10.

42. Florida Third District Court of Appeal, Judge Joseph Nesbitt, https://3dca.flcourts.gov/Judges/All-Judges/Judge-Joseph-Nesbitt.

to the Southern District of Florida, "the first lady of the court."[43] At age sixty-nine while on senior status, Judge Carrero Nesbitt passed on October 6, 2001. Colleagues described her as "a cross between a renaissance woman and a force of nature."[44] In 2001, Judge Carrero Nesbitt was inducted posthumously into the Florida Women's Hall of Fame.[45] The Lenore Carrero Nesbitt Public Service Scholarship was established at Miami Law in her honor in the manner she wanted to be remembered, as a devoted public servant.[46]

3. Sonia Sotomayor, Southern District of New York, 1992–1998

1976	B.A., History, *summa cum laude*, Princeton University, *Phi Beta Kappa*
1979	J.D., Yale Law School, Editor of the Yale Law Journal, Pyne Prize Recipient
1980	Admitted to New York Bar
1979–1984	New York County Assistant District Attorney
1983–1986	Owner, Sotomayor & Associates
1984–1992	Pavia & Harcourt, LLP Associate April 1984–December1987, Partner January 1988–August1992[47]
1992–1998	District Court Judge, Southern District of New York
1998–2009	Article III Judge, Second Circuit Court of Appeals
2009–Present	111th Associate Judge, U.S. Supreme Court

The first Puerto Rican on the mainland to become a federal judge, Sonia was born in the Bronx, New York, on June 25, 1954, to Juan and Celina (*nee* Báez) Sotomayor. Celina was born in Lajas, Puerto Rico, and upon her mother's death was raised by *Titi Aurora* and *Tito Mayo.* At seventeen, Celina joined the Women's Army Corps (WACs) and was sent to Georgia where she met Juan. "Her parents came to the U.S. during WWII, in the words of the Bard, 'bearing their birthrights proudly on their

---

43. *Judge Lenore C. Nesbitt Dies at 69*, Tampa Bay, September 10, 2005; *Posthumous Endowed Scholarship from 'First Lady of the Court' Honors Distinguished Alumna's Legacy*, Miami Momentum 2: Promoting Public Service, 2002, http://www.momentum2.miami.edu/feature_promoting_public_service.html.

44. *Id.*

45. Florida Women's Hall of Fame, https://flwomenshalloffame.org/bio/lenore-carrero-nesbitt/; http://www.momentum2.miami.edu/feature_promoting_public_service.html.

46. *Celebrating Endowment of Lenore Carrero Nesbitt Scholarship for Public Service*, Miami Alumni Magazine LV, no. 1 (2002): 12, https://media.law.miami.edu/alumni/pdf/barrister/barrister-summer2002.pdf.

47. Nominee Sonia Sotomayor, Senate Judiciary Committee Hearings, One Hundred Second Congress 1991–1992, Second Session, Part 9, Serial No. J-102-7, June 4, 1992:202-204, 215, 281–317, 282 (Sotomayor District Court Confirmation).

backs, to make a hazard of new fortunes here.'"[48] And, so they did. Juan worked in a "tool-and-die factory" and Celina as a telephone operator, eventually becoming a nurse shortly after Sonia was born. In 1957, the family moved from a tenement in the South Bronx to a housing project in the East Bronx. "Her relatively close proximity to Yankee Stadium led her to becoming a lifelong fan of the New York Yankees." At age seven, Sonia was diagnosed with type 1 diabetes and began daily insulin injections. Two years later, Juan died at age forty-two of heart problems developed during WWII. Celina's friend Ana was Sonia's babysitter and "the one [her] mother entrusted to tell ... of her father's death." Sonia attended Catholic schools, graduating valedictorian of both Blessed Sacrament School and Cardinal Spellman High School. Inspired by Nancy Drew and Perry Mason, she reflected in 1998: "I was going to college and I was going to become an attorney, and I knew that when I was ten. Ten. That's no jest."[49] Celina returned to school to obtain her registered nurse license when Sonia and her younger brother, Juan, were in high school. Her extended family visited frequently, and Sonia regularly visited Puerto Rico during summers. Sonia married her high school boyfriend in 1976; they amicably divorced in 1983.[50]

Fresh out of law school, Sonia was hired by Manhattan District Attorney Bob Morgenthau and litigated criminal cases for almost five years as an assistant district attorney. Thereafter, she acquired nine years of civil experience at Pavia & Harcourt as an associate and then partner. For the last three months leading up to January 1990, the firm's managing litigation partner David Botwinik, lobbied Sonia to apply for the federal bench, which she repeatedly refused to do. Botwinik finally pulled rank, gave her the application to Senator Patrick Moynihan's Judicial Selection Committee, removed her caseload, and gave her one week to complete the application.[51] In 1992, Sonia became the first Puerto Rican woman on the mainland to become a federal judge for which she has been widely honored. She is the recipient of Woodrow Wilson Award from Princeton University and Katherine Hepburn Medal from Bryn Mawr College, twelve honorary law school degrees, and several national awards such as the Hispanic Heritage Award. For her historic career, she was inducted in 2019 into the National Women's Hall of Fame.

---

48. Induction Proceedings for Circuit Judge Sonia Sotomayor, 1–58 (November 6, 1998) at 25, remarks by Circuit Judge Jose Cabranes (Sotomayor Induction Ceremony), https://judicial-discipline-reform.org/SCt_nominee/98-11-6JSotomayor_induction_proceedings.pdf.

49. Antonia Felix, *Sonia Sotomayor, The True American Dream* (Penguin Publishing Group, 2010) (Felix), Felix chptr. 4 at 56; Felix's book contains a detailed information about the justice's family background.

50. *Id.*

51. *Id.* Felix chptr. 7 at 147, 149.

4. Lourdes Gillespie Baird, Central District of California, 1992–1998

1954	Secretarial School, Certificate
1966–1971	A.A., Los Angeles City College
1973	B.A., Sociology, University of California, Los Angeles (UCLA)
1976	J.D., UCLA School of Law Admitted to California Bar
1977–1983	Assistant U.S. Attorney (AUSA), U.S. Attorney's Office, Central District of California
1983–1984	Attorney, Partner, Baird & Quadros
1984–1986	Attorney, Partner, Baird Munger & Myers
1986–1988	Judge, East / Los Angeles Municipal Court
1988–1990	Judge, Los Angeles Superior Court
1986–1990	Adjunct Professor, Loyola Law School, Los Angeles
1990–1992	U.S. Attorney, Central District of California (C.D. CA)
1992–2004	Article III Judge, C.D. CA[52]
2004	Senior Status May 12, 2004
2005	Retired April 15, 2005 Joined Judicial Arbitration and Mediation Services (JAMS)

On May 17, 1935, Maria Lourdes was born abroad in Quito, Ecuador, the youngest of seven children and four daughters. Josefina Delgado Espinosa and James C. Gillespie married in 1921. James, born in Philadelphia, was an accountant; Josefina did domestic housekeeping. In 1936, James moved the family to Los Angeles where Lourdes was raised. She received a Catholic education, graduating from the all-girls Immaculate Heart High School where the nuns modeled their independence. She left for Europe—taking classes at the University of Madrid—returned to Los Angeles and took secretarial classes earning a certificate in 1954.[53] Two years later at age twenty-one, she married William T. Baird and had three children. Lourdes decided to return to school. She once recalled, "I had three kids, a station wagon, a shaggy

52. U.S. Attorney nomination, PN1263—Lourdes G. Baird—Department of Justice, https://www.congress.gov/nomination/101st-congress/1263?s=2&r=28; Nominee Lourdes Gillespie Baird, Senate Judiciary Committee Hearings, One Hundred Second Congress 1991–1992, Second Session, Part 9, Serial No. J-102-7, June 1, 1992:661-695, at 661-662; PN1024—Lourdes G. Baird—The Judiciary (Baird Art III Confirmation), https://www.congress.gov/nomination-102nd-congress/1024?s=5&r=2761.

53. Henry Weinstein, *Wilson Nominates Woman—a Democrat for U.S. Attorney*, Los Angeles Times, November 30, 1989.

dog and did a lot of volunteer work. After my youngest was in school, I started with one night class at Los Angeles City College."[54] Initially, Lourdes "had no intention of going to law school. It was like stepping on a train that continued to accelerate."[55] In 1975 while in law school, Lourdes divorced but retained Baird and became known professionally as Gillespie Baird. Lourdes started her legal career at age forty-one and soared through the ranks during her six years as an AUSA in the Los Angeles District Office. She tried cases in the Fraud and Special Prosecutions Unit and was promoted to assistant division chief supervising economic crimes. Lourdes was in private practice for three years before her first judicial appointment by Governor George Deukmejian. She presided over two municipal courts before elevation to the Superior Court of Los Angeles as a juvenile court judge. Promoted by Republican California Governor Pete Wilson, Judge Baird was surprised when asked to submit her application for U.S. attorney.[56] Lourdes—a Democrat—was appointed in 1990 by President George H. W. Bush to the Central District of California, Los Angeles as "[o]ne of only five female U.S. attorneys in the country and one of the few who sp[oke] Spanish fluently. She also [wa]s the first grandmother ever selected for the post."[57] The new U.S. Attorney assumed the job in the largest jurisdiction in the country, "at a time when the area is considered one of the major national centers of drug crime, money laundering, savings and loan scams and defense contracting fraud."[58] U.S. Attorney Baird served only two years before being nominated in 1992 to the federal bench. While on the bench, Judge Baird earned a reputation for "cut[ting to the heart of complex cases... [due to her] impressive command of civil and criminal law."[59] She retired on July 15, 2005, and, at almost seventy, joined JAMS as a private mediator and arbitrator.[60]

5. Irma Elsa Gonzalez, Southern District of California, 1992–2013

1966–1967	Study at Stephens College
1970	B.A., History, Stanford University
1973	J.D., University of Arizona School of Law Admitted to Arizona Bar

54. *Id.*

55. Richard D. Aldrich, *Who's Who: 25 of the Most Influential, High-Profile Judges in L.A.*, Los Angeles Business Journal, January 30, 2000.

56. *Id.*; the speculation was that Baird's selection would help Governor Wilson win his 1990 gubernatorial campaign.

57. Henry Weinstein, *Slow Start, Fast Pace for New U.S. Atty. Baird: Appointment: She Came Late to the Legal Profession. Now She'll Head the Biggest Federal Judicial District in the Country*, Los Angeles Times, July 19, 1990.

58. *Id.*

59. *Supra* note 52, Baird Art. III Confirmation.

60. Ashlea Ebeling, *Just a Phase?*, Forbes Magazine, September 11, 2008.

1973–1975	Law Clerk, District of Arizona Judge William C. Frey
1975–1979	AUSA, Criminal Division, U.S. Attorney's Office, District of Arizona
1979	Trial Attorney, U.S. Department of Justice (C.D. CA) Antitrust Division
1979–1981	AUSA, U.S. Attorney's Office (C.D. CA) Criminal Division, Los Angeles
1980	Admitted California Bar
1981–1984	Associate Attorney, Seltzer Caplan Wilkins & McMahon (Seltzer Caplan)
1984–1991	U.S. Magistrate Judge, Southern District of California
1991–1992	Superior Court Judge, County of San Diego
1992	Adjunct Professor, University of San Diego School of Law
1992–2005	Article III Judge, Southern District of California Chief Judge 2005–2012[61]
2013	Senior Status March 29–October 25, 2013 Retired October 25, 2013
2013–2021	Mediator/Arbitrator/Special Master/Referee, JAMS

Irma Gonzalez is the first woman of Mexican American descent to become an Article III judge. She was born in Palo Alto, California, on March 29, 1948, while her father-surgeon Dr. Humberto Gonzalez was in medical school at Stanford. Among the first Latino doctors in the state of Arizona, Humberto was born in Nogales, one of eight children who were orphaned and the sole child to acquire a formal education. Irma's mother Lydia (*nee* Espinosa), was born in Mexico and became a U.S. citizen when Irma was five. Lydia earned a GED at age forty-five and became a realtor. Irma and Humberto raised nine bilingual children (seven daughters) who all earned graduate degrees. While growing up, Irma was the target of racial discrimination. She reflected,

> What was it like growing up as a Latina of Mexican American heritage up in the southwest? Well, I never thought I was different until one day, boys in the neighborhood, when I was in grade school called me a "dirty Mexican." And then in high school, boys told me, they couldn't date me, their parents wouldn't let them date me because I was Mexican.[62]

61. Nominee Irma E. Gonzalez. Senate Judiciary Committee Hearings, One Hundred Second Congress 1991-1992, Second Session, Part 9, Serial No. J-102-7, July 1, 1992: 597–726, at 696-699; PN1044—Irma E. Gonzalez—the Judiciary, https://www.congress.gov/nomination/102nd-congress/1044?s=10&r=2759.

62. ABA Margaret Brent Award 2021 Judge Irma Gonzalez, https://www.youtube.com/watch?v=GVB_vbT5rZw; https://www.americanbar.org/groups/diversity/women/margaret-brent-awards/pasthonorees/, (ABA Gonzalez Video) at 8:00-8:50.

> You were different.... You cannot get away from the fact that you wonder whether people looked at you differently. There is always this feeling that you have to prove yourself because maybe people are saying, "she only got into law school because she is a woman or because she is Latina." Even if that is true, you still have to prove yourself.[63]
>
> Well, what does a woman of color do? Set out to prove yourself. And you have to work extra hard. I am convinced that women of color have to do this with all their endeavors.[64]

One of Irma's grandfathers was a lawyer in Mexico, but she had no knowledge of his work. Irma planned to attend medical school but thanks to organic chemistry and her parents' inspiration, Irma changed her plans to law school.[65] She was one of two Latinas in her law school class and had no women professors; less than 10 of the class's 175 students were women.[66] Irma considers herself "part of the women's movement...during a challenging time...it was a man's world." With her career trajectory, Irma is "an example of what a woman can do in a man's world."[67] Irma was among the first Latinas to serve as an AUSA in Los Angeles where she met her colleague and future husband, Robert Brewer. Despite her federal clerking history and six years of trial experience, only one of the fifty law firms to which Irma applied interviewed and hired her: Seltzer Caplan in San Diego. There, she further refined and added depth to her criminal and civil litigation portfolio.[68] The combined experience netted a federal magistrate judgeship, with Irma among the first Latinas so employed. In 1991, she was appointed by Governor George Deukmejian to the San Diego Superior Court—a short-lived tenure. State Judge Gonzalez became federal Judge Gonzalez. She expanded the court's participation in, and initiated programs designed to promote public accessibility, including the Plan for the Representation of Pro Se Litigants in Civil Cases that matches clients with pro bono lawyers. The judge was responsible for obtaining funding to finish the construction of a new courthouse, completed in 2012. Throughout her career, Judge Gonzalez was actively involved in bar association work. In 2013, she co-founded the nonprofit organization Latinas in the Law, which provides mentoring and resources to Latina lawyers, law students,

---

63. Brooke Ruth, *First Person: Becoming The First Mexican-American Woman Federal Judge*, KPBS, March 13, 2017), https://www.kpbs.org/news/midday-edition/2017/03/13/first-person-first-mexican-american-judge.

64. ABA Gonzalez Video, *supra* note 62 at 8:00–8:50.

65. Amanda C. Fitzsimmons, Federal Bar Association, *Judicial Profile Hon. Irma E. Gonzalez U.S. District Judge for the Southern District of California*, https://www.fedbar.org/wp-content/uploads/2019/10/GonzalezSept2012.

66. *Id.*

67. Women's Museum of California, Irma Gonzalez, San Diego's Women's Hall of Fame 2017, 0:46:00–1:15, https://www.youtube.com/watch?v=RtiyvaMcsVk.

68. Alex Riggins, *Irma Gonzalez: Retired Judge Blazed Trail, Continues Supporting Latinas in Law*, San Diego Union-Tribune, January 29, 2022, https://www.sandiegouniontribune.com/phenomenal-women-series/story/2022-01-29/phenomenal-women-irma-gonzalez.

and prospective attorneys.[69] Upon retiring from the federal bench in October 2013, Judge Gonzalez served as a mediator and arbitrator for at JAMS ADR for eight years.[70] The judge is the recipient of prestigious awards and recognition, notably, the ABA Margaret Brent Award (2021),[71] San Diego County Women's Hall of Fame (2017), HNBA Lifetime Achievement Award (2013), and Outstanding Jurist Award by the San Diego County Bar Association (2008).

6. Martha Alicia Vázquez, District of New Mexico, 1993–2021

1972	Study at St. Mary's College, Notre Dame
1975	B.A., University of Notre Dame
1978	Law Clerk, Human Services Department, State of New Mexico
1979	J.D., Notre Dame School of Law Michigan Migrant Legal Services Admitted to New Mexico Bar
1979–1981	Assistant Public Defender, State of New Mexico
1981–1993	Partner, Jones, Snead, Wertheim, Rodriguez & Wentworth, P.A.[72]
1993–2023	Article III Judge, District of New Mexico, Chief Judge 2003–2010
2023	Senior Status December 31, 2023

Martha Vázquez was the first woman and Mexican American appointed to the federal bench in New Mexico (D.N.M.). She was born to Consuelo (*nee* Mendez) and Remigio Vázquez in Santa Barbara, California, on February 21, 1953. Remigio was an accountant and professional soccer player for the Chivas in Guadalajara when he met Consuelo. Remigio "crossed over" in 1948 to be with Consuelo, and together, they picked the "lemon and avocado fields of Central California."[73] Her parents worked multiple jobs and started a business in Guadalajara. Martha grew up there, spending time in her father's village, until the family returned to the United States when she was six years old. She attended Catholic school as a native Spanish speaker without the benefit of a bilingual education (tuition was covered from

---

69. Fanny Miller, *Latinas in the Law, Changing the Face of Justice*, Celebrando Latinas Magazine, July 23, 2021, https://celebrandolatinas.com/2021/07/latinas-in-the-law/.

70. Chris Poole, *Q&A with Hon. Irma E. Gonzalez*, Mediate, September 20, 2021, https://mediate.com/qa-with-hon-irma-e-gonzalez-ret/; https://www.jamsadr.com/gonzalez/.

71. *Supra* note 62, ABA Gonzalez Video at 3:03-4:00.

72. Nominee Martha Vázquez, Senate Judiciary Committee Hearings, One Hundred Third Congress 1993-1994, First Session, Part 1, Serial No. J-103-28, September 23, 1993:89–119, 89–91; PN539—Martha A. Vazquez—The Judiciary, https://www.congress.gov/nomination/103rd-congress/539?s=4&r=4.

73. Alejandra Vázquez Baur, *How My Family's Immigration Story Connects to Integration*, The Century Foundation, https://tcf.org/content/commentary/how-my-familys-immigration-story-connects-to-integration/.

the sales of her mother's tamales). Growing up in Santa Barbara, Martha worked the "gardens of rich people in Montecito" alongside her parents and brother.[74] Martha did well in school, learning English before her parents and thus, became the family translator.[75] In third grade, she decided to become a lawyer. Attributing the influence of her "patriotic, naturalized father who had this great faith in [the U.S.] legal system," she concluded "we need to have more lawyers who speak Spanish so they can fix things legally."[76] This was her dream.

In the fall of 1972 when Notre Dame University became co-ed, Martha entered as the only woman in most of her undergraduate classes. It was this experience, being one of few women in a male-dominated environment, that she later drew on in navigating the all-male court.[77] Her decision to practice in New Mexico was triggered by the Spanish spoken throughout the state, and the familiarity of the land and terrain of Albuquerque and Santa Fe that was reminiscent of her father's village where she spent her early childhood. In the summer of 1978, she clerked in Albuquerque, and it rained, "poured" like it did in Mexico. "The water on the hot earth creates this smell"... "just like the song Guadalajara, Guadalajara, 'hueles a pura tierra mojada,' you smell like pure wet earth... that mariachis sing all over the place." Martha "was home."[78]

After service as one of two public defenders amongst the Luminaria federal judges, Martha was appointed to the District Court as the first Latina Article III Judge in New Mexico. The job was not as glamorous as perceived. Duty included the three-hundred-mile/three-month court rotations to Las Cruces, New Mexico. As a mother of four young children, it created additional hardship in raising the children with her husband-attorney whom she met in law school. At that point, the children were aged three, five, seven, and nine, but this did not deter her professional agenda. "As a new judge and first woman in my district, I wasn't about to say 'guys, can you do this for me cause my children are too little.'"[79] Though difficult, the new judge "never had the guilt about leaving to go to work because all the generations of my family of women always had to go to work. They did not have the luxury of staying at home."[80] On December 31, 2023, Judge Vázquez assumed senior status, enabling her to give back to her children by devoting time to her eight grandchildren.[81]

---

74. Attorney Michael L. Stout interview of Judge Martha Vásquez (June 8, 2021), Parts 1, 2 and 3 (Vásquez Interview), Part 1, 26:40, 30:00–32:35, 34:59–35:46; available at: https://mlstoutlaw.com/home/true-believers-and-the-road-to-hell/hon-martha-vazquez/.

75. Vásquez Interview Part 1, 35:48–36:56.

76. Vásquez Interview Part 2, 41:03–42:00.

77. Vásquez Interview Part 1, 9:00–9:46.

78. Vásquez Interview Part 2, 2:50–5:44.

79. Vásquez Interview Part 1, 6:23–8:18.

80. Vásquez Interview Part 1, 26:14.

81. Vásquez Interview Part 3, 6:45–7:54.

7. Rosemary Barkett, Eleventh Circuit Court of Appeals, 1994–2013

1994–2013	Article III Judge, Eleventh Circuit[82] Retired (from the federal bench), September 30, 2013
2013	Judge, Iran–U.S. Tribunal, The Hague, October 1, 2013

Judge Barkett's biographical summary that includes her appointment to the Florida Supreme Court is captured in chapter two. She is the only Luminaria state supreme court justice elevated to a Circuit Court and the only Latina to serve on the Eleventh Circuit—until December 2019 when Florida Supreme Court Justice Barbara Lagoa was appointed, replicating Judge Barkett's path. Judge Barkett served on the Eleventh Circuit for nearly twenty years and in that time, was regarded as the most liberal judge. Like her tenure on the supreme court, Judge Barkett participated in thousands of cases, between 5,360 (Westlaw) and 7,004 (Lexis). She voiced her views and analysis through dissenting opinions (at least 128) in cases as diverse as the death penalty, the right of gay parents to adopt, discriminatory impact of purging black voters from voting rolls and transgender discrimination. In chapter five, on the Luminaria circuit court judges, select cases of Judge Barkett will be discussed.

While serving on the Eleventh Circuit, Judge Barkett co-taught international seminars at Columbia Law School on Constitutionalism and Human Rights and Comparative Constitutions. She also lectured on substantive and procedural issues, as well as court administration throughout the world, including Algeria, China, Egypt, Dubai, Haiti, Kuwait, Kyrgyzstan, Mexico, Morocco, Qatar, Syria, and Tunisia, and Turkey. As a board member of the ABA Rule of Law Initiative, some of these seminars were taught in conjunction with that service and its Committee on the Middle East and North Africa Division. This work caught the attention of the State Department which offered her the opportunity to serve on an international court. Thus, Judge Barkett retired from the Eleventh Circuit in 2013 to assume an appointment to The Hague on the Iran–U.S. Tribunal (Tribunal). The Tribunal was established pursuant to the Algiers Accords of January 19, 1981 (Algiers was asked by both countries to serve as an intermediary). The purpose of the accord was to address disputes between the two countries arising from the 1979–1981 Iran hostage crisis and other incidents involving the U.S. Embassy in Tehran. The Tribunal accepts cases involving disputes that arose prior to November 14, 1979. It is comprised of nine members. Three are appointed by the U.S. (Judge Barkett among them), three by Iran and three neutral arbiters selected by the appointees.[83] The U.S. Supreme

82. Nominee Rosemary Barkett, One Hundred Third Congress 1993–1994, Second Session, April 14, 1994, https//www.senate.gov/legislative/LIS/roll_call/votes/vote1032/vote_103_2_00092.htm; PN683—Rosemary Barkett—The Judiciary (Barkett Art. III Confirmation), https://www.congress.gov/nomintion/103rd-congress/683?s=1&r=149.

83. State Department Press Release announcing the appointment of Judge Barkett to The Hague, https://2009-2017.state.gov/r/pa/prs/ps/2013/08/213477.htm; *see also* https://iusct.com/rosemary-barkett/.

Court upheld the constitutionality and legitimacy of the Algiers Accords in *Dames & Moore v. Regan*, 453 U.S. 654 (1981). The filing deadline of new private claims expired on January 19, 1982. In 2015, President Obama appointed Judge Barkett to the Panel of Conciliators for the International Centre for the Settlement of Investment Disputes. In 2016, the judge was elected as Honorary President of the American Society of International Law. Judge Barkett also serves as an *ad hoc* judge on the World Court. Judge Barkett is the Luminaria who has served on the most courts—state trial court, intermediate appellate court and supreme court, federal appellate court, international tribunal, and World Court. Reflecting on her journey, the judge stated:

> ...I think we are the sum of all of our experiences, and I don't know that you can separate out threads and attribute some view...to a particular thread. I think you're—the totality of what you've seen, what you've experienced, what you've done. And so I...think clearly, all of the experiences: my convent experience and the way people treated each other, my family experience and my being an immigrant has...made me care about people. It's made me understand more realistically what people go through than maybe somebody else who hasn't experienced it, although I think...I have a sense of what people experience.[84]

8. Kim Anita McLane Wardlaw, Central District of California, 1995–1998

1972–1973	Study at Santa Clara University
1973–1974	Foothill Community College (no degree)
1976	A.B., Communications, *summa cum laude*, UCLA, Phi Beta Kappa
1978	Legal Intern, U.S. Court of Appeals, Ninth Circuit Law Clerk, O'Melveny & Myers
1979	J.D., UCLA School of Law, Articles Editor, UCLA Law Review
1979–1980	Law Clerk, U.S. District Court Central District of California
1980–1992	O'Melveny & Myers Associate 1980–1987, Partner 1987–1992
1992–1998	Article III Judge, C.D. CA[85]
1998–Present	Article III Judge, Ninth Circuit, Pasadena[86]

84. *Supra* chptr. 2 note 66, Barkett Interview at 1:56:14–1:56:52.

85. Nominee Kim McLane Wardlaw, Senate Judiciary Committee Hearings, One Hundred Fourth Congress 1995-1996, First Session, Part 1, Serial No. J-103-28, June 19, 1998:830, 843–844, 955–1011; PN597—Kim McLane Wardlaw—The Judiciary (McLane Wardlaw USA Confirmation), https://www.congress.gov/nomination/104th-congress/597?s=1&r=40.

86. Nominee Kim McLane Wardlaw, Senate Judiciary Committee Hearings, One Hundred Fifth Congress, Part 4, Serial No. J-105-4, July 18, 1998: 287–358, 305–307; PN829-Kim McLane Ward-

Kim McLane Wardlaw was born in 1954 in San Francisco to Soledad Jimenez, a "Mexican, Catholic, and Republican," and her father McLane, a "Scottish-Irish Presbyterian and a loyal Democrat."[87] Soledad, a California native raised in San Jose, was from a Mexican (Jalisco) immigrant family. Kim's father grew up in Rhode Island, working as a door-to-door furniture salesman and her mother as a bookkeeper. They met in San Francisco in the 1950s. The judge recalls experiencing discrimination due to their mixed race, prompting the family to move after her sixth grade: "[W]e finally moved to San Jose to be near my mother's large family, or, as one of my schoolmates tauntingly put it, 'to be with our own kind.'"[88] Neither parent attended college but encouraged her to obtain undergraduate and graduate degrees. Kim was politically active, including during Bill Clinton's California presidential campaign and as a member of the Clinton-Core Transition Team-DOJ. She also served on one of Richard Riordan's Los Angeles mayoral transition committees. In 1984, she married William M. Wardlaw Sr. and became known as McLane Wardlaw. Kim was active in the ABA and California and Los Angeles Bar Associations. She served as president of the Women's Lawyers Association of Los Angeles (1993–94). Judge McLane Wardlaw has received numerous awards from the HNBA (Judicial Award, 2008) and the California and Los Angeles Women's bar associations.[89] In July 2007, Judge McLane Wardlaw was on the historic first panel of Latino judges that conducted oral argument in Seattle, Washington, joining Judges Arthur Alarcón and Ferdinand Fernandez. This first Latino panel occurred twenty-six years following the first all-woman circuit panel.[90]

9. Hilda Gloria Tagle, Southern District of Texas, 1998–2012

1968	A.A., Del Mar College
1969	B.A., East Texas State University (ETSU, since 1996 A&M University-Commerce)
1971	Master of Library Science, North TSU
1971–1975	Librarian, Strake Jesuit College Preparatory
1974	Teaching Certification secondary schools, ETSU
1977	J.D., University of Texas School of Law Admitted Texas Bar
1977–1978	Assistant City Attorney, Corpus Christi, TX

law—The Judiciary, https://www.congress.gov/nomination/105th-congress/829; Ninth Circuit Judges, https://www.ca9.uscourts.gov/judicial-counsil/judges-seniority-list/.

87. First Women Series: *Judge Kim McLane Wardlaw*, Ms. JD, March 11, 2009.

88. *Id.*, First Woman Series.

89. *Supra* note 85 McLane Wardlaw USA Confirmation, at 958–960.

90. *Supra* note 87; *see also 40 Years Later, Pioneering Women Judges Savor Place in History, United States Courts*, August 14, 2019, https://www.uscourts.gov/news/2019/08/14/40-years-later-pioneering-women-judges-savor-place-history.

1978–1980	Assistant County Attorney, Nueces County
1980–1981	Assistant District Attorney, Nueces County District Attorney
1981–1985	Solo Practitioner, Corpus Christi, TX Instructor Legal Assistant Program, Del Mar College
1984	Intern, Congressman Solomon P. Ortiz
1985–1994	Judge, Nueces County Court
1995–1998	Judge, 148th District Court, Corpus Christi
1998	Article III Judge, Southern District Texas (S.D. TX), Brownsville[91]
2012	Senior Status December 31, 2012–December 21, 2018
2018	Inactive Status

The country's fourth Mexican American female federal judge was born on December 18, 1946, in Corpus Christi to Manuel and Dolores ("Lola," *nee* Cipriano) Cisneros Tagle. Hilda was the first Mexican American female federal judge in Texas and on the Nueces County Court. The eldest and only daughter grew up with four brothers in Robstown, Texas. Upon returning from World War II, Mr. Tagle worked as a mechanic; her mother was a beautician. Though Lola's formal education ended at eighth grade, Hilda described her as "brilliant... but very practical," "*un abogada sin libros*" (a lawyer without books) who owned a beauty shop, Lolitas, in Robstown.[92] At sixteen, Hilda became a licensed beautician to fulfill her mother's demand that she "have something to fall back on."[93] Lola also wanted Hilda to become a "social butterfly." Hilda was a self-described "bookworm," reading through almost all the books at the two local libraries, prompting her mother to bus Hilda to the Lara Toma Library in Corpus Christi. While obtaining an education and practicing law, Hilda became active with several bar associations and women's political/networking groups. She was a founding member of the Women's Bar Association and the Mexican American Bar Association of Coastal Bend. In 1991, Hilda was appointed by Governor Ann Richards to the Texas Commission for Women.[94] In an oral interview about the selection process for the Nueces County judgeship, Judge Tagle stated, "One of the commissioners, bless his heart, had told me that I should forget about being a judge because the job of a judge was too stressful for a woman."[95]

91. Nominee Hilda Gloria Tagle, Senate Judiciary Committee Hearings, One Hundred Fifth Congress 1997-1998, Second Session, Part 3, Serial No. J-105-4, February 25, 1998, 340-344, 477–628, 478-480; PN254—Hilda G. Tagle—The Judiciary (PN254) (Tagle Art. III Confirmation), https://www.congress.gov/nomination/105th-congress/254?s=7&r=2270.

92. The Portal to Texas History, Oral History Interview with Hilda Tagle by Moisés Acuña and James Wall, July 10, 2016 (Tagle Interview), Clip One at 2:30–43, 03:27–48, 5:27–46, 9:28, 9:52–11:07, https://texashistory.unt.edu/ark:/67531/metapth987571/m1/.

93. *Id.*, note 92, Tagle Interview Clip One at 5:29–5:38.

94. *Supra* note 92, Tagle Interview Clip Four at 12:57–13:06.

95. *Id.*, Tagle Interview Clip Four at 5:16 and 9:09–24.

Committed to the advancement of women and Latinos, Hilda had to build a political base for future judicial elections. "When you're an elected judge, you have to be involved in politics, because you run for office."[96] Judge Tagle was twice married but had no children until 1985, when she became mother to her nine-year-old nephew, Santiago.[97] Hilda was appointed to the Nueces County Court in 1985. She ran unopposed in 1986 as well as 1990 when she experienced her first Democratic opponent and defeated him with 55 percent of the vote compared to his 45 percent.[98]

The judge's next campaign was against the incumbent Latino judge for the 148th District Court, which led to a runoff election that she won. Encouraged by "personal friends, the Mexican American Legal Defense Fund (MALDEF), prominent attorneys," and others, the judge applied for the federal bench.[99] As early as 1993, Judge Tagle submitted a questionnaire for the federal judiciary. On January 12, 1995, she wrote to the White House, informing the administration of her interest in the federal bench and sought the support of Congressman Henry B. Gonzalez.[100] With the support of the Texan Democratic delegation, Judge Tagle was nominated by President Clinton on August 10, 1995, but her nomination was returned without consideration by the Senate Judiciary Committee. The judge was renominated on April 21, 1997, and confirmed on March 11, 1998.[101] Judge Tagle was honored with multiple awards, including the Good Gals Award (1990). She assumed senior status effective December 21, 2012 (through 2018).

10. Maria Christine Armijo, District of New Mexico, 2001–2018

1972	B.A. History, *cum laude*, University of New Mexico (UNM)
1975	J.D., UNM School of Law
1976	Admitted to New Mexico Bar
1976–1978	Staff Attorney, Sandoval County Legal Services-Bernalillo
1978–1996	M. Christina Armijo Attorney at Law, Las Vegas, NM Contract, New Mexico Public Defender 1979–198 Contract, New Mexico Children, Youth and Families Department 1985–1992 Contract, New Mexico Department of Education/due process hearing officer 1994–1996

96. *Id.*, Tagle Interview.

97. *Id.*, Tagle Interview Clip Three at 4:08–4:11, Clip Four at 7:15–21 and 12:57–13:06.

98. Sharon A. Navarro, *Moving On Up: The Political Incorporation of Hispanic Women into the Federal Judiciary of Texas*, Latino Studies 11 (2013), 1–20, 12, (Navarro Article), at www.palgrave-journals.com/1st/.

99. *Id.*, Navarro Article at 13.

100. January 26, 1995, letter from Judge Tagle to Veronica Biggins, Director, Office of Presidential Personnel.

101. *Supra note 91, Tagle Art. III confirmation at PN254.*

1996–2001 Judge, New Mexico Court of Appeals

2001–2018 Article III Judge, District of New Mexico, Chief Judge 2012–2018[102]

2018 Inactive Senior Status February 7, 2018

A twelfth-generation New Mexican dating back to colonial times, Christina was born on January 17, 1951, to Mary (*nee* C de Baca) and Luis Felipe Armijo, "a family of significant historical distinction."[103] Luis's father, Luis Enrique Armijo, served as district attorney and was one of the longest tenured judges in New Mexico (thirty-five years).[104] "The Armijo family of Las Vegas... left... a legacy to the legal community" with no less than a court clerk, six lawyers, two district attorneys, and two Court of Appeals judges.[105] Prior to marrying, Mary attended secretarial school and became a "career woman," working through retirement as a supervisor at the New Mexico Department of Human Services.[106] Mary and Luis had four children; Christina was the oldest of three daughters. Through his family, the law was deeply ingrained in Luis, a tradition he carried in his work as a court clerk. He passed when Christina was eleven years old. Her paternal grandmother, Eugenia Delgado Armijo—the judge's widow—helped raise and influenced Christina.[107] Christina continued the family tradition as a career woman and lawyer, extending the legacy to the federal level. She was the first Latina solo practitioner in Las Vegas, New Mexico. The local newspapers that printed front-page features of the new male lawyers in town failed to do so when Christina opened her practice. Only after informal lobbying via a press release by her friends did the newspaper publish an article, which was placed in the shopping-grocery section.[108] This, however, did not deter the feminist pioneer.

In February 1996, Christina became the first Latina appointed to the New Mexico Court of Appeals by Governor Gary Johnson. She followed in the footsteps of her

---

102. Nominee M. Christine Armijo, Senate Judiciary Committee Hearings, One Hundred Seventh Congress 2001-2002, First Session, Part 1, Serial No. J-103-28, October 18, 2001:14, 79–111, 249–274, 79–82; PN905—M. Christina Armijo—The Judiciary, https://www.congress.gov/nomination/107th-congress/905?s+1&r=1995.

103. UNM Distinguished Achievement Awards Dinner—Honorable M. Christina Armijo, October 21, 2019, New Mexico Supreme Court, https://www.youtube.com/watch?v= X1yNb116IaE (UNM Armijo Video), remarks by New Mexico Supreme Court Senior Justice Barbara J. Vigil, 2:38–2:41.

104. Judge John W. Pope, *New Mexico's Man For All Seasons Judge Luis Armijo of Las Vegas*, N.M. Bar Journal 15 (May/June 1996), 16–20, https://www.sbnm.org/Portals/NMBAR/AboutUs/committees/Historical/New_Mexico's_Man_For_All_Seasons_Judge_Luis_Armijo_of_Las_Vegas.pdf?ver=70ZwyP72W-inMqijcJMSyg%3D%3D.

105. *Id.* at 20.

106. Albuquerque Journal Obituaries Luis Armijo, Mary L., March 31, 2005, https://www.newspapers.com/article/albuquerque-journal-obituary-for-a-rmijo/37336303/.

107. *Supra* note 103, UNM Armijo Video remarks by lawyer Norm McDonald at 2:58–3:39.

108. *Id.*, UNM Armijo Video, remarks by U.S. District Magistrate Judge Kirtan Khalsa, 1:26–2:29.

uncle Roberto L. Armijo who was Luis's brother and the first Latino appointed to the appellate court (1967–1968).[109] A Republican, Christina was elected to the New Mexico Court of Appeals in November 1996 to an eight-year term during which time she presided on the first all-woman panel of the court.[110] During her tenure, she authored more than fifty opinions and sat (at times) on the New Mexico Supreme Court by designation to preside over cases. One of those cases was the landmark case of *NM Right to Choose/NARAL v. Johnson*, 986 P.2d 450 (1999), in which the Supreme Court applied the state's equal rights amendment to support a woman's right to choose/reproductive freedom. Judge Armijo concurred with Judge Pamela Minzer's majority opinion. *NM Right to Choose*, at 458, 460.[111]

As an appellate jurist, Judge Armijo earned a reputation as a serious and scrupulous judge who analyzed and protected due process on behalf of the state's citizens—guided by a core belief that all are equally entitled to respect and equal treatment under the law. Advancement of justice in every case was her goal.[112] Judge Armijo did not fulfil her tenure as she was appointed in 2001 as an Article III judge to the District of New Mexico. While on the bench, Judge Armijo (a self-described avid student of history), authored a law review article about the sole woman executed in New Mexico, interweaving her family's connection to the case in *Territory of New Mexico v. Paula Angel: One Woman's Tragic Journey through Territorial Justice in 1861*.[113] The judge transitioned to senior status in 2018. Judge Armijo was honored in 2019 by the University of New Mexico as a beacon for women in the law.[114]

11. Consuelo María Callahan, Ninth Circuit Court of Appeals, 2003–Incumbent

1972	B.A., English, *cum laude*, Stanford University
1975	J.D., McGeorge Pacific School of Law Admitted to California Bar Stockton City Attorney's Office
1975–1986	Supervising/Assistant District Attorney San Joaquin County District Attorney's Office

109. Pamela B. Minzner, *History of the New Mexico Court of Appeals*, N.M. L. Rev. 22 (1992): 595, 600–601.

110. *Supra* note 103, UNM Armijo Video, photos at 3:40–3:57.

111. *See also* Linda M. Vanzi, *Freedom at Home Revisited: The New Mexico Equal Rights Amendment after New Mexico Right to Choose, Naral v. Johnson*, N.M. L. Rev. 40 (2010): 215, https://digitalrepository.unm.edu/cgi/viewcontent.cgi?referer=&httpsredir=1&article=1134&context=nmlr.

112. *Supra* note 103, UNM Armijo Video, remarks by Mark Fine, Esq. 7:15–7:42 and Justice Vigil, 7:45–8:49.

113. 42 N.M. L. Rev. 301 (2012), https://digitalrepository.unm.edu/cgi/viewcontent.cgi?article=1144&context=nmlr.

114. *Supra* note 103, UNM Armijo Video, remarks by Judge Kirtan Khalsa at 12:38–12:40.

1986–1992	Commissioner, Stockton Municipal Court
1992–1996	Judge, San Joaquin County Superior Court
1996	Justice, Third District California Court of Appeals
2003	Article III Judge, Ninth Circuit, Sacramento[115]
2004	M.L.S., University of Virginia School of Law

The oldest of three children, Consuelo was born June 9, 1950, in Palo Alto, California. She was raised in Los Altos and Fremont and attended public schools. Her Irish father, J. Raymond Callahan, was a Spanish teacher who earned a doctorate degree and became an administrator. Consuelo's mother, Hortense Calvo, was Spanish (her family hailed from Spain) and was her inspiration.[116]

Consuelo was one of fewer than ten women enrolled at McGeorge Pacific School of Law. She interned at the public defender's office as a law student. Upon graduating, she moved to Stockton to take an assistant city attorney job. Shortly thereafter, Consuelo passed the bar exam and received offers from both the public defender and district attorney (DA) offices, accepting the DA's offer because it was offered first by a day. As an assistant district attorney at the San Joaquin County District Attorney's Office, she established and later supervised its first Child Abuse-Sexual Assault Unit.[117] She tried more than fifty jury trials. In 1985 at age thirty-five, she married Randy Haight with whom she had a son and stepdaughter. Her judicial career began in 1986 as commissioner of the Stockton Municipal County Court. Consuelo was the first Latina and woman appointed to the San Joaquin County Court. With no appellate expertise but extensive trial experience, Judge Callahan was the first judge from the San Joaquin Court "in 73 years" appointed to the Third District Court of Appeals (Third District). Judge Callahan spent considerable time in the community, especially with young schoolchildren and those who suffered child abuse. She is a former board member and president of the San Joaquin County Child Abuse Prevention Center.

Parroting her law school experience, she was the sole woman among ten men on the Third District. All supported Judge Callahan's appointment to the Ninth Circuit as the first judge from the Third District so nominated.[118] The judge did not seek the Ninth Circuit position but was instead contacted "out of the blue" and agreed to undergo the vetting process. At the time, she was a Republican in a state with two

115. Nominee Consuelo Callahan, Senate Judiciary Committee Hearings, One Hundred Eighth Congress 2003-2004, First Session, Part 1, Serial No. J-108-1, May 7, 2003:248–288, 250–251; PN342—Consuelo Maria Callahan—The Judiciary, https://www.congress.gov/nomination/108th-congress/324?s=3&r=1686; Ninth Circuit Judges, https://www.ca9.uscourts.gov/judicial-counsil/judges-seniority-list/.

116. California Appellate Court Legacy Project, Video Interview Transcript: Justice Consuelo Callahan (Callahan Interview), at 1, 2.

117. *Id.*, Callahan Interview, 12 at 30:38, 15–16 at 40:00, 20 at 54:51.

118. *Id.*, Callahan Interview, introductory remarks at 1, 24–25 at 1:04:55, 26 at 1:09:55.

Democratic senators, Dianne Feinstein and Barbara Boxer, who supported her nomination.[119] During the confirmation hearing, Senator Feinstein described Judge Callahan as "incredibly uncontroversial for someone coming out of our state."[120] Senator Hatch commented that Judge Callahan had an "exemplary legal career as a successful prosecutor and esteemed jurist." Senator Boxer requested the Senate approve Judge Callahan's confirmation upon unanimous consent that it granted on a 99–0 vote.[121] Judge Callahan was one of two finalists considered by President George W. Bush to replace Sandra Day O'Connor on the Supreme Court; the other candidate, Harriet Miers, had her nomination withdrawn. The vacancy was filled by Samuel Alito.

12. Dora Lizette Irizarry, Eastern District of New York, 2004–2020

1976	B.A., Political Sociology, *cum laude*, Yale University
1979	J.D., Columbia Law School
1981	Admitted to New York Bar
1979–1987	Assistant District Attorney, Bronx County 1979–1987 Appeals Bureau 1979–1981 Office of Special Narcotics Prosecutor 1981–1987
1987–1995	Assistant District Attorney, New York County, Office of the Special Narcotics Prosecutor
1995–1997	Judge, New York Criminal Court
1997–2002	Acting Justice, New York Court of Claims, Kings County 1997–1998, New York County 1998–2002
2002–2004	Private practice, Of Counsel, Hoguet Newman & Regal, LLP
2004	Article III Judge, Eastern District New York (EDNY), Chief Judge 2016–2020[122]
2020	Senior Status January 26, 2020

The first Latina judge to serve on the EDNY bench was born in San Sebastian, Puerto Rico, on January 26, 1955, to Rosario and Anselmo Irizarry. She was raised in

---

119. *Id.*, Callahan Interview, 33 at 1:29:52, 34 at 1:35:09, 36 at 1:40:27, 2:20–5:18, and 12:24–14:34.

120. *Id.*, Callahan Interview, 33 at 12:52–56.

121. Senate Judicial Hearings, May 22, 2003, https://www.c-span.org/video/?176514-1/judicial-nominations.

122. Nominee Dora Irizarry, Senate Judiciary Committee Hearings, One Hundred Eighth Congress 2003-2004, First Session, Part 4, Serial No. J-108-1, October 1, 2003:993-1046, 994-999, 1017, 1033, (Irizarry Art. III Confirmation), https://www.congress.gov/108/chrg/shrg92637/CHRG-108shrg92637.pdf; PN541—Dora L. Irizarry—The Judiciary, https://www.congress.gov/nomination/108th-congress/541?s=3&r=1654.

the tenements and Morrisania Heights projects of South Bronx, the latter referred to by police officers as "Little Rikers." From her early days in public school with Justice Thurgood Marshall her hero, Dora knew at age ten she wanted to become a lawyer dedicated to public service.[123] During all three years of law school, she was a Charles Evans Hughes Fellow/scholarship recipient for public service. All but her last two years of practice were criminal law.[124] In 2002, Dora was the Republican Party and Conservative Party candidate for New York State attorney general—an election she lost.[125] In October 2022, Judge Irizarry was interviewed by the White House Counsel's Office for the Article III judicial vacancy in the EDNY.[126] In January 2003, Judge Irizarry was interviewed by the Federal Judicial Screening Committee created by New York Governor George Pataki. A month later, on February 7, 2003, the judge was interviewed by New York U.S. Senator Charles Schumer who supported her nomination to the federal bench.[127] Judge Irizarry has received the Puerto Rican Bar Woman Pioneer Award (2023), the New York City Police Department Hispanic Society Special Recognition Award (2003), the San Sebastian Award for Outstanding Achievements and Distinction from the Mayor of San Sebastian (1998), and recognition from the DOJ and New York law enforcement.

13. Judith Claire Herrera, District of New Mexico, 2004–2019

1976	B.A., University of New Mexico
1979	J.D., Georgetown University Law Center Admitted to New Mexico Bar
1979–1980	Assistant Prosecutor, First Judicial District Attorney's Office
1980–1986	Shareholder, Jones Gallegos, Snead & Wertheim, P.A.
1981–1986	City Councilwoman, Santa Fe City Council
1987–2004	Partner, Herrera, Long, Pound & Komer, P.A.
2004–2019	Article III Judge, District of New Mexico[128]
2019	Senior Status July 1, 2019

123. Judge Irizarry Acceptance Speech to NY County Lawyers Association, November 7, 2018; *View from the Bench: Chief Judge Dora L. Irizarry of the Eastern District of New York*, Thomas Reuters Practical Law, December 1, 2017, https://content.next.westlaw.com/practical-law/document/I0fe5f0c0d6a311e79bef99c0ee 06c731/Q-A-with-Chief-Judge-Dora-L-Irizarry-of-the-Eastern-District-ofNewYork?viewType=FullText&transition Type=Default&contextData=(sc.Default).

124. *Supra* note 122 Irizarry Art. III Confirmation at 1017.

125. *Id.*, Irizarry Art. III Confirmation at 1030.

126. *Id.*, Irizarry Art. III Confirmation at 1040.

127. *Id.*, Irizarry Art. III Confirmation at 1041.

128. Nominee Judith Claire Herrera, Senate Judiciary Committee Hearings, One Hundred Eighth Congress 2003-2004, First Session, Part 1, Serial No. J-103-28, November 12, 2003:262–334, 262–267, 295; PN967—Judith C. Herrera—The Judiciary (Herrera Art. III Confirmation, https://www.congress.gov/nomination/108th-congress/967?s=3&r=1614.

Among the Luminaria Article III judges, Judith Herrera is one of two elected to public office. Born on April 28, 1954, in Chicago, Illinois, to Santa Fe native Dr. William Reymundo and Corine (*nee* Sanchez) Herrera who, since childhood, lived in Santa Fe. While a dental student, William (who grew up in modest means) met Corine during his summer break in Santa Fe. Upon marrying, they moved to Chicago where William completed his last year of dental surgery at Northwestern University and Judith was born. Months later, they returned to Santa Fe and Dr. Herrera launched his dental practice. Corine eventually obtained an accounting degree and managed the books for her husband's dental practice. They raised their five children, four daughters and a son, passing along their love of sports. (One daughter became an assistant football coach.) The children attended Catholic schools and traveled with their parents domestically and abroad to Canada, Europe, and Mexico. Dr. Herrera was proud to financially support the children through undergraduate and graduate schools, including Judith.[129] Judith was an assistant district attorney for one year. She spent the remaining years in private practice, the majority in her own firm, litigating civil cases in state and federal courts. In 1981, Judith was appointed to the Santa Fe City Council, which was a part-time position. In 1982, she was elected to a four-year term. Notably, Judith served on the Federal Advisory Committee, which studied the federal district court in New Mexico and formulated the plan for compliance with the Civil Justice Reform Act. In 2003, Judith was contacted with an inquiry about her willingness to be considered for the federal district court—requesting she send a resume to New Mexico's Republican Senator Pete Domenici. Upon submitting her resume, she was contacted by the White House and the vetting process ensued.[130] In 2024, Judge Herrera became the third Luminaria judge to serve with Judges Vázquez and Armijo, their tenures overlapping.

14. Virginia Maria Hernandez-Covington, Middle District of Florida, 2004–2020

1973	Rollins College, Spain Abroad Program
1976	B.S., *cum laude*, University of Tampa, Outstanding Female Graduate Award Founding Member, *La Alianza de Derecho*
1977	Master of Business Administration (M.B.A.), University of Tampa
1980	J.D., Georgetown University Law Center, *Tax Lawyer Law Review* Admitted to Florida Bar
1980–1981	Trial Attorney, Federal Trade Commission

129. Obituary of Corine S. Herrera (1931–2021) and Obituary of William Reymundo Herrera (1927–2021), Santa Fe New Mexican; *Toughing It Out: Texas Wesleyan Female Football Coach Takes the Field*, Fort Worth Business Press, November 24, 2017.

130. *Supra* note 128, Herrera Art. III Confirmation at 266, 276, 282.

1982–1983	Assistant State Attorney, Thirteenth Judicial Circuit, Florida
1983–1988	AUSA, Civil Division, U.S. Attorney's Office Middle District of Florida (M.D. FL)
1989–2001	AUSA, Chief Asset Forfeiture Section, Criminal Division, U.S.A. Office M.D. FL
2001–2004	Judge, Second District Court of Appeals
2004–2020	Article III Judge, Middle District, Florida[131]
2020	Senior Status July 12, 2020

Virginia was born on July 12, 1955, in Tampa, Florida and raised in a Spanish-speaking household. Her parents, Sofia Hernandez and James W. Covington, married in 1954. Professor Covington taught history at the University of Tampa for nearly forty years, and was a renowned author and community member.[132] Her grandfather, Ramiro Hernandez, was a Cuban landowner who immigrated to Tampa from Havana in 1953 upon learning he was to be arrested and executed for his political beliefs (i.e., for "get[ting] on the wrong side of [Cuban dictator] Fulgencio Batista"). Virginia's grandmother, Esperanza Bolivar, and her mother, Sofia, immigrated a few days thereafter. "By the late 1960s, almost [her] entire family had come from Cuba."[133] The future judge recalled her first visit to the federal district court was in 1966 when her mother became naturalized.[134] In 1978, Virginia married lawyer Douglas M. Bagge; they have two children. As AUSA/chief of the Asset Forfeiture Section, she prosecuted drug and money laundering criminal cases and civil forfeiture (fraud) cases. Virginia lectured extensively on these subjects domestically and abroad, especially in Latin American countries. She was one of few judges selected by the DOJ to the Team Leader, Evaluation, and Review Section responsible for evaluating other districts.[135] Appointed to the Florida bench by Governor Jeb Bush in 2001, the judge was retained in 2002 to a six-year term that ended in 2009. Virginia was deeply involved in the community, chairing the Diocesan Cuban Immi-

131. Nominee Virginia Hernandez Covington, Senate Judiciary Committee Hearings, One Hundred Eighth Congress 2003–2004, Second Session, Part 7, Serial No. J-108-1, June 16, 2004:416–462, 416–418; PN1539—Virginia Maria Hernandez Covington—The Judiciary (Hernandez Covington Art. III Confirmation), https://www.congress.gov/nomination/108th-congress/1539?s=4&r=1579.

132. Obituary of James W. Covington, Tampa Bay Times, February 29, 2004, https://www.newspapers.com/newspage/329455468/.

133. Alejandro Fernandez, *Judicial Profile of Hon. Virginia M. Hernandez Covington*, The Federal Lawyer (July/August 2019): 26–30, 26, 28.

134. *Id*, at 28; *Covington to Receive Distinguished Federal Judicial Service Pro Bono Award*, Florida Bar News, January 27, 2021, https://www.floridabar.org/the-florida-bar-news/covington-to-receive-distinguished-federal-judicial-service-pro-bono-award/#:~:text=Covington%20to%20receive%20Distinguished%20Federal%20Judicial%20Service%20Pe%20Virginia%20M.,Distinguished%20Federal%20Judicial%20Service%20Award.

135. *Supra* note 131 Hernandez Covington Art. III Confirmation at 422–425, 430.

gration Commission, serving as a member of *El Consejo de Necesidades y Servicios para Hispanos*, and in her work as a board director of Tampa Hispanic Heritage, Inc. She was equally involved in the legal profession.[136] Judge Hernandez Covington is the recipient of many awards from community Hispanic and women's groups and professional awards, including seventy DOJ written commendations.[137]

15. Aida Milagros Delgado-Colón, District of Puerto Rico, 2006–2018

1977	B.S., *cum laude*, Business Administration, UPR
1980	J.D., *cum laude*, Pontifical Catholic University of Puerto Rico School of Law, *Pontifical Law Review* Editor
1980–1982	Commonwealth of Puerto Rico, Governor's Advisory Council on Labor Law, Department of Labor and Human Resources 1980–1981, Lead Investigator 1981–1982, Director of Research and Investigations
1982	Admitted to Puerto Rico Bar
1982–1993	Federal Public Defender Office District of Puerto Rico
1991	Acting Federal Public Defender
1988–1993	First Assistant Federal Public Defender
1982–1988	Assistant Federal Public Defender
1993–2006	U.S. Magistrate Judge, District of Puerto Rico (D.P.R.)
2003–2004	Adjunct Professor, Pontifical Law (January–May each year)
2006–Present	Article III Judge, D.P.R.[138]
2011–2018	Chief Judge
2018	Incumbent

The first federal female public defender on the island was born on August 31, 1955, in Lares, Puerto Rico. Aida was the first of four children of Luz Colón, a teacher, and José Delgado, a farmer and owner of a small-scale agro business where she learned the importance of assisting others. This influenced her decision to become a lawyer.

> As a young child, raised in a rural, agricultural town in Puerto Rico, I perceived the needs of the underprivileged for legal assistance. People of sparse economic means were compelled to pay 'legal fees' to individuals simply ren-

136. *Id.*, Hernandez Covington Art. III Confirmation at 427, 430.

137. *Id.*, Hernandez Covington Art. III Confirmation at 418–420.

138. Nominee Aida Milagros Delgado-Colón, Senate Judiciary Committee Hearings, One Hundred Ninth Congress 2005-2006, Second Session, Part 3, Serial No. J-109-4, February 7, 2006, 88–139, 88–89, 91; PN1006—Aida M. Delgado Colon—The Judiciary (Delgado-Colón Art. III Confirmation), https://www.congress.gov/nomination/109th-congress/1006?s=1&r=23.

dering clerical services and completing forms for various federal programs. Then and there, I understood that the legal profession ought to behave differently, and throughout my career I have strived to make that difference."[139]

Attending Catholic schools, she participated in community service that further revealed to her issues confronting Puerto Ricans, amplified by her work at the Department of Labor.[140] In 1982, Aida became the first woman hired as a federal assistant public defender at a time when few women were specializing in criminal law. She became and has remained dedicated to education and rehabilitation. From Assistant Public Defender to First Assistant to Acting Public Defender, Aida forged a leadership path traditionally closed to women. In 1987, the Public Defender received an award for Professional and Humanitarian Services by the Cuban Society of Puerto Rico for her pro bono service to Cuban immigrants. Aida was a charter member of the Puerto Rican Association of Criminal Defense Lawyers (September 1991). In 1993, Aida started her judicial career as the first female federal magistrate judge, appointed to two eight-year terms. In 2016, upon the retirement of Judge Cerezo, Judge Delgado-Colón succeeded Judge Cerezo as the second woman Article III judge in the District of Puerto Rico. She continued volunteer service within the community, in the legal profession, and especially with students—all for which she has been honored. In 2004, the Student Federal Bar Chapter of Pontifical Law was renamed the Hon. Aida Delgado Student Division. Earning a reputation for giving back to her community and profession, the judge was among other judges who nominated their staff for the U.S. Courts Director's Award for Extraordinary Actions. The staff of the Office of the Clerk for the District Court in Puerto Rico received the 2018 honor for their response to two major hurricanes, Irma and Maria, that disrupted operations on the island.[141]

16. Christine Marie Arguello, District of Colorado, 2008–2022

1977	B.S., *Special Honors*, University of Colorado at Boulder (CU)
1980	J.D., Harvard Law School Admitted to Florida Bar
1980–1985	Associate, Valdes-Fauli, Cobb & Petrey, Miami, Florida
1985	Admitted to Colorado Bar
1985–1991	Holland & Hart, Colorado Springs, Colorado Equity Partner 1988–1991 Senior Associate 1985–1988

139. *Id.*, Delgado-Colón Art. III Confirmation at 133.

140. Natalia Morales-Echeverría, *Judicial Profile Hon. Aida M. Delgado-Colón Chief Judge, District of Puerto Rico*, Federal Bar Association, https://www.fedbar.org/wp-content/uploads/2019/10/Delgao-ColonOctNov2012-pdf-3.pdf.

141. https://www.uscourts.gov/news/2018/11/26/2018-directors-awards-presented-leadership-excellence.

1991–1997	Owner, Professional Fee Examiners, Inc.
1991–1999	University of Kansas School of Law (KU Law) 1998–1999, Full Professor 1991–1998, Associate Professor
1999–2002	Colorado Attorney General (AG) Office 2000–2002, Chief Deputy 1999–2000, Deputy for State Services Visiting/Adjunct Professor, CU Law School
2000–2002	Nominated to Tenth Circuit Court of Appeals; nomination returned
2003	Visiting Professor, University of Denver College of Law Admitted to Iowa Bar
2003–2004	Shareholder & Managing Partner, Duncan Green Brown & Langeness, P.C.
2004–2006	Equity Partner, Davis Graham & Stubbs, LLP
2006–2008	Managing Senior Associate Counsel, CU
2008–2022	Article III Judge, District of Colorado[142]
2022	Senior Status July 15, 2022
2025	Retired

Christine was born on July 15, 1955, in Thatcher, Colorado, and raised in Buena Vista, along with six siblings. Her parents, Felipe and Emelia (Emily) Martinez, were poor. Felipe was a railroad worker and the family, including Christine, lived in a railway car. Felipe became a barber and operated Phil's Barber Shop. Christine was the first in her family to attend and graduate from college and then law school. In 1980, she passed the Florida Bar and practiced in Miami for five years before returning to Colorado and large law firm practice at Holland & Hart. At age thirty-two, Christine won a seat in 1987 to the Colorado Springs Board of Education District 11, the second of two Luminarias elected to public office." Education was an interest she would pursue professionally and through volunteer work, starting in 1991. Christine became Professor Arguello at KU Law where she founded the Lawrence High School Partnership program and co-founded the Hispanic Network of KU. With her supportive Colorado connections, she was hired by Kenneth Salazar, the newly elected Colorado AG. She served the AG first as Deputy Chief Assistant AG and then as Chief Deputy. In 2000, she was nominated to the Court of Appeals (Tenth Circuit), but her nomination was not acted on by the Senate. In 2002, Christine returned to teaching, this time at her university alma mater, CU Law. A year later, in 2003, she

142. Nominee Christine Marie Arguello, Senate Judiciary Committee Hearings, One Hundred Tenth Congress 2007–2008, Second Session, Part 4, Serial No. J-110-8, September 9, 2008:459, 625–665, 625–627, 631; PN1843—Christine M. Arguello—The Judiciary (Arguello Art. III Confirmation), https://www.congress.gov/nomination/110th-congress/1843?s=1&r=29.

returned to private practice in Denver. In 2008, Christine was nominated and confirmed as the first Hispanic to the federal bench in the U.S. District of Colorado. Ever committed to expanding higher education opportunities for Latino students, Judge Arguello created a successful mentoring/law school pipeline program in 2014, *Si Se Puede/Yes We Can*.[143] The program pairs college students interested in becoming lawyers with mentors, provides skill-building and exposure programming, demystifies the law school application process, and provides an intensive LSAT preparation course. The judge has been honored with two outstanding lifetime achievement awards and was inducted into the Colorado Women's Hall of Fame (2014) and Latino Hall of Fame (2019).[144]

17. Nitza Quiñones Alejandro, Eastern District of Pennsylvania, 2013–Incumbent

1970–1971	Exchange Student, University of Central Michigan, School of Business Administration
1972	B.B.A., Business Administration, *cum laude*, University of Puerto Rico
1973–1974	Legal Intern, Legal Aid Society, University of Puerto Rico
1975	J.D., University of Puerto Rico Law School Admitted to Puerto Rico Bar (inactive status)
1976	Admitted to Pennsylvania Bar
1975–1977	Staff Attorney, Community Legal Services, Inc., Philadelphia
1977–1979	Attorney Advisor, U.S. Department of Health and Human Services
1979–1991	Staff Attorney, U.S. Department of Veterans Affairs
1980–1991	Arbitrator, Philadelphia Court of Common Pleas
1991	Solo Practitioner, Law Office of Nitza Quiñones
1991–2013	Judge First Judicial District of Philadelphia, Court of Common Pleas[145]
2013	Article III Judge, Eastern District of Pennsylvania

Nitza was born in 1951 in Hato Rey, Puerto Rico as the youngest "daughter of a First Sergeant in the [U.S.] Army and a homemaker.

143. Arguello Dream Catchers, https://lawschoolyeswecan.org/thewhy.

144. Colorado Women's Hall of Fame, Christine Arguello, 2014, https://www.cogreatwomen.org/project/christine-marie-arguello/; Colorado Latino Hall of Fame, https://www.youtube.com/watch?v=JA_8hSQhXmU.

145. Nominee Nitza I. Quiñones Alejandro, Senate Judiciary Committee Hearings, One Hundred Thirteen Congress 2013–2014, Second Session, Part I, Serial No. J-113-1, February 13, 2013:422–425, 528–580, 711–716, 723–724, 745–752; PN25—Nitza I. Quinones Alejandro—The Judiciary (Quiñones Alejandro Art. III Confirmation), https://www.congress.gov/nomination/113th-congress/25.

> [She] grew up on a series of military bases, attended the finest schools, and was surrounded by a community of military families...fortunate to have grown up in a world where the only apparent distinction between individuals was military rank. Throughout...adolescence, [she] never would have predicted that someday it would matter in [her] professional and social interactions that [she] was a woman...Latina [and] gay."[146]

Nitza received her Bachelor of Business Administration degree in 1972 from the University of Puerto Rico, having attended Central Michigan University as an exchange student for part of her undergraduate education. The influence to attend law school came from her mother who expressed disappointment that Nitza was seeking a job as an accountant: "Yo esperabe más de ti. *I expect more of you.*"[147] Nitza explained that her sister was acquiring a master's degree in urban planning and brother was in dental school. "The sting of [her] mother's disapproval, while painful at the time, successfully guilted [her] into applying for graduate studies—a decision that would lay the groundwork for a career [she] would treasure for the rest of [her] life."[148] Nitza decided to attend law school. Of that experience she captured what Luminarias and non-Luminarias (as well as what most first-generation law students) faced:

> In my class at the University of Puerto Rico School of Law, there were approximately twenty-five women and one hundred men. While this statistical disparity certainly did not surprise me, the divide I felt most prominently was not between genders, but rather between the students who came from families of lawyers and those of us who would be first-generation attorneys. This professional disparity was not only significantly numerically, but also significant in its practical effects. Those of us who weren't fulfilling a legacy were unfamiliar with the jargon that permeates the legal world, did not know the logistics of how court systems worked, and certainly did not know how to network without any personal connections in the field. I unexpectantly found myself in a discrete minority and, because of that classification, I felt disadvantaged."[149]

In 1975, Nitza received her law degree and moved after graduation from Puerto Rico to Philadelphia to pursue her passion for public service. She became a staff attorney for Community Legal Services, Inc. in Philadelphia from 1975 to 1977. She transitioned to federal practice with the U.S. Department of Health and Human Services from 1977 to 1979 (HHS) and the Department of Veterans Affairs (VA) from 1979 to 1991 as the first female attorney in that office. It was at the VA that Nitza encountered her first pay disparity. Her HHS position was a GS-11 level (soon to in-

---

146. Nitza I. Quiñones Alejandro, *A Personal Essay,* Univ. of Penn.L.Rev., Vol. 168, No. 6, 1455, at 1458.

147. *Id.*

148. *Id.* at 1459.

149. *Id.*

crease to a GS-12). The VA's job offer was at a GS-9 level which Nitza rejected twice, before accepting the modified GS-12 offer.[150]

In May 1990, Nitza was nominated by Governor Robert P. Casey to the Philadelphia Court of Common Pleas, which occurred partly due to the advocacy of the Pennsylvania Hispanic Bar Association. The nomination was controversial with local Democratic and Hispanic leaders because Nitza was a political novice whose earlier employment by the federal government had barred her from participating in party politics—thus, she was an unknown who had not earned her way through the party. Consequently, Nitza's nomination languished for a year in the Pennsylvania Senate. In 1991, she was in solo practice while attempting to secure her judicial seat.[151] Nitza overcame the controversy and placed tenth out of thirty-four candidates seeking sixteen vacancies, winning the general election in November. In December 1991, Nitza was confirmed by the Senate as the first Latina to serve on the Court of Common Pleas.[152] She later said that running for office gave her the "thick skin" required of a judge. From 1991 to 2013, Judge Quiñones presided over approximately 300 civil trials and 1,500 criminal trials, including cases of first impression.[153] The judge retained her seat in the 2001 and 2011 elections. She was an active member of the Philadelphia bar and community, having served on the boards of organizations and city task forces, such as the Girard Medical Center, Private Industry Council of Philadelphia, the Hunting Park Community Development Corporation, the Ladies Executive Golf Group, and the Mayor's Election Reform Task Force.

On November 27, 2012, President Barack Obama nominated Judge Quiñones Alejandro to the Eastern District of Pennsylvania, to fill the seat vacated by Judge Richard Barclay Surrick. The nomination was made on the recommendation of Pennsylvania Senator Bob Casey, Jr. She is the first Latina lesbian to be nominated to a federal judgeship.[154] The judge has received honors from state and national organizations on the mainland and from the Commonwealth, including from the U.S. Army Corps of Engineers, DOJ, Rutgers, Temple and Villanova University Law Schools, and Pennsylvania Governor Tom Ridge's Advisory Commission on Latino Affairs, Pride Award in 1997.

150. *Id.* at 1460.

151. *Supra* note 145, Quiñones Alejandro Art. III Confirmation at 568; note 146 at 1462.

152. *Supra* note 145, Quiñones Alejandro Art. III Confirmation at 541.

153. *Id.*, Quiñones Alejandro Art. III Confirmation at 542, 543–554.

154. *Id.*, Quiñones Alejandro Art. III Confirmation at 1465–1467.

C. The Roadblocks

1. The Nomination and Confirmation Process "of Judges Is a Political Process"[155]

Beyond education, experience and intellect, political acumen is required of Luminarias (and all Article III judges) to be nominated and confirmed as federal judges. The hurdles through which they must successfully navigate extend beyond the formal Senate Judiciary Committee hearing and full Senate vote. These include securing a nomination that may involve balancing the political interplay between the White House and senators, navigating through investigative scrutiny by the Federal Bureau of Investigation (FBI) and the Senate Judiciary Committee, obtaining passing ratings from the ABA, and successfully navigating the local, state, and national politics of the time—garnering sufficient support and momentum to override any opposition. The possibility of derailment exists from the time of nomination or date of referral (the date when the Senate Judiciary Committee receives the nomination from the White House) to confirmation—due to senatorial holds and filibusters to outside partisan conflict, contrived or substantive. Much has been written about this process and statistics compiled on nominees from the time of nomination-referral to actual confirmation but not specifically on Luminarias. Table 4 reflects the number of days the Luminaria nominees had to wait from the date of their referrals to their confirmation.

155. Stephan O. Kline, *The Topy-Turvey World of Judicial Nominations*, Dickinson L.Rev. 103, no. 2 (1998–1999), 246–342, at 256, quoting former U.S. Senator Paul Simon (D-Ill.); *see also, supra* note 98, Navarro Article.

Table 4 **Number of Days from Nomination to Confirmation**

Nominee District Court	ABA Rating[156]	Referred	Hearing	Confirmed	Commission	Vote[157]	Days
Cerezo[158]	Q	5/14/1980	6/10/1980	6/26/1980	6/30/1980	UC	46
Carrero Nesbitt	WQ	10/31/1983	11/7/1983	11/15/1983	11/16/1983	UC en bloc	43
Sotomayor	Q/WQ	11/27/1991	6/4/1992	8/11/1992	8/12/1992	UC	281
Baird	WQ	4/2/1992	7/1/1992	8/11/1992	8/12/1992	UC	131
Gonzalez	Q	4/9/1992	7/1/1992	8/11/1992	8/12/1992	UC	124
Vázquez	WQ/Q	8/6/1993	9/23/1993	9/30/1993	10/1/1993	VV	55
McLane Wardlaw	Q/WQ	8/10/1995	10/24/1995	12/22/1995	12/26/1995	VV	134
Tagle	Q	8/10/1995 4/21/1997	RETURNED 2/25/1998	3/11/1998	3/17/1998	VV	(943)[159] 324

156. ABA Ratings of Article III and Article IV Judicial Nominees ("ABA Ratings"), Q=Qualified, WQ=Well Qualified, NQ=Not Qualified, https://www.americanbar.org/groups/committees/federal_judiciary/ratings/. Source of Judge Cerezo's ABA rating was obtained by the Author on May 7, 2024, from Denise Cardman, ABA Deputy Director, Governmental Affairs (1980–present). Source of Carrero Nesbitt ABA rating: Ronald Reagan Presidential Digital Library Collections, Baker, James A. Counsel's Office (Jan. 1984–June 1982, 1–44, 18, https://www.reaganlibrary.gov/public/digitallibrary/smof/cos/bakerjames/box-007/40-028-6914302-007-002-2016.pdf; and https://www.congress.gov/nomination: 103rd Congress (1993–1994).

157. UC=Unanimous Consent, VV=Voice Vote, RV=Roll Call Vote.

158. *Refer supra to* PN cites for each judge at https://www.congress.gov/nomination: Carrero Nesbitt PN 551/98th-congress; 102nd-congress: Sotomayor PN402, Baird PN1024, Gonzalez PN1044; Vázquez PN 939/103rd-congress, McLane Wardlaw PN829/104th-congress, Tagle PN254/105th-congress, Armijo PN905/107th-congress, 108th-congress:Herrera PN967, Irizarry PN541 and Hernandez Covington PN1539; Delgado-Colón PN1006/109th-congress, Arguello PN1843/110th-congress and Quiñones Alejandro PN15/113th-congress.

159. Cong. Rec. Vol. 148, No. 129, October 4, 2002, remarks by Senator Patrick Leahy confirming Judge Tagle's waiting period of 943 days, https://www.govinfo.gov/content/pkg/CREC-2002-10-04/html/CREC-2002-10-04-pt1-PgS9975-2.htm.

continues

continued

Armijo	Q	9/4/2001	10/18/2001	11/6/2001	11/12/2001	RV 100–0	63
Herrera	WQ/Q	9/23/2003	11/2/2003	6/3/2004	6/13/2004	RV 93–0	264
Irizarry	NQ/Q	4/28/2003	10/1/2003	6/24/2004	7/8/2004	VV	423
Hernandez Covington	WQ	4/20/2004	6/16/2004	9/7/2004	9/10/2004	RV 91–0	140
Delgado-Colón	WQ/Q	10/25/2005	2/7/2006	3/6/2006	3/17/2006	UC	132
Arguello	Q	7/10/1008	9/9/2008	9/26/2008	10/21/2008	VV	42
Quiñones Alejandro	Q/NQ	(11/27/2012)[160] 1/4/2013	2/13/2013	6/13/2013	6/19/2012	VV	162
Nominee Circuit Court[161]							
Barkett	WQ	9/24/1993	2/3/1994	4/14/1994	4/15/1994	61–37	202
Sotomayor	WQ/Q	6/25/1997	9/30/1997	10/2/1998	10/7/1998	67–29	464
McLane Wardlaw	Q	1/27/1998	6/18/1998	7/31/1998	8/3/1998	VV	185
Arguello	Q	7/27/2000	RETURNED	N/A	N/A	N/A	N/A
Callahan	WQ/Q	2/12/2003	5/7/2003	5/22/2003	5/28/2003	99–0	99

160. Quiñones Alejandro's nomination is an example of when the date of nomination differs from the date of referral, the date the nomination is received by the U.S. Senate.

161. Barkett PN683/103rd-congress; 105th-congress: Sotomayor PN402 and McLane Wardlaw PN829; Callahan PN342/108th-congress.

For the seventeen Article III Luminaria judges, a median number of 228.7 days passed from the date of their referrals to the date of their confirmations. The median number for the fifteen District Court judges is 193.26 days while the median for the Luminaria Circuit Court Judges is 237.5 days. Judge Hilda Tagle waited the longest to be confirmed—943 days from her initial nomination of August 10, 1995, to re-nomination on April 21, 1997, to confirmation March 11, 1998. Judge Irizarry waited 423 days from her date of referral to her confirmation. Judge Arguello had the shortest waiting period of 42 days (but *see* Arguello discussion). Among the four Circuit Court nominees, Judge Sotomayor was the longest at 464 days, while Judge Callahan was the shortest at 99 days.

Table 5 is a macro representation of all District and Circuit Court nominees (male and female) from referral date to confirmation. Organized by presidential administrations from Carter to G. W. Bush, Table 5 compares the median number of days for Luminaria judges to all nominees.[162] President Nixon did not appoint a single Latina Article III judge. Notably, Luminarias comprised 1.6 percent of all District Court nominees and 1.30 percent of all Circuit Court nominees.

162. Source of data for all nominees by U.S. president: CRS, Judicial Nomination Statistics and Analysis: U.S. Circuit and District Courts, 1977–2022, updated April 3, 2023, https://crsreports.congress.gov/product/pdf/R/R45622. Original data for Luminaria judges compiled by author.

Table 5 **District and Circuit Court Judges**

Days from Nomination to Confirmation (1977–2017)

President	District Court	No. of Luminarias	Median # of Days	Median # of Days for Luminarias	Circuit Court	No. of Luminarias	Median # of Days	Median # of Days Luminarias
Carter 1977–1981	**202**	1	56.5	47	**56**	0	N/A	N/A
Reagan 1981–1989	**290**	1	41.0	43	**83**	0	N/A	N/A
G. H. W. Bush 1989–1993	**148**	3	93.0	119.75	**42**	0	N/A	N/A
Clinton 1993–2001	**305**	3	99.0	373.33	**65**	3	139	283.66
G. W. Bush 2001–2009	**261**	6	141.0	177.33	**61**	1	216	99
Obama 2009–2017	**322**	1[163]	215	162	**68**	0	N/A	N/A
Total	**1,528**	15 0.98%	645.5	922.41[164]	**307**	4 1.30%	355	382.66

163. President Obama appointed one Luminaria to the District Court and no Luminarias to the Circuit Courts, to be distinguished from his appointment of Latina attorneys who were not Luminarias.

164. The total median number of 928.41 days includes the two years and seven-month delay of Judge Tagle's first nomination in 1995 to confirmation in 1998.

Twelve of the seventeen Article III judges ultimately were approved by a unanimous vote or by unanimous consent to the District Court: Cerezo, Carrero Nesbitt, Sotomayor, Baird, Gonzalez, Vázquez, McLane Wardlaw, Armijo, Herrera, Hernandez Covington, Delgado-Colón; and Callahan to the Circuit Court. Their Senate Judiciary Committee hearings consisted of *pro forma* questions. Eight of the twelve sailed through their confirmation processes to the District Court without delay or controversy: Cerezo, Carrero Nesbitt, Vázquez, McLane Wardlaw, Armijo, Herrera, Hernandez Covington, and Delgado-Colón. Seven encountered political obstacles, not of their making and one of the seven received an ABA rating that ultimately delayed her confirmation: Sotomayor (District and Circuit Courts), Baird, Gonzalez, Barkett, Tagle, Irizarry, and Arguello.

Senator Joe Biden was chairman of the Senate Judiciary Committee during the confirmation processes of nominees Sotomayor, Baird, Gonzalez, and Vázquez for the District Court and Barkett for the Eleventh Circuit. Senator Hatch served as chairman (the most times) during the confirmation processes of Judges Sotomayor and McLane Wardlaw (Circuit Court), Tagle, Callahan, Herrera, Irizarry, and Hernandez Covington (District Court). Senator Specter switched his party affiliation back to Democrat in 2009, after the last Luminaria judge was confirmed. Senator Patrick Leahy was the chairman of the Senate Judiciary Committee when Judge Quiñones Alejandro secured her confirmation.

2. Nominees Arguello and Tagle, Return of Nominations

Two of the seventeen Luminarias nominated, Christine Arguello and Hilda Tagle, did not receive Senate support. Arguello was nominated initially for the Tenth Circuit and was not renominated for that circuit seat but ultimately was confirmed to the District Court. Tagle was renominated and confirmed to the District Court but only after nearly two years.

a. Nominee Christine Arguello: Nomination Controversy, Inter and Intra Disputes

The controversy ensnaring Judge Arguello concerned vacancies on the Tenth Circuit and District Court of Colorado and involved a Democratic intra-party squabble, dueling Colorado Democratic-Republican nominating committees, and outcry from the Latino community. During the relevant period, Colorado was represented by two Republican senators, Ben Nighthorse Campbell (1993–2005) and Wayne Allard (1997–2009), and Republicans had the majority in the U.S. Senate. A Democrat, Arguello sought a District Court position but was nominated to the Tenth Circuit by a Republican nominating committee.

On September 22, 1999, President Clinton nominated accomplished Denver attorney James M. Lyons for the Tenth Circuit whose nomination languished because of his service to and financial support of the president.[165] While the senior Colorado senator supported Lyons's nomination, junior Senator Allard blue-slipped his nomination, calling Lyons a "political operative of the president."[166] The White House withdrew Lyons from consideration at his request in December 1999; the position remained vacant until 2003.[167] As there were no Colorado Democratic senators, per protocol at the time, the responsibility of forming a local nominating committee fell on the senior Democratic elected congressperson in the state.[168] Diane DeGette (District 1-Denver, 1997–Incumbent), Dave Skaggs (District 2-Boulder, 1987–1999), Mark Udall (District 2-Boulder, 1999–2009), and former Governor Roy Romer formed a nominating committee (Committee) to which Arguello applied. Arguello was not selected by the Committee as one of the four finalists. U.S. Magistrate Judge Patricia A. Coan emerged as the favored candidate. The Committee's decision not to include Arguello as one of the four finalists ignited a backlash from the Latino community against, primarily, Congresswoman DeGette.[169] While not a member of the president's party, Senator Allard formed his own committee to which Arguello also applied, becoming one of five candidates submitted to the White House. Arguello then was Deputy Attorney General and had the support of Colorado Attorney General Kenneth Salazar. Recognizing the impasse, President Clinton offered to nominate Arguello to the District Court and Coan to the Tenth Circuit. Senator Allard refused.[170] President Clinton nominated Arguello to the Tenth Circuit on July 27, 2000, months before the November election. She never received a hearing, a matter raised by Senator Leahy years later during confirmation hearings on February 12 and March 27, 2003. Arguello's nomination was returned, as she did not withdraw from

---

165. White House Press Release (September 22, 1999), https://www.govinfo.gov/content/pkg/WCPD-1999-09-27/pdf/WCPD-1999-09-27-Pg1819.pdf. Lyons was general counsel for the Clinton Transition Foundation, counsel in the Office of President-Elect Clinton, and on several U.S.–Ireland-related initiatives. At Clinton's request during the presidential campaign, Lyons investigated the Whitewater real estate investment in which he found no wrongdoing as did the subsequent independent counsel's report. Senator Allard and others deemed the nomination "political payoff" and wrongfully alleged Lyons covered up the Clintons' role in Whitewater to obstruct his nomination. *See* Robert E. Boczkiewicz, *Imhofe, Others to Block Judge Appointee*, Oklahoman, December 11, 1990; *see also* Oral Interview of Jim Lyon (Aug. 2022) and the Denver Post article referred to therein, "Report Vindicates Denver Lawyer," at 72, 103–104.

166. Robert Boczkiewicz, *Allard to Block Federal Nominee Lyons*, Pueblo Chieftain, December 10, 1999.

167. Tim Tymkovich confirmation to the Tenth Circuit PN16 (Apr. 1, 2003), https://www.congress.gov/nomination/108th-congress/16?s=1&r=33.

168. *See supra* note 98, Navarro Article at 14.

169. Tom Mcavoy, *Hispanics Rally for Arguello Court Nomination*, Pueblo Chieftain, August 31, 2001, https://www.chieftain.com/story/news/2001/08/31/hispanics-rally-for-arguello-court/9026730007/.

170. Bill McAllister, *Allard Rejects Clinton Offer of Judge Swap*, Denver Post, May 12, 2000, https://extras.denverpost.com/news/news0512f.htm. Senator Allard asserts he was not consulted by the Democratic Nominating Committee or the White House in the selection process; *see also, Trouble Brewing over Federal Court Bench Vacancy*, Pueblo Chieftain, (August 16, 1988, https://www.chieftain.com/story/special/1998/08/16/trouble-brewing-over-federal-court/8718438007/.

consideration, and she was not renominated for the Tenth Circuit by newly elected President G. W. Bush. Eight years later on July 10, 2008, President G. W. Bush nominated Arguello to the District Court. Her nomination was stalled for months due to a dispute over judicial candidates between (now) Senator Salazar and Senator Allard; Senator Salazar opposed the Republican nominee.[171] The feud was resolved. On September 26, 2008, Arguello became the first Latina appointed to the District of Colorado. While, amongst the Luminaria judges, Judge Arguello experienced the shortest wait—forty-two days—to receive her commission, she in fact, waited eight years to receive commission as an Article III judge.

b. Nominee, Judge Hilda Tagle: Unexplained, Prolonged Delay to Confirmation

Judge Hilda Tagle was not confirmed for 943 days starting from her August 10, 1995 nomination to the Southern District of Texas (S.D. TX) by President Clinton. From the date of her renomination on April 21, 1997, to confirmation on March 11, 1998, 324 days passed. Senator Hatch presided over the Senate Judiciary Committee from Judge Tagle's initial nomination, to renomination, to confirmation.[172] During her confirmation (and only) hearing on February 25, 1998, the Senate Judiciary Committee asked *pro forma* questions of Judge Tagle and Sam Lindsay (N.D. TX.), the other District Court nominee at hearing that session. Six questions were asked of both nominees about imposing the death penalty, how to reconcile U.S. Supreme Court decisions with which they did not agree, following precedent on racial preferences in contracting, employment, and college admissions, and analysis they would apply to decide cases of first impression.[173] There were no questions asked of Judge Tagle suggesting any controversy, impropriety, inadequate experience, or unsatisfactory performance during her judicial experience—or any other issue relating to or justifying the delay. This fact, coupled with the delay, prompted Senator Leahy to publicly and repeatedly protest Judge Tagle's delay, including in 2003, five years after the fact:

> I recall that Senator Hatch said in September of 1997 that 103 vacancies (during the Clinton administration) did not constitute a "vacancy crisis." He also repeatedly stated that 67 vacancies meant "full employment" on the fed-

---

171. Felisa Cardona, *Judicial Nominee Caught Up in Senators' Dispute*, Denver Post, September 4, 2008, https://www.denverpost.com/2008/09/04/judicial-nominee-caught-up-in-senators-dispute/; and Felisa Cardona, Senate Benches Judicial Feud by Filling 2 Federal Vacancies, Denver Post, September 26, 2008, https://www.denverpost.com/2008/09/26/senate-benches-judicial-feud-by-filling-2-federal-vacancies/.

172. Senator Hatch considered himself a friend to the Latino community. "Tell them I'm sorry," he told a reporter upon deciding not to vote for Supreme Court nominee Sonia Sotomayor. "The Hispanic people are very important to me.... I feel really badly, because I wanted to...." Gebe Martinez, *Why Is the GOP Slighting Hispanics?*, Politico, August 4, 2009, https://www.politico.com/story/2009/08/why-is-the-gop-slighting-hispanics-025745.

173. *Supra* note 91 Tagle Art. III Confirmation at 340–344.

> eral courts.... This is in great contrast to the fate of many of President Clinton's nominees from Texas who were blocked and delayed by the Republican majority, including Enrique Moreno, nominated to the Fifth Circuit Court of Appeals who never got a hearing, never got a vote; Jorge Rangel, nominated to the Fifth Circuit Court of Appeals who never got a hearing, never got a vote, and; Hilda Tagle to the District Court, whose confirmation was delayed nearly two years for no good reason.[174]
>
> We are moving down judicial vacancies. As we can see, starting in 1994, judicial vacancies increased actually under Republican control of the Senate. It went from 63 up to 110. When Democrats took control and I became chairman, we cut that almost immediately from 110 to 60, with nominees of President Bush, notwithstanding all of President Clinton's nominees who had been blocked. Circuit court nominees went from 16 vacancies under Republican Senate leadership up to 33. When I became chairman, we cut it immediately to 25. I note that because we did move to cut those vacancies even though, in this case, it is Cuban-American women, there were many Hispanics and women nominated by President Clinton who were blocked or delayed by the Republican majority. We were told that unless every single Republican agreed, even if one disagreed, they would not get a hearing or a vote.
>
> We had nominees such as Christine Arguello, Jorge Rangel, Enrique Moreno, and Ricardo Morado who were never given hearings, including Judge Richard Paez, Judge Sonia Sotomayor, and Judge Hilda Tagle who were stalled for no good reason. Even though President Clinton's nominees had been blocked, we, the Democrats, when we took over, moved President Bush's nominees for the same spots.[175]

The delay and treatment of the Clinton nominees and delay by the Senate Judiciary Committee under Chair Hatch have been the subject of extensive analysis, with most mentioning Judge Tagle's delay as the longest of those nominees.[176] For her

---

174. Senate Judiciary Committee, Judicial Nominations Hearing July 9, 2003, Statement of Senator Patrick Leahy at 1221. *See supra* note 92, Tagle Interview Clip Five at 5:49–5:55, confirming hearing was non-controversial.

175. Cong. Rec. Vol. 149, No. 66, May 6, 2003, Executive Session, comments of Senator Leahy, at S5756.

176. *See e.g.*, Sheldon Goldman, *The Judicial Confirmation Crisis and the Clinton Presidency*, Presidential Studies Quarterly 28, no. 4 (Fall 1998), 838–844, documenting Judge Tagle "waited the longest at 929 days." *See also* Tagle Interview supra note 92, Clip Three 10:04–11:15 recalling Senator Arlen Specter's niece was nominated a month before her hearing and whose hearing occurred on the same date as her own. Judge Tagle stating, "... I'd been waiting three years, she'd just been nominated the month before." (The senator's niece was Judith M. Barzilay nominated March 27, 1998, for the U.S. Court of International Trade.) Judge Tagle also recalled Senator Strom Thurmond's statement which the record captured: "Thank you Mr. Chairman, I have no questions of this witness. I am going to vote for her. She is the niece of the distinguished Senator Specter. Laughter." *Supra* note 92 Tagle Interview at 319.

part, Judge Tagle attributed the delay to political controversies, unrelated to her qualifications.[177] The official Senate Judiciary Committee records support Judge Tagle's conclusion.

c. Nominee, Judge Dora Irizarry: ABA Judicial Rating

Only one Luminaria judge, Dora Irizarry, did not receive an approval rating from the ABA Standing Committee. The judge was nominated on April 28, 2003, and confirmed fourteen months later on July 8, 2004. Judge Irizarry received a majority rating of "Not Qualified" and a minority vote of "Qualified" based upon judicial temperament during her seven-year combined tenure on the New York Criminal Court (Bronx, Brooklyn) and in Kings County.[178] At her confirmation hearing, the ABA Standing Committee presented complaints that arose during its investigation about the judge's lack of judicial temperament. The investigation consisted of seventy confidential interviews of fifty lawyers (prosecutors and defense counsel) and seventeen judges. The complaints described the judge as "short-tempered," "gratuitously rude, abrasive," "rigid and dismissive," and consisting of demeaning behavior, that included screaming and, in one instance, throwing a pen. Representatives from the ABA Standing Committee relayed there had not been such "consistent and negative" complaints about a nominee since before "President Reagan was in office."[179] The ABA confirmed "there [was] nothing in the public file that indicates any... complaints against the nominee." Then Presiding Justice Michael L. Pesce (Judge Irizarry's supervisor in Brooklyn) testified that no official complaints or reports were filed against Judge Irizarry but that he had received informal complaints about how she ran her courtroom. He never heard of Judge Irizarry throwing anything at attorneys. Justice Pesce described the stress and pressure of the New York Criminal Court as "tremendous," requiring judges to be "tough" and admitted to his own instances of "flying off the handle," getting angry with attorneys, and rudeness.[180] The justice relayed,

> the common description by attorneys about Dora Irizarry was that she is trying to run the courtroom as if it was the Federal bench.... Dora had 8,230-something appearances in 1 year... and when you have hundreds of appearances in 1 day, it is tough.... I can assure you—that the manner in which Brooklyn, Kings County, runs because of the volume, sheer volumes, is unparalleled.... Kings County is quite a place to be.... I have to repeat that if the problem were as serious as [the ABA] found it to be, Dora Irizarry would not have lasted in

177. Navarro Article, *supra* note 98 at 14 and Tagle Interview, *supra* note 92, Clip Five at 3:46–4:10.

178. *Supra* note 122 at 1046–1047 and ABA Ratings *supra* note 156.

179. *Supra* note 122 at 1085–1094.

180. *Id.* Judge Pesce testimony at 1054, *see also* ABA reply at 1068–1069 regarding failure to interview Judge Pesce.

> that part. I would have replaced her. The district attorney of Kings County would have spoken out loud.[181]

Senator Durbin asked the ABA Standing Committee why they did not interview Justice Pesce during its investigation and asked for a response to Justice Pesce's testimony at hearing that he never received complaints about Judge Irizarry's conduct. In its written response to Senator Durbin, the ABA Standing Committee described its interview selection process but did not explain why Justice Pesce was not interviewed.[182]

Judge Irizarry denied she lacked the appropriate judicial temperament, relaying that no complaints ever were filed. She also denied ever throwing objects at anyone in her courtroom and in subsequent written responses to Senator Durbin's questions, provided a contextual explanation of a "passing of a pen" to an attorney in her courtroom.[183] Judge Irizarry described the heavy docket and demands on the criminal court, with upward of 150 to 200 cases daily. She testified:

> As a judge, my only agenda is to make sure that the cases are handled properly, that everyone is heard. Sometimes you're dealing with litigants who are mentally ill. In the criminal term where I sat, sometimes you have defendants who are violent. And so you have safety concerns for everyone in the courtroom, including the attorneys as well... it takes a very firm and tough judge to be able to take control of the courtroom, and at the same time be mindful that you have to be fair... just and... compassionate, and that the appropriate amount of time has to be taken for each case... handle it properly. At times, it takes modulating the tone of your voice, and certainly there could be some who could mistake that as yelling or screaming. Everybody has a different opinion as to what is yelling and what is screaming. And it may be that people are unhappy with the ruling that I have made. In an adversarial system, not everyone is going to be happy with the outcome. So I am truly sorry to know that anyone felt offended, that someone might have been hurt by anything that I might have done in the courtroom. Certainly, that was not my intention. I firmly believe that—in the 7 years that I sat on the bench, there was a mellowing-out process... and learned what techniques... worked better. You learn to be a bit more patient with attorneys who are brand new, and you try to work within that framework and try to follow those kinds of high, lofty goals that I just outlined for the Committee with respect to what is appropriate judicial temperament.[184]

---

181. *Supra*, note 122, Irizarry Art. III Confirmation at 1071–1074.
182. *Id.*, Irizarry Art. III Confirmation at 1068–1069.
183. *Id.*, Irizarry Art. III Confirmation at 1082–1084.
184. *Id.*, Irizarry Art. III Confirmation.

A diverse and supportive New York legal community filed its support of Judge Irizarry through numerous letters and testimony.[185] Senators Leahy and Hatch, respectively, expressed concerns over the ABA findings while identifying key jurists and lawyers not interviewed by the ABA and supportive of Judge Irizarry.[186] Ultimately, the Senate confirmed Judge Irizarry by a voice vote on June 24, 2004.[187]

d. A Hold on Three Historic District Court Nominations: Sotomayor, Baird, and Gonzalez

Almost ten years after the confirmation of the first Luminaria Article III judge on the mainland, a historic vote was taken on August 11, 1992, confirming at once three Luminarias to the District Court. They received their commissions the following day. Sotomayor, Baird, and Gonzalez arrived at the same destination having taken different paths. Baird, relatively unknown as a Democrat, had been confirmed and was serving as U.S. Attorney for the Central District of California when she was referred on April 2, 1992. Gonzalez was a respected sitting judge in San Diego who was referred on April 9, 1992. Sotomayor, an independent, was backed enthusiastically by Senator Daniel Moynihan (D-NY, 1977–2001), a fierce liberal, and Republican Senator Alfonse D'Amato (R-NY, 1981–1999). When she was referred on November 22, 1991, presciently, Senator Moynihan predicted Sotomayor's ascension to the U.S. Supreme Court. They did not then know that it would take twenty-two months to secure her confirmation to the District Court.

President G. H. W. Bush occupied the White House, the Democrats controlled the Senate, and Senator Biden was chair of the Senate Judiciary Committee. Politics overshadowed and converged on their historic appointments. In a 1998 speech to the Cervantes Society, Sotomayor recalled that:

> "[I] was only nominated—and only received a Senate floor vote—because of political horse-trading by Mr. Moynihan...." "Mr. Bush," Judge Sotomayor added, "was far from an enthusiastic advocate for [my] nomination. Over the next twenty months, Senator Moynihan cajoled and pushed the Republican White House to nominate me. He traded other nominees in other states—some circuit and other district court—with the [White House] to get me ultimately nominated by President Bush."[188]

---

185. *Id.* Irizarry Art. III Confirmation at 1052–1054, 1064–1066, 1072–1081, 1099–1101.

186. *Id.*, Statements of Utah Senator Orrin Hatch and Vermont Senator Patrick Leahy (October 1, 2003), 1082–1084, 1095–1098.

187. *See* Robert Raben, "The ABA Ratings and Minority Nominees: Shedding Light on Disparate Impact," American Constitution Society, November 29, 2011, https://www.acslaw.org/expertforum/the-aba-ratings-and-minority-nominees-shedding-light-on-disparate-impact/.

188. Tom LoBianco, *Sotomayor Less Partisan than Thought*, Washington Times, June 6, 2009, https://www.washingtontimes.com/news/2009/jun/06/bipartisan-backing-not-in-98-speech/.

By spring 1992, Governor Bill Clinton's presidential bid gained such momentum that the Senate Judiciary Committee slowed the confirmation process of President Bush's nominees. Caught in the crosswinds were the three Luminaria nominees plus three other Latino judicial and two attorney general nominees.[189] The senatorial stall prompted the HNBA to stage press conferences throughout the country, including in New York City with Congressman Jose Serrano, simultaneously distributing its first survey of Latino Article III judges, and pressing the immediate confirmation of the Latino nominees. In its press release, the HNBA wrote:

> awaiting confirmation hearings before the... Senate Judiciary Committee are six (6) highly qualified Hispanics who have been nominated by President Bush for federal judgeships around the nation and are endorsed by the HNBA. [HNBA Leadership] urges Senator Biden and the Senate Judiciary committee to expedite confirmation hearings for these individuals immediately. The next 60 days are critical for these candidates. We are deeply concerned that as the presidential election draws nearer with each passing day, the more likely it is that the Senate Judiciary Committee and Congress will be inclined to postpone action on any confirmation indefinitely. It is time for [partisan] politics to be set aside in favor of achieving ethnic diversity on the federal bench.[190]

After the press conference, U.S. senators pledged their commitment to and prioritization of women and minority judicial nominees.[191]

On June 4, 1992, Sotomayor's confirmation hearing was held, along with those of Judge Susan Black (Eleventh Circuit), Loretta Preska (S.D.N.Y.), and Irene Keely (D.VA.). All four were voted out of Committee by unanimous consent on June 11, 1992.[192] Baird and Gonzalez were approved by the Committee on June 30, 1992. Thereafter, holds were placed on Sotomayor, Black, Preska, and Keely by several Republican senators in response to those placed by Democratic Senator Howard Metzenbaum and others on Edward Carnes, Republican nominee for the Eleventh Circuit.[193] In placing the hold on Judge Black, Sen. Richard Shelby's office publicly stated, "Shelby has 'no problems with Ms. Black,'... but placed the hold out of 'a sense of fairness.' The nomination of fellow Alabaman Carnes, ready for floor con-

---

189. *Supra* note 1, Atencio HNBA Article at 9. The date of confirmation is mistakenly recorded as August 12 instead of August 11.

190. May 18, 1992, HNBA press statement; Deborah Pines, *Group Urges Appointment of More Hispanics Judges*, N.Y.L.J. (May 18, 1992).

191. *Supra* note 1, Atencio HNBA Article at 10, fn. 22.

192. Black PN933, Preska PN1003 and Sotomayor PN807 at https//www.congress.gov/nomination/102nd-congress/933, 1003 and 807 respectively. *See also, U.S. Courts, Law Dean Said, "You'll Change Your Mind," Susan Black Proved Him Wrong*, September 11, 2019, https://www.uscourts.gov/news/2019/09/11/law-dean-said-youll-change-your-mind-susan-black-proved-him-wrong.

193. Neil A. Lewis, *4 Women Delayed in Rise to Bench*, New York Times, July 14, 1992; John Wagner, 4 Women Caught in Judgeship Fight, Washington Post, June 22, 1992.

sideration for some time, is being 'held hostage' by death penalty opponents."[194] Throughout 1992, the HNBA met with the Senate Judiciary Committee—specifically Senators Biden, Kennedy, and Hatch—and their respective staff, pressing confirmation of the Latino nominees. A "bipartisan package" lifted all holds."[195] On August 11, 1992, Sotomayor, Gonzalez, Baird, Black, Preska, and Keely, were confirmed by unanimous consent. (Carnes later was confirmed in September 1992.) The identity of the senator(s) who placed the anonymous hold on Judge Sotomayor never was publicly revealed.

e. The Secret Hold on Judge Sotomayor's 1998 Nomination to the Second Circuit

Obstruction to Judge Sotomayor's District Court confirmation paled in comparison to her nomination for the Second Circuit. Open opposition to her Circuit Court nomination resulted in a sixteen-month delay, four months less than the District Court. Judge Sotomayor was nominated by President Clinton on June 25, 1997, with the full support of New York Senators Moynihan and D'Amato. Republicans held the majority in the Senate, with Senator Trent Lott serving as majority leader and Senator Hatch as chair of the Senate Judiciary Committee. On March 5, 1998, on a 16–2 vote, Judge Sotomayor passed out of Committee.[196] That day, Rush Limbaugh devoted his show to Judge Sotomayor's nomination calling her an ultraliberal on a rocket ship to the Supreme Court. Anonymous or confidential holds[197] were placed on Judge Sotomayor's confirmation.

> The holds were so secretive that sometimes it [was] difficult to tell exactly which nominees have had holds placed on them.... What they're doing in their court-blocking strategy is really unprecedented. We've never had a Senate majority leader [Trent Lott] allowing so-called holds on people who have been cleared and moved to the full Senate for a vote. This is a personal humiliation of Orrin Hatch. The whole Senate committee system is being challenged.[198]

The reason for blocking Judge Sotomayor's confirmation generated much attention. News outlets reported Republican Party concerns that Judge Sotomayor's next

---

194. *Id.*

195. Phil Schatz, *Judicial Profile Hon. Loretta A. Preska Chief Judge, Southern District of New York*, Federal Bar Association, December 2013, https://www.fedbar.org/wp-content/uploads/2019/10/Preska-Dec2013_4-pgs-pdf-5.pdf.

196. *Supra*, note 47, PN402, https://www.congress.gov/nomination/105th-congress/402.

197. Cong. Rec. S8477, Vol. 149, No. 24 (February 10, 1998), Senator Leahy statement, https://www.congress.gov/108/crec/2003/02/10/ CREC-2003-02-10.pdf. *See supra* note 188, LoBianco writing that news reports "say Alabama Sen. Richard C. Shelby, then a Democrat [who later switched parties], had blocked the nominations (Black/Preska/Sotomayor) because of a separate hold placed on an Alabama prosecutor who supported the death penalty." *See also,* Neil A. Lewis, *G.O.P. Its Eyes On High Court, Blocks a Judge*, The New York Times, June 13, 1998 at https://www.nytimes.com/1998/06/13/nyregion/gop-its-eyes-on-high-court-blocks-a-judge.html.

198. *Supra* note 47, Sotomayor District Court Confirmation at 309.

appointment would be the U.S. Supreme Court. Fueling the concern were rumors that Supreme Court Justice Breyer Stephens would retire at the end of the Court's session (he did not retire until four years later in 2022). On February 10, 2003, during the confirmation fight over nominee Miguel Estrada, Senator Leahy recalled the 1998 opposition to Judge Sotomayor:

> Let me share with the Senate an account of Republican use of ideology in connection with judicial nominations. There was a column in the Wall Street Journal in the summer of 1998 explaining the anonymous Republican holds on the nomination of Judge Sonia Sotomayor to the Second Circuit Court of Appeals. I worked hard for 2 years on that nomination. It is my circuit. It is the circuit court I argued in front of when I was in private practice. I was astounded when Republicans held her up for months without a vote. I could not understand why such an outstanding nominee was being stalled by Republicans. After all, she initially was appointed to the Federal bench by a Republican President. Not only that, she had an outstanding record as a judge and, before that, an outstanding record in private practice and an outstanding record as a prosecutor.
>
> What was not to like about this Hispanic woman appointed initially by a Republican and now nominated by a Democrat? She had been confirmed by the Senate to the U.S. District Court for the Southern District of New York in 1992 after being nominated by the first President Bush.... So then Mr. Gigot explained to all what was the problem behind the closed doors of the Republican Cloakroom. Republicans were fearful, if she were confirmed quickly, she could be in line to be nominated to the U.S. Supreme Court. Mr. Gigot wrote: 'If liberals do prevail, the president could turn to 43-year-old district court judge Sonia Sotomayor. She's every Republican's confirmation nightmare—a liberal Hispanic woman put on the district bench by George Bush.'[199]

While the concern in 1998 was unfounded as there were no openings on the Supreme Court, history proved it to be as prescient as Senator Moynihan's 1991 prediction, *albeit* premature by eleven years. The HNBA, Latino elected officials, and MALDEF advocated on behalf of Judge Sotomayor, which included meetings with the majority leader and the Senate Judiciary Committee. In meetings with the HNBA, Senator Lott repeatedly stated the basis of his refusal to allow a vote was "because the next step was the Supreme Court." The *Nation* documented Senator Lott's "Latina strategy":

> Senate majority leader Trent Lott has established a new rule for the federal judicial selection process. There can be one, and only one, Hispanic woman

199. *Supra* note 197, Sen. Leahy statement at S2073. Paul Gigot is a well-known conservative political commentator and editor of the editorial pages for the Wall Street Journal who wrote the Potomac Watch column.

on the United States Courts of Appeals. Since there is already one such judge (Rosemary Barkett, on the 11th Circuit) other Hispanic women can serve on trial courts, but the appellate courts are officially off limits.

Too bad for Judge Sonia Sotomayor.... After all, rules are rules, even if they are quotas. The majority leader can't just make an exception for Judge Sotomayor. It is too dangerous, according to reports citing Senate Republican staff aids, to confirm another Hispanic woman as an appellate judge. Confirming her would be an admission that she is a highly qualified jurist. (Never mind that she is a highly qualified jurist.)... Once they admit that, the Senate majority would be sunk.... You can see that the risk simply is too great.[200]

On April 9, 1998 senators representing the Second Circuit wrote the majority leader about the vacancy crisis erupting on the court and the need to expedite Judge Sotomayor's confirmation.[201] Senators included Alfonse D'Amato, James Jeffords (R-VT, 1989–2001), Daniel Moynihan, Christopher Dodd (D-CT, 1981–2011), and Joseph Lieberman (D-CT 1989–2012, I-CT 2013). The Senate returned from recess on April 20. To force a vote on Judge Sotomayor's nomination, Senator Leahy placed a hold on Charles Straub, nominee to the Second Circuit at the end of May 1998 but withdrew it in June.[202]

In June 1998, the *Wall Street Journal* announced the "Souter Strategy," theorizing the Clinton administration intended to fast-track Judge Sotomayor by elevating her to the Second Circuit first, then as soon as a vacancy occurred, appoint her to the Supreme Court.[203] The Republican block persisted. To move the Senate, several Hispanic organizations organized a petition drive in New York State, generating hundreds of signatures from New Yorkers. "Over ten thousand people from across the country sent letters to the Senate on [her] behalf"[204] to push a Senate vote. "Hundreds of lawyers... not only sent letters but called upon their personal contacts to assist.... An extraordinarily long list of bar associations expended their own resources to send letters and representatives to Washington to meet with various Senators."[205] Among her supporters were Latino elected officials, including Puerto Rican

200. *Supra* note 1, Atencio HNBA Article at 18–20 citing Deborah Goldberg, Lott's Hispanic Quota, The Nation, October 5, 1998, at 8. HNBA President Lillian Apodaca, board member Ramona Romero, Congressman Rudy Beccera (D-CA), and MALDEF President Antonio Hernandez met with Senator Lott.

201. Cong. Rec., Vol. 140, S7920-21 (July 17, 1998), statement of Senator Leahy; letter entered into congressional record June 2, 1998, at S5568, https://www.congress.gov/105/crec/1998/06/02/CREC-1998-06-02-pt1-PgS5568.pdf.

202. Frank J. Murray, *Leahy Pushes in Public, Undermines in Private*, Washington Times, May 29, 1998, at A4.

203. *The Souter Strategy*, Wall Street Journal, June 8, 1998.

204. *Supra*, note 48, Sotomayor Induction Ceremony at 46, remarks by Circuit Judge Sotomayor.

205. *Id.*; see e.g., Coalition letter of bar associations (Sept. 29, 1998), Puerto Rican, Dominican, NE Cuban, HNBA, National Conference of Women's Bar Associations, NY Asian and Women's Bars, LULAC, NALEO.

Governor Pedro Rossello and New York state Senator Efrain Gonzalez (D-31st District, the Bronx). The state senator refused to endorse Senator D'Amato in his reelection, "unless he got [Sotomayor] a vote," a fact Senator D'Amato acknowledged later to Judge Sotomayor.[206] Senator D'Amato, in need of Latino support and then trailing among crucial Hispanic voters, convinced Majority Leader Lott to schedule a vote on Judge Sotomayor's nomination.[207] By this time, the judge had been waiting sixteen months. One week short of adjournment on October 2, 1998, the Senate confirmed Judge Sotomayor to the Second Circuit by a vote of 67–29; 25 nay votes were Republican senators which included Chairman Hatch.[208] Judge Sotomayor received her commission on October 7, becoming the sixtieth judge on the Second Circuit. She was inducted on November 6, 1998, as "the first *Puertorriquena* ever to sit on a Federal Court of Appeals." "Enhorabuena."[209]

f. Justice Barkett: Controversy within the Senate Judiciary Committee

The opposition against Justice Rosemary Barkett for the Eleventh Circuit was the same she encountered in 1992 for retention to the Florida Supreme Court: that she was too liberal. Justice Barkett was retained by nearly 61 percent of Floridians. During her eight-year tenure on the Florida Supreme Court, Judge Barkett issued 3,000 opinions, joining the majority (her male justices) on the Florida Supreme Court in 91 percent of all cases (who did not face the same opposition upon retention). Justice Barkett reviewed approximately 600 death penalty cases, voting with the majority in upholding 275 death penalty cases involving 150–200 defendants.[210] (Under Florida law, the Florida Supreme Court is required to review all final orders imposing death sentences.) As noted in chapter two, the justice wrote the majority opinion in thirty-eight first-degree murder cases where the death penalty was imposed. The justice's opinions, notably in death penalty cases, fueled the opposition.

The state opposition which migrated to the federal stage, consisted of "right-wing special interest groups" and socially conservative lobbyists that included the National Rifle Association (NRA). This opposition was aided partly by Senator Orrin

---

206. *Supra* note 48, Sotomayor Induction Ceremony at 51.

207. 105th Congress, U.S. Senate Executive Calendar, September 28, 1998 at 2, https://www.senate.gov/legislative/LIS/executive_calendar/1998/09_28_1998.pdf; *see* Joan Biskupic, *Breaking In: The Rise of Sonia Sotomayor and the Politics of Justice* (Farrar, Straus and Giroux, 2014) at 97, 114; 105th Congress, U.S. Senate Executive Calendar, September 28, 1998 at 2,

208. U.S. Senate: Senate Roll Call Votes, 105th Congress, 2nd Session, https://www.senate.gov/legislative/LIS/roll_call_lists/vote_menu_105_2.htm.

209. *Supra* note 48, Sotomayor Induction Ceremony at 5–6, 13, remarks by Luminaria Margarita Rosa (1977 Harvard Law), and at 19 remarks by Circuit Judge Jose Cabranes: "The word enhorabuena is a composite of three words that, idiomatically, convey the sense that a landmark event has taken place 'at a happy and opportune time.'"

210. Nominee Rosemary Barkett, Senate Judiciary Committee Hearings, One Hundred Third Congress, Second Session, Part 2, Serial No. J-103-28, Feb. 3, 1994:359–522, 429–438 (Barkett Art. III Confirmation). *See* questioning by Senators Orrin Hatch at 365–374 and 399–420, Strom Thurmond at 380–389 and Chuck Grassley at 392–397 and 421–424.

Hatch's office whose chief of staff distributed anti-Barkett materials to conservative columnists, editorial boards and newspapers throughout the country urging them to oppose the justice's nomination. The justice learned about the senator's staff involvement through a Florida conservative columnist supportive of Justice Barkett. [211] At the confirmation hearing, Illinois Democratic Senator Paul Simon (1985–1997) cited two ironic and inapposite articles that illustrated the liberal and conservative views held of Justice Barkett. One, was an editorial in the *Washington Times*, stating, "[th]e Clinton administration would be wise to withdraw her name before her radical views become an embarrassment." In contrast, the second was a statement issued by the National Association of Police Organizations relaying they "wholeheartedly support" Justice Barkett's appointment to the Eleventh Circuit.[212] Every major newspaper in Florida endorsed Justice Barkett and published editorials supporting her confirmation to the Eleventh Circuit, encouraging the Senate to rely on the Floridian majority and ignore the minority in-state opposition.[213] Both Florida U.S. senators, Democrat Bob Graham (1987–2005) and Republican Connie Mack (1989–2001), supported the justice.

Primarily at issue was her interpretation of the death penalty, pornography and legislation, and her dissents on these cases and others. At the confirmation hearing, Republican members of the Senate Judiciary Committee focused on select cases in which the justice interpretated the U.S. Constitution vis-à-vis the Florida Constitution that expanded certain rights to its citizens. As Senator Hatch confirmed during the hearing, there was no "doubt as to [her] competence and capability," rather the crucial concern was Justice Barkett's "judicial philosophy."[214] In an attempt to prove Justice Barkett's unsuitability for the Eleventh Circuit, the Senate Judiciary Committee engaged in intense questioning about her judicial record on death penalty cases. Entered into the record was a "scholarly analysis" which concluded the former nun "makes decisions on the basis of personal 'empathy,'" and that she was overly empathetic to criminal and capital defendants. "Rule by empathy" was the pivot point in the growing opposition to Justice Barkett's confirmation and claims were introduced at the hearing that she was outside the mainstream, hobbled law enforcement through the issuance of her opinions, and was engaged in reflexive activism.[215]

In response to the focus of on select cases over the vast bulk of her work, the justice stated:

---

211. Barkett Interview *supra* note 84 at 58:56–1:00:21. Senator Hatch later apologized to Justice Barkett relaying he knew nothing of his staff's involvement.

212. *Supra* note 210, Barkett Art. III Confirmation at 374-375.

213. *Id.*, Barkett Art. III Confirmation at 356–357, Statement of Senator Graham; see also 484-509, editorials and newspapers included in the record affirming Florida's majority support of Justice Barkett's nomination.

214. *Id.*, Barkett Art. III Confirmation, Statement of Chairman Hatch at 351.

215. Cong. Rec. Vol. 140, No. 40, April 14, 1994, analysis *Beyond Judicial Activism* made part of the record; remarks by North Carolina Republican Senator Jesse Helms (1973-2003) during the Senate floor debate on Barkett's nomination at 7539–7540.

> I also have to take pains to add that the selective use of cases is, in my judgment, unfair when one recognizes that I am—I think my critics sometimes are using selective cases to suggest that I am not in the main stream, but my record reflects otherwise, when you recognize that my court is unanimous approximately 70 percent of the time, that I have been in the majority in about 91 percent of the time on my court, and approximately 85 or so percent on criminal cases, so I am hardly out of the main stream.[216]

The Republican Senator from Maine, William Cohen (1979–1997), amplified the justice's point in his statement:

> I was interested in your opening remarks. You said that for all the things you have done right in your life, you owe it to the advice of your family, and that for all the mistakes you have made, you assume personal responsibility. As you said that, I could not help but remember the lines that go something like, 'In my life's dying embers, these are my regrets, when I was right, no one will remember and when I was wrong, no one will forget." You will find that during the course of this confirmation hearing, we will look at when we think you were wrong and omit the hundreds, if not thousands, of times when you were right.
>
> I would also note that many people are under some delusion about the court system. When they look at judges and justices they see black robed oracles who sit in quiet chambers alone dispensing judicial wisdom, unencumbered by personal views, biases, or predilections.
>
> Of course, you know and we all know that is a fiction. Judges are real people, and they are brushed by the wing of experience, as all of us are. They look out at the world through lenses that are clouded, or that are at least covered by a thin film of passion, of preference. It is a measure of judicial temperament to restrain those emotional components that make us human beings.
>
> That rigorous discipline, both in personal behavior and professional thinking, distinguishes those who wish to serve on the bench. There is no way to adhere to this fiction that you and all the others who come before us are looking through an absolutely clear lens which is unencumbered by any past experiences. In Justice Cardozo's little book, "The Nature of the Judicial Process" there is a footnote in which he quotes a French author as saying "In the final analysis, there is no guarantee except the personality of the judge." So we are looking at the personality of the judge, and I suspect that the people of Florida have already done that. They have looked at your personality very closely and at your philosophy and have not found it particularly wanting...

Notwithstanding the opposition, the Senate Judiciary Committee voted favorably on the justice's nomination. Senator Specter was one of seven who voted against

216. *Id.*, Barket Art. III Confirmation at 374.

Justice Barkett from passing out of Committee, stating her record "shows a result-oriented approach that goes beyond judicial activism."[217]

The hearing of February 3, 1994 (five months after referral), also showcased the amiability of Justice Barkett, appreciated by those who supported her—and even those in opposition, which partly explained the justice's popularity. The following snippets capture the Justice's wit.

> **The Chairman (Senator Biden):**... When you were a nun in the Sisters of St. Joseph, were you issued a clicker?
>
> **Justice Barkett:** No, Senator, just a ruler to rap appropriate knuckles. I hope it will not be necessary this morning. [Laughter.]
>
> **The Chairman:** My ears were never this long before I went to Catholic school, and my small hands were in fact not as rough on the back before I attended Catholic school, so I understand. If I ask you anything or if I—the press will know I have had a flashback, if I start saying, "yes, sister," or "no, sister" to your responses, but I will try not to do that. I will try to remember my role.
>
> **Justice Barkett:** Senator, there were, I am told, some judges on the fifteen judicial circuit [of Florida] when I was chief judge there who sometimes had the tendency to refer to me as "mother superior." [Laughter.]...
>
> [After introducing her 35 family members that attended the hearing]:
>
> **Justice Barkett:**... My father is 94, and my mother is 88. They would have been here, had the cold weather and my mother's failing health not precluded it, and then I surely would have worried about any hostile question that may have been asked, I have to tell you.
>
> **Senator Hatch:** You think you would worry, you can imagine how we would feel. [Laughter.][218]

[In a discussion of the differences between the U.S. and Florida state constitutions]:

> **The Chairman:**... so by any reading of the Federal Constitution and the State constitution, Florida's Constitution is more expansive... And it is [sic] that part of your rationale [in analyzing obscenity cases]?
>
> **Justice Barkett:** That is precisely correct, Senator. Under my obligation as a Supreme Court Justice, it includes applying the Florida Constitution to Florida citizens.
>
> **The Chairman:** You have no idea how unusual this is to me. Never did I think when I was in Holy Rosary grade school I would be required to defend a nun against the charge she was soft on pornography. [Laughter.]

217. *Supra* note 210.
218. *Id.*, note 210 at 359, 362.

During the Senate's debate of Justice Barkett's nomination on April 14, 1994, Senator Jessie Helms (R-NC, 1973–2003) stated the following:

> Well, I remember thinking—knowing that Mr. Clinton had nominated the chief justice of Florida's Supreme Court to sit on the U.S. Court of Appeals for the Eleventh Circuit—I thought mercy, is he [President Clinton] really going to put this lady on the U.S. Court of Appeals feeling as he says he does about crime?...
>
> This liberal lady judge has also endorsed a capital punishment theory that would make it impossible to impose the death penalty unless it is carried out according to racial quotas. She has attempted at every turn to make excuses for the acts of brutal criminals based on the fallacious liberal philosophy that criminals are the victims of society—you know, the old society-is-to-blame game.
>
> In the case of *Stall v. Stone*...for example, Chief Justice Barkett joined a dissent that called for striking down a State obscenity statute. She stated, "A basic legal problem with the criminalization of obscenity is that it cannot be defined." I say to the lady, with all respect, you are crazy as the devil. It can and has been defined by the U.S. Supreme Court...the bottom line is that Congress can—as called upon by President Clinton—pass history's toughest crime bill—but that will not make any difference in the world if the President turns around and appoints to the Federal bench individuals such as Rosemary Barkett, the pending nominee. If this lady is confirmed and brings these points of view to the Federal judgeship to which she has been nominated, she is not going to help crime in the streets. She is going to help build up the incidence of crime in the streets and everything else. That is the reason I shall not and cannot support her nomination.[219]

The written submissions, testimony, and arguments presented by both parties at Justice Barkett's confirmation hearing and Senate floor debate depict the controversy surrounding her nomination. Despite the opposition, Justice Barkett was confirmed to the Eleventh Circuit by a 61–37 vote. She served on the Eleventh Circuit, just shy of two decades.[220] Senator Bob Dole, thirty-five Republican senators, and one Democrat voted against Justice Barkett's confirmation. Two years later during the 1996 presidential campaign, Senator Dole included Judge Barkett in his "Judicial Hall of Shame."[221] Reflecting on the Senate floor debate, Judge Barkett did not take the attacks personally, given the strong support she had in Florida, that included the law enforcement community.[222] Interviewed in 2022, Judge Barkett offered the following about the death penalty:

---

219. *Supra* note 215, Senator Helms remarks.

220. *Id.*

221. Ed Whelan, *Bob Dole Puts Judges At Center of 1996 Presidential Campaign*, Confirmation Tales, September 28, 2023, https://www.confirmationtales.com/p/bob-dole-puts-judges-at-center-of.

222. *Supra* note 84, Barkett Interview at 57:58.

> I was very concerned about the death penalty.... I became very concerned about the procedural difficulties of applying the death penalty fairly and equally. First of all, I, I had this overarching impression once I got to the court and we began hearing death cases, that an overwhelming number of them involved very poor people and very mentally disabled people. I thought it would be racial, but—and I've never done an actual study, but, but what hit me was again the poverty that these people came from and the mental disabilities that many of them had. And to that bothered me, and the criteria for applying the death penalty became very—well, it defied definition really.... Florida had the, the aggravating factor of "cold, calculated and premeditated murder." And in conference with the boys [Florida male supreme court justices], I, I said well, what is "'cold, calculated and premeditated? How can that be different than premeditated murder?"...what murder isn't—doesn't occur with utter disregard for human life...[applying the death penalty while on the Eleventh Circuit]...it was just really difficult and, unfair, and a checkerboard pattern of applications of all of these [criteria] across the states made it very unfair to me.... If I were confronted with a case that clearly, clearly met all the criteria, then I...felt I had an oath and had to apply the law. But I think that I applied the law more carefully than others might have.[223]

Ironically, those who opposed Justice Barkett during her 1992 retention election and confirmation process to the Eleventh Circuit failed to recognize (or simply ignored) that they were dealing with a former Catholic nun who profoundly valued life—a professed tenet of the opposition's beliefs.

Conclusion

Over a decade passed from 1980 when Carmen Cerezo became the first Latina Article III judge to 1992 when Judges Sotomayor, Baird and Gonzalez were confirmed and nine years since Judge Carrero Nesbitt was confirmed in 1983. The passage of nearly a decade raises the question why there were no Latinas nominated or confirmed to the federal bench during this time or for that matter, why none were nominated before Judge Cerezo. While the answer will not change history, it is an important part of the judicial story in our country. Between the first two appointments and the three in 1992, there were two Republican presidents, Ronald Reagan (1981–1989) who nominated Judge Carrero Nesbitt and G.H.W. Bush (1989–1993) under whose tenure, Judges Sotomayor, Baird and Gonzalez were confirmed. As a practical matter, there was not a critical mass of Latina attorneys until the 1980s when Luminarias constituted 2.5% (nearly 1,400) of all women lawyers in the country.[224] This means most Luminarias were new attorneys licensed during the decade

223. *Supra note 84, Barkett Interview at 38:44–42.*

224. Luminarias Study, findings on file with the author. *See* Luminarias Article at 31, Table 1 Women Lawyers and Luminarias by the Numbers | 1880–1980 and discussion at 31–34.

of 1970–1980, lacking the requisite years of experience for the federal bench. Nevertheless, there were 260 Latina attorneys who had the necessary credentials and experience, including some with proven judicial records. Among them were the Luminaria Supreme Court Justices Comstock Riley, Naveira Merly, Barkett, Beauchamp Ciparick, Liana Fiol Matta, and Jimenez Maes, state/territory judges Alma Lopez, Irma Santaella Edna Abruna, Zulema Zayas and Jeannette Tomasini-Gomez and the first Latina United States Attorney Andrea Sheridan, as well as Puerto Rico practitioners attorneys Carmen Badillo Martinez, Alma De Torres Delgado and Nilita Vientós Gastón, and mainland attorneys Edna Cisneros, Carmen Dominguez, Vilma Martinez, and Lola Miranda Coles—to name a few.[225] Simply put, the Luminarias were a small but mightily accomplished group of attorneys who provided the opportunity to increase the number of Latina federal judges starting in the 1970s and continuing—up to the present time.

Strikingly, the Luminaria District Court nominees who faced the greatest obstacles and delays were Democratic nominees. None were opposed because of their credentials or ability to fulfill the judicial duties awaiting them as their respective confirmation hearings confirm. Nominees Tagle and Arguello who waited years to be confirmed as Article III judges faced neither obstacles nor difficult questions when they appeared before the Senate Judiciary Committee. The records of the Senate Judiciary Committee and articles cited in this chapter establish that the opposition was purely political and included intra-party fights. Regrettably, the political pressure became even worse (*aún peo*r, even worse) when the Luminaria nominee, Sonia Sotomayor, was considered exceptionally qualified. Scholars on both sides of the political divide have cried foul to the political machinations that prevent or delay well qualified attorneys from being confirmed to the bench. Perhaps there is no better time than the present to confine political battles to the election of public officials.[226]

The fifteen Luminaria District Court Judges represent our country's first generation of Latina federal judges. A review of their cases illustrate they performed their duties well and consistent with that expected of all Article III judges. Unlike other federal judges, however, they bore the extra duty of forging acceptance among their peers and the public. The appointment of double the number of successive Latina federal judges confirms this first generation was successful.

---

225. Luminarias Study, findings on file with the author.

226. Former SCOTUS Justice Sandra Day O'Connor fought for judicial reform due to the nature and purpose of the judiciary. *See*, Institute for the Advancement of the American Legal System (IAALS), four-part blueprint to reform the election of state court judges, IAALS The O'Connor Judicial Selection Plan, June 2014, https://iaals.du.edu/sites/default/files/documents/publications/oconnor_plan.pdf.

Part Two

Luminaria Article III Judges Constructing the Law

Four

Cases and Issues of First Impression

A. Original Federal Jurisdiction of the District Courts

Section 2 of the U.S. Constitution, Art. III, Section II establishes federal jurisdiction:

> The judicial Power shall extend to all Cases, in Law and Equity, arising under this Constitution, the Laws of the United States, and Treaties made, or which shall be made, under their Authority;—to all Cases affecting Ambassadors, other public Ministers and Consuls;—to all Cases of admiralty and maritime Jurisdiction;—to Controversies to which the United States shall be a Party;—to Controversies between two or more States;—between a State and Citizens of another State,—between Citizens of different States,—between Citizens of the same State claiming Lands under Grants of different States, and between a State, or the Citizens thereof, and foreign States, Citizens or Subjects.

There are ninety-one Article III district courts, which are the federal trial courts of general jurisdiction (district courts) within the federal judiciary. Eighty-nine district courts exist within the fifty states with at least one district and judge per state, one in the District of Columbia (D.C.) and one in Puerto Rico. A Provisional Court in Puerto Rico was created in 1899, superseded by the Foraker Act of 1900, which provided a new civil government and territorial court.[1] Judges were appointed to eight-year terms, not lifetime tenures as the other Article III judges until 1966 with Congress's enactment of Public Law 89-571. A year later, the first Article III judge for the District of Puerto Rico (D.P.R.) was appointed.[2] Federal courts have original jurisdiction over cases limited to the U.S. government, U.S. Constitution, or federal laws or controversies between states or between the U.S. government and foreign governments. "Cases or controversies" is a well-known legal requirement or predicate for cases to be tried in federal court. The district courts have jurisdiction to hear

1. 31 Stat. 77 (Apr. 12, 1900), 13 C.F.R. 312.

2. 80 Stat. 764 (Sept. 12, 1966), Federal Judicial Center (FJC), https://www.fjc.gov/node/1390311; see Aid M. Delgado-Colón, Chief Judge, USDC-PR, "Federal Bar Association, Hon. Raymond L. Acosta Puerto Rican Chapter," *From the Bar: 50th Anniversary Special Issue* 57 (Summer 2016): 3–5.

federal civil and criminal cases. Parties may appeal decisions of a federal district court to their respective circuit courts of appeals.

District court judges are responsible for managing the court and supervising court employees. They can be impeached and removed by Congress. There are over 670 district court judges nationwide. Federal magistrate judges handle some of the district court duties. They are appointed by the district court upon a majority vote of the judges to an eight-year term (full-time) and four years if part-time and may be reappointed. In criminal matters, magistrate judges may oversee certain cases, issue search warrants and arrest warrants, conduct initial hearings, set bail, and decide certain motions (e.g., motion to suppress evidence). In civil cases, magistrates often oversee a broad array of issues such as pre-trial motions and discovery. Of the seventeen Luminaria district court judges, two—Gonzalez and Delgado Colón—served as a magistrate judge. Eleven were state appellate or trial court judges before elevation to the federal bench, and five had no prior judicial experience before becoming Article III judges.

The District of New Mexico is the sole federal district court in which three Luminarias served concurrently for fourteen years, from 2004 to 2018: Judge Vázquez (1993–2023), Judge Armijo (2001–2018), and Judge Herrera (2004–2019). All but four Luminaria district court judges retired and/or assumed senior status as of 2023. The five active judges as of 2025 are U.S. Supreme Court Justice Sotomayor, Circuit Court Judges McLane Wardlaw and Callahan, and District Court Judges Delgado-Colón and Quiñones. The ability of the Luminaria judges to navigate the intense bureaucratic and political processes to become the country's first Article III Latina judges paved the path for the thirty-nine others who have since been appointed to the federal district court bench. *See* Appendix B, List of Luminaria & Latina Article III Judges, 1980 | 2025.

B. Type of Cases Handled by Luminaria District Court Judges and Cases Appealed

Generally, the types of cases handled by the Luminaria district court judges (not appealed) appear uniform across the federal districts in which they served. The top six cases[3] were: (1) criminal law, (2) prisoners' rights, (3) civil rights, (4) labor and employment, (5) torts and negligence, and (6) contracts. Following these six categories were (7) other (undefined), (8) real property, and (9) practice and procedure. Intellectual property and technology, class action, and practice and procedure appear as one of the top five cases for at least one of the Luminaria district court judges.

---

3. Westlaw Tools, Litigation Analytics. As of the date this book went to press, Westlaw did not have the same data for the district court tenures of Judges Sotomayor and McLane Wardlaw but attempted to retrieve the data at the author's request. The author obtained their data from a review of their cases.

Types of District Court Cases

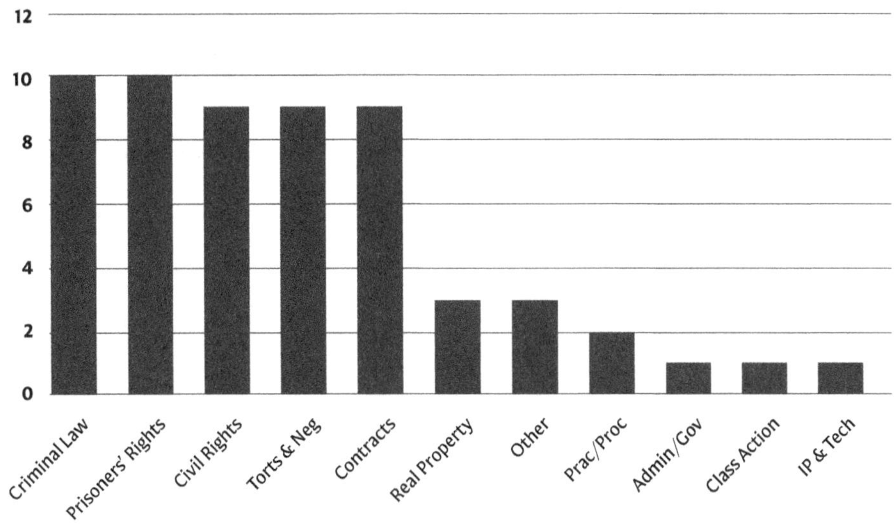

The top three types of cases—criminal law, prisoners' rights, and civil rights—appear uniformly across the districts with no discernible difference in geography. Real property appeared as a top issue for three judges, Judge Carrero Nesbitt in Florida and Judges Cerezo and Delgado-Colón in Puerto Rico. Intellectual property and technology were among the top five cases for Judge Baird (C.D. Cal.). Class actions were in the top five for Judge Irizarry (EDNY).

The top three types of cases appealed were criminal justice, employment/labor, and civil rights, followed by torts/negligence, constitutional law, government, communications, immigration, writs (mostly habeas corpus writs), and legal services. Commercial law/contracts and domestic relations were the top two cases appealed of four of the judges. Immigration cases arose more frequently in the districts of California (Judges Baird and Gonzalez), New Mexico (Judges Vázquez, Armijo, and Herrera), New York (Judge Irizarry), Puerto Rico (Judges Cerezo and Delgado-Colón), and Texas (Judge Tagle), and at a lesser frequency in Colorado (Judge Arguello) and Florida (Judge Hernandez Covington). (With the recent administration and immigration deportations, this trend may have changed.) Appeals involving Indigenous peoples appeared most often in the District of New Mexico.

The Luminaria district court cases presented in this chapter primarily are cases of first impression that were appealed; those that are not of first impression contain unusual facts or legal issues.[4] Table 6 presents statistical data on cases that were appealed.[5]

4. As these are cases that were appealed, the respective district court case citation is given, where available, to provide easier access to those opinions, which are followed by the federal reporter citations.

5. Raw data retrieved from Westlaw Litigation Analytics Report for each Luminaria Article III judge (last reviewed May 28, 2024) further analyzed by the author to produce this table.

Table 6 **Luminaria District Court Judges (15)**
Cases on Appeal

Judge	Total Dockets	Cases Appealed	Affirmed (Includes Remands)	Mixed Outcome	Reversed (Negative)	Other
Cerezo	7,253	252	194	11	40	7
Carrero Nesbitt	1,643	33	23	2	6	2
Sotomayor[6]	439	5	2	0	5	0
Baird	4,247	39	22	7	9	1
Gonzalez	8,486	450	365	22	44	19
Vázquez	7,093	279	211	9	41	18
McLane Wardlaw[7]	230	21	2	0	7	12
Tagle	12,824	1,055	959	19	49	28
Armijo	5,218	214	127	8	16	3
Herrera	5,102	231	185	11	20	15
Irizarry	8,611	223	175	11	17	20
Hernandez Covington	12,427	473	392	18	31	32
Delgado-Colón[8]	9,242	209	163	9	26	11
Arguello	6,316	398	324	17	33	24
Quiñones	3,253	117	86	6	8	17

6. Westlaw identifies 439 cases at the district court level while other sources list 460 cases. There is a difference in the number of cases reported by Westlaw and Lexis.

7. For unexplainable reasons, Westlaw and LexisNexis databases did not provide Litigation Analytics for Judges Sotomayor and McLane Wardlaw at the district court level. For Judge McLane Wardlaw, 230 cases appear for Judge Wardlaw during her tenure relatively short tenure on this bench.

8. Judge Delgado-Colón's analysis excludes the forty-three decisions issued as a magistrate judge.

Collectively, the Luminaria district court judges interpreted and applied federal acts in issuing decisions. Often, particularly in cases where a violation of constitutional rights was asserted, parties invoked both state and federal law. The federal legal landscape was broad and included both civil and criminal laws.[9] The judges rendered decisions pursuant to the following federal acts with select cases provided as examples.[10]

1. Contract Disputes Act (1978), 41 U.S.C. § 607(d), *Southwest Marine Inc. v. Danzig*, 217 F.3d 1128 (9th Cir. 2000), *aff'd*, Gonzalez.

2. Employee Retirement Income Security Act (1974), 29 U.S.C. §§ 1001–1461
   a. *Gomez-Gonzalez v. Rural Opportunities, Inc.*, 626 F.3d 654 (1st Cir. 2010), Delgado-Colón.
   b. *Santana v. Metropolitan Life Insurance Company*, 919 F.3d 691 (1st Cir. 2019), *aff'd*, Delgado-Colón.
   c. *American Chiropractic Ass'n v. American Specialty Health, Inc.*, 625 Fed. Appx. 169 (2nd Cir. 2015), *aff'd and vacated in part*, Quiñones Alejandro.
   d. *Horneland v. United of Omaha Insurance Company*, 717 Fed. Appx. 846 (11th Cir. 2017), *aff'd and rev'd in part*, Hernandez Covington.

3. Equal Employees Occupational Illness Compensation Program Act of 2000, 42 U.S.C. §§ 7384–7385s-15, *Gomez v. U.S.*, 459 Fed. Appx. 701 (10th Cir. 2012), *aff'd*, Vázquez.

4. Fair Debt Collections Practices Act (1946), 15 U.S.C. § 1692 *et seq.*
   a. *George v. Equifax Mortg. Services*, 375 Fed. Appx. 76 (2nd Cir. 2010), *aff'd and rev'd in part*, Irizarry.
   b. *King v. Midland Credit Management, Inc.*, 549 Fed. Appx. 791 (10th Cir. 2013), *aff'd*, Arguello.
   c. *Miljkovic v. Shafritz and Dinkin, P.A.*, 791 F.3d 1291 (11th Cir. 2015), *aff'd*, Hernandez Covington.

5. Fair Labor Standards Act (1938), 29 U.S.C.A. § 207(a)(1), *Espinoza v. San Benito Consolidated Ind. School District*, 753 Fed. Appx. 216 (5th Cir. 2018), *aff'd*, Tagle.

6. Federal Administrative Procedures Act (1946), 5 U.S.C. § 704: *Alto v. Black*, 738 F.3d 1111 (9th Cir. 2013), *aff'd, dismissed and rem'd in part*, Gonzalez.

7. Federal Tort Claims Act (1946), 28 U.S.C. § 1346 *et seq.*
   a. *Salas v. U.S.*, 756 F.3d 1196 (10th Cir. 2014), *aff'd*, Arguello.
   b. *MacDonald v. U.S.*, 578 Fed. Appx. 641 (9th Cir. 2014), *aff'd*, Gonzalez.

---

9. The list is intended to convey a sampling of the federal acts and cases decided by the judges and is not exhaustive.

10. Citations to the federal acts are to those sections at issue in their respective decisions.

   c. *Awad v. United States*, 807 Fed. Appx. 876 (10th Cir. 2020), *aff'd*, Vázquez.

8. Freedom of Information Act (1966), 5 U.S.C. § 552 *et seq.*
   a. *Robert v. Dept. of Health & Human Services*, *aff'd*, 217 Fed. Appx. 50 (2d Cir. 2007), Irizarry.
   b. *MacLean v. U.S. Dept. of Defense*, *aff'd*, 240 Fed. Appx. 751 (9th Cir. 2007), Gonzalez.
   c. *Statton v. Florida Federal Judicial Nominating Commission*, 959 F.3d 1061 (11th Cir. 2020), *aff'd*, Hernandez Covington.
9. Indian Gaming Regulatory Act (1988), 25 U.S.C. §§ 2701–2721, *Navajo Nation v. Dalley*, 896 F.3d 1196 (10th Cir. 2018), *rev'd*, Vázquez.
10. Medicare Inpatient Prospective Payment System (1965), 42 U.S.C. § 1395 *et seq.*, *Asociacion Hospital Del Maestro, Inc. v. Becerra*, 10 F.4th 11 (1st Cir. 2021), *aff'd*, Delgado-Colón.
11. National Environmental Policy Act of 1969, 42 U.S.C. § 4321 *et seq.*, *WildEarth Guardians v. Conner*, 920 F.3d 1245 (10th Cir. 2019), *aff'd*, Arguello.

Criminal cases over which the judges presided, whether in bench or jury trials, were handled under diverse federal laws such as:

1. Computer Fraud and Abuse Act (1986), 18 U.S.C.A. § 1030(a)(2)(B), (e)(6), *Maye v. United States*, 769 Fed. Appx. 882, (11th Cir. 2019), *aff'd*, Hernandez Covington.
2. DNA Analysis Backlog Elimination Act of 2000, 42 U.S.C. § 14135a (2000), *U.S. v. Reynard*, 473 F.3d 1008 (9th Cir. 2007), *aff'd*, Gonzalez.
3. False Claims Act (1863), 31 U.S.C. § 3729(a)(1(A) and (B)
   a. *United States v. Janssen Therapeutics*, 795 Fed. Appx. 142 (3rd Cir. 2019), *vacated*, Quiñones Alejandro.
   b. *Cho on behalf of States v. Surgery Partners, Inc.*, 30 F.4th 1035 (11th Cir. 2022), *aff'd*, Hernandez Covington.
4. Federal Juvenile Delinquency Act (1938), 18 U.S.C. § 5032, *United States v. Vargas-De Jesus*, 618 F.3d 59 (1st Cir. 2010), *aff'd*, Delgado-Colón.
5. Federal Wiretap Act (1968), 18 U.S.C. § 2520 (a), *Zinna v. Cook*, 428 Fed. Appx. 838 (10th Cir. 2011), *aff'd*, Arguello.
6. Foreign Sovereign Immunities Act (1976), 28 U.S.C. § 1330 *et seq.*, *Adler v. Federal Republic of Nigeria*, 219 F.3d 869 (9th Cir. 2000), *aff'd*, Gonzalez.
7. International Child Abduction Remedies Act (1988), 42 U.S.C.A. § 11603(b)

a. *Fernandez v. Bailey*, 909 F.3d 353 (11th Cir. 2018), *vacated and remanded*, Hernandez Covington.

b. *Calixto v. Lesmes*, 909 F.3d 1079 (11th Cir. 2018), *remanded with instructions*, Hernandez-Covington.

8. Racketeering Influenced and Corrupt Organizations Act (1970), 18 U.S.C. § 1961, *et. seq.*

a. *Humphrey v. GlaxoSmithKline PLC*, 905 F.3d 694 (2nd Cir. 2018), *aff'd*, Quiñones Alejandro.

b. *Gilberti v. Adurra Group*, 810 Fed. Appx. 806 (11th Cir. 2020), *aff'd*, Hernandez Covington.

c. *United States v. Munoz-Martinez*, 79 F.4th 44 (1st Cir. 2023), *rev'd*, Delgado-Colón.

9. Religious Freedom Restoration Act of 1993, 42 U.S.C. § 2000bb (Supp. 1994), *Campos v. Coughlin, III*, 854 F. Supp. 194 (S.D.N.Y. 1994), Sotomayor.

10. Religious Land Use and Institutionalized Persons Act (2000), U.S.C.A. § 2000cc(1)(a)

a. *Rogers v. Giurbino*, 625 Fed. Appx. 779 (9th Cir. 2015), *aff'd and rev'd in part*, Gonzalez.

b. *Blair v. Raemisch*, 804 Fed. Appx. 909 (10th Cir. 2020), *aff'd and rev'd in part*, Arguello.

c. *Khan v. Barela*, 808 Fed. App. 602 (10th Cir. 2020), *aff'd and rev'd in part*, Vázquez.

11. Social Security Act (1935), 42 U.S.C. § 402(d), *Steele v. Commissioner of Social Security*, 51 4th 1059 (11th Cir. 2022), Hernandez Covington, *question certified.*

12. Trafficking Victims Protection Act (2000), as amended by Trafficking Victims Protection Reauthorization Act, 18 U.S.C. § 1595

a. *Francisco v. Susano*, 2011, 525 Fed. Appx. 828 (10th Cir. 2013), *aff'd and rev'd in part*, Arguello.

b. *Roman v. Tyco Simplex Grinnell*, 732 Fed. Appx. 813 (11th Cir. 2018), *aff'd*, Hernandez Covington.

13. Violent Crimes in Aid of Racketeering Act (1970), 18 U.S.C. § 1959 (a)(5), *United States v. Ramos*, 987 F.3d 27 (1st Cir. 2021), *aff'd*, Delgado- Colón.

14. Wartime Suspension of Limitations Act (1921, amended 1948), 18 U.S.C. § 3287: *United States v. Melendez Gonzalez*, 892 F. 3d 9 (1st Cir. 2018), *aff'd*, Delgado-Colón.

The criminal cases of the Luminaria district court judges tracked the national trend in types of cases handled at the federal level (ranked from highest to lowest): 1) drugs, 2) economic offenses, 3) immigration offenses (smuggling and illegal entry), 4) firearm trafficking and possession, 5) violent crimes, and 6) sex crimes.[11]

Across all federal districts in which the judges served, a large percentage of the cases appealed involved sentencing issues. The Sentencing Reform Act of 1984[12] (Sentencing Act) created the U.S. Sentencing Commission (Commission), which promulgated the Federal Sentencing Guidelines (Guidelines) that judges had to follow in imposing sentences. The Guidelines included mandatory minimum penalties. Implementation of the Guidelines, however, did not start until the Commission passed constitutional muster in *Mistretta v. United States*, 488 U.S. 361 (1989).[13] *See, U.S. v. Bogle*, 689 F. Supp. 1121 (1988), Judge Carrero Nesbitt's dissent discussed *infra*. According to the Commission's 2004 report on federal sentencing, "Between November 1987 and 1992, the average prison term served by federal felons more than doubled. Since fiscal year 1992, there has been a slight and gradual decline in average prison time served, but federal offenders sentenced in 2002 will still spend almost twice as long in prison as did offenders sentenced in 1984, increasing from just under 25 to almost 50 months in prison for the typical federal felon."[14] For Luminaria judges, the primary issue on appeal[15] was the length of the sentences imposed, followed by challenges to sentencing enhancements and the types of enhancements imposed that lengthened prison terms such as:

- Official victim, *U.S. v. Garcia-Lopez*, 49 Fed. Appx. 737 (2002), Gonzalez.
- Sentence imposed included time served after revocation of probation, *United States v. Montepeque-Peralta*, 116 Fed. Appx. 853 (2004), Gonzalez.
- Use of sophisticated means, *United States v. Reyes-Rivera*, 2016 WL 373931, *aff'd.*, 813 F.3d 414 (1st Cir. 2016), Delgado-Colón.
- Abuse of position of trust, *United States v. Throne*, 702 Fed. Appx. 765 (2017), Gonzalez.

---

11. United States Sentencing Commission (Commission Report), *Fifteen Years of Sentencing Guidelines, An Assessment of How Well the Federal Criminal Justice System is Achieving the Goals of Sentencing Reform*, November 2004, at vi–x, 47, 55, 61, 65, 68, and 72, covering the period starting 1989, https://www.ussc.gov/sites/default/files/pdf/research-and-publications/research-projects-and-surveys/miscellaneous/15-year-study/15_year_study_full.pdf.

12. Pub. L. No. 98-473, Title II, 98 Stat. 1976 (1984), amended by Sentencing Act of 1987, Pub. L. No. 100–182, 101 Stat. 1266 (1987).

13. *Supra* note 11 Commission Report, Executive Summary, at iv.

14. *Id.*, Commission Report, Executive Summary, at vi and vii. The passage of the Anti-Drug Act of 1986 further complicated and increased sentences that the judges had to consider and implement as it created mandatory five and ten-year minimum penalties. See also Report, Rules Having Significant Adverse Impacts, at 131–133.

15. 18 U.S.C. § 3742; Commission Report, *Appellate Review*, at 33–34.

- Crimes of violence, *United States v. Baez*, 720 Fed. Appx. 984 (2017), Hernandez Covington.
- Terrorist conviction, *United States v. Ansberry*, 976 F.2d 1108 (10th Cir. 2020), Arguello.
- Possession of a firearm, *United States v. Tirado-Nieves*, 982 F.3d 1 (1st Cir. 2020), Delgado-Colón.
- Obstruction of justice, *U.S. v. Grabsky*, 2009 WL 1505141, *aff'd*, 330 Fed. Appx. 259 (2009), Irizarry and *United States v. Rivera-Nazario*, 2023 WL 3642084, *aff'd*, 68 F.4th 653(1st Cir. 2023), Delgado-Colón.

In the area of immigration law, most of the cases handled by the judges involved illegal entry and on appeal, sentencing. According to the Commission's Report, the number of sentencing cases for smuggling and illegal entry between 1990 and 1993 was 1,000 to 2,000 per year. That number began to increase starting in 1995:

> ...after the implementation of Operation Gatekeeper—the Immigration and Naturalization Service's southwest border enforcement strategy—the number began to soar, reaching a peak of just under 10,000 cases in 2000. Along with the phenomenal growth in the size of the immigration offense docket, a series of policy decisions by Congress and the Commission have steadily increased the severity of punishment for the two most common classes of immigration offenses: alien smuggling and illegal entry, sentenced under USSG §§2L1.1 and 2L1.2, respectively.[16]

Typically, the cases resulted in penalties that produced harsh results. For example, in a case decided by Judge Carrero Nesbitt, *San Pedro v. United* States, 79 F.3d 1065 (11th Cir.1996), at issue was the authority of United States Attorneys (USA) and AUSAs to promise non-deportation to an undocumented criminal defendant during plea negotiations. The judge granted summary judgment to the defendants. She recognized the authority of the U.S. Attorney General to offer non-deportation during plea negotiations but ruled that in the absence of such authorization, the USA/AUSAs lacked the authority to offer non-deportation. The Eleventh Circuit upheld the judge's ruling, enabling the Immigration and Naturalization Service to initiate deportation proceedings against San Pedro. Of precedential value, the case was cited in eight subsequent cases. On a related issue, *United States v. Garcia-Tirado*, 86 Fed. Appx. 277 (9th Cir. 2004). Judge Gonzalez held the due process rights of the undocumented person were violated for failure to inform him that he was eligible for discretionary relief. Notwithstanding this violation of his rights, the judge ruled Garcia-Tirado was not entitled to relief from deportation pursuant to 8 U.S.C. § 1326 (212)(c). The Ninth Circuit affirmed her ruling. In *U.S. v. Aguirre-Tello*, 324 F.3d 1181 (10th Cir. 2003), Judge Vázquez dismissed the indictment against the undocument-

16. *Supra*, note 11 Commission Report at 61–62.

ed person who was charged with illegal entry into the country, on the grounds that his deportation proceeding was fundamentally unfair. Sitting *en banc*, the Tenth Circuit reversed her dismissal in *United States v. Aguirre-Tello*, 353 F.3d 1199 (10th Cir. 2004), holding that the undocumented person did not have a constitutional right to be advised of discretionary relief from deportation.

The judges also handled qualified immunity cases that covered governmental institutions and positions. For example, in a case of first impression, *United States v. Potes Ramirez*, 260 F.3d 1310 (11th Cir. 2001), the Eleventh Circuit upheld Judge Carrero Nesbitt's ruling that recognized sovereign immunity protected the government from money damages as a remedy for destruction of property. In other decisions, the judges recognized qualified immunity, or their decisions were reversed to recognize immunity, for:

- District attorneys, *Rios v. Reidel*, 456 Fed. Appx. 720 (10th Cir. 2007), Armijo.
- County clerk of court, *Barthlow v. Jett*, 2008, WL 5233097, *aff'd*, 303 Fed. Appx. 723 (11th Cir. 2008), Hernandez-Covington.
- Child protection agency employees, *V.S. v. Muhammad*, 2010 WL 536719, *rev'd*, 595 F.3d 426 (2d Cir. 2010) ordering absolute immunity, Irizarry.
- Secret Service agents, *Howards v. McLaughlin*, 2009 U.S. Dist. LEXIS 68526 (D. Colo. July 28, 2009), *rev'd*, 634 F.3d 1131 (10th Cir. 2011), Arguello.
- Postal inspector, *Mitan v. United States Postal Inspection Service*, 656 Fed. Appx. 610 (2d Cir. 2016), *reversing* judge's decision dismissing the complaint, Quiñones Alejandro.
- University professor and department chair, *Pompeo v. Board of Regents of the University of New Mexico*, 852 F.3d 973 (10th Cir. 2017), *aff'd*, Armijo.
- County sheriff, *Shew v. Horvath*, 712 Fed. Appx. 949 (11th Cir. 2017), *aff'd*, Hernandez-Covington.
- Tribal police officer, *Clema v. Colombe*, 676 Fed. Appx. 801 (10th Cir. 2017), *aff'd*, Vázquez.
- Federal judges, *Fletcher v. Tymkovich*, 786 Fed. Appx. 826 (10th 2019), *aff'd*, Arguello.

No qualified immunity was found for the category of persons in the following cases:

- Building inspector, *Mimics, Inc. v. Village of Angel Fire*, 394 F.3d 836 (10th Cir. 2005), *aff'd* and *rev'd in part*, Vázquez.
- California police officer, *Flores v. JC Penny Corp.*, 2008 SL 187050, *aff'd*, 256 Fed. Appx. 979 (9th Cir. 2007), Gonzalez.

- Paramedic, *Mitchell v. County of San Diego*, 243 Fed. App. 242 (9th Cir. 2007), *rev'd*, Gonzalez.
- City attorney, *Sandberg v. Englewood*, 727 Fed. Appx. 950 (10th Cir. 2018), *rev'd*, Arguello.
- Deputy sheriff, *Wate v. Kubler*, 839 F.3d 1012 (11th Cir. 2016), *aff'd*, Hernandez-Covington.

C. Select Luminaria District Court Decisions

Combined, the Luminaria district court judges issued hundreds of cases, too great a number to capture in one book. Cases were chosen because they are district court decisions that were appealed, resulting in Circuit Court opinions from which students and scholars can learn. Second, most of these cases involved issues of first impression. They are presented in chronological order based on the year the appellate opinions were issued in the categories of constitutional rights, government cases, voting rights, labor and employment, criminal law, terrorism cases, environment and health cases, and entertainment and sports cases. The cases provide an overview of the scope of the judges' legal rulings. Some of the cases reveal the judges' visceral reactions to the offenses they were challenged to dissect; other cases convey the cool, seemingly unaffected scrutiny of judges bridging the gap between the facts and the law.

1. Constitutional Rights

1. Sotomayor, J., *Campos v. Coughlin, III*, 854 F. Supp. 194 (S.D.N.Y. 1994), Freedom of Speech and Free Exercise of Expression Pursuant to the Religious Freedom Restoration Act.

Campos v. Coughlin presented an issue of first impression under the Religious Freedom Restoration Act (RFRA), 42 U.S.C. § 2000bb (Supp. 1994). Two inmates imprisoned at New York's Sing Sing Correctional Facility were practitioners of the Santeria religion. They challenged a 1993 directive (Directive 4202) of the Department of Corrections (DOC) that provided, "[i]nmates will be permitted to wear only traditionally accepted religious medals, crucifixes, or crosses. The religious medal, crucifix, or cross shall be affixed to a chain only. It is not acceptable to wear religious medals, crucifixes or crosses that are affixed to beads, leather, strings, or rope." *Campos*, 854 F. Supp. at 199. Previously, the DOC allowed inmates to wear their beads and display their shrines, once the facility determined an inmate was a genuine adherent of the faith. Upon enactment of Directive 4204 on January 1, 2004, the inmates' beads were confiscated, forcing them to wear beads under their clothing and to forego altogether displaying shrines in their cells. Directive 4202 permitted inmates to seek permission to possess but not to wear proscribed religious items. Under the directive, certain religious artifacts were treated preferentially with, for example, inmates being allowed to publicly display crucifixes and wear crosses, while other items such as Dhikr beads and black rosaries were treated less favorably in that they could be possessed but not worn. Santeria beads were not recognized. DOC implemented the directive based on its conclusions that there was system-wide use by gang members of religious items as symbols of gang membership, especially beads with colors that signified membership in particular gangs. DOC claimed it adopted Directive 4202 to stop the violence and prevent further violence worn by the colored religious beads. Campos filed the lawsuit alleging a violation of First Amendment rights of religious freedom and expression under the RFRA. Lance, the second inmate, received a misbehavior report for possession of the contraband religious items that was upheld upon a hearing. Campos and Lance both filed grievances, alleging infringement of religious beliefs; they were denied. Ultimately, DOC alleged in their pleadings that they could not verify the genuineness of the inmates' Santeria religious beliefs, despite both relaying and describing themselves also as Catholic and Christian.

Judge Sotomayor defined the inmates' lawsuit as follows:

> This case raises significant constitutional and statutory issues about the protections accorded fundamental First Amendment rights of freedom of religious expression in a prison setting. It underscores the complex nature and difficulty of accommodating various religious belief systems and tenets within a prison system, wherein violence is a real and daily threat. Plaintiffs herein challenge DOC, and our society, to acknowledge their religious beliefs, no matter how unfamiliar they may be to prison officials, and to refrain from over-broadly burdening the practice of a non-mainstream religion. To that end, plaintiffs seek from this Court protection of their First Amendment rights. *Campos*, 854 F. Supp. at 197.

Judge Sotomayor held that the plain language of the RFRA applies to the free exercise of religious claims,[17] the focus turning to the legitimacy of Santeria as a religion. The judge summarized the nature and rituals of Santeria religious beliefs, recognizing Santeria as a legitimate religion with Catholic underpinnings. The judge characterized the wearing of beads as not only a religious symbolic act, but as "a

17. SEC. 3 FREE EXERCISE OF RELIGION PROTECTED, (a) IN GENERAL. Government shall not substantially burden a person's exercise of religion even if the burden results from a rule of general applicability, except as provided in subsection (b). (b) EXCEPTION. Government may substantially burden a person's exercise of religion only if it demonstrates that application of the burden to the person (1) is in furtherance of a compelling governmental interest; and (2) is the least restrictive means of furthering that compelling governmental interest. (c) JUDICIAL RELIEF. A person whose religious exercise has been burdened in violation of this section may assert that violation as a claim or defense in a judicial proceeding and obtain appropriate relief against a government. Standing to assert a claim or defense under this section shall be governed by the general rules of standing under article III of the Constitution.

focus of spiritual presence, as protection against misfortune, and as markets of spiritual identity," quoting from one of the affidavits submitted for her consideration. *Campos* 854 F. Supp. at 202. DOC's attempt to cast doubt on the sincerity of the inmates' Santeria religious beliefs was rejected. Verified by its own submissions and testimony, Judge Sotomayor concluded that the DOC did not understand the Santeria religion, writing that the DOC "at best, [was] ill-informed and indifferent." *Campos,* 854 F. Supp. at 211. The judge acknowledged that the directive's resulting harm to the inmates was great as they had no other mode of expressing or practicing their religion but through wearing beads and displaying shrines. Conversely, she held the impact to DOC of accommodating these requests by permitting the inmates to wear the beads under their clothing was constitutionally insignificant. She accepted the reasonableness of DOC's evidence of gang usage of different colored beads that were not the color of the Santeria beads used by the inmates in practicing their religion. The DOC's rationale of gang-related usage of colored beads, she found, was speculative and an exaggerated response to prison concerns, writing the DOC could adopt less restrictive means of furthering its purpose of quelling violent friction or "penological institutional safety goals." *Campos,* 854 F. Supp. at 207. As the inmates established a likelihood of success on the merits of their First Amendment claims under the RFRA, Judge Sotomayor ordered preliminary injunctive relief, enjoining DOC from preventing inmates from possessing or wearing beads underneath their clothing or placing them in cell shrines.

2. Arguello, J., *Mountain States Media, LLC v. Adams County, Colo.*, 2010 WL2169267, *aff'd and vacated in part,* 389 Fed. Appx.829 (2010), Free Speech and Regulation of Advertising.

The First Amendment guarantee of free speech and the equal protection clause were at issue in this case of first impression before Judge Arguello. The plaintiffs (MSM), an outdoor advertising company, and its owner (Wayne Osterloo) planned to build a 672-square-foot placard for civic events posters and announcements. They were denied a permit to construct the billboard by Adams County pursuant to its Development Manual, § 4–15, which exempted placards from its sign regulations. Pursuant to Section 1983, plaintiffs asserted that private parties are barred absolutely from erecting signs promoting civic events, violating their rights under the First Amendment, Freedom of Speech, and Equal Protection under the Fourteenth Amendment. The plaintiffs sought a declaratory judgment that the exemption was applicable to both governmental and private entities. Judge Arguello granted summary judgment in favor of the defendants. Plaintiffs appealed her decision. Writing for the Tenth Circuit, Judge Carlos F. Lucero agreed with Judge Arguello that § 4–15 of the Development Manual established reasonable standards to guide a decision maker in determining whether a conditional use permit is appropriate. The court found no violation of the plaintiffs' freedom of speech. It held that the county's refusal to apply the civic event poster exemption to plaintiffs did not violate the Equal

Protection Clause. As a matter of first impression, the Tenth Circuit further held that the county's grandfathering of non-conforming billboards also did not violate the Equal Protection Clause. The Tenth Circuit vacated and remanded the case back to her with instruction to dismiss the plaintiffs' claim for declaratory judgment for want of jurisdiction.

3. Delgado-Colón, J., *O'Connell v. Marrero-Recio*, 2012 WL 3561921, *aff'd*, 724 F.3d 117 (1st Cir. 2013), Free Speech and Freedom of Association.

This lawsuit was filed by a former employee of two Puerto Rico governmental agencies against former supervisors under Section 1983 and Puerto Rico law, alleging constructive discharge at one agency and unlawful termination at the second agency. The plaintiff claimed she was terminated due to her political beliefs and allegiance with a faction of the New Progressive Party (NPP) disfavored by her supervisor Marrero and in retaliation for asserting her right of free speech and freedom of association. She also claimed relief as a whistleblower. The NPP won Puerto Rico's November 2008 general election. As long-time NPP members, defendants were appointed as the Commonwealth's Human Resources Director (Marrero) and the first (Recio) and second persons (Garcia) in charge of the Permits and Regulation Administration (ARPE). The NPP had two candidates running in the May primary election; one was supported by Marrero, the other by O'Connell. Marrero demanded that O'Connell not vote for her candidate. Thereafter, he directed her to carry out job duties that O'Connell believed were unlawful, such as falsifying personnel records, ignoring an Office of Government Ethics request for information on possible unethical conduct at the agency, disregarding personnel inquiries made by NPP employees, and arbitrarily transferring an ARPE employee as punishment for supporting the opposing party. O'Connell expressly told Marrero that his requests were not legal and that she would file a whistleblower complaint, which plaintiff never did. O'Connell submitted a resignation letter effective two months thereafter, but within a few days received an offer to become the human resources and labor relations director at another Commonwealth agency. She accepted the offer and changed the effective date of her resignation. During O'Connell's first day at the new job, the new supervisor informed O'Connell that she was being terminated immediately because Marrero had threatened to cause problems if she remained employed.

Judge Delgado-Colón dismissed some claims and granted defendants' motion for summary judgment. The judge held that O'Connell failed to properly plead her claims, including the misuse of public property or public funds and protected whistleblowing activity, and failed to file complaints about Marrero. The judge also found that plaintiff did not engage in speech protected by the First Amendment but rather found that the speech identified by plaintiff as protected speech consisted of responses to Marrero's directives in the course of her employment. Judge Delgado-Colón accepted the defendants' claims that O'Connell's positions were trusted, policy-making positions exempted from the protection of the First Amendment.

O'Connell appealed. The First Circuit Court upheld Delgado-Colón's decision that O'Connell's speech was not protected by the First Amendment. Applying the three-part test under *Decotiis v. Whittemore*, 635 F.3d 22, 29 (1st Cir. 2011), the court found plaintiff did not speak as a citizen on a matter of concern pursuant to her official duties but rather that she engaged in unprotected speech owing to her professional responsibilities. The court held that the plaintiff did not predicate her retaliation claim on her First Amendment allegations of protected speech or participation in the elections, but rather upon her refusal to carry out Marrero's orders, concluding that Judge Delgado-Colón had no reason to factor into her analysis O'Connell's retaliation claims. Lastly, the court concluded that political affiliation was an appropriate requirement for an employee's position as a human resources director.

4. Gonzalez, J., *Peruta v. County of San Diego,* 758 F. Supp. 1106 (2010), *rev'd,* 742 F.3d 1144, *aff'd en banc*, 824 F.3d 919 (9th Cir. 2016), Second Amendment Right to Bear Arms.

This matter consolidated two cases in which plaintiffs asserted violations of their Second Amendment right to bear arms predicated on two county ordinances; Judge Gonzalez was assigned to one of the two cases, *Peruta*. The Second Amendment provides: "[a] well regulated Militia, being necessary to the security of a free State, the right of the people to keep and bear Arms, shall not be infringed." Plaintiffs were residents of two California counties, and gun rights advocacy groups challenged the county's definition of the good cause requirement to obtain and carry concealed (and loaded) weapons in public.[18] California Penal Code §12050 prohibits permits in counties where the population is 200,000 or more and contains exceptions for categories of law enforcement or security guards, plus it excludes certain activities such as hunting. The plaintiffs lived in counties with less than 200,000 inhabitants and were unable to obtain permits from the local sheriffs who make the determinations. The plaintiffs relied on *District of Columbia v. Heller*, 554 U.S. 570 (2008), in which the Supreme Court recognized that the Second Amendment protects the individual right to keep and bear arms for self-defense. They argued that *Heller* extended the right to carry concealed weapons in public. Judge Gonzalez rejected the plaintiff's argument in *Peruta* and granted the county's summary judgment motion, finding no constitutional violations. Her colleague, Judge Morrison England, also granted the county's summary judgment motion in the second case, *Richards v. County of Yolo*, 742 Fed. Appx. 681 (2011). When Judge Gonzalez's decision was reversed (742 F.3d 1144), the sheriff declined to petition for rehearing and the State of California (State)

18. The section requires showing: (1) the applicant is of good moral character, (2) good cause exists for issuance of the license, (3) the applicant is a resident of, or his/her business is located in, the county or city within the county and (4) the applicant has completed a course of training as described in Section 26165. The sheriff's department averred good cause was defined as a person with a set of circumstances that distinguishes him/her from the mainstream and is in harm's way. *Peruta at 296.*

moved to intervene in the case. Luminaria Circuit Court Judge Callahan denied the State's motion. *Richards*, thereafter, was reversed (560 Fed. Appx. 681) based on the reversal of Judge Gonzalez's decision in *Peruta*. The Ninth Circuit consolidated *Peruta* and *Richards*, hearing both cases *en banc*; Circuit Court Judges Carlos Bea, Consuelo Callahan and Richard Paez sitting. The Ninth Circuit undertook a thorough and interesting analysis on the history of the right to bear arms—reaching back to England, colonial America, pre- and post-Civil War—bringing the analysis up to the present. It acknowledged *Heller* and concluded that *Heller* did not extend the right to bear arms to carrying concealed weapons, noting the Supreme Court's recognition that the Second Amendment was not unlimited. The Ninth Circuit held that the Second Amendment right to keep and bear arms does not include the right of any member of the public to carry concealed firearms in public. The court ruled that the State had the absolute right to intervene, rejecting Judge Callahan's earlier decision. The summary judgment rulings of Judges Gonzalez and England were affirmed. The majority opinion spurred concurring and two dissenting opinions, including one by Judges Callahan which Carlos Bea joined. The essence of Judge Callahan's dissent was that the majority misinterpreted and misapplied *Heller* which extends the right to bear arms beyond the home. *Peruta,* 824 F. 3d at 945–956.

5. Cerezo, J., *Arroyo v. Rosselló*, 305 F. Supp. 3d 327 (D.P.R. 2018), Right to Privacy for Transgender People.

Among Judge Cerezo's most celebrated cases is the landmark case of *Arroyo v. Rosselló*. Judge Cerezo ordered the Commonwealth must allow transgender people to change their gender marker on their birth certificate. In April 2017, the transgender plaintiffs filed an action for declaratory relief against defendants Governor Ricardo Rosselló Nevares (Rosselló), the Secretary of the Department of Health, and the Director of the Division of Demographic Registry and Vital Statistics of the Commonwealth of Puerto Rico (Commonwealth). They sought a ruling in compliance with 24 L.P.R.A. § 1136,[19] ordering the Commonwealth to permit transgender persons born in Puerto Rico to correct their birth certificates consistent with their gender identity and an order eliminating the correction procedure of 24 L.P.R.A. § 1231 that consisted of striking out names. In denying the Commonwealth's motion for summary judgment, Judge Cerezo issued detailed findings of fact (Findings) that included finding the plaintiffs proved their transgender identities and that they suf-

19. If the birth of an adoptee had previously been registered in the Vital Statistics Registry, the registration certificate of such birth shall be substituted for another showing the new juridic status of the registered child, as if he were a legitimate child of the adopters; Provided, that the original registration certificate of the birth of the adoptee, the decision of the court, and other documents, shall be kept in the Registry in a sealed envelope and shall be confidential documents. In no registration certificate issued by the Registry shall the fact of the original registration be set forth, unless the petitioner of said certificate has expressly required the showing of such facts and a competent court has so ordered for justified causes; Provided, that such authorization shall not be required when the applicant be the adopter or the adoptee.

fered from gender dysphoria caused partly by the Commonwealth's discrimination of transgender persons. Findings #1 and #2 at 329–330, #20–21, *Arroyo,* 305 F. Supp. at 330. Of transgenderism, the judge specifically documented:

> Transgenderism is an immutable characteristic determined by the hormonal balance a person is born with. It is an innate trait caused by an individual's biological features and genetic makeup.... The incongruence between a transgender person's gender identity and sex assigned at birth is associated with gender dysphoria...a serious medical condition recognized in the American Psychiatric Association's Diagnostic and Statistical Manual of Mental Disorders, Fifth Ed. (2013). Findings # 16 and #20, *Arroyo,* 305 F. Supp. at 329.

Judge Cerezo recognized that the plaintiffs had changed their personal identification records in accordance with Commonwealth law, OE-2008-57, requiring the Department of Public Works to reflect correct gender markers in issuing identification cards. She found the plaintiffs had changed their Social Security records, passports, and drivers' licenses, OE-2015-029, but not their birth certificates. The judge's order recognized "the importance of a Commonwealth birth certificate as a primary identification document...needed to obtain a driver's license, a marriage license, a U.S. passport, a Social Security card, a voting card, and generally as proof of identification to conduct banking transactions and other business." Findings #13, *Arroyo,* 305 F. Supp. at 330.

> Disclosing that one is transgender involves a deep personal choice which the government cannot compel, unless disclosure furthers a valid public interest. 'These matters, involving the most intimate and personal choices a person may make in a lifetime, choices central to personal dignity and autonomy, are central to the liberty protected by the Fourteenth Amendment. At the heart of the liberty is the right to define one's own concept of existence, of meaning, of the universe, and of the mystery of human life. Beliefs about these matters could not define the attributes of personhood where they formed under compulsion of the State.' *Arroyo* 305 F. Supp. at 333, citing *Planned Parenthood of Southeastern Pa. v. Casey,* 505 U.S. 833 (1992).

Judge Cerezo took judicial notice of Commonwealth law expressly prohibiting discrimination in rendering public services, specifically by the Department of Registry in OE-2008-57. Findings # 32, *Arroyo,* 305 F. Supp. at 332. The judge found the Commonwealth's birth policy "categorically requires that birth certificates reflect the sex assigned at birth—determined solely on genitalia—and prohibits transgender persons from correcting the gender marker in their birth certificates." Findings # 15, *Arroyo,* 305 F. Supp. at 329. Accordingly, she found the plaintiffs' birth certificates did not reflect their true transgender identities but rather were incongruent with their female/male identities and expression. Judge Cerezo found that permitting plaintiffs to change their birth certificates while prohibiting them to change their gender markers forced disclosure of their transgender status in violation of their right to privacy guaranteed by the Fourteenth Amendment. Quoting from *Planned Parenthood*, 505 U.S. at 851 (1992), Judge Cerezo wrote:

> The right to identify our own existence lies at the heart of one's humanity. And so, we must heed their voices: "the woman that I am," "the man that I am." Plaintiffs know they are not fodder for memoranda legalese. They have stepped up for those whose voices, debilitated by raw discrimination, have been hushed into silence. They cannot wait for another generation, hoping for a lawmaker to act. They, like Linda Brown, took the steps to the courthouse to demand what is due: their right to exist, to live more and die less. *Arroyo,* 305 F. Supp. at 334.

The judge ordered the Commonwealth to adopt the criteria of the Department of Transportation and Public Works[20] and issue new birth certificates containing the applicant's true gender without using a strike-out line or "otherwise including any information that would disclose a person's transgender status on the face of the birth certificate." *Arroyo,* 305 F. Supp. at 334.

6. Hernandez-Covington, J., *Young Israel of Tampa, Inc. v. Hillsborough Area Regional Transit Authority*, 582 F. Supp.3d 1159 (M.D. Fla. 2022), *aff'd and remanded*, 89 F.4th 1337 (11th Cir. 2024), Religious Free Speech in a Transit Setting.

The Hillsborough Area Regional Transit (HART) is a public transit agency that provides mass transportation to the public in the Tampa, located in Hillsborough County. For a fee, HART places advertisements on its vehicles and property. It implemented a policy in 2013 prohibiting advertisements that primarily promote a religious faith or religious organization; the policy did not define the terms "primarily promote" or "religious." Out of concern for public safety and so as not to offend riders or potential riders in a multicultural and religiously diverse community, HART refused to accept primarily religious advertisements. HART selected a contractor to conduct an initial review of proposed advertisements, and where there is a dispute, the matter may be appealed to, and is resolved by, HART's chief executive officer. HART did not provide training to its contractors or employees about interpreting or deciding whether to place ads by religious groups. One of HART's employees proffered testimony that the determination of whether an ad is "primarily religious" is informally made and based on whether religious symbols are used. The plaintiff Young Israel of Tampa (Young Israel) hosts an annual Chanukah on Ice celebration and attempted to place an ad with HART that included the event information and images of a menorah and skaters. The ad was rejected on the basis that it was religious. Young Israel filed its lawsuit alleging violations of Free Speech under the First Amendment and Due Process and Equal Protection Clauses of the Four-

20. She ordered the Commonwealth to use the specific "Request to Change Transgender Persons' Gender Marker, DTOP-DIS-324."

teenth Amendment. Both parties moved for summary judgment after discovery was completed. Young Israel argued HART's policy constituted an unreasonable content-based restriction and that it was singled out for disfavored treatment. Judge Hernandez Covington held that Young Israel's constitutional rights were violated upon a finding that HART's policy discriminated based on viewpoint. As authority, the judge relied on rulings in three cases that addressed and rejected viewpoint as a defense to a First Amendment Free Speech violation, including *Lamb's Chapel v. Ctr. Moriches Union Free Sch. Dist.*, 508 U.S. 384, 386–390 (1993), *Rosenberger v. Rector & Visitors of the Univ. of Va.*, 515 U.S. 819, 829 (1995), and *Good News Club v. Milford Cent. Sch.*, 533 U.S. 98 (2001). In dispensing with the need for HART to conduct a threshold forum analysis determination (public vs. nonpublic forum), Judge Hernandez Covington cited as authority the ruling in *Northeastern Pennsylvania Freethought Society v. County of Lackawanna Transit*, 938 F.3d 424 (2019). The judge further held that even if HART's viewpoint was neutral, it was unreasonable because it lacked objective and workable standards, with inconsistent application and haphazard enforcement, applying the analysis in *Minnesota Voters Alliance v. Mansky*, ___ U.S. ___, 138 S. Ct. 1876, 201 L.Ed.2d 201 (2018). She entered summary judgment and a permanent injunction in Young Israel's favor, enjoining HART from rejecting ads on the grounds that it primarily promotes a religious organization. *Young Israel*, 2022 WL 1819250.

On appeal before the Eleventh Circuit, the court chose not to undertake the analysis of a forum determination relied on by Judge Hernandez Covington but assumed that HART was a nonpublic forum. The circuit court proceeded to address *Mansky* in the context of advertising in a public transportation setting, which it had not previously decided. It held Judge Hernandez Covington's analysis under *Mansky* was correct and consistent with its ruling in a case involving political advertisements, *Cambridge Christian Sch., Inc. v. Fla. High Sch. Athl. Ass'n, Inc.*, 942 F.3d 1215 (11th Cir. 2019), but declined to decide whether HART's policy constitutes impermissible viewpoint discrimination. The circuit court concluded the terms "primarily promote" and "religious" were too vague and devoid of workable standards and that, therefore, the policy was unreasonable under *Mansky*. Accordingly, the circuit court remanded the matter back to the judge to assess whether HART's current policy is consistent with the permanent injunction issued.

2. Constitutional Issues Involving State and Federal Agencies

1. Sotomayor, J., *Dow Jones & Co., Inc., v. U.S. Dept. of Justice*, 880 F. Supp. 145 (S.D.N.Y. 1995), *vacated in part*, 907 F. Supp. 79 (S.D.N.Y. 1995), Freedom of Information Act.

The Freedom of Information Act (FOIA), 5 U.S.C. § 552, was at issue in *Dow Jones*, stemming from the suicide of Vince Foster (Foster), then Clinton Deputy White House Counsel. Two investigations had been conducted and reports issued, one by the U.S. Park Police and the second by the Department of Justice (Reports). During the investigation and days after his passing, a note handwritten by Foster (Note) was found torn in his briefcase. At the August 10, 1993, DOJ press conference, parts of the Reports were read to the media, and they were advised the Note would be available to review and to file FOIA requests for copies of the Reports. In January 1994, Attorney General Janet Reno appointed Independent Counsel Robert Fiske (IC Fiske) to investigate the Madison Guaranty Savings & Loan, Whitewater Development Corporation (Whitewater Matter). Under that authority IC Fiske denied release of the Reports to the media, asserting 5 U.S.C. §§ 552(b)(7)A) and (c) exempted the Reports and the Note from disclosure as they would "substantially prejudice his investigation of the events." Exemption 7(A) excludes from the FOIA's mandatory disclosure requirements: "records or information compiled for law enforcement purposes, but only to the extent that the production of such law enforcement records or information (A) could reasonably be expected to interfere with enforcement proceedings." *Dow Jones,* 880 F. Supp. at 148. IC Fiske determined releasing the Note would not impair his investigation, but DOJ withheld disclosure.

Plaintiffs filed the instant action to compel release of the Reports and the Note, arguing DOJ had waived Exemption 7(A) through its disclosures at the press conference. Both parties moved for summary judgment. DOJ thereafter released ninety-one pages of its report, and IC Fiske released portions of the Park Police report. The IC was also near completing his investigation into Foster's death. A new IC was appointed, Kenneth W. Starr, who argued any further releases would impair his investigation. Judge Sotomayor ruled that DOJ established the unreleased portions of the DOJ report fell within Exemption 7(A). She determined that the release of the Park Police report raised the issue whether the unreleased portions of that report were waived. Based on IC Starr's affidavit averring the withheld portions were relevant to other investigatory matters, Judge Sotomayor held those portions fell within Exemption 7(A) as well. She dismissed plaintiffs' request for an *in camera* examination of the withheld portions ruling *in camera* reviews were the exception, not the rule, and was unnecessary in this case given those portions are exempt, and further, that the plaintiffs failed to establish a prima face case that DOJ waived the 7(A) exemptions, citing *Mobil Oil Corp. v. EPA*, 879 F.2d 698 (9th Cir. 1989), among other caselaw authority. *Dow Jones,* 880 F. Supp. at 153. Next, the judge considered whether the public interest outweighed the personal privacy of the widow precluding disclosure of the Note. The widow and DOJ filed declarations averring that such disclosure would constitute an unwarranted intrusion of personal privacy. Judge Sotomayor ruled that the public interest outweighed the privacy interest and ordered the disclosure of the Note. In so doing, she distinguished the two primary cases relied on by the defendants. She concluded the public interest outweighed any violation of the family's privacy, citing *New York Times v. NASA*, 782 F. Supp. 628 (D.D.C. 1991) (audiotape of astronauts prior to their deaths were exempt), and *Katz v. National Archives & Records Administration*, 862 F. Supp. 476 (D.D.C. 1994) (privacy interest of Kennedy family outweighed public interest in release of President John Kennedy's autopsy reports). Upon stipulation of the DOJ and Foster's widow that the matter was moot due to the plaintiffs' procurement of and publishing the Note. Judge Sotomayor granted DOJ's motion to vacate portions of her opinion and order requiring the DOJ to release a photocopy of the Note. *Dow Jones,* 907 F. Supp at 83.

2. Tagle, J. *In re Hearst Newspapers, L.L.C.*, 2011 WL 1844189, *rev'd*, 641 F.3d 168 (5th Cir. 2011), First Amendment, Denial of Press Access Sentencing Proceedings

Cardenas-Guillen, a former Mexican leader of the Gulf Cartel was convicted of conspiracy with intent to distribute cocaine and marijuana. Due to the notoriety of Cardenas-Guillen (responsible for killing up to 2,000 people), most pleadings were sealed and remained under seal. Sentencing was moved from Brownsville to Houston which the judge scheduled at a covert time due to safety concerns. Prior notice to the public or press of the scheduled sentencing hearing was not provided. One Houston Chronicle reporter learned of the sentencing hearing, attempted to enter the closed proceedings and filed a motion to gain access. The judge did not address the motion and within hours of the sentencing, Judge Tagle made available to the public, the recording of the hearing and a transcript. Publisher Hearst Newspapers moved to intervene, requesting uncontested documents to be unsealed; the Chronicle filed a second motion to intervene. Judge Tagle denied the motions as moot but also denied notice of future hearings, whether publicly held or closed. Because the issue was capable of repetition (denial of public and press access), the Fifth Circuit concluded it had jurisdiction and that the issue fell into the exception of mootness, relying upon numerous Supreme Court decisions, including *Globe Newspaper Co. v. Super. Ct.*, 457 U.S. 596 and *Richmond Newspapers, Inc. v. Virginia*, 448 U.S. 555 (1980). The Fifth Circuit recognized the First Amendment rights of the press and public to attend sentencing proceedings and held the judge's exclusion of them (the Chronicle) from the sentencing violated their right of access. It further noted the importance of a court notice to be heard on issues, deeming such public access as possessing "community therapeutic value," and held the First Amendment required public notice and an opportunity to be heard before sentencing proceedings could be sealed.

3. Irizarry, J., *United States v. Ortiz*, 2010 WL 3419898, *aff'd*, 621 F.3d 82 (2d Cir. 2010), Ex Post Facto Clause

In this appeal of Judge Irizarry's decision, the defendant pled guilty to being a felon in possession of a firearm and narcotics with intent to distribute pursuant to 18 U.S.C. §922(g)(1) and 21 U.S.C. § 841(a)(1). He was sentenced by to 120 months' imprisonment, a sentence that fell 48 months below Guidelines, but which included Judge Irizarry's application of enhancements of prior felony convictions, obliteration of a serial number from a gun, and an attempted burglary conviction to the firearms offense, with upward adjustments. In appealing his sentence, defendant raised an issue of first impression, that the sentence violated his constitutional rights under the Ex Post Facto Clause, U.S. Const. Article I, Section 9, that provides "no bill of attainder or ex post facto Law shall be passed." Specifically, defendant argued the attempted burglary conviction was not a crime of violence and that he was unaware of the obliterated serial number from the gun and, therefore, this enhancement should not have been applied. Summarily, the Second Circuit disposed of defendant's enhancement arguments on the burglary and obliterated serial number issues. The Circuit Court analyzed defendant's novel argument that the Guidelines (or adjustments thereunder applied by Judge Irizarry) should not have been applied because they were amended after the date of his offense. On this issue, the circuit courts were divided as noted in the Second Circuit's opinion. *Ortiz,* 621 F. 3d at 86–87. The Second Circuit adopted the substantial risk approach of the D.C. Circuit Court in *United States v. Turner*, 548 F.3d 1094 (D.C. Cir. 2008), in large part due to its nuanced approach that was faithful to the Supreme Court's ruling in *Garner v. Jones*, 529 U.S. 244 (2000). That case also involved the imposition of a non-Guideline sentence (the amendment adopted after the defendant was sentenced) that, at its lowest, was still a higher penalty than Guidelines existing before the defendant was sentenced. Applying the substantial risk test to defendant resulted in a finding that Judge Irizarry's non-Guideline sentencing fell below the unamended Guidelines. The Second Circuit found no violation of the Ex Post Facto Clause in this case.

4. Hernandez Covington, J. *Gardner v. Mutz*, 360 F. Supp. 3d 1269 (2019), *aff'd and vacated in part,* 962 F.3d 1329 (11th Cir. 2020), Confederate Statute, First Amendment Free Speech.

The City of Lakeland (City) decided to relocate a privately funded Confederate cenotaph monument honoring dead Confederate soldiers from Munn Park (nationally registered historic public park) to another, Veterans Park. "In 1908, the City granted the United Daughters of the Confederacy's petition to erect the monument in Munn Park. The cenotaph is huge at twenty-six feet in height, weighing fourteen tons, and is engraved with the words 'Confederate Dead,' a poem, and images of Confederate flags." *Gardner*, 962 F.3d at 1335. Complaints from the public triggered the relocation of the monument. Plaintiffs were citizen-taxpayers and various Confederate organizations whose purposes are to "vindicate the cause." *Gardner,* 360 F. Supp. at 1273. The judge wrote that the "[p]laintiffs are united by their shared concern for the preservation of history 'from a Southern perspective.'" *Id.* The plaintiffs objected to the City's relocation of the monument, arguing it violated the City's Historic Preservation Ordinance, and filed suit alleging their First Amendment free speech and Fourteenth Amendment due process rights were violated. The judge undertook an analysis of the plaintiffs' standing, specifically analyzing whether they suffered an injury-in-fact under the applicable state and federal caselaw, and concluded the monument constituted government speech over which the plaintiffs had no standing. Judge Hernandez Covington granted the defendant's motions to dismiss for failure to state a claim and lack of standing. Plaintiffs failed to file a stay pending appeal, therefore, while their appeal was pending, the monument was relocated. The Eleventh Circuit affirmed the judge's decision that the plaintiffs lacked standing to pursue their First Amendment Article III and Fourteenth Amendment due process claims. It vacated the dismissal with prejudice and remanded requiring the district court to determine whether plaintiffs had Article III standing before proceeding to consider the merits of claim. The circuit court held the taxpayers had no standing.

5. Hernandez Covington, J., *Cho on behalf of States v. Surgery Partners, Inc.*, 2020 WL 5076712, *aff'd*, 30 F.4th 1035 (11th Cir. 2022), Government—False Claims Act, Medicare Reimbursements.

The False Claims Act (FCA) permits private parties, qui tam relators, to bring lawsuits on behalf of the United States against persons who have submitted false claims to the government. In a case of first impression, physician recruiter Baker and pain specialist Dr. Cho (together, Relators) brought a qui tam action alleging that H.I.G. entities (HIG) and Surgery Partners, LLC (Surgery Partners), owned by HIG, submitted false claims for reimbursement to Medicare and other government payors; they filed an amended complaint. Surgery Partners owned a network of surgery and pain management centers. It also operated a diagnostic testing business under the name Logan Laboratories, Inc. that specialized in urine drug testing (UDT). There are two types of UDTs—one that detects the presence of drugs (quantitative UDT), the second that detects how much drug is in the body's system (qualitative UDT), which is not often medically necessary. The Relators alleged Surgery Partners pressured its medical providers to refer patients to Logan Labs for qualitative UDTs and that such excessive tests were run. Reimbursements for these tests formed the basis of the Relators' lawsuit, alleging fraudulent reimbursements were submitted to Medicare that generated millions of dollars. A separate group of relators had filed a fraud action against Surgery Partners and Logan Labs eight months prior to the Relators' filing. This suit resulted in a $41 million settlement that contained a general release for Logan Labs but not to HIG as the relators failed to plead fraud with respect to HIG. Notwithstanding, HIG was released from liability per the settlement agreement. By the time the Relators filed their amended complaint, the other lawsuit had been settled.

Based on the initial complaint, Judge Hernandez Covington dismissed their action without prejudice under FCA's first-to-file bar provision[21] because another matter was pending, 2020 WL 5076712. The Relators appealed arguing the judge

21. 31 U.S.C. § 3730(b)(5) provides: "When a person brings an action under [the FCA], no person other than the Government may intervene or bring a related action based on the facts underlying the pending action."

incorrectly based her dismissal on the initial complaint, instead of the second amended complaint, and that the pending action was unrelated to their action. The Second Circuit upheld the judge's dismissal on both grounds. The circuit court rejected the Relators' argument that the second, amended complaint was controlling based on *Rockwell International Corp. v. United States*, 549 U.S. 457 (2007) (amended complaint premised on original source of information that cannot be ignored), and *Makro Capital of America, Inc. v. UBS AG*, 543 F.3d 1254 (11th Cir. 2008) (original complaint was not a qui tam action), concluding the issue was one of timing. It concluded that the first-to-bar provision is applicable when the action is initiated (initial filing) in a qui tam filing, not when an amended complaint is filed. To resolve the issue whether the two qui tam lawsuits are related, the circuit court had to adopt a new rule. On this issue of first impression, it adopted the "same material/essential elements" test, applied by other circuits, here, the same essential elements of fraud. Accord, *United States ex rel. Chovanec v. Apria Healthcare Grp. Inc.*, 606 F.3d 361, 363 (7th Cir.), and *United States ex rel. Heath v. AT&T*, 791 F. 3d 112, 121 (D.C. Cir. 2015). HIG argued that Judge Hernandez Covington's analysis was flawed because she dismissed the complaint as to Surgery Partners but not HIT. Under the authority cited, the circuit court summarily concluded that the first-to-bar test does not require a defendant-specific approach. Lastly, the circuit court considered HIG's argument that the addition of a new defendant to the complaint in their later-filed qui tam action did not include the broader, more pervasive, or distinct scheme (i.e., conspiracy), therefore, lacking notice to the government. Conducting a side-by-side analysis of both cases, the circuit court held the material essential elements were substantively the same.

3. Voting Rights

1. Herrera, J., *Valdez v. Squier,* 2012 WL 547404 (2012), *aff'd*, 676 F.3d 935 (10th Cir. 2012), National Voter Registration Act

In a case of first impression, the plaintiffs in *Valdez* alleged past and continuing violations by the New Mexico Human Services Department (HSD) that interpreted Section 7 of the National Voter Registration Act of 1993 (NVRA), 42 U.S.C. 1973gg-5, as an "opt in" provision to receive voter registration information upon applying for public benefits. Section 7 mandates all state offices that provide public assistance to distribute voter registration application forms, assist applicants in completing those forms if requested, accept completed voter registration forms, and transmit those forms to the appropriate state election official. Plaintiffs asserted that HSD's history of non-compliance warranted injunctive relief and court supervision to ensure meaningful relief in the future. HSD contended that it is currently in compliance with its obligations under the NVRA. The secretary of state contended her office has different obligations under the NVRA than HSD, and that her office has met those obligations and cannot be held responsible for any noncompliance by HSD.

Both Judge Herrera and the Tenth Circuit held that the NVRA's Section 7 requirements apply to each transaction conducted in an office overseen by HSD. Conversely, HSD interpreted and applied Section 7 as an "opt in" to receive voter registration information based on marking "yes" on the HSD's benefit application forms. Judge Herrera concluded the plain language of Section 7, NVRA's remedial purpose and legislative history, requires public assistance agencies to provide benefits applicants with a voter registration application unless they explicitly refuse. Plaintiff's motion for partial summary judgment was granted. Rejecting HSD's arguments on appeal (including one not raised before), the Tenth Circuit held that when the provisions of 1973gg-5(a)(6) are considered together, the most reasonable interpretation is the one urged by the plaintiff and adopted by the district court. If an applicant does not check either the "YES" or "NO" box on the declination form, HSD must, in accordance with the mandate of subsection (A), still provide him or her with a voter registration form but is relieved from providing the applicant with assistance in completing that form. On the other hand, if an applicant checks the "NO" box on the information form, he or she would be deemed to have declined, in writing, the opportunity to receive a voter registration form, and HSD would be relieved from providing the applicant with a voter registration form under subsection (A).

2. Cerezo, J., *Colón-Marrero v. Velez,* 2016 WL 386428, *aff'd,* 813 F.3d 1 (1st Cir. 2016), National Voter Registration Act.

In *Colón-Marrero*, the plaintiff invoked the NVRA, § 20507(b)(2), to challenge the purging of 300,000 voters from the Puerto Rico voter registration list under § 1983. Plaintiff sued the Puerto Rico State Elections Commission (SEC), seeking declaratory relief and compliance with the Help America Vote Act (HAVA), 52 U.S.C. § 21083(a). Plaintiff and others were removed for failing to vote in one general election and filed an interlocutory appeal in 2012, just before election day. (In Puerto Rico, federal elections are held every four years instead of every two years.) Judge Cerezo initially denied the plaintiff's petition, but the First Circuit remanded. The judge thereafter held in favor of the plaintiff, holding the NVRA did not apply to Puerto Rico and that HAVA must be given deference over the NVRA. HAVA created an individual private right of enforcement through a § 1983 claim that superseded Puerto Rico law.[22] HAVA did not authorize the removal of voters unless they failed to vote in two preceding general elections, not one as in the NVRA. Judge Cerezo enjoined the SEC from removing voters that met HAVA's requirements. SEC's president Velez appealed Judge Cerezo's decision asserting HAVA, like the NVRA, did not apply to Puerto Rico. Alternatively, Velez argued that HAVA creates no private right of action. Plaintiff counter-sued seeking a declaration that the

22. Article 6.012, P.R. Law Ann. Tit. 16 § 4072 (2011), which section provides in pertinent part: "If a voter fails to exercise his/her right to vote in a general election, his/her file in the General Voter Registry shall be inactivated."

NVRA applied to Puerto Rico and the exclusion of its applicability to Puerto Rico would violate the equal protection clause. The First Circuit affirmed an earlier ruling—and Judge Cerezo's second decision—that Congress did not expressly include Puerto Rico as a state under the NVRA but held the NVRA was superseded by HAVA. It adopted Judge Cerezo's interpretation that Puerto Rico was specifically included under HAVA's definitions, making HAVA applicable to Puerto Rico elections from the preliminary relief stage through the federal elections. While agreeing with the SEC that HAVA does not specifically include a private right of action, it upheld Judge Cerezo's finding that HAVA section 303(a)(4)(A) created such a right asserted when brought pursuant to § 1983.

4. Challenges to Campaign Expenditure Limits on First Amendment Grounds

1. Gonzalez, J., *Thalheimer v. City of San Diego*, 2011 WL 2400779, 706 F. Supp. 2d 1065 (2010), *aff'd*, 645 F.3d 1109 (9th Cir. 2011), *overruled* by *Board of Trustees of Glazing Health and Welfare Trust v. Chambers*, 941 F.3d 1195 (9th Cir. 2019) *en banc*, Mootness.

Judge Gonzalez partly granted relief to plaintiff-residents, political action committees (PACs), and a local political party, who sought invalidation of municipal campaign finance ordinances[23] on First Amendment grounds. *Thalheimer*, 706 F. Supp. 2d 1065. Thalheimer is a San Diego resident considering running for office who believes he may not be able to raise sufficient funds and wants to use his own money for advertising. The remaining plaintiffs are PACs and the Republican Party. To address the anti-corruption public interest of expenditure restrictions, Judge Gonzalez cited caselaw authority, including *Citizens United v. Fed. Election Comm'n*, 558 U.S. 310 (2010), as authority for the proposition that "independent expenditures do not give rise to corruption or the appearance of corruption." *Thalheimer* at 1072. Against this legal backdrop, the judge addressed the issue whether the $500 limitation in § 27.2935 may be too low such as to harm the electoral process. Judge Gonzalez recognized the appropriate standard was the five factors enunciated in *Randall v. Sorrell*, 548 U.S. 230 (2006); the low limits: (1) would significantly restrict funding available for challengers, (2) threatened the right to associate in a political party, (3) possibly impeded the effective use of volunteers, (4) were not adjusted for inflation, and (5) there was no "special justification" to warrant these burdens. The plaintiffs did not dispute the validity of the City's public interest in preventing corruption but

23. San Diego Municipal Election Campaign Control Ordinance (ECCO), § 27.2935, $500 contribution limit; § 27.2936, money spent by committees must be attributable to individuals not over $500; § 27.2938, no solicitations or donations twelve months before primary election; § 27.2950, no contributions from PACS and corporation; and § 27.2952, prohibitions on accepting contributions drawn against checking account or credit card not belonging to a person.

argued the $500 limit is not closely drawn because it restricts both small and large contributions. *Thalheimer* at 1073. Judge Gonzalez ruled that the record was insufficiently developed to permit an assessment of whether the $500 was too low and declined to so rule.

Adopting the caselaw authority from the Second and Fourth Circuits (while rejecting *McConnell v. Fed. Election Comm'n*, 540 U.S. 93 (2003)), Judge Gonzalez found it "implausible" that contributions by PACs corrupt or create the appearance of corruption, prohibited by § 27.2950. Accord, *North Carolina Right to Life, Inc. v. Leake*, 525 F. 3d 274 (4th Cir. 2008). Thus, the judge found it likely the plaintiffs would prevail on the issue of PAC contributions. Turning to the twelve-month restriction on solicitations and donations in § 27.2938, the judge concluded the City demonstrated its likelihood to prevail on this issue due to the attenuation between the end of contributions and the election. Her conclusion also was based partly on the plaintiffs' inability to overcome the City's interest in reducing corruption and appearance of corruption. Judge Gonzalez found in the City's favor on this challenge. Conversely, the judge found the City could not overcome the plaintiffs' rationale that contributions to oneself does not pose a risk of corruption and concluded the plaintiffs demonstrated a likelihood of success on this issue, citing as authority *Buckeley v. Valeo*, 424 U.S. 1 (1976) (finding caps on personal expenditures by a candidate to his/herself interferes with constitutionally protected freedoms). As the City submitted no evidence to prove this provision was valid, the judge found the plaintiffs demonstrated a likelihood they would prevail in this challenge as well. She also found the plaintiffs would prevail on their challenge to bans on contributions from political parties, § 27.2936, based partly on caselaw and in other part because the City did not successfully demonstrate a sufficiently important interest that was closely drawn to the prohibition. The judge did, however, find caselaw supported the ban on contributions from corporations, holding *Citizens United, supra*, did not specifically address the issue in this case. Relying on *Fed. Election Comm'n v. Beaumont*, 539 U.S. 146 (2003) (upheld federal statute barring corporate contributions to candidates), the judge concluded the City likely would prevail on this issue. Judge Gonzalez ruled partly in favor of the plaintiffs, preliminarily enjoining the City from enforcing the $500 limitation on individuals and PACs, the ban on contributions by political parties, and the ban from accepting donations from a political party's account.

On appeal to the Ninth Circuit, Luminaria Circuit Judge McLane Wardlaw began her majority opinion with the following:

> The modern era of campaign finance reform began in 1972, following the infamous break-in at the Watergate hotel. Congress responded to the ensuing scandal by overhauling the Federal Election Campaign Act to impose new caps on political spending, as states and cities followed suit with laws of their own.... Recent Supreme Court decisions, notably *Citizens United* [citation omitted], have once again placed the constitutionality of campaign finance re-

> form in flux, inspiring new challenges to election laws across the country. This is one such case. Plaintiffs mount a First Amendment challenge to San Diego's campaign finance laws. The district court considered the constitutionality of five provisions and generally upheld the City's pure contribution limits but enjoined a provision that restricts both the fundraising and spending of independent political committees. The district court correctly recognized that even as the campaign finance reform landscape has shifted, nearly four decades after the Watergate break-in *Buckley*'s expenditure-contribution distinction continues to frame the constitutional analysis of campaign finance regulations. Because the district court properly applied the applicable preliminary injunction standard in the context of the presently discernible rules governing campaign finance restrictions, we affirm. *Thalheimer*, 645 F.3d at 1113–1134.

Circuit Judge Wardlaw's decision contained slight modifications to Judge Gonzalez's ruling, including a finding that a specific showing of actual or perceived corruption was not required for a temporal ban on traditional direct campaign contributions. She ruled the plaintiffs did not have a substantial likelihood of success on the merits of their First Amendment claim and further, that the municipality's adoption of a new provision in direct response to the earlier issuance of a preliminary injunction did not moot the appeal. Judge Wardlaw concluded that Judge Gonzalez did not abuse her discretion by concluding that plaintiffs were likely to succeed on the merits of their challenge to application of campaign finance provisions to political parties.

2. Vázquez, C.J., *Homans v. City of Albuquerque*, 217 F. Supp. 2d 1197 (2004), *aff'd*, 366 F.3d 900 (10th Cir. 2004), Limits on Contributions and Expenditures.

Mayoral candidate Homans brought a challenge under the First and Fourteenth Amendments to Albuquerque's (City) mayoral-candidate expenditure restriction. Homans had qualified as a mayoral candidate for the election in October 2021. Though Homans lost, he garnered nearly 10,000 votes; the winner won with one vote shy of 11,000 votes. Specifically, Homans asserted that Article XIII, Section 4(d)(2) of the City's Charter (Charter), specifically the following language, violates his free speech, "[n]o candidate shall allow contributions or make expenditures in excess of the following for any election: [t]o a candidate for the office of Mayor contributions or expenditures equal to twice the amount of the annual salary paid by the City of Albuquerque to the Mayor as of the date of filing of the Declaration of Candidacy." In the first hearing, Chief Judge Vázquez found that Homans established a likelihood of success on the merits that the Charter violated the First Amendment and that he would suffer irreparable harm if the Charter was not enjoined from implementation. Under the Charter, Homans was exposed to $500 fines for each offense. The chief judge concluded that the balance of harms and the public interest weighed in his favor. During the second hearing, the City introduced expert witness testimony about election reform that favored campaign limitations.

The parties thereafter agreed no trial was necessary, filed an expedited motion for a decision on the merits, and stipulated to facts that formed the basis of Judge Vázquez 's review and detailed findings of fact in this decision. Those findings included the campaign contributions made by each of the eight candidates. Three of the eight candidates, including Homans, exceeded the Charter limitation of $174,200 by generating contributions of more than $300,000. While the judge still recognized Homans's potential irreparable harm, she ruled the public interest weighed in favor of the City and denied the preliminary injunction. In reaching her decision, the chief judge recognized *Buckley v. Valeo*, 424 U.S. 1 (1976), as the seminal case on campaign expenditure limitations in which it ruled that *expenditure* limitations "impose direct and substantial restraints on the quantity of political speech" and "limit political expression 'at the core of our electoral process and of the First Amendment freedoms.'" *Homans,* 217 F. Supp. 2d at 1205, citing *Buckley,* 424 U.S at 39. Accounting for ongoing Supreme Court debate about the scope of those limitations. she relied on the following dicta in *Landell v. Vermont Pub. Interest Research Group*, 300 F.3d 129, 144–145 (2nd Cir. 2002), "an unyielding interpretation of *Buckley* that expenditure limits are *per se* unconstitutional ... would require us to ignore not only *Buckley's* own language, but also over three decades of experience as to how the campaign funds race has affected public confidence and representative democracy." *Homans,* 366 F. 3d at 1204. Thus, the chief judge concluded *Buckley* was not a complete bar to campaign expenditure limitations and that the City Charter was not *per se* unconstitutional. She concluded the City's restrictions were narrowly tailored to fit the governmental purpose for which it was enacted. Notwithstanding, Chief Judge Vázquez noted the Tenth Circuit's disagreement with her conclusion that the Supreme Court was divided over the scope of the limitation and further that the Tenth Circuit favored no limitations. Ultimately, she ruled in favor of Homans noting her obligation to follow the Tenth Circuit's rulings, prompting the City's appeal. *Homans,* 217 F. Supp. 2d 1197. A Tenth Circuit panel had granted the temporary injunction filed by Homans on an emergency basis, enjoining the campaign expenditure limit pending appeal of the chief judge's decision.

Meanwhile, a city council candidate for the City's district five, Sander Rue, brought a similar suit challenging the expenditure limit for city council candidates. Upon obtaining a favorable summary judgment, the City appealed that ruling. The Tenth Circuit consolidated the two cases. Circuit Judge Carlos Lucero[24] held that the Tenth Circuit panel that granted the temporary injunction against the campaign expenditure limit pending appeal was not binding under the law of the case doctrine. The City asserted on appeal that the two governmental interests were anti-corruption, or undue influence as perceived by the public and preserving incumbents' time, enabling them to perform official duties, rather than campaigning in the face

24. Judge Lucero was the first Hispanic nominated to the Tenth Circuit by President Clinton (1995–2021, status Senior Judge). No Latina attorneys have been appointed to the Tenth Circuit though Judge Arguello was nominated, see chapter. three.

of increased funded opposition. Judge Lucero rejected both of the City's public interest arguments, including that the restriction promotes electoral competition (equalization of candidates' resources argument). The judge held the City's candidate campaign expenditure limits for both mayoral and city council elections violated the free speech clause of the First Amendment, concluding the City's Charter was not necessary to further a governmental interest. The Tenth Circuit ruled the restriction also violated Homan's First Amendment claim and affirmed Chief Judge Vázquez's ruling. A permanent injunction was issued.

3. Armijo, J., *Greenbaum v. Bailey*, 2015 WL 1432985, *dism'd*, 781 F.3d 1240 (10th Cir. 2015), Constitutionality of Campaign Contributions by Business Entities.

In *Greenbaum*, Judge Armijo resolved a dispute involving campaign contributions by business entities. Four citizens filed a lawsuit against the Albuquerque city clerk and the Board of Ethics and Campaign Practices (Board) alleging that Article XIII § 4 (f) of the city charter[25] prohibited candidates from accepting contributions from business entities in violation of the First and Fourteenth Amendments. The Board is responsible for enforcing Albuquerque's Election Code. The Committee to Elect Pete Dinelli for Mayor intervened as a party defendant (Committee) and sought a declaration that § 4(f) was constitutional. It argued that the plaintiffs lacked standing to challenge § 4(f)'s ban on contributions from any corporation or similar business entity. As there was no representation by a business or corporation, Giant Cab Company (Giant Cab) then moved to intervene as an additional plaintiff. Judge Armijo added Giant Cab as a plaintiff and dismissed the original plaintiffs from the suit, concluding they lacked standing as § 4(f) did not prohibit individual contributions. Accordingly, only Giant Cab remained as a plaintiff. Judge Armijo held § 4(f) was unconstitutional, concluding the City Council failed to show that § 4(f) was closely drawn to further the interests of eliminating or reducing corruption and preventing the circumvention of individual campaign contribution limits. The Committee appealed but original defendants did not. The Committee filed a notice of appeal asserting it had the right to enforce the limitation on campaign contributions, thereby constituting a personal stake in the outcome. Appellee Giant Cab challenged the appeal arguing that the Committee lacked standing because it did not have a direct stake in the outcome of the appeal. The Tenth Circuit held that the Committee lacked standing to appeal and dismissed the appeal.

---

25. § 4(f) provides: No candidate shall accept a contribution in support of the candidate's campaign from any corporation, limited liability company, firm, partnership, joint stock company or similar business entity or any agent making a contribution on behalf of such a business entity. No candidate shall accept a contribution in support of the candidate's campaign from any person, other than a City employee, who at the time of the contribution is in a contractual relationship with the City to provide goods or services to the City.

5. Restrictions on Nonprofit Organizations and Candidates to Qualify for the Ballot and Voting Restrictions

1. Armijo, J., *The American Civil Liberties Union of New Mexico v. Santillanes*, 506 F. Supp. 2d 598 (D.N.M. 2007), *rev'd*, 46 F.3d 1313 (10th Cir. 2008), Constitutionality of Requirement on the Homeless to Provide Photo Identification.

On behalf of Albuquerque city residents (City) and organizations representing voters and homeless individuals, the ACLU filed an action challenging the constitutionality of an amendment to the City's charter approved by the voters in 2005 (Amendment). The Amendment required non-absentee voters to display a current and valid photographic identification card to vote in municipal elections.[26] Plaintiffs asserted that the amendment violated the First and Fourteenth Amendments, the Civil Rights Act of 1964, and the Voting Rights Act of 1965. The parties agreed to dismiss all but the equal protection and First Amendment claims. At trial, the plaintiffs introduced evidence that they and their members intended to vote in-person in future elections and that individual plaintiffs possessed photo identifications (IDs) that may or may not be deemed current or valid by an Albuquerque election official. The New Mexico Coalition to End Homelessness entered testimony that homeless populations have a particularly difficult time obtaining and keeping photo IDs. Judge Armijo granted in part and denied in part cross-motions for summary judgment, and issued a permanent injunction, enjoining the City from enforcing the Amendment in future elections. She ruled that the Amendment violated the federal equal protection guarantees. The City appealed.

After Judge Armijo issued her opinion but before oral argument in the Tenth Circuit, the Supreme Court decided *Crawford v. Marion County Election Board*, 533 U.S. 181, 128 S.Ct. 1610, 170 L.Ed.2d 574 (2008), which involved an equal protection challenge that altered the judge's ruling. SCOTUS upheld an Indiana photo identification requirement mandating in-person voters to present a government-issued photo ID, like the City's. The Indiana law required all in-person voters to present a government-issued photo identification. Chief Justice Stevens held that the appropriate standard for evaluating constitutional challenges to a regulation affecting the right to vote is to balance the restrictions imposed by the regulation against its justifications. *Crawford*, 128 S. Ct. at 1616. In his concurring opinion, Justice Scalia held that any burden imposed by the photo identification law was "minimal and justified.... The burden of acquiring, possessing, and showing a free photo identification is simply not severe in comparison to the usual burdens associated with voting." *Id.* at 1625, 1627. Justice Stevens held that the burden of presenting a photo identification at a polling place imposes only a "limited burden on voters' rights" and that the

26. Albuquerque, N.M., City Charter, art. XIII, § 14 (as amended Oct. 4, 2005).

justifications for Indiana's law were both neutral and sufficiently strong to uphold the law. *Crawford* at 1623 (quoting *Burdick*, 504 U.S. at 439).

Relying upon recently decided *Crawford*, the Tenth Circuit held that the differentiation between absentee and non-absentee voters did not violate equal protection and that the law did not impose a substantial burden on a person's right to vote. It further ruled that the prevention of voter fraud and voting impersonation were sufficient justifications for the law and thus, passed constitutional muster. Judge Armijo's decision was reversed.

2. Herrera, J., *New Mexico Youth Organized v. Herrera*, 2010 WL 2598314, *aff'd*, 611 F.3d 669 (10th Cir. 2010).

Judge Herrera held that the New Mexico Campaign Reporting Act (Act) was unconstitutional and that the secretary of state's attempt to regulate the organizations also was unconstitutional. The Southwest Community Resources Center (SWOP) served as the sponsor of the New Mexico Youth Organized (NMYO) for tax purposes. NMYO was formed to educate the public about public interest issues and to participate in nonpartisan get out the vote efforts. NMYO and SWOP mailed advertisements criticizing several incumbent state legislators and a state senator complained to the secretary of state that SWOP-NMYO was not a registered political committee. The secretary of state sent letters to NMYO and SWOP mandating their compliance with N.M. Stat. Ann. §1-19-26.1(A)–(B) or they would face mandatory fines. NMYO and SWOP filed a complaint seeking declaratory and injunctive relief. Judge Herrera found that the Act's definition of "political purpose"[27] was substantively identical to the Federal Election Campaign Act that was held unconstitutional by the Supreme Court in *Buckley v. Valeo*, 424 U.S. 1, 78–79 (1976), followed by its progeny, *Colorado Right to Life Committee, Inc.*, 498 F.3d 1137 (10th Cir. 2007). Relying on *FEC v. Wisc. Right to Life, Inc.*, 551 U.S. 449 (2007), the judge ruled that the phrase "political purpose" may be applied only to reach contributions or expenditures for communications that constitute express advocacy for the election or defeat of a clearly identified candidate, or its functional equivalent. She held that the NMYO and SWOP did not satisfy this narrow definition of political purpose on three grounds: the speech was not express advocacy, the ads did not constitute the functional equivalent of express advocacy, and the ads were not electioneering communications as they were not mailed within thirty days of a primary election or sixty days of a general election. Judge Herrera deemed the Act was overbroad and vague and granted summary judgment to NMYO and SWOP. The Tenth Circuit affirmed, agreeing with Judge Herrera's ruling that the secretary of state could not regulate the organizations.

---

27. NMSA. §1-19-26(M), provides: "'political purpose' means influencing or attempting to influence an election or pre-primary convention, including a constitutional amendment or other question submitted to the voters."

3. Herrera, J., *Woodruff v. Herrera*, 2010 WL 3989114, *aff'd*, 623 F. 3d 1103 (10th Cir. 2010), New Mexico Election Code, Campaign Reporting Act.

Woodruff v. Herrera was filed by a New Mexico resident who was not a registered voter but was a potential candidate for the U.S. House of Representatives. New Mexican resident Daniel Fenton sought a seat in the U.S. House of Representatives but was not a registered voter. He and the Green Party (Plaintiffs) sued the secretary of state to challenge the New Mexico Election Code, specifically, §§1-8-2(B) and 1-8-31(C). Judge Herrera held the provisions were invalid, concluding it is unconstitutional to require a person running for Congress to register to vote, citing as direct authority *Campbell v. Davidson*, 233 F.3d 1229, 1234 (10th Cir. 2000). As to the Green Party's issue, Judge Herrera held that the provision requiring signers of petitions to state their address of residence or their address as registered was internally inconsistent and unconstitutionally vague. *Woodruff* at 899. She ruled that petition signers could provide one or the other—the residence address or the registration address—but not both. Judge Herrera issued a remedial order that granted the plaintiffs relief except the specific relief requested by Fenton—to be placed on the ballot; and the Green Party—that it should not be required to file petitions as a minor party. This formed the basis of appeal to the Tenth Circuit, which ruled *en banc*.

The Tenth Circuit affirmed Judge Herrera's ruling of unconstitutionality of the two provisions at issue but agreed with the judge that the two specific remedies requested by the plaintiffs were not suitable. It specifically noted that Judge Herrera did not invalidate the entire Election Code, leaving intact the remaining provisions with which the plaintiffs must comply. Pointedly, the Tenth Circuit underscored that Judge Herrera did not expressly order that Fenton be placed on the ballot or that the Green Party was exempted from the statutory obligation of filing petitions or that it be recognized as a qualified party, in the absence of meeting the statutory requirements. The Tenth Circuit held that Judge Herrera's remedial orders were appropriate and upheld her order granting summary judgment.

4. Vázquez, J., *Parker v. Winter*, 2014 WL 7653394, *aff'd*, 645 Fed. Appx. 632 (10th Cir. 2016), Additional Requirement on Independent Party Candidate.

Parker, an independent registered voter, sought to appear on the November 2014 ballot as an independent candidate for secretary of state. As a minor party candidate, Parker had to obtain 732 signatures, but as an independent candidate, more signatures (2,196) were required. Parker obtained 1,379 signatures, 817 short of the minimum signatures required. Consequently, Parker was deemed ineligible to be placed on the ballot. Parker sought injunctive relief from New Mexico's Election Code[28] that required a prospective independent party candidate to obtain more signatures

28. NMSA 1978 § 1-8-45; NMSA §§ 1-8-51, 1-8-51, further requiring a petition must bear signatures of a number of voters equal to at least 3 percent of the total number of votes cast in the district for governor in the last preceding election.

on a nominating petition than a minor party candidate. Parker also sought a declaration that these provisions of the Election Code were unconstitutional. Parker alleged the statutes violated the First and Fourteenth Amendments of the U.S. Constitution and the New Mexico Constitution.

Applying the rationale of *Burdick v. Takushi*, 405 U.S. 14 (1972), and *Anderson v. Celebrezze*, 460 U.S. 780 (1983), the judge recognized the State's right to regulate its elections on behalf of the voters and candidates does not compel close scrutiny. The judge identified the appropriate balances of rights and interests. She wrote the court "must weigh 'the character and magnitude of the asserted injury to the rights protected by the First and Fourteenth Amendments that the plaintiff seeks to vindicate' against 'the precise interests put forward by the State as justifications for the burden imposed by its rule.'" *Parker*, 645 Fed. Appx. at 5, quoting *Anderson*, 460 U.S. at 789. Judge Vázquez cited Tenth Circuit cases in which substantively similar challenges were raised and rejected, including *Populist Party v. Herschler*, 746 F.2d 656 (10th Cir. 1984), and *Arutunoff v. Okla. State Election Bd.*, 687 F.2d 1375 (10th Cir. 1982) (signature requirements). She emphasized that minor party parties are required to meet other state requirements that independent candidates are not required to meet that have been upheld. Accord, *Kuntz v. N.Y. State Senate*, 113 F.3d 326 (2nd Cir. 1997). Lastly, Judge Vázquez addressed the state interests, citing *Munro v. Socialist Workers Party*, 479 U.S. 189, 193 (1986), for the proposition that States may impose minimum conditions on an independent candidate to demonstrate a "modicum of support among the potential voters for the office." *Parker*, 645 Fed. Appx. at 8. Upon a balance of the state and public interest, Judge Vázquez determined the greater harm to the public exceeded the plaintiff's individual harm and interest. She concluded Parker was not likely to succeed on the merits. Plaintiff's motion for a temporary restraining order and injunctive relief were denied. The Tenth Circuit upheld Judge Vázquez's decision for the reasons delineated her order (outlined here). Notwithstanding that the election had passed, the Tenth Circuit held that a case or controversy continued to exist, permitting it to exercise its jurisdiction over the appeal on the basis that the issue may arise in the future.

6. Labor and Employment Cases

The judges handled many labor and employment cases that covered the range of traditional issues that more commonly arise, as well as cases with distinct issues or parties.

1. Carrero Nesbitt, J., *O'Connor v. PCA Family Health Plan, Inc.*, 2000 WL 348388, *aff'd*, 200 F.3d 1349 (11th Cir. 2000), Family Medical Leave Act, Retaliation (Interference) Claim, and Res Judicata.

Judge Carrero Nesbitt was required to resolve an issue of first impression in the Eleventh Circuit, regarding the scope of employment protection afforded by the

Family Medical and Leave Act of 1993 (FMLA), 29 U.S.C. §§ 2601–2654—namely, whether an interference or retaliation claim may be brought. O'Connor, a former account executive for PCA Family Health Plan, Inc. (PCA) who was a new mother, filed suit against PCA for refusing to grant her request for leave without pay for birth and postnatal care of her newborn. PCA had instituted a reduction in force (RIF), laying off 190 employees, and set aside those on leave, but mistakenly failed to set aside O'Connor. She was terminated in phase I of the RIF. PCA's human resources department advised O'Connor's supervisor that O'Connor should not have been terminated, and O'Connor was offered reinstatement, which O'Connor declined. The trial court granted PCA's motion for summary judgment. O'Connor appealed. O'Connor filed a second action alleging, *inter alia,* sex and pregnancy discrimination and retaliation for having requested pregnancy leave pursuant to Title VII of the Civil Rights Act of 1964 (Title VII), as amended, 42 U.S.C. § 2000e. Essentially, O'Connor alleged PCA pled the RIF as a pretext for discriminating and terminating her. Judge Carrero Nesbitt granted PCA's summary judgment, concluding PCA terminated O'Connor based on a legitimate RIF. O'Connor appealed and both of her appeals were consolidated. The Eleventh Circuit affirmed Judge Carrero Nesbitt's rulings, that 1) an employer may discharge an employee on FMLA leave and 2) deny reinstatement when the employer demonstrates it would have discharged employee even had employee not been on leave. The court cited as authority *Diaz v. Fort Wayne Foundry Corp.*, 131 F.3d 711 (7th Cir. 1997) and *Illhardt v. Sara Lee Corp.*, 118 F.3d 1151 (7th Cir. 1997) (employer may terminate employee on FMLA leave as part of a RIF). The Eleventh Circuit found O'Connor had established a prima face case but failed to overcome the employer's evidence and affirmed the judge's order granting summary judgment to PCA predicated on the RIF. Judge Carrero Nesbitt further held that O'Connor's discrimination suit was barred under the doctrine of res judicata. The Eleventh Circuit agreed, concluding the judge properly analyzed and applied the elements of res judicata that were present in the case. Accord, *Citibank, N.A. v. Data Lease Fin. Corp.*, 904 F. 2d 1498 (11th Cir. 1990).

2. Vázquez, J., *N.L.R.B. v. Pueblo of San Juan*, 30 F. Supp. 2d 1348 (1998), summary judgment *aff'd by divided panel*, 280 F.3d 1278 (10th Cir. 2002), *aff'd* on rehearing *en banc*, 276 F.3d 1186 (10th Cir. 2002).

The National Labor Relations Board (NLRB) brought action for declaratory and injunctive relief challenging the right of the Pueblo of San Juan (Pueblo Tribe), a federally recognized tribe, to enact and enforce an ordinance prohibiting union security agreements for companies engaged in commercial activity on tribal lands. Local Union No. 1385 intervened as a plaintiff. Judge Vázquez granted summary judgment for the tribe, 30 F.Supp.2d 1348, prompting the NLRB's appeal. Judge Vázquez held the Pueblo Tribe's right-to-work ordinance was a valid exercise of its sovereign governmental authority over commercial activity on tribal lands considering statutory authority, which permits state and territorial governments to regulate union security agreements. On appeal, the NLRB and the Union claim that the enactment of the right-to-work ordinance and the inclusion of the provision within a lease violated the National Labor Relations Act (NLRA), 29 U.S.C. §§151–169. Through federally approved leases, the Pueblo Tribe rents certain portions of its tribal land to a non-tribal business as a source of generating tribal income and as a means of employment for tribal members. For almost twenty-seven years, Duke City Lumber Company (Duke City) owned and operated a sawmill on the Pueblo Indian Reservation, pursuant to a lease approved by the Department of the Interior (DOI). Duke City operated under a collective bargaining agreement (CBA) with the Union, which contained a union security clause that required all bargaining unit employees to become and remain members of the union and pay union dues; the Pueblo Tribe never once objected to the CBA.

Circumstances changed when Duke City sold the sawmill and assets to Idaho Timber Company for use by Idaho Timber's subsidiary, Rio Grande Forest Products Industry (Rio Grande). The Pueblo agreed to release Duke City from the lease in exchange for a commitment by Idaho Timber to enter a new lease. The DOI approved the arrangement. The Pueblo Tribe and Idaho Timber negotiated a new lease containing a preferential employment hiring provision for Pueblo members and a provision forbidding Rio Grande from adopting a CBA requiring Pueblo Tribe employees to become union members before they could obtain the benefits of the employment preference. The DOI approved the lease. Rio Grande hired approximately eighty employees, twenty-eight of whom are Pueblo Tribe members. After the lease was executed, the Union demanded Rio Grande to enter a CBA with it as the exclusive bargaining agent for employees. Rio Grande was unwilling to recognize the Union, and the Union filed an unfair labor practice complaint with the NLRB. The Pueblo Tribe enacted Labor Organization Ordinance No. 96-63 (Ordinance), expanding the lease by affording to all employees on tribal lands the freedom of choice regarding union membership. The Ordinance relates only to compulsory membership; it does not prohibit employees from voluntarily joining a union or from voluntarily organizing or participating in union activities on tribal lands. To settle the unfair practice complaint, the Union and Rio Grande entered a CBA, conditioned on a federal court determining the validity of the Ordinance. The NLRB and the Union assert the NLRA preempts tribal law.

Judge Vázquez recognized that section 14(b) of the NLRA demonstrates that federal policy was not exclusive or uniform regarding union security agreements and that any ambiguities in federal law should be construed to comport with the federal policy of encouraging tribal independence, citing *White Mountain Apache Tribe v. Bracker*, 448 U.S. 136, 143–144 (1980). She ruled, and the Tenth Circuit agreed, that notwithstanding federal law (e.g., NLRA § 8(a)(3)), Indian tribes retain the sovereign power to enact right-to-work ordinances and, furthermore, CBAs with such provisions.

3. Cerezo, J., *Acosta-Ramirez v. Banco Popular de Puerto Rico*, 2013 WL 1320411, *vacated*, 712 F.3d 14 (1st Cir. 2003), FIRREA.

In a case of first impression, the First Circuit upheld Judge Cerezo's ruling that severance pay claims were barred jurisdictionally under the FIRREA[29] and that the bar triggered by plaintiffs' failure to comply with the FDIC administrative claims process could not be avoided by failing to name the FDIC as a defendant. The First Circuit vacated Judge Cerezo's entry of summary judgment for the defendants and remanded with instructions to dismiss the case for lack of subject-matter jurisdiction. Seventy-six former employees of Westerbank (employed from 1978 to 2005) filed suit in a territorial court, asserting relief for severance pay under Puerto Rico Law, Law 80, P.R. Law Ann. tit. 29 185A *et seq.* Westerbank was a failed bank subject to receivership by the FDIC. The plaintiffs filed against the bank's successors, Banco Popular de Puerto Rico (BPPR), a bank that acquired Westerbank's deposits and certain assets. The Puerto Rico Office of the Commissioner for Financial Institutions closed Westerbank and appointed the FDIC receiver. *See Benson v. JP Morgan Chase Bank, N.A.*, 673 F.3d 1207, 1211 (9th Cir. 2012) (FIRREA gives the FDIC authority to act as receiver). On the same day, the FDIC informed all employees of their termination and notified them of their right to submit claims against Westerbank or the FDIC under the mandatory administrative claims process, 12 U.S.C. § 1821(d)(3)–(13), that was established under FIRREA. Plaintiffs neither initiated nor exhausted the administrative claims process. Many became temporary employees of Banco Popular, which the FDIC agreed to indemnify for severance/enhanced severance pay claims. Thereafter, the plaintiffs were terminated and sued Banco Popular for unjust termination, seeking severance pay. Upon motion by Banco Popular, the action was removed to federal court with the FDIC intervening as a defendant. FDIC asserted lack of jurisdiction under 12 U.S.C. 1821(d)(13(D) based on plaintiffs' failure to file claims or challenge the FDIC's disallowance of their administrative claims. Judge Cerezo granted defendants' motion for summary judgment, who had appealed. At oral argument, the plaintiffs conceded the FDIC's position. The First Circuit agreed with Judge Cerezo that severance pay claims were barred jurisdictionally under FIRREA, which were triggered by the plaintiffs' failure to comply with the FDIC administrative claims process, and they could not be avoided by failing to name FDIC as defendant. As the judge failed to first address subject-matter jurisdiction, the First Circuit did so and held that when the plaintiffs failed to adhere to the FDIC's mandatory administrative process, the court (and Judge Cerezo) did not have jurisdiction to substantively rule on the matter, citing *Simon v. FDIC*, 48 F.3d 53, 56 (1st Cir. 1995). Thus, it was on this basis that the First Circuit vacated the summary judgment order and instructed Judge Cerezo to dismiss the case for lack of subject-matter jurisdiction.

29. Pub.L. No. 101-73, 103 Sta. 183 (1989).

4. Hernandez Covington, J. *Brotherhood of Locomotive Engineers and Trainmen General Committee of Adjustment CSX Transp. Northern Lines v. CSX Transp., Inc.*, 2007 WL 1469383, *aff'd*, 522 F. 3d 1190 (11th Cir. 2008).

In this case of first impression, Judge Hernandez Covington resolved a claim for back wages under the Railway Labor Act, 42 U.S.C. § 151 *et seq.* (Act). The issues were whether an enforcement action accrues under the Act's statute of limitations and whether a request for interpretation of an arbitration award tolls the limitations period. In November 2002, Pitzen who was employed by CSX Transportation (CSX), claimed he suffered an off-duty neck injury that prevented him from operating a train and missed work. After nearly a three-week absence, Pitzen told a supervisor that during his absence, he had driven from Ohio to Panama City, Florida, and participated in a karate tournament, winning the heavy-weight title. CSX charged Pitzen with dishonesty, claiming injury under false pretenses, and terminated him. The union challenged Pitzen's dismissal on his behalf and requested his reinstatement. The matter was referred to the arbitrator who determined that CSX failed to prove Pitzen had been dishonest. In June 2004, the arbitrator reinstated Pitzen and ordered CSX's compliance within thirty days. CSX reinstated Pitzen but did not pay him back wages for the period of his dismissal. For nearly a two-year period from June 2004 until February 2006, the union did not request the arbitrator to clarify whether the award included back wages. On April 7, 2006, the arbitrator clarified that, although the award did not provide for back wages expressly, the CBA terms mandated payment of back wages. The union waited another four months until August 1, 2006, to file an enforcement action with the district court. CSX moved to dismiss pursuant to the two-year statute of limitations barring the union from enforcing the payment.

Judge Hernandez Covington concluded that the enforcement action accrued on July 3, 2004, and that the union filed outside the two-year limitations period. She granted CSX's motion for summary judgment. The judge additionally decided that the Board had issued an interpretation of the award under § 152 First (p) of the Act on April 7, 2006, which did not toll the statute of limitations. The union appealed the judge's order. The circuit court held that the Act permits the Board to enforce actions in federal district court and requires an enforcement action to be filed within two years from the time the cause of action accrues. It upheld Judge Hernandez Covington's interpretation and application of the Act, citing *Lekas v. United Airlines*, 282 F.3d 296, 300 (4th Cir. 2002), and *Transportation Commc'ns Int'l Union v. CSX Transp., Inc.*, 30 F.3d 903, 905 (7th Cir. 1994). The Eleventh Circuit rejected the Board's argument of equitable tolling, holding there were no extraordinary circumstances beyond its control such as to delay and toll the limitations period as Judge Hernandez Covington found. *Arce v. Garcia*, 434 F.3d 1254 (11th Cir. 2006).

7. Criminal Law

During their tenures, the Luminaria district court judges handled significant and complex cases, including in jury trails and trials to the bench—not all captured in appellate opinions. Some of the cases reflect the important trials and proceedings below, other are more purely legal analyses of the issues that arose during the litigation.

1. Carrero Nesbitt, J. *dissenting, United States v. Bogle*, 689 F. Supp. 1121 (S.D. Fla. 1988), Constitutionality of the Sentencing Act, Separation of Powers.

Eight cases were consolidated in which defendants were found guilty and were awaiting sentencing under the Guidelines.[30] "Because of the paramount importance of the issue to [the] district... as well as [the] desire to promote procedural uniformity and avoid disparate sentencing," the Southern District of Florida considered, *en banc*, whether the separation of powers was violated when the executive installed the U.S. Commission on Sentencing (Commission) within the judiciary function. *Bogle*, 689 F. Supp. at 1123. The majority found the Sentencing Act unconstitutional except Judge Carrero Nesbitt who dissented. The district court held that the constitutional challenge was ripe with respect to Florida defendants who had pleaded or had been found guilty, but not with respect to defendants who had been indicted but had not pled guilty or found guilty. It found the Sentencing Act placed legislative and executive functions within the judicial branch that violated the separation of powers as it conferred substantive and unprecedented rule making authority upon the judiciary—a congressional and legislative function. The district court also concluded that the Sentencing Commission cannot be viewed as part of the executive, and even if so viewed, the service of federal judges on the Commission would further violate the separation of powers principles. Judge Carrero Nesbitt wrote the following dissent:

> I respectfully dissent. It would serve no useful purpose to repeat the statutory framework and the various challenges to the Sentencing Act which have been well reviewed by Judge Marcus in the majority opinion. My view is that the Sentencing Reform Act of 1984 is constitutional. The reasons for this conclusion are expressed in the fully-explored opinion of Chief Judge Rothstein of the Western District of Washington which rejects the constitutional and statutory challenges to the Act and concludes that "the Commission's placement, composition and authority are constitutionally permissible as being in aid of the performance of a judicial function assigned to the Judicial Branch by Congress, rather than the Constitution." *United States v. Amesquita-Padilla*, 691 F. Supp. 277 (W.D. Wash. 1988), Order Denying Motion to Preclude Use of Sentencing Guidelines, at 290. *Bogle*, 689 F. Supp. at 1165.

30. *Supra note 11, see Sentencing Act and Commission Report.*

The Supreme Court upheld the constitutionality of the Sentencing Act in *Mistretta v. United States*, supra. In *Mistretta*, Justice Harry Blackmun writing for the majority concluded the Sentencing Guidelines were neither an excessive delegation of legislative power of a violation of the separation of powers, as stated by Judge Carrero-Nesbitt. (Justice Scalia filed a dissent.) The justice wrote that appointing judges to the Commission, asking for their expert input did not offend the separation of powers principle.

2. Gonzalez, J., *U.S. v. Montero-Camargo*, Nos. CR-96-2233-1 and 2-IEG, *aff'd by split panel,* 177 F. 3d 1113, *aff'd en banc,* 208 F. 3d 1122 (9th Cir. 2000), Reasonable Suspicion Based on Hispanic Appearance.

The defendant was convicted upon a guilty plea with intent to distribute and the second defendant was convicted by a jury trial of the same offenses, as well as the offense of being an "illegal alien" in possession of ammunition, by Judge Gonzalez. The defendants appealed. A split panel affirmed, and the Ninth Circuit reheard the case *en banc* on the sole issue of whether there was reasonable suspicion to stop the defendants. While the *en banc* affirmed Judge Gonzalez's ruling and the split panel, it rejected some of the factors relied upon in determining reasonable suspicion.

A passing driver at the Highway 86 permanent checkpoint in El Centro, California, relayed the to the border patrol that two cars heading north with Mexicali plates had made U-turns on the highway shortly before the checkpoint. Border patrol agents Johnson and Fisher drove south in unmarked cars to investigate. The defendants were driving separate automobiles and in tandem made U-turns on the highway at the only place, according to the two border patrol agents, where the view is obstructed from the agent manning the checkpoint. The U-turns occurred shortly after the cars passed a sign stating that the previously closed Border Patrol facility was now open. According to the patrol agents, the defendants stopped briefly in an area that is often used as a drop-off and pick-up point for undocumented aliens and contraband. Based on these and other factors, the district court concluded that the stop, which occurred some fifty miles north of the Mexican border, was justified, as did the majority of the three-judge panel that initially considered the question.

At the suppression hearing, Agent Johnson testified that a large percentage of Hispanics lived in the area and that the defendants appeared to be Hispanic. He further offered that one of the defendants, who noticed the agents parked behind him, picked up a newspaper and began reading, which further aroused his suspicion. Agent Fisher followed the second defendant and testified that the driver appeared to be Hispanic. Their searches produced marijuana and a .32-caliber pistol. Judge Gonzalez conceded the government's case was weak but denied defendants' suppression motion, concluding there was a sufficient foundation of suspicion to make an investigatory stop. One of her findings was "the fact that the occupants of both cars appeared to be of Hispanic descent." This finding also was noted by the three-judge panel in affirming Judge Gonzalez's decision not to grant defendants' motion to suppress. *Montero* at 1129. The Ninth Circuit held that the defendants' Hispanic appearance was not a proper factor to consider in determining whether the Border Patrol agents had reasonable suspicion to stop them, in light of large number of Hispanics living in area, The circuit court held that "[re]asonable suspicion requires *particularized* suspicion, and in an area in which a large number of people share a specific characteristic, that characteristic casts too wide a net to play any part in a particularized reasonable suspicion determination." *Montero*, 208 F. 3d at 1134. The court agreed that the remaining circumstances constituted sufficient reasonable suspicion for an investigatory stop and affirmed Judge Gonzalez's ruling with the modification that being or looking Hispanic in a highly populated Hispanic community were not appropriate factors that supported reasonable suspicion.

3. Carrero Nesbitt, J., *U.S. v. Potes Ramirez*, No. 94-00642-CR-LCN, *rev'd and remanded*, 260 F.3d 1310 (11th Cir. 2001), Return of Property and Sovereign Immunity.

After criminal proceedings for importation of cocaine terminated, the defendant moved for return of his identification cards—military card, Colombian citizenship card, and navigation license. The government informed the court that the items were destroyed by the Drug Enforcement Administration. Judge Carrero Nesbitt denied his motion, relaying in her order only that the items had been destroyed. In this case of first impression in the circuit, the circuit court held that, upon termination of a criminal proceeding, a motion for return of property is a civil proceeding for equitable relief subject to the sixty-day appeal period for civil cases against the government under the Federal Rule of Appellate Procedures.[31] Accord, *United States v. Bein*, 214 F.3d 408, 412 (3rd Cir. 2000), *United States v. Garcia*, 65 F.3d 17, 18 (4th Cir. 1995), and *United States v. Madden*, 95 F.3d 38, 39 (10th Cir. 1996) (all adopting the sixty-day period for filing a civil action for return of property). The court rejected the government's argument that the ten-day rule applied, pursuant to Rule 4(b)(1)(A(i), and further held it did not meet its burden of showing that property was destroyed. On the second issue of first impression, the circuit court concluded that under sovereign immunity the government was protected from an imposition of money damages under the Federal Tort Claims Act, 28 U.S.C. § 2680(c), as a remedy for destruction of property but that the doctrine of laches could be considered in fashioning an equitable remedy. The court recognized as authority *Thomas v. Covington*, 47 F. 3d 974 (8th Cir. 1995) (a case is not mooted by the government's assertion that it cannot find the property because the court has the power to fashion equitable relief), and other cases cited in the opinion. It concluded, "For these reasons, we agree with the Third, Fourth and Fifth Circuits and hold that sovereign immunity protects the government from money damages sought under rule 41(e)." *Potes*, 260 F. 3d at 1316.

---

31. FRAP, Rule 4(a)(1)(B).

4. Baird, J. *Taylor v. Delatorre*, 2021 WL 1749901, *aff'd and rev'd in part*, *Delatorre v. Donovan*, 281 F.3d 844 (9th Cir. 2002), Prison Litigation Reform Act, in *forma pauperis* proceedings.

In a case of first impression, Judge Baird summarily dismissed prisoner Taylor proceeding in *forma pauperis.* Taylor filed a § 1983 action alleging he had been badly beaten by a prison guard and was refused medical attention. He failed to pay the initial partial filing fee of $6.62 due to lack of funds and throughout the thirty-day extension, his account balance was at $0. A provision of the Prison Litigation Reform Act (Act), 28 U.S.C. § 1915(b)(4), provides a prisoner cannot be prohibited from bringing a civil action on the grounds that he lacks assets and no means to pay the initial filing fee. Known as the safety valve provision, it allows monthly payments equal to 20 percent when the prisoner's account exceeds $10. Notwithstanding, the magistrate judge dismissed the prisoner's appeal, which Judge Baird approved. Prisoner Taylor appealed. As a matter of first impression, the Ninth Circuit held the filing fees provisions of the Act are constitutional, and although Judge Baird's assessment of the filing fee was proper, Taylor's civil rights action should not have been dismissed for failure to pay the initial filing fee. Judge Baird's dismissal was reversed and the matter remanded.

5. Baird, J., *United States v. Gurolla*, 2003 WL 21435741, *rev'd*, 333 F.3d 944 (9th Cir. 2003), Entrapment Defense pled upon *ex parte* sealed declarations.

Operation Checkmark was part of Operation Casablanca, an international investigation of a money laundering sting by the U.S. Custom Service conducted from November 1995 to May 1998. Operation Checkmark targeted Mexican banks which the Customs Service believed used bank drafts to launder money for the Cali and Juarez drug cartels. Forty international defendants were indicted, including the three defendant bankers. The issue of first impression on appeal was whether Judge Baird erred in refusing to allow defendant Ortega to present an entrapment defense to the jury—his declarations had been submitted *ex parte* under seal to the judge. At issue was the government's objections that Ortega's sworn declarations remained under seal to which they had no access, preventing it from preparing arguments in its opening brief. The government filed a motion in *limine* to prohibit defense counsel from discussing entrapment in their opening statements. Only one defendant "Kissel" initially opposed the motion. Judge Baird issued an order that was broader than the motion and prohibited all defendants, except Kissel, from presenting evidence of an entrapment defense during their case-in-chief. Ortega moved for reconsideration and filed *ex parte* and under seal, a sworn declaration explaining the factual basis for his claims that Judge Baird denied. Ortega renewed his motion, and the judge permitted Ortega to submit a more detailed offer of proof on entrapment. Ortega filed a second *ex parte* declaration that was also sealed, but Judge Baird held that Ortega did not make a prima facie showing of entrapment. As a result of Judge

Baird's ruling, Ortega did not testify at trial. Kissel presented an entrapment defense and was acquitted. The Ninth Circuit held that Ortega's sealed declarations are protected from disclosure on appeal and that in filing an appeal, Ortega did not waive the confidentiality of his testimony under seal, citing *United States v. Poehlman*, 217 F.3d 692, 693 (9th Cir. 2000), as further authority that the government was not entitled to review or rely on sealed evidence. It also held that Judge Baird erred when she refused to allow Ortega to present a defense of entrapment and discussed the elements of entrapment. Ortega's conviction was reversed and the matter remanded for a new trial.

6. Cerezo, J., *United States v. Collazo-Castro*, 2009 WL 6319546, *aff'd*, 660 F.3d 516 (1st Cir. 2011), Warrant Clause, Delayed Revocation Statute, necessity of sworn oath or declaration.

In this case of first impression arising under the Delayed Revocation Statute, 18 U.S.C. § 3583(i),[32] Judge Cerezo was asked to resolve the question of whether an arrest was proper on a warrant that was executed without an oath or affirmation under the Warrant Clause of the Fourth Amendment.[33] The defendant, Collazo-Castro, pled guilty to one count of conspiracy to smuggle undocumented aliens into the United States in violation of 8 U.S.C. § 1324(a)(1)(A)(i), (v)(I). She was sentenced to twelve months and one day of imprisonment, followed by a three-year term of supervised release. The probation officer filed a motion to revoke supervised release and requested a warrant that was not made under oath, in which she alleged that Collazo-Castro had abandoned her drug treatment program and failed to report after abandoning the treatment. The district court issued an arrest warrant pursuant to 18 U.S.C. § 3606 that permits arrests of a person on supervised release without an arrest warrant. Over four years later, Collazo-Castro was arrested. At the revocation hearing, Collazo-Castro's attorney argued that the district court lacked jurisdiction to revoke her term of supervised release and requested a dismissal because the government did not arrest Collazo-Castro for over four years. Thereafter, the defendant filed a motion to dismiss the revocation proceedings, asserting the original arrest warrant was invalid under the Delayed Revocation Statute because it was not based on a finding of probable cause supported by a statement made under oath or affirmation. Judge Cerezo found the defendant's term of supervised release was tolled while she was a fugitive under the doctrine of fugitive toll-

32. That section provides: "The power of the court to revoke a term of supervised release for violation of a condition of supervised release, and to order the defendant to serve a term of imprisonment and, subject to the limitations in subsection (h), a further term of supervised release, extends beyond the expiration of the term of supervised release for any period reasonably necessary for the adjudication of matters arising before its expiration if, before its expiration, a warrant or summons has been issued on the basis of an allegation of such a violation."

33. U.S. Const. amend. IV, provides that "no Warrants shall issue, but upon probable cause, supported by Oath or affirmation."

ing and denied her motion without addressing the Warrant Clause argument. Subsequently, in *United States v. Hernandez-Ferrer*, 599 F.3d 63, 69 (1st Cir. 2010), the First Circuit rejected the doctrine of fugitive tolling and Collazo-Castro moved for reconsideration of Judge Cerezo's order denying the motion to dismiss. Judge Cerezo then issued an order on April 23, 2010, finding that Collazo-Castro's fugitive status did not toll her term of fugitive release, but that the motion to dismiss was properly denied on other grounds.

The First Circuit affirmed Judge Cerezo's authorization of an arrest warrant without an oath or affirmation because of the status of Collazo-Castro as a supervised releasee, adopting the rulings by sister circuits. Accord, *United States v. Garcia-Avalino*, 444 F.3d 444 (5th Cir. 2006). In essence, the circuit court reasoned that, given her status, a warrant may be triggered for ordinary offenses without an oath or affirmation and that the situation does not require the heightened scrutiny of the Warrant Clause.

7. Quiñones Alejandro, J., D.C. No. 2:15-cr-00241-002 (2019), *aff'd, United States v. Renteria*, 903 F. 3d 326 (3d Cir. 2018), *writ denied, Renteria v. U.S.*, Venue for Conspiracy Charges, furtherance of the acts initiated in one state, concluding in a second state.

Following a denial of his motion for a change of venue, the defendant, who was a California resident, was convicted by a jury of drug trafficking conspiracy charges to distribute heroin and methamphetamine in Pennsylvania and California. At trial, Judge Quiñones Alejandro gave a venue instruction pursuant to 18 U.S.C. § 3237(a) that stated the defendant did not have to be in the Pennsylvania district, even if the defendant did not know or did not reasonably foresee that the act occurred in Pennsylvania. She sentenced the defendant to 153 months' imprisonment and five years of supervised release. Defendant appealed, arguing that the Eastern District of Pennsylvania was not a proper venue for his case because it was not reasonably foreseeable to him that his conduct in furtherance of the conspiracy would have occurred in Pennsylvania. Homeland Security Investigations Special Agent Jeffrey Kuc posed undercover in May 2015 as a methamphetamine and heroin trafficker in southeastern Pennsylvania to two men, Cejas and Juan. Per their agreement, Cejas and Juan sent per two kilograms of methamphetamine to a mailbox in Springfield, Pennsylvania, in exchange for $30,000. Kuc deposited $2,000 into a bank account provided by Cejas. As arranged, Kuc flew to Los Angeles to purchase more drugs and spoke to Cejas, who informed him that he would direct his contact in the area to reach out to Kuc. Later that day, the defendant called Kuc and devised a plan to exchange the methamphetamine and heroin for $146,500—the value of the new drugs Kuc would receive plus the $28,000 he owed for the prior Pennsylvania methamphetamine shipment. The next day, they met at a fast-food restaurant in Huntington Beach, California. There, the defendant was arrested after Kuc saw the drugs and the prearranged signal to other agents. As a matter of first impression, the Third Circuit,

Judge Julio Fuentes[34] writing, upheld Judge Quiñones Alejandro's venue instruction and the defendant's conviction. He held that to establish the proper venue for a conspiracy charge, the defendant initiating the conspiracy in one venue (California) is not required to have reasonably foreseen that an act in furtherance of the conspiracy would have been committed in another venue (Pennsylvania). Stated otherwise, the Third Circuit declined to adopt the reasonable foreseeability test in the context of § 3237(a), noting the statute does not require the test, explicitly or implicitly. He further noted it was rejected by the Ninth Circuit within the context of § 3237(a), by the Fourth Circuit involving venue statute 15 U.S.C. § 78aa, and the problems experienced by the Second Circuit within the context of § 3237(a). *See e.g.*, *United States v. Svoboda,* 347 F. 3d 471 (2d Cir. 2003).

8. Vázquez, J., *United States v. Chavez*, 460 F. Supp. 3d 1225 (2022), *rev'd and remanded*, 29 F. 4th 1223 (10th Cir. 2022), Federal Bank Robbery of an ATM.

This case presents an issue of first impression: whether a defendant's attempt to rob two victims by having them unsuccessfully withdraw money from an ATM by armed force constitutes federal bank robbery. The defendant, armed with a rifle, ran up to the passenger side of an occupied vehicle parked at a Wells Fargo ATM in Albuquerque, New Mexico. The ATM was not located on the premises of a Wells Fargo bank branch. He demanded money from the vehicle's two occupants. As they did not have any cash, defendant demanded they put a bank card into the ATM, not on bank property, and make a withdrawal. A law enforcement officer arrived on the scene and disrupted the robbery, causing the defendant to ask for cigarettes and then leave. He was later arrested and charged with federal bank robbery by force, attempting to take property from Wells Fargo Bank, pursuant to 18 U.S.C. § 2113(a) and (d) and § 924(c)(1)(A)(ii). Section 2113(a) provides in pertinent part that whoever, "by force and violence, or by intimidation, takes ... from the person or presence of another ... money ... belonging to, or in the care, custody, control, management, or possession of, any bank" commits federal bank robbery. The defendant pled a legal impossibility defense, i.e., that he did not attempt to take money from a bank and therefore could not commit federal bank robbery which abrogated federal jurisdiction. Judge Vázquez dismissed the charges as a matter of law, on the basis that the defendant, had he been successful, would have stolen money from the victims and not the bank. She also reasoned that the bank would no longer have a property interest in the money, once it was withdrawn and transferred to the victims. In so ruling, the judge relied on the Fifth Circuit's ruling that the conduct does not qualify as federal bank robbery. *United States v. Burton*, 425 F.3d 1008 (5th Cir. 2005) holding the funds were not in the care, custody, control, or management of the bank once the victim with-

34. Judge Fuentes was the first Hispanic appointed to the Third Circuit (2000–2016, Senior Judge status). As of April 2025, there are no Latina Circuit Court judges on this circuit court.

drew the money from the ATM—the defendant took the money from the bank customer, not the bank. At the time, the circuit courts were divided on the issue. The government appealed. The Tenth Circuit reasoned that the appeal turned on whether, had the accountholders withdrawn the money, defendant would have committed federal bank robbery. If so, it concluded, defendant's charges could not be dismissed as a matter of law. Choosing instead to adopt the rationale of the Seventh Circuit, the Tenth Circuit held that directly forcing bank customers to withdraw money from an ATM qualified as federal bank robbery. *United States v. Parker*, 508 F.3d 434, 440–441 (7th Cir. 2007). Judge Vázquez's dismissal was reversed and remanded.

8. Terrorism Cases

1. Irizarry, J., *U.S. v. Ibrahim*, 529 Fed. Appx. 59 (2013), *aff'd*, *U.S. v. Kadir*, 718 F.3d 115 (2d Cir. 2013), Rulings on Evidence.

Ibrahim and *Kadir* involved multiple defendants who were convicted of several charges relating to terrorism conspiracy to blow up the JFK International Airport. *Kadir* involved the convictions of the co-conspirators in *Ibrahim*. Their plot was revealed through confidential informant, Steven Francis (Francis), who provided information to the FBI. Early on, Kadir expressed interest in the plot to Francis. Ibrahim was brought into the conspiracy to present the plot to his contacts in Iran. Kadir and Ibrahim and Nur (the third accomplice), were arrested in June 2007. They were charged with conspiracy to attack a public transportation system in violation of 18 U.S.C. § 2332(a)(2) and other federal crimes of terrorism. Defendants were sentenced to life in prison. Judge Irizarry severed Ibrahim's case and Nur pled guilty to other charges and was sentenced to 180 months in prison. Ibrahim was convicted and, upon adding an enhancement of terrorism, Judge Irizarry sentenced him to life imprisonment. Kadir was convicted on all counts except the surveillance count and was sentenced to life imprisonment. The judge issued numerous evidentiary rulings upon which the defendants' appeals were based, including empaneling an anonymous jury, admission of photos of Kadir holding a machine gun and expert witness testimony, exclusion of Kadir's tape recordings and refusal to declassify other portions of a report introduced at trial. The Second Circuit held that Judge Irizarry properly empaneled an anonymous jury, precluded submission of a complete version of a redacted affidavit, admitted documents seized during a search of the co-conspirator's home, admitted the testimony of a terrorism expert as probative of the intent element of the charged conspiracies, and properly applied both the terrorism and obstruction of justice enhancements.

2. Irizarry, J., *Weiss v. National Westminster Bank PLC*, 2014 WL 4667348, *vacated*, 768, F.3d 202 (2d Cir. 2014), *vacated and remanded*, 2021 WL 1287174, *aff'd*, 993 F.3d 144 (2d Cir. 2021), Liability of Bank in Funding Terrorist Attacks.

Victims who suffered injuries and estates of victims who were killed in over fifteen terrorist attacks in Israel and Palestine by Hamas filed suits against the United Kingdom Bank NatWest. Pursuant to the Antiterrorism Act (ATA), 18 U.S.C. §§ 2331(1)(A), 2333(a) and 2339B(a)(1), plaintiffs asserted the bank aided and abetted the murders and attempted murders of approximately 200 Americans. The aiding and abetting emanated from, plaintiffs alleged, by maintaining accounts and collection of funds by National Westminster Bank (NatWest) for the Palestine Relief & Development Fund (Interpal) that were used to finance the terrorist acts. In August 2003, the U.S. Treasury Department designated Interpal as a Specially Designated Global Terrorist. In September, Interpal's accounts were frozen. A report subsequently was issued concluding there was inadequate evidence to show Interpal had links to Hamas and recommended its accounts should be unfrozen. NatWest was informed that any payments to Hamas were prohibited. While conducting a review in May 2005, NatWest uncovered a payment by Interpal to the Bank of England and other organizations, which were suspected of supporting terrorism. There was no evidence, however, that NatWest was aware of Interpal payments to organizations designated as terrorist organizations. The cases were consolidated, and Judge Irizarry granted the NatWest's motion for summary judgment, concluding there was insufficient evidence, proximate cause, to show NatWest acted with the "requisite scienter" to support civil remedies under the ATA. On appeal, plaintiffs claim Judge Irizarry applied the wrong standard in assessing whether NatWest acted with the requisite *mens rea,* actual knowledge or deliberate indifference to whether Interpal funded terrorist activities. The Second Circuit remanded on this issue, ruling Judge Irizarry imposed a higher standard of proof that involved financing activities. It held that the appropriate focus was not activities but whether NatWest had actual knowledge of or deliberate indifference to Interpal providing material support to a terrorist organization, in this case, Hamas. Its analysis included balancing the First Amendment right of freedom of association and mental state required to find an ATA violation. The Second Circuit found there was adequate evidence to create a triable issue of fact whether NatWest met the more lenient standard and remanded on this basis and for consideration of NatWest's additional grounds for summary judgment. Upon remand, Judge Irizarry again found inadequate evidence of aiding and abetting by NatWest and that plaintiffs failed to submit sufficient evidence warranting trial. Her decision was affirmed.

3. Arguello, J., *Ghailani v. Sessions*, 2015 WL 430375 (2015), *rev'd and remanded*, 859 F.3d 1295 (10th Cir. 2017), Special Administrative Measures.

Ahmed Khalfan Ghailani was an al-Qaeda operative and part of the terrorist 1998 embassy bombings in Kenya and Tanzania in which 224 people were killed. Ghailani was captured in 2004 and transferred to Guantanamo Bay Detention Center until 2009 when he was transferred to the high security penitentiary in Florence, Colorado upon his conviction. He was subjected to Special Administrative Measures

(SAMs) that limited his contact with the outside world due to his past terrorist activities and his connections with terrorist groups. SAMs are tools used to limit privileges for certain federal inmates, 28 C.R.R. §501.3(a). One of the restrictions included a prohibition against participating in group prayer. Ghailani filed a pro se challenge to the SAMs, seeking injunctive relief from his ban from group prayer and a declaratory judgment pursuant to the Religious Freedom and Restoration Act (RFRA) that the restrictions violated various constitutional rights. Ghailani alleged his First (religious freedom), Fifth and Eighth (deprivation of basic human needs) Amendment rights were violated; he also pled a violation under the RFRA. Judge Arguello granted the government's motion to dismiss Ghailani's suit with prejudice which he appealed. While his case was pending on appeal, the government allowed Ghailani's SAMs to expire but still prohibited him from participating in group prayer due to the housing restrictions at a high security prison. Ghailani's SAMs expired on June 10, 2015, and they were not renewed. The government therefore contended Ghailani's claims were moot. The Tenth Circuit held that mootness did not apply because the SAMs, though capable of repetition, was unlikely given the government's voluntary cessation of them (for two years by time of oral argument) and thus mooted Ghailani's action. While it held that Ghailani failed to state a claim for violation of his First Amendment right to religious freedom, the Tenth Circuit concluded the judge erred in dismissing his claim under the RFRA, concluding the government failed to show that banning group prayer was in furtherance of compelling governmental interest and in the least restrictive manner.

4. Delgado-Colón, J., *United States v. Morales Negron*, 2020 WL 5361647, *aff'd and remanded,* 974 F.3d 63 (1st Cir. 2020), Statements of Reasons (SOR).

This was a case of first impression on the statement of reasons (SOR). Without a plea agreement, defendant pled guilty to being a felon in possession of a firearm and ammunition and unlawfully possessing machine gun, 18 U.S.C. 922(g)(1) and 922(o). He was apprehended in February 2016 by Drug Enforcement Administration agents and U.S. Marshals Service deputies. Defendant fled from the agents, throwing a fanny pack onto the roof of a nearby residence as he tried to escape by running across adjacent rooftops. The agents arrested Morales and seized the fanny pack which contained one loaded Glock pistol modified to fire as a machine gun and later seized four Glock magazines. A background check revealed that Morales had an outstanding arrest warrant for a state probation violation. Judge Delgado-Colón imposed an above-Guidelines sentence and denied defendant's motion to access the SOR for her imposition of sentence. Denial of SORs was the customary practice in Puerto Rico. The defendant appealed. The First Circuit Court held that while Judge Delgado-Colón did not abuse her discretion in imposing the above-Guidelines sentence, she erred in denying the defendant's access to the SOR. Factoring in that defense counsel was entitled to the SOR, the First Circuit concluded withholding the SOR did not warrant vacating the defendant's sentence. The sentence was affirmed but remanded for disclosure of the SOR. Judge Juan Torruella[35] sat on the panel but did not issue the opinion.

9. Environmental and Health Cases

1. Armijo, J., *Chevron Mining, Inc. v. United States*, 139 F. Supp. 3d 1261 (2015), *aff'd and rev'd in part,* 863 F.3d 1261 (10th Cir. 2017), CERCLA Strict Liability for Cleanup Costs.

Judge Armijo was asked to determine the strict liability of the federal government in cleaning up contaminated land under the Comprehensive Environmental Response, Compensation and Liability Act of 1980 (CERCLA), 42 U.S.C. §§ 9601–9675. At issue was the Questa, New Mexico, Site (Questa Site) that had been placed on the National Priorities List (NPL) in 2011 by the Environmental Protection Agency (EPA) pursuant to 42.U.S.C. § 9605(a)(8). The United States owned national forest lands in New Mexico that were mined (molybdenum mining operation) over several generations by Chevron Mining Inc. (Chevron) near the Questa Site. The mining generated significant amounts of hazardous substances, triggering a costly cleanup of $1 billion. Chevron acknowledged its status under CERCLA as a "Potentially Responsible Party" (PRP) for the hazardous substance contamination of the site, before and after the Questa Site was placed on the NPL. Throughout the lawsuit, Chevron sought financial assistance for the cleanup. It sought a declaratory judgment that the government was a PRP and strictly liable as an owner of portions of the Questa Site and as an arranger of hazardous substance disposal. It relied on 42 U.S.C. §§ 9607(a) and 9613(f)(3)(B), for a ruling that the government must bear its equitable share of past, present, and future cleanup costs. Judge Armijo granted and denied in part Chevron's motion for summary judgment; both parties appealed. The question before the Tenth Circuit was whether the United States was a PRP for the environmental contamination located on the Questa Site. The Tenth Circuit held that the government was an owner and PRP, and strictly liable for its equitable share of the cost of cleanup. The circuit court concluded the United States was not an "arranger" of hazardous substance disposal because it did not own or possess the substances in question and, therefore, bore no arranger liability. Judge Armijo's ruling was remanded for further proceedings to determine the United States' equitable share, if any, of the cleanup costs.

2. Herrera, J., *Cuba Soil and Water Conservation Dist. V. Lewis*, 2008 WL 2221815, *aff'd,* 527 F.3d 1061 (10th Cir. 2008), Federal Mineral Leasing Act creates implied cause of action to challenge states over royalties.

---

35. Judge Torruella (a four-time Olympian and former district court judge) was the first Hispanic appointed by President Reagan to the First Circuit (1984–2020). Even though Puerto Rico is in the circuit, no Latinas have been appointed to the First Circuit and none currently sit.

In this case of first impression before Judge Herrera, soil and water conservation districts (Districts) filed a lawsuit against the State of New Mexico (State) for certain royalties received pursuant to the Federal Mineral Leasing Act of 1920 (Act), 30 U.S.C. §§181–287. At issue was whether the Act created an implied cause of action to challenge the State's allocation of federal mineral royalties. Judge Herrera held the Act did not confer an implied right of action on the Districts and dismissed their complaint, and the Districts appealed her decision. Under the Act, §191, Disposition of moneys received, the federal government must return 50 percent of federal mineral royalties generated from the lease of public lands to the Districts. In conflict was state law that required the larger portion of money received by the State under the Act to be distributed to the public-school fund, NMSA, §22-8-34.1. The Districts' claimed the State was violating §191 and sought to enjoin the state treasurer to comply with the Act. Judge Herrera dismissed the lawsuit on the ground that the Act did not confer an implied right of action on the Districts. The Tenth Circuit held that, absent congressional intent, the enactment of a benefit did not create either an explicit or implicit right of action or remedy. Judge Herrera's decision was affirmed.

3. Arguello, J., *WildEarth Guardians v. Conner*, 2019 WL 1592314, *aff'd*, 920 F.3d 1245 (2019), National Environmental Act, Failure to File Impact Statement.

The Canadian lynx was at issue in this case filed against the U.S. Forest Service (USFS) by WildEarth, an environmental organization. WildEarth alleged the USFS violated the National Environmental Policy Act (NEPA), 42 U.S.C. §4321 *et seq.*, by not preparing an environmental impact statement (EIS). Specifically, the group was concerned that the USFS had not adequately assessed the effect on the Canadian lynx from a project in the San Isabel and White River National Forests to protect the forest from insects, disease, and fire, improve wildlife habitat, and maintain watershed conditions. USFS did an evaluation of how the project would affect Canadian lynx but chose not to specify, in its environmental assessment (EA), the sizes, locations, and treatment planned for each treatment unit. USFS also did not disclose in the EA the locations of its preidentified precommercial thinning units. As part of the EA, the USFS assessed snowshoe-hare availability as the key factor in determining the Canadian lynx winter habitat. The USFS concluded in the EA that the project would not adversely affect Canadian lynx but did not quantify the denning habitat in drawing this conclusion. Based on this evidence, Judge Arguello granted summary judgment in favor of the USFS, and WildEarth appealed. The Tenth Circuit affirmed the judge's decision, holding that the EA did not have to include more baseline data to monitor USFS's commitment not to treat areas of mapped lynx habitat. It further concluded that the project, involving over 2,000 acres of clearcutting and 7,000 acres of thinning, did not require an EIS. The circuit court found USFS was not arbitrary and capricious in reaching its findings, including that an EIS was unnecessary.

4. Hernandez Covington, J., *SA Palm Beach, LLC v. Certain Underwriters at Lloyd's London Insurance*, 515 F. Supp.3d 1218 (2022), *aff'd and rev'd in part*, 34 F.4th 1002 (2022), COVID-19, Liability of Insurance Company, Scope of Coverage.

Judge Hernandez Covington addressed the extent of insurance coverage due to the COVID-19 pandemic in *SA Palm Beach*. Insured restaurants and retailers brought actions seeking coverage under all-risk commercial property insurance policies for losses they incurred as result of the Florida governor's executive orders restricting on-premises operations of non-essential businesses during the COVID-19 pandemic. Judge Hernandez Covington and three other judges assigned to cases involving similar issues dismissed the plaintiffs' complaints for failure to state a claim. All the insurance policies contained provisions addressing Business Interruption, Extra Expense, Contingent Business Interruption and Loss Adjustment Expenses. The plaintiffs appealed and their cases were consolidated before the Eleventh Circuit. They presented a question of first impression, whether under Florida law, all-risk commercial insurance policies providing coverage for "direct physical loss of or damage to" property or "direct physical loss or damage to" property insure against losses and expenses caused by the COVID-19 pandemic. The Eleventh Circuit upheld the judge's ruling that under Florida law there is no coverage because COVID-19 did not cause a tangible alteration of the insured properties. In so ruling, the Eleventh Circuit reviewed and cited cases reaching the same conclusion from the Fourth, Fifth, Sixth, Seventh, Eighth, Ninth, Tenth Circuits plus numerous state cases. The circuit court further held that the claims did not fall under the scope of the businesses' income or business interruption. Of significant, the business interruption provisions were predicated upon the covered property requiring repair, rebuilding or replacement. Stated otherwise, the Eleventh Circuit held to obtain coverage, material destruction or material harm to the covered premises must be shown. It further held that the need to disinfect the premises did not constitute direct physical loss or damages. Judge Hernandez Covington's order was wholly affirmed as were three other cases; one case was remanded for further proceedings.

10. Entertainment and Sports Cases

1. Sotomayor, J., In *Silverman v. Major League Baseball Player Relations Committee, Inc.*, 880 F. Supp. 246 (S.D.N.Y. 1995),[36] Collective Bargaining Agreement, Unfair Labor Practices.

The National Labor Relations Board (NLRB) sought temporary injunctive relief against the baseball owners for unfair labor practices under the National Labor Re-

36. Daniel Silverman was the NLRB Regional Director for Region 2 under whose name the NLRB filed the action against the Owners.

lations Act (Act), 29 U.S.C. §§151–169, as amended (1988). The parties were the Major League Player Relations Committee, Inc. that was the collective bargaining representative for the twenty-eight major league clubs (Owners) and the Major League Baseball Players Association, which was the collective bargaining association for the forty-two rosters of each of the Major League Clubs (Players). During the negotiations for a collective bargaining agreement (Basic Agreement) and before an impasse was reached, the Owners eliminated salary arbitration for certain reserve players, competitive bargaining for certain free agents, and the anti-collusion provision. A player becomes a free agent after completing six seasons playing for a major league and permits the free agent to set wages between himself and the club owner under the anti-collusion provision. (The free agent then must play an additional five seasons before becoming eligible for free agency.) Reserve players are those with less than six years of major league experience whose rights are included in the Uniform Player's Contract (UPC) that is incorporated into the Basic Agreement. Those with three but less than six years are eligible for salary arbitration. The Basic Agreement expired on December 31, 1993, and negotiations began in March 1994. The new season began in April 1994 with both parties operating under the terms of the expired Basic Agreement, *N.L.R.B. v. Katz*, 369 U.S. 736 (1962) (expired mandatory terms remain intact until parties reach an impasse). Without an agreement reached, the Players began striking on August 12, 1994, but continued to discuss terms. The Owners wanted a salary cap, which the Players opposed; the Players submitted a new tax proposal that the Owners opposed. The Owners did not submit a counterproposal and announced an impasse, as well as a salary cap. Despite the impasse, negotiations continued. But by February 1995, the Owners advised the Board of their rescission of the prior changes to the Basic Agreement. They also informed the Players that until a new Basic Agreement was ratified, the Major League Clubs had no authority to negotiate or execute Players' contracts.

The NLRB determined a violation of the Act occurred—that the Owners failed to negotiate in good faith—and that injunctive relief was warranted. The parties stipulated that the only issues before Judge Sotomayor were questions of law. The judge recognized that section 10(j) of the Act authorized district courts to grant temporary injunctions pending the resolution of NLRB proceedings, writing, "Provision 10(j) reflects Congress's recognition that, absent injunctive relief, the Board's often lengthy administrative proceedings could allow an unfair labor practice to go unchecked and thereby render a final Board order ineffectual." *Silverman* at 254. Judge Sotomayor was required to determine whether the Owners' unilateral recission of the salary arbitration clause constituted a mandatory or permissive provision. If a mandatory provision, the unilateral recission of that term constituted an unfair labor practice and violated the duty to bargain collectively in good faith. Regarding the nature of salaries and free agency, the judge wrote:

> Courts in addressing the antitrust area of law have easily recognized, however, that the essence of collective bargaining in professional sports is the establish-

> ment and maintenance of reserve and free agency systems in which owners agree to bid competitively for some players and collectively for others. The Owners' argument has a superficial appeal in its attempt to harken back to the unionizing cry of employees when they banded together to create this nation's labor laws. What the Owners have missed here, and the NLRB has not, is that the statutory right to join collective bargaining units belongs to employees, not to employers. *The NLRA gives only employees the section 7 right to bargain collectively through an elected representative.* The only reciprocal statutory right the Act imposes on employers and employees is that they bargain with the other in good faith. In other words, the term "employer union" for collective bargaining purposes is not meaningful. *Silverman,* 880 F. Supp. at 256.

Judge Sotomayor concluded that the provisions in question were mandatory, including for reserve Players. She found the NLRB had reasonable cause to conclude the Owners engaged in an unfair labor practice and that finding required the issuance of a temporary injunction. Public interest, the restoration of bargaining equality, the loss of free agency to Players, and non-monetary considerations, buttressed the judge's conclusion that a temporary injunction was warranted. Judge Sotomayor's injunction required the Owners to restore the expired Basic Agreement, rescind its written notice, and bargain in good faith, absent unilateral changes to the Basic Agreement. *Cf. infra chapter. four*, Sotomayor J., concurring opinion as a Second Circuit judge in *Major League Baseball Properties Inc. v. Salvino, Inc.*, 542 F.3d 290 (2d Cir. 2008), in which she proposed that the ancillary restraint doctrine would be the better approach to determine violations of antitrust laws in disputes involving Major League Baseball exclusive licensing agreements.

2. Baird, J., *Laws v. Sony Music Entertainment, Inc.*, 294 F. Supp.2d 1160 (2006), *aff'd*, 448 F.3d 1134 (2006), Copyright Act, Preemption of Common Law Rights, and Remedies.

The plaintiff Debra Laws (Laws) was a professional vocalist and recording artist. Laws entered into a recording agreement with Spirit Productions (Spirit) to produce master recordings of her performances for Elektra. Under that agreement, Elektra had the sole, exclusive and worldwide right to copyright the master recordings in perpetuity and to use and permit others to use her name and likeness. Elektra's agent, Warner Special Products, Inc. (Warner), entered into an agreement with Sony Music Entertainment, Inc. (Sony), granting Sony a non-exclusive license to use a sample of Laws' "Very Special" recording by Jennifer Lopez and L.L. Cool J. Warner did not seek permission from Laws or Spirit before it released the disc and video to Sony, and they were not compensated. Laws filed a lawsuit against Sony pursuant to the Copyright Act (2010), 17 U.S.C. §101-1332, for misappropriating her voice and name in the song "All I Have" by Jennifer Lopez and L.L. Cool J. "All I Have" included ten seconds of Laws' recording at the beginning of the song and in the background; it became a number one song in the United States. Judge Baird found that

Sony had obtained a license to use a sample of Laws' recording of "Very Special" and that the claims for violation of common law right to privacy and statutory right of publicity were preempted by the Copyright Act. The Ninth Circuit agreed with Judge Baird's ruling and affirmed her decision. *See also* Baird, J. *Three Boys Music Corp. v. Bolton*, 212 F.3d 477 (2000), *affirmed* (copyright jury award of $5.4 million for infringement of song "Love is a Wonderful Thing").

3. Delgado-Colón, J., *Latin American Music Co., Inc. v. Media Power Group, Inc.*, 2011 WL 1261534, *aff'd,* 705 F.3d 34 (1st Cir. 2013), Copyright Infringement Amendment of Summary Judgment Order.

The Latina American Music Company (LAMCO) sued Media Power Group (MPG) for copyright infringement for twenty-one broadcasting songs it allegedly owned. MPG owns four radio stations and broadcasts programming that its affiliates rebroadcast. MPG moved for summary judgment as to twelve of the twenty-one songs which was granted by Judge Delgado-Colón. Claims on the remaining nine songs went to trial, resulting in a jury verdict for the MPG, primarily because there was inadequate evidence of LAMCO's ownership of the songs The judge ruled certificates of recordation of songs were not evidence of copyright registration. After the trial, the judge amended her summary judgment order to revive the issue of song ownership. LAMCO appealed the amended order. The First Circuit held that the judge was not precluded from revising her order. It further held that LAMCO was not prejudiced by the judge's failure to give formal notice of the amended order because LAMCO was collaterally estopped from relitigating ownership. *See also Curet-Velazquez v. ACEMLA de Puerto Rico, Inc.*, 656 F.2d 47 (2012), involving another copyright lawsuit by a composer's heirs. Upon a bench trial, Judge Delgado-Colón granted summary judgment in favor of the heirs. The judge imposed the maximum statutory damages against the music publisher and performance-rights society. The First Circuit upheld her decision. It ruled the judge acted within her discretion in reopening discovery and ordering simultaneous disclosure of expert reports, refusing to exclude testimony by the heirs' expert as a sanction against the music publisher for failing to supplement an expert report, and in awarding the maximum statutory damages.

4. Arguello, J., *Willliams v. National Football League*, 2012 WL 2366636, *aff'd,* 495 Fed. Appx. 894 (10th Cir. 2012), Federal Arbitration Act, Substance Abuse Program.

Denver Broncos football player Genos "D.J." Williams filed in state court seeking to vacate an arbitrator's decision to suspend him for alleged steroid use. Williams pursued his complaint under the Labor Management Relations Act (LMRA), 29 U.S.C. § 185, and the Federal Arbitration Act (FAA), 9 U.S.C. §§ 1–16. Accordingly, the matter was moved to federal court and the National Football League (NFL) moved for summary judgment. The NFL implemented a Policy on Anabolic Steroids and Related Substances (Policy) and the Substances of Abuse Program (SAP). Pursuant to the Policy, in August 2011, Williams provided a urine specimen that did not contain endogenous steroids, which meant the specimen was not physiologically (naturally) produced human urine. In November, Williams was notified of his suspension for six games for attempting to manipulate a specimen or test in violation of the Policy. Plaintiff filed an appeal to overturn his suspension asserting the chain of custody was incomplete, and that the specimen was neither collected nor handled in accordance with protocol and the suspension should be dismissed. A decision was to be issued within five calendar days of the disciplinary action, but the NFL asked for a delay to reach resolution of the dispute. Plaintiff then moved to have the case dismissed for failure to issue a timely decision, which was denied.

Judge Arguello ruled that the NFL established its compliance with the Policy's protocol in collecting and testing the specimen and made prima facie showing that the Policy was violated by Williams. Williams established a gap in the chain of custody for approximately three hours. The judge ruled that the gap did not materially affect the validity of the test, and that Williams failed to prove the specimen was manipulated. Judge Arguello held that her authority to reverse the arbitration award under the LMRA or FAA, 9 U.S.C. §10(a)(1)–(4), was not triggered, because Williams did not establish that: (1) the award was procured by corruption, fraud, or undue means; (2) there was evident partiality or corruption by the arbitrator; (3) the arbitrator was guilty of misconduct in refusing to postpone a hearing, in refusing to hear evidence, or in misbehaving in some other way; or (4) the arbitrator exceeded his powers or imperfectly executed them. Citing *Sheldon v. Vermonty*, 269 F.3d 1202, 1206 (10th Cir. 2001) as authority, she concluded Williams did not prove any of the grounds established by caselaw, including a violation of public policy, manifest disregard of the law, or denial of a fundamentally fair hearing. Williams appealed Judge Arguello's order granting the NFL's motion for summary judgment. The Tenth Circuit upheld the judge's order, writing, "We conclude, for substantially the same reasons announced in the district court's thorough and well-reasoned order granting summary judgment, that Mr. Williams has failed to show such a wholesale abandonment of the collective-bargaining agreement." *Williams,* 495 Fed. Appx. at 898–899.

Conclusion

These cases demonstrate the malleability required of the Luminaria (and all) district trial court judges to promptly and simultaneously master substantive areas of the law on diverse issues while fulfilling highly demanding administrative tasks. What struck a chord in reviewing the hundreds and hundreds of cases decided by these Luminaria judges, was their attempt to align the evolving law and current appellate rulings with the facts and circumstances presented in each case, that is, to reconcile the human element with the philosophical. From a historical lens, it bears reminding that this generation of first Latina/Luminaria Article III judges were educated at a time when the country was experiencing great social change and upheaval that, for most, resulted in the opportunity to secure a law degree. In cases evincing serious constitutional violations or simply unjust outcomes, their analyses appear to sharpen with more thoughtful consideration of the facts and the law. Their cases (especially those of first impression) illustrate the ingenuity and intellectual capacity of the judges to define and register legal rulings that have shaped our jurisprudence.

At the front line of the federal system where 80% of all cases are heard and resolved, these trailblazing jurists had to adjust to a legal system of litigators unfamiliar with them while forging their acceptance by the juridical elite. Successful at their craft, the number of Latina federal judges has more than doubled with the appointment of the second generation of Article III judges who face even greater threats to the rule of law and their personal safety.[37] Given the harsh reality of today's political climate which increasingly intrudes and attempts to sway the federal judiciary, Justice Sonia Sotomayor recently stated to Georgetown University Law Center students that they, judges, must "remain fearlessly independent if the rule of law is to survive."[38] The Luminaria judges are at the forefront of this fight.

---

37. Though not a Luminaria but of the second generation of Latina Article III Judges, it is appropriate to acknowledge the personal sacrifice of Judge Esther Salas (D.N.J.) who lost her son by a litigant's crime of violence. Through herculean effort, she pursued the adoption of legislation to protect judges. *See*, the Daniel Anderly Judicial Security and Privacy Act, Pub. L. 117-263, 136 Stat. 3458 (2022).

38. Adam Liptak, *Sotomayor: Judges must be "fearlessly independent,"* The New York Times, March 28, 2025, https://www.nytimes.com/2025/03/28/us/sotomayor-remarks-georgetown.html, the Justice borrowing from former Canadian Supreme Court Justice Rosalie Silberman Abella who remarked: "[t]hey need to remain fearlessly independent, protective of rights and ensure that the state is respectful of both."

Five

The Luminaria Judges on the Circuit Courts of Appeals

The cases in this chapter were curated to present a cross-section of legal work and appellate issues decided by the first Luminaria Circuit Court of Appeals (Circuit Court) Judges over thirty years, from 1994 to 2024. Summaries of select cases offer a guide to the judge's jurisprudence. They contain essential facts and rulings necessary to understand the crux of the decisions. These summaries do not contain all the nuanced procedural strategies or facts in every case; selecting from over 1,200 majority opinions made this task difficult. To appellate purists, understandably, this is less than ideal as those who have practiced appellate law (the purest form of legal practice) know sculpting an appellate case depends upon skillful chiseling that rests, at times, on the smallest but most significant details. A good faith attempt has been made to capture relevant detail. Citations to other cases on same or similar issues are provided to assist with additional research. This chapter may be viewed as the beginning of an important study worthy of further dissection and writings, made more compelling with the ongoing circuit work of two Luminaria judges and that of another who was elevated from the Circuit Court to the U.S. Supreme Court. The purpose of this chapter was to chronicle their work and create a foundation from which future study could be launched.

A. Overview of the Circuit Courts of Appeal

The Circuit Courts are organized into thirteen regional circuits, which hear criminal, civil, and bankruptcy cases. Eleven circuits are composed of two to several states with a few circuits encompassing U.S. territories. Puerto Rico is a part of the First Circuit Court of Appeals. The Twelfth Circuit covers only the District of Columbia. The Thirteenth Federal Circuit exercises jurisdiction over the Court of Appeals for Veterans Claims, Court of Federal Claims, Court of International Trade, and administrative agencies. The thirteen Circuit Courts have been assigned 179 authorized judgeships: 167 for the twelve regional circuit courts and twelve judges for the Thirteenth Federal Circuit.[1] Each Circuit Court has multiple judges, ranging from six on the First Circuit to twenty-nine on the Ninth Circuit. Circuit Court judges are appointed for life by the U.S. President and confirmed by the U.S. Senate.

1. U.S. Courts, Court Role and Structure, https://www.uscourts.gov/about-federal-courts/court-role-and-structure.

Once a federal district court (District Court) has issued a final decision, the case may be appealed to a Circuit Court with one exception. Interlocutory appeals are those filed before a final decision is rendered. Interlocutory appeals seek resolution of issues involving a controlling question of law where there is a substantial ground for differing opinions and where the decision rendered may materially advance the litigation, 28 U.S.C. 1292(b). For all appeals, briefs are filed by both parties advancing their respective opinions to affirm or overturn a District Court's decision. A panel of three Circuit Court judges presides over oral arguments and issues its decision. One Circuit Court judge is designated to write the panel opinion for the majority panel. Once the opinion is published, no future panel of the same circuit can overrule the previous decision. A Circuit Court may consider certain appeals *en banc* (before all judges of a circuit) but only after the initial panel has heard the case; it may also decline to consider a case *en banc*. 28 U.S.C. § 46.[2] *En banc* opinions are viewed as having greater authority and significance because the entire court hears the case and issues a decision.

The Supreme Court of the United States (SCOTUS) has original jurisdiction over appeals from the federal circuits. Thus, Circuit Court panel decisions are directly appealable to SCOTUS. The vote of four Supreme Court justices is required to accept a writ of certiorari (the "Rule of Four").[3] This chapter includes discussion of cases decided by Luminaria Circuit Court judges that were reversed by SCOTUS.

B. Circuit Court Luminaria Judges

Of the nearly 1,400 licensed Luminarias, only four were appointed to a Circuit Court:

Judge	Circuit	Tenure
Rosemary Barkett	Eleventh Circuit	1994–2013
Sonia Sotomayor	Second Circuit	1998–2009
Kim McLane Wardlaw	Ninth Circuit	1998–Incumbent
Consuelo Callahan	Ninth Circuit	2003–Incumbent

Judge Barkett was the first Latina elevated to the Circuit Court in 1994 where she served as the sole Latina appellate judge in the country for four years until Judge McLane Wardlaw was confirmed in August 1998. As discussed in chapter

2. Due to its size, the Ninth Circuit has a different process for *en banc* hearings than the other circuits consisting of a limited panel composed of the chief judge and ten other judges selected at random for each case, a "limited *en banc court." 28 U.S.C. § 46(c); 9th Cir. R. 35-3.1.*

3. The Supreme Court Case Selections Act of 1988 (Pub. L. 100-352, 102 Stat. 662, enacted June 27, 1988), Judiciary and Judicial Procedure, 28 U.S.C. § 1257. This Act eliminated appeals as of right from state courts to SCOTUS except as set forth in 28 U.S.C. § 1253. The Rule of Four emanated out of tradition and is implemented through writs of certiorari.

three, Judge Sonia Sotomayor was nominated to the Second Circuit on June 25, 1997, before Judge McLane Wardlaw, but her confirmation was delayed for sixteen months until she was confirmed on October 7, 1998; two months after Judge McLane Wardlaw. The Luminaria Circuit Court judges served concurrently for six years, from 2003 (when Judge Callahan was confirmed) to 2009 when Judge Sotomayor was elevated to the U.S. Supreme Court. The remaining three served concurrently for four additional years from 2009 to 2013, until Judge Barkett joined the Iran–U.S. Tribunal at The Hague. The two remaining on the Ninth Circuit, Judges McLane Wardlaw and Callahan, were joined by seven non-Luminaria Latina Judges: Mary Murguía (2011) Kara Fernandez Stoll (2015), Barbara Lagoa (2019), Myrna Pérez (2021), Ana de Alba and Irma Carrillo Ramirez (2023) and Nancy Maldonado (2024). Starting in November 2023, for the first time in the country's history, the greatest number of Latinas judges have served concurrently on any circuit, the Ninth Circuit: McLane Wardlaw, Callahan, Murguía, and Fernandez Stoll. Judge Murguía became the first Latina chief judge of a Circuit Court on December 1, 2021 (Incumbent). *See* Appendix B, List of Luminaria & Latina Article III Judges, 1980 | 2025.

Combined the four Luminaria Circuit Court judges wrote majority opinions in 1,232 cases:[4] Judge Rosemary Barkett, 286 cases; Judge Sotomayor, 380 cases; Judge McLane Wardlaw, 323 decisions; and Judge Consuelo Callahan, 243 cases. The Luminaria Circuit Judges handled, interpreted and applied a broad range of federal statutes, many are the same as those handled by the District Court Luminaria Judges, such as the Americans with Disabilities Act (ADA), Age Discrimination in Employment Act (ADEA), Title VII, Employee Retirement Income Security Act (ERISA), Foreign Sovereign Immunities Act, Immigration and Naturalization Act (INA), Prison Litigation Reform Act, and the Truth in Lending Act (citations to these federal statutes provided in chapter three). They also encountered lesser-known laws, such as, e.g., the Packers and Stockyards Act, 7 U.S.C.S. § 181 *et. seq.*, Driver Privacy Protection Act, 18 U.S.C. §§ 2721–2725, Torture Victim Protection Act, 28 U.S.C. § 1350, Pub. L. No. 102-256 (1992), Seaman's Wage Act, 46 U.S.C. § 10313, Georgia Trade Secrets Act of 1990, § 10-1-760, Georgia Humane Care for Equines Act, O.C.G.A. § 4-13-1 *et seq.* (2008) and the South Africa's Employment Equity Act 55 of 1998. The Luminaria Circuit Court Judges also issued hundreds of dissents, some lengthy and others summary or brief: Barkett—128, Sotomayor—21, McLane Wardlaw—96, and Callahan—266. The following reflects the number of cases in which Judges Barkett, McLane Wardlaw and Callahan issued opinions by areas of the law[5]:

4. As reported by Westlaw and Lexis, last accessed March 27, 2025, as of this book's publication.

5. Lexis, Opinions by Areas of the Law (based on cases). For unexplainable reasons (per Lexis), these analytics were not available for Judge Sotomayor's tenure on the Second Circuit, despite numerous attempts.

Civil Procedure **937**

Criminal Law & Procedure **825**

Evidence **553**

Governments **460**

Constitutional Law **385**

Business & Corporate Compliance **307**

Torts **222**

Administrative Law **207**

Immigration **110**

Civil Rights **96**

Insurance Law **53**

Real Property Law **51**

There are fewer panel decisions written by Luminaria Circuit Court judges that were reviewed, affirmed or reversed by SCOTUS, as is true with all Circuit Court judges. The cases are presented in chronological order from earliest to more recent. SCOTUS reversed twenty-five circuit cases in which the Luminaria Circuit Judges wrote majority opinions: Judges McLane Wardlaw—12, Barkett—9, Sotomayor—3, and Callahan—1. The Ninth Circuit has the highest number of cases granted certiorari by the Supreme Court. In a study of SCOTUS Circuit Court decisions from 2007 to 2024, the Ninth Circuit bears the highest reversal rate with 192 reversals and 50 cases affirmed over that period.[6] In contrast during the same period, the Eleventh Circuit had 53 cases reversed and 29 affirmed; the Second Circuit had 64 cases reversed and 31 affirmed. To exclusively ascribe liberal leanings as the basis of SCOTUS reversals, especially as to Judges Barkett and McLane Wardlaw, or as their judicial philosophy of choice, does not wholly or accurately portray their body of legal work. An analysis of their opinions, like those of other Circuit Court judges—and for that matter, the Luminaria state Supreme Court justices and District Court judges—reveals a complexity that at times results in unexpected rulings. Their decisions and leanings are far more nuanced and purposeful.

1. Rosemary Barkett, Eleventh Circuit Court of Appeals, 1994–2013

As conveyed in her biographical summary, no one had generated as much attention, excitement or opposition as Justice Rosemary Barkett when she was nominated in 1994 to the Eleventh Circuit. The controversy ignited by the justice's rulings espe-

6. *See, e.g.*, SCOTUS Opinions, The Supreme Court at Work, https://www.scotusblog.com/reference/stat-pack/; https://www.supremecourt.gov/about/courtatwork.aspx.

cially in death penalty cases, the subject of most consternation, were the very ones endorsed by her male colleagues on the Florida Supreme Court. Nevertheless, the hyperbolic words of Senator Jesse Helms conveyed during Justice Barkett's confirmation process,[7] captures the perplexing contradiction (or failure) of some conservative senators to reconcile the justice's upbringing and belief system about the value of life that could be characterized as harmonious. To some, it may beg the obvious question, was the opposition stirred to prevent the first Latina intellectual from securing a Circuit Court appointment due to her rulings in a limited number of cases or because of her gender or race—or a mix of all three? Or arguably, was the opposition triggered by a profound appreciation of the justice's prowess to concisely interpret and apply the law which, if permitted, would bring clarity to contradictory political philosophies adopted in legislation *vis a vis* her legal scrutiny. Clearly, her appointment to the Circuit Court empowered a new segment of Americans—Latinas—to inscribe their juridical mark on appellate law.

To contextualize Judge Barkett's body of legal work, a quick overview of the Eleventh Circuit is helpful. The Eleventh Circuit has had responsibility for part of the deep South—Alabama, Florida, and Georgia since it was created in 1981 when the Fifth Circuit (which had jurisdiction over all southern states) was split in half.[8] Prior to the Reorganization Act, the Fifth Circuit in 1980 divided its work into two panels: Unit A-Louisiana, Mississippi and Texas and Unit B-Alabama, Florida and Georgia. As the second youngest Circuit Court after the Federal Circuit (established in 1982), it is one of the busiest. Title VII, qualified immunity, criminal sentencing and death penalty cases comprise a significant percentage of the circuit's docket with sentencing and death penalty cases commanding the most time; as is the case with the Fifth Circuit (Georgia, Mississippi, Texas and District for the Canal Zone). In contrast, areas such as antitrust and securities cases are filed rarely.[9] In *Bonner v. Prichard*, 661 F. 2d. 1206 (11th Cir. 1981) *en banc*, the Eleventh Circuit adopted as precedent cases decided by the Fifth Circuit on or before September 30, 1981; cases decided after that date are considered persuasive authority unless the decision was rendered *en banc*.[10] Thus, while on the Eleventh Circuit, Judge Barkett continued to adjudicate a high percentage of criminal, sentencing and death penalty cases guided in part by Fifth Circuit precedent and persuasive authority.

---

7. Cong. Rec. Vol. 140, No. 40 (April 14, 1994) comments of Senator Jesse Helms.

8. Fifth Circuit Court of Appeals Reorganization Act of 1980, Pub. L. No. 96-452, 94 Stat. 1994 (1980) (codified at 28 U.S.C. §§ I, 41 (Supp. V 1981) (Reorganization Act); *see* Kevin Golembiewski and Jessica Arden Ettinger, *Advocacy Before the Eleventh Circuit: A Clerk's Perspective*, 73 U. Miami L. Rev. 1221 (2019) (Miami Law article). Of interest, the U.S. Senate considered splitting the Ninth Circuit in 2006 under S. 1845 but was discarded, *see*, Pamela A. MacLean, *Judge from 9th Circuit Protests Proposal for New Breakaway Circuit*, The Legal Intelligence, October 9, 2006.

9. *Id.* Miami Law article at 1223–1224, 1228.

10. Accord, *Stein v. Reynolds Security*, 667 F. 2d 33 (11th Cir. 1982). This is an over-simplification of the complex transition. For an in-depth discussion, *see* Thomas E. Baker, *A Primer on Precedent in the Eleventh Circuit*, 34 Mercer L. Rev. 1175 (1983) at 1182–1184.

During her tenure, Judge Barkett participated in a minimum of 5,360 cases (Westlaw) and up to 7,004 (Lexis).[11] In her opinions, the judge dealt with the following types of law:[12]

1. Civil Procedure **388**
2. Criminal Law & Procedure **373**
3. Evidence **204**
4. Governments **183**
5. Constitutional Law **135**
6. Torts **104**
7. Business & Corporate Compliance **69**
8. Insurance Law **53**
9. Real Property Law **51**
10. Administrative Law **48**

a. Judge Barkett's Eleventh Circuit Majority Opinions

Among the judge's 286 majority opinions were cases involving issues commonly arising such as the appropriateness of sentencing/enhancements and sufficiency of the evidence, as well as more unusual issues which the following select cases reveal. Of first impression before the circuit in *Montes v. Shearson Lehman Bros.*, 128 F.3d 1456 (11th Cir. 1997), was the reversibility of a commercial arbitration award on the ground of violation of public policy. The conduct of an arbitration panel (Panel) of the Fair Labor Standards Act, 29 U.S.C.S. § 201 *et. seq.* gave rise to appellant's appeal of a ruling in favor of the appellee-employer. Appellant submitted irrefutable documentation of her claim for overtime pay. The employer submitted negligible evidence countering her claim. Appellant asserted that the Panel flagrantly and blatantly ignored the law as repeatedly requested by the appellee's counsel. The arbitration record verified appellee's counsel asking the Panel to ignore the law. Citing as authority *Wilko v. Swan*, 346 U.S. 427 (1953) and progeny including *First Options of Chicago, Inc. v. Kaplan,* 514 U.S. 938 (1995), Judge Barkett drew the distinction and grounds for reversal between those with erroneous misinterpretations or misapplications of the law (reversal not permitted) and awards that manifestly disregard the law (reversal allowed). The majority concluded the Panel's decision did not involve a misinterpretation, misstatement or misapplication of the law. Judge Barkett wrote that "[t]o manifestly disregard the law, one must be conscious of the law and deliberately ignore it" as was evidenced in the record in this case. *Montes*, 128 F.3d at 1461. The judge noted the Panel's reference to counsel's pleas in rendering its decision, the absence in the record of any stated reasons by the Panel for its decision and, further,

11. Lexis, last accessed March 27, 2025.
12. Lexis, Barkett Opinions by Areas of Law (based on cases), last accessed March 27, 2025.

the marginal evidence in the record that did not support a decision in appellee's favor. On these narrow grounds for the first time in the Eleventh Circuit, the Judge concluded that the Panel engaged in a manifest disregard of the law. Judge Barkett noted the Fifth Circuit's refusal to set aside arbitration awards on any non-statutory grounds. *Montes*, 128 F.3d at 1460.

Judge Barkett wrote the panel decision in *Dillard v. Baldwin County Comm'nrs*, 225 F.3d 1271 (11th Cir. 2000). In 1986, African American voters, among them John Dillard, sued the Baldwin County Commission (Commission) which then was composed of four members from each of the four districts in the county. The case was one among many Dillard suits in the district courts that challenged at-large election systems used across Alabama (Dillard Plaintiffs). The Dillard Plaintiffs alleged that the at-large system used to elect its members violated section 2 of the Voting Rights Act of 1965, as amended, 42 U.S.C. § 1973 (VRA).[13] Upon the Commission's concession of liability, the district court ordered relief, specifically to increase its membership to seven persons elected from single-member districts to ensure majority-black voting districts. The court's 1988 remedy (Remedial Order) created a district with a black population expected to be over 63 percent in 1990. In October 1996, three private citizens (Intervenors) sought to have the 1988 order vacated based upon the SCOTUS decision in *Holder v. Hall*, 512 U.S. (1994), and the Eleventh Circuit's ruling in *White v. Alabama*, 74 F.3d 1059 (11th Cir. 1996), *cert. denied*, 514 U.S. 1083 (1995) (*en banc*). The Intervenors alleged that the district court exceeded its authority under the VRA through the Remedial Order by increasing the size of the Commission from four to seven members to create a majority-black district and violated the Tenth and Eleventh Amendments of the U.S. Constitution. The district court granted the Intervenors' motion to intervene. In December 1996, the Dillard Plaintiffs moved to dismiss the Intervenors' complaint for lack of standing to challenge the Remedial Order and for failing to state a claim upon which relief could be granted. In June 1999, the district court granted the Dillard Plaintiffs' motion to dismiss. It held the Intervenors had standing to challenge the Remedial Order but failed to state a claim upon which relief can be granted under the Tenth and Eleventh Amendments because their alleged deprivation of rights was the result of state, not federal authority. Writing for the majority, Judge Barkett held the Intervenors had standing to assert Tenth Amendment claims because they established standing to assert a claim alleging a particularized injury under the VRA, citing *Meek v. Metropolitan*

13. 42 U.S.C. § 1973(a) provides: "No voting qualification or prerequisite to voting or standard, practice, or procedure shall be imposed or applied by any State or political subdivision in a manner which results in a denial or abridgement of the right of any citizen of the United States to vote on account of race or color." Section 2 (b) continues: "nothing in this section establishes a right to have members of a protected class elected in numbers equal to their proportion in the population." The Tenth Amendment provides powers not delegated to the federal government nor prohibited to the states by the Constitution are reserved to the states; the Eleventh Amendment restricts federal court jurisdiction (citizens cannot sue states in federal court) and establishes sovereign immunity.

Dade County, Fla., 985 F.2d 1471 (11th Cir. 1993), as its authority. *Meek* also involved a constitutional challenge by black and Hispanic voter-intervenors to their board of commissioners that elected eight commissioners in at-large elections for eight districts; the Eleventh Circuit held not only that they pled a particularized injury but, in fact, had standing to sue by asserting the allegation. Judge Barkett also found that the Intervenors stated a claim upon which relief could be granted, interpreting their complaint as alleging race discrimination, resulting in injury based on that discrimination. She cited *Dillard v. Baldwin County Comm'n*, 649 F. Supp. 836 (M.D. Ala. 1988), for the proposition that § 2 of the VRA applies equally to black and white citizens. The judge recognized the circuit's rulings in two cases that concluded courts cannot order the size of a district to remediate past discrimination, *White v. Alabama*, 74 F.3d 1058 (11 Cir. 1996), and *Nipper v. Smith*, 39 F.3d 1494 (11th Cir. 1994) (*en banc*), *cert. denied*, 514 U.S. 1083 (1995). Lastly, Judge Barkett disagreed with the district court's reasoning that the instant matter involved state instead of federal action and authority because a federal injunction was being imposed by a state body—the Commission. The judge refused, however, to grant the Intervenors' request to modify the Remedial Order, instead remanding back to the district court to proceed in accordance with the decision.

In *Collier v. Dickinson*, 477 F.3d 1306 (11th Cir. 2007), Judge Barkett concluded Collier and the putative class had a statutory right to pursue a lawsuit against the Florida Department of Highway Safety and Motor Vehicles (Department) pursuant to the Driver Privacy Protection Act (DPPA), 18 U.S.C. §§ 2721–2725 that prohibits sharing personal information to others except as proscribed by the statute. In this case, the Department's executive officials sold to mass marketers the personal information of Collier which he and the putative class provided to the Department to obtain drivers licenses. Judge Barkett wrote that the facts of this case gave rise to an enforceable violation of right to privacy against the state and individuals under the DPPA and Section 1983, thereby rejecting the defendants' claim and the district court's interpretation. The judge wrote such claims were distinct from claims of a constitutional violation under Section 1983 that were not tenable based upon circuit precedent, *Pryor v. Reno*, 171 F.3d 1281, 1288 n. 10 (11th Cir. 1999), *rev'd on other grounds*, 528 U.S. 1111, 120 929, 145 L.Ed.2d 807 (2000) and *Saucier v. Katz*, 533 U.S. 194, 201, 121 S.Ct. 2151, 150 L.Ed.2d 272 (2001). Lastly, Judge Barkett wrote the statutory language was objectively clear such as to reasonably conclude that Department employees should have been aware they violated the DPPA by sharing the appellants' personal information. On this basis, Department officials were not entitled to qualified immunity.

Brewer-Giorgio v. Producers Video, Inc., 216 F. 3d 1281 (11th Cir. 2000), the Elvis case. Plaintiff portrayed herself as the preeminent expert on the theory that Elvis Presley is still alive. She published two books, *The Most Incredible Elvis Presley Story Ever Told* (1988) (later retitled to, *Is Elvis Alive?*) and *The Elvis Files* (1990). Both were copyrighted with rights assigned to plaintiff's privately held corporation, the Arctic

Corporation (Arctic). In 1991, plaintiff filed a copyright application for a third unpublished book about Elvis, the *Operation Fountain Pen.* Arctic contracted with Producer's Video, Inc. (PVI) to produce a home video that was completed, based upon her first book. In November 1990, Arctic and PVI entered into a second agreement that granted to PVI the sole, exclusive and perpetual right to use any information in the possession of Arctic or the plaintiff relating to Elvis for a television special about Elvis. Under the agreement, PVI could produce any additional production relating to the same subject matter but that would require reaching a third agreement with plaintiff. In 1991, PVI produced and broadcast a nationwide television special titled *The Elvis Files* aired by WGNX in Atlanta, Georgia. Plaintiff wrote the script, appeared on the show as a live guest and in a taped interview. A dramatized re-enactment of a telephone call she allegedly received from Elvis after his death also was aired. Due to the show's success, PVI and All American Television, Inc. (AAT), decided to produce a sequel called *The Elvis Conspiracy*. Plaintiff worked on a script that later became the focus of this appeal, but she was not involved further. Before broadcasting, a dispute arose over payments due to plaintiff and Arctic from the first television special which was not resolved. Plaintiff refused to sign a proffered written agreement covering the sequel and informed PVI and AAT she would not authorize the sequel's broadcast. PVI and AAT broadcast the show nationally in January 1992, again aired by WGNX. Plaintiff was mentioned and a portion of the (alleged) phone call from Elvis was replayed. At the end of the show, the host conveyed his belief that Elvis died on August 16, 1977. Two days before the limitation period lapsed, plaintiff filed a lawsuit against numerous parties, with defendants AAT, WGNX, Micki Guzman (major stockholder of PVI), and Syd Vinnedge (AAT officer) remaining. The remaining counts alleged domestic and foreign copyright infringement, invasion of privacy, misappropriation of right of publicity, constructive trust, and fraudulent conveyance. The sole issued addressed by Judge Barkett was plaintiff's motion to amend the complaint to include her new script. The motion was filed over a year after her initial complaint was filed and eight months after the deadline to amend her complaint had passed. The district court denied plaintiff's motion finding no good cause to grant leave to amend. Though Guzman and Vinnedge had yet to file responsive pleadings, the trial court ruled that the expiration of the statute of limitations prevented plaintiff from filing new claims. The district court's denial was upheld by Judge Barkett, the judge further noting that plaintiff had not registered her copyright on the new script by the time the limitation period lapsed.

Glenn v. Brumby, 663 F.3d 1312 (2011) was a Title VII discrimination case in which appellant claimed she was terminated due to her sex, as well as her medical condition known as gender identity disorder. At issue was whether discrimination on the basis of gender non-conformity constitutes sex-based discrimination under the Equal Protection Clause. Glenn was undergoing gender transition which she reported to her supervisor and, as part of that transition, wore women's clothing to work. It was uncontroverted that employer fired Glenn due to her gender transition. He gave deposition testimony that he terminated Glenn for inappropriate appearance at work dressed as a woman, that he found it unsettling and unnatural that the employee would appear wearing women's clothing and admitted his decision to terminate was based on the sheer fact of the transition. The district court ruled against the employee on the gender identity disorder claim but granted summary judgment on the claim of sex discrimination. Upon discussing relevant authority, Judge Barkett concluded that sex discrimination includes discrimination against transgender persons because of their failure to comply with stereotypical gender norms, citing other circuit rulings and *Price Waterhouse v. Hopkins*, 490 U.S. 228, 109 S.Ct. 1775, 104 L.Ed. 2d 268 (1989) (holding that discrimination based upon gender stereotyping constitutes sex discrimination). *Glenn v.* 663 F.3d at 1317. She wrote that the employer advanced no governmental purpose in firing Glenn, "... much less an important governmental purpose, and even less than that, a sufficiently important governmental purpose was achieved by firing the employee because of her gender non-conformity." *Glenn v.* 663 F.3d 1312 at 1317.

Other notable majority opinions issued by Judge Barkett that involved discrimination issues include *Rendon v. Valleycrest Prods.*, 294 F.3d 1279 (11th Cir. 2002), finding a potential ADA violation in a class action suit where game show failed to accommodate disabled individuals from participating because its telephone hotline contestant selection process screened out hearing-impaired or upper body mobility impaired persons. In *Chappell v. Chao*, 388 F.3d 1373 (11th Cir. 2004), writing that appellant with a mixed case involving discrimination and non-discrimination claims was required to file in federal district court rather than the circuit when appealing a decision of the Merit Systems Protection Board pursuant to 5 U.S.C.S. §7702. In a case of first impression, *Adams v. Fla. Power Corp.*, 255 F.3d 1322 (11th Cir. 2001), Judge Barkett specially concurred that a disparate impact theory of liability is not available under the ADEA, 29 U.S.C. §621 *et seq.* Another factually interesting case in which the judge wrote a special concurrence was *Simmons v. Conger*, 86 F. 3d 1080 (11th Cir. 1996), involving a challenge by a trial court judge of an injunction prohibiting him from denying public access to divorce proceedings.

In *United States v. Pouty*, 303 F. 3d 1249 (11th Cir. 2002), reversible error was found when the district court failed to allow defendant to allocute. *Geddes v. Am. Airlines, Inc.*, 321 F.3d 1349 (11th Cir. 2003) raised the preemption issue of whether a complaint brought under the Railway Labor Act (RLA), 45 U.S.C.S. §151, 184, could be moved to federal court. Judge Barkett wrote the federal courts lacked jurisdiction because the doctrine of complete preemption did not apply to the RLA and reversed and remanded the case back to state court. *Jean v. Dorelien*, 431 F.3d 776 (11th Cir. 2005), involved claims brought by appellants against a Haitian military colonel for death and torture under the Alien Tort Claims Act, 28 U.S.C. §1350 (1948) and the Torture Victim Protection Act (TVPA), 28 U.S.C. §1350 (1992). Judge Barkett wrote that the victims were not barred by the TVPA's 10-year statute of limitations because the period was equitably tolled until the colonel was disempowered and present in the U.S. In *Ocwen Orlan-*

do Holdings Corp. v. Harvard Prop. Trust, LLC, 526 F.3d 1379 (11th Cir. 2008) the judge interpreted an agreement to purchase property in Florda that contained a forum selection clause in which Ocwen waived the right to transfer venue. Treated as a hybrid clause—a permissive jurisdiction clause to sue in one forum that becomes mandatory in the forum chosen by the suing party once suit is filed—is subject to interpretation the judge wrote under contract law, the plain language of the contract.

a. Dissents

Judge Barkett wrote 128 dissenting opinions that conveyed her sense of justice, starting with one of her earlier cases. *Jennings v. BIC Corp,* 181 F.3d 1250 (11th Cir. 1999), was a case that presented an interesting procedural twist with which Judge Barkett had extensive experience. At issue was whether the unintended use by children of defendant's BIC lighter was reasonably foreseeable as to warrant the application of strict liability. BIC had not included on its lighters a warning that the product could be dangerous to children. As there was no binding precedent in Florida law on the issue, the judge concluded the question should be certified to the Florida Supreme Court instead of being speculated upon and decided by the majority panel. Based upon the statistical data that established hundreds of children dying annually from the use of BIC lighters, Judge Barkett concluded the use was reasonably foreseeable and that both causes of action—strict liability and negligence—were warranted against the manufacturer.

The judge objected to: the imposition of the death penalty on persons determined to be mentally incompetent, *Hill v. Humphrey,* 662 F.3d 1335 (11th Cir. 2011), *In re Hill,* 715 F.3d 284 (11th Cir. 2013), and *Holsey v. Warden, G. Diagnostic Prison,* 694 F.3d 1230 (11th Cir. 2012); the sentencing of juveniles to life without parole, *In re Morgan, supra*; unreasonable searches on the person: *Evans v. Stephens,* 407 F.3d 1272 (2005), two black college students strip-searched for a speeding ticket and *In re Morgan,* 717 F.3d 1186 (11th Cir. 2013), the judge concluding the case warranted an *en banc* hearing, because the panel opinion made a "critical mistake" in applying *Miller v. Alabama,* 567 U.S. 460, 132 S.Ct. 2455, 183 L.Ed.2d 407 (2012) as procedural. She wrote that the *Miller* rule, which prohibits mandatory life sentences without the possibility of parole for juvenile offenders, is substantive rather than procedural and was a basis for a second or successive habeas petition. Judge Barkett also objected to warrantless entries into the home, *Coffin v. Brandau,* 642 F.3d 999 (11th Cir. 2011) and *United States v. Rodriguez,* 530 Fed. Appx. 908 (11th Cir. 2013).

The judge dissented in cases where the evidence was insufficient to sustain the conviction: *United States v. Warden,* 175 Fed. Appx. 308 (11th Cir. 2006) ("absolutely no evidence defendant" had knowledge of the presence of controlled substances) and *United States v. Rodriguez, supra* (insufficient evidence). She objected to the prosecutor's closing statements that, in her opinion, violated the defendant's Fifth Amendment right against self-incrimination, *Duke v. Allen,* 663 F.3d 1205 (11th Cir. 2011), and to sentences which exceeded the offense, *In re Morgan, supra, United*

States v. Hales, 236 Fed. Appx. 505 (11th Cir. 2007), *United States v. Gainous*, 298 Fed. Appx. 853 (11th Cir. 2008) (defendant complied with all conditions of supervised release but majority still required him to sell his home), and *Gilbert v. United States*, 640 F. 3d 1293 (11th Cir. 2011) (the Suspension Clause was violated by majority's ruling denying Gilbert a meaningful opportunity to bring a habeas corpus petition to show he was being held pursuant to the erroneous application or interpretation of relevant law). She dissented in *Boyd v. Allen*, 592 F.3d 1274 (11th Cir. 2010), concluding the failure of counsel to investigate and be present during sentencing prejudiced the defendant.

Judge Barkett demonstrated, literarily, the advantage and import of an immigrant background and experience in evaluating asylum cases. *See especially*, *Garcia v. United States AG*, 217 Fed. Appx. 855 (11th Cir. 2007) in which she departed from the majority decision that landowner Jenny Garcia, who sought asylum from Columbia, was targeted because she refused to pay the "war tax" and not because she was a member of a protected class. Upon providing a historical overview of the two major guerilla groups, the ELN and Revolutionary Armed Forces of Columbia and how they operated in that country, Judge Barkett concluded Garcia was a member of a protected group targeted by the Marxist ELN gang. In *Akapo v. United States AG*, 377 Fed. Appx. 901 (11th Cir. 2010), the majority denied asylum to Akapo who sought refuge from Sierra Leone on the basis that the death threats were unsigned. Judge Barkett noted in her dissent that Akapo's testimony was corroborated by witness testimony before the Board of Immigration Appeals (BIA). Her immigrant roots, however, did not prevent her from affirming the BIA's denial of asylum where warranted by the facts such as in *Barreto-Clara v. United States AG*, 275 F. 3d 1334 (Cir. 2001) (alien lied on asylum application and his testimony deemed incredible), *Bonhomme-Ardoin v. Unites States AG*, 291 F. 3d 1289 (11th Cir.) (concurred in denying temporary stay because clear and convincing evidence not submitted; she further discusses the appropriate standard to be applied in such cases) and *Nreka v. United States AG*, 408 F. 3d 1361 (Cir. 2005) (insufficient evidence of persecution).

b. Judge Barkett's Florida Supreme Court Decisions Reversed by SCOTUS

SCOTUS reversed decisions written by Justice Barkett when she served on the Florida Supreme Court in the following four criminal cases. In *Riley v. State*, 511 So. 2d 282 (Fla. 1987), *rev'd*, 488 U.S. 445 (1989), Justice Barkett wrote that the defendant had a reasonable expectation of privacy in his greenhouse from aerial observations by police which were conducted by flying a helicopter 400 feet over his greenhouse. Based up an anonymous tip, the police conducted the aerial observations (as they could not see into the greenhouse from the ground) and recovered marijuana. Justice Barkett wrote that the aerial observations constituted a search and an unlawful one under the Fourth Amendment and that the marijuana should be suppressed. The Supreme Court disagreed and reversed. Justice Byron White held that the aerial observations constituted a lawful search because police traveling in the public airways that permits observing what is visible to the naked eye does not require a warrant. He further wrote that such aerial observations (or helicopters flying at 400 feet) are not so rare such that Riley could have not have reasonably anticipated such aerial observations.

In *Bostick v. State*, 554 So.2d 1153 (Fla. 1989), *rev'd, Florida v. Bostick*, 501 U.S. 429, 111 S. Ct. 2382, 115 L.Ed.2d 389 (1991), at issue was a question certified by the district court over the standard "working the buses" procedure used by the Broward County Sheriff's Department (Department). The procedure applied in Bostick's case revealed cocaine in his luggage. Under this procedure, sheriffs randomly approached bus passengers and intentionally asked potentially incriminating questions that often resulted in consent to conduct searches of their baggage. The certified question (rephrased) was, "[d]oes an impermissible seizure result when police mount a drug search on buses during scheduled stops and question boarded passengers without articulable reasons for doing so, thereby obtaining consent to search the passenger's luggage?" *Bostick*, 554 So.2d at 1154. The answer supplied by Justice Barkett was yes, the police conducted an unconstitutional search of Bostick's luggage. The facts included the police boarding the bus in raid jackets carrying a recognizable zipper pouch containing a pistol, and partially blocking the bus exit when questioning Bostick. The state argued that initial contact by the police did not constitute a stop or detention, rather it was a consensual encounter. The judge analyzed what constitutes police intrusion, stops and seizures (concluding a seizure was not limited solely to physical custody), as well as voluntary consent to police intrusion and searches. She wrote that the officers' stop of Bostick amounted to a seizure. The judge wrote that Bostick's consent (if actually given) did not overcome and was not "free from the taint of the illegal detention." *Bostick*, 554 So.2d at 1156. Justice Sandra Day O'Connor issued the Supreme Court's decision reversing the case, ruling there is no *per se* rule that the investigative technique used was unconstitutional and held each case must be decided on the totality of the circumstances. On remand in *Bostick v. State*, 593 So.2d 494 (1992) in a *per curiam* decision, the Florida Supreme Court summarily upheld the district court's ruling which denied Bostick's motion to suppress. Justice Barkett dissented for the reasons delineated in her majority opinion, that there was an unlawful detention and the totality of the circumstances and specific facts in this case warranted suppression of the evidence.

There are several iterations of *Gaskin v. State*, involving Gaskin's initial convictions and appeal to the Florida Supreme Court, remand from SCOTUS on a jury instruction and subsequent postconviction relief proceedings. Judge Barkett rendered the majority opinions in *Gaskin v. State*, 591 So.2d 917 (Fla. 1991) and *Gaskin v. State*, 615 So.2d 679 (11th Cir. 1993) (*Gaskin II*). The defendant was convicted of first-degree murder, armed robbery and related charges. Gaskin killed Robert and Georgette Sturmfels and robbed their home; thereafter, he tried unsuccessfully to kill another. Gaskin confessed and led police to additional evidence of stolen items. The jury was given an instruction to determine whether the crime was "especially heinous, atrocious or cruel." He was convicted of multiple counts of premeditated and felony murder for the two victims and was sentenced to death. Gaskin moved for change of venue, challenged the jury instruction on "cold, calculated and premeditated" aggravating circumstances, conviction on multiple counts of first-degree murder, and the proper weighing of aggravating and mitigating circumstances. Judge Barkett delivered the majority opinion in the first appeal, finding no error in denying the motion for change of venue or in the weighing of circumstances. She summarily concluded Gaskin was wrongfully convicted of premeditated and felony murder for each victim, writing that each death supported only one adjudication. In *Gaskin*, ___ U.S. ___, 112 S.Ct. 3022, 120 L.Ed.2d 894 (1992), SCOTUS vacated the case finding error in the "especially heinous, atrocious or cruel" jury instruction, and remanded for reconsideration based upon its ruling in *Espinosa v. Florida*, 505 U.S. 1079, 112 S. Ct. 2926, 120 L.Ed.2d 854 (1992). *Espinosa* invalidated the instruction asking the jury to determine if the crime was heinous, atrocious, or involved cruel aggravating circumstances. In *Gaskin II*, Justice Barkett held the defendant failed to preserve the issue of unconstitutional vagueness as to this jury instruction and even if had he done so, the error here was harmless. The two death sentences were affirmed.

Certiorari was denied by SCOTUS in *State v. Slappy*, 522 So.2d 18 (11th Cir. 1988), *cert. denied*, 487 U.S. 1219 (1988). In this case, Justice Barkett defined the appropriate procedure when a claim of racial discrimination is raised through the exercise of peremptory challenges. Slappy, who was black, was tried for carrying a concealed firearm. Four of the state's six peremptory challenges were used to exclude black people from the panel, although all four had indicated an ability to serve as fair and impartial jurors. After the fourth challenge, the defense objected, and an exchange between the trial court and prosecutor ensued. When pressed, the prosecutor gave vague and unpersuasive reasons for the challenges, including that two potential black jurors were excused because they were teachers and more liberal, after the state accepted a teacher for the jury. Another potential black juror was excused because the state deemed her in "poor health." The trial court accepted the proffered "neutral" excuses, as did the intermediate appellate court even though it concluded the explanations were not supported by the record. At the outset of her analysis, Judge Barkett wrote,

> Despite continuing efforts, racial and other discrimination remains a fact of this nation's evolving history. The United States Supreme Court has characterized it as a problem needing unceasing attention. *McCleskey v. Kemp*, ___ U.S. ___, 107 S. Ct. 1756, 1775, 95 L. Ed. 2d 262, rehearing denied, ___ U.S. ___, 107 S. Ct. 3199, 96 L. Ed. 2d 686 (1987). As the Supreme Court elsewhere has noted: [W]e ... cannot deny that, 114 years after the close of the War Between the States ..., racial and other forms of discrimination still remain a fact of life, in the administration of justice as in our society as a whole. Perhaps today that discrimination takes a form more subtle than before. But it is not less real

or pernicious. *Rose v. Mitchell*, 443 U.S. 545, 558–559, 99 S.Ct. 2993, 3001, 61 L.Ed. 2d 739 (1979). *Slappy*, 522 So.2d at 20.

Judge Barkett's analysis included *Batson v. Kentucky*, 476 U.S. 79 (1986), the Florida Constitution and Florida caselaw. She wrote that Florida law exceeded the guarantees under federal law in protecting against bias in jury selection. Accord, *State v. Castillo*, 486 So.2d 565 (1986), clarified and reinforced in *State v. Neil*, 457 So.2nd 481 (Fla. 1984), which further addressed the "impossible" burden of proof imposed by *Swain v. Alabama*, 380 U.S. 202 (1965), rehearing denied, 381 U.S. (1965). *Swain* required defendants to show discriminatory practices employed systematically in a number of cases or contexts. The test employed by Judge Barkett was that enunciated in *Neil*: a party concerned about the other side's use of peremptory challenges must make a timely objection and demonstrate on the record that the challenged persons are members of a distinct racial group and that there is a strong likelihood that they have been challenged solely because of their race. *Slappy*, 522 So.2d at 21–22. In applying the challenges in the instant case to *Neil*, Judge Barkett found the explanations proffered by the state were facially neutral but under deeper examination, concluded the explanations were pretextual. For example, she noted the state failed to ask any questions of the two excluded teachers about their perceived "liberalism." Judge Barkett held the pretextual excuses combined with the pattern of excluding four black potential jurors constituted reversible error.

c. Judge Barkett's Eleventh Circuit Opinions Reversed by SCOTUS

Judge Barkett wrote the majority panel in ten Eleventh Circuit cases reversed by SCOTUS.

1. *Joiner v. GE*, 78 F.3d 524 (11th Cir. 1996), *rev'd, General Electric Co. et al. v. Joiner*, 522 U.S. 136 (1997). Joiner was an electrician employed by the Water Light Department of the City of Thomasville (City). Joiner worked around and fixed the City's transformers which used a coolant mineral-oil based dielectric fluid. PCB contamination was found though PCBs were not used in the coolant as they were banned under federal law, 15 U.S.C. §2605(a)(2)(A). The City found one in five transformers were contaminated. Joiner was a smoker with a family history of lung cancer. After he was diagnosed with small-cell lung cancer at age 37, Joiner and his wife sued in Georgia state court, alleging, *inter alia,* that his disease was promoted by his workplace exposure to chemical PCB's and derivative furans and dioxins that were manufactured by, or present in materials manufactured by, the petitioners. The petitioners moved the case to federal court and filed for summary judgment. Joiner responded with the depositions of expert witnesses who testified that PCB's, furans, and dioxins can promote cancer, and opined that Joiner's exposure to those chemicals was likely responsible for his cancer. This expert testimony was founded on animal studies. The district court held there was a genuine issue of material fact as to whether Joiner had been exposed to PCB's but granted summary judgment for

petitioners. It ruled there was no genuine issue as to whether Joiner had been exposed to furans and dioxins, and that his experts failed to establish a link between exposure to PCB's and small-cell lung cancer. It excluded all of Joiner's expert witness evidence. In reviewing whether the lower court abused its discretion, Judge Barkett applied a "particularly stringent standard of review" to the district court's exclusion of the expert witness testimony based upon *Frey v. United States*, 293 F. 1013 (D.C. Cir. 192) which favored a general acceptance test. For authority, the judge cited *Daubert* v. *Merrell Dow Pharmaceuticals, Inc.*, 509 U.S. 579, 113 S.Ct. 2793 (1993) which held Federal Rule of Evidence 702 superseded the general acceptance test enunciated in *Frey* and adopted a two-part test for courts to ascertain whether: (1) the testimony is scientific and (2) assists the trier of act to understand the fact in issue. *Daubert* also enunciated several factors to aid in a court's deliberation. Judge Barkett wrote that the expert witness testimony met the *Daubert* test and that there was sufficient evidence that the district court's ruling was in error as the proper review was whether Joiner's expert testimony was scientific, not whether it was correct. SCOTUS disagreed with Judge Barkett's application of a more stringent standard to review the district court's decision. Justice William Rehnquist wrote that Fed.R.Evid 702 did not alter the general rule of abuse of discretion which was the applicable standard by a lower court to assess the admissibility of scientific evidence. He concluded *Daubert* did not address the appellate review standard for evidentiary rulings and that a court of appeals abuse-of-discretion review to such rulings may not categorically distinguish between rulings allowing or excluding expert testimony. The Supreme Court concluded the Federal Rules of Evidence while permitting district courts to admit a somewhat broader range of scientific testimony than did pre-existing law, left in place the trial judge's gatekeeper role of screening such evidence to ensure that it is not only relevant, but reliable. *Daubert,* 509 U.S. at 589. Justice Rehnquist concluded that the animal and epidemiological studies relied upon by Joiner's experts were different from and irrelevant to Joiner's case and found no error in the trial court's order granting summary judgment.

2. In a case of first impression, *Zimring v. Olmstead*, 138 F.3d 893 (11th Cir. 1998), *rev'd and rem'd in part*, *Olmstead v. L.C.*, 527 U.S. 581, 119 S. Ct. 2176 (1999), Judge Barkett remanded in an ADA case, 42 U.S.C. § 12101 *et seq*. The appellant was held in a Georgia state-run psychiatric facility and segregated with others possessing mental disabilities. She sought removeable from state confinement and integrated care that addressed her needs. The judge wrote that the ADA and the Department of Justice's integration regulation prohibited Georgia from confining a disabled individual in a state-run institution where that individual could be appropriately treated in a more integrated community setting. She further found that confinement of the patients in a state psychiatric hospital in a segregated environment violated the ADA, notwithstanding the state's claim of lack of funding. The judge remanded to the district court the issue whether requiring the state to make additional expenditures would fundamentally alter the service it provided. SCOTUS

remanded and reversed Judge Barkett's decision in part. Justice Ruth Bader Ginsburg held that though the patients were qualified for community-based treatment, the state could consider the available resources in determining whether patients were entitled to immediate community placement. Justice Ginsburg's opinion generated two concurring opinions and a dissenting opinion by Justice Thomas, joined by Justices Rehnquist and Antonin Scalia.

3. In *Jones v. State Board of Pardons and Paroles*, 164 F.3d 589 (11th Cir. 1999), *rev'd*, *Garner v. Jones*, 529 U.S. 244, 120 S. Ct. 1362 (2000), the judge ruled that the Ex Post Facto Clause[14] was violated by the retroactive application by the Georgia Parole Board. At issue was the amendment to the parole reconsideration rule, Board Rule 475-3-.05(2), which changed the frequency of required reconsideration hearings from three to every eight years. The Supreme Court reversed Judge Barkett's decision, Justice Kennedy writing that the change from three to eight years did not necessarily violate the Ex Post Facto Clause but further, that the Eleventh Circuit failed to demonstrate how the Board's Rule created a significant risk of increased punishment. Justice David Souter issued a dissenting opinion joined by Justices Paul Stevens and Ginsburg, concluding the Eleventh Circuit made no error.

4. *Covad Communications Co. v. BellSouth Corp*, 299 F.3d 1272 (11th Cir. 2002), *vacated and rem'd, BellSouth Corp. v. Covad Communs. Co.*, 540 U.S. 1147, 124 S.Ct. 1143, 157 L.Ed.2d 1040 (2004). Covad appealed the district court's dismissal of its case alleging violations of the Sherman Antitrust Act (Sherman Act), 15 U.S.C. §§ 1–38 and the Telecommunications Act of 1996, 47 U.S.C. §§ 251, 252 (together, the Acts), as well as Florida anti-monopoly and unfair competition statutes. The Telecommunications Act imposes duties upon incumbent local exchange (telephone) companies (ILECs) to facilitate the market entry by competitors, Congress recognizing that new companies could not compete if they had to duplicate ILEC networks. From AT&T's breakup, BellSouth assumed monopoly control in a nine-state region. Covad was a seller of high-speed digital subscriber line (DSL) internet service. Covad and BellSouth entered into an interconnection agreement that enabled Covad to provide DSL service to its customers over BellSouth's existing telephone lines. Covad alleged BellSouth breached its agreement, engaged in misleading advertisement and misused Covad's customer information. Relying as authority on *Goldwasser v. Ameritech Corp.*, 222 F.3d 390 (7th Cir. 2000), the district court dismissed Covad's Sherman Act claims, concluding that claims based upon duties proscribed by the Telecommunications Act could not be pursued under the Sherman Act. Judge Barkett wrote the opinion which reversed the district court's dismissal, finding Covad properly pled claims under the Acts, including the monopoly leveraging and essential

14. U.S. Const. Art. I, § 10, cl. 1 which states: "No State shall...pass any...ex post facto Law" interpreted by caselaw to mean laws that change the punishment and inflicts a greater punishment than the law annexed to the crime when committed. Accord, *Atkins v. Snow, 922 F.2d 1559 (11th Cir. 1991).*

facilities doctrines and refusal-to-deal theory. The judge wrote that the Telecommunications Act did not preempt all Sherman Act claims, relying on the plain language of the act that was buttressed by its legislative history documenting Congress' intent that LECs remained subject to antitrust enforcement. BellSouth conceded that the district court's dismissal of Covad's breach of contract claim was inconsistent with Florida caselaw with which Judge Barkett agreed. The Supreme Court vacated Judge Barkett's decision and remanded it back to the Eleventh Circuit for reconsideration in light of its decision in *Verizon Communications Inc. v. Law Offices of Curtis V. Trinko, LLP*, 540 U.S. 398 (2004), holding Respondent's claim alleging breach of contract failed to state a claim under § 2 of the Sherman Act.

5. At issue in *Plaintiffs v. Humana Ins. Co. (In re Humana Inc. Managed Care Litig.)*, 285 F.3d 971 (11th Cir. 2003), *rev'd, Pacificare Health Systems, Inc. v. Book*, 538 U.S. 401, 123 S. Ct. 1531 (2003), was whether health care management organizations could be compelled to arbitrate under the Racketeer Influenced and Corrupt Organizations Act (RICO), physicians' demand for reimbursement for patient services they provided. Judge Barkett upheld the district court's ruling that a managed health care organization could not be forced to arbitrate under RICO where treble damages could be awarded. SCOTUS reversed. Justice Scalia held physicians could be forced to arbitrate, even where the arbitration agreement suggested the arbitrator's authority to award treble damages was limited.

6. *Scott v. Harris*, 433 F.3d 807 (11th Cir. 2005), *rev'd, Scott v. Harris,* 550 U.S. 372 (2007). Judge Barkett authored the initial panel decision reversing and affirming in part, the decision of the district court which granted the officer's motion for summary judgment based on qualified immunity. The Eleventh Circuit, *sua sponte*, vacated its initial decision and replaced it with *Harris v. Coweta County*, 433 F.3d 807 (11th Cir. 2005), the decision considered by SCOTUS. *Harris* was a case of first impression that involved a six-minute chase of Harris by a Coweta County deputy that covered nine miles, ending in Peachtree City in Fayette County, Georgia. The deputy was trying to stop Harris for speeding, the reason unknown to Harris. That deputy radioed for help but did not disclose that the chase was for speeding. Deputy Timothy Scott (Scott) responded taking the lead on the chase. Harris sped away in his vehicle, clocked at between 70 and 90 miles per hour. Scott had no training on Precision Intervention Techniques (PIT) which was a driving technique used to stop a fleeing motorist by hitting it at a certain specific point that causes a vehicle to spin. Notwithstanding, Scott received permission from his supervisor to employ the PIT and take Harris out though the supervisor had no detailed information about the scene. When Scott hit Harris's vehicle, Harris lost control causing the vehicle to run down an embankment and crash; Harris was rendered a quadriplegic. Harris filed a Section 1983 action against Scott alleging the deputy used excessive force with his cruiser. The district court rejected Scott's qualified immunity claim, finding the deputy seized Harris when he rammed into Harris's car—a finding the deputy did not dispute. Judge Barkett ruled that Scott's actions could constitute deadly force and thus,

constituted an unreasonable seizure in violation of the Fourth Amendment. She found there was no imminent threat because Harris remained in control of his vehicle (signaling and using his blinkers to ward other drivers away), factoring in that the roads were relatively empty. The judge concluded not only that Scott's use of deadly force was unconstitutional but, for the first time among the circuits, held that the use by an officer of his police vehicle in a high-speed chase constituted deadly force. Judge Barkett applied the factors in *Tennessee v. Garner*, 471 U.S. 1, 3 (1985), as support for the panel's decision. In *Garner*, the Supreme Court held that the reasonableness of a seizure depended on the circumstances, including how the seizure is carried out. With respect to a fleeing suspect, it held deadly force may not be used unless necessary to prevent the escape and there is probable cause to believe the suspect poses a significant threat of death of serious physical injury to the officers or others. The Supreme Court viewed a videotape of the incident which the majority interpreted very differently from those described in the summary judgment motion. After viewing, it concluded Harris posed a substantial and immediate threat of serious physical injury to others, considering the number of bystanders, the danger of causing injuries to others, and Harris's culpability, citing *United States v. Place*, 462 U.S. 696, 703 (1983). Justice Scalia wrote, "*Garner* did not establish a magical on/off switch that triggers rigid preconditions whenever an officer's actions constitute 'deadly force.' The Court there simply applied the Fourth Amendment's 'reasonableness' test to the use of a particular type of force in a particular situation. That case has scant applicability to this one, which has vastly different facts." *Garner*, 550 U.S. at 382. The Supreme Court reversed and held Scott was entitled to qualified immunity because his use of his vehicle to stop Harris's threat was reasonable. Justice Stevens dissented noting that the majority wrongly concluded Judge Barkett's description of the facts was "blatantly contradicted by the record" as the video actually confirmed, not contradicted, Judge Barkett's recitation of the facts. *Garner*, 550 U.S. at 390–391.

7. *Obasohan v. U.S. Attorney General*, 479 F. 3d 785 (11th Cir. 2007), *rev'd* by *Nijhawan v. Holder*, 557 U.S. 29 (2009), involved the appeal by a lawful permanent resident of the BIA's removal order. Obasohan appealed BIA's ruling that his prior conviction qualified as an aggravated felony under the INA, 8 U.S.C. §1101(a)(43)(M)(i) because it involved fraud or deceit with a loss over $10,000. Obasohan pled to one count of conspiracy to produce, use and traffic in counterfeit credit cards but did not admit to any loss. While entering the plea, the government's counsel affirmed there was no loss because the new credit card was being sent to the recipient and had not been used, to which the court replied, "so the loss would be zero." *Obasohan*, 479 F. 3d at 787. The Presentence Investigation Report (PIR) uncovered Obasohan's use of other credit cards that caused losses exceeding $37,000 to financial institutions which was used as the predicate for the 41-month sentence. Removal proceedings were initiated and the Immigration Judge (IJ) determined Obasohan was removable for conviction of an aggravated felony based upon the additional fraud contained in

the PIR. Obasohan objected and challenged this determination. Judge Barkett concluded that the BIA and IJ erred because, in determining Obasohan had been convicted of an aggravated felony, they relied on conduct that had not been charged, proven or admitted and granted the petition for reconsideration. She wrote, "[t]he INA does not authorize removal on the basis of the relevant conduct that may be considered at sentencing. Rather, what constitutes an 'aggravated felony' for purposes of the INA must be tethered to convicted conduct." *Obasohan*, 479 F. 3d at 790. SCOTUS granted certiorari as several circuits—the Fifth, Seventh, Eighth, and Eleventh—plus California appellate courts reached different conclusions. These courts adopted and applied a fact-based approach in their decisions, i.e., the crimes of fraud or deceit were never charged. The Supreme Court reversed *Obasohan* (and other cases), with Justice Stephen Breyer delivering the unanimous decision. He wrote that the words "fraud" or "crime" may refer either to a generic crime (categorial interpretation) or specific acts ("circumstance-specific" interpretation) and bootstrapped this distinction onto the $10,000 threshold used to find cause for removal. He concluded that the $10,000 threshold refers to the particular circumstances in which an offender committed a fraud or deceit crime on a particular occasion *rather than* to an element of the fraud or deceit crime actually committed. (Emphasis added.) Under this interpretation, SCOTUS held it was permissible for immigration judges to review the underlying circumstances of the loss to determine if it exceeded the threshold for purposing of removing individuals from the country, whether or not the crimes were charged.

8. *Siebert v. Allen*, 480 F. 3d 1089 (11th Cir. 2007), *rev'd, Allen v. Siebert*, 552 U.S. 3 (2007). An Alabama death row inmate filed a writ of habeas corpus, pursuant to 28 U.S.C.S. § 2254 which the district court dismissed as untimely filed. Judge Barkett issued the majority opinion reversing the district court's dismissal, writing the state limitation was not jurisdictional because Alabama state courts had discretion in enforcing the limitation. The matter was remanded to the district court to consider the merits of Siebert's petition in accord with Judge Barkett's panel opinion. In a *per curiam* opinion, SCOTUS reversed based upon its ruling in *Pace v. DiGuglielmo*, 544 U.S. 408, 125 S.Ct. 1807, 161 L. Ed. 2d 669 (2005). *Pace* held a state postconviction petition that is rejected by a state court as untimely is not properly filed within § 2244(d). SCOTUS applied the one-year limitations period of the Antiterrorism Death Penalty Act of 1996 (AEDPA) which may be tolled where an inmate is pursuing state postconviction relief that is pending. It concluded that the inmate was not entitled to tolling the limitation because his petition for state postconviction relief was filed three months after expiration of that filing period. AEDPA had yet to become effective when Siebert's direct appeal became final. Justices Ginsburg and Stevens dissented, distinguishing limitations that "go to the very initiation of a petition" (as in *Pace*) and those, like the one in *Siebert*, that create an affirmative defense as noted by Judge Barkett.

9. *United States v. Fowler*, 603 F. 3d 883 (11th Cir. 2010), *rev'd, Fowler v. United States*, 563 U.S. 668 (2011). Petitioner and several other men were preparing to rob a bank when a local police officer came upon the group, whom petitioner shot and killed. The petitioner was convicted of violating the federal witness tampering statute, 18 U.S.C.S. § 1512, which makes it a crime to kill another person with intent to prevent communication of a crime to a law enforcement officer. Petitioner argued there was insufficient evidence to prove he killed the police officer intending to prevent him from communicating with a federal officer. Judge Barkett affirmed the conviction, concluding there was sufficient evidence of a possible or potential communication to federal authorities. SCOTUS reversed, ruling there must be a reasonable likelihood that a relevant communication would have been made to a federal officer to convict of witness tampering. Justice Breyer wrote that a remand was warranted for the lower court to determine whether, and how, the standard applied in petitioner's case. Interestingly, Justice Alito dissented with Justice Ginsburg joining, writing that the majority inserted a new element rather than applying the statutory text. Justice Alito concluded there was sufficient evidence to prove three elements 1) a killing, 2) intent to prevent person from communicating and 4) information concerning commission of the (possible) crime were met. The remaining third element that a person was a federal law enforcement officer was also met but it was this element, he wrote, that caused the majority concern. Justice Alito outlined what element three did not include and wrote that the focus of this element rests solely on the defendant's intent which did not require that the defendant had any particular officer in mind or that he knew an officer was a federal official. On this basis, Justices Alito and Ginsburg would affirm Judge Barkett's panel decision.

2. Sonia Sotomayor, Second Circuit Court of Appeals, 1998–2009

In the summer of 2010, the Hispanic National Bar Association (HNBA) published a special edition of its Journal on Law and Policy dedicated to the nomination and appointment of the nation's first Hispanic Supreme Court Justice, Sonia Sotomayor.[15] The journal contained several articles, including the due diligence report on Judge Sotomayor's judicial record (HNBA Report). The HNBA Report summarized Judge Sotomayor's tenure and experience on the Second Circuit:

15. *Supra*, Chapter 1, fn. 162, HNBA Law Journal at 77-182 (HNBA Report or HNBA Journal), Editors in Chief, Circuit Judge Jimmie V. Reyna and Benny Agosto, Jr., (Houston). Disclosure: the author is a former HNBA president and was a member of the HNBA Supreme Court Committee that approved the HNBA Report, upon which the HNBA's support of nominee Sotomayor partially was based.

> Judge Sotomayor has been a federal judge for 17 years, serving with distinction on the Southern District of New York for six years and on the Second Circuit Court of Appeals for 11 years. She decided over 450 cases as a trial judge and on the Court of Appeals she has participated in over 3000 panel decisions, authored approximately 400 published opinions, and hundreds more unpublished opinions. If confirmed, she will be the only sitting member of the Court with experience as a trial judge.[16]

Since nominated to the Supreme Court, much has been written about Judge Sotomayor's personal and professional life. As she prepared for the Senate Judiciary confirmation hearing, numerous assessments were made of her work as a federal trial court judge and as an appellate judge with primary focus on her Second Circuit tenure. Organizations such as the ABA, American Civil Liberties Union (ACLU), National Association of Women Lawyers (NAWL), and other organizations listed in the congressional record.[17] The ABA gave Judge Sotomayor the highest rating of "well qualified."[18] The consensus of most reports about her Second Circuit tenure was that captured by the Congressional Research Service (CRS), "[p]erhaps the most consistent characteristic of Judge Sotomayor's approach as an appellate judge has been an adherence to the doctrine of *stare decisis*, i.e., the upholding of past judicial precedents. Other characteristics appear to include what many would describe as a careful application of particular facts at issue in a case and a dislike for situations in which the court might be seen as overstepping its judicial role."[19] The HNBA Report summarized what most other reports concluded:

> A review of Judge Sotomayor's opinions indicates that her decisions are well written, detailed, fact specific and adhere closely to Circuit and Supreme Court precedent. She is also a strong proponent of judicial restraint and often decides cases narrowly, avoiding opining on matters not before the Court or matter unrelated to unnecessary to the Court's legal analysis. Her decisions

---

16. *Id.*, HNBA Report at 92; Scholars who undertook and prepared the due diligence report included New York Court of Appeals Judge Jenny Rivera (a former law clerk of Judge Sotomayor, then a CUNY law professor), and law professors Lauren Gilbert-formerly at St. Thomas Law, Laura E. Gómez-University of New Mexico Law, Elizabeth Iglesias-Miami Law, Solangel Maldonado-Seton Hall and Catherine Sandoval-Santa Clara Law.

17. *Report of the ACLU on the Nomination of Judge Sonia Sotomayor to be Associate Justice of the United States Supreme Court* (ACLU Report), https://www.aclu.org/wp-content/uploads/publications/sotomayor_report.pdf; Nominee Sonia Sotomayor to U.S. Supreme Court, Senate Judiciary Committee Hearings, One Hundred Eleventh Congress, 2009–2011, First Session, Serial No. J-111-34, July 13-16, 2009, NAWL Letter at 1148, press release at 1158, see https://news.temple.edu/news/law-dean-testifies-supreme-court-confirmation-hearings.

18. July 7, 2009 letter from ABA Chair of the Standing Committee Kim J. Askew to Senator Patrick J. Leahy, https://www.americanbar.org/content/dam/aba/administrative/government_affairs_office/sotomayor-rating-letter.pdf; *see also* Letter from former law clerks at https://obamawhitehouse.archives.gov/the-press-office/letter-support-senators-sotomayor-law-clerks.

19. Legislative Attorneys Anna C. Henning and Kenneth R. Thomas, CRS Judge Sonia Sotomayor Analysis of Select Opinions, June 19, 2009, Summary https://sgp.fas.org/crs/misc/R40649.pdf.

> reveal a strong commitment to judicial deference to legislative mandates as well as a fair approach to the balancing of government and private interests... The recurring theme in [her]... majority opinions, concurring decisions and dissents are her methodical and narrow application of the law to the specific facts of the case and her careful application of *stare decisis*. Her opinions are also distinguished by her careful reading of statutory text and her vigorous application of the plain language of statutes.[20]

Clearly, Judge Sotomayor's approach continues as reflected in some of the most recent SCOTUS decisions, for example, her dissent regarding the role of the executive in *Trump v. United States*, 603 U.S. ___ (2024), Justice Sotomayor dissent at 1–30. The cases selected in this chapter reveal the judge's balanced, thoughtful and thorough discourses, whether in cases involving private citizens, cases of first impression, or those bearing significant national implication. As the HNBA Report observed, "[a]s both a lawyer and as a judge, she distinguished herself by her commitment to excellence.[21]

a. Majority Opinions

The HNBA Report found that immigration cases comprised a significant percentage of the 3,000 cases in which she participated. Over a ten-year period, from 1999 to 2009, the judge was involved in "over 800 cases involving appeals of asylum decisions pursuant to 8 U.S.C. § 1158, withholding of removal decisions under 8 U.S.C. § 1231(b)(3), and under the Convention Against Torture."[22] Noting the hundreds of cases in which Judge Sotomayor upheld BIA decisions, the HNBA concluded her "published decisions depict her insistence on holding the BIA and the IJs accountable to the respondents who appear[ed] before her."[23] The following cases in which Judge Sotomayor issued majority opinions exemplify the HNBA's conclusion.

The judge vacated and remanded the BIA's denial of asylum to a Guatemalan native in *Alvarado-Carillo v. INS*, 251 F. 3d 44 (2d Cir. 2001), partly because the BIA failed to apply its own standard in assessing petitioner's claim of persecution by the Guatemalan military. That failure included the mischaracterization of part of the evidence, reliance on inaccurate translation of the petitioner's testimony, ignoring significant parts of evidence of persecution for nearly ten years by the Guatemalan military and erroneous conclusions. The BIA further ignored or discounted, *inter alia*, the petitioner's union leadership, activism and university employment which made him a target which, when combined with the other BIA failures, warranted setting aside the BIA decision. Judge Sotomayor found impermissible in *Dickson v. Ashcroft*, 346 F.3d 44 (2nd Cir. 2003) the BIA's use of facts contained in a pre-sen-

20. *Supra* note 15 HNBA Report, Executive Summary at 92–93.
21. *Id.* HNBA Report at 97.
22. *Supra* note 15 HNBA Report, at 138.
23. *Id.*, HNBA Report at 139.

tence report and vacated the Jamaican native's removal order and remanded it back to the BIA. In *Alrefae v. Chertoff*, 471 F.3d 53 (2d Cir. 2006), the judge remanded the case back to the IJ to explain an *in absentia* removal order when the lawful permanent resident presented himself voluntarily. The petitioner provided evidence that his wife refused to sign the required joint petition to remove the conditional basis of his permanent resident status. This document also would establish the legitimacy of their marriage which ended due to her drug addiction, thus establishing a showing of exceptional circumstances.

Judge Sotomayor wrote the majority opinion in three of the four following asylum cases involving forced sex-related proceedings on two victims, an alleged perpetrator of the forced proceedings and (concurring opinion) a case extending asylum to boyfriends and spouses of petitioners who underwent forced procedures. In *Zheng v. Gonzales*, 497 F.3d 201 (2d Cir. 2007), the judge remanded back to the BIA the case of a Chinese female national to determine whether the forced insertion of an intrauterine device IUD constituted persecution. The judge noted the BIA had yet to articulate whether this circumstance constituted persecution and had adopted conflicting positions that provided no reliable guidance to the court. *Jiang v. Bureau of Citizenship and Immigration Services*, 520 F.3d 132 (2d Cir. 2008), also was remanded back to the BIA for the same reasons articulated in *Zheng*. Jiang, a Chinese female national, was a former employee of a family-planning clinic who allegedly participated in the forcible insertion of IUDs on other Chinese female nationals. The judge remanded the issues, 1) whether participation in these procedures constituted persecution and 2) whether the extent of Jiang's involvement constituted persecution such that she should be denied asylum. Forced genital mutilation was at issue in *Bah v. Mukasey,* 529 F. 3d 99 (2d Cir. 2008). In this consolidated case, the judge found that the BIA again had failed to follow its own regulations, writing the Guinea victims were entitled to same presumption as others. In the *en banc* decision of *Shi Liang Lin v. United States Department of Justice,* 494 F. 3d 296 (2d Cir. 2007), Judge Sotomayor concurred with the majority opinion holding that asylum does not extend to the fiancés, or boyfriends of unmarried applicants who underwent forced abortions or involuntary sterilization but dissented to extending the ruling to spouses. She concluded it was inappropriate to recognize such an extension since the petitioner was not married and, therefore, the issue was not properly before the court. In a non-asylum case involving abortion, *Center for Reproductive Law and Policy v. Bush*, 304 F. 3d 183 (2d Cir. 2002), Judge Sotomayor addressed abortion funding. The judge ruled against the Center in its challenge of the Mexico City Policy which prohibited foreign organizations receiving U.S. funds from promoting or funding abortion. *Cf., Port Washington Teacher's Association v. Bd. of Educ.*, 478 F. 3d 494 (2d Cir. 2007) turned on the standing of the teachers' association to bring suit. The substantive issue, whether teachers had to implement a school policy which required school employees to inform parents that their daughters were pregnant when the students' refused to do so never was considered. The case was dismissed.

In *Wala v. Mukasey*, 511 F.3d 102 (2d Cir. 2007), the judge wrote that a conviction for third-degree burglary under Connecticut law did not constitute a crime of moral turpitude within the meaning of INA, 8 U.S.C. §1182(a)(2)(A)(i)(I). Further, she wrote the BIA could not infer as much from the plea colloquy to affirm the removal of the Polish lawful permanent resident as it "has no expertise in construing... state criminal statutes..." (emphasis hers). *Wala*, 511 F.3d at 105. The judge reached the same conclusion in *Dulal-Whiteway v. U.S. Dept. of Homeland Security*, 501 F. 3d 116 (2d Cir. 2007), writing that the Trinidad native's conviction for making false statements in procuring a firearm did not establish fraud of deceit with loss exceeding $10,000, justifying removal. That portion of the BIA's decision was reversed but removal for the firearms conviction was upheld. This ruling was abrogated by SCOTUS in 2009 by *Nijhawan, supra,* the case which also effectively reversed Judge Barkett's *Obasohan* asylum case. Judge Sotomayor cited the *Obasohan* case, concluding the statute in that case was similar to the one in the instant case, rendering the statute here "*divisible*." *Dulal-Whiteway,* 501 F. 3d at 128, footnote 7. In *Mendis v. Filip*, 554 F. 3d 335 (2d Cir. 2009), Judge Sotomayor returned the asylum case back to the IJ for an explanation why the Sri Lankan native was ordered removed to the United Kingdom. Mendis was in that country for only a few hours en transit from Sri Lanka to Qatar and to England before arriving in the U.S. Mendis did not designate a country of origin after two hearings; the BIA finding this an adequate basis to return him to the United Kingdom. Mendis offered evidence of persecution. Because the judge found the IJ's decision ambiguous, she concluded the case could not be heard on the merits and vacated and remanded the case. Lastly, the judge also took the district court to task in *Paul v. I.N.S.*, 348 F.3d 43 (2d Cir. 2003), for writing a letter to Paul informing him that he had filed in the wrong court and that the Second Circuit was the appropriate forum. She wrote that the district court abused its discretion under 28 U.S.C. §1631 by failing to docket and transfer Paul's case to the Second Circuit. Paul's petition for a review of BIA's deportation decision to return him to Jamaica was timely filed under these circumstances.

Defining her as neither pro-defendant nor pro-prosecution, the HNBA Report concluded Judge Sotomayor seriously evaluates the constitutional rights of defendants seriously while simultaneously and appropriately balancing the government's interest. The following select cases illustrate the point. in *Cassidy v. Chertoff*, 471 F. 3d 67 (2d Cir. 2006), the judge evaluated the Maritime Transportation Security Act of 2002, 46 U.S.C. §§70101–70119, that was passed after the 9/11 terrorist attack. At issue were screenings of certain vessels and searches of passengers' vehicles or bags conducted by the U.S. Coast Guard. The plaintiffs were two Vermont residents who regularly commuted on ferries that were stopped and searched, though they did not object to the searches, claiming fear of retaliation. Judge Sotomayor applied the special needs doctrine and found the government's interest outweighed the intrusion on their privacy. In *Farrell v. Burke*, 449 F. 3d 470 (2d Cir. 2006), Judge Sotomayor addressed the due process rights under Section 1983 of a former state parolee convicted of sexual crimes involving minors. Farrell alleged his parole officers violated his rights by imposing a special condition prohibiting him from viewing "pornographic material" that depicted lurid pictures of men and boys having sex, asserting the term was inherently vague. The judge wrote that the condition imposed upon the parolee was not unconstitutionally vague as applied to his criminal conduct. Another case of child pornography, *United States v. Falso*, 544 F. 3d 110 (2d Cir. 2008), involved Falso's guilty plea to 243 counts of child pornography and traveling with intent to engage in illicit sex with minors. Falso was sentenced to thirty years' imprisonment. The district court denied the motion to suppress evidence seized from Falso's home and computer. The panel unanimously agreed that the search warrant was not supported by probable cause but upheld the search based upon the good-faith exception to the exclusionary rule enunciated in *United States v. Leon*, 468 U.S. 897 (1984) and *Arizona v. Evans*, 514 U.S. 1 (1995). *See also United States v. Santa*, 180 F. 3d 20 (2d Cir. 1999), an earlier case in which the judge also upheld the search of a man known by a police officer from a prior criminal investigation who relied upon a vacated search warrant to conduct a search of the person that resulted in the discovery of crack cocaine. In a criminal case involving a related First Amendment issue, *United States v. Quattrone*, 402 F. 3d 304 (2d Cir. 2005) during the Internet boom in the late 1990s, Frank Quattrone was tried twice for obstructing investigations into the handling of initial public offerings of technology companies by Credit Suisse First Boston Bank. When the jury deadlocked in the first trial, the judge issued an order forbidding the media from publishing the names of jurors during the trial disclosed in open court. Judge Sotomayor wrote that the judge's order amounted to an unjustified prior restraint in violation of the First Amendment. Judge Sotomayor ruled in the defendant's favor in *U.S. v. George*, 386 F. 383 (2d Cir. 2004), issuing a unanimous opinion reversing the district court for applying the erroneous *mens rea* standard where defendant was convicted of making a false statement on a passport application.

Unlike Judge Barkett, Judge Sotomayor issued no majority opinions in death penalty cases during her tenure on the Second Circuit. (A few others are discussed below in her dissents.) As a district court judge, she handled one case that involved the interim payment of attorneys' fees relative to the defendant's right to counsel, *United States v. Heatley*, 2001 WL 6728 (S.D.N.Y. Jan. 2, 2001), providing an instructive note, relevant today in the climate of political prosecutions:

> While this Court would hope that no member of the U.S. Attorney's office would reject a cooperation agreement and pursue a prosecution solely for the purpose of getting his or her first death sentence, it is far from clear that such a motive would be unconstitutional, provided that the prosecution could in good faith assert that the defendant had committed a capital crime which was of sufficient unusual severity to 'warrant' the death penalty.[24]

---

24. *Supra* note 17 ACLU Report at 67 quoting Heatly.

The ACLU reported twenty-two published habeas corpus opinions issued by Judge Sotomayor in which she ruled in favor of the government, some of those cases were discussed in its report. The report included a contrast with her tenure on the district court in which she granted the petitions pursuant to AEDPA. *See* ACLU Report at 68–72. In cases involving the Fourth and Fifth Amendment, the ACLU found the judge ruled predominantly in favor of the government but found unconstitutional violations especially as regards searches of the person and property. *See* for example, *Walczyk v. Rio,* 496 F. 3d 139 (2d Cir. 2007) (the judge specially concurring with the majority that the search warrant was not supported by probably cause).

According to the HNBA Report, the judge's six antitrust opinions, "evidenced a nuanced command of the statutory scope of antitrust laws"[25] that are often cited by other scholars and appellate judges. Among those cases reviewed were *Todd v. Exxon Corp.*, 275 F.3d 191 (2d Cir. 2001), a case of significant precedential value, in which the judge interpreted the standard of review applicable to antitrust claims for dismissal on the alleged failure to state a claim. The HNBA noted *Todd* has been cited in 185 cases and the Supreme Court relied on it in *Twombly v. Bell Atlantic,* 425 F.3d 99, 106 (2005). In *Clarett v. National Football League (NFL),* 369 F.3d 124 (2d Cir. 2004), *cert. denied,* 544 U.S. 961 (2005), the judge reversed the summary judgment order entered against a player who challenged under the Sherman Act, the NFL's draft requirement to complete three college football seasons played out of from high school. Judge Sotomayor wrote a concurring opinion in *Major League Baseball Properties, Inc. v. Salvino, Inc.*, 542 F.3d 290 (2d Cir. 2008), agreeing the summary judgment was properly granted. She evaluated the joint exclusive licensing agreement differently from the majority—through the lens of the ancillary restraints doctrine under the rule of reason. In another antitrust case recognized for its precedential value, *Innomed Labs, LLC v. Alza Corporation,* 368 F. 3d 148 (2d Cir. 2004), Judge Sotomayor concluded that intangible services, like tangible products, fell under the Robinson-Patman Act, 15 U.S.C. §13(a) (Act) and were covered under the semi-exclusive agreement between the parties. Here, the parties entered into an agreement involving the distribution of patented pharmaceutical products (Agreement). The Act addresses those instances where a seller charges different prices to different buyers for the same commodity or service resulting in an anti-competitive effect. Innomed charged Alza with committing price discrimination for charging it higher prices than prices charged to other semi-exclusive distributors, and with tortious interference and other contract breaches. The district court dismissed most of Innomed's contract claims and tort claim; the jury found against Innomed on the remaining claims. Innomed appealed citing two faulty jury instructions, by 1) instructing the Patman Act would not apply if the jury found the Agreement involved distribution rights of intangible services and 2) too narrowly defining entitlement to

25. *Supra* note 15 at 93, 98, see generally 98–106, the antitrust analysis written by Professor Sandoval.

treble damages. These issues required the judge to examine and determine the applicability of the Act where the dominant nature or purpose of an agreement is intangible services and how damages should be assessed. The judge reviewed the caselaw interpreting the Act, including those that applied the strict view that the Act covers only tangible commodities. Alza asserted the dominant nature of the Agreement was the sale of intangible distribution rights. Judge Sotomayor held that the district court's jury instruction was faulty because it instructed the jury that if it found the dominant nature was intangible, here distribution rights, the Act did not apply. Stated otherwise, the district court concluded that intangible services could alter the nature of an agreement where this was the dominant purpose of an agreement. The judge determined that in cases where the elements are fused, "[i]t would therefore make little sense to attempt to parse a contract price for a finished product into separate charges when the parties themselves have agreed that the tangible and intangible elements are but two aspects of the product that is the object of the contract. The dominant nature test is simply the means by which to determine whether the tangible element is incidental to the intangible object of the contract, or vice versa." *Innomed,* 368 F. 3d at 158–159. If, as in the instant case, the elements are not fused, the appropriate question is whether the inclusion of exclusive distribution rights renders the Act inapplicable (a case of first impression), making the dominant nature test inapplicable to commodity distribution cases. She wrote, "…the grant of the right does not diminish the fact that the parties have bargained for the transfer of the commodity. Although some portion of the contract payments presumably represents the value of the right to distribute on an exclusive or semi-exclusive basis, this element of the contract does not change the basic object of the contract, because the distribution right would be meaningless without the transfer of the commodity itself." *Innomed,* 368 F. 3d at 159–160. In a footnote, the judge concluded the factfinder must first determine the price of the commodity. On this basis, she concluded that the Act was intended to apply to all commodities distribution contracts in the distribution chain and further, that the jury instruction given by the district court was erroneous. Notwithstanding, Judge Sotomayor decided there was no fundamental error because the district court's jury instruction was limited to treble damages; Innomed having failed to raise this particular challenge.

Cases involving civil and constitutional rights and employment discrimination claims, according to the HNBA Report, "illustrate her commitment to a close and faithful reading of the plain language of federal statutes and adherence to precedent, and also illustrate her opposition to judicial overreaching."[26] In two important employment cases, Judge Sotomayor employed her brand of "heavy fact-specific analysis."[27] *Parker v. Columbia Pictures,* 204 F.3d 326 (2d Cir. 2000) was a case of first impression in which Judge Sotomayor applied a mixed motive theory to claims

26. *Supra* note 15 HNBA Report at 93.
27. *Id.* HNBA Report at 114.

under the ADA. Plaintiff sued Sony Pictures Entertainment (Sony) alleging his firing was in retaliation for filing an EEOC complaint and that his firing, non-rehiring, and retaliation violated the ADA and New York State's Human Rights Law, N.Y. Exec. Law § 296 (1993 & Supp. 1999). Plaintiff injured his back while working at Sony and eventually had back surgery. The trial court granted Sony's motion for summary judgment, in part due to claims made on the Social Security and long-term disability benefits applications in which plaintiff stated he was completely incapacitated and unable to work. Judge Sotomayor ruled that the inconsistent statements were insufficient on their face to defeat an ADA claim as caselaw required a deeper inquiry into the inconsistency, citing *Cleveland v. Policy Mgmt. Sys. Corpo.*, 526 U.S. 795 (1999) as authority. She reasoned a jury could find the plaintiff disabled at the time he sustained his injury, while recovering and able to return to work with reasonable accommodations. The district court also granted summary judgment to Sony because the plaintiff failed to demonstrate he was fired due to his disability by injecting another possible motive for his firing, that his supervisor wanted to hire another, more loyal employee. Judge Sotomayor disagreed with this finding and applied for the first time, the mixed-motive analysis to the ADA.[28] She relied on cases from sister-circuits, thus aligning the Second Circuit with the First, Fourth, Fifth, Seventh, Eighth, and Eleventh Circuits. *Parker* 204 F.3d at 337. The judge concluded this was a close question but one that raised issues of fact for a jury and therefore was sufficient to survive summary judgment. *See also Bartlett v. New York State Board of Law Examiners*, 970 F. Supp. 1094 (S.D.N.Y. 1997) in which the judge found the plaintiff suffered from a learning disability that impaired her ability to read and work as a lawyer but was entitled to reasonable accommodation to take the New York bar examination.

In *Cruz v. Coach Stores*, 202 F.3d 560 (2d Cir. 2000), Judge Sotomayor affirmed the district court's summary judgment except for the plaintiff's hostile work environment claims. As to that claim, the judge concluded plaintiff established a history and culture of: 1) impermissible touching by a supervisor that was condoned by Coach Stores, 2) supervisor Bloom and co-worker's regularly used racial epithets, including use of the words "spics," "Colored People's time," and the "n" word, 3) racist statements to the effect, "the only other job you [Hispanics] can do is sweep the floors at McDonalds," as well as 4) repeated sexist remarks by Bloom that women should be barefoot and pregnant, these comments accompanied, at times, by Bloom looking women employees "up and down" and standing uncomfortably close to her. There was an allegation of a physical altercation in which a coworker made a sexual comment to the plaintiff and got into her face, whereupon plaintiff slapped him, and the coworker put her in a neck hold. Both were terminated. Judge Sotomayor concluded that the complaint, while not artfully drafted, contained the essential elements of a gender and racial hostile work environment from which a jury

28. 42 U.S.C. § 2000e-2(m)(1994), mixed-motive theory of causation.

could find in plaintiff's favor. *Cruz*, 202 F.3d at 570–571. The judge rejected the district court's conclusion that an epithet was made one time citing as authority, *Harris v. Forklift Sys., Inc.*, 510 U.S. 17 (1993). The judge reached a similar conclusion in *Raniola v. Bratton*, 243 F. 3d 610 (2d Cir. 2001), dismissing all but the hostile work environment and retaliation claims of the female New York police officer.

b. Dissents

Judge Sotomayor dissented in an international custody dispute case involving a minor child that was subject to the Hague Convention arising from the International Child Abduction Remedies Act (Act) in *Croll v. Croll*, 229 F. 3d 133 (2d Cir. 2000). The district court ordered the minor to be returned to the father in Hong Kong and the Second Circuit reversed, holding the district court lacked the jurisdiction to enter such an order. The majority premised its conclusion that the father had no custody rights on a *ne exeat* (s/he may not depart or let them not leave) provision in the Hong Kong custody order that mandated the child could not leave until reaching 18 years of age. The mother, however, had removed the minor child from Hong Kong without the father's permission. The judge dissented asserting that under the Hague Convention, the father had custody rights that were further eroded with the mother's breach of the custody agreement.

In criminal law cases, the judge wrote dissents on diverse issues, some favoring the government and in others, favoring the defendants. In *United States v. Gori*, 230 F. 3d 44 (2d Cir. 2000), the judge disagreed with the majority, writing it failed to apply the heightened protection required in the search of a person's home, relying on two SCOTUS cases and agreeing with Justice Alito's conclusion that preservation of the home is worthwhile. In *N.G. ex rel. S.C. v. Connecticut*, 382 F. 3d 225 (2d Cir. 2004), the judge wrote that the strip search of a teenager in a juvenile detention facility did not bear a sufficiently close and substantial relationship to meet the special needs test. In *U.S. v. Yakobowicz*, 427 F. 3d 144 (2d Cir. 2005), she objected to the majority's reversal of defendant's conviction for filing false tax returns based upon the prosecutor's comments. The prosecutor commented following eleven of twenty-six witnesses' testimony, the judge concluded this was harmless error. In *U.S. v. Cavera*, 550 F. 3d 180 (2d Cir. 2008) Judge Sotomayor objected to the majority's affirmance of district court sentences of a septuagenarian army veteran who entered a guilty plea to one count of conspiracy to deal in and transport firearms. The veteran was sentenced to 24-month's imprisonment, instead of the 12–18 months under the sentencing guidelines. The defendant in *U.S. v. Blackburn*, F. 3d 259 (Cir. 2006), was sentenced to 37-months imprisonment and three year's supervised release upon entering a plea of guilty to one count of being a felon in possession of a firearm. The judge dissented due to the district court's erroneous calculation under the guidelines.

U.S. v. Huezo, 546 F. 3d 174 (2d Cir. 2008), is a sound example of the judge's adherence to *stare decisis* as revealed by her dissent. At trial, the government introduced evidence of an international money-laundering conspiracy involving Columbia drug suppliers. Huezo was tried and convicted for money laundering and conspiracy to launder money based principally on the use of his jeep, possession of a black bag containing money and socializing with the two other co-conspirators after the drop-off. There was no direct evidence Huezo knew what the bag contained, the purposes of trips he took in the jeep or a connection between the bag containing the money and the conspiracy. Huezo's two convictions were set aside when the district court granted his motion for post-verdict motion for judgment of acquittal on the grounds that there was insufficient evidence to support the knowledge and specific intent elements of both offenses; the government appealed. The majority reversed the district court, applying the slight evidence formulation (once a conspiracy is shown, only slight evidence is needed to link another defendant with it), concluding there was significant circumstantial evidence establishing a conspiracy and Huezo's connection to that conspiracy, especially as regards the concealment of the crimes, citing as authority, *Regalado Cuellar v. United States*, 128 S.Ct. 1994, 170 L.Ed.2d 942 (2008). The judge agreed there was "ample evidence" establishing the conspiracy but disagreed that there was sufficient evidence to establish Huezo's guilt in the conspiracy beyond a reasonable doubt. Characterizing as weak the majority's inference of Huezo's actual knowledge from the circumstantial evidence produced at trial, Judge Sotomayor argued Huerzo's case was more similar to *United States v. Rodriguez*, 392 F. 3d 539 (d Cir. 2004) (insufficient evidence introduced, including the use of his car, to sustain conviction of possession of heroin). *Cuellar* provided clear guidance that the majority here should have applied, the judge argued, to affirm the district court's ruling of inadequate evidence to establish knowledge as it did in *Rodriguez*.

In a case involving the applicability of the Religious Freedom Restoration Act (Act) to an ADEA case, *Hankins v. Lyght*, 441 F. 3d 96 (2d Cir. 2006), Judge Sotomayor dissented. She objected to the majority ruling that the Act applied on the ground that defendants had waived this defense. Pastor John Paul Hankins claimed he was discriminated against because the New York Annual Conference of the United Methodist Church (Conference) forced him into retirement at age 70, that was further exacerbated by Bishop Lyght's policy not to reappoint mandatory retirees. The EEOC issued a Right to Sue Letter that contained errors. The district court granted a 12(b)(6) motion based on the ministerial exception to the ADEA—a rule adopted by several circuits that civil rights laws cannot govern church employment relationships with ministers without violating the free exercise clause because they substantially burden religious freedom. It cited as authority, *McClure v. Salvation Army*, 460 F.2d 553, 560 (5th Cir. 1972), concluding that applying Title VII to the church-minister relationship «would result in an encroachment by the State into an area of religious freedom into which it is forbidden to enter by the Free Exercise Clause. The Second Circuit underwent a thorough analysis of the RFRA to conclude that its statutory language was clear and on point as restricting the courts from applying the

ADEA under the ministerial exception. In her dissent, Judge Sotomayor wrote the RFRA was not relevant because the appellees did not raise an RFRA defense and thus, the statutory protections were waived. As a third ground, she wrote, "we should affirm the judgment of the district court without reaching the RFRA issue on the ground that Supreme Court and Second Circuit precedent compels a finding that the [ADEA]...does not govern disputes between a religious entity and its spiritual leaders. The majority's opinion thus violates a cardinal principle of judicial restraint by reaching unnecessarily the question of RFRA's constitutionality." *Hankins v. Lyght*, 441 F. 3d at 114–115.[29]

Hayden, et al. v. Pataki, 449 F. 3d 305 (2d Cir. 2006) *en banc*, involved the right of felons and parolees on parole for felony convictions to vote under Section 2 of the VRA) and New York Election Law, § 5-106(2). Due to substantially similar issues, *Hayden* was consolidated with *Muntaqim v. Coombe*, 366 F.3d 102 (2d Cir. 2004). The *en banc* court entered an order deconsolidating the *Muntaqim* and *Hayden* cases and filed a separate opinion vacating the district court's opinion in *Muntaqim* on the ground that the plaintiff in that case lacked standing to bring a claim. *Hayden* involved twenty-one plaintiffs and was a class action lawsuit of Black and Latino prisoners (six who were incarcerated and four who were on parole for felony convictions) who were U.S. citizens of lawful age to vote in New York. The prisoners/parolees alleged they are denied an equal opportunity to participate in the political process in New York State because of the disproportionate disfranchisement under New York State Election Law of Black and Latino persons who are incarcerated or on parole for a felony conviction. In the opinion written by Judge Jose Cabranes, the Second Circuit applied the clear statement rule (applied when the statute is ambiguous, "admits of an interpretation that would alter the federal balance") and upheld their disenfranchisement. *Hayden*, 449 F. 3d at 325. Four dissents were filed in the case, including a lengthy one by Judge Barrington Parker which Judge Sotomayor joined. Her brief dissent to the majority's decision was to address one point, that the "duty of the judge is to follow the law, not to question its plain terms...or to invent exceptions to the statutes it has created." The judge's observation was made in response to the majority's conclusion that "there was a wealth of persuasive evidence that Congress intended disenfranchisement laws to be immune from scrutiny under the Act." *Hayden*, 449 F. 3d at 367–368.

c. Judge Sotomayor's Second Circuit Opinions Affirmed and Reversed by SCOTUS

SCOTUS granted certiorari in seventeen of Judge Sotomayor's cases: thirteen were of precedential value and four non-precedential. Certiorari was denied by

---

29. For further discussion *see*, Steven M. Shepard, *The RFRA Defense to Federal Discrimination Claims*, Yale Law & Policy Review, Vol. 26, No. 1 (Fall, 2007), pp. 359–366, available at: https ://www-jstor-org.du.idm.oclc.org/ stable/pdf/40239696.pdf?refreqid=fastlydefault%3A1c5f468e5c 621013704c28b5075c1feb&ab_segments=&initiator=&acceptTC=1.

SCOTUS in 340 cases in which the judge wrote the majority opinions: 125 were of precedential value and 215 were non-precedential.[30] Only five of her decisions were reviewed by the U.S. Supreme Court: two were affirmed and three were reversed. SCOTUS upheld the judge's majority opinions in *Empire Healthchoice Assur., Inc. v. McVeigh,* 396 F. 3d 136 (Cir. 2005), *aff'd,* 547 U.S. 677 (2006) (writing that Empire's case arose under state law and not under the Federal Employees Health Benefits Act of 1959, 5 U.S.C. § 8902(a), and could only arise under federal common law, the judge concluded, if federal law governed the Empire's claim in the first instance) and *William Rudkin Testamentary Trust v. Comm'r,* 467 F. 3d 149 (2d Cir. 2006), aff'd, *Knight v. Comm'r,* 552 U.S. 181, 128 S.Ct. 782, 169 L. Ed. 652 (2008) (the judge writing that investment-advice fees incurred by a trust created upon the sale by Pepperidge Farm to the Campbell Soup Company, are subject to the two-percent floor of 26 U.S.C. § 67(a) and thus, are not fully deductible). In two of the three reversals, a few of the more liberal justices dissented, agreeing with Judge Sotomayor's rulings, including in a *Bivens* action.

1. *Correctional Services Corporation v. Malesko,* 229 F.3d 374 (2d Cir. 2000), *rev'd,* 534 U.S. 61, 122 S. Ct. 515 (2001), was a 5–4 decision in which the Supreme Court reversed Judge Sotomayor's ruling that an inmate, John Malesko, could sue a private contractor who operated a halfway house on behalf of the Bureau of Prisons (BOP) over injuries he sustained. Petitioner Correctional Services Corporation (CSC) contracted with BOP in the operation of its Le Marquis Community Correctional Facility (Le Marquis), which houses federal inmates. Le Marquis adopted a policy that mandated inmates residing below the sixth floor of the facility to use the stairs, rather than the elevator. Malesko was assigned a room on the fifth floor and had a heart condition that impaired his ability to take stairs, therefore, he was exempted from the policy. CSC forbade Malesko from using the elevator and directed him to take the stairs when he suffered a heart attack, fell, and sustained injuries. Malesko filed a damages action against the petitioner. The district court treated Malesko's case as raising a *Bivens* issue, *Bivens v. Six Unknown Fed. Narcotics Agents,* 403 U.S. 388 (1971). In *Bivens* for the first time, the Supreme Court recognized a private right of action against federal officers who violated a citizen's constitutional rights. Relying on *FDIC v. Meyer,* 510 U.S. 471 (1994), the district court dismissed Malesko's action against CSC as a corporate agency, which was not recognized by *Bivens.* On appeal to the Second Circuit, Judge Sotomayor, while recognizing *Bivens* sanctioned private actions against federal agents but not agencies, nevertheless expanded the private right of action against private entities. She reasoned those agencies, acting under color of federal law, which engage in constitutional deprivations should be held liable under *Bivens.* This interpretation would accomplish the goal of providing citizens a remedy to address constitutional violations. The judge reversed the district court's ruling in part and remanded. Justice Rehnquist, writing for the majority, held

30. *Supra* fn. 17, Sotomayor Questionnaire at 249–269.

that *Bivens* was decided to provide remedy against individual federal agents for engaging in unconstitutional violations, not agencies. The justice identified the only two exceptions made—both involving individual officers, *Carlson v. Green*, 446 U.S. 14 (1980), and *Davis v. Passman*, 442 U.S. 228 (1979)—for a plaintiff to sue where no other alternate remedy existed. He stressed, "*Meyer* made clear… that the threat of suit against an individual's employer was not the kind of deterrence contemplated by *Bivens*… [f]or if a corporate defendant is available for suit, claimants will focus their collection efforts on it, and not the individual directly responsible for the alleged injury." *Malesko* 534 U.S. at 63. Justices Souter, Ginsburg, and Breyer joined in Justice Stevens's dissent.

2. *Entergy v. Riverkeeper*, 475 F.3d 83 (2d Cir. 2007), *rev'd* 556 U.S. 208, 129 S. Ct. 1498 (2009), involved the Clean Water Act (Act), 33 U.S.C. § 1326 (b). Judge Sotomayor ruled in favor of Respondent environmental groups and various states, writing that the Environmental Protection Agency (EPA) could not use a cost-benefit analysis under the Act to determine the best technology available for minimizing adverse environmental impact. Upon a 6–3 vote in an opinion written by Justice Scalia, the Supreme Court reversed the judge, concluding it was well within the EPA's discretion to determine whether to employ a cost-benefit analysis that is not forbidden under the new regulations. At issue were regulations promulgated by the EPA pursuant to the Act, § 1326 (b), Phase I and Phase II regulations. Section 1316 of the Act requires the EPA to essentially choose the best technology for minimizing the adverse environmental impact on aquatic life. Departing from thirty years of employing a case-by-case analysis to determine the best technology, the EPA passed the Phase I and II regulations to govern their choices in selecting new cooling water intake structures. Such cooling structures threaten aquatic life by squashing or suctioning them into the cooling systems through intake screens. Phase I regulations governed new cooling water intake structures, while Phase II regulations applied to certain large existing facilities that adopted new national standards to reduce impingement mortality for aquatic organisms. Phase II regulations also included baseline calculations and percentages that had to be met. The EPA declined to mandate closed-cycle cooling systems for existing facilities, as the cost would be exorbitant and because other technologies could approach the performance of closed-cycle operation. The Phase II rules also permitted site-specific variances from the national performance standards, provided other conditions were met in accordance with §125.94(a)(5)(i), (ii). Concluding that the Phase II cost-benefit analysis was impermissible and unlawful under § 1326 (b), Judge Sotomayor remanded the matter back to the EPA to clarify whether it had relied on cost-benefit analysis in setting the national performance standards.

In his majority opinion, Justice Scalia adopted the opposite view—a cost-benefit analysis in setting national performance standards in Phase II regulations, relying on *Chevron U.S.A., Inc. v. Natural Resources Defense Council, Inc.*, 467 U.S. 837 (1984) (Chevron defense). The justice reasoned that the term, "minimizing adverse environmental impact," in contrast to the plain language of other statutes mandating certain outcomes or technology, suggested the EPA had some discretion to determine the extent of the reduction warranted. He similarly interpreted the word "plausibly" used in the regulations to buttress his conclusion that a consideration of the cost and benefits was permissible. Justice Stevens filed a dissenting opinion, joined by Souter and Ginsburg; Justice Breyer dissented in part. The essence of the justices' dissents who agreed with Judge Sotomayor was that the Act was mandatory, not discretionary. The justices concluded that the EPA misinterpreted its obligation under § 1326(b) based on the plain language that the EPA "shall require" that the cooling structures "reflect the best technology for minimizing adverse environmental impact." *Entergy,* 556 U.S. at 237–238. The justices also based their interpretation of the Act on the legislative history that established Congress purposefully withheld cost-benefit authority from EPA regulations governing the type of technology chosen and the standards by which it chose such technology. Based on that same history, the justices noted that Congress intended the EPA to adopt regulations that required facilities to adopt the best available demonstrated control technology that reflected the greatest degree of "effluent reduction." *Entergy,* 556 U.S. at 245. The justices thus concluded that Congress forbade the EPA to implement a cost-benefit analysis. Ironically, Justice Alito concurred with the majority opinion in *Loper Bright Enterprises v. Raimondo,* ___ U.S. ___, 144 S. Ct. 2244 (2024), that overruled *Chevron.* Chief Justice Roberts ruled that courts need not, and under the APA, may not defer to an agency's interpretation of the law simply because a statute is ambiguous.

3. *Dabit v. Merrill Lynch, Pierce, Fenner & Smith,* 395 F. 3d 25 (2d Cir. 2005), *vacated, Merrill Lynch, Pierce, Fenner & Smith v. Dabit,* 547 U.S. 71 (2006), were two consolidated appeals (oral argument and opinion) to decide a preemption issue of first impression in the circuit involving the Securities Litigation Uniform Standards Act of 1998 ("SLUSA"), Pub.L. No. 105-353, 112 Stat. 3227. SLUSA preempts certain class actions based upon state law brought by private parties alleging a misrepresentation or omission "in connection with the purchase or sale" of certain nationally traded securities, that do not assert reliance upon the defendant's alleged misconduct. SLUSA § 101(b), 112 Stat. at 3230 (codified at 15 U.S.C. § 78bb(f). Upon investigation by the New York Attorney General into conflicts of interest that arose within Merrill Lynch Co., Inc. and Merrill Lynch Pierce Fenner Smith, Inc. (Merrill Lynch), the plaintiffs sued. Plaintiffs claimed Merrill Lynch issued investment recommendations based upon biased research that was designed to garner investment banking business. Plaintiff Dabit brought a putative class action against Merrill Lynch in federal court in Oklahoma on diversity grounds. Plaintiffs-appellants IJG Investments Limited Partnership ("IJG Investments") and Irlys Guy (IJG) brought a putative class action against Merrill Lynch in Minnesota state court. After removal of the IJG action to federal court and subsequent coordinated proceedings in the Southern District of New York, the district court dismissed the lawsuits under Federal Rule of Civil Procedure 12(b)(6) as preempted by SLUSA. The Second Circuit reversed,

Judge Sotomayor writing that SLUSA should be interpreted to give standing only to purchasers of sellers of securities and not holders. The judge wrote this application was consistent with other circuits deciding the issue and further with the holding in *Blue Chip Stamps v. Mano Drug Stores,* 421 U.S. 723 (1975). She concluded that this approach enhanced judicial efficiency as only claims for which there was a federal remedy would be preempted. SCOTUS reversed the Second Circuit. Justice Stevens wrote the near-unanimous decision (Justice Alito took no part) that SLUSA should continue to preempt claims by holders of securities even if they had no federal remedies because SLUSA does not pre-empt all claims but denies only the use of the class-action device to vindicate certain claims.

Two additional cases in which Judge Sotomayor participated were overturned by SCOTUS. *Lopez Torres v. N.Y. State Bd. of Elections*, 462 F. 3d 161 (2d Cir. 2006), *rev'd,* 128 S. Ct. 791, 169 L. Ed. 2d 665 (2008), involved a challenge to New York's election law governing the selection of judges, N.Y. Elec. L. §§ 6-106–124. The law required successful judicial candidates to recruit and manage slates of delegates in each assembly district, to conduct individualized voter education campaigns because the delegates could not be associated with the judicial candidate, among other responsibilities. The Second Circuit agreed with the district court that the law imposed severe burdens on the First Amendment associational rights of candidates and voters. Focusing on the associational rights of political parties, SCOTUS reversed concluding it was the right of political parties to structure procedures to select candidates, regardless of the burden imposed on candidates who were not endorsed by the party leadership.

Ricci v. Destefano, 264 Fed. Appx. 106 (2d Cir. 2008), was the initial panel decision issued by Judge Sotomayor that was replaced with an *en banc* decision in which Judge Sotomayor participated, 530 F.3d 88 (2d Cir. 2008), *rev'd,* at 557 U.S. 557 (2009). This case is notable for the new test adopted by SCOTUS. An employment discrimination lawsuit was filed by seventeen white firefighters and one Hispanic firefighter when the New Haven (City) Civil Service Board (Board) refused to certify their promotional tests for vacant lieutenant and captain positions. Among the plaintiffs was a firefighter who had dyslexia and put in additional work to pass the test. No black firefights and few other Latinos passed the promotional test, but some had qualified in tests taken in prior years. Confronted with arguments for and against certifying the test results—and threats of a lawsuit either way—the City threw out the results based on the statistical racial disparity. The plaintiffs alleged discrimination under Title VII and violations under the Equal Protection Clause of the Fourteenth Amendment. Judge Sotomayor upheld the Board's right to throw out the test and start anew. Before the district court, the Board asserted that if they certified the test results, they could have faced Title VII liability for adopting a practice which had a disparate impact on the City's minority firefighters. On this basis, the district court granted summary judgment in favor of the defendants. A Second Circuit panel that included Judge Sotomayor issued a brief, unsigned summary order affirming the lower court's ruling, 264 Fed. Appx. 106 (2d Cir. 2008). This order was replaced with an expanded *per curiam* decision that was reviewed by SCOTUS. Circuit Judge Jose Cabranes filed a strongly worded dissent and objected to the handling of the case and requested that the circuit court hear the case *en banc*. Judge Sotomayor joined six other colleagues who voted (7–6) to decline rehearing the case.

In a 5–4 decision, SCOTUS reversed with Justice Kennedy writing the opinion. He wrote the decision to cancel the promotions violated the Equal Protection Clause of the Fourteenth Amendment as well as Title VII which guarantees equal employment opportunity. The justice concluded the Second Circuit's ruling would allow the city to "experiment" with tests until they found one that produced "a more desirable racial distribution." A new test was adopted to address the predicament and tension in *Ricci* to eliminate government-imposed discrimination on others. Justice Kennedy wrote, "All the evidence demonstrates that the City rejected the test results because the higher scoring candidates were white. Without some other justification, this express, race-based decision-making is prohibited. The question, therefore, is whether the purpose to avoid disparate-impact liability excuses what otherwise would be prohibited disparate-treatment discrimination." The justice recognized cases which held that certain governmental actions to remedy past racial discrimination is possible and constitutional where there is a "strong basis in evidence," that the remedial actions were necessary citing, *Richmond v. J.A. Croson Co.*, 488 U.S. 469 (1989), and *Wygant v. Jackson Bd., of Ed.*, 476 U.S. 267 (1986). Justice Kennedy noted that the Wygant plurality reasoned that "[e]videntiary support for the conclusion that remedial action is warranted becomes crucial when the remedial program is challenged in court by nonminority employees." Wygant, 476 U.S. at 277. He concluded that the same interests exist between Title VII's disparate-treatment and disparate-impact provisions, especially regarding the prohibition on adjusting employment-related test scores based on race, §2000e–2(l), and the protection of bona fide promotional exams, see §2000e–2(h). The justice held that before an employer can engage in intentional discrimination to avoid unintentional disparate impact, the employer must have a strong basis in evidence to believe it will be subject to disparate-impact liability if it fails to take the race-conscious action. He concluded the City was not facing disparate-impact liability because the promotional tests were job related and consistent with its business necessity. The justice held that the defendants could not satisfy the strong-basis-in-evidence standard, nor did the defendants submit evidence of an equally valid, less discriminatory testing alternative. He concluded the City's refusal to certify the promotional results violated Title VII.

Judge Sotomayor remained on the Second Circuit until 2009 when she was nominated and confirmed to the U.S. Supreme Court. The HNBA endorsed Judge Sotomayor for the country's highest court. Testifying before the Senate Judiciary Committee, then HNBA President Ramona Romero stated:

While the HNBA is proud that Judge Sotomayor is Latina, we support her confirmation because she is unquestionably well-qualified under the objective and subjective standards that have traditionally been applied to Supreme Court nominees. We base our endorsement on our due diligence evaluation of her credentials, judicial record, and reputation. Judge Sotomayor offers an unquestionable integrity, temperament, commitment to equal justice and record of service to the American public and the Hispanic community. Moreover, Judge Sotomayor has extraordinary academic credentials, a varied professional background and more judicial experience than any of the current members of the Supreme Court at the time of confirmation.

The HNBA has been looking forward to this moment for decades. For a variety of reasons, including our interest in preserving public trust in the Supreme Court, the HNBA has long advocated for the appointment of a Justice of Hispanic descent... All [past HNBA presidents] have worked to educate the public on the importance of a diverse judiciary and on the practical, intellectual and symbolic significant of Hispanic presence on the Supreme Court.[31]

3. Kim McLane Wardlaw, Ninth Circuit Court of Appeals, 1998–Incumbent

In describing the Ninth Circuit Judge, one legal news journal wrote:

Kim McLane Wardlaw worked closely with both former President Bill Clinton, a Democrat, and former Los Angeles Mayor Richard Riordan, a Republican. It is telling that both politicians were accused by members of their own party as gravitating toward the opposition. While it is perhaps not prudent to compare politicians to judges, Wardlaw shares something with both men: She is comfortable holding views that are not in lockstep with the expectations of prevailing wisdom. Put another way, Judge Wardlaw can be unpredictable. The Clinton appointee has a wicked curveball. [32]

The judge has been described as a "natural born judge," "sharp-eyed pragmatist" and a highly prepared judge who marches, on some issues, to the beat of her own drum. Among those appearing before her, she is known as a "stickler for procedure" who sets a high bar. Her expectations of lawyers are to "know the appropriate law better than [she does]," as well as to answer her questions directly, else they will be

31. *Supra* note 15 HNBA Law Journal at 172–173, Written Statement of the Hispanic National Bar Association In Support Of The Confirmation Of The Honorable Sonia Sotomayor As Associate Justice Of The Supreme Court Of The United States, Submitted On July 15, 2009 By Ramona Romero, National President.

32. *Judicial Profile: Kim McLane Wardlaw; Ninth Circuit Court of Appeals,* The Recorder, November 7, 2001.

called to task.[33] The judge's humor and light heartedness may be gleaned from certain majority opinions that extends to (non-binding) opinions in non-judicial arenas. *See* for example, "Judging A Book, Wardlaw Reviews 'Hamilton and the Law: Reading Today's Most Contentious Legal Issues Through the Hit Musical." In her review, the judge opined, "'Hamilton and the Law' has the seemingly incongruous effect of drawing the reader into America's formative history while also contemplating the intractable issues facing us today, including racial justice, immigration and gender equality."[34] A survey of Judge McLane Wardlaw's work reveals a thoughtful, thorough jurist who, as noted, marches to her own drum.

Circuit Court Judge McLane Wardlaw participated in a minimum of 7,937 cases and up to 10,104.[35] She authored the majority opinion in 336 cases and wrote or joined in 97 dissents. The judge's opinions by areas of law[36] are:

1. Civil Procedure **268**
2. Criminal Law **164**
3. Constitutional Law **147**
4. Governments **146**
5. Evidence **134**
6. Bs/Corporate Compliance **180**
7. Administrative Law **79**
8. Immigration Law **62**
9. Torts **51**
10. Civil Rights **50**

The judge rendered opinions in cases involving issues as diverse as the landscape of the Ninth Circuit itself. From the Hawaiian harbor to Alaskan forests to major government agencies in large California cities, the judge applied her judicial skills (and humor) to answer the questions at hand. At the outset of a copyright case, the judge wrote, "Inspector Jacques Clouseau, famously unable to crack the simplest of murder cases, would most certainly be confounded by the case we face. While Inspector Clouseau searched for the answer to the question, "Who did it?", we must search for the answer to the question, "Who owns it?" *Richlin v. MGM Pictures, Inc.*, 531 F. 3d 962, 964 (9th Cir. 2008).

33. *Id.*

34. Author Lisa Tucker's essays, Law360, December 1, 2020, https://www.law360.com/articles/1299572.

35. As of March 27, 2025, Westlaw reports 7,937 cases while Lexis reports 10,104 cases.

36. Lexis, Judge McLane Wardlaw Opinions by Areas of Law (based on cases).

a. Majority Opinions

During her tenure, Judge McLane Wardlaw has issued majority opinions and participated in *en banc* decisions whose rulings had precedential value nationally, with a few garnering international attention. Writing for the majority in *Altmann v. Republic of Austria*, 317 F. 3d 954 (9th Cir. 2002) Judge McLane Wardlaw ruled that the Foreign Sovereign Immunities Act (FSIA), 28 U.S.C. §§1602–1611, conferred jurisdiction in U.S. federal courts over Austria and its state-owned gallery. The ruling permitted Mrs. Altmann to recover her family's Gustav Klimt's paintings taken during WWII that were stolen by the Nazis.[37] The judge analyzed and applied principles of sovereign immunity and retroactivity in rendering the decision. *Compare Von Saher v. Norton Simon Museum of Art*, 897 F. 3d 1141 (9th Cir. 2018), in which Judge McLane Wardlaw concurred with the majority ruling against Marei von Saher in her quest to recover two Renaissance oil paintings (Adam and Eve) painted by Lucas Cranach the Elder. The Cranachs were taken from her father in law in a forced sale by the Nazis during WWII. The paintings were restored to the Dutch government which had established a claims process to which von Saher declined to participate upon advice of counsel, unlike the circumstances involving Mrs. Altmann. This was one of several cases in which the judge rendered majority opinions involving other countries.

While the judge did not write the opinion, she was part of an important Ninth Circuit case, *Summerlin v. Stewart*, 341 F. 3d 1082 (9th Cir. 2003). The majority reversed the death sentence of Summerlin because it was imposed by a judge rather than a jury giving retroactive effect to *Ring v. Arizona*, 536 U.S. 584, 122 S.Ct. 2428, 153 L.Ed.2d (2002). The court in *Ring* vacated a death penalty sentence imposed by a judge in violation of the Sixth Amendment right to a trial by jury. In so doing, the Ninth Circuit overturned slightly more than 100 death sentences in Arizona, Idaho, Nevada and Montana.[38] In *Ellis v. U.S. District Court*, 356 F. 3d 1198 (9th Cir. 2004), Judge McLane Wardlaw wrote the majority for a split *en banc* panel. The case was remanded back to a new judge because the sentencing judge reinstated a first-degree murder against the sixteen-year-old defendant that had been negotiated away between the prosecutor and defense counsel. Concluding that the trial court judge exceeded his authority, she wrote, "[w]hile the district court did not violate Rule 11's proscription against participating in plea negotiations, it effectively and improperly inserted itself into the charging decision by vacating Ellis' plea and reinstating the first degree murder indictment. The procedures contemplated by Rule 11 guard

---

37. *See* Lisa Iadevaia, *Atlmann v. Republic of Austria,* 317 F.3d 954 (9 Cir. 2002), 13 DePaul J. Art, Tech. & Intell.

Prop. L. 481 (2003); the 2015 motion picture *Woman in Gold* depicts a part of the district court proceeding.

38. Jason Hoppin, *9th Circuit Voids More Than 100 Death Sentences,* Daily Report, September 4, 2003; *see also* Terrance E. Egland, *Summerlin v. Stewart* 341 F.2d 1082 (9th Cir. 2003), 16 Cap. DEF J. 319 (2003).

against an intrusion of this nature into the separate powers of the executive branch." *Ellis*, 356 F. 3d at 1209. The writ of mandamus was granted.

Judge McLane Wardlaw issued the split panel decision affirming the district court's decision to grant a writ of habeas corpus to Isaac Ramirez in *Ramirez v. Castro*, 365 F. 3d 755 (9th Cir. 2004). Ramirez was sentenced to 25-years-to-life in prison for stealing a $199 video cassette player from a Sears Department Store. The State of California (State) appealed the district court ruling that its Three Strikes Law, Cal. Penal Code §§ 667, 667.5 and 1170.12 violated the Eighth Amendment's right to be free from cruel and unusual punishment. Both the California Supreme Court and Court of Appeals denied Ramirez's petition. The federal magistrate judge's order concluded there was a constitutional violation and that the denial of Ramirez's petition by the California Court of Appeals to reduce his sentence was objectively unreasonable under 28 U.S.C. §§ 2254(d)(1). Ramirez was released from prison on June 17, 2002 after having served five and half years and returned to work for his church. The State appealed that order. In 1991, five years before the Sears theft, Ramirez pled guilty to two nonviolent shoplifting counts charged as second-degree felonies. Ramirez was sentenced to one year in county jail. In this case, Ramirez was charged with petty theft with a prior felony known as a "wobbler" offense for which he was convicted (the crime could have been charged as a misdemeanor). Upon a bifurcated trial in 1997, the jury found that the two 1991 convictions were strikes pursuant to the Three Strikes Law. The lower state superior court judge considered Ramirez a "professional theft" because he had taped up the VCR box and found a seller who had a "constant pattern" of stealing. He was incarcerated in a security level III prison for inmates with several prison terms or significant behavioral problems. Judge McLane Wardlaw noted that the sentence imposed upon Ramirez for three, nonviolent shoplifting offenses (the prior two were outside of the Three Strikes Law) was more severe than had the crimes been murder, manslaughter or rape. The judge evaluated the relevant federal and state law on sentencing disproportionality, including *Rummel v. Estelle*, 445 U.S. 263, 100 S.Ct. 1133, 63 L.Ed. 2d 382 (1980), *Ewing v. California*, 538 U.S. 11, 123 S.Ct. 1179, 155 L.Ed. 2d 108 (2003), *Andrade v. Attorney General*, 270 F. 3d 743 (9th Cir. 2001) and *Lockyer v. Andrade*, 538 U.S. 63, 123 S.Ct. 1166, 155 L.Ed.2d 144 (2003) ("*Andrade II*") recently decided by SCOTUS. The panel asked Ramirez to brief the effect of *Andrade II* on his case. (During the federal court appeal proceedings, Ramirez appeared *pro se*.) She also undertook a thorough interjurisdictional comparative analysis of sentences, contrasting what Ramirez would have been sentenced to under both California and federal law. Judge McLane Wardlaw computed the maximum sentence Ramirez would have received under federal law was seven months in prison. Judge McLane Wardlaw addressed the dissent's concern by writing that such analysis did not "trample" upon California's authority because "there does not appear to be any other jurisdiction in the country that would have imposed a sentence...". *Ramirez*, 365 F.3d at 773. She noted, "Ramirez's sentence of 25 years to life in prison is grossly disproportionate to the offenses he committed. The California appellate court's decision to the contrary is an objectively unreasonable application of clearly established federal law because it erroneously characterizes and otherwise fails to consider the unique, objective factual circumstances of Ramirez's case." *Ramirez,* 365 F.3d at 775. The panel found Ramirez's sentence violated the Eighth Amendment. The dissenting opinion admitted the sentence was harsh but not unreasonable under AEDPA and further, turned on the deference that should be given to the State.

Judge McLane Wardlaw wrote the panel decisions in other criminal cases alleging constitutional violations. In *Bryan v. McPherson*, 630 F.3d 805 (9th Cir. 2009) a case of first impression nationwide, the judge wrote that the use of tasers and similar devices must be justified by a strong government interest that "compels" the employment of such force—no justification, no warning given here for the use of force. In *United States v. Chapman,* 524 F. 3d 1073 (9th Cir. 2009), she affirmed the district court's dismissal of 64 charges and refusal to grant a new trial. She wrote that the two federal Nevada prosecutors unconstitutionally withheld 650 pages of exculpatory evidence in a stock fraud case, concluding it was the highest form of prosecutorial misconduct. At issue in *Sassounian v. Roe,* 230 F. 3d 1097 (9th Cir. 2000), was improper jury deliberation. The jurors deliberated the defendant's guilty during a phone conversation with a reporter. The ethnic Armenian defendant was convicted of assassinating the Turkish Consul General in Los Angeles with a special circumstance of nationality and was sentenced to life without the possibility of parole. The Justice Commandos for the Armenian Genocide claimed responsibility for the assassination though there was no evidence submitted at trial that Sassounian was a member of that group. The issue was discussed during a sidebar but not admitted into evidence. Judge McLane Wardlaw wrote that the jury may have improperly found a special circumstance of killing because of nationality due to the conversation with the journalist that required reversal.

Protesters filed a lawsuit against the U.S. Coast Guard for establishing a security zone to protect and ensure Hawaii's Superferry's operation could dock ferries in the Nawiliwili Harbor in Kauai. In *Wong v. Bush*, 542 F. 3d 732 (9th Cir. 2008), the protesters asserted their First Amendment rights were violated by the zone because it prevented them from accessing and stopping the docking—from protesting effectively. Further, they alleged the security zone violated the National Environmental Policy Act (NEPA), and the law governing the Coast Guard's authority to create security zones in U.S. waters and harbors, specifically 50 U.S.C.S. § 191 and 33, and 33 C.F.R. § 165.30. While recognizing the First Amendment rights of the protesters, Judge McLane Wardlaw wrote that the Coast Guard did not exceed its authority or violate NEPA because its purpose was to secure the safety of those involved; the acts were neither arbitrary nor capricious.

Judge McLane Wardlaw wrote the majority opinion in *Mann v. City of San Diego*, 907 F. 3d 1154 (9th Cir. 2018), finding that the county violated the parents' Fourth and

Fourteenth Amendment rights pursuant to § 1983 by violating their privacy rights and failing to provide due process notification. The parents were professionals, the father a director at a university and the mother, a nurse. Upon an allegation of child abuse, the county removed four children from their home. The triplets were aged four and the older child was six. Two incidents prompted removal; one was a red mark found by the preschool on the back of one of the triplets which the father admitted he caused with a wooden spoon in a "misguided" effort to calm the child. The father cooperated with the preschool's mandatory reporting to the county's health and human services agency (HHSA) and the parents signed a voluntary safety plan. The second, a bruise on the forehead of another child, was noticed during an HHSA visit. Ultimately, the examining physician determined that the bruise was accidentally caused when the child hit his forehead on a kitchen counter as reported by the mother. Notwithstanding their cooperation, HHSA prepared a dependency application which omitted exculpatory information which resulted in the children's removal to Polinsky Children's Center (Polinsky). The district court later concluded that the omitted evidence would have rendered the application insufficient. The parents appeared at a detention hearing where the county obtained their consent to treatment by a private physician. During this time and without the parents' knowledge, the children underwent gynecological and rectal exams that involved visual and tactile inspections at Polinsky—the exams were described more graphically in the opinion. The children were released to their parents the following day and the dependency proceedings were dismissed due to insufficient evidence. The parents were not notified of the medical exams by the county, only learning from one of the children that she was touched "down there." Relying as authority on *Wallis v. Spencer*, 202 F. 3d 1126 (9th Cir. 2000), the judge wrote that the parent's Fourteenth Amendment substantive due process rights were violated by the county's examination of the children and by its failure to notify and obtain parental consent, noting there were no exigent circumstances warranting such exams. The county argued Wallis was inapplicable because it involved investigatory exams, unlike the "assessment exams" conducted here, The judge wrote, "[t]he County's attempts to parse a purely non-investigatory purpose out of the Polinsky medical examinations are not persuasive." *Mann*, 907 F. 3d at 1161. She concluded the exams conducted were not routine pediatric exams and that, absent parental notice, consent and/or court order, *Wallis* applied to investigatory and dual-purpose examinations. *Wallis*, 202 F. 3d at 1162.

Other cases authored by Judge McLane Wardlaw involving or impacting minors include *Flores-Chavez v. Ashcroft*, 362 F. 3d 1150 (9th Cir. 2004) (deportation proceedings reopened for juvenile alien where custodian adult had not received notice and order to show cause and where notice was defective), *Redding v. Safford Unified Sch. Dist. #1*, 531 F. 3d 1071 (9th Cir. 2008) (school officials violated student's constitutional rights by conducting a strip search for pain relievers based upon an uncorroborated tip from a fellow student), *Sklar v. Comm'r*, 549 F. 3d 1252 (9th Cir. 2008) (upheld decision by the U.S. Tax Court ruling that the IRS disallowance of deductions for children's Orthodox Jewish day schools was not deductible because the payments were for purely religious benefits and did not constitute an exception), *C.W. v. Capistrano Unified Sch. Dist.*, 779 F. 3d 956 (9th Cir. 2015) (attorneys' fees improperly awarded to school district where parents' IDEA claims were not frivolous) and *Grizzell v. San Elijo Elem. Sch.*, 110 F. 4th 1177 (9th Cir. 2024) (upheld adjudication by district court that plaintiff could not represent her children pro se and dismissal of plaintiff's claims brought on their behalf because plaintiff was not an attorney).

In a copyright case involving the limited use of plaintiff's photo, *Bell v. Wilmott Storage Servs., LLC,* 12 F. 4th 1065 (9th Cir. 2021), the issue was whether the number of times of the infringement—*de minimus* concept—eradicated the infringement or, whether it was a defense to an infringement action. Richard Bell, an attorney, took a photo of the Indianapolis skyline and posted it on his firm's website and another one of his websites. The photo was appropriated without Bell's permission and posted on a rarely used and hard to access website. Interpreting 17 U.S.C.S. § 106 (Exclusive rights in copyright works), Judge McLane Wardlaw wrote, "[t]he de minimis concept is properly used to analyze whether so little of a copyrighted work has been copied that the allegedly infringing work is not substantially similar to the copyrighted work and is thus non-infringing." *Bell,* 12 F. 4th at 1068. She concluded that *de minimus* use was not a defense once an infringement was established. The district court's grant of summary judgment in favor of the defendant on the *de minimus* use theory was reversed. In another copyright case, *Richlin v. MGM Pictures, Inc., supra*, the judge ruled that the heirs of the author who created a story treatment used to create the motion picture, The Pink Panther, had no interest in the copyright. She recognized that the ancestor did not co-own the treatment or motion picture and failed to file for copyright protection, thus, the treatment was never "invested with statutory copyright. Lastly, the judge concluded the right to renew the original term of the copyright had not vested in the ancestor nor reverted to the plaintiffs. In a case involving another set of beneficiaries—those of Marilyn Monroe—*Milton H. Greene Archives, Inc. v. Marilyn Monroe LLC,* 692 F. 3d 983 (9th Cir. 2012), the judge held the beneficiaries of her estate under California law did not inherit a right of publicity through a residual clause in her will because the executors asserted Ms. Monroe was domiciled in New York at the time of her death.

In a Title VII case, Judge McLane Wardlaw recognized in *Okonowsky v. Garland,* 109 F. 4th 1166 (2024), that conduct occurring entirely off the jobsite and unrelated to the workplace may still constitute a sexual hostile work environment, abrogating an inapposite nonpublished ruling. A federal prison psychologist left her job after the prison failed to act on her complaint about a co-worker who posted online sexually hostile materials targeting her. These postings were viewed by and generated comments from co-workers. In assessing whether the postings were sufficiently severe or pervasive to alter the conditions of employment, the judge determined that under the totality of the circumstances, the postings created a hostile work environment for Okonowsky. In reaching this conclusion, the judge specially noted the digital aspect of the work environment and the "workplace ratification of or acquiescence to offsite conduct by employees." *Okonowsky*, 109 F.4th at 1181.

The judge was required to interpret South Africa's Employment Equity Act 55 of 1998 (Act) in *Gormley v. Ashcroft*, 364 F. 3d 1172 (Cir. 2004). The judge found no reverse discrimination in the application of that law. In June 1999, Michael and Edith Gormley visited the United States as non-immigrant "B-2" visitors that was extended to November. On August 6, 1999, Mr. Gormley filed asylum applications for himself and his wife citing as grounds actual and imputed political opinion—they feared persecution if returned to Africa because they are white. In his affidavit, Mr. Gormley stated that under the Act, the new South African government gave job preferences to blacks, rendering him unable to obtain employment. He further alleged that with the fall of apartheid, crime escalated and he was the victim of two robberies. In the first robbery, his cell phone was taken and six months later in a second robbery held up by "steak knives," his cell phone and watch were taken. Mr. Gormley alleged a third attempted but averted robbery. The crimes, according to Mr. Gormley, were committed by black men and/or black teenage youths. Mr. Gormley last asserted he was laid off as a scaffolding contract supervisor after 27 years of service because the company adopted an affirmation action production policy pursuant to the Act. The denial of asylum by the BIA was upheld. Judge McLane Wardlaw noted in her opinion that there was no credible, direct or specific evidence the robberies were based on race, i.e., they offered no subjectively genuine fear of persecution or evidence that could be construed as objectively reasonable to support a finding of persecution. Mr. Gormley's own statements established that members of his social group found work after being fired, both black and white blue-collar workers in South Africa experienced job loss and had difficulty finding jobs, and that their two sons were employed there. While the judge acknowledged the Gormleys' fear of adverse economic consequences and potential future criminal attacks, the evidence did not amount to persecution warranting asylum. Contrast *Gormley* with the inapposite result in *Kaiser v. Ashcroft*, 390 F. 3d 653 (9th Cir. 2004) where the judge found a Pakistani family met the burden of proof required to establish eligibility for asylum based upon concrete evidence of future persecution directed to the family because of the father's military service as a commissioned officer in the Pakistani Army.

Judge McLane Wardlaw delivered the panel's unanimous decision involving the Deferred Actions for Childhood Arrivals (DACA) in *Regents of the Univ. of Cal. v. United States Dept. of Homeland Sec. (Regents)*, 875 F. 3d 476 (9th Cir. 2017), *rev'd Trump v. United States Dist. of N. Cal.*, 875 F. 3d 1200 (9th Cir. 2017). The judge captured the underlying relevant facts of the case by summarizing the life of a Dreamer:

> It is no hyperbole to say that Dulce Garcia embodies the American dream. Born into poverty, Garcia and her parents shared a San Diego house with other families to save money on rent; she was even homeless for a time as a child. But she studied hard and excelled academically in high school. When her family could not afford to send her to the top university where she had been accepted, Gar-

> cia enrolled in a local community college and ultimately put herself through a four-year university, where she again excelled while working full-time as a legal assistant. She then was awarded a scholarship that, together with her mother's life savings, enabled her to fulfill her longstanding dream of attending and graduating from law school. Today, Garcia maintains a thriving legal practice in San Diego, where she represents members of underserved communities in civil, criminal, and immigration proceedings. On the surface, Dulce Garcia appears no different from any other productive—indeed, inspiring—young American. But one thing sets her apart. Garcia's parents brought her to this country in violation of United States immigration laws when she was four years old. Though the United States of America is the only home she has ever known, Dulce Garcia is an undocumented immigrant. *Regents supra* at 485–486.

Under the Obama administration on June 15, 2012, the Secretary of Homeland Security Janet Napolitano announced the DACA program granting non-citizens such as attorney Garcia "who unwittingly entered the [U.S.] as children" to apply for two-year renewal periods of deferred action to remain in the U.S. DACA recipients or "Dreamers" as they have become known, must have been under sixteen when they entered the country, continuously lived in the U.S. for at least five years preceding the start of the program, present in the country and in school, graduated from high school, obtained a general education development certificate or is an honorably discharged Coast Guard or Armed Forces veteran, has a clean criminal record and was not above the age of thirty when the program began. Dreamers are permitted to work legally and pay taxes. The deferred action is revocable. With the change in administrations in 2017, the government moved to end the DACA program. "Why? According to the Acting Secretary of Homeland Security, upon the legal advice of the Attorney General [Jeff Sessions], DACA was illegal from its inception and could no longer continue" and upon challenge by Garcia and others, "the government adopted the position that its fundamentally legal determination that DACA is unlawful is *unreviewable* by the judicial branch." [Emphasis added.] Judge Wardlaw, *Regent,* 875 F. 3d at 486.

The judge reviewed the history of deferred action by the U.S. government, DACA, and the Obama administration's adoption in 2014 of the Deferred Action for Parents of Americans and Lawful Permanent Residents program (DAPA). DAPA permitted noncitizen parents of American citizens and lawful permanent residents to remain in the country and also expanded DACA from two to three-year extensions. DAPA and the DACA extension were challenged in court by twenty-six state attorney generals. Its implementation was enjoined by the district court's imposition of a nationwide injunction. (DAPA ultimately was rescinded, significantly, as an exercise of discretion.) Texas Attorney General Paxton (AG Paxton) wrote Attorney General Sessions threatening he would amend the lawsuit then pending in the Fifth Circuit unless DACA was rescinded. One day before AG Paxton's deadline expired, Attorney General Sessions rescinded DACA. The challenge was upheld by a divided Fifth Circuit panel and affirmed by an equally divided

SCOTUS. The Fifth Circuit held that DAPA exceeded Homeland Security's statutory authority and would irreparably harm Texas. *Texas v. United States*, 809 F. 3d 134 (5th Cir. 2015), was affirmed by an equally divided court in 597 U.S. 547 (2016). The original DACA program remained in effect.

Against this backdrop, the legal issue before Judge McLane Wardlaw was whether the decision by Homeland Security to end DACA was reviewable, the government asserting that the APA and the INA, 8 U.S.C.§ 1252(g), precluded judicial review. Judge McLane Wardlaw analyzed the issue of reviewability under the APA and INA and concluded neither precluded judicial review. The judge cited black letter law to conclude that Homeland Security could not rely on its opinion that the DACA program was illegally formed as the basis for asserting its recission was not judicially reviewable. The judge scrutinized each of the reasons asserted by Attorney General Sessions for DACA's recission, concluding the reasons were based upon an incorrect interpretation of executive power, rather than act of discretion that made it reviewable under the APA, 5 U.S.C.S. §702, Right of judicial review. Further, she wrote that DACA was a permissible exercise of executive discretion pursuant to 6 U.S.C.S. § 202(5), Border, Maritime, and Transportation Security:

> With due respect for the Executive Branch, we disagree. The government may not simultaneously both assert that its actions are legally compelled, based on its interpretation of the law, and avoid review of that assertion by the judicial branch, whose "province and duty" it is "to say what the law is." *Marbury v. Madison,* 5 U.S. (1 Cranch) 137, 177, 2 L. Ed. 60 (1803). The government's decision to rescind DACA is subject to judicial review. And, upon review, we conclude that plaintiffs are likely to succeed on their claim that the rescission of DACA—at least as justified on this record—is arbitrary, capricious, or otherwise not in accordance with law. *Regents,* 875 F. 3d at 486.

Next, the judge addressed the merits of the preliminary injunction granted by the district court on the grounds that plaintiffs met all four standards for granting the injunction, including the likelihood of success on the merits. The government responded to only this latter standard, asserting that because it determined its decision was not judicially reviewable, the plaintiffs could not prevail. Turning to the scope and necessity of a nationwide injunction, Judge Wardlaw McLane quoted the Fifth Circuit's rationale in *Texas v. U.S., supra,* to conclude that the very same rationale used to support a nationwide injunction in that case was as applicable here. "As the Fifth Circuit stated when it affirmed the nationwide injunction against DAPA, 'the Constitution requires a *uniform* Rule of Naturalization; Congress has instructed that the immigration laws of the United States should be enforced vigorously and *uniformly*; and the Supreme Court has described immigration policy as a comprehensive and *unified* system.' *Texas,* 809 F. 3d at 187-88. Allowing uneven application of nationwide immigration policy flies in the face of these requirements." *Regents,* 875 F. 3d at 511. She held that the district court did not abuse its discretion in granting the nationwide injunction. In his concurrence, Judge John B. Owens added:

> .... I would hold that Plaintiffs have plausibly alleged that the rescission of DACA was motivated by unconstitutional racial animus in violation of the Equal Protection component of the Fifth Amendment, and that the district court correctly denied the government's motion to dismiss this claim... As the majority details, the record assembled at this early stage is promising. Plaintiffs highlight (1) the disproportionate impact DACA's rescission has on "individuals of Mexican heritage, and Latinos, who together account for 93 percent of approved DACA applications"; (2) a litany of statements by the President and high-ranking members of his Administration that plausibly indicate animus toward undocumented immigrants from Central America; and (3) substantial procedural irregularities in the challenged agency action. *Regents,* 875 F. 3rd at 524.

b. Dissents[39]

In her twenty-seven year tenure on the Ninth Circuit, Judge Wardlaw has issued 96 dissents. *Free Speech Coalition v. Reno,* 198 F. 3d 1083 (9th Cir. 1999), *rev'd Ashcroft v. Free Speech Coalition,* 535 U.S. 234 (2002), struck down the Child Pornography Prevention Act of 1996 ("CPPA") by ruling that the First Amendment prohibits Congress from enacting laws that proscribes as child pornography and makes criminal the generation of virtual images of fictitious children engaged in imaginary, explicit sexual conduct. In *Free Speech Coalition v. Reno,* 220 F. 3d 1113 (2000), Judge McLane Wardlaw objected to the majority's decision denying an *en banc* rehearing of the split-panel decision. She reasoned that the majority disregarded the physical and psychological welfare of minors and ignored the real harm caused by virtual pornography, as well as decisions of sister-circuits on this issue—the Supreme Court had yet to address virtual pornography. The judge cautioned the future use of technology such as to impair ability in the future to distinguish between real and virtual child pornography.

Taylor v. United States, 143 F. 3d 1178 (9th Cir. 1998), involved a lawsuit by two inmate-plaintiffs, two inmates who challenged the Arizona's inmate behavior and discipline rules and procedures, and deprivation of two-for-one good behavior time. On December 22,1972, the parties entered into a consent decree and a final order was issued on October 19, 1973 (Judgment). Defendants moved to terminate the consent decree asserting that the Prison Litigation Reform Act of 1995 (PLRA), 18 U.S.C.A. § 3626(b)(2), specifically, the termination provisions to prospective relief were applicable. (Congress passed the PLRA to oust the judiciary from day-to-day prison management and authorizes prison officials to obtain immediate termination of prospective relief granted under consent decrees.) Defendants further argued that a final prospective order does not represent the last word of the judicial department on a particular case or controversy. Plaintiffs contended that a consent decree imposing

39. Lexis, last accessed March 27, 2025.

prospective relief is a final judgment and moved to declare this section of the PLRA unconstitutional. The lower court found the order was not the final judgment, that the motion to terminate was moot as there was no consent decree left to be terminated once judgment was entered and declared the PLRA's termination provisions unconstitutional. A Ninth Circuit panel affirmed the district court's invalidation of the termination provision. Thereafter, the Ninth Circuit heard the case *en banc* and affirmed the lower court's denial of the motion to terminate the consent decree. In the majority's opinion, there was no separation of powers issue (as the dissent argued) because the matter was rendered moot by the 1973 order. Judge McLane Wardlaw objected because the Ninth Circuit was the only court that declared the PLRA unconstitutional. She wrote, "...the majority today firmly entrenches the Ninth Circuit outside the judicial mainstream of PLRA interpretation. Worse, it effectively precludes Congress from limiting prospectively a discrete kind of federal district court expropriation of power from democratically-elected state governments." *Taylor*, 143 F. 3d at 1028. The judge disagreed that the matter was moot as the consent decree provisions were embodied in the Judgment and further, noted it continued to provide prospective relief.

The judge wrote several dissents in cases involving minors, including *Camfield v. Bd. of Trustees of Redondo Beach Unified Sch. Dist.*, 800 Fed. Appx. 491 (9th Cir. 2020). The judge dissented in part to the majority's finding that the plaintiff did not established a prima facie case of retaliation (conceded by the district) under the ADA and Rehabilitation Act. She concluded the mother submitted sufficient evidence of pretext to overcome the school district's evidence including that they offered inconsistent justifications. The evidence of pretext included use of a Disruptive Parent Letter (DPL) to substantiate its adverse action against her when the acts complained of in the DPL consisted of advocacy on behalf of her disabled son. In *Tobias v. East*, 803 Fed. Appx. 93 (9th Cir. 2020), the judge disagreed with the majority finding Fifth and Fourteenth Amendment violations. She wrote that the interrogation tactics used by police against a thirteen-year-old juvenile who invoked his right to counsel throughout and later was exonerated from the murder, violated his constitutional rights. The judge's dissent in *Martinez-Cedillo v. Sessions*, 896 F. 3d 979 (9th Cir. 2018) has been cited as authority on the issue of adjudicating a separation of families as child abuse. Martinez, a legal resident alien for twenty-five years, was convicted of driving under the influence (DUI) on two occasions (one year apart). He pled guilty to a vehicle violation and DUI. The crimes to which Martinez pled were not deportable felonies. Both times, Martinez's younger son was in the car not wearing a seat belt, but he was not injured. Homeland Security thereafter instituted deportation proceedings charging Martinez had been convicted of a crime of child abuse, neglect or abandonment pursuant to 8 U.S.C. §1227(a)(2)(E)(i) which Martinez appealed. The BIA found Martinez's conviction was the categorical equivalent of child abuse and upheld his removal even though its definition of child abuse at the time of Martinez's conviction required physical injury. Martinez left behind his two

American born children. Throughout, the defense asserted Martinez's conduct was neither felonious nor met the BIA's changing definition of child abuse. The Ninth Circuit held that the BIA was entitled to the *Chevron* defense and deferred to its definition of child abuse. Judge McLane Wardlaw objected, concluding the majority strayed far from Congressional intent. She issued a comprehensive and lengthy analysis, pointedly and persuasively challenging the majority's findings and highlighting faulty rationale that included relying on civil law to define a criminal child abuse offense. (The judge noted the BIA admitted reliance upon civil child endangerment statutes to define child abuse.) The judge found the BIA's definition was ever-changing such as to render it justiciably unadministrable and overly vague. Noting BIA's definition required physical injury at the time Martinez-Cedillo pled guilty, the judge further objected to the Ninth Circuit's retroactive application of the BIA's definition of child abuse (stating it was particularly underserving of retroactivity). The current version did not require physical injury to the child to Martinez. Judge McLane Wardlaw noted that the BIA's deportation of Martinez resulted in a family separation for lapses in judgment in childrearing, not envisioned by enactment of the statute. She wrote:

> The majority's willfully blind characterization of the Board's dithering definitions of this deportable offense does not match reality. It should not be lost on us that, while we fault Martinez for endangering his son, we simultaneously condone the separation of a family, exiling a father of two children who has resided in the United States lawfully for more than twenty-five years. That Congress did not intend such a result is apparent from these facts. *Martinez-Cedillo,* 896 F. 3d at 1002.

Issuing another lengthy dissent in *Desire, LLC v. Manna Textiles, Inc.*, 986 F. 3d 1253 (2021), Judge McLane Wardlaw objected to the majority ruling in a textile infringement copyright case that reduced multiple statutory awards down to one. At issue was the number of damages that could be awarded pursuant to the Copyright Act, 17 U.S.C.S. § 504(c)(1). Desiree LLC won $480,000 against Manna Textiles which took Desiree's flower design and sold knockoffs to retailers such as Burlington Coat Factory; it resulted in multiple damages awards. The majority decided, contrary to Ninth Circuit precedent, that under joint liability, only a single award per case could be awarded.

In *Friends of Alaska National Wildlife Refuges v. Haaland*, 29 F.4th 432 (9th Cir. 2022), Judge McLane Wardlaw objected to the majority's ruling over a land exchange which pitted environmental preservation concerns against the economic interest of the Alaskan Native village of King Cove. The exchange would allow access to Cold Bay City by building a road through the Izembek National Wildlife Refuge. In 2013, under the Obama administration, former Interior Secretary Sally Jewell rejected the land exchange that was later approved in 2019 by successor Interior Secretary David Bernhardt. The majority overturned the district court's set aside of the land-exchange agreement deciding Bernardt had supplied the necessary justification and did not arbitrarily contradict Secretary Jewell's findings. Judge McLane Wardlaw concluded Secretary Bernhardt violated both the APA and the Alaska National Interest Lands Conservation Act,[40] by failing to provide justification for reversing the earlier administration's decision and further, failing to adequately justify the change under the APA. The judge wrote, "Congress ... did not give carte blanche to the Interior Department to depredate Alaska's irreplaceable natural wonders under the guise of pursuing the economic and social needs of Alaskans." *Friends,* 29 F.4th at 451.

c. Judge McLane Wardlaw's Ninth Circuit Majority Opinions Reversed by SCOTUS

Of the Luminaria Circuit Court judges, Judge McLane Wardlaw has had (to date) the most cases reversed by the Supreme Court. With the current composition of the highest court and the Ninth Circuit considered the most liberal, it may not be surprising. In these cases, the judge tackled complex and original issues that continue to address the issues confronting North American society. Her opinions reveal thoroughly researched and well-reasoned decisions.

1. *Department of Transp. v. Public Citizens,* 316 F.3d 1002 (9th Cir. 2003), *rev'd,* 541 U.S. 752 (2004). In this case, unions and environmental groups petitioned the Court for review of an order of the Department of Transportation (Department) and the Federal Motor Carrier Safety Administration (FMCSA), regarding the promulgation of three regulations. The regulations were promulgated when the moratorium imposed by Congress in 1982 was lifted by President G.W. Bush in 2001. The moratorium prohibited Mexican motor carriers from obtaining operating authority in the United States; lifting the moratorium fulfilled one of the obligations of the United States under the North American Free Trade Agreement (NAFTA). The regulations established the application form for such carriers, and another addressed a safety-inspection regiment. Congress thereafter passed a provision that no funds would be appropriated or obligated to fund a review or process Mexican motor carrier applications until FMCSA passed safety-monitoring requirements. Judge McLane Wardlaw granted the petition, concluding the Department failed to prepare in-depth Environmental Impact Statements and conformity determinations required under the National Environmental Policy Act of 1969 (NEPA) and the Clean Air Act (CAA).[41] She remanded the matter back to the Department. Justice Clarence Thomas held that because FMCSA lacked the discretion to prevent cross-border operations of Mexican motor carriers, the FMSCA was not required to evaluate the environmental effect of such operations under the National Environmental Policy Act (NEPA) or the Clean Air Act (CAA), 42 U.S.C. § 7506(c)(1).[42]

---

40. Pub.L. No. 96-487, 94 Stat. 2371 (1980).

41. NEPA, Pub. L. No. 91-190, 83 Sta. 852 (1970), 42 U.S.C. §§ 4321–4370f; and CAA, 42 U.S.C. §§ 7401–7671q; NAFTA, Dec. 17, 1992, U.S.-Can.-Mex., 32 I.L.M. 289 (chptrs. 1–9), 32 I.L.M. 605 (chptrs. 10–22) (1993).

42. 42 U.S.C. § 7401 *et seq. (1970).*

2. *Whitman v. Dept. of Transportation*, 382 F.3d 938 (9th Cir. 2006), *rev'd*, 547 U.S. 512 (2006) (per curiam). Terry Whitman was an employee of the Federal Aviation Administration (FAA) and was subject to its drug and alcohol testing program. Without first pursuing internal grievance procedures under the collective bargaining agreement (CBA), Whitman filed suit in the District of Alaska. He alleged the FAA tested him in a nonrandom manner in violation of his constitutional rights and 49 U.S.C. §45104(8), Alcohol and Controlled Substances Testing. The FAA adopted certain sections of the Civil Service Reform Act of 1978 (CSRA), including Chapter 71 of Title 5, which sets forth the rules for grievances under 49 U.S. C. § 40122(g)(2)(C) (Section 5). The district court held that under CSRA, it did not have jurisdiction to consider the Whitman's claims. Judge Wardlaw affirmed the district court's conclusion that Whitman's claims were precluded, because she interpreted Section 5[43] as not expressly conferring federal court jurisdiction over employment-related claims covered by the grievance procedures negotiated by the federal employees' CBA. The Supreme Court acknowledged that Judge McLane Wardlaw correctly interpreted Section 5 but identified 28 U.S.C. § 1331 (Section 1331) as conferring jurisdiction to "all civil actions arising under the Constitution, laws, or treaties of the United States." The question became whether the federal courts are divested completely of jurisdiction or if the CSRA removes the jurisdiction given to the federal courts under Section 1331. To address that inquiry, it cited *Verizon Md. Inc. v. Public Serv. Comm'n of Md.*, 535 U.S. 635 (2002), holding that even if the statute at issue does not *confer* jurisdiction, "it at least does not *divest* the district courts of their authority under Section 1331 to review the Commission's order for compliance with federal law." *Whitman* 382 F.3d at 514. The Supreme Court remanded to the Eleventh Circuit to decide the question of jurisdiction and preclusion, by first determining where Whitman's claims fit within the CSRA's statutory scheme (i.e., to ascertain if his claim was a prohibited personnel practice since the CSRA proscribes different treatment for grievances depending on the nature of the claim). On remand, the Ninth Circuit was instructed to address the remaining issues, including whether Whitman challenged final agency action, exhausted his administrative remedies, and whether exhaustion is required given the CSRA statutory scheme pursuant to the Administrative Procedure Act, as interpreted in *Darby v. Cisneros*, 509 U.S. 137 (1993), and whether the government has forfeited its exhaustion-of-remedies argument. The Supreme Court hinted that resolution of any of these questions may not warrant an analysis of preclusion.

3. Judge McLane Wardlaw's decision in *McDaniel v. Brown*, 525 F.3d 787 (2007), was reversed and remanded by the SCOTUS, 558 U.S. 120, 130 S. Ct. 665 (2009) (per curiam). Nine-year-old Jane Doe was sexually assaulted in her trailer home in Carlin, Nevada; the assault occurred sometime between approximately midnight and 12:40 a.m. Jane was home alone with her four-year-old sister while their mother,

43. 5 U.S.C. § 7121(a)(1), as amended in 1994.

Pam, was drinking at a bar. Troy Brown (Brown), the brother of Pam's friend Trent, was arrested, tried, and convicted for this crime. There was conflicting testimony from Pam and bartenders as to when Brown was last seen at the bar, from between 11 p.m. up to 1:30 a.m. Between midnight and 12:30 a.m., Jane called Pam at the bar and explained that some man was at the trailer looking for Pam and had hurt her. When Pam arrived home, she found Jane covered in blood from the waist down and called 911. A police officer and the paramedics responded. Jane told the paramedic that she felt pain in her vaginal area. Pam told police that her ex-husband had done this because he previously threatened to assault Jane to get at her (Pam). (The father was at work during the assault.) At the hospital, the assault was confirmed; a vaginal smear was taken because sperm was present. Jane had bruises on her neck and scratches on her face. Debris was collected from Jane's teeth because she stated she had bitten the assailant's hands. Jane described the assailant that matched the description of Brown, including his clothing. Brown's trailer was ten trailers away from Pam's trailer. Two witnesses testified that, at 1:05 a.m. that morning, they saw a man near Jane's trailer wearing a cowboy hat, dark jeans, and a black satin jacket with a bright green emblem on the back that looked like a skull or bandit. Brown stated he had been drinking steadily that night and, while walking home to his trailer, had vomited and soiled his pants and shirt. When Brown arrived home, Travis awoke from sleeping on the couch around 1:32 a.m. Travis stated he did not see any traces of blood in the house. Brown washed his clothes as soon as he returned home because he was leaving for Utah for a week. When a police officer arrived at 5 a.m. to question Brown, he saw no blood on Brown or his boots and no evidence of bite marks. Jane stated she fell asleep with a night light on, but that the man who assaulted her must have turned it off because it was off when the man left. Brown's fingerprints were not found anywhere in Jane's trailer, and the one fingerprint found on the night light did not match Brown's. Thereafter, Jane gave conflicting accounts of her assailant, including that it was Trent, not Brown. Brown requested a full-body examination to be conducted by a nurse to record his physical condition. In early February 7, Brown voluntarily surrendered to the police and was arrested. Throughout the proceedings, Brown repeatedly denied involvement in the crime.

At trial, DNA expert Renee Romero testified there was a 99.99957 percent chance that Brown was the assailant. The jury found Brown guilty of two counts of sexual assault on a child under the age of fourteen and one count of abuse or neglect of a child resulting in substantial bodily harm. Brown appealed to the Nevada Supreme Court, claiming the district court abused its discretion when sentencing him, the bar against double jeopardy was violated by the duplicative convictions for sexual assault and abuse or neglect of a child, the DNA evidence was improperly admitted, and the evidence was insufficient to sustain his conviction. The Nevada Supreme Court vacated one charge and remanded for resentencing on the second sexual assault count. The trial court resentenced Brown to life with the possibility of parole after ten years on both sexual assault counts, to run consecutively. Brown unsuccessfully appealed a second time to the Nevada Supreme Court and then filed a state petition for post-conviction relief. The judge allowed Brown to expand the record with an uncontested report by Dr. Laurence Mueller (Mueller Report) that discredited Romero's testimony and report. The state court denied relief. Judge McLane Wardlaw agreed with Brown that in the absence of Romero's discredited testimony, there would have been insufficient evidence to convict him. She also agreed with the district court that the Nevada Supreme Court decision was contrary to and an unreasonable application of established U.S. Supreme Court precedent, *Jackson v. Virginia*, 443 U.S. 307 (1979). The judge further held that there was no error in allowing Brown to supplement the record under 28 U.S.C. § 2254(e)(2), even though none of the conditions were met pursuant to an exception where, as here, Brown exercised due diligence to develop the factual basis for his claims in state proceedings. *Cooper-Smith v. Palmateer*, 397 F.3d 1236, at 1241 (9th Cir. 2005). Judge McLane Wardlaw concluded that the prosecutor's fallacy occurred in Brown's case in that Romero's testimony conflated random match probability with source probability—the prosecutor elicited statistical testimony from Romero to suggest the DNA indicates the likelihood of Brown's guilt, rather than the odds of the evidence having been found in a randomly selected sample. *Brown* at 795–796. She also concluded that Romero minimized the possibility that the DNA would match one of his four brothers. Judge Wardlaw affirmed the district court's grant of Brown's habeas petition on due process grounds.

The Supreme Court reversed and remanded Judge McLane Wardlaw's decision on numerous grounds, including that the district court erred in admitting Mueller's report to evaluate Brown's *Jackson v. Virginia* claim; the state supreme court's rejection of defendant's insufficiency of the evidence claim was not an unreasonable application of federal law to federal habeas relief; and Brown forfeited his claim that errors by the state' constituted unnecessarily suggestive identification testimony in violation of due process.[44] It granted certiorari to consider two issues: the proper standard of review for a *Jackson* claim on federal habeas and whether outside evidence outside the trial record that goes to the reliability of the evidence may be considered. Before rendering its decision, the parties agreed that the circuit court erred by resolving Brown's claim under *Jackson*; nevertheless, the Supreme Court held there was sufficient evidence to sustain Brown's conviction. The Supreme Court agreed that the state fell into the prosecutor's fallacy but found the two errors made by Romero were insufficient to warrant a reversal. In so ruling it rejected Brown's claim that under *Manson v. Brathwaite*, 432 U.S. 98 (1977), a reversal is required because, due to Romero's errors, he was denied due process of law—the Court ruling this alternate ground was waived by Brown.

4. *AT&T Corp. v. Hulteen*, 556 U.S. 701 (2009), reversed Judge McLane Wardlaw's decision in *Hulteen v. AT&T*, 498 F. 3d 1002 (9th Cir. 2007). She delivered the major-

44. The state was represented by Catherine Cortez Masto, then Nevada's attorney general.

ity opinion finding that AT&T's retirement credit policy violated the Pregnancy Discrimination Act (PDA) because AT&T failed to count pregnancy leave when determining retirement eligibility. This case was discussed previously in Chapter 1, Luminaria Irma Herrera and the Equal Rights Advocate. *Hulteen* is one of the rare cases that involved Luminarias from lower court litigation to appeal—from Luminaria activistas to the Circuit Court. Arguably, it represents a consensus among the leading Luminarias practicing at the time of how the PDA should be interpreted and applied to benefit women in the country, with Justice Ginsburg concurring.

5. *Quon v. Arch Wireless Operating Co., Inc.*, 529 F. 3d 892 (9th Cir. 2008), *rev'd*, City of *Ontario v. Quon*, 560 U.S. 746, 130 S.Ct. 2619, 177 L Ed. 2d 216 (2010). Arch Wireless was contracted by the city of Ontario (City) to provide to Ontario's Police Department (OPD) wireless text-messaging services through alphanumeric pagers. The pagers were distributed to Sergeant Quon (Quon) and other OPD employees. The City had only a general policy on computer usage, internet and e-mail (Policy) which limited usage to City related business; the pagers had a monthly word limitation. In 2000, the sergeants signed a form indicating that (1) the City reserved the right to monitor and log all network activity including e-mail and Internet use, with or without notice, (2) users should have no expectation of privacy or confidentiality when using these resources and (3) they had read and fully understood the City's Policy. Two years later, Quon attended a meeting during which Lieutenant Steve Duke (also an administrator), informed those present that the pager messages were considered e-mail, and such messages would fall under the Policy as public information, and were eligible for auditing which Quon only vaguely remembered. Quon (and others) exceeded the monthly charges three to four times and paid for the overages upon appraisal by Lt. Duke. In another meeting, Lt. Duke stated he was tired of overages and would request an audit and obtain transcripts of messages, including from Quon. An audit was conducted and sexually explicit messages sent by Quon to his wife Jerilyn Quon, Sergeant Steve Trujillo and OPD dispatcher April Florio were discovered and transcribed. These were reviewed by OPD Chief Lloyd Scharf in late 2001–early 2002. The sergeants sued the company and the City, alleging invasion of their privacy and those to whom the messages were sent, unreasonable search in violation of the Fourth Amendment and Article I, Section 1 of the California constitution, as well as violation of the Stored Communications Act (SCA), 18 U.S.C. §§ 2701–2711 (1986). The SCA prevents providers of communication services from divulging private communications to certain entities and/or individuals but is exempted from liability as a remote computing service (RCS) under SCA § 2702(a) in contrast to an electronic communication service (ECS) under SCA §§ 2701–2711. Both, however, may release private information with lawful consent of the addressee or intended recipient pursuant to § 2702(b)(1), (b)(3), but only RCS may release messages with the consent of the subscriber, SCA § 2702(a)(2).

The district court ruled Arch Wireless was an RCS and exempt from liability which Judge McLane Wardlaw wrote was an error as the nature of the services was dispositive. She described Arch Wireless' services as facilitating communication, text messaging between pagers over radio frequencies. Upon concluding the City was subscriber and that OPD was not an addressee or intended recipient, she wrote that the City violated the SCA and reversed the district court's ruling. Relying upon *O'Connor v. Ortega,* 480 U.S. 709, 107 S.Ct. 1494, 94 L. Ed. 2d 714 (1987), the district court found Quon had a reasonable expectation of privacy. The judge agreed, writing that the City violated Quon's Fourth Amendment and California constitutional rights of privacy, concluding the search was unreasonable at the outset, noting employees do not lose such rights working for a public employer, citing *O'Connor* as authority. She found Quon's argument persuasive, namely that the informal overage usage procedure implemented by Lt. Duke established for Quon a reasonable expectation of privacy—no audit if overage paid. For purposes of the appeal, SCOTUS assumed Quon had a reasonable expectation of privacy, the search was unreasonable and that the rules of privacy apply to the electronic sphere but refused to address the constitutional privacy issues. It reversed the Ninth Circuit on a narrower basis—legitimate work purpose—concluding that the City's audit of text messages was based upon a legitimate interest in determining whether the City's contract for services with Arch Wireless was sufficient.

6. *Safford Unified School Dist. No. 1 v. Redding,* 557 U.S. 364 (9th Cir. 2009), *reversed* Judge McLane Wardlaw's panel decision in *Redding v. Safford Unified Sch. Dist. #1,* 531 F.3d 1071 (9th Cir. 2008). A middle school student, by her mother and legal guardian, brought a Section 1983 action against the school district, assistant principal, administrative assistant, and school nurse alleging that the strip search to which she was subjected violated her Fourth Amendment rights. The district court granted summary judgment in favor of defendants that was affirmed by Judge Wardlaw at 504 F.3d 828. On rehearing *en banc,* Judge McLane Wardlaw affirmed in part, reversed in part, and remanded. Certiorari was granted. Justice Souter held that the assistant principal had reasonable suspicion that the student was distributing contraband drugs, which did not justify the strip search. As the law on student strip searches was not clearly established, the officials were entitled to qualified immunity. The Supreme Court affirmed and reversed in part and remanded.

7. *National Aeronautics and Space Admin. (NASA) v. Nelson,* 563 U.S. 134 (2011), *reversed* Judge McLane Wardlaw's panel decision in *Nelson v. NASA,* 530 F.3d 865 (2008). The employees at NASA are federal civil servants and contract employees. Contract employees were not subject to the background checks conducted by the National Agency Check with Inquiries (NACI) that involves completing a questionnaire for non-sensitive positions known as the Standard Form 85 (SF-85) until 2011 when President Obama imposed the requirement. Employees filed suit alleging the background check violated a constitutional right to informational privacy as required by SF-85. Judge McLane Wardlaw reversed the district court's decision not to issue a preliminary injunction, ruling that SF-85's questions about drug involvement furthered the government's interests in combatting illegal drug use but concluded

the questions about treatment or counseling did not further that interest. Justice Alito held that the Constitution protects a right to informational privacy but that the questions about employees' treatment or counseling for recent illegal drug use did not violate this right. Lastly, he held that the open-ended questions on the form sent to employees' landlords and designated references also did not violate any such right. As authority, the justice relied on *Whalen v. Roe*, 429 U.S. 589 (1977), and *Nixon v. Administration of General Services*, 433 U.S. 425 (1977), that recognized a constitutional privacy interest in avoiding disclosure of personal matters.

8. *Mercado-Zazueta v. Holder*, 580 F. 3d 1102 (9th Cir. 2009) *rev'd, Holder v. Martinez Gutierrez and Holder v. Sawyers* (*Holder v. Martinez*), 566 U.S. 583, 132 S.Ct. 2011, 182 L.Ed. 2d 922 (2025). *Holder v. Martinez* involved two individuals seeking cancellation of their removal upon imputation of the residency requirement of seven years which the BIA historically had done. This case overrules the Ninth Circuit's rulings on imputation, including *Mercado-Zazueta*. The INA, 8 U.S.C. § 1229(b)(a), establishes the requirements for lawful permanent residency (LPR) and requires presence in the U.S. for five continuous years, which renders one eligible to seek cancellation of a removal order. In *Holder v. Martinez Gutierrez* and *Mercado-Zazueta*, the appellants and Jose Luis Mercado (Mercado) requested cancellation by imputing the seven-year residency requirement based upon their parents' legal status. The Ninth Circuit in *Cuevas-Gaspar*, 430 F. 3d 1013 (9th Cir. 2005) imputed the lawful permanent resident status of a parent to a child, an imputation decision also adopted by the Second and Third Circuits. Mexican native Mercado came into the country at the age of seven in 1992 and lived with his mother who married Ramon Mercado Cuevas that year. Cuevas acquired LPR in 1983 and adopted Mercado in 1998, when he was thirteen years old. Mercado has three siblings, two who are U.S. citizens and a sister who also has LPR. In 2002 at age seventeen, Mercado obtained independent lawful permanent resident status. In 2006, he pled guilty in Arizona to aggravated assault and conceded removability pursuant to section 237 of the INA which covers removal based on crimes involving moral turpitude that are committed within five years after the date of admission. Mercado was determined ineligible for cancellation and his removal was ordered; Mercado timely applied to the BIA for cancellation of removal pursuant to INA § 240 (a), 1229(b(a). In an unpublished case, the BIA expressed disagreement with the Ninth Circuit's decision in *Cuevas-Gaspar* and declined to impute the five-year requirement, instead deciding Mercado had to meet the statutory LPR requirements on his own. Writing for the majority, Judge McLane Wardlaw held that the BIA was compelled to impute under *Cuevas-Gaspar* and its decision to decline was unreasonable. Citing *Cuevas-Gaspar* she wrote, "both the BIA and this court repeatedly have held that a parent's status, intent, or state of mind is imputed to the parent's unemancipated minor child in many areas of immigration law, including asylum, grounds of inadmissibility, and legal residency status." *Mercado-Zazueta v. Holder*, 580 F. 3d at 1104. As to BIA's last objection, Judge McLane Wardlaw noted that the BIA mistakenly asserted that al-

lowing imputation is inconsistent with the purpose of the INA and Congress's intent, writing that silence in the INA regarding imputation suggests acquiescence practice. What the judge found inconsistent was BIA's inconsistent rulings on imputation, and the incongruity of its decision when Mercado acquired LPR and further, could demonstrate continuous presence in the country for more than ten years. She wrote:

> Mercado has spent almost his whole life within the United States. When Mercado was legally adopted at the age of thirteen, he easily could have adjusted his own status with the assistance of his parents. Not only is it absurd to penalize Mercado for his parents' failure to assist him with the adjustment process, but it flies in the face of common sense to conclude that a lawful permanent resident such as Mercado... cannot be eligible for cancellation of removal, which is premised on the longstanding 'congressional policy of recognizing that presence in the United States of an extended length gives rise to such strong ties to the United States that removal would result in undue hardship.

Mercado-Zazueta v. Holder, 580 F. 3d at 1110. The Supreme Court affirmed BIA's decision as consistent with the statutory language and therefore, permissible and held it was within BIA's discretion to require the child to meet the eligibility requirements of the INA. SCOTUS rejected the idea that the Congress ratified an imputation requirement when it adopted § 1229(b)(a) and thus the Ninth Circuit rationale.

9. The consolidated and thrice-appealed case of *Rodriguez v. Robbins*, 804 F. 3d 1060 (9th Cir. 2015)[45], *rev'd, Jennings v. Rodriguez*, 583 ___ U.S. ___, 138 S. Ct. 830 (2018). In this third *Rodriguez* case, Judge McLane Wardlaw delivered the majority opinion. This was a putative class action brought by detained noncitizens against the Immigration and Customs Enforcement (ICE) and others. Under the INA, 8 U.S.C. §§ 1225(b), 1226(a) and (c) and 1231(a)(6) governing detentions, they challenged prolonged detentions without individualized bond hearings and determinations to justify their continued detention.[46] The district court entered a preliminary injunction requiring bond hearings before an IJ that was appealed. Invoking the canon of constitutional avoidance, the judge interpreted the INA as implicitly requiring bond hearings every six months, writing that equity and the public interest would be served by the mandatory bond hearings. Detention beyond the six-month period, she wrote, required the government to prove by clear and convincing evidence that further detention was justified. The panel decision concluded that the attorney general's authority to place aliens in custody for as long as removal proceedings are "pending" cannot be read to authorize mandatory detention with no limit on the duration, opining that unlimited detentions were likely to cause irreparable harm. The panel reached this decision after reviewing Ninth Circuit and SCOTUS cases

45. *See also Rodriguez v. Hayes* (*Rodriguez I*), 591 F. 3d 1105 (9th Cir.) appealing the denial of class certification and *Rodriguez v. Robbins*, 715 F.3d 1127 (2013), *Rodriguez II*, appealing affirming the injunctions and bond hearings.

46. 8 U.S.C. § 1225(b) and (c).

"grappling in piece-meal fashion" with the question of whether federal law authorizes prolonged detention, *Rodriguez*, 804 F. 3d at 1067, as well as other such cases recognizing the constitutional deprivation of rights arising from indefinite detention. In its review of this collective precedent, Judge McLane Wardlaw recognized the implicit and "reasonable limitation" in §1231(a)(6). SCOTUS reversed. Justice Alito rejected the Ninth Circuit's detention limitation. He concluded that the INA could not plausibly be interpreted as implicitly placing a six-month limit on detention or requiring periodic bond hearings.

10. *Cuero v. Cate*, 827 F. 3d 879 (9th Cir. 2016) *rev'd, Kernan v. Cuero*, 583 U.S. 1, 138 S. Ct. 4, 199 L.Ed. 2d 236 (2017). The Supreme Court ruled that the Ninth Circuit mistakenly interpreted and applied federal law by ruling that, upon withdrawal of a guilty plea, the state court must impose the lower sentence that the parties originally expected. In the Ninth Circuit case of parolee Michael Cuero (Cuero), Cuero was charged with two felonies and a misdemeanor stemming from serious injury to a pedestrian with a car while driving under the influence of drugs, without a license and carrying a gun. Cuero pleaded guilty to two felony counts in an amended criminal complaint that included a 14-year, 4-month sentence. Cuero acknowledged the amendment would lead to a higher sentence. The state trial court scheduled a sentencing hearing but before that hearing, the state learned of Cuero's four additional prior convictions that qualified as an additional strike (to the one included in the amended complaint) and moved to amend the criminal complaint. The district court granted the state's motion but also permitted Cuero to withdraw his guilty plea. The state then amended the criminal complaint to one felony count and two strikes upon to which Cuero pled guilty. The district court imposed a minimum 25 year-sentence was imposed which was affirmed on direct appeal; the California Supreme Court and federal district court denied Cuero's petitions for habeas relief. Cuero appealed to the Ninth Circuit, arguing that the agreed upon 14-year, 4-month sentence should have been honored. Delivering the majority's decision, Judge McLane Wardlaw held that the California court made a mistake interpreting federal law and that Cuero was entitled to specific performance of the 14-year, 4-month sentence. Citing as authority the AEDPA, the Ninth Circuit's ruling was reversed, the Supreme Court ruling, *per curiam*, that there was no Supreme Court precedent that clearly established specific performance as a remedy. "Circuit precedent does not constitute "clearly established Federal law." *Kernan v. Cuero*, 583 U.S. at 9.

11. *Dept. of Homeland Sec. v. Regents of the Univ. of Cal*, 591 U.S. 1 (2020), *rev'd Trump v. United States Dist. of N. Cal.* (In re United States), 875 F. 3d 1200 (9th Cir. 2017). This case consolidated three cases which addressed the legality of the DACA recission, *Regents v. United States Dept. of Homeland Sec.* (Regents) *supra, Batalla Vidal v. Nielsen*, 291 F. Supp. 3d 260 (EDNY 2018) and *NAACP v. Trump*, 298 F. Supp. 3d 209 (2018). Chief Justice Roberts delivered the court's opinion. The Supreme Court vacated and reversed *Regents* in part concluding the equal protection guarantee of the Fifth Amendment was not violated based upon the record in the case

which he declared insufficient to support this challenge. Ironically, SCOTUS granted the government's request for a writ of mandamus to abrogate the district court's order in *Regents, supra* that it complete the administrative record which, at that time consisted of—per Judge McLane Wardlaw, only 256 pages used to reverse the legal status of 800,000 people. *Regents,* 875 F. 3d at 493. Ultimately, it was this scant record upon which the Ninth Circuit was required to evaluate and issue its decision and upon which SCOTUS drew its finding of insufficiency. The Supreme Court upheld the *Regents* finding that the DACA recission was reviewable under and violated the APA as it was arbitrary and capricious. Justice Sotomayor concurred with the finding that the DACA recission violated the APA but dissented with the majority on the plaintiffs' equal protection claim. She found the ruling to preclude a challenge to the DACA recission on equal protection grounds was premature based upon the incomplete record and at that preliminary stage of the litigation and would grant plaintiffs the opportunity to develop the record.

12. In *Vega v. Tekoh*, 597 U.S. 134 (2022), the Supreme Court reversed Judge McLane Wardlaw's panel opinion in which she held a suspect's Fifth Amendment right against self-incrimination was violated. The suspect brought an action pursuant to 42 U.S.C. § 1983 against a sheriff's deputy. Deputy Vega did not advise Tekoh of his *Miranda* rights before or during his questioning about touching a patient's genitals, *Miranda v. Arizona*, 384 U.S. 436 (1966). Tekoh alleged the deputy violated his rights by obtaining incriminating statements from him (a written confession) in violation of *Miranda* rights that later were used in criminal proceedings against him. Justice Alito, citing *Dickerson v. United States*, 530 U.S. 428 (2000), held that a *Miranda* violation does not constitute a constitutional deprivation enforceable under § 1983. The justice wrote that assuming the *Miranda* rule protects the Fifth Amendment right against compelled self-incrimination, the rule was not a federal law securing such rights and did not include the right to sue for damages under § 1983.[47]

4. Consuelo Maria Callahan, Ninth Circuit Court of Appeals, 2013 | 2025

Beyond the Ninth Circuit, Judge Callahan sits as president of the Anthony M. Kennedy Inn of Court.[48] Justice Kennedy who sat on the Supreme Court from 1988 to 2018, initially was known as a conservative jurist until 1992 when he co-authored the majority opinion in *Planned Parenthood of Southeastern Pennsylvania v. Carey,* 505 U.S. 833 (1992), upholding the right to abortion in *Roe v. Wade* but permitted state regulation of abortions, issued the majority opinion in *Romer v. Evans,* 517 U.S.

47. Section 1983 provides a cause of action against any person acting under color of state law who subjects a person "to the deprivation of any rights, privileges, or immunities secured by the Constitution and laws."

48. Melanie Padgett Powers, *Judge Consuelo M. Callahan, President American Inns of Court,* September/October 2024. https://home.innsofcourt.org/AIC/AIC_About_Us/Our_President_Consuelo_Callahan.aspx.

620 (1996) striking down Colorado's anti-LGBT state constitutional amendment and was the swing vote in *Obergefell v. Hodges, supra* upholding same-sex marriage. Thereafter, Justice Kennedy became recognized as the swing vote on the court and proponent of individual rights. A review of Judge Callahan's cases shows a conservative bent, expected of a former prosecutor, but defender of individual rights—upon thoughtful scrutiny of the facts and the law. This precisioned and agile approach suits the judge, well known for her love of dance.[49]

a. Majority Opinions

Circuit Judge Callahan authored the majority opinions in 237 cases and dissents in 266 cases. She participated in a minimum of 7,563 (Westlaw) and as many as 9,662 (Lexis). The judge's opinions by areas of law[50] include:

Criminal Law & Procedure **288**

Civil Procedure **281**

Evidence **215**

Governments **131**

Constitutional Law **103**

Administrative law **80**

Torts **67**

Business & Corporate Compliance **58**

Immigration Law **48**

Civil Rights Law **46**

Criminal law and procedure (87) and immigration (39) were the dominant areas of the law in cases comprising more than half—126, of her 237 decisions. The judge evaluated Title VII cases, in criminal law and procedure consisting of constitutional challenges to searches, double jeopardy, ineffective counsel, sentencing/enhancements, and revocation of supervised relief. Immigration matters upon which she opined included multiple asylum cases involving issues of evidence of persecution, continuous presence in the country, need for court-appointed counsel, violation of a protected order, crimes of moral turpitude or nonturpitudinous conduct, illegal reentry, and fundamental changes in the law, as well as cases involving complex procedural matters. *See* for example, *Duran Gonzales v. United States Dept. of Homeland Sec.,* 659 F. 3d 930 (9th Cir. 2011) (*Duran Gonzales III*), involving three iterations of the same issue. In *Duran Gonzales II,* 508 F. 3d 1227 (9th Cir. 2007), six un-

49. Brendan J. Begley, *Courtly Jubilee Celebrates Judge Callahan's 20 Years on the Ninth Circuit,* Sacramento Lawyer, Vol. 2.2023, https://issuu.com/milenkovlais/docs/sacramento_lawyer_mag_cover_publish_2-2023/s/28810487.

50. Lexis, Judge Callahan Opinions by Areas of Law (based on cases), last accessed March 27, 2025.

documented persons who were removed from the country and reentered illegally, filed applications for adjustment of status disclosing these facts and claimed relief under 8 U.S.C. § 1255. They relied upon *Perez–Gonzalez v. Ashcroft,* 379 F. 3d 783 (9th Cir. 2004) which held plaintiffs could file for relief (readmission) inside, rather than outside, the country. The district court certified plaintiffs' proffered class and issued a preliminary injunction on this basis. The government successfully appealed. The Ninth Circuit concluded that it was bound to follow, *In re Torres-Garcia,* 23 I. & N. Dec. 866 (BIA 2006), where it determined that individuals like the plaintiffs were not eligible for relief, notwithstanding the statutory interpretation in *Perez–Gonzalez.* The district court's injunction was vacated and the matter remanded. At issue in *Duran Gonzales III,* was whether the ruling in *Duran Gonzales II* required retroactive or prospective application, the plaintiffs asserting prospective application was appropriate. The majority adopted and applied retroactively *Duran Gonzales II* and affirmed plaintiffs' ineligibility to adjust their legal status which rendered them ineligible to receive I-212 waivers. Judge Callahan wrote retroactivity was especially proper here because the same plaintiffs were involved and another Ninth Circuit panel ruling that *Duran Gonzales II* was retroactive. Accord, *Morales–Izquierdo v. Dep't of Homeland Sec.,* 600 F. 3d 1076 (Cir. 2010).

Ramos v. Wolf, 975 F. 3d 872 (9th Cir. 2020), involved an equal protection challenge to the Trump administration's elimination of the Temporary Protected Status program (TPS), 8 U.S.C. § 1254a(b), to four countries—El Salvador (three earthquakes), Haiti (earthquake), Nicaragua (Hurricane Mitch) and Sudan (civil war) by the Homeland Security Department (Department).[51] Filed by individual citizens, the putative class alleged the Department departed from previous practices and failed to provide adequate explanations for termination under the APA, and that the countries selected was based upon discriminatory animus. Based upon plaintiffs' proffered evidence of Trump's animus against non-European immigrants and his influence over the decision makers, the district court found numerous instances where the White House applied pressure on the Department and individual decision-makers to end TPS for these four countries. TPS provides widescale nationality-based humanitarian harbor for nationals of designated countries stricken by natural disaster, armed conflict or extraordinary and temporary conditions. Under TPS, the Department has the authority to designated which countries come within the ambit of the program's protections if certain criteria are met; those protections lasting from between six to eighteen months. The Department determined summarily that the temporary conditions in each of the four countries no longer merited protection and revoked TPS. Pursuant to § 1254(b)(5)(A), the TPS provides no judi-

51. On March 31, 2025, an order granting injunctive relief was issued by the Ninth Circuit in *NTPSA v. Noem,* Case No. 25-cv-01766-EMC, that enjoins the Trump administration's revocation of existing TPS (never done in 31 years of TPS) for Venezuela on behalf of 600,000 Venezuelan TPS holders, asserting violation of the APA and racial animus. https://www.aclusocal.org/sites/default/files/2025.03.31_93_order_granting_postponement_motion.pdf.

cial review of the Department's designations, extensions or terminations. The district court entered the preliminary injunction finding the statute did not bar general collateral practices or colorable constitutional claims. Applying the Arlington Heights standard (even if no animus is shown to be harbored by deciding officials, their actions could rise to an equal protection violation if they were influenced or manipulated by President Trump's animus),[52] the district court found circumstantial evidence of race as a motivating factor in the TPS terminations. The jurisdictional question was whether the APA conferred jurisdiction to entertain an equal protection challenge. Judge Callahan found the TPS bars judicial review of the Department's country-specific determinations but not over general collateral challenges to the constitutionality of agency's procedures or practices used to make such determinations (*McNary* determinations). *McNary v. Haitian Refugee Center, Inc.*, 498 U.S. 479, 111 S.Ct. 888, 112 L.Ed.2d 1005 (1991). She noted the presumption favoring judicial review over colorable claims but concluded that the plaintiffs failed to genuinely allege or establish a collateral action under the APA and vacated the district court's preliminary injunction. Judge Callahan disposed of the dissent by writing that reconstruction of the plaintiffs' APA claim to fit a *McNary determination* does not save the claims.

The following cases were selected to provide a general survey of Judge Callahan's decisions.

Doe v. Kelly, 878 F. 3d 710 (9th Cir. 2017) concerned the rights and treatment of detainees confined in 2015 under the Obama administration by the U.S. Customs and Border Protection in their facilities along the 262-mile border of Tucson, Arizona and the U.S. (Border Stations). The Defendants represented that between 2009 and 2016, 31,432 apprehensions were made in March 2009, to a low of 4,071 apprehensions in July 2015. Consequently, detainees were held in overcrowded and unsanitary cells at eight different Border Stations. Plaintiffs claimed it took up to three days to process them before being transferred and that they are packed into overcrowded and filthy holding cells, stripped of outer layers of clothing, and forced to endure brutally cold temperatures. They are denied beds, bedding, and sleep and deprived of basic sanitation and hygiene items like soap, sufficient toilet paper, sanitary napkins, diapers, and showers and forced to go without adequate food, water, medicine, and medical care. The class was certified in 2016 and plaintiffs sought injunctive relief. The district court noted that of 16,992 detainees, only 115 detainees were given shows and only 122 received a mat. It concluded the Border Stations simply could not accommodate the number of detainees longer than twelve hours as that duration requires sleep which was the basis of the district court's order to provide mats and blankets. The district court also found that the conditions of confinement imposed by the Border Stations did not meet the National Standards on Transport, Escort,

52. *Arlington Heights v. Metro. Housing Dev. Corp.*, 429 U.S. 252, 97 S.Ct. 555, 50 L. Ed. 2d 450 (1977).

Detention and Search (TEDS standards) and violated the Fifth and Fourteenth Amendments. This determination was based partly upon the testimony of the Assistant Chief Patrol Agent George Allen who admitted that in comparison, criminal detainees at the Santa Cruz County jail had "bed[s], blanket[s], clean clothing, showers, toothbrushes and toothpaste, warm meals and opportunity for uninterrupted sleep." *Doe*, 878 F. 3d at 715. The district court granted the preliminary injunction requiring the Defendants to provide mats and blankets after twelve hours, to provide "some means" for washing or maintaining personal hygiene if held longer than twelve hours and to ensure the medical screening form was used at all eight Border Stations. It denied the parties' motion for reconsideration of the order to impose additional relief. As authority, the district court relied upon *Bell v. Wolfish*, 441 U.S. 520, 99 S.Ct. 1861, 60 L.Ed. 2d 447 (1979) which requires evaluating the totality of pretrial detention conditions to determine whether they amount to punishment and on *Demery v. Arpaio*, 378 F. 3d 1020 (9th Cir. 2004) holding that in evaluating the conditions of the Border Stations, one can infer an intent to punish if the conditions are not reasonably related to a legitimate governmental objective or are excessive in relation to the legitimate governmental objective.

Plaintiffs filed an appeal because the district court failed to order beds and mattresses, showers, and adequate medical care. Defendants appealed, alleging the order was too rigid and burdensome and that the district court erred in applying the *Bell* standard. Judge Callahan upheld the order, noting the district court considered the (temporary) duration of the detention, that the holding cells were not designed for sleeping and have no beds, security/safety reasons compelled that clothing be removed and lights kept on, and that the Plaintiffs submitted persuasive testimony that their human needs were not being met in accordance with TEDS standards. The judge noted there was insufficient evidence of deliberate indifference to the detainees' medical needs as found in the authority cited by plaintiffs, including *Toussaint v. McCarthy*, 801 F. 2d 1080 (9th Cir. 1986). She wrote that the district court "sculptured the relief granted to reflect the unique feature of the Border Patrol stations and field operations" and that "[t]he limited injunction reflects the district court's careful consideration... in light of *Bell*." *Doe*, 878 F. 3d at 720.

In the case of *Scheehle v. Justices of the Supreme Court of Arizona*, 508 F. 3d 887 (9th Cir. 2007), tax attorney Mark Scheehle (Scheehle) appealed his court appointment for a third time as an arbitrator asserting it was an unconstitutional taking of his attorney property rights and deprived him of the economic benefit of his labor. Scheele was admitted in 1981 and had been a certified tax specialist since 1988. The Local Rules of Practice for the Superior Court of Maricopa County, Arizona Revised Statutes §12-133, require all attorneys who are members of the bar for five years and reside in the county must serve as arbitrators twice a year for a flat fee (Appointment System). Those who have served twice may be excused from further service. When appointed a third time, Scheele elected to challenge the Appointment System instead of filing for relief for good cause as suggested by the lower court. The Arizona Supreme Court reaffirmed the district court's summary judgment in favor of the state. Judge Callahan evaluated Scheehle's claims under the Takings Clause of the Fifth Amendment and the regulatory takings test adopted in *Penn Central Transportation Company v. City of New York*, 438 U.S. 104, 98 S.Ct. 2646, 57 L.Ed. 2d 631 (1978). The panel ruled there was no *per se* taking because Scheele was compensated, the economic impact was negligible and admission to the bar included service owed to the court. In *Harger v. DOL*, 569 F. 3d 898 (9th Cir. 2009), Judge Callahan also addressed attorneys' fees, denying an attorney's request to secure a security interest via an equitable fee lien against lump sum payments to be made to claimants under the Energy Employees Occupational Illness Compensation Program Act, 42 U.S.C.S. § 7384 *et seq*.

Allen v. Boeing Co., 784 F. 3d 625 (9th Cir. 2015) involved the local single event exception to the Class Action Fairness Act of 2005, 28 U.S.C.S. § 1332(d)(1)(B)(ii)(I) (CAFA). For decades, from the 1960s to the 1990s, Boeing used and allegedly discharged solvents into the groundwater that contained hazardous chemicals derived from its aircraft parts manufacturing plant in Auburn, Washington. In 1987, the Washington Department of Ecology (Department) initiated requirements for Boeing to treat, store and handle the hazardous materials. In 2002, Boeing entered into an agreement with the Department to investigate and remediate releases of hazardous substances and retained Landau Associates (Landau), an environmental remediation company, to conduct the investigation and remediation. In November 2013, plaintiffs filed an action against Boeing and Landau in King County Superior Court alleging they incurred property damages from the groundwater contamination. They further alleged that Boeing and Landau, were liable for a decade of negligent investigation, remediation, and cleaning and for failing to warn plaintiffs of the contamination. Plaintiffs pled state claims of negligence, nuisance, and trespass against Boeing and negligence against Lanau. Boeing removed the action to federal court, asserting diversity jurisdiction pursuant to CAFA and further alleged Landau had been fraudulently joined to defeat complete diversity. The district court remanded the case to state court holding that (1) Landau was not fraudulently joined, and thus there was not complete diversity, and (2) plaintiffs' action came within the local single event exception to CAFA's federal jurisdiction. Boeing appealed and the Ninth Circuit reversed. Judge Callahan wrote that plaintiffs' action did not come within CAFA's local single event exception and thus, the district court lacked federal jurisdiction under §1332(d)(4)(A). The judge upheld the district court's finding that Boeing failed to establish that Landau was fraudulently joined.

Doe v. Snyder, 28 F. 4th 103 (4th Cir. 2022), was a putative class action involving a sex discrimination lawsuit brought by two transgender teenagers (Doe and D.H.), born female, who sought male chest reconstruction surgery for functional (not cosmetic) purposes. Plaintiffs sought a mandatory preliminary injunction claiming they would suffer irreparable harm if the surgeries were delayed. Both had been undergoing medical treatment for gender dysphoria consisting of hormone therapy and counseling. Their health care providers recommended male chest reconstruction to ameliorate their gender dysphoria. The teenagers sought coverage of their surgeries from the Arizona Health Care Cost Containment System (AHCCCS), and under the Affordable Care Act (ACA), Section 1557 and the Medicaid program. They asserted that Arizona Administrative Code R9-22-205(B)(4) which precluded coverage for gender reassignment was unconstitutional under the Medicaid Act, 42 U.S.C. §§1396a(a)(10)(B) and the Equal Protection Clause of the Fourteenth Amendment. Plaintiffs relied on *Bostock v. Clayton County*, 140 S.Ct. 1731, 207 L. Ed. 2d 218 (2020) to support their claim that denial of benefits under the AHCCCS because they are transgender constituted discrimination. The district court found that the surgeries were neither medically necessary nor effective for correcting or ameliorating their gender dystopia. Its ruling was based *inter alia* upon conflicting endocrinologist and psychiatric expert testimony that the surgeries were medically necessary, the age of one of the minor plaintiffs gave rise to the court's concern that he may not sufficiently appreciate the consequences of irreversible surgery, and the serious psychiatric issues suffered by *Doe,* then 15 years old. Upon filing the appeal, the plaintiffs withdrew their motion for class action and D.H. dismissed his case. Writing for the majority, Judge Callahan first addressed the higher standard for issuing a preliminary mandatory injunction that required a finding of clear error in the district court's factual determinations plus a likelihood of irreparable harm. She concluded the district court's ruling was erroneous, citing as authority *Edmo v. Corizon, Inc.*, 935 F. 3d 757 (9th Cir. 2019) (finding gender confirmation surgery was medically necessary). Judge Callahan did not reach the constitutional arguments pending litigation in the lower court but affirmed the standard of scrutiny adopted in *Karnoski v. Trump*, 926 F. 3d 1180 (9th Cir. 2019)—more than rational basis but less than strict scrutiny. Applying this standard, the judge found the district court's interpretation of *Bostock* was too narrowly interpreted as pertaining only to sex discrimination under Title VII. The judge construed the sex discrimination protections of Title IX and Title VII and found both were consistent and aligned with the protections of Section 1557 of the ACA, prohibiting the denial of benefits on the basis of sex discrimination.

At issue in *Mohammad v. Gen. Consulate of the State of Kuwait in L.A.*, 28 F. 4th 980 (9th Cir. 2022), was diplomatic immunity pursuant to FSIA, 28 U.S.C.S. §1605(a)(2). Plaintiff was of Syrian national origin and worked as an administrative assistant for the State of Kuwait's Consulate in Los Angeles (Consulate) when she was discharged. She filed suit in Los Angeles Superior Court and alleged under California's employment laws, twenty-three claims of discriminatory constructive termination based on her religion, gender and national origin. Plaintiff asserted her claims fell under the FSIA exceptions of commercial activity, expropriation and tort. The Consulate removed the action to federal district court and asserted plaintiff was part of Kuwait's civil service, that her duties included powers peculiar to sovereigns and invoked immunity under FSIA. Addressing the Consulate's motion to dismiss, the district court found partly in plaintiff's favor, ruling she was not part of Kuwait's civil service as her duties and benefits were clerical in nature, not diplomatic or those provided by foreign service officers or those involving public policy and therefore could pursue her claims under California law. The district court further ruled that the claims fell under FSIA's commercial activity exception relying on *Holden v. Canadian Consulate*, 92 F. 3d 918 (9th Cir. 1996). Judge Callahan affirmed the district court's finding that the commercial activity exception applied, but distinguished between the nature of the act or course of conduct that she wrote was determinative, rather than the purpose. She concluded plaintiff was not a servant as her duties did not include "powers peculiar to sovereigns" but were clerical and fell within FSIA's commercial activity exception. Accordingly, the judge found sovereign immunity was properly denied. The judge reaffirmed the Ninth Circuit's ruling in *Holden*, "that the employment of diplomatic, civil service, and military personnel is entitled to immunity." *Holden*, 92 F. 3d at 921.

The judge delivered the majority opinion in *Doe v. Regents of the Univ. of Cal.*, 23 F. 4th 930 (9th Cir. 2022). Doe was a Chinese national Ph.D. chemistry/biochemistry graduate student at UCLA accused of harassing a female student. Doe met a female student in a chemistry class. They began dating, became engaged and planned to marry in June 2017 upon Doe's graduation. The relationship soured when Doe learned his fiancé had been unfaithful during the relationship and broke off in February 2017. They planned to meet to exchange belongings on February 13 after work; by this time, the fiancé was no longer a student. On the morning of February 13, the fiancé appeared unannounced at Doe's office while Doe was meeting with another student. She pounded on the door, refused to leave when Doe opened the door, stood with outstretched arms causing Doe to move around to get to class and followed him to class. She called the University police to report Doe pushed and grabbed her. Doe was arrested for misdemeanor domestic battery. Thereafter, Doe learned that the fiancé withdrew the entire balance of $8,000 from their joint bank account. The ex-fiancé then filed a complaint with the University charging Doe with numerous acts (some dating back to 2014), including having suffered a broken rib which proved untrue. In filing, the ex-fiancé misrepresented to the University that she was still a student. The University charged Doe initially with thirteen violations of its dating violence/policies (four additional charges later were added), including placing the fiancé in fear of bodily harm. During the investigation, Doe was given limited information and brief opportunity to comment or provide new information. He was found guilty of four charges and twelve allegations were dismissed. Over Doe's objections, the University Dean accepted the investigator's findings and suspended Doe for two years which Doe timely appealed. Doe lost his teaching assistant job, housing, ability to complete his Ph.D., and student visa. Doe sued the University alleging discrimination during its Title IX disciplinary proceeding. In February 2018, Doe filed a writ of mandamus, and the judge assigned granted a stay of the decision and sanction, finding the evidence did not support the University's findings. In May, the Regents filed a Confession of Judgment. The matter was set aside and remanded back to the Regents. By this time, Doe lost his student visa. In December 2019, Doe filed the instance matter (later amended) alleging sex discrimination under Title IX, under the erroneous outcome and the selective enforcement theories. The district court concluded that Doe›s allegations were insufficient to state a Title IX claim under either theory and granted the University's motion to dismiss. Judge Callahan delivered the Ninth Circuit's panel decision, disagreeing with the district court. She emphasized that the inquiry was whether the facts raised a *plausible* inference that the University discriminated on the basis of sex citing as clarifying authority, *Schwake v. Arizona Board of Regents*, 967 F. 3d 940, 947 (9th Cir. 2020). The judge determined that Doe was not required to meet the "doctrinal tests superimposed by some circuit's because 'at bottom,' they all ask the same questions," whether the complaint met the appropriate standard. *Doe v. Regents*, 23 F. 4t at 935, quoting *Schwake* 967 F. 3d at 947. She found Doe's first amended complaint established sufficient facts (outlined here) to support allegations of external pressures that when combined with those supporting an internal pattern and practice of bias plus specific instances of bias, presented a plausible case of sex discrimination under Title IX to survive a motion to dismiss. The asymmetrical enforcement allegations identified by the appellate court, Judge Callahan concluded, further buttressed Doe's Title IX claims of plausible discrimination by the University. The judge reversed the district court's dismissal of Doe's complaint.

Other Title VII cases by Judge Callahan include *Porter v. Cal. Dept. of Corr.*, 383 F. 3d 1018 (9th Cir. 2004)(inference of causal link not foreclosed by lapse of time) and *Arizona ex rel. Horne v. Geo Group, Inc.*, 816 F. 3d 1189 (9th Cir. 2016) (holding EEOC satisfied the conciliation process in a class action suit involving sexual discrimination, harassment and retaliation by prison facility employees because it made a reasonable cause determination and sent determination letter, invited employer to conciliate and proposed a settlement).

In *Mendocino Ry. v. Ainsworth*, 113 F. 4th 1181 (9th Cir. 2024), the City of Fort Bragg (City) and the California Coastal Commission (Commission) filed a declaratory and injunctive relief action in Mendocino Superior Court to require the Mendocino Railway (Railway) to comply with local laws in the use and maintenance of Railway properties. The Railway operated a railroad line between the City and Willits, California and acquired an estimated 300 acres of land within the City that were adjacent to the Fort Bragg railway station, some bearing dilapidated structures. In 2017, the Commission started discussions with the Railway to obtain permits pursuant to the California Coastal Act of 1976 (Act), Cal. Pub. Res. Code § 30000 *et seq.* The Railway moved the matter to federal district court seeking a declaration that the City and Commission were preempted from regulating its operations under federal law. Upon analyzing the Railway's claim under the Colorado River doctrine, the district court dismissed the federal case finding there was concurrent state jurisdiction and pending parallel state court proceedings. *See Colorado River Water Conser-*

vation Dist. v. United States, 424 U.S. 800, 96 S.Ct. 1236, 47 L.Ed.2d 483 (1976). Judge Callahan also applied the eight-factor balancing test of the Colorado River doctrine to the Railway's claims. She determined that the first two factors, specific property and forum inconvenience, did not apply and that the third factor, piecemeal litigation by different tribunals, favored dismissal of the federal case. Consideration of remaining factors also militated against dismissal: factor four, order in which the forums gained jurisdiction with the state having filed first; fifth factor, the parties agreed federal preemption applied but here, the state had concurrent jurisdiction; and the sixth factor whether the state action adequately protects the rights of all parties favored dismissal based upon the Railway's concession that its federal preemption issue could be resolved by the state court. In reviewing the seventh factor, forum shopping, Judge Callahan while acknowledging that both parties took "a somewhat opportunistic approach to the litigation," also considered the Railway's attempt to disqualify the state court judge. As to factor eight, the judge found the state and federal cases were substantially similar (but not exact) proceedings and that this was the proper analysis, rejecting the Railway's overreliance on exact parallelism enunciated in *Ernest Bock, LLC v. Steelman*, 76 F.4th 827, 836 (9th Cir. 2023). Judge Callahan concluded a balancing of the Colorado River factors favored the state proceeding and upheld the district court's dismissal of the Railway's federal case was upheld.

b. Dissents

Judge Callahan issued dissents in 266 cases, a percentage of them on procedural grounds. For example, in a sex reassignment case of a female prisoner who was released, *Norsworthy v. Beard*, 802 F. 3d 1090 (9th Cir. 2015), the judge dissented because she believed the mandatory preliminary injunction should also have been vacated in addition to the majority's dismissal because the case was moot. In *Dickens v. Ryan*, 744 F. 3d 1147 (9th Cir. 2014), the judge dissented because she concluded the *en banc* opinion should have been vacated instead of declaring the case moot based upon the inmate's death. In a case involving the adequacy of notice, *Lopez v. Barr*, 925 F. 3d 396 (9th Cir. 2019), the judge disagreed with the majority that a notice to appear in an asylum case that is defective under *Pereira v. Sessions*, 138 S.Ct. 2105, 201 L. Ed. 2d 433(2018) cannot be cured by a subsequent notice. Judge Callahan wrote that she did "not read *Pereira* as holding that the notice of time and place must be provided in a single document." *Lopez v. Barr*, 925 F. 3d at 407.

The judge issued dissents in discrimination cases, such as *Vangieson v. Austin*, 2024 U.S. App. LEXIS 4312 (9th Cir. 2024), in which she concluded the plaintiff who suffered from Aspergers and severe anxiety successfully performed his job for years and thereby raised genuine issues of material fact in a disability discrimination under the Rehabilitation Act. In *O'Brien v. R.C. Willey Home Furnishings*, 748 Fed. Appx. 721 (9th Cir. 2018) the judge opined that Plaintiff was properly terminated in an ADA case on the basis of being at work with a blood alcohol level of .04% and not, as the majority decided, for his lawful off-duty drinking, and in *Guthrey v. Alta Cal. Reg'l Ctr.*, 2024 U.S. App. LEXIS 22111 (9th Cir. 2024), she objected to the majority's finding of a physical nexus as the predicate for reversing the district court's dismissal of plaintiffs' ADA claim. Judge Callahan found that two visits by the plaintiffs to defendant's office to receive social services was inadequate to establish defendant's office as a place of public accommodation.

In criminal cases, Judge Callahan objected to the majority's refusal to rehear *en banc*, *Ileto v. Glock, Inc.*, 370 F. 3d 860 (9th Cir. 2004). Upon illegally purchasing a Glock, the defendant killed postal worker Ileto and seriously injured others. The majority determined that Glock failed to exercise reasonable care to protect the public from risk created by its distribution and marketing schemes such as to create an illegal secondary market. She wrote that the majority improperly interpreted and applied California's negligence and public nuisance law to extend liability to Glock whose guns (made and sold outside California) were used by a man (prohibited from owning guns). *Dirks v. Grasso*, 449 Fed. Appx. 589 (9th Cir. 2011) involved the arrest of Professor Charles Dirks who was arrested by three officers for verbal comments which was recorded and videotaped. Professor Dirks objected to the planned interrogation of a student sheriff's cadet and refused to immediately leave but rather stood at the entrance of the sheriff's station, speaking to the officers from there. The officers arrested the professor for disturbing the peace and obstruction of justice. The district court denial the officers' motion for qualified immunity because it found there was no probable cause to arrest Professor Dirk and, therefore, the arrest was unlawful. The majority ruled that verbal opposition to police action does not constitute probable cause for arrest. Judge Callahan dissented concluding there was probable cause to arrest Professor Dirk and, therefore, qualified immunity should have been granted. In *Wood v. Ryan*, 759 F. 3d 1076 (9th Cir. 2014) the majority granted a conditional stay of Wood's execution with lethal drugs by the state of Arizona (State). In so doing, it reversed the district court's denial of an injunction on the basis of a First Amendment violation by the State for failing to provide information about the manufacturer. Dissenting from the majority's decision denying an *en banc* hearing, Judge Callahan wrote, "[e]xecutions historically have been open to the public, but this does not mandate revealing the manufacturer of the lethal drugs. Similarly, it is a stretch to argue that the identity of the manufacturer is critical to the public discussion of the process." *Wood*, 759 F. 3d at 1104.

The judge dissented in *Niz-Chavez v. Garland*, 2021 U.S. App. LEXIS 28043 (9th Cir. 2021), in a case where the majority reversed the BIA's denial of asylum to a Guatemalan woman. The majority found the BIA failed to consider Guatemalan women as a protected group, particularly those who are viewed as property of which petitioner was a member. Judge Callahan expressed her sympathy for the Guatemalan woman seeking asylum but concluded there was inadequate evidence submitted to BIA and insufficient evidence presented by Niz-Chavez to establish a nexus between her past harm and membership in the protected group. In an earlier asylum case, *Gui Xiang Zheng v. Sessions,* 720 Fed. Appx. 394 (9th Cir. 2018), Judge Callahan departed from the majority who remanded the case back to the BIA to consider whether China's enforcement of its coercive family-planning policies constitutes changed country conditions such that petitioner had a well-founded fear of future persecution. The judge took issue with the petitioner's illegal entry into the U.S. and 11-year delay in raising her claim that she was in violation of China's one-child policy. *See* a 2025 dissent, *Barron v. Bondi,* 2025 U.S. App. LEXIS 5594 (9th Cir. 2025), in which Judge Callahan disagrees with the majority that the undocumented person can establish meritorious grounds to stay in the country.

c. Judge Callahan's Ninth Circuit Majority Opinions Reversed/Affirmed by SCOTUS

Judge Callahan authored four opinions that were appealed and reviewed by the Supreme Court. Of the four appealed, three were affirmed and one was reversed.

1. *Video Software Dealers Ass'n v. Schwarzenegger,* 556 F. 3d 950 (2009), *aff'd, Brown v. Entertainment Merchants Assn.*, 564 U.S. 786, 131 S. Ct. 2729, 180 L.Ed.2d 708 (2011), involved violent video game content and the Obscenity to Minors Exception under the First Amendment. On October 7, 2005, California Governor Schwarzenegger signed into law Assembly Bill 1179 (Act). The Act states that "[a] person may not sell or rent a video game that has been labeled as a violent video game to a minor and further defines violent video games. Civil penalties up to $1,000 may be imposed upon violators of the Act." Cal. Civ. Code § 1746.1(a)(4).[53] The Act also defines the terms "cruel," "depraved," "heinous," and "serious physical abuse."[54] Labels are mandated to inform the public of the nature of the violence in the video games. Violators are subject to a civil penalty of up to $1,000. *Id.* at § 1746.3. The Act identifies the State's compelling interests as preventing violent, aggressive, and antisocial behavior and harm to minors. The State supplemented the record with material and studies on the impact of violent video games on minors. In California, the video game industry adopted a voluntary rating system. Additionally, an independent body, the Entertainment Software Rating Board (ESRB), rates the content of video games in one of six age-specific categories. Before the Act's effective date, the plaintiffs—consisting of associations of companies that create, publish, distribute,

53. Civil Code §§ 1746–1746.5.3; § 1746(d)(1) defines a violent video game: a video game in which the range of options includes killing, maiming, dismembering, or sexually assaulting an image of a human being, if those acts are depicted in the game in a manner that does either of the following: (A) Comes within all of the following descriptions: (i) A reasonable person, considering the game as a whole, would find appeals to a deviant or morbid interest of minors. (ii) It is patently offensive to prevailing standards in the community as to what is suitable for minors. (iii) It causes the game, as a whole, to lack serious literary, artistic, political, or scientific value for minors.

54. §1746(d) (B)(2) and (3), violates the Act if it "[e]nables the player to virtually inflict serious injury upon images of human beings or characters with substantially human characteristics in a manner which is especially heinous, cruel, or depraved in that it involves torture or serious physical abuse to the victim."

sell, and/or rent video games—filed an action for declaratory judgment to invalidate the Act, asserting the Act violated Section 1983 and the First and Fourteenth Amendments. The State appealed when the district court granted the plaintiffs' motion and enjoined it from implementing the Act. On a content-based analysis, Judge Callahan held that the State's concession that its definition of "violent video game" was unconstitutionally broad did not invalidate the entire Act. She concluded that the State did not have a compelling interest in preventing psychological or neurological harm to minors allegedly caused by violent video games and even if it did, that interest was not narrowly tailored to further its interest. Judge Callahan cited *R.A.V. v. City of St. Paul*, 505 U.S. 377 (1992), and *United States v. Playboy Entm't Group, Inc.*, 529 U.S. (2000), as guiding her analysis under the strict scrutiny test which she concluded was the appropriate standard in this case.

As a matter of first impression, Judge Callahan considered whether violent video games fell within the legal definition of obscenity under the First Amendment and the proper standard for analyzing the issue. The State argued that the Act should be analyzed under the "variable obscenity" or "obscenity to minors" standard enunciated in *Ginsberg v. New York*, 390 U.S. 629, 88 S.Ct. 1274, 20 L.Ed.2d 195 (1968). It further asserted that the holding in *Ginsberg*, which affirmed a state's prohibition of sale of sexually explicit material to minors, should be extended to violent video material in video games. Judge Callahan distinguished *Ginsberg* on the basis that at issue was sexually explicit material (not violent material) that did not create a new category of expression excepted from First Amendment protection. She identified and discussed other circuit cases that refused to broaden *Ginsberg* beyond sexually explicit material, even when such material was a part of violent material, accord, *American Amusement Machine Association v. Kendrick*, 244 F.3d 572, 574–575 (7th Cir. 2001), *Video Software Dealers Association v. Webster*, 968 F.2d 684, 688 (8th Cir. 1992), and *James v. Meow Media, Inc.*, 300 F.3d 683, 698 (6th Cir. 2002). The judge declined to extend the ruling in *Ginsberg* and analyzed the Act under the strict scrutiny standard, affirmed the district court's summary judgment in favor of defendant. SCOTUS affirmed Judge Callahan's ruling, also declining to extend *Ginsberg* to violent material in video games and create a new exception, citing *United States v. Stevens*, 559 U.S 460 (2010), as controlling. *Stevens* involved a federal statute that criminalized the creation, sale, or possession of certain depictions of animal cruelty. Justice Alito wrote, "[W]e held [in *Stevens*] that new categories of unprotected speech may not be added to the list by a legislature that concludes certain speech is too harmful to be tolerated." *Brown*, 131 S. Ct. 2729, at 2734. The justice agreed that the state failed to satisfy its burden that the Act was narrowly drawn to serve its purpose of protecting minors. Justices Thomas and Breyer filed dissenting opinions.

2. *Kimble v. Marvel Entertainment, LLC*, 727 F. 3d 856 (9th Cir. 2013), *aff'd*, 576 U.S. 446, 135 S. Ct. 2401 (2015), focused on the payment of patent royalties beyond the expiration of the patent. On an issue of first impression involving a hybrid licens-

ing agreement with patent and non-patent rights, Judge Callahan ruled that the agreement was unenforceable beyond the expiration date of the underlying patent. The Supreme Court upheld Judge Callahan's ruling. The facts that gave rise to the appeal are as follows. Appellant Stephen Kimble invented a Spider-Man toy in approximately 1990. A child could role-play with the toy by mimicking Spider-Man's web shooting with foam string that was activated by a valve connected to a can of foam through a flexible line. A patent was granted that expired on May 25, 2010 (Patent). In December Kimble met with the president of Marvel's predecessor, Lou Schwartz, to discuss the idea covered by then-pending application. Kimble contends that at the meeting, Schwartz verbally agreed that Marvel would compensate him if it used any of his ideas. Marvel subsequently told Kimble that it was not interested in his ideas. Despite its supposed lack of interest, Marvel thereafter began manufacturing a similar Spider-Man role-playing toy called the "Web Blaster." The Web Blaster allowed that toy's user to shoot foam string from a can mounted on the user's wrist by activating a trigger in the user's hand. The only difference between the two toys was the Web Blaster contained a purely cosmetic plastic glove that was not needed to activate the valve. Seven years later, in 1997, Kimble sued Marvel for patent infringement and breach of contract, claiming that Marvel misappropriated his idea without compensating him. Marvel denied Kimble's claims. The district court granted Marvel's motion for summary judgment on the patent infringement claim but not on the contract claim as it found there were genuine issues of material fact. In a subsequent jury trial on the contract claim, the jury found in favor of Kimble, whereupon the district court entered a judgment awarding him 3.5 percent of past, present, and future Web Blaster net product sales (excluding sales of foam string refills). Kimble appealed the court's decision on the patent infringement claim, and Marvel appealed the verdict on the contract claim.

The parties entered a settlement in 2001 while the appeal was pending in which Marvel agreed to pay Kimball $516,214.62 for the patent and "3% of 'net product sales' (as such term is used in the Judgment) excluding refill royalties made after December 31, 2000. For purposes of this paragraph 3.b, 'net product sales' shall be deemed to include product sales that would infringe the Patent but for the purchase and sale thereof pursuant to this Agreement as well as sales of the Web Blaster product that was the subject of the Action and to which the Judgment refers." *Kimble,* 727 F. 3d at 859–860. Kimble released Marvel and they agreed to dismiss the pending appeal. Accordingly, the district court entered an order vacating the judgment and dismissing the action with prejudice. Marvel paid Kimble more than $6 million in royalties until 2006 when Marvel entered into a licensing agreement with Hasbro to produce the Spider-Man toy. The parties had disputes regarding royalties and Kimble filed suit in Arizona. Marvel's position was it no longer had an obligation to pay Kimble royalties due to expiration of the patent. The district court granted summary judgment to Marvel, concluding Kimble could not recover royalties under the Settlement Agreement upon expiration of the patent.

Judge Callahan affirmed the district court's decision that the royalty provision was unenforceable in a hybrid agreement, containing inseparable patent and non-patent provisions, based on *Brulotte v. Thys Co*, 379 U.S. 29 (1964). *Brulotte* is the seminal case holding patents were unenforceable beyond the scope of the patent. Judge Callahan also cited as authority *Aronson v. Quick Point Pencil Co*, 440 U.S. (1979), in which SCOTUS held royalty payments could be paid indefinitely where no patent had been issued and distinguished the instant case on that basis. The judge also cited as support other circuit cases that reached the same decisions, *Meehan v. PPG Indus., Inc.*, 802 F.2d 881, 884–86 (7th Cir. 1986). Justice Elena Kagan affirmed Judge Callahan's decision, citing *Brulotte* as the seminal authority and discussed *stare decisis* that compelled the high court to affirm the decision. (Justice Sotomayor was part of the majority.) Justice Alito dissented with Chief Justice Roberts and Justice Thomas joining.

3. *Hana Financial, Inc. v. Hana Bank*, 735 F. 3d 1158 (9th Cir. 2013), *aff'd*, 574 U.S. 418, 135 S. Ct. 907, 190 L.Ed.2d 800 (2015), was a trademark priority and tacking case decided by a jury. The parties went to trial over their common usage of the word "hana" (which means first/top/unity or number one in Korean). At issue was whether the infringer's mark "Hana Bank" infringed on its "Hana Financial" mark. The plaintiff, Hana Financial, Inc. (HFI), was a U.S. financial corporation, incorporated in California in 1994. The defendants' bank, Hana Bank, adopted its name in 1991 and is the fourth largest bank in Korea. The principals of the businesses knew one another since 1985, Charles Kim (HFI's former CEO), Sunnie Kim (HFI's current CEO), and the Bank's Chairman, Seoung-Yu Kim. Charles and Sunnie Kim were working at an American bank in 1991 when the Bank was considering offering services to Korean Americans living in Los Angeles through a partner. The three principals met to discuss an alliance and executed a non-binding memorandum of understanding, but the deal never was completed. In May 1994, the Bank extended its services to the United States, establishing the "Hana Overseas Korean Club" (the "Club") to provide financial services to Korean expatriates. HFI came into existence one month later to engage in enterprises other than banking. It began using its trademark in 1995 and, in July 1996, obtained a federal trademark registration for a pyramid logo with the words "Hana Financial." In 1995, Charles Kim showed Seoung-Yu Kim a copy of his HFI business card; Seoung-Yu Kim asked why "Hana" was being used without his permission. Charles Kim explained that HFI would be engaged in factoring and not banking, so there would be no overlap in the two companies' services. In 2000, the Bank changed its name to the "Hana World Center." In 2001, The Bank sought to register its trademark in 2001 but was unable to do so, due partly to HFI's mark. The Bank contacted HFI about the issue, but they were unable to resolve it. In 2002, the Bank began operating an agency in New York under its own name. In March 2007, HFI filed its complaint alleging trademark infringement. The Bank sought cancellation of HFI's trademark based on HFI's alleged awareness of the Bank's superior rights, and the Bank also asserted the equitable defenses of laches

and unclean hands. In January 2008, the district court granted the Bank's motion for summary judgment on trademark priority and granted HFI's motion for summary judgment on the Bank's cancellation counterclaim. Both parties appealed.

The Ninth Circuit reversed the appeal on the issue of priority and remanded for trial on that issue; it affirmed the court's summary judgment cancelling the Bank's counterclaim. The jury found in favor of the Bank, finding it had priority since it used its mark in commerce in the United States prior to April 1, 1995, and continuously since that date. The jury also issued an advisory that the Bank had proven its laches but not an unclean hands defense. The court issued its findings, determining that HFI's claims were barred by both laches and unclean hands. Judge Callahan started her legal analysis with a description of the applicable law:

> A party claiming trademark ownership must establish that it was the first to use the mark in the sale of goods or services. This concept is known as trademark "priority." One of the ways that a party may establish priority is through the constructive use doctrine known as "tacking." Tacking allows a party to "tack" the date of the user's first use of a mark onto a subsequent mark to establish priority where the two marks are so similar that consumers would generally regard them as being the same... We have previously indicated that tacking only applies in "exceptionally narrow" circumstances, *Brookfield Communications, Inc. v. West Coast Entertainment Corp.*, 174 F.3d 1036, 1047 (9th Cir. 1999), and is properly resolved "as a matter of law if reasonable minds cannot differ and the evidence permits only one conclusion," *One Industries, LLC v. Jim O'Neal Distributing, Inc.*, 578 F.3d 1154, 1160 (9th Cir. 2009). Nonetheless, the rule in our circuit is that tacking "requires a highly fact-sensitive inquiry" generally reserved for the jury. *Hana Financial, Inc. v. Hana Bank*, 735 F. 3d at 1158, 1161.

After assessing the facts in the case, Judge Callahan concluded that reasonable minds could differ on the result. She concluded the issue whether the marks conveyed the same commercial impression was for the jury, and further, that the issue of whether the alleged infringer abandoned its "Hana Overseas Korean Club" mark when it switched to its "Hana World Center" mark also was for the jury. The judge held the jury was entitled to find that the doctrine of tacking applied. Justice Sotomayor, writing for the Supreme Court opinion, agreed with Judge Callahan that the issue of tacking must be decided in a trademark case by a jury where, as here, the facts do not warrant summary judgment as a matter of law. The justice defined the issue as whether two trademarks may be tacked for purposes of determining priority. She rejected HFI's assertion that the question was a matter of law, not to be resolved by a jury.

4. In *Reed v. Town of Gilbert, Ariz.*, 587 F.3d 966 (9th Cir. 2009), *rev'd*, 576 U.S. 155, 135 S. Ct 2218, 192 L.Ed.2d 236 (2015), the First Amendment's freedom of speech was at issue over ordinances regulating signage. Justice Clarence Thomas (joined by

Justice Sotomayor) reversed Judge Callahan's decision in which she affirmed summary judgment for the Town of Gilbert, Arizona (Town). At issue was the Town's ordinances that permit signage (Code), defined in twenty-three categories, with three directly relevant to petitioners' case: ideological (20 square feet), political (32 square feet), and temporary directional signs (six square feet not to exceed four signs on a single property). Temporary directional signs cannot be displayed more than twelve hours before the event and one hour after the event. The petitioners were Good News Community Church (Church) and its pastor, Clyde Reed. Sunday services are held in the town at different temporary locations; services and locations are posted on signs in and near the Town each Sunday. The Church was cited for exceeding the time limits for displaying temporary directional signs and for failing to include an event date on the signs. As the parties could not resolve the dispute, petitioners filed suit, claiming that the Code abridged their freedom of speech. The district court denied the petitioner's motion for a preliminary injunction, and the Ninth Circuit affirmed. Judge Callahan held that the Code's sign categories were content neutral, and that the Code satisfied the intermediate scrutiny accorded to content-neutral regulations of speech. Justice Thomas defined the Code as a content-based law, which is presumed to be unconstitutional and analyzed under the strict scrutiny standard. He disagreed with Judge Callahan that the Code's categories were not content based but were "a paradigmatic example of content-based discrimination," that singled out specific subject matter for differential treatment. The justice based his conclusion on the three categories of ideologic, policy, and temporary directional—holding that no matter the sponsor, speaker or event—they are regulated differently from the remaining categories and are therefore constitutionally impermissible.

Conclusion

This chapter does not allow for a deeper examination of the opinions of the Luminaria Circuit Court judges beyond an introduction of their work. The current political landscape has revived legal battles that were the subject of college student protests in the 1970s and 1980s, in areas such as sex discrimination, reproductive rights, immigration, and religious freedom. The legal issues of today's America are being evaluated and addressed by the few remaining active Luminaria judges and the second generation of Latina (and Latino) Article III judges. A deeper and focused study of their collective work would be instructive. Of interest, for example, may be an analysis of SCOTUS reversals, from the lens of its current composition, of the majority opinions of Judges McLane Wardlaw, Callahan and the incumbent Latina circuit court judges. A focus on those cases where Justice Sotomayor concurs, or dissents may be illuminating. A review of the cases where more than one Luminaria judge is on a circuit panel to ascertain similarities and differences would be helpful to litigators, such as comparing *Lavan v. City of Los Angeles*, 693 F.3d 1022

(9th Cir. 2012), Judge McLane Wardlaw finding the possibility of success on the merits of a homeless person's due process rights against the city with Judge Callahan dissenting, or *Ibrahim v. U.S. Department of Homeland Security*, 912 F.3d 1147 (9th Cir. 2019), Judge McLane Wardlaw affirming the *Bivens* action of an undocumented person for airport detention and erroneous inclusion in a terrorist database with Judge Callahan dissenting in part. From a gender lens, a review of cases where the Luminaria Circuit Court judges differ from their male colleagues would be insightful, such as Judge Sotomayor's *Ricci v. Destefano* case and *Bringas v. Rodriguez v. Sessions*, 850 F.3d 1051 (9th Cir. 2017) in which Judge McLane Wardlaw found the undocumented appellant presented compelling evidence of presumptive eligibility for asylum, with Judge Carlos Bea dissenting. The number (albeit small) of Latino/a judges currently sitting on the Ninth Circuit provides the opportunity to review cases where they disagree or agree as in *Meza Diaz v. Garland*, No. 23-973 (9th Cir., October 8, 2024) majority opinion delivered by Judge Richard Paez,[55] joined by Judge McLane Wardlaw, in which the BIA's denial of asylum was reversed on the grounds that cartel violence including murder, kidnapping and death threats made over a number of years constituted persecution against a Mexican immigrant mother and daughter. A cross-circuit analysis of cases where majority opinions by any of these judges—especially on select issues—would be both germane and beneficial to the study of appellate law. The possibilities are endless.

Studies of their collective work may (most likely will) result in the conclusion that the Luminaria and Latina Circuit Court judges render their decisions like most other fair-minded Circuit Court judges, from the facts and law presented, undeniably infused with a blend of their unique backgrounds, experiences and vision of the law—and therein lies the fun and challenge in the exploration. One thing not in doubt is their appointment to the Circuit Courts of Appeals made and continue to make a profound difference to American society and appellate jurisprudence. Such is the goal of perfecting our Union.

55. While the *Luminarias Project* focuses on Latina attorneys and judges, the journey of the Latino Article III judges is equally compelling. For example, U.S. District Court Judge Paez had to wait four years (from 1996 to 2000) to be elevated to the Ninth Circuit. "The story goes that that... Senator Barbara Boxer used two words to break the logjam on... Paez's nomination to the Ninth Circuit... Senate Majority Leader Trent Lott wanted a friend, the mayor of Tupelo, Miss. named to the Tennessee Valley Authority. Boxer blocked the mayor, whom she had never heard of, causing a Lott aid to ask what possible interest the Californian would have in the TVA. Boxer is said to have replied, 'Richard Paez.' *Supra* note 15 HNBA Journal at 20, fn. 55.

Appendix A

List of Luminaria and Latina State Supreme Court Justices 1982–2025

NO.	LUMINARIA JUSTICES	COURT	APPOINTING AUTHORITY	TENURE	STATUS
1.	Dorothy Comstock Riley 1949 LL.B. Wayne State	Michigan Supreme Court Chief Justice 1987–1991	Gov. William Milliken Elected, Reelected	12/9/1982–2/15/1983 1/1/1985–9/1/1997	Retired, Deceased
2.	Miriam Naveira Merly LL.B. 1960 UPR	Puerto Rico Supreme Court Chief Justice 2003–2004	Gov. Rafael Hernández Colón	6/11/1985–7/28/2004	Mandatory Retirement, Deceased
3.	Rosemary Barkett JD 1970 Florida	Florida Supreme Court Chief Justice 1992–1994	Gov. Bob Graham	10/14/1985–7/1/1994	Elevated
4.	Carmen Beauchamp Ciparick JD 1967 St. John's	New York Court of Appeals	Gov. Mario Cuomo	1/4/1994–12/31/2012	Mandatory Retirement
5.	Vanessa Ruiz JD 1975 Georgetown	D.C. Court of Appeals	Pres. Bill Clinton	7/12/1994–8/31/2011	Retired
6.	Petra Jimenez Maes JD 1973 New Mexico	New Mexico Supreme Court Chief Justice 2003–2005, 2012–2014	Gov. Gary Johnson	12/3/1998–12/31/2018	Retired
7.	Liana Fiol Matta JD 1970 UPR	Puerto Rico Supreme Court Chief Justice 2014–2016	Gov. Sila Calderon	2/19/2004–1/31/2016	Retired
8.	Carmen Espinosa JD 1976 George Washington	Connecticut Supreme Court	Gov. Daniel Malloy	3/6/2013–7/16/2017	Retired

continues

continued

NO.	LATINA JUSTICES	COURT	APPOINTING AUTHORITY	TENURE	STATUS
9.	Anabelle Rodríguez JD 1985 UPR	Puerto Rico Supreme Court	Gov. Sila Calderon	8/19/2004–12/10/2020	Retired
10.	Mildred Pabón JD 1983 UPR	Puerto Rico Supreme Court	Gov. Luis Fortuño	2/4/2009–Current	Incumbent
11.	Eva Guzman JD 1989 South Texas	Texas Supreme Court	Gov. Rick Perry	10/8/2009–6/11/2021	Retired Private Practice
12.	Monica Márquez JD 1997 Yale	Colorado Supreme Court Chief Justice 7/2024–Incumbent	Gov. Bill Ritter	12/10/2010	Incumbent
13	Barbara J. Vigil JD UNM 1985	New Mexico Supreme Court	Gov. Michelle Lujan Grisham	11/6/2012–6/30/2021	Retired
14.	Jenny Rivera JD 1985 NYU	New York Court of Appeals	Gov. Andrew Cuomo	2/11/2013–2/10/2027	Incumbent
15.	Maite Oronoz Rodríguez JD 2002 UPR	Puerto Rico Supreme Court Chief Justice 2/2026–Incumbent	Gov. Alejandro García Padilla	7/15/2014–2/22/2016	Incumbent
16.	Barbara Lagoa JD 1992 Columbia	Florida Supreme Court	Gov. Ron DeSantis	1/9/2019–12/6/2019	Elevated
17.	Dalila Argaez Wendlandt JD 1996 Stanford	Massachusetts Supreme Court	Gov. Charlie Baker	12/4/2020–Current	Incumbent
18.	Julie J. Vargas JD UNM 1993	New Mexico Supreme Court	Gov. Michelle Lujan Grisham	1/1/2021–12/21/2028	Incumbent
19.	Briana H. Zamora JD 2000 UNM	New Mexico Supreme Court	Gov. Michelle Lujan Grisham	7/6/2021–12/31/2032	Incumbent
20.	Patricia Guerrero JD 1997 Stanford	California Supreme Court Chief Justice 7/2024–Incumbent	Gov. Gavin Newsom	3/2022	Incumbent

NO.	LATINA JUSTICES	COURT	APPOINTING AUTHORITY	TENURE	STATUS
21.	Camille Rivera Pérez JD 2000 Pontifical Catholic	Puerto Rico Supreme Court	Gov. Jennifer González Colón	1/17/2025	Incumbent
22.	Maria Elena Cruz JD 2001 Arizona	Arizona Supreme Court	Gov. Katie Hobbs	1/29/2025	Incumbent

As of publication date, no Latinas/os have served on the state Supreme Courts of:[1] Alabama, Alaska, Arkansas, Delaware, Georgia, Hawaii, Illinois, Idaho, Indiana, Iowa, Kansas, Kentucky, Louisiana, Maine, Maryland, Minnesota, Missouri, Montana, Nebraska, Nevada, New Hampshire, North Carolina, North Dakota, Ohio, Oklahoma, Pennsylvania, Rhode Island, South Carolina, South Dakota, Tennessee, Utah, Vermont, Virginia, West Virginia, Wisconsin, Wyoming. The first Ohio Court of Appeals Judge Marilyn Zayas has served on the supreme court by special assignment. Latinos also have been appointed to the state supreme courts of Colorado, Florida, Mississippi, New Jersey, New Mexico, New York, Oregon, Texas, Washington and Puerto Rico.

1. The list was compiled from state websites and historical records and the Luminarias database on file with the Author.

Appendix B

Article III Luminaria and Latina Judges

NO.	LUMINARIA JUDGES	DISTRICT COURT	PRESIDENT	TENURE	STATUS
1.	Carmen Cerezo	D.P.R.	Carter	6/30/1980–2/28/2021 Chief Judge 1993–1999	Retired
2.	Lenore Carrero Nesbitt	S.D. Fla.	Reagan	11/16/1983–10/6/2001	Deceased
3.	Sonia Sotomayor	S.D.N.Y.	H.W. Bush	8/12/1992–10/8/1998	Elevated
4.	Lourdes Gillespie Baird	C.D. Cal.	H.W. Bush	8/12/1992–4/15/2005	Retired
5.	Irma Gonzalez	S.D. Cal.	H.W. Bush	8/12/1992–10/25/2013 Chief Judge 2005–2012	Retired
6.	Martha Vazquez	D.N.M.	Clinton	10/1/1993–12/31/2023 Chief Judge 2003–2010	Senior Status
7.	Kim McLane Wardlaw	C.D. Cal.	Clinton	12/26/1995–8/3/1998	Elevated
8.	Hilda Tagle	S.D. Tex.	Clinton	4/17/1998–12/31/2012	Inactive Senior Status
9.	M. Christina Armijo	D.N.M.	G.W. Bush	11/12/2001–2/18/2018 Chief Judge 2012–2018	Inactive Senior Status
10.	Judith Herrera	D.N.M.	G.W. Bush	6/13/2004–7/1/2019	Retired
11.	Dora Irizarry	E.D.N.Y.	G.W. Bush	7/8/2004–1/26/2020 Chief Judge 2016–2020	Senior Status
12.	Virginia Hernandez Covington	M.D. Fla.	G.W. Bush	9/10/2004–7/12/2020	Senior Status
13.	Aida Delgado-Colón	D.P.R.	G.W. Bush	3/17/2006 Chief Judge 2011–2018	Incumbent

continues

continued

14.	Christina Arguello	D. Colo.	G.W. Bush	10/21/2008–7/15/2022	Retired
15.	Nitza Quiñones Alejandro	E.D. PA.	Obama	6/19/2013 Chief Judge 2016–2020	Incumbent
NO.	**NON-LUMINARIA JUDGES**	**DISTRICT COURT**	**PRESIDENT**	**TENURE**	**STATUS**
16.	Alia Moses	W.D. Tex.	G.W. Bush	11/15/2002 Chief Judge 2022–Present	Incumbent
17.	Cecilia Altonaga	S.D. Fla.	G.W. Bush	7/1/2003 Chief Judge 2021–Present	Incumbent
18.	Micaela Alvarez	S.D. Tex.	G.W. Bush	12/13/2004–6/8/2023	Senior Status
19.	Marcia Morales Howard	M.D. Fla.	G.W. Bush	2/20/2007 Chief Judge 2024–Present	Incumbent
20.	Gloria Navarro	D. Nev.	Obama	5/6/2010 Chief Judge 2014–2019	Incumbent
21.	Diana Saldaña	S.D. Tex.	Obama	2/9/2011	Incumbent
22.	Esther Salas	D.N.J.	Obama	6/14/2011	Incumbent
23.	Nelva Gonzales Ramos	S.D. Tex.	Obama	8/4/2011	Incumbent
24.	Marina Garcia Marmolejo	S.D. Tex.	Obama	10/4/2011	Incumbent
25.	Yvonne Gonzalez Rogers	N.D. Cal.	Obama	11/21/2011	Incumbent
26.	Analisa Torres	S.D.N.Y.	Obama	4/23/2011	Incumbent
27.	Rosemary Márquez	D. Ariz.	Obama	5/19/2014	Incumbent
28.	Silvia Carreño-Coll	D.P.R.	Trump	2/26/2020	Incumbent
29.	Aileen Cannon	S.D. Fla.	Trump	11/13/2020	Incumbent
30.	Regina Rodriguez	D. Colo.	Biden	7/1/2021	Incumbent

31.	Linda Lopez	S.D. Cal.	Biden	12/21/2021	Incumbent
32.	Ruth Bermudez Montenegro	S.D. Cal.	Biden	3/30/2022	Incumbent
33.	Cristina Dionne Silva	D. Nev.	Biden	4/7/2022	Incumbent
34.	Evelyn Padin	D.N.J.	Biden	6/24/2022	Incumbent
35.	Ana de Alba	E.D. Cal.	Biden	7/7/2022–11/16/2023	Elevated
36.	Nancy Maldonado	N.D. Ill.	Biden	8/10/2022–7/11/2024	Elevated
37.	María Antongiorgi-Jordán	D.P.R.	Biden	12/1/2022	Incumbent
38.	Camille Vélez-Rivé	D.P.R.	Biden	12/9/2022	Incumbent
39.	Mia Roberts Perez	E.D. PA.	Biden	12/16/2022	Incumbent
40.	Ana C. Reyes	D.D.C.	Biden	2/21/2023	Incumbent
41.	Gina Méndez-Miró	D.P.R.	Biden	2/24/2023	Incumbent
42.	Margaret R. Guzman	D. Mass.	Biden	3/3/2023	Incumbent
43.	Araceli Martinez-Olguin	N.C. Cal.	Biden	3/3/2023	Incumbent
44.	Monica Ramirez Almadani	C.D. Cal.	Biden	11/21/2023	Incumbent
45.	Jacqueline Becerra	S.D. Fla.	Biden	2/29/2024	Incumbent
46.	Angela M. Martinez	D. Ariz.	Biden	5/22/2024	Incumbent
47.	Jeannette A. Vargas	S.D.N.Y.	Biden	11/6/2024	Incumbent
48.	Cynthia Valenzuela Dixon	C.D. Cal.	Biden	12/10/24	Incumbent
49.	Serena Raquel Murillo	C.D. Cal.	Biden	12/20/24	Incumbent

continues

continued

NO.	LUMINARIA JUDGES	CIRCUIT COURT	PRESIDENT	TENURE	STATUS
50.	Rosemary Barkett	Eleventh State Department	Clinton	4/15/1994–9/30/2013 10/1/2013	Retired The Hague, Iran–U.S. Tribunal (Non-Art. III)
51.	Sonia Sotomayor	Second	Clinton	10/7/1998–8/8/2009	Elevated
52.	Kim McLane Wardlaw	Ninth	Clinton	8/3/1998	Incumbent
53.	Consuelo Callahan	Ninth	G.W. Bush	5/28/2003	Incumbent
NO.	**NON-LUMINARIA JUDGES**	**CIRCUIT COURT**	**PRESIDENT**	**TENURE**	**STATUS**
54.	Mary Murguía	Ninth	Obama	1/4/2011 Chief Judge 2021–Present	Incumbent
55.	Kara Fernandez Stoll	Federal	Obama	7/9/2015	Incumbent
56.	Barbara Lagoa	Eleventh	Trump	12/6/2019	Incumbent
57.	Myrna Pérez	Second	Biden	11/12/2021	Incumbent
58.	Ana de Alba	Ninth	Biden	11/15/2023	Incumbent
59.	Irma Carrillo Ramirez	Fifth	Biden	12/8/2023	Incumbent
60.	Nancy Maldonado	Seventh	Biden	7/11/2024	Incumbent
NO.	**LUMINARIA JUDGE**	**U.S. SUPREME COURT**	**PRESIDENT**	**TENURE**	**STATUS**
61.	Sonia Sotomayor	111th Associate Justice	Obama	8/8/2009	Incumbent

As of publication date, no Latinas have served on the following Circuits:[1]

- First Circuit: Maine, Massachusetts, New Hampshire, Puerto Rico, Rhode Island
- Third Circuit: Delaware, New Jersey, Pennsylvania, Virgin Islands
- Fourth Circuit: Maryland, North Carolina, South Carolina, Virginia, West Virginia
- Sixth Circuit: Kentucky, Michigan, Ohio, Tennessee
- Eighth Circuit: Arkansas, Iowa, Minnesota, Missouri, Nebraska, North Dakota, South Dakota
- Tenth Circuit: Colorado, Kansas, New Mexico, Oklahoma, Wyoming
- Twelfth Circuit: District of Columbia

1. This list of Luminaria and Latina Article III Judges was compiled in collaboration with Dr. Jill Lynch Cruz, https://www.jlc.consulting/about.

Acknowledgments

In writing this book about the first Latina judges and public interest litigators, I have often thought of former law professor Michael Olivas, University of Houston Law Center, whom I first met in 1990. A few years ago, Professor Olivas offered to introduce me to the CAP editor, which I declined with gratitude as the research was not completed. By the time the research was completed in 2023, we had lost Professor Olivas the year prior. One of his colleagues, constitutional law scholar and law professor Gilbert Carrasco (Willamette Law School), stepped in and made the introduction. To Professor Carrasco, also a long-time colleague and friend, I am forever grateful. I thank CAP and staff for publishing this book about our first generation of Luminaria judges and activistas.

Over the past ten years while conducting the Luminarias Study and research, I developed a deep appreciation for our librarians and archivists. The staff at the University of Denver Law library have provided tremendous assistance, sometimes with last-minute requests that were never minor. I thank Assistant Director Katrina Condra, Faculty Services Librarians Andy Stamm and Michael Whitlow, Research Librarian Rebecca Plevel, and 3L student Sasha Shandrina—who under the leadership of Associate Dean of the Library Catherine Dunn and Law Dean Bruce Smith provided critical support.

I hold these same sentiments for DU Law Professor Tom Romero and DU Latinx Center Director Dr. Debora Ortega, who ensured the Luminaria Project had a home. They had long-game faith in my scholarship. I also thank Leslie Poston, A Draft Supreme, LLC., for her editing and calm guidance and assurance during the earliest drafting phase.

As much of the content involved appellate law, I fondly remember those who first taught me to research, write, and prepare written and oral arguments as a newbie Colorado Assistant Attorney General (AG)—lifelong skills that culminated in this book. I am grateful to former Assistant Deputy AG and retired Colorado Court of Appeals Judge John Dailey and AG colleague Valerie J. McNevin, both brilliant lawyers with masterful appellate skills from whom I learned much. Two dear friends and colleagues must be mentioned and thanked, Dr. Jill Lynch Cruz, my 15-year collaborator on the status of Latina lawyers, and my dear friend Mary T. Hernández, Garcia Hernández Sawhney, LLP, for her unwavering support. It was she who in 1993 first conceived of honoring our earliest Latina lawyers. No documentation about Luminarias may be published without recognizing the community of Latina attorneys and colleagues within the HNBA and the Latina Commission. Through inter-generational leadership, hard and enduring work, the body of literature on Latina attorneys is becoming a reality.

At the most personal level, I acknowledge my grandfather, George Solorzano, Sr., an immigrant and legal U.S. resident who shared his love of reading, learning, and for his adopted country. It was he to whom my heart turned while plowing through the hundreds of immigration cases handled by our Luminaria judges. I thank my husband, Alfredo Peña, who lived through this journey. As a fellow lawyer, he provided the opportunity to engage as only lawyers can about legal theories, cases, and the contradictions of the law that proved invaluable. I thank the Luminaria litigators and jurists who crafted the law that is now part of our legal history. Their personal stories and work provided illumination and inspiration. I dedicate this book to my daughter Simone, son-in-law Jorge and grandchildren Jorge Julian and Lilia—as well as to my nieces and nephews—to carry on the legacy of the Luminarias.

Dolores S. Atencio

Table of Principal Cases

United States v. Svoboda, 347 F.3d. 471 (2d Cir. 2003), 301

Table of Statutes

Index